Form pp 48-49, 51
Gunkel + Gressman
210-214
221-224
Cassuto 226

IN SEARCH OF HISTORY

IN
SEARCH
OF
HISTORY

HISTORIOGRAPHY IN THE ANCIENT WORLD AND THE ORIGINS OF BIBLICAL HISTORY

JOHN VAN SETERS

YALE UNIVERSITY PRESS
NEW HAVEN AND LONDON

Designed by Sally Harris
and set in Sabon type.
Printed in the United States of America by
Vail-Ballou Press, Binghamton, N.Y.

Library of Congress Cataloging in Publication Data

Van Seters, John.
  In search of history.

  Bibliography: p.
  Includes indexes.
1. Near East—History—To 622—Historiography.
2. Bible. O.T. Historical books—Criticism,
interpretation, etc. I. Title
DS62.2V35 1983   939′.4   82–48912
ISBN 0–300–02877–6
    0–300–03633–7 (pbk.)

11 10 9 8 7 6 5 4 3 2

To Peter and Deborah

CONTENTS

PREFACE

The impetus for writing this book came from a faculty seminar on the theme "Histories and Historians of the Ancient Near East," which was held during the 1974–75 academic year by the Department of Near Eastern Studies at the University of Toronto. The seminar was chaired by John W. Wevers (see his "Preface" in *Orientalia* 49 [1980]: 137–39). I want to make special mention of the papers presented by A. Kirk Grayson on Mesopotamia, Harry Hoffner on the Hittites, and Donald Redford on Egypt, because it will be clear in the following chapters which deal with the historiography of these regions how much I am indebted to their studies. The contributions of Grayson and Hoffner have appeared subsequently in *Orientalia* 49 (1980): 140–95 and 283–332. Redford's study will be published as part of a larger work on Egyptian historiography, entitled *King-lists, Annals, and Day-books*. My own paper in the Toronto seminar, which dealt with Israelite historiography, has also appeared in print in *Orientalia* 50 (1981): 137–85, and is reflected, with some modifications, in chapters eight and nine.

Most of the research and writing for the present volume was done during a study leave in 1979–80, made possible by a fellowship from the John Simon Guggenheim Memorial Foundation. I am grateful to the foundation for its support. The University of North Carolina also deserves my sincere thanks for supplying me with research assistants, for a publication subvention through the James A. Gray trust fund, and for the use of the facilities of the Institute for Research in the Social Sciences.

A number of scholars have seen various parts of the manuscript and have offered suggestions and encouragement. Special thanks are due to William A. Hallo of Yale University, to Hans H. Schmid of Zurich, to Phillip A. Stadter and William C. West, my colleagues in the Classics Department, and to Jack M. Sasson, my colleague in the Department of Religion. None of these scholars, however, should be held responsible for the views expressed in this book or any errors that may still remain in it.

I wish also to thank my research assistants, Teresa Smith and Flora

Taylor, for their help in the preparation of the manuscript. My thanks are due to Yale Press and especially to its editor, Charles Grench, who has encouraged me in this project over the past three years. Finally, a word of gratitude must go to my wife, Elizabeth, who always helps out in so many ways.

The book is dedicated to my children, Peter and Deborah.

John Van Seters
Chapel Hill, N.C.
September 1982

ABBREVIATIONS

ABC	Grayson, A. K. *Assyrian and Babylonian Chronicles.* Locust Valley, N.Y., 1975.
AEL	Lichtheim, M. *Ancient Egyptian Literature: A Book of Readings.* Berkeley, Los Angeles, and London, 1973–80.
AfO	*Archiv für Orientforschung.*
AIPHO	*Annaire de l'Institute de Philologie et d'Histoire Orientales.*
ANEP²	Pritchard, J. B., ed. *Ancient Near Eastern Pictures Relating to the Old Testament.* 2d ed. with supplement. Princeton, N.J., 1969.
ANET³	Pritchard, J. B., ed. *Ancient Near Eastern Pictures Relating to Old Testament.* 3d ed. with supplement. Princeton, N.J., 1969.
AnBib	Analecta Biblica.
AnSt	*Anatolian Studies.*
AOAT	Alter Orient und Altes Testament.
AOATS	Alter Orient und Altes Testament-Sondereihe.
ARAB	Luckenbill, D. D. *Ancient Records of Assyria and Babylonia.* 2 vols. Chicago, 1926–27.
ARI	Grayson, A. K. *Assyrian Royal Inscriptions.* 2 vols. Wiesbaden, 1972–76.
ASTI	*Annual of the Swedish Theological Institute.*
AThANT	Abhandlungen zur Theologie des Alten und Neuen Testaments.
AThD	Acta Theologica Danica.
BA	*The Biblical Archaeologist.*
BARE	Breasted, J. H. *Ancient Records of Egypt.* 5 vols. Chicago, 1906–07.
BASOR	*Bulletin of the American Schools of Oriental Research.*
BBB	Bonner Biblische Beiträge.
BHLT	Grayson, A. K. *Babylonian Historical-Literary Texts.* Toronto and Buffalo, 1975.
Bi Or	*Bibliotheca Orientalis.*
BJRL	*Bulletin of the John Rylands Library.*

BTAVO   Beihefte zum Tübinger Atlas des Vorderen Orients.
BWANT   Beiträge zur Wissenschaft vom Alten und Neuen Testament.
BZ   *Biblische Zeitschrift.*
BZAW   Beihefte zur Zeitschrift für die Alttestamentliche Wissenschaft.
CAH³   *The Cambridge Ancient History.* 3d ed. Cambridge, 1973–75.
CBQ   *Catholic Biblical Quarterly.*
CJT   *Canadian Journal of Theology.*
CSSH   *Comparative Studies in Society and History.*
DOTT   Thomas, Winton. *Documents from Old Testament Times.* London, 1958.
FRLANT   Forschungen zur Religion und Literatur des Alten und Neuen Testament.
GG   von Fritz, K. *Die Griechische Geschichtsschreibung.* Berlin, 1967.
HAT   Handbuch zum Alten Testament.
HKAT   Handkommentar zum Alten Testament.
HTR   *Harvard Theological Review.*
ICC   The International Critical Commentary.
IDB   *The Interpreter's Dictionary of the Bible.* Edited by G. A. Buttrick. 4 vols. New York, 1962.
IEJ   *Israel Exploration Journal.*
JAOS   *Journal of the American Oriental Society.*
JARCE   *Journal of the American Research Center in Egypt.*
JBL   *Journal of Biblical Literature.*
JCS   *Journal of Cuneiform Studies.*
JNES   *Journal of Near Eastern Studies.*
JSOT   *Journal for the Study of the Old Testament.*
KAI   Donner, H., and Röllig, W. *Kanaanäische und aramäische Inschriften.* 3 vols. Wiesbaden, 1962–64.
KAT   Kommentar zum Alten Testament.
LCL   Loeb Classical Library.
MDAIK   *Mitteilungen des Deutschen Archäologischen Instituts, Abt. Kairo.*
MT   Massoretic Text.
M V–A G   Mitteilungen der Vorderasiatischen-Aegyptischen Gesellschaft.
OLZ   *Orientalistische Literaturzeitung.*
OTS   *Oudtestamentische Studiën.*
PAPS   *Proceedings of the American Philosophical Society.*
PEQ   *Palestine Exploration Quarterly.*
RA   *Revue d'Assyriologie et d'Archéologie Orientale.*
RB   *Revue Biblique.*

RGG	*Die Religion in Geschichte und Gegenwart.* 1st, 2d, and 3d editions.
RLA	*Reallexikon der Assyriologie.* Edited by Ebeling and Meissner.
SAT	Die Schriften des Alte Testament.
SB	Sources Biblique.
SBL	Society of Biblical Literature.
SBT	Studies in Biblical Theology.
SKL	Sumerian King List.
SSI	Gibson, J. C. L. *Textbook of Syrian Semitic Inscriptions.* 2 vols. Oxford, 1973–75.
SVT	Supplement to Vetus Testamentum.
TAPA	*Transactions of the American Philological Association.*
ThR	*Theologische Rundsau.*
TLZ	*Theologische Zeitschrift.*
UF	*Ugarit-Forschungen.*
ÜS	Noth, M. *Überlieferungsgeschichtliche Studien.* Tübingen, 1943.
VT	*Vetus Testamentum.*
WMANT	Wissenschaftliche Monographien zum Alten und Neuen Testament.
WO	*Die Welt des Orients.*
WuD	*Wort und Dienst.*
YGC	Albright, W. F. *Yahweh and the Gods of Canaan.* Winona Lake, Ind., 1968.
ZA	*Zeitschrift für Assyriologie.*
ZAS	*Zeitschrift für Ägyptische Sprache und Altertumskunde.*
ZAW	*Zeitschrift für die Alttestamentliche Wissenschaft.*
ZDP–V	*Zeitschrift des deutschen Palästina-Vereins.*
ZThK	*Zeitschrift für Theologie und Kirche.*

CHAPTER ONE

INTRODUCTION

a. A DEFINITION OF HISTORY WRITING

A study of the rise of history writing in the ancient world immediately confronts the problem of defining the terms *history, history writing,* and *historiography.* To define the concept of history it is not necessary to discuss the philosophical question of how one can have a knowledge of past events, or to compare various states of "historical consciousness." Nor is it necessary to set up scientific criteria by which to judge whether a piece of writing is sufficiently historical to pass for history. What I am looking for is an adequate definition of history as a form of the narration of past events. Not all literary forms having to do with past events can be classified as histories; greater precision is needed than simply regarding all reference to the past as history. The noted Dutch historian J. Huizinga has addressed the question of form and has proposed the following definition: "History is the intellectual form in which a civilization renders account to itself of its past."[1] Huizinga's definition, which includes ancient historiography as well as modern, is well suited as a guideline for the discussion of historiography in this work.[2]

The first observation that may be made about Huizinga's definition is that the "intellectual form" is what is meant in this study by the term *history writing.* Consequently, in conformity with Huizinga's definition, this work examines the development of national histories and the history of the Israelites in particular. Because most historical texts of the ancient Near East do not really fit this nationalistic sense of history writing, some schol-

1. "A Definition of the Concept of History," in *Philosophy and History: Essays Presented to Ernst Cassirer,* p. 9.
2. This definition could be taken to mean that every civilization had a form that one could call its history. Thus J. J. Finkelstein has identified Mesopotamia's omen texts as its particular form of history writing (see "Mesopotamian Historiography," *PAPS* 107 [1963]: 461–72). But it is difficult to see how the omen literature really fits the sense of a civilization rendering account to itself of its past. Consequently, I would argue that not all civilizations developed an intellectual form that one can rightly designate as history.

ars may object to this definition as being too narrow. How are all the texts outside this definition that make reference to past events or that reflect a certain consciousness about the past to be considered? For the sake of discussion, all historical texts may be subsumed under the term *historiography* as a more inclusive category than the particular genre of history writing.[3] In this way one can still speak about the contribution of historiographic texts to the development of histories while at the same time keeping quite distinct the study of history writing itself.

The notion of a people or nation rendering account to itself has a dual connotation that will be quite useful in this discussion. On the one hand, to render account has a forensic sense of assessing responsibility for, and passing judgment upon, a nation's past actions and their consequences for the present state of affairs.[4] Herodotus and Thucydides, for example, wanted to determine who was responsible for provoking the hostilities leading to the Persian and Peloponnesian wars. However, another aspect of a civilization rendering account to itself has to do with corporate identity. A national history expresses what a nation is and what principles it stands for. Now, these two ways of a people rendering account to itself are not mutually exclusive but frequently occur in the same history. The national history is the presentation of the people's essential character or constitution followed by praise or condemnation (implicit or explicit) of its subsequent corporate actions. Some period in the past is usually taken as the ideal beginning, the constitutional age, the point of departure on the basis of which subsequent periods are to be judged and the nation's present circumstances accounted for.

The concerns for personal identity and self-justification lie at the heart of many historiographic documents, broadly understood. But in the ancient Near East, in most cases, these concerns involve the person of the king—his right to rule or his giving of an account of political actions before gods and men. Yet, unless we are to assume that the king was universally recognized as the embodiment of the state, we cannot speak of such texts as history. It may even be argued that history writing arises at the point when the actions of kings are viewed in the larger context of the people as a whole, so that it is the national history that judges the king and not the king who makes his own account of history.

History writing is also a genre of tradition.[5] Tradition is a broad cate-

3. See also J. J. M. Roberts, "Myth *versus* History: Relaying the Comparative Foundations," *CBQ* 38 (1976): 3, n. 15.
4. How far the development of law had an impact on the development of historiography cannot be pursued here. But see the study by J. G. A. Pocock, "The Origins of Study of the Past: A Comparative Approach," *CSSH* 4 (1962): 209–46.
5. For a general treatment of tradition see E. Shils, "Tradition," *CSSH* 13 (1971): 122–59.

gory encompassing not only verbal forms handed down from the past but also modes of action and behavior. Specific reference to the past may even be a rather small part of the whole body of traditional "texts." Verbal forms of tradition may be either written or oral. In recent years so much attention has focused upon *oral* tradition that any discussion about tradition invariably becomes a discussion about oral tradition. But tradition is not restricted to "primitive" societies or to the illiterates in society. All societies are traditional to some degree, and the literate society may, in fact, have many more, and more complex, traditional texts than the illiterate society.

The functions of tradition—the uses of the past—are so varied and numerous that no simple formula can cover them all. The tendency of many biblical scholars to confine the role of tradition in ancient Israelite society to the religious realm and to see all narrative texts about the past as cult functional is far too restrictive. Tradition is used to fortify belief, explain or give meaning to the way things are, invest persons and institutions with authority, legitimate practices, regulate behavior, give a sense of personal and corporate identity, and communicate skills and knowledge. The forms that the verbal tradition may take—whether poetry or prose, whether sung, spoken, or written—are almost endless in number. Many traditional forms—laws, proverbs, genealogies—have rather specific functions. But some are more complex and their function more embracing: such is the genre of history, which may contain within it many different kinds of traditional material. But a history is not merely the sum of its parts, and to analyze a history by taking it apart in order to discern the original functions of the various elements will never yield the meaning of the whole. History, as a distinct genre of tradition, has its own function; any particular history can be appreciated only when its proper limits are discerned, and its audience and time of writing are correctly identified.

History writing is a literate form of tradition, the product of literacy (although not all literate societies attained to true history writing). Jack Goody and Ian Watt observe in a recent article[6] that in a nonliterate society the cultural tradition tends to be "homeostatic"; that is, it maintains a kind of organic equilibrium by the very process of oral transmission, which forgets or transforms those parts of the tradition that cease to be either necessary or relevant. In this way oral tradition allows for social change with little sense of discontinuity. On the other hand, in a literate society the cultural tradition continues to grow, so that it accumulates, without forgetting or discarding, older levels of the tradition. A consequence of literary accumulation is some awareness of the historical process

6. "The Consequences of Literacy," in *Literacy in Traditional Societies,* ed. J. R. Goody, pp. 27–68. See also Goody's introduction, pp. 1–26.

in the development of the tradition and of the fact of change. History writing answers to the needs to account for social change and to provide a basis for new meaning, new authority, and new legitimation for those traditional forms that have become dysfunctional in changing social circumstances. [7]

History writing is not accidental, either in its composition or in its preservation. It is not the result of an accidental accumulation of data but is a literary work that is written for, and becomes part of, the society's "stream of tradition." Leo Oppenheim, who coined this phrase,[8] draws a distinction between the great mass of written documents preserved from ancient Mesopotamia dealing with day-to-day business and those literary texts that were meant to be preserved and handed down to posterity. One can speak of the former as the business and legal archives, while the latter "traditional" texts belong to the library collections. What served as oral tradition in an illiterate society had its counterpart in the scribal tradition of the literate society. The greatest known example of such a scribal tradition in the Near East before Alexander was the library of Ashurbanipal. But Israel also, as a literate society, developed its own scribal tradition, and that accounts for much of the character and variety of the Old Testament.

The histories of Greece and Israel were preserved as part of the larger literary tradition of the people. Their composition, however, was also traditional in the sense that historians used sources within the scribal tradition as well as from the great lore of oral tradition. However, archival material, even though it contained information from the past, was not used even if it was accessible.[9] Historians were more likely to use older literary works than to try to reconstruct a period "from scratch," using archival materials. This highly traditional aspect of history writing must be given due weight when we consider the development of historiography in ancient Israel.

On the basis of this discussion I would propose the following criteria by which to identify history writing in ancient Israel:

1. History writing is a specific form of tradition in its own right. Any explanation of the genre as merely the accidental accumulation of traditional material is inadequate.

2. History writing is not primarily the accurate reporting of past events.

---

7. For my earlier application of these observations to Israelite historical traditions, see J. Van Seters, "Tradition and Social Change in Ancient Israel," *Perspectives in Religious Studies* 7 (1980):96–113, esp. pp. 98–99.

8. See A. Leo Oppenheim, *Ancient Mesopotamia: Portrait of a Dead Civilization,* p. 13. See the full discussion, pp. 7–30, as background for the discussion here.

9. For Greek historiography see A. Momigliano, "Historiography on Written Tradition and Historiography on Oral Tradition," in *Studies in Historiography,* pp. 211–20.

It also considers the reason for recalling the past and the significance given to past events.

3. History writing examines the causes of present conditions and circumstances. In antiquity these causes are primarily moral—who is responsible for a certain state of affairs? (It goes without saying, of course, that modern scientific theories about causation or laws of evidence cannot be applied to the ancient writer.)

4. History writing is national or corporate in character. Therefore, merely reporting the deeds of the king may be only biographical unless these are viewed as part of the national history.

5. History writing is part of the literary tradition and plays a significant role in the corporate tradition of the people.

All these criteria are quite in keeping with Huizinga's definition of the concept of history, and this understanding of history and history writing will be used in the study that follows.

The approach that I have adopted here is in rather marked contrast to the recently published work of Herbert Butterfield.[10] His treatment of the origin of history focuses on the rise of a historical consciousness about "the process of things in time." He is not concerned with the question of genre, or with writing " 'The History of Historiography', the mere story of the development of a branch of literature, but [with] the unfolding of a whole great aspect of human experience." For Butterfield, history's origin is to be seen in the gradual evolution of human consciousness in thinking about the past. "The emergence of a feeling for history and a sense of the past could come only as part of the development of the whole human outlook." Basic to the development of a historical mentality, in Butterfield's view, is an increasing sophistication in dealing with the question of the causality of events, from the "religious outlook" of antiquity to the scientific and worldly-mindedness of modernity.

The disadvantages of such an approach are considerable, especially when it is applied to the historical documents from early antiquity. It is quite possible to see in certain texts of ancient civilizations a great concern for the past and for the meaning or consequence of that past for the present. But that significance or use of the past is almost entirely circumscribed by the nature of the genre of text in which it is found. Some types of texts express a sense of continuity and causality that is quite secular in outlook, while other historical texts of the same culture and period reflect a strong religious outlook. Some civilizations that have long and varied traditions of historical texts never developed histories until the Hellenistic era, whereas Israel and Greece, which produced histories, also produced philo-

10. H. Butterfield, *The Origins of History*. The quoted remarks are taken from the preface, pp. 13–16.

sophical and theological texts that seem to deny the very notion of taking the past seriously. One must pay close attention to the matter of the genre and function of historical texts, for it is in the transformation of such limited forms of historiography into a particular form of literature that the origin of history is to be found.

b. THE METHOD OF INVESTIGATION

While the primary concern of this book is to understand the origins and nature of history writing in ancient Israel, such an investigation must be undertaken against the background of the Near Eastern and classical world. The comparative method has often been employed in studies of Israelite historiography, but the selection of sources for comparison has been rather narrow and too many scholars merely repeat broad generalizations about the nature of historical texts from the rest of the Near East. To avoid these weaknesses it seems advisable to lay out a broad survey of all the historiographic material that might have some relevance for the study of Israel's own writing of history. This will at least enable the reader to make an informed judgment on the significance of such comparisons and to evaluate the scholarly discussion of Israelite historiography that will be undertaken in the last part of this work.

The first order of business will be to review the current discussion about early Greek historiography from the fragments of the earliest prose works down to Herodotus. In doing so it will become apparent that many opinions about Greek historiography, often repeated in Old Testament studies, are quite out-of-date. Very important, in my view, are the current studies on Greek historical prose, which I believe will be useful for Old Testament narrative studies. Furthermore, classical scholars are becoming increasingly aware that ancient Greece belonged to the eastern Mediterranean world including the Near East, and that literary forms, styles, and interests were therefore not so distinct between the two regions.

The second task will be a survey of Near Eastern historiography, and here the concern will be somewhat different. Instead of the evolution of a particular form like Herodotus' history, we are faced with an almost overwhelming volume and variety of historical texts from a number of different regions and covering a very long time span. The several chapters devoted to this survey are intended to convey just this sense of rich diversity. The approach, first of all, is to concentrate on genre analysis and the literary history of certain forms. Especially important are those forms that might have some relevance to Israelite historiography. But as with the Greek texts, we must give some attention to the study of narrative prose composition. In these texts one finds many of the same kinds of puzzles and problems that are common to Old Testament prose. It seems only reasonable that in the analysis of biblical texts and in the search for solutions to literary problems, we should turn to this rather large body of material. Yet on matters of narrative composition the Near Eastern texts have been almost totally ignored. On the other hand, in contrast to some earlier surveys, no attempt will be made to reconstruct the mind of "Mesopotamian man," or the Egyptian view of history, because such a complete uniformity cannot be imposed on any culture, and certainly not on those of the Near East and ancient Greece. Only in attempting to understand the function or special character of a certain genre will it be necessary to discuss its use of the past.

Finally, we will take up the question of Israel's own historiography. The current status of the discussion will be reviewed in the light of the comparative survey and with a view to setting forth the various issues that need to be addressed. It will not be possible, however, to deal with all the historical prose of the Old Testament within the scope of this volume. Instead, the investigation will attempt to uncover the first Israelite historian—the one to inaugurate the historical tradition in Israel—and, by implication, the first in the intellectual tradition of the West.

CHAPTER TWO

EARLY GREEK
HISTORIOGRAPHY

a. THE RISE OF HISTORIOGRAPHY IN GREECE

It would appear to be self-evident and entirely natural for biblical scholars who treat the subject of the origins of history writing in ancient Israel to give some attention to the corresponding rise of history writing in Greece and to the work of Herodotus in particular. But this has not been the case, and the neglect of Greek historiography for any comparative study has been almost total, for at least two major reasons. First, it has been customary for a long time now to understand the rise of history writing in Israel as an inner Israelite development quite independent of Near Eastern influence and as something that anticipated the emergence of the Greek historians by five hundred years.[1] But the present study will seek to date the earliest Israelite histories in the sixth century B.C., not in the tenth, and will try to show that there is evidence of considerable foreign influence. Besides, it seems ironic that the exponents of the prevailing view have drawn upon Greek analogies of the sixth and fifth centuries without, however, making such a comparison explicit.

The second reason for resistance to any comparison with Greek historiography is that for many years Old Testament scholars fostered the conviction that Hebrew thought was to be contrasted with Greek, that the two ways of viewing reality were entirely different. And this difference was thought to be most acute in their respective understanding of time and history.[2] The supposed contrast between Hebrew and Greek thought has recently been thoroughly exposed as untenable, especially as it relates to the respective historians of these two peoples.[3] For instance, no cyclical view of time is evident in the Greek histories, whatever the philosophers might say, and there is no eschatology in the Israelite histories, whatever prophet

---

1. See below, chap. 7.
2. See T. Boman, *Hebrew Thought Compared with Greek*.
3. J. Barr, *Biblical Words for Time*; A. Momigliano, "Time in Ancient Historiography," in *Essays in Ancient and Modern Historiography*, pp. 161–204.

and apocalyptist might propose. The way is open, therefore, to undertake a preliminary comparison of the development of the two historical traditions.

Herodotus is the earliest Greek historian whose work has come down to us intact; he was recognized by later Greek historians themselves as the "father of history," a title that few would deny him today. Yet he was anticipated by a number of writers, and was a contemporary of still others, whose works are known to us only by name and by fragments that survived in the quotations of later authors.[4] These earlier writers are grouped together under the rubric of *logographers,* a term that is meant to suggest that they were something less than historians, that they were primarily storytellers whose subjects were drawn mostly from myths, legends, and anecdotes. During the height of the period of *Quellenstudien* in classical studies in the late nineteenth century, Herodotus was regarded as merely a collector and final redactor of materials gleaned from these older sources.[5] But the careful collection and publication of all the fragments of these early writers and their comparison with Herodotus have made this approach obsolete. Even the term *logographer* is seriously questioned as misleading.[6] It is generally accepted today that Herodotus did, in fact, investigate directly and gather firsthand the largest part of his work, and that he tested where possible the views he inherited from other writers. Above all, the way in which he employed new critical methods and set his "researches" down as a unified whole was what made him so superior to all his predecessors and contemporaries.

But this still does not answer these questions: who were Herodotus's predecessors and what was the nature of the influence they had upon him? Or, to put the questions in a somewhat different form: what were the factors and influences that gave rise to historiography in ancient Greece? For the development is by no means a straight line or a single impulse, and the product even beyond Herodotus remained quite diversified.[7] The first important factor was the transmission of the art of writing

4. These have been collected by F. Jacoby in *Die Fragmente der griechischen Historiker.* See also L. Pearson, *Early Ionian Historians.*

5. For brief surveys of earlier Herodotean studies see J. L. Myres, *Herodotus: Father of History,* pp. 17–31; C. W. Fornara, *Herodotus: An Interpretive Essay,* pp. 1–23; R. Drews, *The Greek Accounts of Eastern History,* pp. 36ff.

6. See the discussion of this term by K. von Fritz, *Die griechische Geschichtsschreibung,* vol. 1: *Anmerkungen,* pp. 337–47. He is particularly critical of the use of this term by Pearson (see above, n. 4).

7. My survey in what follows is heavily dependent upon the discussion by von Fritz, *Die griechische Geschichtsschreibung,* vol. 1: *Text,* pp. 23–522; idem, "Herodotus and the Growth of Greek Historiography," *TAPA* 67 (1936):315–40. See also F. Jacoby, "Greichische Geschichtsschreibung (1926)," in *Abhandlungen zur griechischen Geschichtsschreibung,* pp. 73–99; and C. G. Starr, *The Awakening of the Greek Historical Spirit.*

to the Greeks from the Phoenicians and the consequent growth of literacy from the late eighth to the sixth century B.C.[8] Besides short dedication inscriptions and the like, the first literature to be committed to writing was the epic poetry of Homer (the *Iliad* and the *Odyssey*), the poetic works of Hesiod (the *Theogony* and the *Works and Days*), and, following these, other closely related works in the heroic and mythological traditions set forth in epic verse. Such presentations of the tradition, particularly Homer's epics and Hesiod's *Theogony*, took on a canonical character for the Greek people as a whole and ordered their local traditions accordingly.[9]

On the other hand, a critical spirit developed that tried to free itself from the religious world view represented in the epic and to explain the cosmos in rationalistic and naturalistic terms. This was the so-called Ionic enlightenment centered in the Greek states of Asia Minor. Its products were philosophy, mathematics, astronomy, geography, and ultimately historiography. Two of the strongest impulses toward this new spirit were the opening up of these Greek states to the other cultures of the eastern Mediterranean with their own long traditions of learning and the voyages of maritime exploration throughout the Black Sea, the Mediterranean, the west coast of Africa and Europe, and the Indian Ocean. This was an altogether different world from that conveyed by the fantasy voyage of the *Odyssey*.

The impact of this new age of discovery can be seen on Anaximander. He developed a "scientific" counterpart to the mythical theogony in his cosmology in which life originated from the sea and man derived from a particular kind of fish. He also explained the rest of the cosmos, but for him the earth was the center of the universe. He was interested in geography and attempted to construct a map of the world, perhaps with the aid of a Babylonian model. The development of maps showing the divisions of lands, seas, and rivers in the spatial sphere suggested a corresponding treatment of the history of mankind in its various divisions in the temporal sphere. Now the method applied to cosmology and geography was the test of experience, and this critical principle gradually demythologized the study of the cosmos, the world of science, and eventually, human history.

Hecataeus was recognized in antiquity as a true disciple of Anaximander even though he was too young to have been his student.[10] His floruit was the last two decades of the sixth century. His major achievements were his

8. On this point see also J. Goody, *Literacy in Traditional Societies*, pp. 40ff.
9. On the significance of Homer and Hesiod in the Archaic period see Starr, *Awakening*, pp. 12–36.
10. On the fragments of Hecataeus see also Pearson, *Early Ionian Historians*, pp. 25–106.

attempts to fill in the details of geography and history of the families of nations according to the principles and outline of Anaximander. He prepared an improved map and a descriptive world geography, *Periēgēsis,* or *Periodos Gēs,* which included the ethnography of various peoples and places as well. Much of this work was based on travels to various lands in the region of the Black Sea, to the lands of the Eastern Mediterranean, and to Egypt. It emphasized the principle of investigation—*historiē*—as well as rationalistic deduction, such as the scheme of the continental division of Europe, Asia, and Africa, the attempt to impose simple geometric configurations upon regions and continents, and a rather primitive attempt to use a two-dimensional coordinate system for establishing the location of places.

The other major work of Hecataeus, the counterpart to his geography, was his *Geneēlogiai,* a rationalistic history of mankind. In it he attempted to relate to each other in a complex genealogical structure the great mass of place names and peoples from his geography, and to trace the relationship back in time in a great family tree to the heroic age. The extant fragments of this work are too sparse to permit us to know for certain just how much synchronistic connection Hecataeus developed among various *Stammbaumen,* but the way was certainly open for those who came later to continue to develop this schematization. The analogy between geography and "history," however, was not entirely complete. For the geography could operate with a fixed and absolute spacial schema—that of the circular map of the world which it inherited from the epic tradition. But Hecataeus could not establish in the same way an absolute temporal reckoning of the beginning of mankind as we find it in the mythical cosmogony and theogony because Anaximander had ruled out for him this way of thinking. So he limited his genealogical and chronological extension into the past to the heroic age. If one may judge from Herodotus's use of this basic scheme from Hecataeus, it would appear that the latter's ultimate point of departure was Heracles, three generations before the Trojan War.

Hecataeus included within his work on genealogies references to stories about heroes—hence the name *Hērōologia,* which later authors as well applied to the work. But, as he indicates in his proem, he wants to tell the truth about these stories, so he applies to them the rationalistic critique of what is believable from experience. The result was to present such stories as trivial and commonplace and to make the heroic age seem little different from the present historical period.

Among his predecessors who attempted to write history, Herodotus mentions directly only Hecataeus. Herodotus was strongly influenced by Hecataeus's work and tried to emulate its method of personal investigation into the geography and customs of foreign lands—*historiē*[11]—as well as to go beyond it in correcting what he viewed as its major deficiencies. For instance, Herodotus took exception to his adopting the traditional notion that the earth was a circular disc with water around the outer limits because no one had yet actually explored those limits and could say what lay beyond the known world. Herodotus's clear dependence upon Hecataeus has given rise to one of the primary approaches to understanding Herodotus in twentieth-century scholarship, which is to see him early in his career as a geographer and ethnographer in the tradition of Hecataeus; according to this view, only subsequently did he develop into a historian.[12] The major reason for this view is the long digression in book 2 on the geography and customs of Egypt and a parallel treatment in the first half of book 4 on the geography and customs of the regions inhabited by the Scythians. These two sections present theories of world geography and the views of Hecataeus and may be seen as the primary motivation for Herodotus's early travels. Herodotus used the discoveries of his travels to criticize Hecataeus for starting the *Geneēlogiai* with Heracles, since the genealogy of the Egyptian priesthood and the early history of its kings, along with the early dating for the temple of Heracles at Tyre, prove that history did not begin with Heracles. These questions have only a loose connection with the theme of Persian imperial expansion and the Persian wars with Greece.

But Herodotus's reaction to Hecataeus was not entirely negative. On the contrary, he was in agreement with much of his work, particularly his method of investigation, *historiē*. It was in the very nature of this method to scrutinize and correct previous views as well as to gather new information firsthand. Herodotus also seems to have taken over the general scheme of the genealogical chronology of Hecataeus back to the era of the Trojan War and to have combined it with the various national chronologies that he encountered—though he did not do this in a wholly systematic fashion.[13] Since Hecataeus rationalized heroic deeds, Herodotus gave very little place to such events of earlier times. He seems to replace the heroic marvels with the "historic" marvels of ancient Egypt, Babylon, and other foreign places.[14] Indeed, it is suggested that in the course of his geographic research and travels he became impressed with historical won-

11. For discussions of this term in Herodotus see Starr, *Awakening*, pp. 6–7, 111ff.; Lloyd, *Herodotus: Book II, Introduction*, pp. 81ff.

12. For the statement of this theory see von Fritz, "Herodotus and the Growth of Greek Historiography," *TAPA* 67 (1936): 315–40; idem, *Die griechische Geschichtsschreibung*, pp. 442–75.

13. On the development of genealogical chronologies see D. W. Prakken, *Studies in Greek Genealogical Chronology*.

14. On the frequent reference to *thōmata* in book 2 see Lloyd, *Herodotus*, pp. 141–47.

ders, and his interest shifted or broadened to include historical investigation as well. It is further argued that not until he took up residence in Athens did he fasten on the particular theme of the Persian Wars as an event of epic dimensions, one that was comparable to the Trojan War and could be used to bind all his researches together.[15]

It would be misleading, however, to suppose that there was only one line of development from Hecataeus to Herodotus and the rise of historiography, or that there were no approaches to the traditions of the past other than a rationalistic critique. Some of the primary concerns of prose writers in the sixth and fifth centuries were in the areas of mythology and genealogy and the interrelationship of these two. Hesiod in his *Theogony* had already set about to systematize Greek mythology by constructing a genealogy of the gods interspersed with mythological digressions, and the followers of this tradition sought to continue this schematization for the heroes as well.[16] These attempts were made not only in poetry, but by the mid sixth century they were also being put forward in prose. Such versions would deal, for instance, with the origins of man down to the time of the Trojan War, often with special emphasis on those deities or heroes associated with the paternal city-state of the author. Another type of *Genealogia* was the tracing of ancestors and family trees back from the time of the author to the heroic age. This was particularly important for aristocratic families and powerful clans. Pherecydes of Athens did this for the major families of that city. In his description of this type of genealogy F. Jacoby states:

> So far as we can judge genealogical works had a certain scheme or arrangement: they gave the pedigree, which is naturally dry because it consisted almost exclusively of proper names, and they interrupted this sequence of names by digressions, short remarks, and circumstantial tales; they consisted, one may say, of στέμματα and μῦθοι.[17]

It is possible that *in form* Hecataeus's *Geneēlogiai* was quite similar. Herodotus tells us that, being of an aristocratic family in Miletus, Hecataeus himself had a pedigree which he traced back to Heracles, but that he was disabused of the notion of family pedigrees by the great antiquity of the

---

15. In *The Greek Accounts of Eastern History*, pp. 20–44, Drews disputes that Herodotus was the first to develop the theme of the Persian Wars in a history. But the various books entitled *Persica* by Dionysius of Miletus, Hellanicus of Lesbos, and Charon of Lampsacus, which Drews argues were precursors of Herodotus, are either of uncertain content or dated by others such as Jacoby and von Fritz after Herodotus. See esp. the remarks by von Fritz, *GG, Text*, p. 103, and *Anm.*, p. 78.

16. On works in the Hesiodic tradition see M. L. West, *Hesiod: Theogony*; H. G. Evelyn-White, *Hesiod: The Homeric Hymns and Homerica*.

17. "The First Athenian Prose Writer," *Mnemosyne* III, 13 (1947):41.

Egyptians. In content, however, the two types were quite different: most of
the other genealogies retained the myths and legends in their miraculous
form without any sign of the rationalization that marks the work of
Hecataeus. And it is likely that Hecataeus used the form of genealogy to
structure in a new way the interrelationship of peoples and nations as well
as their dynasties.

The relationship of this sort of material to Herodotus and to Greek historiography in general is quite limited. One can see a certain resemblance
in form to Hesiod in the way in which Herodotus often departs from the
main account of a series of events to give an anecdote or longer digression.
Herodotus may also have used the genealogies as source materials for information about the leaders and important families of the Greek states.
But he was highly critical of their treatment of myth and the heroic age.

On the other hand, Hellanicus of Lesbos,[18] a near contemporary of Herodotus, did follow very much in the line of these early prose mythographers and genealogists, even though he was inclined to use some rationalistic criticism in the manner of Hecataeus. In this way he attempted
to make history out of the whole heroic age and to tie it to historical times
with a comprehensive genealogical-chronological system. In order to make
the system work he had to synchronize numerous mythological strands by
duplicating names and events, filling in blank spaces with stories invented
on the model of other accounts.[19] He attempted where possible to eliminate the miraculous by offering naturalistic explanations. He also had a
great love for finding the etymologies of the names of peoples and places
and for making eponymous heroes into *Stammväter* or founders of states.
In spite of such efforts to integrate the mythological and heroic tradition
with historiography, mythography retained a largely parallel existence to
historiography.

An aspect of Hellanicus's work that was much more important for the
development of historiography was his attempt to devise a comprehensive
chronology based on one chronological system to which all other systems
could be related. This he attempted to do with the chronology of the
priestesses of Hera, which he traced back to heroic times; he then "dated"
significant events in relation to them. He also tried to do the same thing
with the early kings and the later archon list of Athens. The system that ultimately won general acceptance was to date according to the Olympic
games.

Another near contemporary of Herodotus was Xanthus of Lydia, who

18. For discussions of Hellanicus see von Fritz, *GG, Text,* pp. 476–522; Pearson, *Early Ionian Historians,* pp. 152–235.
19. Cf. my treatment of the Isaac stories of Gen. 26 in *Abraham in History and Tradition,* pp. 175ff.

wrote a work on Lydian history.[20] This is clearly a much fuller account than Herodotus's, containing much more "history" for the older period, including the heroic age. But here again there is a tendency to rationalize stories, often with reference to geological observations. Interesting linguistic arguments are used in order to decide between different traditions of past events. It is also likely that Xanthus combined the royal chronicle of Sardis with anecdotes and traditions in order to produce his history. Of all these early mythographers and historians, apart from Hecataeus, Xanthus seems to stand closest to Herodotus in the way he combines sober history with anecdote. But which author came first is impossible to determine on the basis of such fragmentary evidence. Herodotus seems to suggest that he has access to much more material on Lydian history than he cares to use; this may be a reference to Xanthus. Although most scholars think there is no direct connection, at least one suggests that the work was meant to fill out Herodotus's brief treatment with a history that went from before the time of Gyges back to the heroic age.[21]

One other writer is worthy of some comment. Ion of Chios, who dates to the mid fifth century, was noted primarily for his tragedies, comedies, and other poetic works. He also wrote a local history dealing with the founding of Chios which consisted of an account from the island-state's mythical origins to historical times. Such local histories, of which there were perhaps many, were not chronicles but stories set down in a chronological sequence. Ion also wrote a work of anecdotes about political figures with whom he was acquainted, a remarkable instance of an early memoir.

This brief survey of prose writers of the sixth and fifth centuries B.C. is by no means complete since it excludes the most famous successor of Herodotus, namely, Thucydides, as well as a number of other writers who are little more than names.[22] My purpose has been to indicate in a general way the literary and intellectual milieu in which Herodotus did his own work. Some of the authors mentioned would seem to deserve a closer examination were it not for the fact that their preserved works are so fragmentary. Further attention must therefore be focused primarily upon Herodotus himself as both the product of this literary development and as a skillful author in his own right. In fact, a rather strong tendency exists in Herodotean studies to pay less attention to, or even discount, the efforts of *Entwicklungstheorien*, and to focus on the high literary quality of the *Histories* and the masterful unity that Herodotus has created out of the diver-

20. See von Fritz, *GG, Text,* pp. 97ff.; *Anm.,* pp. 348–77; Pearson, *Early Ionian Historians,* pp. 109–37.
21. Drews, *Eastern History,* pp. 100–03.
22. See von Fritz, *GG, Text,* pp. 96ff.

sity of his material. Yet these two approaches may be viewed as complementary, the one explicating the reasons for the diversity and variety in terms of past development both in the subject of history and in the author's own career, and the other concerning itself with the final extant product and its proper appreciation as a work of literature.[23]

The study of the historical books of the Old Testament has gone through a number of similar phases. In Herodotean studies the role of *Quellenstudien* has largely receded into the background and has been replaced by a more form-critical approach toward the variety of source material, both written and oral, that Herodotus might have utilized. Likewise, in Old Testament studies a documentary analysis for the prose works from Joshua to 2 Kings has little support, and even for the Pentateuch the documentary hypothesis (that the work is an edited combination of independent documents) is largely viewed as obsolete. Here too form criticism now plays a major role in the discussion of sources. It is used to account for the variety of genres and diversity of styles from one unit to the next, and the primary interest of form criticism has been in the oral forms of the traditions. At this point, however, Old Testament and classical studies seem to diverge and to have much less in common with each other. One could perhaps suggest a parallel between the developmental approach in classics and the traditio-historical method of Old Testament studies, but they are clearly not the same at all. Old Testament scholars have focused not on the development of authors but rather on the separate units of tradition, especially in their oral form, as if the traditions they contain had a life of their own.[24] The authors become even less important than they were in the heyday of the documentary hypothesis. The extant works of the Old Testament, it is suggested, are the result of an accumulative communal process in which the whole notion of an author may be dispensed with.

Such a conception of tradition-history applied to the development of Greek historiography, it seems to me, would make very little sense. We know this early historiography only in the works of numerous individual authors who shared some common genres but who were all quite different in their own way. They drew upon a large body of traditional material, some of it "fixed" in epic poetry—although they were not above changing it radically—and some of it consisting of an amorphous body of oral traditions of all kinds with no uniformity or coherence. The early prose writers were not transmitters of a fixed or single-stranded communal tradition.

23. See esp. the remarks by Fornara, *Herodotus*, pp. 1–23.
24. For an extensive review of the traditio-historical method see D. A. Knight, *Rediscovering the Traditions of Israel*; and see my earlier critique of this method in *Abraham in History and Tradition*, pp. 139ff.

They did their own systematizing for their own purposes and by means of their own externally constructed schemes, their favorite being the genealogy.[25] Their work does not manifest any obvious evolution in oral form from the simple to the complex that would enable us to distinguish the older, more primitive layers of tradition from the later, more advanced. An author could recount a simple etiological legend, a miraculous myth, a hero story, or a "modern" romantic novella, simply because he chose for his purpose to do so and not because they were already fixed in some communal tradition. He could have heard from separate sources all these types of stories in his own day. The same author could also invent new stories based on old ones in the same form and style. How is it possible to apply the traditio-historical method, used in Pentateuchal studies today, to this kind of literary phenomenon? The answer is not to dismiss the early Greek prose writers as irrelevant to biblical studies but rather to see if their forms and methods can provide a more controlled and more adequate explanation for early prose historiography in ancient Israel.

The analogue to Herodotus in the Old Testament would be the Deuteronomistic historian of Joshua to 2 Kings, seen not simply as a redactor of previously compiled blocks of material—the end of a long and complex traditio-historical process—but rather as a historian who gathered his own material, much of it in the form of disparate oral stories, but some from records and from the royal chronicles. The same approach would be entirely applicable to the Yahwist (J) of the Pentateuch as well. It would be consonant with form-critical analysis while at the same time rejecting the traditio-historical method as it is usually employed. It would also give new impetus to the literary appreciation of the prose authors in the Bible especially in the understanding of the structure and unity of their work.

We noted above the current emphasis upon the structure and unity of Herodotus's work. The trend in biblical studies is also toward a literary approach with the same disinterest in source analysis and theories of development and with a special emphasis upon "structure." But in Herodotean studies the new literary approach is not incompatible with the form-critical or the developmental approach, whereas in biblical studies all three are for the most part completely at odds.[26] This is because many of the literary analyses in biblical studies give little regard to the integrity of separate literary works, and the structuralism they employ is often imposed from

25. I am reminded here of the scheme suggested by M. Noth, *A History of Pentateuchal Traditions*, pp. 54ff., whereby the various traditions about the individual patriarchs were arranged secondarily into a genealogical scheme of three successive generations: Abraham, Isaac, and Jacob. Noth accounts for this development by a vague traditio-historical process. But is it not possible to view it as the work of a particular author, even the Yahwist?

26. I do not include in this criticism such structural analysis as that discussed in W. Richter, *Exegese als Literaturwissenschaft*, pp. 82ff., or in the work of N. Lohfink.

without, for example, using the methods of E. Leach and Claude Levi-Strauss.[27] In Herodotean studies an effort is made to elucidate the form and structure from within the work itself and as a quality of that particular author as distinct from others.

If the relevance of a comparative study of early Greek and Hebrew historiography may be accepted on the basis of this preliminary sketch, we may then consider a number of specific topics that would seem helpful for solving problems in Old Testament studies. I do not intend to give a comprehensive treatment of all the current issues in Herodotean studies or a detailed analysis of the *Histories*. What I hope to demonstrate is the possibility of using this method of comparative analysis as a control on the study of Old Testament prose narrative. Here the comparative data will not be anthropological or sociological materials, helpful as these may be for form critical analysis, but literary ones, using a body of literature closely related in time and space to that of the Hebrews but largely ignored.

b. THE RELATIONSHIP OF EPIC TO HISTORIOGRAPHY

One question that is closely related to the preceding discussion is the relationship of epic to historiography, both in ancient Greece and in the Old Testament. It has become rather common to hear American biblical scholars speak of an epic tradition lying behind the present form of the Pentateuch. This would make epic an important source for the development of historiography. The present prose narrative is viewed as heavily dependent upon an original epic in poetic form. An exponent of this position is D. N. Freedman, who writes:

> The precise character of G[28] can hardly be determined now; it was composed of older poetic materials, perhaps a sequence of patriarchal sagas, and a continuity dealing with the exodus-conquest cycle. Behind these are the individual stories, legends, etiological tales, cult narratives, the original data which formed the oldest traditions of Israel. G may have been a connected poem or series of poems orally transmitted and recited in whole or in part at the sacred festivals of

27. See R. C. Culley, "Structural Analysis: Is It Done with Mirrors?" *Interpretation* 28 (1974):165–81.

28. The notion of G (*Grundlage*) is taken over from M. Noth, *A History of Pentateuchal Traditions,* pp. 38ff., and represents the hypothetical basis for the earliest sources of the Pentateuch, J (Yahwist) and E (Elohist). Noth was uncertain whether it was oral or written and says nothing about the possibility of its being epic poetry.

"all Israel." Or it may have been a prose document derived from such an oral poetic collection. The former would seem more likely for the period of the judges. We conclude that G was a poetic composition, orally transmitted, relating the official story of Israel and its forebears. It is to be dated in the twelfth-eleventh centuries B.C. and finds its cultic locus in the amphictyonic festivals.[29]

One becomes puzzled, however, when a little further on the same author draws a contrast between Israelite and Greek epic.

[Like pagan myth][30] the pagan epic was a self-enclosed entity describing a distinct era of the past: the age of the heroes and their great deeds. But Israel, even with the "epic" tradition reflected in G, could not simply look back to the glorious past, but was concerned with the continuing actions of God. Even G may have been expanded and revised during the period of the amphictyony.[31]

This leaves virtually no point of similarity between epic and the Old Testament. Freedman has first explained away the difference between the poetic form of epic and the prose narrative of the Pentateuch by means of a hypothetical poetic G. He then offers a reason why the content of the Bible is fundamentally different. How then do we know that there ever was a Hebrew epic? It is by no means certain that all peoples had epic traditions.[32] Where is the evidence that points clearly to an epic tradition in Israel? No satisfactory evidence has ever been produced. An attempt made in the past to find a poetic form underlying the Pentateuch has been rejected as completely unconvincing.[33] The existence of a Hebrew epic tradition is based entirely upon the frequent repetition of such a notion by "authorities" such as W. F. Albright and F. M. Cross. The latter, in his book *Canaanite Myth and Hebrew Epic,* makes frequent reference to the "Epic sources" of the Pentateuch but gives no explanation for his use of the term *epic.* His short definition of "Epic sources" is similar to Freedman's.

29. *IDB* 3, p. 714.

30. Freedman emphasizes in the preceding paragraph the contrast between pagan mythical thinking and Hebraic historical thinking, a contrast we have already had reason to question.

31. *IDB* 3, p. 714.

32. See H. M. and N. K. Chadwick, *The Growth of Literature,* 3 vols., for an extensive collection of epic materials. For an earlier critique of the notion of a Hebrew epic see S. Talmon, "The 'Comparative Method' in Biblical Interpretation—Principles and Problems," *SVT* 29 (1977):352ff.

33. E. Sievers, *Metrische Studien,* vol. 2: *Hebräische Genesis* (1904–05). See Gunkel's rebuttal of Sievers in *Genesis*³ (1910), pp. xxviiff. Albright's statement (in the introduction to a new edition of H. Gunkel, *The Legends of Genesis* [1964], p. viii) that "Gunkel saw that the narratives of Genesis were a prose form of earlier poetic tradition" is quite incorrect.

We prefer to speak of J and E as variant forms in prose of an older, largely poetic Epic cycle of the era of the Judges. . . . No doubt the Epic cycle was originally composed orally and was utilized in the cult of covenant renewal festivals of the league, taking on variant forms at different sanctuaries and in different times.[34]

Both Cross and Freedman depend implicitly upon the position taken by their teacher, W. F. Albright, who outlined this scheme in his work *From the Stone Age to Christianity*. He states:

In many cases we can show that our present prose form of an orally transmitted document is the result of a secondary adaptation or abstract [from poetry]. This secondary prose stage is found in many Graeco-Roman logographers and historians who narrate Homeric or other saga; . . . it is clearly present in the prose version of certain biblical stories which also occur wholly or partly in poetic form (e.g., the Song of Deborah).[35]

The reference to the classical model is noteworthy because the same scheme was put forward in the nineteenth century by F. Creuzer, who also saw the "logographers" as a transition from the *Sagendichtung* of the epic cycle to prose history-writing.[36] This position has been sharply criticized by K. von Fritz, who has shown in his own work, as summarized above, that the relationship of early prose writers to the epic tradition was quite different from that suggested by Creuzer.[37] Von Fritz also disputes the use of the term *logographer*, invented by Creuzer and still in common use, as misleading because it suggests a uniformity that did not exist.[38] In antiquity the term *logographoi* simply meant prose writers as distinguished from poets; they could belong to almost any period, and the term could cover a broad range of prose genres. This leads us to attempt a brief outline of what the attitude or relationship of early prose writers was to Greek epic.

34. *Canaanite Myth and Hebrew Epic*, p. 293. See also pp. 67, 124n. The title of Cross's book suggests a distinction between the two literatures but he does not spell this out anywhere, and in fact he also uses the term epic for the Ugaritic myth-literature, including the Baal cycle. This seems to do away with the classical distinction between myth and epic.

35. *From the Stone Age to Christianity*, p. 35. See also the reference in n. 33 above and in *Yahweh and the Gods of Canaan*, chap. 1.

36. *Die historische Kunst der Griechen in ihrer Entstehung und Fortbildung*. Creuzer makes a parallel with Scandinavian epic (see pp. 265ff.) that is also picked up by Albright.

37. *GG, Anm.*, pp. 337–38. See also A. Momigliano, "Friedrich Creuzer and Greek Historiography," in *Studies in Historiography*, pp. 75–90 but especially pp. 79–90, for a discussion of this schema in Creuzer and its origins.

38. Von Fritz is particularly critical of the discussion on "logographers" by Pearson in *Early Ionian Historians*, chap. 1.

Because the term *epic* is vague and imprecise, an exact definition may be arbitrary. Let us begin, at least, with a dictionary definition: "an epic is a long, formal, narrative poem in elevated style, typically having as its subject heroic exploits and achievements or grandiose events."[39] The primary examples from Greek antiquity are Homer's *Iliad* and *Odyssey*. They have a rather limited time span and each focuses primarily upon the deeds of one great hero to which the others and their deeds are largely complementary. They manifest a distinctive poetic style and language.[40] Recent analysis of this style by Milman Parry and Albert Lord has made it appear likely that the Homeric epics depended heavily upon certain formulaic techniques and other devices used in the oral composition of the works.[41]

Hesiod's works also give evidence of the same elevated poetic style, but in other respects they constitute a problem for the understanding of epic. Although it is far from certain, it nevertheless appears quite probable that Hesiod was directly dependent upon Homer, and his poetic style along with a number of formulaic expressions are evidence of his dependence. In most other respects, such as subject matter, his works do not easily fit the category of epic. The *Theogony* is a divine genealogy used as an explanation of cosmology into which have been fitted various mythological episodes in the form of digressions. The *Works and Days* is largely a gnomic work that falls into the class of didactic wisdom literature. Even though it begins with two myths about the origins of evil, it can hardly be considered an epic. It is only because both poems employ the poetic form of Homer and the elaborate proem with its appeal to the Muses that they can be considered epics at all.

To judge by the standards of Near Eastern literature, the Homeric epic would correspond most closely to the Gilgamesh Epic[42] in terms of its time span and focus upon the exploits of one main hero. Hesiod's *Theogony*, on the other hand, comes closer to such mythological texts as the Enuma Elish and may in fact be heavily dependent upon such Near Eastern materials.[43] The fragmentary texts from Ugarit also contain epics about the heroes Keret and Aqhat as well as mythological texts dealing

39. *Funk & Wagnalls Standard College Dictionary*, 1966, s.v. "epic."
40. For several additional features see esp. H. M. and N. K. Chadwick, *The Growth of Literature*, vol. 1, pp. 64–95.
41. A. B. Lord, *The Singer of Tales*. See also W. Whallon, *Formula, Character, and Context: Studies in Homeric, Old English, and Old Testament Poetry*.
42. A. Heidel, *The Gilgamesh Epic and Old Testament Parallels*. See also *ANET*[3], pp. 72–99, 503–07.
43. For the Mesopotamian creation myths see *ANET*[3], pp. 60ff., 501ff. The term epic is used indiscriminately of both myths and epics in this work without explanation or definition. For comparisons of Hesiod with Near Eastern materials see P. Walcot, *Hesiod and the Near East*, pp. 27ff.; M. L. West, *Hesiod: Theogony*, pp. 1–3.

only with the deeds of the gods.[44] These mythological texts, however, do not appear to be theogonic, whatever their meaning might be.[45]

The earliest Greek prose writers used the Homeric epic, as well as the epic cycle and the myths and legends preserved in Hesiod and his followers, as a rich source of information for their many books. They continued the systematic collection and arrangement of the myths and legends, often as a background for nationalistic traditions, in order to establish heroic connections with royal dynasties and for genealogical "research" into the distant past. But they made no effort to reproduce epic works in prose. There are no prose versions of the *Iliad* or the *Odyssey* or of the works of Hesiod. Nor did the prose writers feel any need to stick very close to the "facts" as presented by Homer and Hesiod. They were often busy discovering new legendary events or inventing new connections between the heroes through genealogical constructions. At the same time, in the sixth century, the Ionic enlightenment encouraged a critical approach to these traditions that rationalized their miraculous elements and also corrected them by new information. Thus Herodotus argues, from supposedly Egyptian sources (2.112–20), that the ship of Paris and Helen strayed off course and came to Egypt. There it was learned that Helen had been abducted from her true husband, Menelaus. The king of Egypt, therefore, kept Helen in Egypt but sent Paris off without her to Troy. Thus, according to this account, the Greeks fought the Trojan War for nothing.

The degree to which the early historians made use of the epic tradition varies greatly. Herodotus gives very little attention to it, apart from some chronological allusions to the Trojan War and to the heroic founding of some dynasties and cities. However, his contemporary Hellanicus was especially well known for his use of mythological and legendary material. Two of his works, known only in fragmentary form, are most instructive: the *Phoronis* and the *Deucalioneia*. The former is named after Phoroneus, who was regarded as the "first man" and to whom the autochthonous population of Greece, for example, the Pelasgians, trace their origin. The remarks of L. Pearson on this work are most instructive.

The main thesis of the *Phoronis* undoubtedly was to show that the Greek families of mythical times originated in the Peloponnese. It evidently was intended to bring some of the chaos of Greek mythology

44. See *ANET*³, pp. 129–55. The Baal cycle is often lumped together with Keret and Aqhat as epic (cf. Albright, *Yahweh and the Gods of Canaan*, pp. 4ff.), but it would seem to me more helpful to keep them distinct.

45. Cross's interpretation of these myths as "cosmogonic" (*Canaanite Myth*, pp. 40, 120) is certainly debatable.

into order. Obviously this could not be done unless the writer used his own imagination, and invented his own solution of difficulties.[46]

The other work, the *Deucalioneia*, begins with Deucalion, who was the first to survive the deluge; the two works are thus complementary. Deucalion was the father of the three major Greek tribes—Dorian, Ionian, and Aeolian—but it appears that the focus of the work was entirely upon the last tribe, the Aeolians, to whom Hellanicus's native island of Lesbos belonged.[47]

We have, then, two tendencies in early Greek historiography. The first, represented by Herodotus, is to deal primarily with recent events while making only casual allusion to the distant past. The second, represented by Hellanicus, is to make a "history" out of myths and legends of the distant past and to bring them into some genealogical and chronological connection with present realities. This is not to dispute that in many other ways Herodotus was dependent upon the Homeric epics as models for his own work. For the very process of rationalizing the heroic age meant that the events of the distant past were regarded as no different in kind from those of recent times. Thus what Homer did for the Trojan War through epic poetry Herodotus did for the Persian Wars through the medium of prose narration.[48] The contrast between the heroic perspective and the new scientific age can also be seen in the subject of world geography. Through the travels and accounts of Hecataeus and Herodotus the strange places and customs of other peoples are made part of the known world instead of the fantasy lands of the *Odyssey*.

The middle ground between the heroic age of epic and the recent past of historiography was occupied by genealogies and eponyms. The Homeric epic shows little interest in genealogy and uses it only to identify the immediate ancestry of the heroes. It also shows no concern for eponyms. Hesiod employs genealogy in his *Theogony* as a way of ordering the gods and explaining their powers. But it was not until the prose writers Hecataeus and Pherecydes of Athens that the attempt was made to establish by means of genealogies a connection between the heroic age and various national dynasties or aristocratic families. At the same time there were increasing attempts to ascribe eponymous heroes to Eastern peoples and to bring their origins into a larger genealogical framework. As R. Drews states:

---

46. Pearson, *Early Ionian Historians,* p. 170.
47. Ibid., pp. 170ff.
48. See Starr, *Awakening,* pp. 12ff. This seems to me a more balanced view than the one presented by H. Strasburger, *Homer und die Geschichtsschreibung,* Sitzungsberichte der Heidelberger Akad. der Wissen., Phil.-hist. Kl. 1972, 1 Abh., pp. 5–44.

The Greeks invented eponymi and included them in the heroic genealogies because they wished to account for present realities. The etiologist started with an awareness of such realities as the Apis bull or the city of Nineveh and furnished for them an explanation based on probability. He sought no new information, but attempted to order and schematize the information which he already had.[49]

This kind of speculation led to the interconnection of the "histories" of many different peoples and the possibility of an elaborate interrelated chronological scheme based upon genealogical chronologies.[50] Such a scheme became a prerequisite for the wide-ranging history that Herodotus ultimately produced. But it is not the concern of epic; it is historiographic, and even though it is unhistorical in content it at least leads to the sense of a need for an absolute chronology and universal history, which is important for the development of historiography.

Prominent in Hesiod's *Theogony* are the etiological myths, and this is true also of the Enuma Elish, because the very nature of the cosmogony is to explain the origin of the gods and the world. By contrast, Homer's epics contain very little etiology. Yet popular folklore associated the origins of many things with the heroic age and this finds some reflection in later epic tradition. The *aitia*—"cause" or "explanation"—is most often understood in terms of the beginning, *archē*, so that "natural" causes would be sought in mythology, whereas "historical" causes having to do with man and society would more likely be associated with the heroic age.[51] For this reason some of the prose writers before Herodotus include so much mythological and legendary explanation in their histories. Herodotus, in his proem, lays great stress on his presentation of the causes (*aitiai*) of the Persian Wars. However, he dismisses rather briefly (1. 1–5) the whole matter of causes from the heroic age and raises the question of responsibility within the time and scope of the historical period itself. In fact, Herodotus's treatment of the causes is his most important organizing principle and the reason B. A. van Groningen characterizes his type of history writing as etiological.

This form of historiography establishes a hierarchy of facts; not the significance of the fact in itself determines the place in the order, but the value which it has as an aetiological, elucidating element. One

49. *The Greek Accounts of Eastern History*, p. 10.
50. See the work of Prakken, *Studies in Greek Genealogical Chronology*.
51. See esp. the remarks about etiology as it relates to history, philosophy (or science), and religion by B. A. van Groningen, *In the Grip of the Past*, pp. 25ff., 69ff., 88ff.

traces a line of development, by preference up to the last *aition,* the *arche,* and establishes what must be put on that line.[52]

Of course, alongside this sophisticated etiology Herodotus has many stories that reflect the popular brand of etiological folktales, especially as they have to do with social customs. Nevertheless, it is true that etiology is a necessary precursor to historiography in much the same way that cosmogony came before the cosmology of Ionian philosophy. Each new kind of explanation was different from that offered by mythology and legend. Yet we must be wary of positing a straight line of evolution from etiological folktale to historiography, since both popular and sophisticated types of etiology could exist side by side.[53]

Closely related to etiology are stories about inventors, *prōtoi heuretai,* "first finders." To quote again from van Groningen:

> Many of these inventions are ascribed to divine or heroic finders: musical instruments, agricultural implements, tools for men's and women's labour, games, sciences and arts. . . . Even when in the course of the fifth century certain theorists try to determine the origin of religion, they are convinced that mankind owes it to an inventor.[54]

This concern, which is evident in the works of Hesiod and the late "epic" tradition of the Homeric Hymns and similar works, also finds frequent mention in the historians, including Herodotus. However, the latter emphasizes the purely human and non-Greek inventions as a contrast and critique of the heroic tradition. While it is clear, therefore, that popular etiologies and stories of inventors were in vogue from the time of the earliest recorded Greek literature and retained their appeal for many centuries, they were not especially characteristic of epic poetry since they find no place in Homer. As such they are not a mark of epic's influence upon later historiography.

From the preceding it should be clear that the sources of Genesis resemble more closely the historiographic tradition of ancient Greece than its epic tradition. While the accounts of creation and the flood story do seem

52. Ibid., p. 30. Commenting on the cosmogonic myths of Hesiod, van Groningen makes a similar statement: "These myths also exhibit a marked aetiological tendency. This tendency is the same as appeared to be normal in historical and scientific literature. But the extreme form of aetiological thought is the form which goes back to the *arche,* that is to say, in genealogical terms to the primogenitor" (p. 88). There would appear to me to be no justification for a distinction between pure etiology, which is only mythical, and historical etiology as Childs has recently argued in "The Etiological Tale Re-examined," *VT* 24 (1974):387–97.

53. This is the fault I see in the approach of von Rad, in "The Beginnings of Historical Writing," pp. 166–204.

54. *In the Grip of the Past,* pp. 33–34. For a discussion of "first finders" in Greek literature see A. Kleingunther, *Protos Heuretes,* Philologus suppl. vol. XXVI/1, 1933.

to have their counterparts in Babylonian myth and epic, and to a lesser degree in Hesiod's *Theogony,* the treatment is hardly epic in character. The priestly version of creation in Gen. 1:1–2:4 has been compared to the demythologized cosmology of Ionic philosophy,[55] while the account of the origin of evil in Gen. 2–3 has some similarity to Hesiod's didactic story of Pandora in *Works and Days,* more in the wisdom tradition than in epic tradition.

But the real test is the attitude expressed by the Yahwist to the notion of a heroic age, an age remote from the historical period in which the heroes performed great deeds and were semidivine or exceptional in some way. The most obvious reference by the Yahwist to such an age is found in Gen. 6:1–4. It speaks of the "sons of God" being attracted to beautiful mortal women and producing offspring who were giants (*nepīlîm*), and warriors and men of great fame. All this points to a heroic age which, however, the Yahwist condemns as evil and the cause of the flood.[56] Here is a remarkable critique of the whole notion of a heroic age, an idea that was very likely foreign to the author. Its special juxtaposition with the deluge makes it a rather sophisticated etiology, as can be seen from the fact that in both Mesopotamian and Greek traditions the heroic age came *after* the flood and had no direct connection with it.

In the preceding section in the Yahwistic source, Gen. 4:17–26, there is a series of statements referring to the founding of a city and its naming, and to inventors or "first finders": the first nomad, the first musician, and the first metalworker.[57] All these inventions, however, are viewed nega-

55. G. von Rad, *Genesis,* p. 63.

56. The recent attempt by Paul D. Hanson ("Rebellion in Heaven, Azazel, and Euhemeristic Heroes in 1 Enoch 6–11," *JBL* 96 [1977]:210, 213ff.) to associate Gen. 6:1–4 with a "rebellion-in-heaven" motif derived ultimately from Hurrian and Ugaritic myths seems to me farfetched. Hanson is probably correct in seeing in Ezek. 32:27 a reflection of a past heroic age that may be related to Gen. 6:1–4 (see p. 210), but this also says nothing about a rebellion-in-heaven motif. What it does do is place the dead heroes with all the foreign nations that have also gone down to Sheol. In Greek tradition the heroes and the rebellious gods are quite separate from one another. See also R. Bartelmus, *Heroentum in Israel und seiner Umwelt,* AThANT 65 (1979).

57. Mesopotamia also had a tradition of first inventors of the arts and skills of civilization in the form of seven sages; see W. G. Lambert, "Ancestors, Authors, and Canonicity," *JCS* 11 (1957):1–14, 112; E. Reiner, "The Etiological Myth of the 'Seven Sages,'" *Orientalia* 30 (1961):1–11. Reference to these sages could occur in various kinds of texts, such as medical remedies said to derive from the sages. One reference in the Epic of Era speaks of the antediluvian sages being protected by Marduk from the flood in order to restore civilization to the world. Other texts speak of sages both before and after the flood, which is quite similar to the placement of the inventors in Genesis. However, the negative attitude toward them in Genesis is in contrast to the Mesopotamian sources. No provision is made for their preservation from the flood. A Phoenician version of cultural inventors is preserved in Philo Byblius within an elaborate genealogical framework of several generations. The strong possibility of a Hellenistic date for this work and the likelihood of Greek influence upon it make its similarity to both biblical and Greek traditions hard to evaluate. On the character and dating of

tively as the products of the sons of Lamech and the descendants of Cain. Even when Noah after the flood is identified as the first one to cultivate the grape, the discovery leads to his shame (9:20ff.). Only in the case of the offspring of Seth—Enosh—is there an exception since he was the first to "call upon the name of Yahweh," thus being the founder of religion. On the whole the sentiment expressed toward the founders of culture and civilization, with the exception of religion, is antiheroic.

It is possible to argue that the deluge constitutes a heroic theme, but in fact it belongs more to the realm of mythology and cosmology as a second beginning than it does to the heroic. Even though the theme occurs in the Gilgamesh Epic it is a digression and a flashback to the time of the beginning and is separated from the time of the hero by an unbridgeable gap. At any rate the treatment of Noah is entirely prosaic and passive. He does not utter a single word in the whole story, he has no emotional reaction or feelings. Only the event is recorded.

Furthermore, like the treatment of the deluge in Hellanicus,[58] we are introduced through the biblical flood story to the three sons of Noah—Ham, Shem, and Japheth—from whom all mankind is descended. The Table of Nations in Gen. 10 has a number of functions in the J account. One is the separation of the remote "heroic" age with its founding of the autochthonous nations from the later period of "history" proper, in which the younger peoples, including Israel, were established. The Yahwist's account does not attempt any genealogical or chronological continuity from one era to the other. It is only in the Priestly Writer (P) with his superimposed genealogical and chronological scheme that the chronology is continuous. However, what the Yahwist does attempt by means of the genealogical structure is to bring some systematization into the geography and ethnography of the world of the sixth century B.C. This combination of geography and ethnography on the one hand and genealogy on the other is evident, as we have seen in Hecataeus, whose tripartite division of humanity is also similar to J, although the latter's perspective is more eastern. Direct geographic statements are also rather limited as in the case of the Canaanites (10:19) and the sons of Joktan (10:30).

One anecdotal digression in 10:8–12 reflects notions of a heroic age. It deals with Nimrod, the first great warrior and hunter, a king of Babylonia and a founder of Assyria and its major cities. No more is made of this hero

---

Philo's "Phoenician History" see below, 6e. On the comparison of the Mesopotamian and Phoenician materials with Genesis see R. R. Wilson, *Genealogy and History in the Biblical World*, pp. 148ff. See also Hanson, *JBL* 96 (1977):227ff.

58. See Pearson, *Early Ionian Historians*, pp. 170ff. Deucalion, the Greek hero of the flood, is the grandfather of Dorus, Xuthus, and Aeolus, the three progenitors of the different Greek tribes.

who seems curiously out of place as a son of Cush (Ethiopia). But the system of relationship employed here is well known from the Greek writers of
the sixth and fifth centuries. A hero or eponymous ancestor departs from
one ancient civilization to found a new one elsewhere and then he in turn,
or his sons, establishes yet other kingdoms and cities.[59]

Thus the account suggests the priority of Cush and Egypt over
Babylonia and Assyria. It is quite unlikely that in this construction the
Yahwist is making use of a foreign epic tradition as a source of information. It is hardly a fragment of Israelite epic. The brief remark in 10:25 to
the effect that one of Eber's sons was called Peleg "for in his days the earth
was divided" may reflect speculation about the division of the world into
continents such as we find in Hecataeus and Herodotus. It should be noted
that both the anecdotal and the geographic digressions within the larger
structure of genealogy represent very well the form and manner of presentation in the various *Genealogiai* of the early Greek writers.

Following the Table of Nations in J is the story of the Tower of Babel.
As frequently noted, it presents a problem because it gives an etiology for
the origin of language that does not fit with the previous division of
mankind into language groups and regions according to the division of the
three sons of Noah. But the story has an important didactic and theological function as a prelude to the story of Abraham, which was intended to
follow it directly. So, in spite of its bad fit, it was appended as a useful
piece of lore. We are reminded, in this regard, of the two opening myths in
Hesiod's *Works and Days,* the Pandora myth and the myth of the five
ages; they do not fit together, but Hesiod uses them together because they
both deal with the common theme of the origin of evil. This method of
combining entirely different materials related to a common theme is certainly not the method and style of epic. It has some affinities with wisdom
literature, but it becomes the primary method of historiography, of which
Herodotus is the chief example.

One of the major contributions of the Priestly Writer to the primeval
history is the genealogical chronology, which he gives in two parts: Gen. 5
and 11:10ff. Now both of these genealogies are in some sense parallel to
those in J, in Gen. 4:17–26 and chap. 10 respectively, but their functions
are quite different. The notices in 4:17–26 tend to fill in the period from
creation to the flood in a rather general way, as do the remarks in 6:1–4;
but there is no strict chronology, with the result that one does not know
Noah's precise origin. The Table of Nations, chap. 10, also does not fur-

59. Cush gained its reputation from its domination of Egypt during the twenty-fifth dynasty in the eighth and seventh centuries B.C. The priority of Babylonia over Assyria probably
reflects the traditions of both its greater antiquity and its political domination in the sixth
century.

nish a chronology. It merely gives the relationship of the various peoples to each other in a segmented genealogy without indicating the length of time from the flood to Abraham; he comes "out of the blue." By contrast, the Priestly Writer provides the chronological links from Adam to Abraham by means of a *linear* genealogy, ascribing dates to each step in the fashion of a king list to arrive at a rather precise chronology. Now P indicates that his information comes from a "book of the generations of Adam," which reminds us of the many similar *Genealogiai* of Greece and the particular efforts in the late sixth and fifth centuries to fill in the space of time from the first man to historic times with genealogical chronologies. It appears to me that both the Yahwist and the Priestly Writer, or his source, represent two distinct phases of this historiographic development, comparable to the phases so evident in the Greek sources.[60]

After the prologue dealing with the wider history of mankind, the focus is narrowed to the forefathers of the nation of Israel. The contrast between the age of the patriarchs and the "heroic" age is sharply drawn. The earlier period was one of continuous curses upon mankind, peoples, and nations; with Abraham, God promises blessing to the "families of the earth." This is the strongest critique of the heroic age. It is entirely likely that the writer, J, was aware of such notions in other cultures—Babylonian, Phoenician, and even Greek—and found this way of repudiating them. Nor is there anything in the treatment of the patriarchs themselves that would suggest an epic. The wanderings are not adventures like those of the *Odyssey,* and the one battle account in Gen. 14 is a very late addition to the stories as a whole.[61] For the most part we have a genealogical succession in which the patriarchs' lives are filled out with folktales, etiological motifs, anecdotes, and novellas. There are stories dealing with the origins of neighboring peoples and some supplementary genealogical digressions. All this belongs to the stuff of the historiographic tradition.

The story of Moses is hardly any closer to a heroic model or an epic presentation. His rescue as a foundling is a folktale that could be used of a hero, but it could also be told of a historic person of recent history, as it was of Cyrus by Herodotus.[62] Moses' youthful attempt at delivering his people by force of arms is a failure, and he flees out of fear of the king's threat. When his call as a deliverer does come he tries very hard to excuse himself from the challenge. His contest with the king of Egypt is by the prophetic word and succeeds when the Israelites flee or are driven from the

60. Cf. the treatment of these genealogies in Wilson, *Genealogy and History,* pp. 138ff. His explanations of the differences are entirely anthropological.
61. See *Abraham in History and Tradition,* pp. 296–308.
62. See B. S. Childs, "The Birth of Moses," *JBL* 84 (1965): 109–22; D. B. Redford, "The Literary Motif of the Exposed Child," *Numen* 14 (1967):209–28.

land. The rebellions of the people in the wilderness and the other trials are hardly akin to the labors of Heracles. And the long digression on the laws hardly fits the epic pattern. Even the battles with Sihon and Og are treated as reports in a manner similar to Israel's own historiographic tradition in Samuel and Kings.

There seems to me no need to belabor the point further. The reason for proposing the scheme of an original poetic epic behind the sources of the Pentateuch is to argue for the great antiquity of its "history" through a long stage of oral tradition. But the scheme proposed by Albright on the supposed Greek model cannot be demonstrated either from the Greek sources or from the Old Testament. It is true that Homer's epics do represent the high point of a certain poetic style and by their popularity became preserved in writing, with the result that his treatment of a few short segments of the heroic age became virtually canonical.[63] But there were many other traditions about the heroes, in prose and in poetry, that did not enjoy that degree of fixity. Nor was the poetic style used in the epic restricted to heroic themes, as is clear from the works of Hesiod. It just happens that in the early phase of Greek literacy poetic works of art were deemed more worthy of being committed to writing than stories in prose. But when the medium of writing became more widely used for other subjects, the prose writers could set down their versions of early "history" as well. These were not epitomes of poetic versions, as we have seen. They were collections of mythological and legendary lore, critical or uncritical according to the viewpoint of the author and drawn from "canonical" and "uncanonical" versions. And from the time of Hecataeus, at least, there was the urge to collect foreign traditions and to use them as a means of criticizing or correcting the stories of the Greeks.

The scheme does not apply to Mesopotamia, Egypt, or Phoenicia-Canaan. No prose versions of their epics and mythology existed until the time of Berossus, Manetho, and Sanchuniathon, all historians of the Hellenistic period, and even then only a small part of their work was devoted to epic. In Mesopotamia, as in Greece, the poetic epics themselves survived through constant recopying, with no known prose version preserved. Yet we are asked to believe that in ancient Israel the opposite was the case—that only the abbreviated prose versions survived and not the original epics.

There seems to me no justification for the notion of an evolution from a Hebrew epic tradition to prose "history" in the Pentateuch. To the extent that the J source is similar to the early Greek historiographic tradition, it would argue against any such conclusion. And this similarity is consider-

---

63. See esp. the treatment of Cedric H. Whitman, *Homer and the Homeric Tradition.*

able. There is first of all the common subject matter: the first man, the flood story and the divisions of the peoples, the first inventors and the lives of the eponymous ancestors. Both early Greek and Israelite historiography employ the techniques of relating peoples and tribes by the use of seg- mented genealogies and of connecting the distant past with more recent times and historic peoples by means of genealogical succession. In both traditions etiology is used extensively as an important historiographic prin- ciple. Like the early Greek historiographers, the Yahwist is a collector of very diverse and even contradictory materials and information. But his skill as an author is, above all, in the organization and thematic struc- turing of these materials into a whole, and in this he seems worthy of com- parison with Herodotus.

c. UNITY IN HERODOTUS AND THE OLD TESTAMENT

In our survey of the rise of historiography in ancient Greece we touched upon the question of Herodotus's own development from geographer to historian. The evidence for such a development is the marked difference in subject matter and manner of presentation in different parts of the work. But the danger of this genetic approach is to focus upon evidence of dis- unity or lack of homogeneity of style and substance at the expense of the work's overall unity.[64] In fact, the evidence for disunity may derive from using false criteria to judge the work's unity. We will therefore give some attention to the nature of unity in Herodotus's work. We do so also be- cause the same tension between a developmental approach and a unitary approach exists in the study of Old Testament prose narrative.

There are two aspects to the problem of unity:[65] one has to do with dis- covering the common theme or subject of the work, the other deals with the structural character and the literary techniques by which the material, collected by Herodotus for his subject, becomes a unified whole. For the sake of analysis it seems best to consider these two aspects separately, al- though they are so closely related that they cannot be kept entirely apart.

The subject or theme of the *Histories* is still a matter of some debate. The point of departure is usually the opening statement of the proem, which is understood as Herodotus's own announced intention for his work.

64. See the remarks of H. Immerwahr, *Form and Thought in Herodotus*, pp. 8–9.
65. Our discussion of unity in Herodotus is heavily dependent upon the work of Immer- wahr cited in the note above. See also J. L. Myres, *Herodotus: Father of History*; H. Wood, *The Histories of Herodotus: An Analysis of the Formal Structure*.

Here are set forth the researches [*historiē*] of Herodotus of Halicarnassus that men's actions may not in time be forgotten nor things
great and wonderful, accomplished whether by Greeks or barbarians,
go without report, nor especially the cause [*aitiē*] of the wars between
one and the other.[66]

This statement may be interpreted in a developmental sense to represent
the loose integration of various aspects of Herodotus's interests into one
work. The term *historiē* ("researches"), from which the present somewhat
erroneous title *Histories* derives, occurs in other introductory statements in
book 2, the Egyptian *logos*. The term suggests particularly that type of research requiring investigation and observation, such as was undertaken in
learning the geography and customs of Egypt. This form of investigation
was adopted from Hecataeus's work on geography, the *Periēgēsis*. Herodotus attempts to legitimize his claim to firsthand information and thus to
establish his right to criticize the views of his predecessors. His use of the
term *historiē* in the opening statement of his work extended its meaning to
include the subject of past deeds as well as investigations on nature and
ethnography. Just how Herodotus thought he was expanding *historiē* to
include traditions of the past is not clear, but it is usually understood that
he felt he was collecting firsthand information based primarily on oral tradition rather than reproducing the work of other prose writers.

Herodotus states that the purpose of his investigation is to report for
posterity the great and wonderful deeds of Greeks and barbarians. The
proper limits of his work he quickly defines as beginning with Croesus, ca.
560 B.C., and he explicitly excludes the heroic age, the usual subject of the
great and wonderful deeds of the Greeks celebrated in epic. On the other
hand, in book 2 Herodotus speaks frequently of the great and wondrous
things in the land of Egypt. These include not only the deeds of man, such
as the construction of the Labyrinth and the digging of Lake Moeris, but
also the unusual customs of the people and the unusual features of nature,
such as the Nile. In size and strangeness there was nothing comparable in
Greece. Herodotus also reports in a similar way about other foreign places
and people, such as Babylon and the Scythians. Yet the great and wonderful deeds of Greeks and barbarians mentioned in the proem must refer not
to these marvels primarily but particularly to the events leading up to and
including the Persian Wars.

This shift in subject matter is made complete by the concluding remarks
of Herodotus's opening statement, in which he says that he will deal especially with the *cause* of the war. He then dismisses any serious discussion
about causes in the heroic age and puts the blame upon Croesus for start-

66. 1.1. This translation is by H. Carter, *The Histories of Herodotus* (2 vols.), vol. 1, p. 1.

ing the hostility between East and West. This shift of subject marks a shift in the nature of the proem as well, from one that seeks to justify the author's qualifications, as in book 2, to one that introduces a series of events in an emphatic way (see 7.20–21).

The opening proem, which presents Herodotus's intention in the final form of the work, does seem to indicate a shift from his intention in individual units (especially as illustrated by book 2) and so to give evidence of the genetic approach. All the various subjects of the work are not included within this statement and some are even in conflict with it. But it is also possible to place too much weight upon the proem to yield the subject for the whole work. It should perhaps be viewed more as a simple justification for writing and as an invitation to his audience to enjoy the stories he has to tell as well as to think with him about some profound human issues —the causes of the great war. The actual subject must be derived from an analysis of the work itself—the way in which all the various units are put together, its structure and plan. Here we must distinguish between the main line of narrative and the numerous digressions, which are, for the most part, clearly marked off from it. Based on such an analysis, H. Immerwahr defines the subject as "the unification of Asia [by the Persians], the attempted extension of empire beyond the borders of the continent, and the failure of this attempt."[67] The period of history covered by this subject begins with Croesus, who first subjugated the Greeks of Ionia. His realm of western Asia was conquered by Cyrus, who thereby also inherited the whole future conflict with the Greeks. It ended when the Greeks checked the Persian expansion in Europe and began the liberation of the Ionian Greeks from Persian rule. This main theme, developed primarily in chronological sequence, allows Herodotus to attach a great many smaller or larger blocks of material in the nature of digressions to fixed points in the Persian chronology at the point when Persia came into contact with, or defeated another nation. Thus the Egyptian *logos* comes at the time of Cambyses' campaign against Egypt, the Scythian *logos* when Darius invades Scythia, etc. Many of the digressions deal with the geography, ethnography, and past history of the nation under consideration, but they may be short anecdotes attached to various names and places as they appear in the course of the larger narrative.

If the general theme and plan of the work as described above seem fairly clear, the actual order of some of the *logoi* and the reason for including still others are not entirely explained by this scheme alone. This is so because Herodotus has another level of thematic concern, above that of tracing the mere course of events, which is reflected in the term *aitiai*,

67. Immerwahr, *Form and Thought*, p. 42.

"causes."[68] This term is used not so much in a temporal or logical sense of one thing leading to another but in a human sense of those responsible. One type of human cause may be "unjust acts," for example, those committed by Croesus, "the first to inflict injustice against the Greeks." Closely related to this is the idea of retribution, *tisis,* which is attributed to the gods. Another parallel notion is that of *hubris,* the pride of men in their accomplishments and the envy of the gods, which inflicts misfortune on them.[69] This principle is spelled out in the speech of Solon to Croesus in 1.32 and is illustrated in the tragic death of Croesus's son. The causes in history for Herodotus, then, are injustice and retribution along with *hubris* and the divine humbling.

Herodotus has a great interest in custom or law (*nomos*) and its practice by various peoples.[70] This grows out of his interest in ethnography and the comparison of Greek and foreign customs. But custom also has a role in affecting the course of events, for a people's way of life determines to some extent their ability to withstand conquest. Even the Persian drive for expansion that leads to the fateful confrontation with the Greeks is described as their *nomos,* so that the subject of customs is integrated into the main theme of the work. Furthermore, since the gods recognize *nomoi,* their intervention in human affairs is also related to them.

Herodotus has a notion of world order that includes the realm of nature as well as the realm of history.[71] The natural order can therefore provide analogues for understanding the affairs of men. In this world order there is a balance between the continents of Asia and Europe, as is illustrated by the discussion of world geography. The Persian Wars may thus be understood as a violation of this balance, which is then set right by the gods. Such divine intervention is suggested in the account of the battle of Artemisium in which the gods intervene with a storm at sea to destroy a large part of the Persian fleet, thus making the forces more nearly equal (8.12).

This brief description of the inner themes does not exhaust the complexity of the implied connections among them and among numerous other subthemes, such as the issue of freedom within the Greek states as opposed to slavery under foreign despotism, the main issue in the struggle between East and West.[72] It was precisely this kind of thematic interest in interpreting historical events that led Herodotus to arrange his work in the way he did and to find connections between events that are not obvious. For

68. On this term see Myres, *Herodotus,* pp. 55ff.
69. For discussion of the terms *tisis* and *hubris* see Myres, *Herodotus,* pp. 49–50, 53; Wood, *Histories,* pp. 15, 24ff., et passim; Immerwahr, *Form and Thought,* s.v. "Hybris" and "Vengeance motif" in the index.
70. Immerwahr, *Form and Thought,* pp. 319–22.
71. Ibid., pp. 15, 102–03, 315; Wood, *Histories,* p. 18.
72. On the theme of "freedom" see Fornara, *Herodotus,* pp. 48–51.

this reason too he included "illustrative" material that did not force all his investigations to fit some precise philosophy of history. The association of his subject matter with a particular theme may be rather loose and somewhat artificial. The material, collected in the course of his lifetime, came first; the effort to give it sense and meaning was the work of his final revision.

The diversity of subject matter in Herodotus is also held together by external literary structures. Immerwahr describes the character of the *Histories* in the following way:

> On the simplest level, Herodotus' work is a prime example of archaic parataxis, by which short individual items are placed in a row to build up larger compositions. In this manner, individual accounts, or parts thereof, are combined in Herodotus into larger pictures, like the pebbles in a mosaic.[73]

Immerwahr uses the term *logos* both for the smaller units and for the larger compositions. He further states:

> In outlining the units of the work we must free ourselves from the notion of subordination, for Herodotus' *logoi* are of every conceivable length; they are in turn composed of other *logoi,* and there is no specific hierarchy of major and minor units. A *logos* is thus basically a series of items, which are themselves smaller *logoi,* held together by certain formal elements signifying in turn a selection (but never the totality) of unifying themes, besides which other elements are left intact.[74]

These chains of *logoi* are bound together by putting them within "framing sentences," that is, an introductory statement at the beginning of the *logos* and a summary statement at the end, thus giving the limits of each unit.[75] This device is also called "ring composition,"[76] a literary technique taken over and adapted from epic style, although the statements at the beginning and end need not be verbally identical in prose. These framing constructions may be of two types, one in which the "ring" refers to the unit within it and the other in which it refers to the main story line broken by a unit, in which case the "ring" or repetition is a way of returning to the previous point in the narrative that was interrupted by a digression. So Immerwahr states: "It is by a simple system of external repeti-

73. Immerwahr, *Form and Thought,* p. 7.
74. Ibid., p. 15.
75. Ibid., p. 12.
76. Ibid., pp. 54ff. See also Wood, *Histories,* pp. 15ff.

tion between semiautonomous parts of his narrative . . . that Herodotus
has created a large unified work."[77]

The particular order of the various *logoi* in the paratactic chain is governed by thematic considerations. The subject of Persian expansion suggested the chronological order, based no doubt upon Persian royal chronicles.[78] For the *logoi* on Lydian history and the Saite period of Egypt,
similar chronicles must also have been utilized since major political events
and the lengths of the reigns of the kings of these nations are fairly clearly
presented. Where such chronicles were deficient for early history, Herodotus inherited a system of genealogical chronology that reckoned forty
years to a generation. In his own independent calculations Herodotus
counted three generations to a century, and it seems evident that there is a
mixture of both systems in his work. He also established a fixed date for
the battle of Salamis by linking the archonship of Calliades of Athens, during which the battle occurred, to Persian chronology (8.51). But Herodotus did not take advantage of this fixed point to establish an elaborate
synchronism of events. He cites only a few such connections (see 3.39;
4.145) and often prefers a rather vague formula, "after this," which has no
real temporal significance.

Chronology is not the only or even the most important organizational
principle, and often certain episodes are described out of turn. For example, the whole Lydian *logos* is presented before the account of Cyrus's rise
to power. This is because the Lydian *logos* serves as a model and analogy
for the conflict between East and West as a whole, and the principle of
analogy is more important than that of chronology. As H. Wood states,
"Analogy is Herodotus' first principle of order in arrangement of material."[79] Such a principle can often lead to an understanding of the thematic relationship between digressions and the main course of the narrative as well as between two *logoi* within the larger unit. Analogy may be
indicated by the balancing of units opposite each other or by the repetition
of the same words in two different and widely separated contexts. The external structural device complements the internal thematic one.

When we consider the narrative style of the individual *logoi*, we are impressed by the number of different patterns that occur.[80] The units are
still built upon the paratactic mode of presentation, as in the larger works,
but their structure varies greatly. The ethnographic *logoi* follow a fairly
definite scheme of presentation that may have been inherited from Heca-

77. Immerwahr, *Form and Thought*, p. 59.
78. On the use of chronicles in Herodotus see ibid., pp. 26ff., esp. n. 34. The pattern is
similar to that used in the biblical tradition.
79. Wood, *Histories*, p. 17.
80. Immerwahr, *Form and Thought*, pp. 67–72.

taeus. The historical sections of national histories, including the basic form of the campaign reports, very likely derive from the chronicles. The account of a battle, however, is specifically dramatized by using the model of "circular composition" derived from epic. This pattern creates a balance around a central point in which "the preceding and following sections correspond to each other in inverse sequence." There is also the dramatic *logos*, which has been strongly influenced by Attic tragedy, for example, in the story of Croesus. We could also include here the large variety of folktale types, anecdotes, and other stories.

Besides these narrative patterns, certain thought patterns help to create a sense of unity.[81] This can be seen in the use of speeches of all kinds. There is, for instance, a strong tendency to couple thought and action in the form of counsel, or advice, and action. A negative parallel might be passion and action, implying thoughtless action. Very similar to the pattern of advice and action is that of warning by oracles, dreams, or even a wise counselor. In most cases these warnings are not heeded or are misunderstood, and the consequences are always disastrous. Such devices are also found in epic and drama, and their utilization by Herodotus is quite deliberate.[82] It is most often in the speeches that the thematic elements come to the fore. Advice and execution or prophecy and fulfillment can also forge a connection that cuts across several minor units.

How is this discussion of unity in Herodotus relevant for the Old Testament? Let us first consider the question of narrative structure as an aspect of unity. It is not difficult to see that biblical prose also has a strongly paratactic style. Scholars have long noted that so much of the Bible's prose narrative is made up of larger or smaller units strung together in a loosely connected chain with little subordination of major and minor items.[83] However, the point at issue is the significance of this style and the nature of the connectives between the units—how the smaller *logoi* are combined to form larger ones and how these in turn form the literary works. Many scholars insist that these combinations could have resulted only from a multistage traditio-historical process, but the parallel phenomena in Herodotus are strong evidence to the contrary. The Greek examples show that any early Greek prose writer using the conventions of his day would have composed his work in a paratactic fashion with varying degrees of unity. Why should early Hebrew prose have been any different? Parataxis does not need to be explained by the traditio-historical method. Furthermore, we have seen in Herodotus that parataxis often links units that are quite

81. Ibid., pp. 72ff.; van Groningen, *In the Grip of the Past*, p. 41.
82. For a full treatment see R. Lattimore, "The Wise Adviser in Herodotus," *Class. Phil.* 34 (1939):24–35.
83. See the "classic" statement by Gunkel, *Genesis*, pp. xxxiff.; *Legends*, pp. 42ff.

different in genre and style, in size and complexity of structure, and in refinement of presentation. This may say more about the author's sources than about the author himself. But it does *not* suggest that the tradition grew in stages, with the simplest forms being the oldest and the most complex the most recent.[84] All the genres in Herodotus were available for his use at virtually the same time, and the form of the unit says nothing about the age of the content.

The connectives between individual units in the Old Testament are often described as "redactional," but this, it seems to me, is a belittling term meant to deny the qualities of authorship to the biblical writers. To describe Herodotus as merely a redactor of received traditions for employing the same techniques would be ridiculous today, although such an opinion was not unheard of in the nineteenth century.[85] It seems to me just as wrong to use the term for the historians of the Old Testament. Even more questionable is the proliferation of redactors whenever a variation in such connectives is evident. A full treatment of all the connective techniques used in the Old Testament must await detailed analysis, but at least some of those used in common with Herodotus may be pointed out here. The use of framing sentences, or "ring composition," has previously been noted by scholars, although it is not as extensive in the Old Testament as it is in Herodotus.[86] Prolepsis is also a feature of both Greek and Hebrew prose.[87] The use of royal chronologies, genealogies, or genealogical chronologies as a way of ordering separate story units is common in early Greek prose in general and Herodotus in particular, and it is also basic to biblical prose. Kings uses a framework explicitly drawn from royal chronicles even though most of the material in Kings is not derived from such a source. For the early history the Yahwist simply uses a genealogy, while in the absence of a chronicle the Deuteronomist uses a succession of generations of forty years' length for the period of the Judges and early monarchy. The Priestly Writer constructs an elaborate genealogical chronology for the period from creation to the time of the Exodus with a system of periodization of antediluvian, postdiluvian, and post-Mosaic ages. The Chronicler combines the genealogy of the early period with the royal chronology of the later period, deriving his system from the earlier biblical

84. Gunkel's fundamental mistake in the works cited above has led subsequent scholars astray. See the discussion by J. A. Wilcoxen, "Narrative," in *Old Testament Form Criticism,* pp. 62ff.

85. See Myres, *Herodotus,* p. 21.

86. See S. Talmon, "The Textual Study of the Bible—A New Outlook," in *Qumran and the History of the Biblical Text,* ed. F. M. Cross and S. Talmon, pp. 363–64. See earlier, C. Kuhl, "Die 'Wiederaufnahme'—ein literarkritisches Prinzip?" *ZAW* 64 (1952): 1–11. The principle has gone by various names, such as "resumptive repetition," "inclusio," etc.

87. Wood, *Histories,* p. 14.

sources. The books of Kings also construct synchronisms between the two kingdoms of Judah and Israel, but only at the points where their reigns begin. An absolute synchronism with a foreign realm, that of Babylon, is given only with the fall of Jerusalem in 598/7 and 587/6 B.C. (2 Kings 24:12; 25:8; see also 25:27).

In order to drive home his basic themes, Herodotus repeats similar events and episodes; these are associated with one another by analogy rather than arranged in logical or temporal sequence. The biblical authors prefer to place similar episodes in a series with interpretive introductions and summary statements, as in Judges and Kings. The result is a much tighter connection within the series but a much looser connection between the series. Yet analogies and comparisons from one block of material to another are sometimes achieved, as in Herodotus, by repeating similar phrases and formulae (e.g., Exod. 1:6–8 and Judg. 2:8–10). Since analogy is a more subtle form of unity than logical or temporal connection, there may be more examples than have hitherto been recognized. At any rate, the use of repetition as a deliberate connective technique must receive more attention in biblical studies.

The thought patterns in Herodotus, described above, are also strongly reminiscent of the Old Testament. Thought and action, word and deed, prophecy and fulfillment, and similar thought patterns abound in the Old Testament and are very important as connectives both within units and between widely separated units. Such patterns and their function as literary techniques within a larger work could certainly be more fully explored. The exact repetition of such patterns or other connective devices is rare in Herodotus, and variation in fact seems to be deliberate. The tendency of some biblical scholars, therefore, to see in any variation of a formula or pattern a distinct stage in the traditio-historical or redactional process seems ill advised and unfounded.

On the basis of narrative style and technique alone the Old Testament and Herodotus share a great deal in common and ought to be studied together. The Old Testament ought also to be compared with Herodotus on the basis of thematic unity. It is of course obvious that they do not deal with the same general subject or period of history; but on the level of interpretive themes—how the events of history are to be understood—some similarities do exist. Like Herodotus, the Old Testament exhibits a dominant concern with the issue of divine retribution for unlawful acts as a fundamental principle of historical causality. Human responsibility and divine justice are frequently stated themes. The law, as the divinely mediated rule for Israel itself, has a decisive role in the explication of what is just and unjust, so that foreign nations are thereby assumed to be in the wrong. It is true that the understanding of *tôrāh* (law) in the Old Testament is different from that of *nomos* in Herodotus. But what is significant is that historiography, whether in its various forms in the Old Testament or in Herodotus, deals extensively with law as an important element in understanding the actions of men and nations and the consequences of those actions. For both, history is theodicy. While the so-called Deuteronomistic historian and the Chronicler are concerned with this issue only on the national level, and so are more restrictive in scope than Herodotus, the Yahwist and the Priestly Writer do indicate the universal dimensions of the problem.

Although Herodotus has other themes in common with one or more historians of the Old Testament, there are many others that are quite distinctive in both bodies of literature. We must beware of making the theme too simple and then judging the unity of the work on the basis of it, or of inventing genetic explanations for its complexity. In both Herodotus and the Old Testament we must deal with an interpretive cluster of themes that are applied piecemeal to the events and traditions as they seem appropriate. The theme is presented in the same paratactic fashion as the narrative units themselves and is never systematized in "periodic" fashion. Only when the full story is told has the message been given. In this respect there is one other interesting similarity between Herodotus and the Old Testament, especially the Book of Kings. Scholars have noted the abrupt ending and the complete lack of anything like an epilogue in both. But this is precisely because both are composed by means of the same paratactic style in which the message is complete with the telling of the story.[88]

d. THE PROBLEM OF SOURCES IN HERODOTUS
AND THE OLD TESTAMENT

The source problem in Herodotus has a special relevance for the discussion of historiography in the Old Testament. What may be broadly defined as historiographical material from the rest of the ancient Near East is based either upon direct contemporary information or indirectly upon a very limited number of sources, or it consists of an indefinite perpetuation of the same genre. Thus royal annals utilize campaign reports and building records, as well as other annals; king lists recopy and extend older lists with every new accession to the throne; omen texts add new observations to the stock of previous collections, etc.[89] But Herodotus and the Old Testament histories share the quite different characteristic of being based upon a variety of sources, both written and oral, using several different genres in each category. Students of the source problem in the Old Testa-

88. Immerwahr, *Form and Thought*, pp. 8–9.
89. All these genres will be discussed in subsequent chapters.

ment have focused too narrowly upon the origin of the individual unit, its genre and *Sitz im Leben,* as if each unit had a certain life of its own prior to, and independent of, the author-historian. Its form and content and even the arrangement into larger combinations is regarded as fixed by tradition, so that the role of the historian as author is viewed as minimal. Not so with Herodotus. The discussion of sources in Herodotus must deal seriously with the questions of what sources Herodotus had available to him from the past—his relationship to tradition, both Greek and foreign—and what freedom he exercised in the use of these sources or in the invention of his own material. Such questions, when applied to biblical authors, raise a new perspective with a new range of possibilities for the biblical histories.

Now it would be very convenient for the biblical scholar if there were a uniformity of opinion among classicists concerning the nature of Herodotus's sources, but there is not. Yet this is no reason to dismiss a consideration of the subject because the issues involved have a direct bearing upon the same problems in biblical studies. I will here try briefly to indicate the major areas of discussion and the range of opinion in the debate over Herodotus's sources.

The *Quellenstudien* of the nineteenth century had as a primary objective the investigation of literary sources behind Herodotus.[90] These were regarded as belonging to the so-called logographers who were Herodotus's predecessors, while Herodotus was viewed as merely a compiler and redactor of these sources. As noted earlier, the systematic publication of the fragments of the early prose writers made such a general scheme about written sources quite unlikely. At the same time that the study of possible written sources was being carried out, other scholars were investigating the character of the smaller units. The application of folkloristic studies to Herodotus by W. Aly and others (much like Gunkel in Genesis) led to a recognition of the oral character of much of the material.[91] Yet Herodotus the author remained the vital means of connection between the individual units (as was not the case in the form-critical approach to the Old Testament), and, as we have seen above, his creative role in fashioning the whole has come more and more to the fore.

Since a broad spectrum of opinion on the question of Herodotus's sources is represented by the brief discussion of von Fritz, I will begin by outlining his views.[92] The use of literary *Vorlagen* by Herodotus has now been reduced to a rather small amount. Book 2 contains evidence of rather close copying of certain passages directly from Hecataeus, and Herodotus appears to have gleaned a certain amount of general information from him

90. See Myres, *Herodotus,* pp. 21–22.
91. W. Aly, *Volksmärchen, Sage und Novelle bei Herodot und seinen Zeitgenossen.*
92. *GG, Text,* pp. 407ff.

as well. But there are also explicit statements in which Herodotus takes issue with his predecessor, based, as he says, upon his own researches. It is likely that Herodotus used the poet Aristeas, directly or indirectly, for information about northern Europe. Whether Herodotus used passages directly from any other writers on the specific subjects he treats is difficult to say. At present this possibility is not supported by the extant fragments of other prose writers. It is likely that Herodotus did borrow some information from the dramatists who dealt with the theme of the Persian Wars, especially Aeschylus, and from some of the lyric poets as well.[93] He quotes a short saying from Pindar and a passage from the *Iliad* but in general takes issue with Homer's treatment of the Trojan War and his and Hesiod's presentation of the gods.

Indirect evidence for literary dependence also exists in a number of units not likely to derive from oral tradition. This is true of the geographical theories that Herodotus discusses, as well as for the genealogies and genealogical chronologies that we know were especially the subject of literary activity before his time. His presentation of the rulers of various nations along with their length of reign and certain political and military activities would strongly suggest that he had access to chronicles of these kingdoms. He also furnishes lists of such things as the Persian satrapies under Darius and the amounts of tribute paid, and a description of the king's highway from Sardis to Susa. Whether Herodotus actually saw the monuments and inscriptions he discusses is more difficult to decide. He explicitly mentions some of these, and the existence of others may be implied by the kind of information he gives. But there are some monuments in foreign lands that Herodotus often claims he saw but could not read. His understanding of their content, which he says he learned from those who could read them, was invariably wrong. In the main, however, von Fritz suggests that the total amount of information or direct quotation from literary sources was a rather small part of the whole.

It is clear that for von Fritz the most important source of information for the *Histories* was oral tradition.[94] This conclusion is not surprising since everywhere in the work itself Herodotus speaks about receiving information in this way. It is most often described as coming from various groups of people, such as the Greeks, the Persians, the Egyptians, or from some particular group within these national designations, such as "the

93. This has recently been emphasized by Drews, *The Greek Accounts of Eastern History,* pp. 32ff. Drews also argues that a number of Persian histories called *Persica* dealing with the Persian Wars were written before the time of Herodotus. But most scholars in the field appear to dispute this claim.

94. On the predominant use of oral tradition in ancient historiography see A. Momigliano, "Historiography on Written Tradition and Historiography on Oral Tradition," in *Studies in Historiography,* pp. 211–20.

priests" or "the learned." As confirmation of the traditions he received, Herodotus couples with these source designations statements of his own investigations (*historiē*) on geography and social customs, as well as on landmarks or monuments. Furthermore, he gives many variants—two or three different versions of a story—usually associated with quite different peoples. At times he gives his own opinion about the variants, deciding in favor of one or the other. But he often simply gives the accounts without offering a judgment, or disclaims any confidence in the versions that he tells. In the absence of any specific source designation we could, of course, assume that Herodotus followed the same basic procedure of gathering and evaluating the tradition; thus we come away with a rather remarkable picture of the "historical research" of Herodotus, even though at times he may seem to lack a good critical sense by modern standards. Most scholars realize, however, that the matter is not quite so simple. The reason is that often a unit of tradition will be attributed to a foreign source, such as the Persians or the Egyptians, but the content of the tradition will be entirely Greek in character, or a unit will represent a serious misunderstanding of a foreign custom or historical period. These problems have led scholars to develop theories about the Hellenization of the foreign sources or the willingness of foreign informers to answer "tourists" according to the visitors' own traditions, or even to deliberately exaggerate or deceive.[95] In the end, at least some degree of "invention" by Herodotus of at least some of the traditions and anecdotes is generally admitted, but on the whole most of the major *logoi* are considered to be based on fairly direct sources of information close to the parties involved or their national traditions.

In a recent study D. Fehling has presented a strong challenge to this confidence in the oral sources of Herodotus.[96] The central focus of his study is to show that the Herodotean source designations cannot be taken as genuine but must instead be viewed as only a literary convention. This convention follows a number of principles and patterns that betray its complete artificiality. For instance, instead of merely offering a rationalistic explanation for a legend or fairy tale in the manner of Hecataeus, Herodotus presents the rationalized version as a separate variant of the "original" and then attributes it to a distant foreign source, making it appear obvious that the rationalized version is the correct one. Herodotus also likes to tell different versions of a story to represent two sides in a dispute. But most often he simply attributes stories or anecdotes about foreign states or nations to sources directly connected with that group with

95. For recent discussion of Herodotus's Egyptian sources see A. B. Lloyd, *Herodotus, Book II: Introduction*, pp. 77–140; J. A. Wilson, *Herodotus in Egypt*. Wilson puts a great deal of emphasis upon conscious deception by the Egyptian priests.
96. *Die Quellenangaben bei Herodot: Studien zur Erzählkunst Herodots*.

little indication of how he actually obtained the information. The fundamental purpose of this practice of source designation would appear to be to bolster his own credibility. To this end Herodotus also frequently cites material evidence (*Beweisstüke*) in support of his accounts, some of which is highly dubious. The convention of using fictitious source designations is apparently well attested in later historiography as well and disguises the fact that the information was merely drawn from a prior literary source. In the case of the Egyptian *logos* we have good reason to believe that some of the items that he says he saw and heard himself he actually took directly from Hecataeus.

If the source designations are fictitious, as Fehling argues, then this calls into question the whole process of a systematic collection of oral traditions and instead raises the possibility of Herodotus's wholesale invention of stories. This is a much easier way of explaining why so many Greek stories are found among his foreign informants: both informants and stories are the product of Herodotus's own imagination. This invention does not mean that Herodotus created everything *ex nihilo* but only that he did not pass traditions on in any fixed form, whether Greek or foreign. The ways in which he might embellish or alter them are numerous and show a great deal of freedom on his part.

Fehling also discusses a literary principle, reflected already in Herodotus's own remarks (6.55), which became standard in later writers: that one could not deal with the same subject about which others had *written* unless one was writing from a different point of view or correcting an earlier presentation. Thus there are many versions of the same event, but they are not the result of new information or "new" oral sources. Instead they derive from the free inventions of the authors. This can be seen in the prose dealing with accounts of the primeval history. The variations in the genealogical schemes containing the mass of eponymic heroes who are supposed to account for the origins of peoples, the naming of places, and the founding of cities are largely the result of creative ingenuity. To the extent that Herodotus deals with such "pseudohistory," he invents his own variation of such genealogical schemes. These genealogies are not oral variants but literary creations.

The nature of Herodotus's literary inventions may be illustrated by a number of examples. Many invented stories, according to Fehling, have a literary function in the composition as a whole. This is the case in 1.56–70, in which Croesus appeals to Athens and Sparta for a treaty against the Persians. The account is an invented doublet based upon the later appeal by Aristagoras in 5.49–51 and has no historical value. Its literary function in book 1 is to introduce Athens and Sparta and to allow for digressions on the histories of these two states near the beginning of the work instead of leaving them to be recounted in book 5, where the two states appear together again. Fehling also points to the principle of economy of narration, according to which the supposed tradition or anecdote recounted by Herodotus contains only what is appropriate to his purpose or theme. Thus, of the seven Persian conspirators who debate what form of government should replace the deposed Magian (3.80–83), only three speak, and each represents one of the classical forms—democracy, oligarchy, and monarchy. Darius, the spokesman for monarchy, immediately receives the support of the remaining four, which decides the issue. Few would argue against the view that the whole scene is a fiction, but it is also important to note that the same principle of economy of story pattern is found in many other places as well.

It is well recognized by scholars that Homer's *Iliad* provided a model for Herodotus, who viewed the Persian Wars as an event worthy of commemoration on the same scale as the Trojan War. This implicit comparison inspired the creation of certain details in the account to make the connection more obvious. Thus the catalogue of Greek ships in the *Iliad* before the invasion of Asia provides the pretext for the review of the fleet by Xerxes before the invasion of Greece, even to the point where the numbers of ships are approximately the same (8.89–99).[97] Herodotus also made use of themes and motifs from tragedy, as well as the tragic structure, in many of his anecdotes. For example, in 3.119, the remarks of the wife of a Persian statesman directly parallel those of Antigone concerning her reason for honoring a brother above husband and son (Sophocles *Antigone* 904ff.).[98]

It appears that Herodotus made rather free use of story themes and simple motifs in the creation of his many anecdotes, often repeating the same motif in different contexts very close to one another. Thus two Egyptian

97. For a discussion of these numbers and their sources see ibid., p. 165. On the device of the catalogue in Homer and Herodotus see also Myres, *Herodotus*, pp. 108ff.

98. This example is not cited by Fehling but it seems to me to fit the case very well. For some time scholars have seen the dependence in the other direction, that of Sophocles upon Herodotus. But this creates numerous difficulties since Sophocles' work was performed in 441 B.C. while Herodotus's work is usually dated to some time after 430 B.C. One would then have to argue that Herodotus was already in Athens prior to 441 and was giving lectures that included the anecdote in question. It was then preserved in his notes to be reproduced at a much later day. A second difficulty is that if Herodotus's account of the story is the original one, the statement of the wife of Intaphrenes seems so much less appropriate to its context than the statement in the *Antigone*. Why would a man's brother-in-law be punished for his rather singular action and not also the man's wife? Herodotus's effort to make a connection between two story themes is rather weak. T. Noldeke, "Zu Herodot 3, 119 (Sophokles Antigone 903–913)," *Hermes* 29 (1894):155–56, was responsible for the view that the story had a Persian or Eastern origin, and R. Pischel, "Zu Sophokles Antigone 909–912," *Hermes* 28 (1893):465–68, cites Indian examples. However, on the basis of these rather late texts I am not convinced that the stories traveled from East to West.

kings prostitute their daughters for their own purposes (2.121, 126). But repeated motifs are sometimes widely separated from each other, in which case they help to create analogies between different events. One such repeated motif is the "warner" or "wise counsellor."[99] There are twenty-one examples of the tragic warner and thirty-seven of the practical adviser. They have the literary function of introducing an episodic unit usually having to do with preparations for a military campaign, or of signaling impending disaster. Oracles and dreams also function in a similar fashion. It is unlikely that any of the anecdotes based upon the warning or advising motifs originated in independent traditions. They are the free creation of Herodotus himself.

Another topic that Fehling discusses is Herodotus's use of typical numbers. He has a great fondness for numbers, such as three, seven, ten, twelve, and their multiples in tens, hundreds, thousands, etc. The number twelve is often associated by Herodotus with groups of states, such as the twelve Ionian cities in Asia Minor that were descended from twelve original Ionian states in the Peloponnesus before they were replaced by twelve Achaean states; twelve original Aeolian cities in mainland Asia Minor as well as six on the island of Lesbos; twelve Phocian cities destroyed by the Persians; and twelve original kings of Egypt ruling over the twelve divisions of the land. It is interesting to see how Herodotus often justifies his count in cases where it could be disputed. In the use of large numbers, such as in the enumeration of troops or of those fallen in battle, the counts are just as artificial. These typical numbers, Fehling argues, are not derived from the sources directly but are part of the artifice of Herodotus himself.

It is clear from this brief survey of Fehling's study that he thinks very little in Herodotus is derived from actual historical or traditional sources and that most of it is free invention. He states:

> Im ganzen kam für so grosse Teile des Werkes freie Erfindung als sicher, wahrscheinlich oder möglich erwiesen werden, dass der Schluss berechtigt ist, Herodot habe nur ein ganz grobes Gerüst echter historischer Nachrichten gehabt und durch eigenes Schaffen ausgefüllt.[100]

Needless to say, such a position ends up with a view of Herodotus the historian that is entirely different from that proposed by von Fritz. Fehling takes Herodotus's travels to Egypt and the Black Sea as fiction and regards Herodotus as a wandering intellectual who lived by his wits. He dismisses as fantasy the notion that Herodotus's *historiē* was a precursor of scientific

99. See especially the treatment by R. Lattimore, "The Wise Adviser in Herodotus," *Class. Phil.* 34 (1939):24–35.
100. Fehling, *Quellenangaben*, p. 181.

research. Everything that Herodotus learned from anyone he completely reworked for his own use. The *Histories* contain source material for certain individual data but not for entire accounts.

The above discussion indicates the wide range of scholarly opinion about the source problem in Herodotus. Yet these differences are more a matter of degree than of kind. Almost all scholars would admit that there is a measure of invention in Herodotus in virtually every category that we have discussed: in the designation of sources, in the creation of anecdotes, and in the use of stereotyped motifs and typical numbers. Furthermore, such an emphasis on literary creativity is quite compatible with the scholarly interests in the thematic and structural unity of Herodotus, which is just another aspect of his literary inventiveness. Scholars also admit that very little of the *Histories* is derived from written sources, especially from "historical" records, and what is is limited primarily to the skeleton of the work. The big difference among scholars is in the assessment of how much Greek and foreign oral tradition Herodotus collected and what kind of use he made of it. The fact that so much of the foreign tradition resembles Greek themes and motifs gives rise, on the one hand, to explanations of the Hellenizing of foreign informants and, on the other hand, to skepticism about the existence of such traditions. A complete resolution of this debate can hardly be expected.[101]

This survey raises many similar questions in biblical studies that are usually overlooked. Consider, for example, the matter of written sources. The situation is clearest for the Book of Kings, which refers to a "Book of the Deeds of Solomon" for the period of Solomon's reign and, for the time of the divided monarchy, "The Chronicles of the Kings of Israel" and "The Chronicles of the Kings of Judah."[102] Yet these three sources, whatever their exact nature may have been, cover only a small part of the actual narrative in Kings. Like Herodotus, the author used only a small amount of these chronicles to provide a political and chronological framework, so that the anecdotes, prophetic legends, and other story material must have come either from unwritten sources or from the author himself. In some cases poems are quoted from books like the "Book of Jashar" or the "Book of the Wars of Yahweh," or perhaps from other unnamed collections. The priestly document mentions a "Book of the Generation of Adam" (Gen. 5:1), which may suggest that the genealogy in Gen. 5 and the other *tôledôt* belonged to the kind of *Genealogia* so common in early Greek prose.

101. For an attempt to respond at some length in support of the older consensus on Herodotus's trustworthiness see J. Cobet, "Fehling, Die Quellenangaben bei Herodot," *Gnomon* 46 (1974):737–46.
102. These literary sources will be discussed at greater length below.

But the problem of literary sources is by no means limited to these explicit references. We must take seriously the possibility of literary dependence whenever parallel texts exist in different literary works. In a literate society as small and closely knit as the Jerusalem religious community we cannot ignore the strong probability that each "history" was well known by subsequent historians. The historians may have dealt with different periods and may therefore have complemented each other, as in the case of the Yahwist and the Deuteronomistic historian, or they may have presented a "revision" of the earlier history, such as the Priestly Writer's work in the Pentateuch and Chronicles vis-à-vis both the Pentateuch and the Deuteronomistic history. It should be noted that the Chronicler goes out of his way to make reference to sources, but they can hardly be taken as genuine.[103] In fact they are all fictitious, and their purpose is to disguise his obvious literary dependence upon the Pentateuch and the Deuteronomistic historian. This was his way of seeking to justify and make credible his numerous additions, alterations, and deletions. Furthermore, the additions are all his own invention and betray in the clearest way his own ideological orientation. In this he seems so close to the Greek historiographic tradition as to suggest that he was directly influenced by it.

Concerning the subject of oral tradition in biblical narrative, most of those genres in Hebrew historiography that are regarded as oral in source and origin also occur in Herodotus and his predecessors.[104] One certainly cannot apply to the *Histories* an evolutionary scheme of historiographic development from the simplest etiological form to the most complex narrative.[105] The simplest forms in Genesis dealing with cultural and national eponyms and ancestors belong to precisely that body of pseudo-history in Herodotus and other prose writers that is most easily recognized as invented. The variations in the genealogical schemes are of the same kind and order that we find between the genealogy of Cain in Gen. 4:17–26 (J) and the genealogy of Seth in Gen. 5 (P). This difference is not due to anthropological factors;[106] it is purely literary.

Furthermore, if it is possible for Herodotus to fabricate stories and anecdotes using little or no traditional material, only popular motifs or themes from other literary works, it is possible for biblical writers to do the same.

103. See a listing of these and a discussion in E. L. Curtis and A. A. Madsen, *The Books of Chronicles*, pp. 21–26; J. M. Myers, *I Chronicles, Anchor Bible*, pp. xlv–xlviii.

104. Compare the categories discussed by Aly, *Volksmärchen, Sage, und Novelle bei Herodot*, with those listed in the Old Testament introductions of O. Eissfeldt, G. Fohrer, O. Kaiser, and others.

105. This scheme will be discussed below, in 7a.

106. See Wilson, *Genealogy and History*, pp. 138–66. It is, to my mind, highly questionable whether functional explanations of variations in genealogies based on anthropological analysis of oral societies can also apply to literary variations. Wilson does not examine the many contemporary literary genealogies in the Greek world.

The assumption that the biblical writers never did this is totally unwarranted. The full range of "oral" forms could be invented by a writer such as Herodotus for his own literary purposes: etiologies, cult legends, anecdotes, and novellas. This also means that identifying a genre does not tell us anything about its "original" *Sitz im Leben* or the process of transmission of a particular story or narrative unit. In spite of its form it may have existed only in literature. Especially suspect of direct fabrication are those stories and anecdotes that are heavily dependent upon a set motif, such as the prophetic warner in the Deuteronomistic history and the preaching Levite in the Chronicler.[107] Nor can we assume that doublets are a clear indication of variants in oral tradition; they may also be literary—a pattern repeated by the same author or a story borrowed by a second author.[108] Repetition in narrative has many literary functions in written compositions. It is not just a phenomenon of oral tradition, and traditio-historical analysis founded upon such a principle is a delusion.

One characteristic mark of oral tradition identified by Gunkel, Alt, and Noth is the statement, found in a number of stories in biblical narrative, that a certain landmark or object that plays a role in the story could still be seen "to this very day." They interpret this statement as a sign of popular etiology such that the stories linked with this formula arose to explain the landmark in question. In a recent study B. S. Childs disputes this claim and points to similar statements in Herodotus and other Greek writers that appear to have a different function.[109] While the statements could appear with etiological material, they could also be associated with non-etiological stories, that is, "historical" material. Childs separates the witnessing formulae from the stories themselves and sees the former as motivated by historiographic interests. Now the similarity of a personal witness element (*historiē*) in both Greek and Hebrew historiography is noteworthy and should remind us of the importance of treating these two bodies of literature together. But Childs's next suggestion, that the witness formula is secondary and "redactional" to the received tradition,[110] raises for Old Testament studies the same issues that we have noted in treating the source problem in Herodotus. The issue in Herodotus is certainly more complex than Childs suggests. First, Herodotus's investigation may relate to geography and ethnography, in which case the witness formula is certainly not intended as secondary confirmation, although in actuality it may be a mere

---

107. See G. von Rad, "The Deuteronomic Theology of History in *I* and *II Kings*" and "The Levitical Sermon in *I* and *II Chronicles*," in *The Problem of the Hexateuch and Other Essays*, pp. 205–21 and 267–80.

108. See my earlier treatment of the doublets of Genesis in *Abraham in History and Tradition*, pp. 161ff.

109. B. S. Childs, "A Study of the Formula 'Until this Day,'" *JBL* 82 (1963):279–92.

110. Ibid., p. 292.

convention to disguise the fact that the material was copied from written sources, that is, Hecataeus. Second, the formula may be linked with "historical" traditions and therefore intended to be secondary confirmation, but instead it could be simply a device to persuade his audience to believe a story that he invented, in which case the witness formula would not be "redactional." Third, the landmarks themselves may or may not be real objects. An element of fiction within the witnessing statement itself cannot be ruled out. Although the witness formula is a historiographic convention, it is difficult to determine whether the "historical" material to which it is linked is received tradition that is merely being confirmed or part of an invented story. The formula thus falls in the same category as source citations, which have the function of raising the credibility of the writer.

The use of typical numbers, discussed by Fehling, is also an important factor in assessing whether a unit in the narrative is dependent upon a traditional source or is a reflection of the author's creativity. Typical numbers in themselves may, of course, be found in oral tradition. But when a larger pattern of numbers is established that cuts across several literary units, the imagination of the author is clearly at work. The different ways in which we might assess a typical number in the narrative of the Old Testament can be seen in the number twelve. Noth observed the rather fixed association of this number with the various groupings of the tribes of Israel as well as of other national and tribal groupings and concluded that these references were all highly traditional no matter what their source and that they reflect an institution in Israel's early history, that of the "amphictyonic league."[111] What persuaded him of this theory was the rather frequent groupings of twelve members to a league in the Greek and Latin sources dealing with such amphictyonic institutions. We are not concerned here with a full critique of Noth's theory of an amphictyonic league in Israel.[112] (We know, for example, that the membership of such leagues in Greece and Italy was not always twelve in number.) But what we can see is that Herodotus for some reason had a strong tendency to use the typical number twelve for "original" groupings of peoples, their ancestors, and their cities. He also used, somewhat less frequently, the number six.[113] Such numbers may be only a convention, which would mean that the groupings are arbitrary and have no historical or traditio-historical significance. The creation of such groupings by the Yahwist and the Priestly Writer for the eponymous ancestors of the Aramaeans, Arabs, Edomites,

111. *Das System der zwölf Stämme Israels,* BWANT 4/1 (1930).
112. See R. de Vaux, *Histoire ancienne d'Israël,* vol. 2, pp. 19–36.
113. See the remarks on the number twelve, ibid., pp. 25–26.

and Horites, as well as for the first kings of Edom,[114] shows the similarity of these writers to Herodotus. The typical number by itself cannot constitute evidence for an ancient institution or for the traditional character of the material containing the number.

The comparison of Israelite historiography with Greek strongly suggests that it was no more the result of a gradual traditio-historical process than was Herodotus's work. It was the product of a complex literary history, the work of authors dependent upon written models and sources who combined genres of great variety and structured the whole with conscious compositional techniques. Oral tradition played a major role in providing source material for such works and in supplying the genres and general character of many of the individual units.[115] This historiography did not consist simply of prose versions of "epic" traditions. We must also admit the possibility that the Bible's authors invented some of the stories which may even resemble the genre of oral tradition but which were based merely on general folklore motifs or similar stories told of other persons, times, and places. How much is invention and how much is received tradition will always be a matter of debate, as it is in the case of Herodotus.

Furthermore, in terms of the scope of subject matter and the themes treated, nothing in the literature of the Near East before the fourth century so closely resembles the biblical histories as the Greek prose histories. Both deal with recent events, such as the Persian Wars or the Exile, and their causes through successive periods of the past. Both reconstruct the distant past through the technique of genealogy development with anecdotal or folkloristic digressions. The combination of "official" sources, such as chronicles, with oral tradition, and of poetic fragments with prose narration in a multigenre product, is not evident in any other body of preserved literature from the Near East in this period.

The very structure of prose composition in both Greece and Israel, using the paratactic style, was a way of moving from oral storytelling to written combinations of stories, and the compositional skill of the author was demonstrated by how he employed certain techniques to overcome the limitations of parataxis and create a unity of his work. To label these techniques as merely "redactional" and then to fragment such a redactional process is to destroy completely the compositional work of the biblical au-

---

114. See Gen. 22:20–24; 25:2, 13–15; 36. For a critical discussion of these lists see Noth, *Das System*, pp. 42ff.

115. For Herodotus oral tradition was important in both respects, but for Thucydides oral tradition was important only as source, not as form.

thors.[116] To my mind, the present studies of Herodotus give no warrant
for such an approach to biblical literature, and no one in recent times has
suggested an alternative model to justify this type of redaction criticism. It
is merely the perpetuation in biblical studies of a scholarly tradition from
the days in which such redactors abounded in classical studies as well.

The similarity of themes in Herodotus and the biblical historians must
also be taken seriously now that we are free of the Greek-Hebrew dichotomy. Comparison would not, of course, reveal complete identity of outlook between the two literatures, for there is a considerable range of diversity even among the Hebrew historians, as there is among Herodotus,
Thucydides, and Xenophon.[117] But the themes of divine providence, of
retribution or salvation, and the use of the past as a mirror for present and
future events in order to deal with the problem of change[118] appear to be
basic concerns addressed by both historiographic traditions and constitute
a major motivation for their existence.

The problem of sources is perhaps the most basic and the most difficult
issue in the study of the Pentateuch and historical books. The nature of the
sources, both written and oral, and the way in which they were used by
the writers are the questions whose answers largely determine the principles and methods of biblical interpretation. It would be hard to find in antiquity a closer analogue to this problem than the source problem in
Herodotus, and yet it is entirely ignored by biblical scholars. Admittedly,
not all these problems have been solved in Herodotus studies, as we have
seen, and the student of the Old Testament may be reluctant to add these
to the ones he already has. But serious consideration of the source problem
in Herodotus would give a whole new perspective to the place and use of
oral tradition and literary sources in the biblical works. As for written
sources, one would have to deal with the use of "official" documents as
well as prior literary works, especially those extant within the Old Testament itself. And the way in which biblical scholars are inclined to view the
oral sources would have to be greatly revised, in terms of both the variety
of types at the disposal of an author and the freedom he could exercise in
using them.

It is time to focus again upon the *authors* of the biblical histories and
upon their respective *audiences*. This is not to say that as works of literature Herodotus's *Histories* and Genesis do not have universal appeal. But
if we take seriously the task of the history of literature and specifically the

116. Cf. the discussion of redaction criticism by K. Koch, *The Growth of the Biblical Tradition*, pp. 57ff.
117. Van Groningen, *In the Grip of the Past*, pp. 24ff.
118. A. Momigliano, "Tradition and the Classical Historian," in *Essays*, pp. 161–77.

rise of history writing, then the dimensions of time and place of writing and of the audience for whom the work was intended cannot be ignored, however difficult these may be to determine precisely. The present literary approach in tradition history and redaction criticism has denied any place or significance to these questions.[119]

This comparison of Greek and Hebrew historiography raises the question whether it is possible to account for the similarities we have suggested. A definitive answer cannot yet be given, but a few points for consideration may be put forward. In a recent study on *Hesiod and the Near East*[120] P. Walcot argues convincingly that Hesiod was strongly influenced by eastern forms and ideas in both his mythological and didactic texts. This influence very likely came into Greece in the eighth century B.C., when the Phoenician alphabet and other cultural features were also introduced into Greek civilization. Two important locations in the Levant for the dissemination of such influence were the ports of Al Mina and Tell Sukas, which had numerous Greek settlers living alongside the Phoenicians from the mid-ninth to the mid-sixth centuries and had active trade communication with the Aegean.[121] In Cyprus too and in the Aegean area itself there were many Phoenician settlements in close proximity to Greeks. The Phoenician coast was dominated politically most of the time throughout this period by the Assyrians and Babylonians, whose interest and presence in the region was rather strong for commercial reasons. So Phoenicia was a natural place for Greeks to encounter cultural influences from the east as well. If such influence is well attested in Hesiod for the late eighth or early seventh century B.C,[122] there is no reason to believe in any great decline in such influence or contact in the subsequent period, except for the interlude of Persian hostilities.

It seems reasonable to assume that the Greeks adopted the use of chronicles and the development of genealogical chronologies from the pattern of the eastern king lists. The question of the origin of other shared features, such as the paratactic style of early prose and the anecdotal digressions within chronologies, is hard to answer on the basis of the extant material from Phoenicia.[123] But it would appear most reasonable that those features clearly shared by Greek and Hebrew historiography also belonged to the Phoenicians, who were in close contact with both regions. It is, of course, doubtful that there was much direct cultural contact between the

119. See especially R. Rendtorff, *Das überlieferungsgeschichtliche Problem des Pentateuch*, BZAW 141 (1977).
120. Cardiff, 1966.
121. Walcot, *Hesiod and the Near East*, pp. 120ff.
122. Hesiod's dates are still very much disputed within the range of ca. 750–650 B.C.
123. See the discussion in 6c and e on the Annals of Tyre and Philo Byblius.

Greeks and the Hebrews before the fourth century B.C.[124] Once we admit
that Phoenicia could serve as a bridge between Israel and the Aegean as
well as a center for the dissemination of culture in both directions, nothing
stands in the way of an intensive comparative study of the Bible and early
Greek historiography.[125]

---

124. The presentation of Near Eastern "contributions" by Starr, *Awakening*, pp. 25–32,
will certainly need some revision in the light of this study.

125. For a comparative study of Greek and Hebrew folklore themes and motifs that seems
to point in the same direction see W. Baumgartner, "Israelitisch-griechische Sagenbeziehun-
gen," in *Zum Alten Testament und seiner Umwelt*, pp. 147–78.

CHAPTER THREE

MESOPOTAMIAN HISTORIOGRAPHY

My intention in this chapter is not to discuss the history of Mesopotamian historiography but to identify certain approaches and concerns that lead to quite different treatments of the subject. There is some confusion as to how these different approaches and concerns are related to each other. The modern historian, for example, is concerned with evaluating the ancient historical writings in terms of their degree of historical reliability. Thus Olmstead's early study, "Assyrian Historiography," focused upon the principles of evaluating the Assyrian royal inscriptions for the purposes of writing a modern history.[1] In a more recent study J. J. Finkelstein made historicity the crucial test of Mesopotamian historiography by searching in the numerous historical texts for highly reliable information about the people's past that was also intended by their authors to be an accurate historical presentation.[2] He suggested that "the omen texts, and the historical information imbedded in them, lie at the very root of all Mesopotamian historiography, and that as a historical genre they take precedence both in time and in reliability over any other genre of Mesopotamian writing that purports to treat of the events of the past."[3] Finkelstein argued that there was a direct connection between omen literature and the development of chronicles, which in his view was the only true historiographic genre because it could meet the tests of historicity and of a proper historical objectivity of the author. He states: "Upon analysis, it would become clear that all genres of Mesopotamian literature that purport to deal with past events, with the exception of omens and chronicles, are motivated by purposes other than the desire to know what really happened, and the authenticity of the information they relate was not in itself the crucial point for their authors."[4] Finkelstein's thesis, especially the suggested connection

1. A. T. E. Olmstead, "Assyrian Historiography," The University of Missouri Studies, Social Studies Series III/1 (1916).
2. "Mesopotamian Historiography," PAPS 107 (1963): 461–72.
3. Ibid., p. 463.
4. Ibid., p. 469.

between omen texts and chronicles, has not gone unchallenged.[5] But the question I wish to raise here is the degree to which historicity and objectivity of presentation must be dominant factors in restricting the range of subject matter under consideration. Even if we admit a wider range of literature as most scholars do, the questions of historical sources of information, objectivity of presentation, and the purpose of the author will be important aspects of the discussion.

A second approach to the subject of Mesopotamian historiography is by contrast a very inclusive one. It takes up the task of analyzing all those genres that reflect a strong interest in the past or preserve the narration of historical events in one form or other. H. Güterbock was the first to categorize the various historical genres, and his study,[6] though modified and extended by many subsequent contributions, still remains the basis of such analysis today. A new attempt at a comprehensive form-critical survey has just been completed by A. K. Grayson,[7] and this work will serve as the basis of my own remarks about Mesopotamian historiography. One aspect of this approach is to examine the history of Mesopotamian literature—the way in which various forms of literature are related to each other. Thus genres that are even marginally historiographic must be brought into consideration.

A third approach, concerned primarily with the history of ideas, deals with "the idea of history" in ancient Mesopotamia, as in the presentation of E. A. Speiser.[8] He held the view that there was a unified Mesopotamian notion of history stemming from the ancient Sumerians and running through the subsequent civilizations of Assyria and Babylonia. Speiser suggested that this interest in the past was motivated by cultic considerations of maintaining the continuity of a "covenantal" relationship between deity and community. For the ancient Mesopotamian the past was made up of alternating periods of bliss and disaster for which the rulers by their actions toward the gods were responsible. This view of history Speiser regarded as normative in the Old Babylonian period and embodied in the so-called Weidner Chronicle, which he dated to this period and which he called "the first Mesopotamian textbook on the idea of history."[9] One

5. See below, 3d; also A. K. Grayson, "Divination and the Babylonian Chronicles," *La Divination en Mésopotamie Ancienne*, pp. 69–76.

6. H. G. Güterbock, "Die historische Tradition und ihre literarische Gestaltung bei Babyloniern und Hethitern bis 1200," *ZA* 42 (1934):1–91; 44 (1938):45–149.

7. "Histories and Historians of the Ancient Near East: Assyria and Babylonia," *Orientalia* 49 (1980):140–94. I am very much indebted to Grayson for the use of a manuscript of this study prior to its publication.

8. "Ancient Mesopotamia," in *The Idea of History in the Ancient Near East*, ed. R. C. Dentan, pp. 35–76.

9. Ibid., p. 59. It now seems much more likely that the Weidner Chronicle is to be dated to the late second millennium B.C. See Grayson, *ABC*, addenda to p. 44, pp. 278–79.

must, however, seriously question whether there was such a uniformity of thought about the past by "Mesopotamian man." This approach also has the weakness of being highly selective in the historiographic works that it considers to the neglect of certain major genres, and also of establishing interconnections between certain bodies of literature on the basis of similarity in historical concept where no literary relationship is apparent. It may be useful, after a form-critical analysis of the various historiographical genres, to discuss the "ideas of the past" reflected in these works as Grayson does in his study,[10] without imposing on the whole of Mesopotamian history a false uniformity.

Whenever comparative historiography has centered on the idea of history in Mesopotamia and in ancient Israel the result has usually been to emphasize the contrast between the two. There is a rather pervasive opinion that Israel was unique in the ancient world in its understanding of history and in its formulation of theology as revelation through history. The contrast was sharpened by characterizing the Mesopotamian world as polytheistic and therefore mythical and cyclic in its view of nature and history. For this reason it could have no sense of history and no historiography.

This view has been strongly challenged by B. Albrektson in his recent book suggesting that in the texts of Mesopotamia and the Hittites the gods are presented as intervening in the affairs of men, directly affecting the historical process.[11] Thus the outcome of historical events such as wars is directly attributed to the activity of the gods, often as a direct consequence of human behavior, whether pious or impious. The king is frequently represented as an agent of the deity in such activity and is often designated with an appropriate title of subordination. The deity's word has the inherent power to command the forces that govern nature and the affairs of men, and to affect the outcome of battles as well as bring about changes in nature. Consequently, one could speak about revelation through history even to the extent that the gods were seen as always supporting the righteous and the pious king and therefore just in their actions, or as merciful in bringing about a return to prosperity after a period of hardship. The greatness of the gods was often reflected in the success of the nation with whom they were primarily associated—for example, Ashur among the As-

Speiser's suggestions were also taken up, with very little change, by H. Gese, "Geschichtliches Denken im Alten Orient und im Alten Testament," *ZThK* 55 (1958):127–45.

10. "Assyria and Babylonia," *Orientalia* 49:188–94; see also J. Krecher and H.-P. Müller, "Vergangenheitsinteresse in Mesopotamien und Israel," *Saeculum* 26 (1975):13–44. This study suggests a variety of "ideas about the past" based on a sampling of genres with little similarity in the comparison between Mesopotamia and Israel.

11. *History and the Gods: An Essay on the Idea of Historical Events as Divine Manifestations in the Ancient Near East and in Israel.*

syrians and Marduk among the Babylonians—as well as in the powers of nature that they represented.

At each point in the discussion Albrektson makes a comparison with the Old Testament and finds very little difference in outlook. At times quite similar formulae are used to express the notion of divine intervention. Thus he points out: "The phrase which the king here uses to express the belief that the course of events was directed by the gods and that his victory over the enemies was a divine gift, 'the gods delivered it into my hand,' seems to have spread all over the ancient Near East and is found in texts from different ages and different areas."[12] Albrektson finds examples of this formula for the divine handing-over of the enemy in the Hittite Old Kingdom, the Amarna period, an inscription of Nebuchadnezzar II, and numerous references in the Deuteronomistic corpus of the Old Testament.

Of course, Albrektson does concede that there is a great difference between a theological world view in which there are numerous gods with different and often competing spheres of activity and the monotheism of the Old Testament, in which all supernatural activity is subordinated to the will and direction of the one deity. It would appear, therefore, that just this difference would be most apparent in the notion of a divine plan in history, and many scholars have emphasized the distinctiveness of Israel's thought precisely at this point. Albrektson's response to this is to say that the notion of a divine plan of history in the Old Testament has been greatly overstated. Such a view does not appear to be the perspective of the historical books, at any rate. The Deuteronomistic history and the Chronicler do not point to any universal goal in history. Whether or not such a view is present in the Yahwist depends upon a rather disputed interpretation of the divine promise of blessing to all the families of the earth. In the prophetic literature Albrektson finds only a vague plan of salvation or restoration for Israel which he describes as a rather diluted sense of the idea of a "plan of history." Only in the apocalyptic literature of the Book of Daniel can one speak in terms of a fixed plan for universal history.

It is at this point that Albrektson's work has come in for criticism. W. G. Lambert,[13] while admitting that there is not much difference between the Deuteronomistic and the Babylonian view of history, nevertheless argues strongly that in the Yahwist as well as in the prophets there is an eschatology and a movement in history toward a goal. But it is still doubtful whether any of the Old Testament histories can be shown to have

12. Ibid., p. 38.
13. See his review "History and the Gods" in *Orientalia* 39 (1970):170–77; idem, "Destiny and Divine Intervention in Babylon and Israel," *OTS* 17 (1972):65–72.

an eschatological perspective. The notion of the election of Israel, upon which Lambert places considerable weight, is not so different from the notion of the divine election of the king that is very common in Mesopotamian thought.[14] One can even speak of a certain democratization of royal ideology if one compares the language of Second Isaiah—being chosen from the womb—with that of the Assyrian and Babylonian royal ideology. Historical thinking does not have to be teleological in order to produce historiographic works, as is evident from the classical histories.

Albrektson's book, it seems to me, goes a long way toward breaking down any prejudice against the comparative study of Israelite and Mesopotamian historiography. It is not necessary for him to prove that all Mesopotamian ideas of history are the same as all Israelite views. What they have in common in their "theologies" of history is enough to warrant a comparison of historiographic genre as well.

This point has also been made in a recent article by J. J. M. Roberts,[15] who agrees with Albrektson and objects to the widely held position that true historiography first developed in Israel. He seeks to counter a definition of historiography that might be particularly appropriate for Israel's historical corpus in its final form but that would exclude the rest of the Near East from consideration. He rightly warns against the confusion of "a *literary* category (historiography), which could include more than one genre, with a particular, though not self-evident, *philosophical* concept of history,"[16] or what we have referred to above as ideas of history. Within the literary category of historiography Roberts would include several genres: king lists, chronicles, annals, epics, and royal apologies, among others,[17] and in this he is in agreement with Grayson. His own work, however, is not to pursue this literary side of the study but to carry forward Albrektson's program on a comparison of the ideas of history in Israel and Mesopotamia.[18] The task in the present study will be to emphasize the comparative literary approach, although it is recognized that the concerns with the forms of history writing and with the expression of the ideas of history are complementary.

14. See H. Frankfort, *Kingship and the Gods*, pp. 239–40.
15. "Myth *versus* History: Relaying the Comparative Foundations," *CBQ* 38 (1976):1–13.
16. Ibid., p. 3.
17. Ibid., p. 3, n. 15.
18. See also J. J. M. Roberts, "Nebuchadnezzar I's Elamite Crisis in Theological Perspective," in *Essays . . . in Memory of J. J. Finkelstein*, pp. 183–87; P. D. Miller and J. J. Roberts, *The Hand of the Lord: A Reassessment of the "Ark Narrative" of I Samuel*.

a. ROYAL INSCRIPTIONS

The simplest form of royal inscription[19] is the "label," which merely indicates the ownership of an object or a building. It may be expanded into either a statement commemorating the construction of a building or a dedication inscription, often called a "votive" inscription,[20] in which a cult object or temple is given to a deity. These forms were known in Sumer, inherited by Babylonia, and in time diffused into Assyria. These forms, in themselves, are not historiographic, but one notion that was put forward many years ago by S. Mowinckel and has often been repeated is that all royal inscriptions derive from "votive" inscriptions,[21] a view that must now be considered doubtful.[22]

More important for this study are the longer commemorative inscriptions recounting royal deeds and inscribed on clay tablets, cones, cylinders, bricks, stone steles, and statues. These were put on display in public places or deposited for safekeeping in palaces and temples, or even buried as a foundation deposit. The commemorative inscriptions of Babylonia, like their Sumerian predecessors, primarily describe building activities and only rarely mention military adventures. The Assyrian commemorative inscriptions, on the other hand, placed great emphasis upon military campaigns as well as upon the construction of temples and palaces. Although the specific styles and patterns of the inscriptions vary, they often contain such elements as the royal name and epithets, a statement of the king's commission by the gods, a prayer, a dedication of a building, blessings, and curses. Some building inscriptions contain a history of the temple being restored, even to the point of estimating the time between the stages of restoration, as well as naming the earlier kings involved in its construction. This indicates that inscriptions that were buried in foundations were intended to be discovered by future renovators of a temple or palace and so were perhaps regarded as a more permanent record than those on display; in this way the original builder would be given his due. Those who discovered such records were obviously interested in the continuity with the past afforded by

19. See Grayson, *Orientalia* 49:150–71, for the form-critical discussion of royal inscriptions with examples. The present order of the discussion does not follow that of Grayson. See also Grayson, *Assyrian Royal Inscriptions*, vols. 1 and 2 with extensive bibliography cited there, and older translations in D. D. Luckenbill, *Ancient Records of Assyria and Babylonia*, vols. 1–2. A sampling of texts may also be found in *ANET*³, pp. 274–301, 556–60.

20. Grayson points out (*Orientalia* 49:156–57, 162–64) that the designation "votive" is questionable; he prefers the term "dedicatory."

21. "Die vorderasiatischen Königs and Fürsteninschriften," *Eucharisterion Gunkel*, vol. 1 (1923), pp. 278–322, esp. 313–16.

22. It was first criticized by W. Baumgartner, "Zur Form der assyrischen Königsinschriften," *OLZ* 27 (1924):313–17.

these texts, a use of the past that strengthened their sense of religious and political identity.[23]

One group of Assyrian royal inscriptions are the annals, which narrate, in the first person of royalty, a single campaign, or two or more arranged in chronological order. These are similar in some respects to Hittite and Egyptian annals of the second millennium B.C., but we do not know of any from Sumer and Babylonia. Since the Assyrian annals begin with the reign of Adad-narari I (1306–1274 B.C.),[24] there may be a relationship between the Hittite or Egyptian and the Assyrian annals. The whole matter, however, is hotly debated.[25] Texts dealing with only one campaign were often set up in the conquered region, whether on a stela or on a prominent rock surface, in order to commemorate the king's victory in that region. No doubt such Assyrian monuments were plentiful in Syria-Palestine. Noticeable in these accounts are references to the role played by the deities in the king's successes. Texts that enumerate more than one campaign are set down in chronological order as yearly campaigns. The material for the various campaigns prior to the last one mentioned has been extracted from earlier annals and often shortened or otherwise changed to fit the requirements of space in the new account.[26] The presentation of the king's building activities that follows in the texts often does not have a clear chronological connection with the other events. Instead it is loosely joined to the preceding material by the simple connective "at that time" (*ina ūmešuma*). We thus get the strong impression, sometimes explicitly stated, that only after all the enemies of the king had been subdued did he construct his palaces and temples. In actual fact, these activities went on side by side. Similar to the annals in most respects are the so-called display inscriptions, some of which recount military campaigns. Their main difference from the annals is that they do not record events in chronological order.

23. Speiser ("Ancient Mesopotamia," in *The Idea of History*, pp. 46–47) rightly notes the interest in the past indicated by these texts. But whether they also suggest a covenantal relationship between god and king (or people) is doubtful. None of the texts indicates that the right of the king to rule or the securing of his dynasty was given by the god in exchange for the construction of the temple. Speiser's suggestion that the clay nail or peg "literally nailed down the agreement" may be clever but it is hardly accurate. For a discussion of such "cones" see R. S. Ellis, *Foundation Deposits in Ancient Mesopotamia*, chaps. 3 and 5.

24. Dates used here are those proposed by J. A. Brinkman, "Appendix: Mesopotamian Chronology of the Historical Period," in *Ancient Mesopotamia: Portrait of a Dead Civilization*, ed. A. Leo Oppenheim, pp. 335–52.

25. See below, 4a.

26. For discussions about the compositional methods of the Assyrian annalists see H. Tadmor, "Observations on Assyrian Historiography," in *Essays . . . Finkelstein*, p. 210; W. de Filippi, "A Reappraisal of the Ashurnasirpal Text in King's College, Halifax," *RA* 68 (1974):141ff.; L. D. Levine, "The Second Campaign of Sennacherib," *JNES* 32 (1973):312–17; M. Cogan and H. Tadmor, "Gyges and Ashurbanipal: A Study in Literary Transmission," *Orientalia* 46 (1977):65–85.

The sources for the royal inscriptions and their manner of composition are of considerable interest to the subject of history writing, even though many questions still remain to be answered.[27] For the Middle Assyrian period there appears to be evidence of some "chronicles" of individual kings, and if this were the case then one could suppose that they would have served as a useful source for the annals. But because these so-called chronicles are in very fragmentary condition, their exact nature and genre identity are not at all certain. It would appear unwarranted to suppose on the basis of these texts that a running chronicle existed throughout Assyrian history.[28] On the other hand, it seems highly likely that booty or tribute lists and campaign diaries were used even though the existence of these sources is completely hypothetical. A feature of the annals that seems to suggest diverse primary sources is the fluctuation at times between first and third person. This can best be explained in most instances as the result of a dependence upon written sources with incomplete editing by the scribe or "author" of the text. We can also speak of "secondary" sources for many of the texts in that scribes often copied directly from earlier inscriptions, either abbreviating earlier accounts or conflating two or more versions of the same event. This would also seem to point to their inability to go back to a standard chronicle of events from which they could compose each new annalistic text directly. Only the most recent events were based upon primary reports, which were apparently discarded after their initial use. Occasionally scribes would use older or even very archaic inscriptions as models for their own texts. Later versions of a particular military campaign would often change and exaggerate the numerical sums for booty items, conquered cities, and captives appearing in the original text.[29]

The nature of Mesopotamian scribal composition and editing can be illustrated by a comparison of the various recensions of the Nabonidus inscriptions, especially those having to do with the building of the temple of Sin, Ehulhul, at Harran.[30] The differences in these texts are significant. The version coming from Babylon (VAB$_4$) speaks of a divine appearance in a dream of the gods Marduk and Sin to Nabonidus in his accession year. Marduk takes the principal role and commands the king to rebuild

27. See Grayson, *Orientalia* 49:164–70.

28. Cf. Tadmor, "Assyrian Hist.," pp. 209–13. For a full discussion of these chronicles see below, 4b.

29. See Olmstead, "Assyrian Historiography," p. 5.

30. For the texts see C. J. Gadd, "The Harran Inscriptions of Nabonidus," *AnSt* 8 (1958):35–92, plates 1–16; and a new translation in *ANET*[3], pp. 562–63. See also W. L. Moran, "Notes on the New Nabonidus Inscriptions," *Orientalia* 28 (1959):130–40; H. Tadmor, "The Inscriptions of Nabunaid, Historical Arrangement," *Assyriological Studies* 16 (1965):351–64.

the temple of Eḫulḫul for Sin. When Nabonidus objects that he cannot do it because the barbarians (*Ummanmanda*) occupy Harran, Marduk prophesies their expulsion by Cyrus, which is then recorded as fulfilled. Whereupon Nabonidus is said to have carried out the gods' command. The Harran version (H2, A–13) contains two important departures from this text. The first is that Sin appears alone to Nabonidus and it is he who commands the king to rebuild his own temple. Now, given the fact that the priests of Marduk were most unhappy with Nabonidus's exaltation of Sin and his temple in Harran over Marduk and his temple, Esagil, in Babylon, the Babylonian version, which has Marduk command the construction of Sin's temple, is clearly a piece of propaganda. The original version must have presented Sin appearing alone to Nabonidus.

The second departure in the Harran text comes after the divine command to Nabonidus to build the temple. In the Babylonian text reference is made to the foreigners in Harran and their expulsion by Cyrus. But in the Harran text this is replaced by a long account of Nabonidus's north Arabian campaign and his ten-year residence in Teima. Only after this long delay does he return to carry out the god's command. The Babylonian version knows nothing of such a delay or of the Teima sojourn. There is, then, both the historical problem of when the restoration of the temple took place and the literary problem of how the two accounts relate to each other.

W. L. Moran has suggested a solution based upon a literary analysis of the two texts.[31] He points out that the Harran text creates a serious difficulty in comprehension[32] because the text that mentions the vision of Sin is rather artificially separated by the long account of the Teima episode from the statement that the command was carried out promptly. Once the interpolation is removed, the resulting version parallels rather closely in abbreviated form the Babylonian version, with identical words in a number of passages. But, as noted above, since the Babylonian version cannot have been the original, it is likely that both go back to an earlier *Vorlage* resembling the Babylonian version more closely but without its reference to Marduk. The extant Harran text created the shorter version of the building inscription so that it could include within it the Teima history. But this explanation still leaves unanswered the question why the scribe should have falsified history by putting the Teima episode where he did in the account if the original inscription suggested that Nabonidus fulfilled the command before his Teima retreat. The answer to this question is based, as Moran indicates, on the dictates of formal conventions of royal inscriptions. Harran differs from Babylon in having had a long and impor-

31. "Notes on the New Nabonidus Inscriptions," pp. 130–40.
32. This problem is smoothed over in the translation in *ANET*[3], p. 563.

tant association with Assyria as one of its major royal cities and with the temple of Eḫulḫul as an important Assyrian temple. As we have already noted above, in the Assyrian commemorative inscriptions notices of military campaigns always came before descriptions of building activity regardless of the chronological order of events. So a scribe who wanted to follow the Assyrian model simply took an earlier Harran text dealing only with the circumstances of the rebuilding of Eḫulḫul and added to it the account of the Teima expedition, inserting it before the mention of the building of the temple even though this was chronologically wrong and created an awkward split between the divine command to rebuild and its prompt fulfillment. It seems clear in this instance that a simple building dedication has been modified by a major addition, following an Assyrian annalistic model, to produce a more complex form that, with its strongly apologetic character, has in itself become something new.[33]

What is important here is that grammatical and form-critical observations as well as comparison with parallel versions allow one to make careful literary-critical judgments. Throughout the Neo-Assyrian and Neo-Babylonian periods the scribes who composed and edited "historical" texts were strongly inclined to use previous versions of texts whenever they dealt with the same subject, to change or edit them to suit their own needs or the particular audience for which they were intended, to conflate various kinds of source material or parallel versions with varying degrees of literary skill, and always to be rather rigidly bound by conventions of style, genre, and formulaic expression. These observations cannot be ignored by anyone concerned with the compositional problems of the historical books of the Old Testament.

One other genre that falls within the general category of Assyrian royal inscriptions is the so-called letter to the god. Because of its distinctive prose style it calls for special consideration. The best example of this type is the letter of Sargon II, a report of his eighth campaign against the land of Urartu (714 B.C.) addressed to the god Ashur and to the gods and citizens of the city of Assur.[34] While the opening lines of address may suggest the letter form, the designation is a misnomer. As A. L. Oppenheim has convincingly argued,[35] it is a text specially composed for a great ceremony

33. Tadmor (see n. 30) has offered a number of arguments for dating the restoration of the temple of Eḫulḫul to the period after Nabonidus's return from Teima. Admittedly the evidence is somewhat ambiguous, but what makes his position difficult to accept is that he still gives no explanation for the literary problem that he is willing to admit does exist.

34. For a translation see Luckenbill, *ARAB*, vol. 2, pp. 73–99.

35. "The City of Assur in 714 B.C.," *JNES* 19 (1960):133–47. My discussion of the text is heavily dependent upon this literary analysis by Oppenheim. For another example not cited by Oppenheim see N. Na'aman, "Sennacherib's 'Letter to God' on His Campaign to Judah," *BASOR* 214 (1974):25–39.

celebrating the triumph of a successful campaign and was meant to be read aloud to the priests and the populace of the city. The ending also turns it into a eulogy for those fallen in battle since it mentions the casualties in stylized form: one charioteer, two cavalrymen, three sappers. Although unnamed, they are called "heroes" and represent the unknown soldiers. Since this same feature is found at the end of the "letter" of Esarhaddon, its stereotyped and ceremonial character seems assured.

In his literary analysis Oppenheim calls attention to the careful structure of the work in which the scribe divides the body of the text (ca. 420 lines) into fifteen sections. "Twelve of the sections begin with the same phrase and even with the same word (*ultu* 'from'): 'I moved from GN and reached GN$_2$' and thus are clearly meant to indicate the stages of the campaign. Most of them are quite stereotyped as to their content: they mention cities, rulers, mountains, and countries without giving much detail; monotonously they report on victories and destructions." In the fourth section a major battle that constitutes a turning point in the war is described. This is followed by eight more stages after which the style changes in order to deal at length with a special surprise attack upon the city of Muṣaṣir, the climax of the entire text.

Oppenheim comments upon the style of the campaign itinerary. "The presentation is inexorably paratactic; the report shifts abruptly from stop to stop, the endlessly repeated verbal forms in the first person sing. offer a monotonous staccato which does not convey the purpose and planning of the action, the realities of the situation . . . and the motives that may have animated the king and his adversaries."[36] The scenery, which has an initial appearance of realism, is in fact highly formulaic and schematized. Nevertheless, the work as a whole achieves "an astonishing sense of drama"[37] by the way in which it leads up to the initial victory over the king of Urartu in the fourth *ultu*-section and then, after eight more stages, to the climax in the attack on Muṣaṣir. But in order to achieve just this effect the author had to slightly alter the chronological facts, which were that Muṣaṣir was not the last battle in the campaign. It was put at the end because it was the most important. Oppenheim also points out that prior to the battle at Muṣaṣir, as the circumstances clearly indicate but the account never openly admits, Sargon was in some military difficulty which caused Urzana, governor of Muṣaṣir, to change his mind about submitting to Sargon. If he had done so the city would have been spared, but his treachery and resistance led to the city's destruction. The author interprets this as "the *hubris* of Urzana and the sweet reasonableness of the Assyrian

36. "The City of Assur in 714 B.C.," p. 134.
37. Ibid., p. 135.

king"[38] and thus uses the occasion to delineate the character of the protagonists. Much attention is also given in the text to three divine signs before the attack on Muṣaṣir in order both to emphasize divine intervention on behalf of the Assyrian king and to justify the subsequent severe action taken against a most holy city, Urartu, and its temple and gods.[39]

Oppenheim also points out another important feature of the text, its digressions from the main action. The topics of the digressions are both geography, including animals and topography, and foreign mores. In the case of the former the emphasis is clearly on the wonder and grandeur of the territory traversed and the hardships that had to be overcome. The traditional attitude of most literary texts toward foreign mores is to hold them up to ridicule as "barbarian." In this text, however, the attitude toward foreign customs is clearly sympathetic, and even achievements in technology are admired. In the latter category are descriptions of the irrigation systems of Urartu, the system of communication by fire signals, the strong military installations, and the raising of horses in the mountain valleys. One major digression, which comes right in the middle of the attack on the city of Muṣaṣir, is a description of the city, its deity Ḥaldia, and the manner of the king's coronation. Both in the sympathetic tenor of its treatment and in the placement of such digressions within battle accounts this text bears a remarkable resemblance to the style of Herodotus.[40]

Oppenheim stresses that the function of this text was directly related to an audience that was to hear the text read and to be immediately responsive to the content.

> The intention to keep the interest of an audience aroused can also be observed on the artistic level. With much sophistication the letter displays fireworks of dramatics solely in order to hold its listeners. The carefully laid out overall structure has already been described . . . with its slow moving exposition, climax, crisis, divine intervention, and triumphal end. In the superstructural ornamentation designed for the same purpose we find interspersed flights of highly poetic comparisons, descriptions of the marvels of nature, and interesting information on foreign mores. . . . In every respect the letter has the marks of having been written by an artist sure of himself and backed by a solid tradition as to style, diction, and inventory of motifs.[41]

38. Ibid., p. 136.

39. One is reminded of a similar justification in the epic of Tukulti-Ninurta, in which the gods of Babylon who were brought to Assur after the destruction of the southern city were viewed as visiting and paying homage to Ashur. So here in lines 315ff. (see Luckenbill, *ARAB*, vol. 2, p. 93, no. 170) the king is given the right to bring the foreign gods into the temple of Ashur to do him homage. The Tukulti-Ninurta precedent seems evident. On the Tukulti-Ninurta Epic see below, 3e.

40. See above, 2c.

41. *JNES* 19:143–44.

The conviction that one is dealing in this text with artistic creativity as well as conventional forms can be tested by a comparison with the so-called Letter of Esarhaddon.[42] While it exhibits many of the same qualities as the Sargon Letter to the God, its author uses different techniques to achieve characterization of the protagonists and dramatic effect. He does this by employing speeches and messages between the two kings; they take up a major portion of the extant text. But these speeches are invented for this purpose in a fashion not unlike that found in the later classical historians. Perhaps the style of the historical epic, in which speeches are important, has had some influence upon the artistic form.[43]

On the basis of this discussion of the Sargon and Esarhaddon texts, two additional observations may be made. First, it has been suggested that these "letters" are related to certain references in texts from Mari that speak about its rulers giving reports or other information to a god about their activities.[44] It is therefore argued that the real origin and motivation for all the royal annals were the letters to the gods. This is unlikely because, first, many centuries intervene between the Mari examples and those of the Neo-Assyrian period, and continuity cannot be assumed. Second, the one clear example of a letter to a god is a kind of apology for the king's authority in Mari based upon the military activity of his grandfather and father, not his own;[45] and it is hardly in the form and style of an annal. It is also very different in form and probably also in function from the Neo-Assyrian texts. Finally, the style of the Neo-Assyrian letters to the god preclude them from being used as the primary reports from which the annals themselves were made. While both annals and the "letters" relied originally on the same kind of primary sources—reports and booty lists—for their composition, their styles are so different as to be totally unrelated to each other. It is not even certain how many such texts of "letters," written for the purpose of a specific performance, were actually retained as literature on their own artistic merits. That so few have survived would indicate that keeping the texts was the exception rather than the rule.

A second observation involves the larger question of historiography. There are many serious objections to considering the "letters to the god" as history writing. The subject matter of the letter is more accurately described as "current events" than history; the dominance of the first-person

42. For a translation see Luckenbill, *ARAB*, vol. 2, pp. 231–37.

43. See the discussion of the Tukulti-Ninurta Epic below, 3e. One finds there the same note of "righteousness" on the part of the Assyrian king and admission of guilt by the enemy king being attacked. See also the possible epic fragment on Kurigalzu in Chronicle P (Grayson, *ABC*, pp. 173–75).

44. See Speiser, "Ancient Mesopotamia," in *Idea of History*, pp. 63–66; followed by Gese, *ZThK* 55:137–38.

45. See Grayson, *ARI*, vol. 1, pp. 27–28, no. 10.

singular hardly presents the perspective of objectivity; the apparent disregard for chronological exactitude violates proper historical method; and the function of a text for a particular occasion is more conducive to achieving certain propagandistic or entertainment goals than to recording the "facts" for posterity. Nevertheless, the style and content of the Sargon Letter to the God do raise some interesting historiographic questions. Where did the author get all the information on geography and topography beyond the usual stereotypes, and where did he learn about the specific customs of foreigners and get other information for his digressions? Was he a member of the expedition who took his own careful notes or did he gather the information from those who had returned?

In either case the author's work must have been a form of "historical" research similar to that practiced by Hecataeus and Herodotus. Furthermore, the scope given to the subject matter by the inclusion of geography and ethnography, the artistic freshness and freedom, the fair-mindedness toward the "barbarians" are all important qualities in the development of the historiographic tradition. Even the presentation of historical events from a particular viewpoint with the intent of persuading an audience to see these events in a certain way is an important facet of history writing. It is perhaps unfortunate and only accidental that so little prose narration of historical events of the quality of these "letters to the god" has been preserved. Consequently, the overwhelming impression from the Mesopotamian royal inscriptions with their wooden and stereotyped prose is that they have little to contribute to the development of historiography. Yet, when these so-called letters are put together with other materials a somewhat different picture of the place of Mesopotamian literature in the rise of historiography will emerge.

b. KING LISTS

According to Grayson, king lists belong to a larger category of historiographic texts called chronographic texts, which include both king lists and chronicles.[46] Grayson groups them together in his classification scheme because they share certain dating formulas and because some king lists include brief narrative notices about important events that resemble chronicles. Nevertheless, this does not mean that one form is derived from the other, and there are good reasons, as I hope my exposition makes plain, why the two types of texts might be fruitfully considered separately.

46. *ABC*, pp. 4ff., 193ff.; *Orientalia* 49:171–82; see also W. Röllig, "Zur Typologie und Entstehung der babylonischen und assyrischen Königslisten," *lišan mithurti. Festschrift W. von Soden*, AOAT 1, pp. 265–77.

It is also clear from Grayson's classification that there was more than one king-list tradition, so that the origins and functions of the lists were not always the same. A general statement about king lists, therefore, could not adequately represent their relationship to the development of the historiographic tradition.

King lists have often been associated with the Mesopotamian list-science mentality, and for one category of king lists this appears to be justified. In the scribal tradition of ancient Mesopotamia there was a great propensity to make useful lists of all kinds: syllabaries, bilingual vocabularies, lists of plants and animals, observations of the heavens, gods, in fact almost anything. Such a list-science was a widespread literary phenomenon and can be witnessed in the onomastica of ancient Egypt[47] and in the Old Testament.[48] Most lists had a practical application, for example, "date lists" were used for the purpose of reckoning the dates of documents.[49] As far back as the Ur III period (ca. 2100 B.C.) there was a standard practice of naming each year after an important event of that year and then using this year name to date documents. In order to keep track of this dating system it was necessary to make lists of year names that one could consult in order to calculate the age of a document and therefore of a legal or business transaction. This practice continued to the end of the Old Babylonian period (ca. 1600 B.C.).

Included in these date lists was the number of the years of a particular king's reign, which corresponded to the sum of all the date names for each king in the list. From the tallies in the date lists it was then possible to make king lists giving the number of years in a reign and the name of the king. While the date lists are not known for a period later than Old Babylonian, the king lists deriving from them do continue on, giving the names of each successive ruler of Babylonia, in one list from the first dynasty of Babylon to the late seventh century B.C.[50] and in another down into Seleucid times.[51] These king lists appear to go beyond the practical function of the date lists and reflect antiquarian interests.

In Assyria a different system for dating was used, called eponym dating.[52] The Assyrians named their years after a high government official,

---

47. A. H. Gardiner, *Ancient Egyptian Onomastica*, 3 vols.

48. G. von Rad, "Job xxxviii and Ancient Egyptian Wisdom," in *Problem of the Hexateuch and Other Essays*, pp. 281–91.

49. A. Ungnad, "Datenlisten," *RLA* 2:131–94.

50. Babylonian King List A. See *ANET*³, p. 272, for translation, and Grayson, *ABC*, p. 269, for bibliography; also Röllig, "Typologie," p. 268.

51. The Uruk King List. See *ANET*³, p. 566; Grayson, *ABC*, p. 268. Besides these lists there were other, shorter lists of the same type but covering more limited periods of time: the Ur-Isin King List, Larsa King List, Babylonian King List C. A school text in a different style covering the first two dynasties of Babylon is Babylonian King List B.

52. A. Ungnad, "Eponym," *RLA* 2:412–57. A small sample is given in *ANET*³, p. 274. See also Grayson, *ABC*, p. 196.

līmu, who changed every year. Lists were then made of the *līmu* or eponym years. Some lists seem to correspond closely with the Babylonian date lists in also citing an important event in the period of office of a particular *līmu.* Yet it is not so easy to see how the Assyrian *līmu* lists could be used as sources to construct king lists since there was no point of connection between the office of *līmu* and the king, at least on a regular basis, until the time of Adad-nirari II (911–891), when the kings began to hold the office of *līmu* for one year during their reign.[53]

Belonging to quite a different tradition of king lists is the Sumerian King List (SKL).[54] This remarkable literary work, which is preserved in a number of copies in the Sumerian language from the Old Babylonian period (ca. 1800–1600 B.C.), tells how kingship came down from heaven and was first established in the city of Eridu. Then follows a list of eight or nine kings, each of whom had very long reigns, who ruled in five cities. This period is brought to an end by the deluge that swept over the earth, after which kingship descended once again to Kish. Again, "dynasties" of various cities given in a single sequence successively exercise rule over the region of southern Mesopotamia. The length of each individual reign, while still very long, is much shorter than the previous period and soon is reduced to "historical" proportions. This series of reigns is traced to the first dynasty of Isin and ends about 1800 B.C.

A few points about this work should be noted. First, as Jacobsen has observed in his major study,[55] the presentation of kingship as a continuous series in which only one king reigned at a time in the whole region of Sumer before the Akkad dynasty is entirely artificial. Through most of this period a number of city-states existed side by side quite independently. The perspective of SKL was produced by combining individual dynastic lists from various city-states into one long list. Because these individual king lists often contained legendary ancestors as well as historical rulers, the legendary and the historical became rather mixed in the Sumerian King List. Second, since the initial section of SKL dealing with the antediluvian kings was not a part of some versions of the text, it seems likely that this was a later addition to the work from a quite separate tradition. The formulaic language used in this section is different from that in the postdiluvian section, and it is also known from other sources where it is independent of SKL.[56] Third, besides the name of the king and length of reign,

53. Röllig, "Typologie," pp. 275–76.
54. T. Jacobsen, *The Sumerian King List; ANET*³, pp. 265–66. For bibliography see Grayson, *ABC,* pp. 197–98, 268–69, 295. On the genealogical material in SKL see R. R. Wilson, *Genealogy and History in the Biblical World,* pp. 73–83.
55. *The Sumerian King List.*
56. See the recent discussion by W. W. Hallo, "Antediluvian Cities," *JCS* 23 (1970):57–67.

SKL also contains a few notes on filiation,[57] occupations or professions other than kingship, political and military achievements, and a few other remarks regarding some of the rulers. Jacobsen suggests that these are most likely derived from legends and epic sources. Some of the notes can be paralleled from extant epics.[58]

Interpretations of the function of SKL rest primarily upon its date. Jacobsen's view is that the original version is to be dated to the beginning of the Ur III dynasty and the text is therefore to be seen as a legitimation of Ur's domination of the whole region of Sumer and Akkad on the theory that kingship can be held rightly only by the ruler of the leading city of the region. Some scholars, however, date the work to the subsequent period, the first dynasty of Isin, as all the exemplars with complete endings would indicate. In that case we would have to modify Jacobsen's interpretation and to see the work instead as the legitimation of rulers of Isin as the rightful successors to the Ur III empire.[59] Either way one understands it, SKL was an attempt to collect various documents about rulers and heroes of the past in order to present the past in a certain way for a specific political and ideological purpose in the author's own time. The facts that it survived in so many exemplars after the fall of Isin and that it was further developed by the addition of the antediluvian kings suggest a shift in its function to that of reflecting antiquarian, or "historical," interest.[60]

Although copies of SKL do not extend beyond the Old Babylonian period, the work does have some interesting descendants. One such text is the Dynastic Chronicle,[61] which stands very close to the SKL tradition. It was composed in a mixture of Sumerian and Akkadian in the Neo-Assyrian period. It contains nine antediluvian kings ruling in five cities, and although the order of the cities is slightly different from that in SKL, the names of the cities and the rulers are so similar that a direct relationship to the earlier tradition cannot be doubted.[62] After the antediluvian kings a

57. Wilson, in *Genealogy*, pp. 82–83, discusses the possible sources for the genealogical notices in SKL.

58. See also W. G. Lambert and A. R. Millard, *Atra-ḫasīs: The Babylonian Story of the Flood*, pp. 15ff. Cf. S. N. Kramer, *The Sumerians*, pp. 43ff. Kramer treats SKL and the epics as mutually independent and confirming historical sources.

59. See Wilson, *Genealogy*, p. 81, for recent discussion and literature on this question.

60. The remarks about SKL here are quite at variance with the discussion by Gese, *ZThK* 55:134–35. There is no evidence whatever that SKL was an outgrowth of "ordering science," that it had anything to do with omens or with the so-called "*narū*" literature. The development that Gese constructs is totally artificial.

61. The text is included by Grayson among his chronicles in *ABC*, pp. 40–42, 139–44, as Chronicle 18, but it certainly belongs to the king-list tradition. For this reason I am treating it here although I follow closely Grayson's discussion of this text. See also Lambert and Millard, *Atra-ḫasīs*, pp. 17–18, who refer to it as a "dynastic list."

62. Jacobsen regarded the text as a late recension of SKL and listed it as such under the siglum K; see *Sumerian King List*, p. 11. However, Lambert and Millard, *Atra-ḫasīs*, p. 18, think it misleading to refer to it as a copy of SKL but treat it as a "descendant."

substantial break occurs in the text with only a few words preserved and then follow some names of postdiluvian kings that again parallel those in SKL. The few words between these two groups of names appear to have been part of a substantial reference to the flood, much longer than the notation in SKL.[63] The rest of the text includes the first dynasty of Babylon down to the "dynasty of Chaldea" but with many lacunae. Throughout, the author attempts to continue both the same type of "dynastic" succession as in SKL and the archaic Sumerian language and terminology. One remarkable feature of the latter part of the text is the notation about the proper or improper burial of the king. This may have been a way of distinguishing legitimate rulers from usurpers.[64]

The function of this text is not easy to determine because of its fragmentary condition. But given the fact that it deals primarily with Babylonia, although it was found at Nineveh, it is possible that its purpose was to show that the authority of the southern region was ultimately transferred to Assyria. The text is badly broken at the end, but enough remains to suggest that the "dynasty" of Chaldea fell and that its kingship was transferred to another power. In the known historical context only Assyria would fit this place.

The same chronographic tradition continues on into later times, as can be seen in a king list of the Hellenistic period.[65] The same archaic terminology of SKL is still preserved in it. Even the Macedonian rulers wished to use this scheme to legitimize the transition of power to their "dynasty." The tradition is also found in Berossus, who employs the framework of antediluvian cities and kings (with Babylon replacing Eridu as the first city), the flood, and subsequent history.[66] Whatever the purpose of the earliest version of SKL might have been, the scheme itself created a conceptual framework for representing universal history that went beyond the borders of Mesopotamia to include Phoenicia, Palestine, and even the Aegean world.

The Assyrian King List (AKL)[67] is another document that, like the Su-

63. Lambert and Millard, *Atra-ḫasīs*, offer cogent reasons why the text probably contained a long account of the flood in the broken portion between the antediluvian and postdiluvian kings.

64. On the reference to burial places see Grayson, *ABC*, p. 41, and idem, *ARI*, vol. 1, p. 25, n. 76.

65. Called a "Seleucid King List" in *ANET*[3], pp. 566–67. See Grayson's remarks on its relation to SKL, *Orientalia* 49:178.

66. Lambert and Millard, *Atra-ḫasīs*, pp. 15ff., 134–37; S. M. Burstein, *The Babyloniaca of Berossus*.

67. I. J. Gelb, "Two Assyrian King Lists," *JNES* 13 (1954):209–30; J. A. Brinkman, "Comments on the Nassouhi Kinglist and the Assyrian Kinglist Tradition," *Orientalia* 42 (1973):306–19; *ANET*[3], pp. 564–66. See bibliography in Grayson, *ABC*, pp. 264–70; also Röllig, "Typologie," pp. 265–77; Wilson, *Genealogy*, pp. 86–100.

merian King List, suggests certain historiographic principles beyond the tendency merely to compile lists. It is a list of the kings of Assyria, reaching back to their earliest ancestors and coming down, in the latest version, to the reign of Shalmaneser V (726–722 B.C.). The first section is a list of seventeen names that are called "17 kings who dwelt in tents." The second section then lists "10 kings who are ancestors" and gives them in genealogical order with the formula RN, son of RN_2, RN_2, son of RN_3. This produces a list in reverse chronological order from the rest of the text. The last two names in section two, Apiashal and Ushpia, are repeated in reverse order from the last two names of section one, thus connecting the two sections. Section three lists six kings and begins with "Sulili, son of Aminu" but then gives five names without any genealogical designation. As earlier, the filiation in the first line is intended to make a connection with Aminu, of the previous section. Section four follows with a series of names using the formula RN_2, son of RN_1, he ruled x years. These are given in correct chronological order and tied to the last name of section three. The formula for section four becomes the fixed formula for the rest of the text.

The list is interrupted again after the first six names in section four by the name "Shamshi-Adad (I), son of Ilu-kabkabi," and a chroniclelike account of how he seized the throne from the previous rulers. Now Ilu-kabkabi, Shamshi-Adad's father, occurs at the beginning of the list of the ten ancestors in section two along with Aminu, who was probably Shamshi-Adad's brother and immediate predecessor. Section two is thus a genealogy of Shamshi-Adad. Aminu's name cannot, therefore, stand at the head of section three as the beginning of a line of thirteen rulers before Shamshi-Adad. The duplication of the names Apiashal and Ushpia in sections one and two is also suspect. This means that the first three sections, which have their own distinct styles, were originally independent, and that the connections made between them were artificial.

The task of unfolding the "tradition-history" of AKL, by which these various blocks of material were brought together, is complex. One important control in this discussion, however, must be the utilization of extant historical and inscriptional information. The texts must also be compared with other relevant king-list and genealogical traditions.[68]

Compared with SKL, AKL says nothing about the antediluvian and postdiluvian kings or the period of Assyria's domination by the Akkad dynasty and the Neo-Sumerian rulers of the third dynasty of Ur. Furthermore, the pattern of kingship transferred from one state to another is not recognized. Instead, kingship is traced back to the hoary antiquity of the

68. See esp. W. W. Hallo, "Assyrian Historiography Revisited," *Eretz-Israel* 14:1–7.

tent-dwelling kings,[69] and the whole list is associated with one place, the city of Assur. On the other hand, the first section of AKL must be related in some way to the recently published Babylonian genealogy of the Hammurapi dynasty,[70] which also has at the beginning a list of eleven or twelve names that parallel rather closely the first twelve names of AKL. Since most of these names are tribal or geographic, the list has the character of a group of eponymous ancestors. A rather widespread opinion is that the names represent a common, oral, West-Semitic ("Amorite") tribal heritage which became the traditional basis for both Babylonian and Assyrian kingships. Shamshi-Adad, the "Amorite," is then credited with introducing this tradition into Assyria.

As indicated above, the "10 kings who are ancestors" in section two have been interpreted by most scholars as a genealogy of Shamshi-Adad. Consequently, it has been suggested that the earliest document was composed in the time of Shamshi-Adad and was created by combining the West-Semitic tribal eponyms (1) and the Shamshi-Adad genealogy (2) with the native traditions of the rulers of the city of Assur (3–4). The purpose of this work was the legitimation of Shamshi-Adad's rule. The rest of the list grew simply by supplementing it with additional names after the accession of each new king.

Hallo, however, has recently raised some serious objections to this reconstruction.[71] He points out that Shamshi-Adad did not rule his empire from Assur but from Shubat-Enlil, and that Assur was not even maintained as the capital of its provincial region. In his inscriptions Shamshi-Adad mentions only his father in his royal descent and claims no succession from the Old Assyrian kings.[72] In fact, for at least a century Shamshi-Adad and his son Ishme-Dagan were not considered legitimate members of the Assyrian royal line, so that the legitimation of Shamshi-Adad and his successor must have come some time later. Furthermore, in comparing AKL with the genealogy of the Hammurapi dynasty, another fact is often overlooked or obscured. In the latter document the list is homogeneous in its form from the beginning through the enumerations of the first dynasty of Babylon. But as we have already noted, section one of AKL, which contains the tribal names, does not belong together with the

69. See Hallo, ibid., p. 5, and n. 49, where he offers a corrective to my statement, in *Abraham in History and Tradition*, p. 14.
70. J. J. Finkelstein, "The Genealogy of the Hammurapi Dynasty," *JCS* 20 (1966):95–118. See also W. G. Lambert, "Another Look at Hammurapi's Ancestors," *JCS* 22 (1968):1–2; A. Malamat, "King Lists of the Old Babylonian Period and Biblical Genealogies," *JAOS* 88 (1968):163–73; Röllig, "Typologie," pp. 269–73; Wilson, *Genealogy*, pp. 107–14; Hallo, "Assyr. Hist.," pp. 4–5.
71. "Assyr. Hist.," pp. 5–6.
72. See inscriptions in Grayson, *ARI*, vol. 1, pp. 18–28.

Shamshi-Adad genealogy.[73] It becomes highly unlikely that we can speak of a common oral tradition that came into Assyria with Shamshi-Adad. Instead it must be viewed as a separate source used by the author of the original version of AKL.

Of the names preceding Shamshi-Adad, Puzur-Ashur I to Puzur-Ashur II are known from inscriptional evidence to belong to the native dynasty of Assur, and they constitute an overlap of sections three and four. But the successor of Puzur-Ashur II, Naram-Sin, was not the former's son as AKL suggests, but an invader from Eshnunna. Erishum II, the next name, may or may not be his son. This period of foreign rule of Assur has been suppressed in AKL by the fiction of genealogical connection.

AKL indicates that there was a rather troubled period after Ishme-Dagan. It omits three additional members of this ruling family who are included in a divergent king-list tradition,[74] and it mentions a number of irregular rulers—"sons of nobodies"—one of whom ruled for six years while six others ruled for less than a year each.[75] Out of this period a new dynastic line is seen to emerge which carries the royal line through the petty kings of the early Middle Assyrian period. Wilson, in a study of the genealogies within this part of AKL,[76] points out a number of discrepancies within the list itself and between the list and extant inscriptional evidence for the period. It would be difficult to account for these errors in AKL if the king list after Shamshi-Adad were merely a running list of kings supplemented after each reign.

Three other factors should be considered in dating the composition. First, there are a series of statements describing the violent seizure of the throne. In three cases, including Shamshi-Adad, the usurper is said to have come from Karduniash (Babylonia).[77] In the case of Shamshi-Adad the terminology and pattern of behavior are clearly fictional and anachronistic, reflecting a later period when Babylonia was actively meddling in Assyrian affairs. Second, the construction of such an elaborate chronographic scheme as one finds in AKL suggests the notion of a national state, an As-

73. Malamat, "King Lists," obscures these literary issues in his treatment, especially by his chart on p. 173. It is difficult for me to see how the extant form of AKL could ever have resulted from a single Shamshi-Adad genealogy such as he proposes. See also R. R. Wilson, "The Old Testament Genealogies in Recent Research," *JBL* 94 (1975):169–89, for a further critique of Malamat's proposals.

74. See Grayson, *ARI*, vol. 1, p. 29, no. 172; also idem, *ABC*, p. 270.

75. See the note by Oppenheim, *ANET*³, p. 565, n. 3.

76. *Genealogy*, pp. 88ff.

77. Brinkman, *Orientalia* 42:315–16, takes the reference to Karduniash as evidence that the "final redaction" was not made before the Middle Assyrian period. I am not sure what is meant by this since all later editions which supplemented the earliest versions were "redactions" and not just copies. It seems preferable to see in this reference a clue to the time of the "author."

syrian kingdom, but this is not reflected in any texts before the time of Ashur-uballit I (1365–1330).[78] So the earliest version of AKL cannot date before the late Middle Assyrian period. Third, Lambert has recently published a text that comes from the time of Tukulti-Ninurta I and refers to the listing of the kings, their division into groups ("dynasties"), and their filiations according to AKL.[79] This suggests a *terminus ad quem* for its composition in the time of Tukulti-Ninurta and a date for AKL in the period just prior to, or in the early part of, Tukulti-Ninurta's reign.

The thorny question of sources for such a document is thus raised. Section one, the "17 kings who dwelt in tents," did not belong either to the Shamshi-Adad genealogy, section two, or to the native Assyrian tradition of section three. Therefore it must have been foreign and its place of origin Babylonia, as is clearly attested by the Hammurapi genealogy. It could have come into Assyria in literary form as a late recension of the earlier tradition in the mid-thirteenth century, when such Babylonian influence in Assyria seems to have been strong.[80] The genealogy of Shamshi-Adad was originally preserved on a monument or in a document as the genealogy of Aminu, whose connection with Shamshi-Adad was therefore not clearly understood. Hence its placement in the list. Whether the rest of AKL could have been constructed from simple king lists, eponym lists, monuments containing genealogical statements, and early chronicles for individual rulers must be a matter of considerable conjecture since some of these possible sources are debatable.[81] But the evidence that we reviewed earlier for its artificial character in its earlier sections strongly suggests that it was a product of research. The author was faced with a number of difficult decisions in constructing his work out of the sources he had. His motive was very likely nationalistic but also to a large extent antiquarian and historiographic. This view of history, which connected the monarchy of Assyria with the distant past, was comparable to southern Babylonian traditions but gave no suggestion that Assur was dominated by outside authority at any time. In spite of occasional genealogical disruptions, the continuity of kingship in Assur seemed to be secure. The scheme and the perspective of AKL took hold in the Assyrian scribal tradition, as the continuation of the work by later scribes attests.[82]

78. A. K. Grayson, "The Early Development of Assyrian Monarchy," *Ugarit-Forschungen* 3 (1971):314 and n. 27; Hallo, "Assyr. Hist.," p. 6.

79. W. G. Lambert, "Tukulti-Ninurta I and the Assyrian King List," *Iraq* 38 (1976):85–94.

80. On Babylonian influence in Assyria in this period see P. Machinist, "Literature as Politics: The Tukulti-Ninurta Epic and the Bible," *CBQ* 38 (1976):460–82.

81. See the discussion of this problem by Röllig, "Typologie," pp. 274–77.

82. See also the concluding remarks by Hallo, "Assyr. Hist.," pp. 6–7.

c. OMENS

Omen texts are often included with king lists as part of the Mesopotamian "list-science," and many of them contain statements about the past of the highest historical value. Because some of these statements are similar to, or identical with, statements made in chronicles, a close relationship between the two forms has also been suggested. Finkelstein has proposed that the omen texts were really at the root of Mesopotamian historiography and that the chronicles developed from them.[83] This position cannot go unchallenged.

It is true that omen collections belong to Mesopotamian list-science, which often has the character of empirical scientific activity. Such lists can reflect in their content the careful observation of nature and human activity, but as collections they also represent the practical needs of social, economic, and religious institutions. The diviner needed reference lists of omens to carry out his art.

A particular omen could be interpreted as the recording of a simple empirical observation. An unusual natural phenomenon was recorded together with an event that was viewed as either fortunate or unfortunate in the life of an individual or the state. This observation was then used to predict good or evil on future occasions when such a natural phenomenon occurred again. Those who were consulted about such phenomena of nature kept lists of omens in order to make their predictions. The diviners, however, could also manipulate omens on demand before important undertakings, such as battles, and on these occasions they used such means as pouring oil on water, releasing birds to examine their flight, or inspecting the viscera of sacrificed animals. The results could be interpreted on the basis of previously recorded observations as boding good or ill.[84]

It would be wrong, however, to overemphasize either the empirical-scientific aspect of the diviners' observations or the amount of historical content in the omens. First, behind the art of divination was the rather unscientific belief that it was "a technique of communication with the supernatural forces that are supposed to shape the history of the individual as well as that of the group."[85] In this way one could take advantage of the good omen and avoid the consequences of the evil one. Thus it was actually the gods who wrote the sign on the viscera of animals at the moment of sacrifice, or who produced certain effects in nature to give a message to the suppliant. Such a superstitious attitude, which turns astronomy

---

83. J. J. Finkelstein, "Mesopotamian Historiography," *PAPS* 107 (1963):461–72; see above, 3a.
84. See the discussion by Oppenheim, *Ancient Mesopotamia*, pp. 206–27.
85. Ibid., p. 207.

into astrology, can hardly be expected to develop the historical consciousness that leads to historiography. Furthermore, no distinction was made
between historical events and natural events. Diviners were interested in
what we might regard as "lucky" or "unlucky." Thus, even omens that refer to royalty "often deal with what we would call accidents."[86] If the
events recorded in omens were political or military they were observed not
as "historical" events but merely as examples of what omens were lucky or
unlucky. It is surely significant that most of the omens with historical content are associated with the dynasty of Akkad and the third dynasty of Ur
(ca. 2350–2000 B.C.), and such observations ended very soon afterward,
as if these periods provided enough political examples for the diviner's
purpose. Lists of historical omens could, by themselves, never produce a
work of history.

The value of omens for modern historians is that they contain a contemporary witness to the event recorded in the same way that royal correspondence and other such data give direct information about a historical
period. But unlike the "day-to-day business" texts, the omen texts became
a major part of the scribal tradition and were preserved with their historical material for later generations.

H. Gese takes a somewhat different approach from Finkelstein and
looks at omen science as expressing a certain idea of history: "In this science one proceeded from the presupposition that there was a finite, although large, number of distinct 'times' which could be defined in terms of
certain phenomena."[87] Thus he sees all omens as related to "times," by
which he means historical events, but this is quite misleading since references to such historical "times" are a rather small fraction of the whole
and are mixed with nonhistorical situations. So the listing of omens cannot
be spoken of as the listing of a sequence of "times." Only much later were
omen collections made that specifically isolated historical omens from
nonhistorical ones, perhaps so that the former could be used by scribes as
source material for historical works.[88] But this probably happened under
the influence of another historiographic genre, the chronicles.[89]

Furthermore, since it was believed that omens were a form of revelation
from the gods, either divine favor or a warning of doom and judgment
could come from them. In any case neither result was inevitable. This
could lead to a certain didactic presentation of history that disregarded the

86. A. Goetze, "Historical Allusions in Old Babylonian Omen Texts," *JCS* 1 (1947):265.
87. H. Gese, "Geschichtliches Denken," *ZThK* 55:131.
88. Finkelstein, "Mesopotamian Historiography," p. 470, n. 37.
89. Finkelstein, ibid., pp. 463, 470–71, argues that omens were the source for chronicles.
This is true in only a few special instances, but the development of the chronicle genre was
quite independent of omens. On this subject see A. K. Grayson, "Divination and the Babylonian Chronicles," pp. 69–76. See also below, 3d.

facts contained in the omens themselves. Thus in the Cuthean Legend of Naram-Sin,[90] which is presented in the form of a fictional autobiography, the king speaks of the continuous disasters that he suffered because he failed to heed the omens. The purpose of this work is to warn future rulers not to do likewise. Yet if we actually consult omen texts referring to Naram-Sin, they speak only of his great success. The literary tradition surrounding the figures of Sargon and Naram-Sin as the symbols of good fortune and bad fortune respectively did not derive from the omens of this period. The belief in divine disclosure through omens, dreams, and oracles prior to important events or undertakings was common in Mesopotamia, Israel, and ancient Greece, and this belief, regardless of the content of omen or oracle, is often a major element in the unhistorical character of these nations' historical traditions.

Another didactic use of the belief in omens can be seen in the text known as Advice to a Prince, or *der Fürstenspiegel*.[91] It contains a series of statements in the style of omens that focus upon the evil behavior of the king and its consequences. Certain rather specific remarks have suggested to some scholars a particular historical background. I. M. Diakonoff, for instance, has interpreted the text as a "political pamphlet" from the time of Sennacherib, ca. 700 B.C.[92] The author's technique is to refer to crimes of recent, but unnamed, monarchs who came to an unfortunate end, and to do this in the style of omens as a way of persuading the present monarch not to repeat such actions. Unlike the historical omens, the historical allusions are veiled in anonymity and can be recognized only by those who already know the "facts." So the purpose of the work is didactic. Because omens were viewed as a way of passing divine judgment on the lives and activities of rulers, lists of political evils could be set down in the protases and their appropriate punishment by the gods in the apodoses. Omens, therefore, did not encourage the collection and preservation of information about the past as such, and any historical information gained from them was only a by-product of other religious concerns.

d. CHRONICLES

In discussions of Mesopotamian historiography the group of texts that come under the rubric of *chronicles* have not received much attention.

---

90. See the remarks by Grayson, *BHLT*, pp. 7ff., and bibliography cited in nn. 10 and 11 of his work.

91. W. G. Lambert, *Babylonian Wisdom Literature*, pp. 110–15.

92. I. M. Diakonoff, "A Babylonian Political Pamphlet from about 700 B.C.," *Landsberger Festschrift*, pp. 343–49.

However, as I hope to show, they are very important for the study of history writing both in Mesopotamia and in Israel. These texts have recently been collected into one volume by A. K. Grayson, whose work constitutes the basis of this study.[93] A chronicle is a narration of political or religious events[94] in chronological order and is closely dated to the years of a king's reign. Since many of them extend over the reigns of several kings they have a close affinity with king lists. Because they often use the same formulaic language in the dating portion of the texts, Grayson has grouped the two genres together under the heading of "chronographic" texts for the purpose of analyzing their basic literary patterns. Furthermore, some king lists include notations that have the character of chronicles. Nevertheless, since their origin and function are different it seems best to maintain a distinction between the two groups.

The term *chronicles* now covers a variety of texts, some of which are quite different from each other and do not have a common origin or function even within this genre. Because the discussion of these texts has become quite complex, we cannot get by here with a simple statement about them. Questions of date, function, sources of information, and interrelationship between extant chronicles are important for the study of these texts and for the rise of historiography in Mesopotamia, but they are fraught with many difficulties. The fragmentary nature of the texts and our inadequate knowledge of the historical background in which some of these texts must be set are the reasons for most differences of opinion.

By far the largest group of extant chronicles is the Babylonian Chronicle Series, containing at present about fifteen texts and fragments which divide rather evenly into two groups. The first deals with events between 747 B.C. and 539 B.C., the year of the Persian conquest. Within the texts each regnal year constitutes one entry, and within each of these the events are dated rather precisely to day and month of the year in most cases. The subject matter, the military and political affairs of the Babylonian king, is similar to that of the Assyrian annals. However, mention of religious matters or divine intervention in human affairs is rare, and the perspective is much more objective than in the annals. There is no glossing over a Babylonian humiliation or an attempt to obscure the facts as they were. The account is presented in the third person rather than in the first-person biographical style of the annals.

It has been suggested that chronicles were derived from omen texts because statements in the former were similar in style to the apodoses of omens.[95] But for the Babylonian Chronicle Series Grayson has put for-

---

93. *Assyrian and Babylonian Chronicles (ABC)*. My nomenclature and numbering of chronicles follow Grayson's. See also Krecher's remarks, *Saeculum* 26:28–30.

94. The exception is the Chronicle of Market Prices, no. 23, to be discussed below.

95. See Finkelstein, "Mesopotamian Historiography."

ward a more likely source, astronomical diaries. He describes these documents in the following way:

> Astronomical diaries are records of various phenomena, each text recording the events of half a specific year. The diaries are divided into sections, each section covering the almost day-to-day events of one month. Most of the phenomena recorded are of an astronomical or meteorological nature but at the end of each section there are statements about market prices, the height of the river, and matters of historical interest.[96]

A primary reason for regarding the chronicles and the diaries as related is the fact that both records begin with the "Nabu-nasir era" (747–734 B.C.). Because the chronicle series simply extracted the historical data from the diaries, the results were often texts precisely dated to day, month, and year of a particular king, with the chronicle continuing through the reign of several kings. It seems clear that the astronomical diaries were a development of the list-science of the Babylonians, but the practical uses of such information are not so obvious. Although one might suppose that they could be used to construct omens, there is no evidence from any omen collection for such use. Yet it is the objectivity of the list-science that is carried over into the chronicles and makes them so different historiographically from the Assyrian annals.[97]

The extraction of historical data from the astronomical diaries to create

---

96. *ABC*, p. 13.

97. Grayson also mentions two other origins for the Babylonian Chronicles which are hard to square with his very convincing proposal here. The first (*ABC*, pp. 6, 194–95) is the Old Babylonian date lists, which, as we have seen, developed into king lists. The reason for the connection is the great similarity in the dating formulas and the fact that year dates often have a chroniclelike character. But the similarity in the dating formula is perhaps exaggerated since the form "year + narrative" is not identical to "year Nth (RN) + narrative," which is, however, the form taken over from the astronomical diaries. The similarity between the date lists and the astronomical diaries is largely accidental and derives from the fact that they are lists in a chronological series. As far as the chroniclelike character of year dates is concerned, the longer entries often resemble annals in the third person rather than chronicles (see examples in *ANET*[3], pp. 269ff.). Also, a chronological gap of close to a thousand years between the date lists and the Babylonian Chronicles makes it difficult to see any connection between them. The second origin Grayson suggests is "a running account of all important events affecting Babylonia" (*ABC*, p. 29), which is identified with the astronomical diaries for the Babylonian Chronicle Series and some other late chronicles, but which is an independent historical source for the earlier period. Here he seems to wed his own proposed source of the astronomical diaries with the earlier view of a "running account source," as expressed by D. J. Wisemann, *Chronicles of the Chaldean Kings (625–556 B.C.) in the British Museum*, pp. 3–4. But the two notions do not fit together. What is surely significant is the new beginning in 747 B.C. of both chronicles and diaries, and only in Babylonia. There is no direct evidence for such a running account before this period, and the indirect evidence is doubtful as we shall try to show below.

chronicles seems to have no other function than to present a careful record of the past. Although such texts became part of an important scribal tradition in Babylon, it was primarily an academic tradition with no propagandist function or use for royal aggrandizement. It was restricted in scope to the activities of Babylonian kings but was objective in its presentation of both victory and defeat. As Grayson states:

> We have, therefore, what seems to be history being written for history's sake as early as the eighth century B.C. Of course this history-writing is parochial. But it is not chauvinistic.[98]

The contrast between the Babylonian chronicles and the Assyrian royal annals, in this regard, could not be greater.

The question arises whether there were chronicles before these Neo-Babylonian exemplars and, if so, whether they had any relationship to this chronicle series. The clearest evidence for earlier chronicles comes from a few fragments of Assyrian chronicles from the library of Tiglath-pileser I that date from the Middle Assyrian period.[99] We must be cautious about making any generalizations on the basis of such fragments. Yet a few observations are in order. First, since the fragments deal with only one Assyrian ruler each, we do not know whether there were chronicles covering several reigns, like the Babylonian chronicles. Second, the dating is largely missing, but what there is does not appear to have the same precise form. Occasional temporal references are made with the vague phrase "at that time," *ina ūmišu*, or "in that year," *ina šattim šiati*, which are typical of royal inscriptions.[100] Third, the reason for identifying the fragments as chronicles rather than annals is the use of the third person. However, it should be pointed out that in the dedication inscription of Yahdun-Lim of Mari the third person is used throughout. On the other hand, there are elements in some of the fragments strongly suggesting a dedication to deities as a consequence of victories won, and there is a hint of divine aid. These raise serious questions about whether we are dealing with chronicles or specific victory accounts commissioned by the king.[101]

Based on the meager evidence of these texts, the so-called Assyrian

98. *ABC*, p. 11. Technically, we cannot say when the notion of abstracting the historical information from the diaries first began. It was very likely not as early as the eighth century and could have been as late as the Persian period, since none of the texts is dated earlier.

99. *ABC*, pp. 66–67, 184–89. Lambert ("Tukulti-Ninurta," n. 2) has recently questioned the notion of a "Tiglath-pileser I library." The texts may be both older and more recent in date.

100. H. Tadmor ("Observations on Assyrian Historiography," in *Essays . . . in Memory of J. J. Finkelstein*, p. 211) conjectures that one text may contain the remains of a līmu date. These were also used on inscriptions of this period.

101. Tadmor (ibid., pp. 210ff.) argues that there are elements of chronistic style in some of the Assyrian annals, but since this is based on comparison with the texts in Grayson's *ABC*, the argument becomes circular if there is any doubt about these chronicles. It is even less

chronicles are much different in character from the Babylonian chronicles. They could hardly derive from the same kind of objective listing process, and they may actually be copies or drafts for commemorative inscriptions. Certainly no chronicle tradition established in Assyria has produced any direct textual evidence in the later periods.

The primary indirect evidence for a continuous chronicle tradition in Assyria is the Synchronistic History.[102] Grayson includes it among the chronicles[103] and describes it thus:

> The Synchronistic History is a concise narration of Assyro-Babylonian relations from the reign of Puzer-Ashur III (first half of the fifteenth century B.C.) to the reign of Adad-nerari III (810–783 B.C.). It is divided by horizontal lines into sections of unequal length each section dealing with one Assyrian king and his Babylonian contemporary or contemporaries. There is an introduction, of which only traces remain, and a conclusion which is almost perfectly intact.[104]

The sources for the work must have been fairly comprehensive because the author includes virtually every known contact between Assyria and Babylonia within the period covered while excluding mention of any Assyrian rulers who did not have some association with Babylon. The bias is obviously in favor of Assyria, and in cases of conflict between the two regions only Assyrian victories and Babylonian defeats are mentioned. In some instances the facts may have been altered or misrepresented to make the outcome appear other than was the case. The primary issue in the hostilities is the violation of border agreements, and Babylonia is always viewed as in the wrong. The document is, therefore, strongly propagandistic, as reflected most clearly in the conclusion, which sings the praises of Assyria and makes the crime of Babylonia known everywhere. In pursuing this line of argument the eighth-century author has very likely invented the notion of frequent border treaties and a specific boundary line between Assyria and Babylonia. He has also suggested the fiction that his text was actually set up as a stele to be witnessed by prince and vizier as a lesson to be remembered.[105]

As indicated above, the problem of sources is of special interest. Grayson argues persuasively that close parallels between the Synchronistic His-

---

likely that Tadmor can push the date for such chronicles back to the time of Shamshi-Adad or bring it down to the later age, as he attempts to do.

102. Tadmor, ibid., pp. 210ff.

103. *ABC*, pp. 50–56, 157–70; listed as Chronicle 21.

104. Ibid., p. 51.

105. For an earlier history of a border dispute between two Sumerian city-states which was commemorated on a clay cylinder see S. N. Kramer, *The Sumerians*, pp. 54–57; idem, *History Begins at Sumer*, pp. 35–44. See also the Cuthean Legend of Naram-Sin for the fiction of a stele and a didactic conclusion as a literary device (Grayson, *BHLT*, pp. 7–8, and *ABC*, p. 169, commentary on iv 23–30).

tory and the extant inscriptions of Tiglath-pileser I, Shalmaneser III, and Shamshi-Adad V argue strongly for direct literary dependence upon such inscriptions.[106] The fact that the first two sections are given in reverse chronological order also speaks against an early continuous chronicle and for dependence on individual inscriptions. In considering the annals we noted the great propensity of scribes to use older inscriptions for their works rather than consult "primary" records. The author of the Synchronistic History has done "research" on a particular theme by investigating either the monuments still extant in his day or a collection of scribal copies of such inscriptions. The Assyrian bias in the treatment of the various events would not necessarily be that of the author of the Synchronistic History but is exactly what we would expect from royal inscriptions. He has simply added to this collection a reason for the hostilities, that of treaty and border violation, and put the blame on Babylonia. Since royal inscriptions rarely give any hint of specific causes of such hostility, it is a remarkable departure to view such a series of events as having a unified cause, even if in this case it may be highly suspect.[107]

It would appear from this review of the Assyrian chronicle fragments and the Synchronistic History that no clear evidence exists that Assyria ever had chronicles comparable to the Babylonian Chronicle Series. In spite of the use of third-person narration, these texts were not significantly different from the royal annals, and, in view of the lack of evidence, all efforts to find such chronicles for Assyria seem to me rather strained.

The evidence for chronicles in Babylonia before the eighth century B.C. is also limited. There are, however, three chronicles that deal with historical events before the Neo-Babylonian period, and they must be looked at together. The first is the Chronicle of the Early Kings, which covers the period from Sargon of Akkad to Agum III, ca. 1450 B.C.[108] The information for the early part of this text was derived primarily from omen texts.[109]

106. Note especially Grayson's statement (ABC, pp. 247–48): "What is particularly significant is that the author of the Synchronistic History has relied upon a later summary of the events rather than a document directly contemporary with them." This is said in connection with his use of the inscriptions of Tiglath-pileser I. See also pp. 240ff. s.v. "Shalmaneser III," "Shamshi-Adad V," "Tiglath-pileser I," and p. 54. Note also the fact that the Synchronistic History constantly uses the indefinite reference to time, ina tarsi, "at the time of," typical of inscriptions rather than precise designations. Only once, at the beginning of the Babylonian Chronicle Series, is the phrase used in connection with an event that the author says is not in his records (Chron. 1. i 608). Cf. Tadmor, "Assyr. Hist.," p. 211, who suggests that both the Synchronistic History and the inscriptions go back to a hypothetical "chronicle" source. On the parallels with Chronicle 24 and Chronicle P see below.

107. On the other hand, the theme of treaty violation in which Assyria is in the right and Babylonia in the wrong is prominent in the Tukulti-Ninurta Epic. For a discussion of this work see P. Machinist, "Literature as Politics," CBQ 38:455–82, esp. 456–58.

108. Grayson, ABC, pp. 45–49, 152–56; Chron. 20.

109. This is the basis for Finkelstein's thesis (in "Mesopotamian Historiography," PAPS 107:470) that chronicles were derived from omens. But the close connection applies only to this one text.

Comparison of this chronicle with collections of omens that were in the Neo-Assyrian and Neo-Babylonian libraries indicates almost verbatim copying from the apodoses of the historical omens. One small section about Sargon and one on Shulgi were not derived from omens but were copied from the Weidner Chronicle, an unusual document of religious propaganda. They deal with the same theme that dominates that work, namely, the offenses of these kings against Marduk's temple in Babylon. One section, dealing with Erra-imitti of the first dynasty of Isin (20 A 31–36), tells the story of how a substitute king gained the throne after the sudden death of the real king. This looks very much like a legend fragment. The sources for the last part of the text are not so obvious. One event, at least, is known from a year date, so some events may have been recorded on monuments from the period.

What seems clear from the highly selective character of the chronicle is that its scope was dictated by the kind of information available to the author rather than by any special bias or plan. He apparently gleaned information from a variety of sources in order to produce a chronicle for the early history of Babylonia. Of course, many questions still remain about the text, but on the basis of what we do know it seems reasonable to assume that the author lived in the Neo-Babylonian period and wrote the work according to the style of chronicle writing in that period.[110]

There is now rather abundant evidence to support such an antiquarian interest in the period of early Mesopotamian history. One example is the Sargon Geography, which Grayson, in his recent study of this text,[111] characterizes in the following way:

> The Sargon Geography is a learned treatise on the geography of the conquests of Sargon of Akkad, based on various traditional and legendary sources, and either first composed or largely re-edited during the Neo-Assyrian period. Further, I would hazard the opinion that it is a Babylonian scribe's attempt to interpret in contemporary terms the geography of the empire of the ancient Sargon for the edification of the reigning Sargon, Sargon II of Assyria.[112]

The later Neo-Babylonian copy of this text shows continued interest and "research" in such matters of ancient geography and history.[113]

110. The dependence of the work on the Weidner Chronicle could, according to Grayson's dating of that work (*ABC*, pp. 278–79), hardly make it older than the twelfth century B.C. at the earliest. The use of omen collections which are known only from the late period, however, would tend to push the date down considerably.

111. A. K. Grayson, "The Empire of Sargon of Akkad," *AfO* 25:56–64. This article contains a new edition of the previously known text based upon a recently discovered exemplar in the British Museum that adds several new lines.

112. Ibid., p. 57.

113. What is the relationship of this Near Eastern geography to the development of geography in ancient Ionia? Note especially the measurement of distances between or around certain

Another chronicle, similar to the one just discussed, is the so-called Chronicle P.[114] This Babylonian chronicle deals with a period of history in the latter half of the second millennium B.C., the Kassite period. It is possible that it actually takes up where the Chronicle of Early Kings left off. While on the surface the text appears to be in the narrative style of a chronicle, certain features about it make this judgment premature. First, it contains a long epiclike section on Kurigalzu's victorious campaigns in which direct speech is employed. This could not be from a regular chronicle source. The first column and the end of the third column (iii 20–22) of Chronicle P are parallel episodes to those in the early part of the Synchronistic History. Because the parallelism is verbatim at many points, the question of their relationship to each other arises. Both works share the highly selective character of the kings and episodes that are recorded. Since it is very unlikely that the Assyrian Synchronistic History used Babylonian sources for these episodes or that Chronicle P used the Assyrian monuments, the relationship between the two works must be one of direct literary dependence. The most likely possibility, it seems to me, is that the author of Chronicle P used the Synchronistic History,[115] for the following reasons:

1. The various events and rulers treated in Chronicle P, with only a few exceptions, correspond to the selection in the Synchronistic History. The principle of selection in the latter work is very clear, to deal with the history of the controversy between Assyria and Babylonia in Assyria's favor. The principle of selection, apart from dependence upon the Synchronistic History, would be quite inexplicable in Chronicle P.

2. As we saw above, the unifying theme of the Synchronistic History is the establishing of treaties between Assyria and Babylonia centered on fixing the boundary line. At the point where Chronicle P begins with a legible text it mentions such a treaty and the fixing of a boundary in exactly the same place in the text as the Synchronistic History.

3. In two places where the texts are parallel there seems to be a serious discrepancy over just who were the rulers at the time in Babylonia and Assyria. In both cases it would appear that the version in the Synchronistic History is correct and that Chronicle P has altered the accounts on the basis of some other information, perhaps a faulty king list. At any rate, the more correct version is more likely to be the original one.

4. The episode in the Synchronistic History dealing with Tukulti-

---

regions, lines 30–40, and an attempt to describe, in lines 51ff., the characteristics of peoples beyond the borders of civilization. On early Greek geography see 2a.

114. Grayson, *ABC*, pp. 56–59, 170–77; Chron. 22.

115. Grayson (*ABC*, p. 58) suggests rather tentatively that the Synchronistic History is dependent upon Chronicle P. I argue for the opposite position.

Ninurta in column ii is broken, but it would surely have been a favorable account of his attack on Babylon.[116] The Chronicle P version is certainly the Babylonian account and strongly condemns Tukulti-Ninurta. It also centers around the Babylonian theme of the cult of Marduk and actions taken against it, as in the Chronicle of the Early Kings, where the terminology is very similar, and in the Weidner Chronicle (19:62). One can hardly say that Chronicle P is more "objective" and reliable than the Synchronistic History.[117]

The Synchronistic History was only one of the sources used by the author of Chronicle P. By also incorporating epic material that glorified Kurigalzu as invincible, he could hardly allow him to suffer defeat at Sugaga (iii 20–22), which Kurigalzu does in the Synchronistic History. So he simply switched victor and victim as well as changed the Assyrian king from Enlil-narari to Adad-narari (I), who had been named in the following section of the Synchronistic History, thereby creating serious chronological difficulties. The epic text about Kurigalzu II seems to have been a rather typical genre for this period in both Assyria and Babylonia.[118] Because of the broken state of the last section on the invasions of the king of Elam, not much can be said about a possible source for it.

On the basis of these observations I think it is fair to say that this text does not represent a Babylonian chronicle of the late second millennium. It appears to be an attempt to fill in a dark period of history from various sources available to the author. While he accepts much of his Assyrian source material, even some that is humiliating to Babylonia, at certain points he attempts to set the matter straight from the Babylonian point of view. This work seems to take up where the Chronicle of the Early Kings left off and to continue the same viewpoint on foreign abuse of the Marduk cult and its inevitable consequences.

A third text that I believe belongs to this group is the so-called Eclectic Chronicle.[119] Even though it is very fragmentary it would appear that the time span covered by it extended from the end of Chronicle P down to the Neo-Babylonian period. It shares with the other texts some important features. In the first section there also appears to be a passage that is parallel to, and dependent upon, the Synchronistic History (24:4–8 = 21:ii 25'–27', 31'). The rest of the chronicle seems to go its own way with other very sparse sources. Even in the period preceding the Na-

---

116. As in the Tukulti-Ninurta Epic; see n. 107, above.

117. Contra Grayson, *ABC*, p. 58. See the discussion by W. Röllig, "Die Glaubwürdigkeit der Chronik P," in *Heidelberger Studien zum Alten Orient*, pp. 173–84; J. A. Brinkman, "Ur: 'The Kassite Period and the Period of the Assyrian Kings,'" *Orientalia* 38 (1969):323, n. 1.

118. An extant fragment of this epic may be published in Grayson, *BHLT*, pp. 47–55.

119. Grayson, *ABC*, pp. 63–65, 180–83; Chron. 24.

bu-naṣir era in the eighth century temporal designations are still very vague—no hint whatever of the form in the Babylonian Chronicle Series. The concern over the cult of Marduk, which had been evident in the previous two chronicles, continues in this one.

It seems to me, therefore, that these three chronicles—the Chronicle of the Early Kings, Chronicle P, and the Eclectic Chronicle—all go together as an attempt to give to the Babylonian Chronicle Series a history stretching back into early times. The authors, if there was more than one, used whatever texts were available for their purpose, and they shared common concerns and a Babylonian viewpoint. This historical "research" into the past seems to me a rather remarkable achievement in its own right, even though it cannot be taken uncritically by the modern scholar.

One of several chronicles that reflect a special interest in the cult of Marduk, the patron deity of Babylon, is the Weidner Chronicle,[120] which covers the time span from the Early Dynastic period of Sumerian history to at least the time of Shulgi, a ruler of the Third Dynasty of Ur. It deals with the attitude of some of the principal rulers of Mesopotamia toward the cult of Marduk and especially toward providing fish for his temple, Esagil. "In fact the whole point of the narrative is to illustrate that those rulers who neglected or insulted Marduk or failed to provide fish offerings for the temple Esagil had an unhappy end while those who did concern themselves with these matters fared well."[121] Such a viewpoint represents a serious anachronism since the cult of Marduk and the city of Babylon did not rise to prominence until long after this time. Like the Synchronistic History, this too is "a blatant piece of propaganda,"[122] in this case on behalf of Babylon and its cult center. Grayson offers several reasons for dating the text in the late Kassite or early Isin II period.[123] Source material for such a document was a problem for its author. Apart from the historical names and the very general scheme of the succession of power, the details are almost certainly fabricated. The fact that it begins with a mythological prologue in which the gods by an oath vouchsafe their protection for the city[124] also makes it different from the other chronicles, and it should not, perhaps, be classed in this genre at all.[125]

---

120. Ibid., pp. 43–45, 145–51; Chron. 19.
121. Ibid., p. 43.
122. Ibid.
123. *ABC*, pp. 278–79 s.v. "Addenda," p. 44.
124. An interesting parallel to this apparent divine oath to protect the city now comes from Mari, where the deities are also put under oath not to harm the city of Mari. See *Archives royales de Mari x: La correspondance féminine*, ed. G. Dossin (Paris, 1967), no. 9. The text was brought to my attention by my colleague J. Sasson.
125. This is the only "chronicle" mentioned in the studies of Mesopotamian historiography by Gese and Speiser. To suggest, as Gese does (*ZThK* 55:136–37), that the religious ideas about relations between the gods and mankind found in this text are basic to "all later histor-

Another text showing a strong interest in the Marduk cult is the Akitu Chronicle.[126] It consists of "a description of interruptions in the Babylonian Akitu festival beginning with Sennacherib's sack of Babylon (689 B.C.) and ending in the accession year of Nabopolassar (626 B.C.)."[127] During this period the regular continuation of the Akitu festival was rather difficult. It appears that the author was interested in the interruption of the festival and gleaned his information from extant documents, such as the Babylonian Chronicle Series and perhaps certain records of the temple itself. The two kinds of information—that dealing with political events and that discussing the interruption of the festival—are not very closely integrated.

The Religious Chronicle appears to be similar.[128] It also deals with interruptions in the Akitu festival but for a much earlier period, during the late eleventh to tenth centuries B.C., and these interruptions are usually associated with political events. Interspersed with these are references to bizarre phenomena in nature and the heavens, which are rather precisely dated. These phenomena closely resemble those found in the protases of omen texts, and a relationship seems to be implied between them and the interruptions of the Akitu festival, even though it is not stated in omen form. I think it is very unlikely, as Grayson suggests, that this material was just taken from a "running account of Babylonian history."[129] The sources for such a text I think were twofold. On the one hand, the text would suggest that a list or record of natural phenomena was kept in scribal circles so that omens and hemerologies could be derived from them. The other source was a temple record dealing with the interruptions of the Akitu festival, a concern that seems to have had a long history. The combination of these two types of material produced the omenlike text that we have. The terminology relating to the interruption of the Akitu festival is so similar to the Akitu Chronicle that this source is very likely late and the text as a whole the product of the Neo-Babylonian period.[130]

The Esarhaddon Chronicle is also written with a bias.[131] In its extant

---

ical and historiographic literature" is a serious oversimplification, even for the genre of chronicles.

126. Grayson, *ABC*, pp. 35–36, 131–32; Chron. 16. See also his "Chronicles and the Akitu Festival," *XVIIe Rencontre Assyriologique Internationale*, pp. 160–70.

127. Grayson, *ABC*, p. 35.

128. Ibid., pp. 36–39, 133–38; Chron. 17.

129. Ibid., p. 38.

130. The author deals (in lines iii 6–10) with the eighth and *nineteenth* years of Nabumukin-apli, in which there were interruptions of the Akitu festival, before he deals (in iii 11–12) with an event of nature in the *sixteenth* year of the same king. This lack of chronological order can best be explained by the author's careless conflation of two sources rather than by his switching around of events if he were drawing from only one source. Cf. Grayson, *ABC*, pp. 38–39.

131. Grayson, *ABC*, pp. 30–32, 125–28; Chron. 14.

form it deals with the reigns of Esarhaddon and his son, Shamash-shuma-ukin. It is very close to the Babylonian Chronicle Series but it contains nothing that could be taken as derogatory toward Esarhaddon. In lines 31ff. a greater emphasis is placed upon the restoration of the Akitu festival than in the Babylonian Chronicle Series; lines 31–32, 35–37 are directly parallel to the Akitu Chronicle and likely dependent upon it.[132] So the religious bias from such texts has influenced the chronicle style, if not so much in the manner of presenting the facts as in the subtle selection of the information presented.

Two other chronicles deserve brief mention. One small, private chronicle deals primarily with some events of the seventh century.[133] The text, however, also has to do with a rather obscure king, Shirikti-Shuqamuna of Babylon, who reigned for three months. The style of this section is different from the preceding chronicle style and resembles that of an item taken from a king list. The next item is a reference to the fifth and sixth years of Nabu-shuma-ishkun (760–48), in which "Nabu did not come for the procession of Bel." This item is clearly derived from a religious chronicle or record of interruptions in the Akitu festival such as we have noted above. The scribe also adds a note at the end, "nonintegrated lines from a writing-board . . . ," which clearly indicates that he chose a number of different items at random from his source.

Also unusual is a Chronicle of Market Prices,[134] which seems to represent a strong antiquarian interest in carrying the theme of market prices, found in the astronomical diaries, back to earlier periods of history. Just what kinds of scattered material the author "dug up" for his work is not known, but it hardly represents a continuous economic record from the past.

It would appear that the genre of chronicle writing, best represented in the Babylonian Chronicle Series, actually began in the Neo-Babylonian period, and its main source was the series of astronomical diaries. There seems to be little evidence for any running account of Babylonian history prior to the eighth century. Yet it is apparent that the Babylonian Chronicle Series did inspire strong antiquarian[135] and historical interests in the

132. Grayson, *ABC*, p. 12, suggests that Chronicle 1, the Esarhaddon Chronicle, and the Akitu Chronicle all were dependent directly upon the astronomical diaries. But his chart, n. 34, certainly allows for the possibility that the Esarhaddon Chronicle used both Chronicle 1 and the Akitu Chronicle.

133. Grayson, *ABC*, pp. 32–34, 128–30; the Shamash-shuma-ukin Chronicle, Chron. 15.

134. Grayson, *ABC*, pp. 60–62, 178–79; Chron. 23.

135. For evidence of strong antiquarian interests in this period see Krecher, *Saeculum* 26:28, n. 47; also the work cited in n. 111 above.

more distant past, with the result that chronicles were constructed out of various kinds of source material that contained historical information.

It must also be stressed that the chronicles do not simply represent the continuous tradition of historical record keeping from the ancient past. There is little evidence that any such records were kept. Instead, in every case before the Neo-Babylonian period such records had to be derived from secondary sources, that is, through historical research, by extracting information and combining it with other materials to produce a new work. This intellectual activity may be strongly biased, as in the case of the Synchronistic History, or it may be merely antiquarian in character. But the increasing development and impetus to this kind of activity in the Neo-Babylonian period is surely significant for the rise of historiography in general in the ancient Near East.[136]

In a recent study Robert Drews raises the question whether the purpose of the chronicles was historiographic, as some scholars have claimed.[137] According to the usual criteria of historiography, that a work should deal with the *res gestae* of kings and that it should give some interpretation of events or indicate their significance, the chronicles fall short. In terms of political consequences they make no distinction between the achievement of one king and the disaster of another, nor do they signal in any special way the passing of one "empire" and the beginning of another. In fact, the "objectivity" of these texts, which is praised by many as the mark of emergent historiography, is viewed quite differently by Drews. He argues that the function of the accurate dating of the chronicles is not to place the event into its historical nexus but rather to fill up each time slot with a good or a bad event. The purpose of such recording activity, Drews believes, was to be able to make predictions about future events based on the records of past experience.

The chronicles are usually regarded as more objective than the Assyrian annals because they lack any suggestion of divine intervention in human affairs. But Drews suggests that for the writers of chronicles all events were assumed to be divinely ordained and therefore none is singled out as especially so. He supports this suggestion by pointing to the fact that the chronicles are closely related to the astronomical diaries, whose function must have been to develop a "judicial" astrology to which the precisely dated events could be related.

The weakness of Drews's position lies in his lack of precision about the

136. Its importance for Israelite chronicles will be dealt with below, 9a.
137. "The Babylonian Chronicles and Berossus," *Iraq* 37 (1975):39–55. Cf. W. G. Lambert, "Berossus and Babylonian Eschatology," *Iraq* 38 (1976):171–73.

relationship of the astronomical diaries to the chronicles. If the chronicles were extracted from the diaries, then the connection between the astronomical observations, which are the basis for any predictions, was broken. Drews may be right in suggesting that the function of the diaries was to develop astrology, but how could the chronicles, which no longer had the astronomical observations tied to the events, serve this purpose? Furthermore, if the diaries are the source for the chronicles then the form of the chronicles has been dictated by its source. Therefore the form of the chronicles can say nothing about its function. In the same way Drews himself is ready to concede that the sources for the chronicles outside the Babylonian Chronicle Series dictated their form, so that in these cases also the form of the sources cannot give a true picture of the chronicles' function. But what is also important is that such chronicles as the Chronicle of the Early Kings and Chronicle P could not have been written for the prognostic purpose Drews suggests because accurate dates such as one finds in the later texts were not available to the authors of these early chronicles. Drews further fails to observe that the Esarhaddon Chronicle has an obvious bias in favor of the king, which makes it quite unsuitable for prognostic purposes.

The antiquarian interest of the Babylonians is so well attested in this period that Drews must take this factor more seriously. This seems to be a more likely explanation for the construction of some chronicles of the older period as well as for the perpetuation of other historiographic genres such as king lists, which lack the precision that Drews's theory demands. But what is most impressive about Babylonian historiography is the evidence of a kind of academic "research"—a gleaning of materials about the past from various sources. This belongs to the very basis of the meaning of history in its classical sense, even if the ability to make critical judgments about the sources is not as yet in evidence.

e. HISTORICAL EPICS

The term *epic* is used in the discussion of Mesopotamian literature in a rather vague way to include a wide range of texts in poetic narration.[138] The designation of a particular text as an epic is a result of quite uncritical usage rather than of the application of a specific set of criteria. The Gilgamesh Epic is a long narrative poem about the legendary king Gilgamesh and his various heroic exploits. There would seem to be little debate about calling it an epic. The text called Enuma Elish, which deals with the themes of creation and conflict among the gods, also has the character of

138. For a general treatment of the discussion of epic in Mesopotamia see K. Hecker, *Untersuchungen zur akkadischen Epik*, AOATS 8.

epic because the god Marduk is the hero among his heavenly fellows when he destroys the threatening goddess Tiamat and her company and wins supremacy over all the gods. This then suggests two types of epics— mythological and legendary—with a number of examples in each group.

But there is yet a third type, the "historical" epic.[139] It centers upon historical figures and historical events with minimal reference to mythological episodes, and it presents its account in high poetic style. The line between the legendary epic and the historical epic is not easy to draw since certain historical figures, such as Sargon of Akkad, could actually be the subject of both. Furthermore, the historical epic could also include legendary elements or present its material in a manner that makes it suspect as a "historical" account of events. Nevertheless, the distinction is useful as a general classification although it should not be construed as a scheme of literary development from one stage to the next. Mythological and historical epics were often composed in the same historical periods and exercised some literary influence upon each other.[140]

Mythological and legendary epics were common in the culture of ancient Sumer and were passed on to the later Babylonian literary heritage. But the earliest extant historical epics, which deal with historical events of the Akkad period, seem to belong to the Old Babylonian period. However, all the historical epic texts are quite fragmentary and therefore difficult to study as a group.

The Epic of Tukulti-Ninurta I is a historical epic that is sufficiently well preserved to merit extensive study. It celebrates the victory of Tukulti-Ninurta of Assyria over Kashtiliash, king of Babylonia. In his recent study, P. Machinist has carefully analyzed the various literary and form-critical components that make up the highly eclectic character of the epic.[141] He states: "It is, in other words, no simple historical narrative, but one which subtly uses . . . the languages, themes, and forms of a variety of sources."[142] Machinist identifies three formative sources or spheres of influence for this epic. The first is the native Assyrian tradition, which is most clearly reflected in the use of the royal commemorative inscription with its tripartite division as a model for the epic structure.[143] Thus the first section of the epic, which glorifies the king and declares his closeness to the gods, corresponds in language and substance to the introductory ep-

---

139. Grayson, *BHLT*, pp. 41–46; idem, *Orientalia* 49:184–87.
140. The Enuma Elish, dated by Lambert to the time of Nebuchadnezzar I (1124–1103), comes at the end of a century in which a number of historical epics were written.
141. P. B. Machinist, "The Epic of Tukulti-Ninurta I: A Study in Middle Assyrian Literature" (Dissertation, Yale University, 1978), esp. pp. 509–48; idem, "Literature as Politics: The Tukulti-Ninurta Epic and the Bible," *CBQ* 38 (1976):455–82.
142. "Epic of T-N," p. 509.
143. Ibid.; *CBQ* 38:458–60.

ithets of the royal inscriptions. The second section, a narration of military activity, is also found as a characteristic feature in more prosaic form in the Assyrian royal inscriptions, although it is lacking in Babylonian royal inscriptions.[144] (The few late examples where it does occur are the result of influence from the Assyrian tradition.) The concluding section of the epic refers to the dedications of booty made to the temples of the gods in order to beautify them. Along with this are some final words of praise for the king as well as curses invoked on oath-breakers. The building inscriptions also conclude with descriptions of the construction and decoration of a temple as a consequence of the king's victory. These are often followed by blessings and curses. The relationship between the epic and the royal inscriptions should not be regarded as moving in only one direction. The elaboration of the royal epithets and descriptions of military exploits in the inscriptions may have been encouraged by epic language and style.

A second sphere of influence upon the style of the Tukulti-Ninurta Epic, according to Machinist, is the Sumero-Babylonian tradition.[145] Evidence of this influence is not unknown in Assyrian culture before this time, but the epic itself tells us that Tukulti-Ninurta, in his raid on Babylonia, carried off to Assyria the literary archives of the south as booty.[146] Among the various indications of Babylonian influence Machinist cites the dramatic use of speeches from the Sumero-Babylonian epic tradition, the motif of the divine abandonment of the doomed southern cities, and the royal hymn that raises the king almost to the level of a deity. The last two features occur in the first section and are used to indicate the relationship of the gods to the protagonists. Another Babylonian element is the confession of guilt by Kashtiliash before the war begins by which he condemns himself as the guilty party. As a parallel Machinist cites the genre of Babylonian penitential prayers, but there is also the use of such penitential laments within the Babylonian epic itself, as is clear from the recent examples published by Grayson.[147] Their use in the Assyrian epic as a means of condemning the Babylonian king and justifying the raid is certainly ironical. There is irony also in the use of the theme of divine abandonment of the Babylonian cities as both a prediction of what is to follow and a legitimation of their overthrow by Tukulti-Ninurta.

A third sphere of influence identified by Machinist is that of international treaty language, and he cites many examples from the Hittite trea-

---

144. On royal inscriptions see above, 3a. On the form of royal inscriptions see Grayson, *Orientalia* 49:150–55, 160–61.
145. "Epic of T-N," p. 510; *CBQ* 38:460–68.
146. "Epic of T-N," pp. 128–29, col. VI rev B 1'–13'.
147. See esp. the Adad-shuma-user epic, *BHLT*, pp. 56–77.

ties with Syrian kings.[148] This also gives the work a strong thematic character in that Tukulti-Ninurta is presented as the generous and righteous king who has always tried to uphold the treaty obligations with Babylonia while its king Kashtiliash has been the blatant and self-confessed violator. The gods as guarantors of the treaty pass judgment through the ordeal of war.

Machinist discusses the epic in the context of a *Kulturkampf* between Assyria and Babylonia in which the attitude of Assyria toward Babylonian culture is one of considerable ambivalence.[149] While the epic is about the conquest of Babylonia by Assyria, its author, at the same time, makes a considerable appropriation of Babylonian religious and cultural influence in an effort to create a unity out of the whole region of Mesopotamia. Machinist suggests that in this program Tukulti-Ninurta may have gone too far and created a residue of resentment by conservative Assyrian elements which ultimately caused him trouble. The epic served as a piece of political and cultural propaganda to legitimate and to articulate the basis for a broader Mesopotamian symbiosis.

The Middle Babylonian epics are too fragmentary for detailed analysis or comparison with the Assyrian tradition, but from what is preserved it appears that they followed quite different models of presentation. The epic of Nebuchadnezzar I begins with the king's lament over the absence of the god Marduk, to which the god replies in a revelation.[150] The text is broken at this point but the rest seems to suggest his commission and subsequent campaign against Elam and the recovery of the statue of the god. Another epic fragment of an earlier king, Adad-shuma-user, describes a rebellion against the king that is attributed to his neglect of the cult of Marduk.[151] The penitent king's confession leads to his restoration. In these epics the god Marduk and the honoring of his cult play a major role, as in the Weidner Chronicle and similar literary texts of the age of Nebuchadnezzar I. The same spirit seems to be present in the revival of epic in the Neo-Babylonian period. Thus the Nabopolassar epic celebrates the founding of the Chaldean Dynasty through the power of Marduk.[152] The Verse Account of Nabonidus[153] is in epic style but is really a propaganda piece against this king for his neglect of the Marduk cult. In Babylonia from the rise of Nebuchadnezzar I to the end of the Neo-Babylonian monarchy the priests of Marduk seem to have played a vital role in the development of this genre as a medium for their concerns.

148. "Epic of T-N," pp. 510–11; *CBQ* 38:460.
149. "Epic of T-N," pp. 515–31; *CBQ* 38:468–77.
150. Grayson, *Orientalia* 49:186.
151. Grayson, *BHLT*, pp. 56–77.
152. Ibid., pp. 78–86.
153. *ANET³*, pp. 312–15.

From this brief survey several observations may be made about epic that will be relevant to the discussion of Israelite historiography. First, epic literature in Mesopotamia does not reflect an oral or preliterate mode of composition. This is so even though the epics were all very likely intended for oral performance before an audience. The use of epic style (and it is more a matter of style than of specific genre) has a very long life, occurring alongside prose genres; it is not necessarily older or more recent. Epic is simply one way among others of writing myth, legend, and history, but in no case is any of these the special domain of epic. Epic employs techniques and conventions of composition different from those of prose forms, but interaction between epic and prose historiography often occurs, with influence going in both directions. Yet when prose genres show some influence from epic it is never simply a "translation" from poetry to prose. The epics themselves continue to be handed down in their original poetic form. The features common to all epics are an elevated poetic style of narration and a strongly tendentious political or religious character. But even within one category of epic, the historical epic, there is wide diversity in form, structure, and sources utilized by the past.[154]

f. PROPHECIES

A different presentation of history is given by a number of texts called "prophecies."[155] Grayson describes their basic form:

> An Akkadian prophecy is a prose composition consisting of a number of "predictions" of past events. It then concludes with either a "prediction" of phenomena in the writer's day or with a genuine attempt to forecast future events. The author, in other words, uses *vaticinia ex eventu* to establish his credibility and then proceeds to his real purpose, which might be to justify a current idea or institution or to forecast future doom for a hated enemy.[156]

The types vary in form. In one type, represented by the Marduk Prophetic Speech,[157] the god speaks in the first person and describes his trav-

154. Cf. the discussion about Israelite epic below, 7b.
155. A. K. Grayson and W. G. Lambert, "Akkadian Prophecies," JCS 18 (1964):7–30; W. W. Hallo, "Akkadian Apocalypses," *IEJ* 16 (1966):231–42; *ANET*³, pp. 451–52 (=606–07); R. Borger, "Gott Marduk und Gott-König Šulgi als Propheten: Zwei prophetische Texte," *BiOr* 28 (1971):3–24; Grayson, *BHLT*, pp. 13–37.
156. *Orientalia* 49:183.
157. Borger, *BiOr* 28:21–22; Grayson *BHLT*, pp. 15–16; see also J. J. M. Roberts, "Nebuchadnezzar I's Elamite Crisis in Theological Perspective," in *Essays . . . Finkelstein*, pp. 183–87.

els to various lands—to the Hittites (with the raid of Mursilis I, ca. 1595 B.C.), to Assyria (with the conquest of Tukulti-Ninurta I, ca. 1235 B.C.), and to Elam (under Kudur-Naḫḫunte, ca. 1160). None of these kings is actually named in the text. Hatti and Assyria are said to receive blessing from the divine presence while Elam experiences only trouble. Then the god Marduk predicts in rather glowing terms the rise of a new king of Babylon, the return of the god to Babylon, the restoration of the cult, and great prosperity. This will begin a new era of social order but will also complete the destruction of the enemy Elam.

The text reflects rather clearly the beginning of the reign of Nebuchadnezzar I (1125–1103 B.C.), when the restoration of the Marduk cult took place and the god's cult was exalted to great prominence. The piece was meant as religious propaganda for Nebuchadnezzar's religious reform program.[158]

Belonging to the same scribal series and very similar in type is the Shulgi Prophetic Speech,[159] in which the god-king describes a revelation from the gods. After presenting his own credentials as an ideal ruler, he portrays, in a "prediction," the history of Babylon and Nippur in the second millennium. He does this in rather vague terms down to the time of Kastilias IV and Tukulti-Ninurta I, at which point the prophecy becomes more specific. It is described as a period of *Unheilzeit* for Babylon. This is followed by another period of devastation of Babylonia which seems to correspond to the Elamite raid mentioned in Chronicle P. Whether the text then shifts to a real "prediction" of restoration or continues with subsequent periods of history is not clear since the text is broken, but it is not likely that too much more was included. The date of the Shulgi Prophetic Speech must be some time in the late Kassite or early Isin II period. It also had a propagandistic character, but here it is rather in favor of the older cults, especially that of Enlil of Nippur. This type of prophecy became part of the scribal literary heritage, as is attested by the later copies of these texts.

Another type of prophecy, represented by Text A,[160] lists its "predictions" in the third person. The preserved portion of this badly broken text is much more restricted in time, to the late Isin II period after Nebuchadnezzar I. Here the kings are given in strict sequence, rather than restricting the account to highlights as in the previous prophecies. The names of the kings are not given but each is introduced by the statement, "a

158. See W. G. Lambert, "The Reign of Nebuchadnezzar I: A Turning Point in the History of Ancient Mesopotamian Religion," in *The Seed of Wisdom*, pp. 3–13.

159. Borger, *BiOr* 28:22–23; Grayson, *BHLT*, p. 16.

160. This is the designation by Grayson and Lambert in *JCS* 18:7ff.; see also *ANET*[3], pp. 451–52 (=606–07); Hallo, *IEJ* 16:235ff.

prince will arise," followed by the length of his reign. The descriptions of these reigns fluctuate irregularly between good and bad periods of rule, with some of the details being stereotyped but others more precise. Since the beginning and the end are broken the purpose of the text is unclear, but no obvious theme or propagandist purpose seems to be reflected in it. The language style is like that of the apodoses of omens, but the protases are lacking and the work seems to have no direct relationship to prognostic literature. One source for the work, however, seems to have been a king list designating the specific length of each reign. Another was a source shared by the Eclectic Chronicle.[161] But for the most part the language seems to be derived from omen style and from the descriptions of "good" and "bad" reigns found in the other prophecies. This combination of the very specific historical allusion to the very general descriptions of the reigns suggests that the work is an academic exercise with no large audience appeal and intended for a small circle of learned persons.[162] Its date is uncertain but it could have been composed long after the events described and may have no connection with the kind of intention and *Sitz im Leben* that produced the previous prophecies.[163]

The Dynastic Prophecy, which dates from the Seleucid period, seems to carry this genre a stage further.[164] The text is "a description, in prophetic terms, of the rise and fall of dynasties or empires, including the fall of Assyria and the rise of Babylonia, the fall of Babylonia and the rise of Persia, the fall of Persia and the rise of the Hellenistic monarchies."[165] The kings are all anonymous but the details given about their reigns leave little doubt as to their identity. Although the ending is fragmentary, Grayson speculates that the "real prediction" in the conclusion is the overthrow of the Seleucids in Babylonia.

A number of interesting features occur in this text. There is a clear recognition of "dynasties," as in the Sumerian King List and the Dynastic Chronicle tradition. The whole is quite schematized, with not all the kings mentioned, only those at the beginning and those at the end of the dynasties. The information on the length of the reigns and the circumstances of

161. Chronicle 24 in Grayson's *ABC*. Hallo (*IEJ* 16:237–38) refers to this as the "New Babylonian Chronicle." He argues for a correspondence between some of the items in the chronicle and certain allusions in the prophecy. See also Borger, *BiOr* 28:23, who accepts Hallo's historical identifications.

162. A similar stylistic use of the omen genre is to be found in the "Advice to a Prince" discussed above, 3d.

163. Hallo's attempt (*IEJ* 16:239–40) to relate all these texts to one series in which text D (=Marduk Prophecy) was the climax must now be revised in the light of Borger's study (n. 155 above). This also removes the "eschatological" element and makes the designation "apocalypses" less appropriate (see Grayson, *BHLT* p. 22, n. 35).

164. Grayson, *BHLT*, pp. 24–37.

165. Ibid., p. 24.

their rise or fall seems to be directly dependent upon the Babylonian Chronicle tradition. There is no longer the mere stereotyping of "good" and "evil" reigns, and the details are much more specific. There is a love of archaisms such that Persia is referred to as Elam and the Macedonians as Hanaeans. A concluding remark restricts the disclosure of the text only to the limited circle of the initiated.[166]

While all these texts may be included under the general rubric of "prophecies" and while they manifest a certain continuity in terminology and the predictive element, there is a danger of seeing features of the latest text as implicit in the earlier ones, especially in their present broken and incomplete state. This is especially true for Text A. There is also a difference in intention and *Sitz im Leben* from public propaganda to secret "wisdom." All this has some relevance for biblical histories, where the predictive element plays a role.[167]

166. The parallel with the historical perspective of Jewish Apocalyptic, especially Daniel, is most noticeable in this text. See Grayson, *BHLT*, pp. 20–21.

167. Drews (in *Iraq* 37:48ff.) has recently suggested that the purpose of the Babylonian Chronicle Series was also prognostic and has closely associated them with the Akkadian prophecies. He is especially impressed by the sequence of successive reigns in "Prophecy A." But it should be pointed out that this text rests upon sources that are not precisely dated and of a much earlier period. The so-called Dynastic Prophecy, which may have used information from chronicles, does not give any evidence of a close correspondence in form or in precise dates. It also stresses the notion of dynastic rise and fall as in the Dynastic Chronicle tradition, but this feature is not found in the Babylonian chronicles. The lack of evidence of any close association between these chronicles and Akkadian prophecies would argue against Drews's theory.

CHAPTER FOUR

HITTITE HISTORIOGRAPHY

In the study of Hittite historiography the criterion of historicity does not play a major role, as it did for Mesopotamia, because there are no genres, such as historical omen texts or chronicles, that contain disinterested historical statements. On the other hand, texts that have a "secular" historical content, or that are critical of the forebears of royal office, or that manifest little dependence upon the miraculous do all receive a higher appraisal of their historiographic qualities from the modern reader. So historicity functions in a supporting role in the consideration of any particular text.[1]

The genre analysis of Hittite historiography has proceeded primarily in terms of rather broad classifications, with agreement on how to identify the nature and function of individual works being more difficult to achieve. H. Güterbock, in his 1938 study of Babylonian and Hittite historiography, begins with a discussion of Hittite indebtedness to the Babylonian "historical" epic tradition, especially to those epics that glorify the deeds of Sargon and Naram-Sin in Hittite translation.[2] The significance of Babylon's cultural impact upon the Hittites was well recognized by Güterbock and must be taken seriously in any assessment of the development of the Hittite historical tradition. Nevertheless, very few historiographic genres of Mesopotamia have counterparts in Hittite literature. There are no king lists, few royal inscriptions, no native "historical" omen texts, no chronicles in the strict sense, no prophecies, and no native epic literature corresponding to the translated "imports." On the other hand, several types of Hittite historical texts have no close parallels in Mesopotamian literature, and the similarities between the Hittite and Assyrian royal annals may be more apparent than real.

1. The reason, perhaps, why the criterion of historicity is not so prominent is that the older texts of the same genre seem to be more objective and less influenced by religious piety than the more recent ones. The principle therefore works against any approach stressing generic development.

2. H. G. Güterbock, "Die historische Tradition," pt. 2: "Hethiter," ZA 44 (1938):45–93.

Güterbock subdivides the native Hittite historiography into works that were the product of "official history writing" (*offizielle Geschichtsschreibung*) and works that developed from oral traditions alongside the official texts.[3] The second type of literary text was his primary concern.[4] The sources for these two groups of texts were also considered to be quite distinct. The "official" historiography was based upon personal anecdotes of the king, while the second type usually depended upon popular legends.[5]

Another approach is to trace a literary history from the Old Hittite Kingdom to the end of the New Kingdom (ca. 1650–1200 B.C.),[6] discussing the major works in chronological order. Annelies Kammenhuber adopted this approach in her 1958 survey of Hittite historiography,[7] although she gave considerable attention to the subject of genre as well. At the heart of her survey is the thesis that Hittite historiography is to be seen in basically two forms: one is a *Chronikliteratur*, which is a hypothetical source providing the basic historical material for the Old Kingdom historical texts and the later state treaties; the other is the self-presentation of the individual kings that comes to the fore in the annals of Muršili II. In these forms Kammenhuber sees "an interest in history as such" beyond any religious expression that the text might also contain.[8]

After another twenty years a new survey of Hittite historiography has been undertaken by H. Hoffner[9] in much the same style as those of Güterbock and Kammenhuber. Hoffner adopts, at the outset, a distinction between "historical" texts, which record contemporary public events or those in the recent past, and "historiographic" texts, which use records of the past to reconstruct an ordered and meaningful history.[10] There is certainly some virtue to this distinction although it is not so easy to make it work in all cases.[11] Hoffner adopts the chronological mode of discussion

3. Ibid., pp. 93–145.
4. Ibid., pp. 101–38 (the Story of the City of Zalpa, the Cannibal text, and the Story of the Siege of Uršu).
5. However, on the relationship of the Story of the Siege of Uršu to official historiography of the period see below. The sources for official historiography would also seem to be more complex than Güterbock indicates.
6. The chronology adopted here is the so-called middle chronology, as reflected in the third edition of the *Cambridge Ancient History*.
7. A. Kammenhuber, "Die hethitische Geschichtsschreibung," *Saeculum* 9 (1958): 136–55.
8. Ibid., p. 146. In this regard she considers Hittite historiography far superior to Israelite and Mesopotamian historiography, which in her view are primarily concerned with ethic and eschatology! This comparison is not very helpful.
9. H. Hoffner, "Histories and Historians of the Ancient Near East: The Hittites," *Orientalia* 49 (1980):283–332.
10. This distinction was suggested by Oppenheim. See his classification of historical and historiographical texts in *ANET*³, pp. 265–317.
11. What does one do with the Greek historians, especially Thucydides?

following the order contained in the catalogue of Laroche.[12] Although Hoffner identifies the genres of the various pieces, he does not provide a study of the genres as such or of their possible interrelationship.[13] On the other hand, he eschews the effort to explicate a unified Hittite philosophy of history. He states that there is not "a single uniform 'view' of history writing held by the Hittites, but many individual viewpoints held by some of the Hittites who undertook to write down portions of their past as they conceived it."[14]

Hoffner departs from Güterbock's approach by not considering the Old Babylonian and proto-Hittite texts in translation on the grounds that they are not native Hittite works.[15] He differs from Kammenhuber both on the existence of a "chronicle literature" and on her treatment of the development of annals in the time of Muršili II. His assessment of this last point is based primarily upon the recent discovery of earlier annals. Our study will be heavily dependent upon the latest survey by Hoffner, even though, for the sake of my own comparative analysis, it seems best to consider the Hittite texts in terms of their genre rather than in strict chronological sequence.

As we discussed earlier in connection with Mesopotamian historiography, some scholars approach the subject by dealing with ideas of history or historical thinking. Along these lines is the first of two works on Hittite historiography by H. Cancik,[16] an investigation of the understanding of historical truth in Hittite texts beginning with the pre-Hittite Anitta document and proceeding chronologically to the Apology of Ḫattušili III. Although he finds a similar degree of historical consciousness and similar notions of causality in Hittite and Israelite historiography, he considers the Mesopotamian sources to have little in common with the Hittites in this area. Yet Albrektson, in the work mentioned above,[17] frequently cites Hittite texts side by side with Mesopotamian as expressing the same notions of divine causality in history that one also finds in the Old Testament. To make subtler distinctions about degrees of historical consciousness would take a much more detailed comparative analysis than Cancik has given us.

12. E. Laroche, *Catalogue des Textes Hittites*.

13. Yet the study does contain a number of comparisons between various texts that are very helpful.

14. *Orientalia* 49:288.

15. *Orientalia* 49:289. In the earlier, unpublished version of this study Hoffner hesitated to include the Anitta inscription on the grounds that it was thought to be derived from pre-Hittite Hattic. But a recent study has changed this view and he now gives careful consideration to it.

16. H. Cancik, *Mythische und historische Wahrheit*.

17. See above, pp. 57–59.

In his second work Cancik adopts a somewhat different approach.[18] He seeks to compare Hittite and Old Testament prose on the basis of a historiographic narrative style (*Erzählstrukturen, Erzählformen*). For this purpose Cancik gives a detailed analysis of a more limited body of Hittite writings, those of Muršili II. In principle this approach seems more promising than one that focuses upon concepts like "truth." It also corresponds more closely with the approach taken in the present study. Nevertheless, Cancik makes a number of statements and claims in the first part of his work that cannot go unchallenged, especially as they form the basis and justification for his study as a whole. His position is that the Hittite texts explain the rise of historiography in both ancient Greece and ancient Israel.[19] In comparison with the Mesopotamian and Egyptian historical traditions—in quality, variety, and level—Hittite historiography is far superior. Can this claim in fact be sustained?

The first question that must be answered is whether it is possible to establish a cultural continuity between the Hittites of Asia Minor in the fourteenth and thirteenth centuries B.C. and the later Israelites of Palestine.[20] The bridge of time does not appear too great if we are able to accept a tenth-century date for the few Old Testament texts that Cancik selects. But reasons will be offered below why these texts should be dated much later.[21] It is even less obvious how one can get from the Hittites to Greek historiography of the sixth century B.C. To propose some vague eastern Mediterranean *koinē* of historical understanding, or to see the agent of cultural mediation through "Canaan" is hardly justified.[22] No evidence for this kind of cultural influence is evident at Ugarit or in any extant Canaanite-Phoenician inscriptions. The most obvious place to look for some clue to cultural continuity would be in the inscriptions of the Neo-Hittite states. But, surprisingly, these manifest closer cultural parallels with Mesopotamia than with anything Hittite.[23] As far as we can understand the Hittite hieroglyphic inscriptions of Syria, they represent building inscriptions similar to those known from Assyria but almost entirely unknown among the Hittites. So there is no evidence that the official historiography of Ḫattuša, the Hittite capital, outlived the destruction of the Hittite empire.

Cancik's argument, however, is not based primarily upon providing a

---

18. *Grundzüge der hethitischen und alttestamentlichen Geschichtsschreibung.*
19. Ibid., pp. 3ff.
20. Ibid., p. 4; see also idem, *Wahrheit*, p. 102.
21. See below, 8d.
22. See n. 20, above.
23. W. F. Albright, *CAH³*, vol. 2, pt. 2, pp. 526–29.

plausible explanation for the continuity between the Hittites and Israel. His case rests upon a literary demonstration that seeks to show that the narrative features of Hittite historiography are found in Israel but not in Mesopotamia. To make categorical statements, as Cancik does, that certain features of narrative style are not found in Mesopotamian literature, is very risky and would have to depend upon a thorough literary survey, either his own or another's. But instead we find a very limited comparison with Assyrian building inscriptions. We can therefore have little confidence in the various negative statements by Cancik about Mesopotamian narrative style. In fact, as I hope to show below, a number of features are well represented in Mesopotamian literature and some are superior in quality to those in Hittite.

Cancik, likewise, discusses various criteria for what he calls *Literarizität*.[24] These criteria are: (1) publication, by which he means a place in the library or scribal collections, (2) being written for a specific audience, (3) having broadly diversified sources, and (4) being a carefully structured composition rather than a compilation. These criteria he finds in the Hittite and biblical literature but not in Mesopotamian texts, such as building inscriptions. But, as we have seen above, several pieces of Mesopotamian historiographic writing could be classed as literature alongside the best of the Hittite examples. Among these are the Tukulti-Ninurta epic, those texts that Grayson describes as "historical-literary," the Synchronistic History, and the Sargon Letter to the God, with others in this genre. None of these texts is considered by Cancik.

Cancik sees many literary features in Hittite texts, such as the use of direct fictitious letters and messenger reports, and the use of metaphor, as dependent upon epic poetry.[25] He therefore proposes that Hittite historiography might go back to some stimulation from an epic tradition. He even mentions evidence of epic and poetic elements in early Hittite historiography and quasi-historical texts.[26] The fact of the matter is, however, that the Hittites did not have an epic literature except in translation from Babylonian epic.[27] So if any of these literary features must be derived from epic, they came by way of Babylonian influence. It is not impossible that Mesopotamian historical epic and the Hittite annals—the king's "manly deeds"—functioned in a similar way.

In his discussion of the relation of politics to history writing Cancik is

24. *Grundzüge*, pp. 52ff.
25. Ibid., p. 59.
26. Cancik's argument is based primarily upon his belief that there is a parallel dependence upon epic in ancient Israel and ancient Greece. For a critique of this notion see above, 2b.
27. Güterbock, "Die historische Tradition," *ZA* 44:45ff.

again rather unfair in his treatment of the Mesopotamian m.terial.[28] The Tukulti-Ninurta Epic, the Synchronistic History, and the Sargon Letter to the God are all propagandistic and deserve some comparison with the Hittite works. On the other hand, a political aspect in Israelite historiography is much more difficult to discern, if it exists at all. In any comparative approach the function of a historical work must be an important consideration.

From this examination of Cancik's work we conclude, first, that there is no evidence of direct continuity between Hittite and Israelite literature, whether through Canaan or in any other way. Second, there is no clear demonstration in his work that such a continuity must be assumed because of literary features unique to the Hittites and ancient Israel but not to the rest of the Near East. Those features of narrative style that he cites as distinctive can be found in Mesopotamian texts, and the indebtedness of Israel to Mesopotamian literature has long been obvious. It is possible that the Hittites did not have any literary heirs and that, contrary to Cancik's claim, Hittite historiography has no relationship to later historiography, whether Israelite or Greek, but simply died out with the demise of the empire.

Nevertheless, we may still profit from looking at Hittite historiography. The question of the relationship between the Hittite and Assyrian annals, for instance, has not yet been settled.[29] Many of Cancik's observations on narrative style are worthy of further consideration, especially as they might be applied to Mesopotamian literature. It is also instructive to examine the nature and use of sources for different kinds of presentations of the past, and to make general observations about various uses of the past in different historical works.

a. ANNALS

The earliest historical record from Anatolia in this genre was an account of the reign of Anitta, a proto-Hittite king of the city of Kuššar who extended his rule over a number of cities of eastern Anatolia in around 1800 B.C.[30] His name, and that of his father Pithana, is otherwise attested in the records of the Old Assyrian trading colonies of Asia Minor. The Anitta

---

28. *Grundzüge*, pp. 59ff.

29. At the time of the Toronto Seminar (1974) the issue was vigorously debated between Hoffner and Grayson. See also Tadmor, "Observations on Assyrian Historiography," in *Essays . . . Finkelstein*, p. 213.

30. See Güterbock, *ZA* 44:139–45; Kammenhuber, *Saeculum* 9:148–51; and for historical background see *CAH³*, vol. 1, pt. 2, pp. 714–15; O. R. Gurney, *The Hittites*, 3d ed., pp. 19ff.; Hoffner, *Orientalia* 49:291–93.

text was found at Ḫattuša (modern Boğazköy), the capital of the Hittites, only in a Hittite version, but it may go back to an older pre-Hittite Akkadian original, since in Anitta's time the language of literacy for the whole region was the Akkadian used by the Assyrian merchants.[31] The content of the Anitta text may be summarized as follows. The author identifies himself as Anitta, king of Kuššar, and then tells, in the third person, of his father's conquest of Neša with the aid of the storm god. Anitta then tells, in the first person, how he continued this military activity and greatly extended the realm. He mentions that these early exploits are noted in a royal inscription in the city gate. He then discusses further military campaigns including the destruction of Ḫattuša and the placing of the curse on the city. Further conquests are mentioned, as well as the fortifying of Neša, the building of temples to various gods, an account of a hunt, and the receipt of special gifts from another ruler.

After its discovery scholars had expressed doubts about the genuineness of the document,[32] but the confirmation provided by the Assyrian texts of Kanesh (Neša) has persuaded most of them that it is genuine. Since Anitta was king of Kuššar and since control of this city was eventually gained by Labarna, first king of the Hittites, it is likely that these royal records came into the possession of the Hittites at an early stage. Yet the initial doubts about the genuineness of the text are quite understandable. How could a long historical text arise in such an early period without any literary tradition in this genre? Some explanation is necessary.

Literacy itself and the use of cuneiform in Anatolia were acquired from the Assyrians in the commercial colonies of the region. Yet there is little in Mesopotamian literature from this period with which to compare the Anitta text, at least in this form. On closer examination, however, it may be noted that the text has the appearance of being a compilation of various earlier texts and inscriptions. This is indicated most clearly by the reference to a royal inscription containing the words of the first part of the account.[33] Also, two sets of curses follow two accounts of military campaigns. The last part of the text seems to be a rather haphazard collection of royal deeds. If indeed the text was a compilation of inscriptions it would be easier to explain its form in terms of Mesopotamian antecedents.

Several features of this text may also be found in Assyrian royal inscriptions. References to military campaigns and to temple building are known

---

31. See the latest treatment of the text by E. Neu, *Der Anitta-Text*, where he suggests that the Hittite version is the original one. See also Hoffner's review, *BASOR* 226:78; idem, *Orientalia* 49:291–92.

32. This is reflected in Gurney, *Hittites*, pp. 19–20; but see his later remarks in *CAH³*, vol. 2, pt. 1, pp. 232–33. See also Güterbock, *ZA* 44:139–45.

33. Lines 33–35.

from inscriptions of the time of Shamshi-Adad I[34] and Yaḫdun-lim, king of Mari,[35] near contemporaries of Anitta. Assyrian inscriptions also commonly contain notices of curses upon future monarchs who deface inscriptions or otherwise violate instructions given in the texts. The theme of the hunt is not found in any later Hittite annals but is a favorite one among the Assyrians, although it is not attested before the time of Tiglath-pileser I.[36] The Assyrians likewise cite the receipt of royal gifts or booty in their inscriptions as well as dedications of such items to their gods. The content of the Anitta text is no different from what may be found in Mesopotamian inscriptions. What is exceptional is the way in which various inscriptional accounts have been combined to give the appearance of a primitive annals text, even though the events are not clearly dated. Yet it may be this rather unartistic compilation that ultimately gave rise to the Hittite annals.

The oldest of the Hittite annals are those of Ḫattušili I.[37] They are preserved in both Hittite and Akkadian versions, the former in the first-person singular, the latter in the third person.[38] The colophon on the tablet identifies the text as the "manly deeds of Ḫattušili," a phrase also used for later annals. The text briefly sets out a series of military actions and describes the conquest of cities and the taking of booty which is then dedicated to the temples. At least four sections, after the first, are introduced by the phrase "the next year," thus giving the whole the appearance of annals. The last major section, however, does not retain this strict chronological sequence, and the whole is not yet an annalistic account in the strict sense. Nevertheless, the pattern of each unit is fairly formal and the subject matter more uniform and more restricted than that in the Anitta text. However, because Ḫattušili declares himself the king of Kuššar in a manner similar to the introductory statement by Anitta, it is not hard to see a connection between the two inscriptions. Apart from the references to temple dedications, the tone of the annals is quite secular, with the exception of the unit for the third year. Here the king speaks of the special protection of the sun goddess of Arinna, who "ran before me in battle." This becomes a rather common cliché in later annals.

In the final unit of the annals Ḫattušili's crossing of the Euphrates is

34. Grayson, *ARI*, vol. 1, pp. 25–26, no. 8. The connection with Shamshi-Adad remains conjectural but the approximate dating to his time seems fairly certain.

35. G. Dossin, "L'inscription de fondation de laḫdum-Lim, roi de Mari," *Syria* 32 (1955):1–28; see also the translation in *ANET³*, pp. 556–57.

36. Grayson, *ARI*, vol. 2, p. 4. The theme of the hunt occurs in Egyptian texts of the empire period from Thutmose III onward; see *ANET³*, pp. 240, 241.

37. Hoffner, *Orientalia* 49:293–99; see also H. G. Güterbock, "Sargon of Akkad Mentioned by Ḫattušili I of Ḫatti," *JCS* 18 (1964):1–6.

38. This rendering in the third person does not make them chronicles or prove that they were derived from chronicle literature. Note above (3d) the discussion about third-person accounts in Mesopotamia in the second millennium B.C.

compared with the example of Sargon the Great. This allusion to the
Sargon epic, King of Battle, is confirmed by fragments of this work found
at Boğazköy,[39] and since the epic deals with a campaign by Sargon in support of merchants from Mesopotamia in Asia Minor it is highly likely that
this epic, as well as a similar one about Naram-Sin, came into the region
through the Assyrian merchant colonies. The reference to Sargon in the
Ḫattušili annals would also suggest that the Akkadian literary tradition of
historical epic had a distinct influence upon the development of such historical genres as "the manly deeds" of the various Hittite kings. Thus,
while the Hittites did not develop a poetic epic genre, the annals may have
been the Hittite equivalent of the Akkadian historical epics.

There is rather fragmentary evidence of a number of annalistic texts of
the Old and Middle Kingdoms.[40] One of the better preserved texts is the
Ammuna Chronicle, which is actually a set of annals belonging to the Old
Kingdom. It begins like the other annals with the characteristic opening
"Thus (says) Ammuna, the Great King," and continues with a narration of
events by dating them to a given year more precisely than the Ḫattušili annals. It avoids any statement about divine assistance or self-praise and
gives details about the activities of the king's lieutenants in third-person
narration. All this suggests a further development of the annalistic style beyond that of Ḫattušili I.

Three major annalistic works come from the reign of Muršili II: the
Ten-Year Annals of Muršili, the Detailed Annals, and the Deeds of
Šuppiluliuma I, composed by Muršili, his son.[41] Until recently it was suggested that the writing of annals actually began at this time,[42] but the evidence of earlier annalistic texts, mentioned above, now makes this position
untenable.[43] The emphasis in all three documents is upon the "manly
deeds" of the rulers. But the ruler, Muršili, also places great importance
upon the aid of the gods. Throughout these accounts there is the stereotyped refrain developed from the remark in the Ḫattušili annals that the
gods ran before him (or his father) and thus brought victory. In addition,
references are made to divine intervention, the manifestation of divine
power (para ḫandandatar), and the notion of ordeal by battle in which the
gods vindicate the just cause of the victor.

39. See Güterbock, *JCS* 18:1–6.
40. See Hoffner, *Orientalia* 49:303–06.
41. Güterbock, *ZA* 44:95–96; Kammenhuber, *Saeculum* 9:151–53; Hoffner, *Orientalia*
49:311–15; for the texts see A. Goetze, *Die Annalen des Muršiliš*; H. G. Güterbock, "The
Deeds of Suppiluliuma as Told by His Son, Mursili II," *JCS* 10 (1956):41–50, 59–68,
75–85, 90–98, 107–30. See also Cancik, *Grundzüge* (pt. 2: "Die historischen Werke 'Mursilis II'"), pp. 101–84.
42. Kammenhuber, *Saeculum* 9:151ff.; but see p. 154, n. 101.
43. See Hoffner's remarks in *Orientalia* 49:321.

The language of the annals is stereotyped in the descriptions of battles, victories, destruction of cities, and booty and captives taken. The provocations for war conveyed in the messages of envoys are similar to each other and probably do not represent actual royal correspondence. The Detailed Annals does give fuller descriptions of the events and the topography and even invites the hearer of the tablet read in public to inspect the fortifications of a particular city, presumably to better appreciate the accomplishments of the king.[44] Another feature of the annals is the presentation of "historical background" that often explains the causes of the revolt of a vassal king against the "great king" of the Hittites. These causes occasionally go back to the time of the king's father but they are never very complex, e.g., a number of revolts and other difficulties arose as a result of Šuppiluliuma's long absence in Syria campaigning against Mitanni. Cancik emphasizes such "historical background" as a criterion of historiography, but in this rather limited form it can hardly compare with the *aitiai* of Greek historiography.[45]

The Ten-Year Annals and the Detailed Annals should be compared here since there is a considerable overlap in subject matter between the two.[46] The Ten-Year Annals covers the first ten years of Muršili's rule while the Detailed Annals covers more than twenty years from the beginning of his reign. Quite apart from this overlap and difference in scope, several other significant differences between the two exist. For instance, even within the period of the first ten years of rule the Ten-Year Annals omits a large block of material that is to be found in the Detailed Annals, most notably a description of military activity in Syria under the direction of Muršili's brother, Šarre-Kušaḫ. But the principle of selection in the Ten-Year Annals is actually explained in the epilogue: "These enemy lands I conquered with my own hands in (those) ten years. The enemy lands which the king's sons and the lords conquered are not included (here)."[47] Even when the same events are related in both texts the description in the Ten-Year Annals is usually in a more abbreviated form. Also, different formulae are used for

---

44. Ibid., p. 315; Goetze, *Annalen*, pp. 98–99. Cancik, *Grundzüge*, pp. 54–55, takes this as evidence of a "reading public" (*Lesepublicum*) and compares it with the notations in Kings in the Old Testament to other written documents. The comparison is weak and misleading, and closer parallels may be cited in the Egyptian annals of the empire (see below, chap. 5). Hoffner, *Orientalia* 49:325–26, argues against any specific audience, suggesting that even the Ten-Year Annals may have been intended specifically for the goddess alone. See below the statement in the Apology of Ḫattušili III about placing an account of the king's deeds (I, 73–74) "before the goddess," and on this cf. Cancik, *Grundzüge*, pp. 116–17.

45. Cancik, *Grundzüge*, pp. 24ff. Also, to classify such *Vorgeschichte* in these texts as *archaeologia* and to compare it with the introduction in Thucydides' history seems to be a great exaggeration.

46. Cf. Cancik's discussion of this comparison, *Grundzüge*, pp. 101ff.

47. § 42 (IV:44ff.).

marking the beginning and end of a year. One reason for this is that the Ten-Year Annals was written with a view to summing up what was accomplished in the first ten-year period and not merely as part of a continuous annalistic record.

The Ten-Year Annals is written from a single point of view, whereas the Detailed Annals is not. The former focuses upon the king's ascension to the throne as a minor and the doubt that he could accomplish manly deeds befitting the royal office and save his country from rebellion. In this crisis he prayed to the sun goddess of Arinna to help him and she answered his prayer by subduing his enemies, giving him victories year by year over a ten-year period. This is the theme of the prologue and epilogue, with frequent allusions to it occurring in the text of the annals itself. Even though the Detailed Annals is fragmentary at the beginning and end, there is no indication that it had such a prologue or epilogue or any such unified perspective.[48] The Ten-Year Annals has some aspects of a theological and political apology similar to the later Apology of Ḫattušili III, to be considered below. For this reason it is not an annal in the strictest sense.

What then is the literary relationship between the Ten-Year Annals and the Detailed Annals? It is quite likely that they were not by the same author or written for the same purpose. Yet it is not helpful to suggest, as Cancik does,[49] that both are independent and self-contained works that go back to the same archival material if by this he means a body of primary material such as royal correspondence, dockets, military logs, booty lists, etc. Instead I would suggest that continuous annals were compiled year by year for the royal archive and that the Detailed Annals represents a compilation of these annals rather late in Muršili's reign. In the course of time slight modifications may have been made in the text from the earlier versions, but the Detailed Annals is hardly a composition "from scratch." The Ten-Year Annals, on the other hand, was a special composition, perhaps for a special public celebration at the end of the first ten years of the king's reign. It was directly dependent for its source of information upon the annals tradition, but its selection of material, its use of different formu-

---

48. Cf. Cancik, *Grundzüge*, pp. 112ff.

49. Ibid., pp. 104–05. Cancik wishes to draw some implications from his view of the Hittite materials for the historical portions of the Old Testament, whether it be the doublets in the Pentateuch and "Former Prophets" or the relationship between Kings and the Chronicler. The reference to W. Rudolph's discussion of the Chronicler's sources (*Chronikbücher*. HAT 21, pp. x–xiii) is quite misleading. Rudolph, like most biblical scholars, does not question the fact that the Chronicler made use of the Pentateuch, Samuel, and Kings, as well as other portions of the Old Testament. Whether he used the extant canonical version of Kings or a slightly different and expanded edition may be an interesting hypothesis worth debating. But this possibility does not deny that one history was directly dependent upon another, nor even that various versions of Kings if there were such were directly related to each other. So nothing in Israelite historiography seems to correspond exactly to Cancik's version of the relationship between the Ten-Year Annals and the Detailed Annals.

las, its changes in actual content at some points were all dictated by its theme and purpose. Even so it still contains much of the style, clichés, and general perspective of the annalistic works. On this understanding of the texts, the Ten-Year Annals would be the piece prepared for "publication," in Cancik's sense, and the Detailed Annals primarily for the archival records. Now, publication is a criterion of historiography for Cancik.[50] Yet in this instance I fail to see how the Detailed Annals can be considered any less historiographic than the Ten-Year Annals, since on a number of points it is a better historical document. In any event all the royal annals were written at the direction of the king and reflect the impress of his piety.[51]

The Deeds of Šuppiluliuma I is like the annals in style except that it was written by his son Muršili II.[52] It also describes the deeds of Muršili's grandfather, Tudḫaliya, and therefore represents more than one generation. It was written in the third person, but since both rulers are referred to as "my father" and "my grandfather," the time of composition under Muršili is fairly certain. This way of reviewing the past is also found in the early part of the Anitta text and in prologues of other historical genres such as treaties, so we see that the antecedents for this style are plentiful. The perspective of these texts, with their frequent references to divine aid, is similar to that of the annals of Muršili.

The overall structure of the work cannot be recaptured because of the fragmentary condition of the extant tablets.[53] For the most part the account uses stereotyped clichés in describing the successive military adventures, many of which also occur in the annals of Muršili. But unlike the latter there is almost no indication of chronology, only a succession of events. It is possible that the Deeds is a compilation made from the annals of the previous two kings by the scribes of Muršili, but why it was written is not clear. One part of the text that seems quite different from the rest is the famous scene in which the widowed queen of Egypt requests a son from Šuppiluliuma to be her husband.[54] Here the text is much more dramatic than the annals, with frequent speeches and exchanges of messages that make it most akin to historical epic while still entirely in a prose tradition. Perhaps this represents an anecdotal tradition alongside the annals tradition.[55]

---

50. *Grundzüge*, p. 53.

51. See remarks by A. L. Oppenheim, "The City of Assur in 714 B.C.," *JNES* 19:144.

52. See edition by Güterbock, *JCS* 10:41–50, 59–68, 75–85, 90–98, 107–30. See also the discussion by Cancik, *Grundzüge*, pp. 151ff.

53. Cancik (*Grundzüge*, pp. 157ff.) tries to impose upon the remaining text a form corresponding partly to Thucydides and partly to Herodotus. The analysis is hardly credible.

54. A translation of this portion is given by Goetze in *ANET*[3], p. 319. Cf. Güterbock, *JCS* 10:94–98, 107–08.

55. Could it have come from royal correspondence? The Amarna letters, which reflect royal diplomacy between the great powers, give some weight to this possibility.

Another late text contains an account of a successful campaign by Tudḫaliya IV against Alašiya (Cyprus) in the first part, and a similar action taken against the same foe by his son Šuppiluliuma II in the second part.[56] In fact it would appear that the text reflects a copy of two royal inscriptions, one for each king. In the first part the text itself states that Šuppiluliuma, the king's son, made an image of the king along with an inscription of his father's "manly deeds." In this instance the later king retained the first-person account of Tudḫaliya's royal deeds drawn directly from the latter's annals. Šuppiluliuma even states that he did not neglect or suppress anything, i.e., he did not make an abridgment of his source.[57] This inscription Šuppiluliuma set up in a sacred place called the Eternal Peak, which was probably within Ḫattuša itself. Güterbock suggests the peak at Boğazköy called Nişantepe.[58] On the rock surface is an inscription in Hittite hieroglyphs that belongs to Šuppiluliuma II and may actually correspond to the second part of this text. A postscript to the whole text indicates that the monuments had something to do with the cult of the dead and the granting of certain privileges to the sacred building connected with the Eternal Peak. A curse is invoked on anyone who violates these provisions.

The first part of the text relating the exploits of Tudḫaliya strongly resembles the annals and this fits the designation as the king's "manly deeds." The same stereotyped language of conquest and the designation of booty to the various temples are very close to the style of the annals of Ḫattušili I. The purpose of recounting the king's deeds was to demonstrate that Tudḫaliya was a "true" king because he performed "real" manly deeds and was therefore worthy of the cult established for his sake.

The second part, on the other hand, with its introduction "I am . . ." followed by the king's name and titles, the short scope of the deeds, the close association between deeds and the building of a cult place, and the invocation of a curse, corresponds more closely to Semitic royal inscriptions.[59] In this respect it is quite similar to the Anitta text, which also resembles a combination of inscriptions covering more than one generation of royal deeds. The purpose of combining the inscriptions into one text

56. H. G. Güterbock, "The Hittite Conquest of Cyprus Reconsidered," *JNES* 26 (1967):73–81.
57. On the meaning of II, 15–16 see ibid., p. 79. Cancik (in *Mythische und historische Wahrheit*, pp. 87ff.) makes much of this statement in terms of a documentary and ontological understanding of truth and associates it with certain biblical references. However, statements about copying documents correctly and warnings about accidentally or deliberately changing documents or inscriptions are so common, especially in Mesopotamia, that there is nothing remarkable about finding such statements either in Hittite or in biblical texts. For a statement on abridgment of sources and truthfulness in Egyptian annals see below, 5e.
58. See also K. Bittel, *Hattusha, the Capital of the Hittites*, pp. 60ff.
59. Güterbock, *JNES* 26:74.

may have been to associate both kings with the same cult place so that with the death of the latter he too would receive the same veneration.[60]

Some important considerations for historiography arise out of a study of this text. Insofar as there is any evidence of commemorative inscriptions among the Hittites, whether early or late, they are not significantly different from Semitic royal inscriptions. Therefore it seems inaccurate and misleading to compare the more elaborate Hittite literary annals with the Mesopotamian inscriptions, as Cancik does, and to disparage Mesopotamian historiography on this account.[61] The form and function of a historiographic work have a great deal to do with the nature and quality of its historiography.

Second, as stated above, the source for the first part of the text was probably the annals of Tudḫaliya, which were viewed as *the* official and complete record of the king's deeds. This record was retained as part of the permanent scribal tradition while the temporary "field" records of the events that were used to compose the annals were probably discarded.

Concerning the general problem of sources, Kammenhuber proposed that a Hittite "chronicle literature" lay behind most historical texts and that such documents already existed in the Old Kingdom.[62] But the evidence for this, like the evidence for chronicles in second-millennium Mesopotamia, is not very convincing. There are some fragmentary texts of the Old Kingdom that recount military campaigns in the third person, as well as an account of the assassination of Muršili I. But since these may be the historical prologues or background to annals in the first person, as Hoffner suggests,[63] it is difficult to base the existence of a chronicle literature on fragments of third-person narration. What is missing, and this is basic to any chronicle, is evidence of a systematic chronological scheme to which events could be closely related. The Hittites do not seem to show any interest in long-range chronologies or dating systems. Even within the annals the chronological scheme is rudimentary at best, but very often entirely missing. This must be viewed as a serious deficiency in Hittite historiography just as it was the great strength of Mesopotamian historical thought.[64]

60. On the cult of the dead king among the Hittites see A. Goetze, *Kleinasien*, 2d ed., pp. 169–71.

61. *Grundzüge*, pp. 46ff.

62. *Saeculum* 9:143–44.

63. See Hoffner, *Orientalia* 49:313–14. It should be pointed out that some texts called chronicles by modern scholars do not really belong to this category, e.g., the Palace Chronicle, on which see below.

64. Cancik seems to have overlooked this deficiency in Hittite historiography. Can there be a real historiography without chronology? Hittite chronology is still completely controlled by Mesopotamian and Egyptian chronology.

b. POLITICAL USE OF THE PAST

A number of Hittite texts refer to the past for political purposes, both as didactic examples for royal or official behavior and as justification for political action.[65] These texts do not fall within one clearly defined genre but they seem, nevertheless, to be related to each other in a literary and conceptual development.

The earliest text of this group, dating to the Old Kingdom, is the Political Testament of Ḫattušili I.[66] In it the king addresses the senate (*pankuš*), the nobles of the land of the Hittites, and members of the royal family. He disavows one of his sons, Labarna, as heir to the throne and in his place establishes another son, the young Muršili, whom he enjoins the nobles to accept. He cites past evil actions by members of his family as the reason for taking certain strict measures to curtail their activities. None of these episodes is given in chronological order. At one point the king warns the royal officials to heed his words, drawing upon a historical example from the time of his ancestor in which the nobles did not carry out the "testament" of the king regarding the rightful heir; as a result all their households perished.

This pragmatic and didactic use of the past does not yield a very systematic presentation of history, but it does suggest, at a rather early stage in the literary development, two prominent aspects of Hittite historiography—associating the past with admonition and using the past for political justification. Both the officials of the realm and the heir, Muršili, are admonished to heed the words of the aged king. But alongside this admonition a case is made, from past behavior, for denying the rights of an heir to the throne as well as for placing other restrictions upon members of the royal family. Thus historical precedent is established both for irregularity in succession, when it could be justified before a political tribunal such as the senate by an examination of the facts, and for leniency toward erring members of the royal family.

The admonitory character of this work finds its continuation in the Palace Chronicle,[67] a collection of anecdotes, not clearly dated or in chronological order, about royal officials and how their good or evil deeds were justly rewarded or punished. Most of the stories relate to the time of Ḫattušili I, but the text was composed in the reign of Muršili I. Intended as

65. See especially H. A. Hoffner, "Propaganda and Political Justification in Hittite Historiography," in *Unity and Diversity*, pp. 49–62. I have broadened the discussion to include a wider range of texts under the general rubric of "political use."

66. Hoffner, *Orientalia* 49:300–02; F. Sommer and A. Falkenstein, *Die hethitisch-akkadische Bilingue des Hattusili I.*

67. Güterbock, ZA 44:100–01: Hoffner, *Orientalia* 49:302–03.

an instruction text for royal officials, it uses historical examples to drive home the lessons of competence and obedience. In contrast to works of the later Empire period, its tone is rather secular, with no hint that the gods are the ones who bring the rewards and punishments.

A text that seems closely related in outlook to the Palace Chronicle but quite different in form is the Story of the Siege of Uršu.[68] As the title suggests, this is an account of the campaign and siege of the city of Uršu by Ḫattušili I. Since the beginning and end of the text are broken, we do not know either the reason for the campaign or the outcome. But most of the text seems to be taken up with numerous mistakes made by the officers of the king that greatly enrage the king. It may, therefore, have the same didactic purpose as the Palace Chronicle although it could be construed as a parody of it, since one could certainly interpret some of the episodes as humorous. This raises the question, suggested by Güterbock,[69] whether the portrayal of the king was influenced by the Mesopotamian motif of the "unlucky" king in the traditions of Naram-Sin, since these traditions were known in Ḫattuša.

The form of the account belongs to what Güterbock classifies as the unofficial historiography, the popular or legendary tradition. It comes closest, of any of the Hittite forms, to the historical epic tradition of Mesopotamia. But its prosaic character and its unflattering presentation of the king hardly make it a real example of the epic form. Although it has similarities to other early legendary tales, such as the Story of the City of Zalpa and the so-called Cannibal text,[70] there are no extant examples of a later development of this genre.

The rather rudimentary way of using the past for political justification in the Political Testament becomes much more developed in the Proclamation of Telepinu.[71] The latter belongs to a period of the Old Kingdom approximately 150 years later and is in the form of a decree, with the first half a historical prologue to a set of edicts in the last half of the text. Unlike the anecdotal character of references to the past in the Political Testament, the historical prologue of the Proclamation of Telepinu is set forth in one unit at the beginning with events in chronological order, and all of it illustrates the theme of the unity of the state by the avoidance of bloodshed and internal power struggle within the royal family. The edicts, to be administered by the senate, are not just a series of special arrangements as in the Political Testament but are generalized rules for succession and the

---

68. Güterbock, ZA 44:113–38; Hoffner, *Orientalia* 49:299–300.
69. Güterbock, ZA 44:137–38.
70. Ibid., pp. 101–13.
71. See text and translation in E. H. Sturtevant and G. Bechtel, *Hittite Chrestomathy,* pp. 183–93; cf. Hoffner, *Orientalia* 49:306–08.

treatment of royal offenders. Nevertheless, the themes of unity and lenien-cy behind the edicts are drawn directly from the Political Testament.

The review of history in the Proclamation of Telepinu begins with a re-cital of the strong and unified rulers from Labarna I to Muršili I—the kingdom as it should be—followed by a series of royal assassinations con-tinuously avenged by the gods until the time of Telepinu.[72] Even though Telepinu was a usurper he put an end to the bloodshed by his leniency and his royal decree. The basic themes presented here are similar to those of the Political Testament: the unworthy are compared with the worthy, the evil and violent are compared with the merciful and lawful, and the wise king sets everything right by issuing just and holy decrees. A similar pat-tern is evident in later works such as the Apology of Hattušili III.[73] The question arises whether these works, by their manner of presentation, are not also written as self-justifications of the king's own actions and therefore constitute a kind of state propaganda. In the Political Testament the king attempts to dissociate himself from the evil actions of other members of the royal family. In the Proclamation of Telepinu the king justifies his usurpation of power, as does Hattušili in the Apology. But nowhere in these texts is this made the explicit point of the presentation.

The period of time encompassed by the Proclamation of Telepinu is the longest among the Hittite texts. But the extensive survey of so much past history was dictated entirely by the pragmatic requirements of the back-ground of the edicts. The Proclamation did not depend upon, nor did it give rise to, a tradition of dealing with the past history of the Hittite peo-ple or the monarchy as such.[74] Much of Telepinu's description of the early history is stereotyped, but certain events from the time of Muršili on-ward do appear to reflect some use of historical documents, such as royal annals. Even so, the viewpoint of these sources, if not the facts themselves, is certainly changed to suit the purpose of the work as a whole.

Another political use of the past is seen in the historical prologues to state treaties dating from the time of Šuppiluliuma I onward.[75] These trea-ties have received much attention because scholars have sought to draw parallels between them and the presentation of law and covenant in the

---

72. The tendentious character of this work is clear when we compare it with such works as the Ammuna Chronicle, which portrays a rather successful reign for this king. See also Güterbock, ZA 44:138–39.

73. See Hoffner's study in n. 65 above in which he makes a detailed comparison between the Proclamation of Telepinu and the Apology of Hattušili III.

74. This is another marked difference from Mesopotamian and Israelite historiography that is not unrelated to the Hittite lack of any clear chronological approach to the past.

75. Hoffner, *Orientalia* 49:311; V. Koresec, *Hethitische Staatsverträge*; E. von Schuler, "Staatsverträge und Dokumente hethitischen Rechts," in *Neuere Hethiterforschung*, pp. 34–53. See the examples translated by A. Goetze in *ANET*[3], pp. 201–06.

Old Testament.[76] But the use of history in these documents must, first of all, be seen in its own Hittite context. The historical prologue deals primarily with those past circumstances leading to the present relationship between the Hittite king and the vassal state. The concern with the past is not so much one of causality, i.e., why a certain state became a vassal of the Hittites, but of precedent, i.e., why it should continue to be a vassal state. A great deal is made of historical precedent as binding upon treaty partners. Precedent argues both for the continuity of the relationship and for the fairness of the obligations imposed.

The historical prologues of treaties functioned as a means of political persuasion, like the curses at the end of the treaties,[77] and this worked best when the past relationship was between the royal family of the vassal and the family of the great king. Where the Hittites had to deal with king-less states, such as the Kashkeans, the matter was more complicated. These treaties contain no historical prologue,[78] even though the Hittites had contact with these peoples for many generations. The prologue to the famous Hittite-Egyptian treaty between Ḥattušili and Ramesses II is also instructive.[79] While it does refer vaguely to a treaty between Egypt and Hatti in the distant past that was interrupted by hostilities between Muwatalli and Ramesses, the basis for the later treaty is the renewal of a relationship that was regarded as mythologically established from the beginning of time by the principal gods of the two lands. The fact that an appeal to mythology could function in the same way as an appeal to past "history" warns us against making strong comparisons between historical thinking among the Hittites and mythological thinking on the part of their neighbors.[80] In antiquity the uses of history and mythology are never very distinct.[81]

If Hittite treaties are historiographic texts, then so are all correspondence that refers to past events, all recorded legal judgments, and much else besides. But if all such material from Mesopotamia is admitted to the discussion, a whole new basis of comparison with the Hittites or any other culture is immediately suggested. Yet it seems doubtful to me that any use-

76. G. E. Mendenhall, "Law and Covenant in Israel and the Ancient Near East," *BA* 17 (1954):26–46, 49–76; K. Baltzer, *Das Bundesformular*, WMANT 4, 2d ed.; D. J. McCarthy, *Treaty and Covenant*, AnBib 21a. The literature on this subject is too voluminous to cite here, but see the recent review by McCarthy.

77. See von Schuler, "Staatsverträge," p. 38, where he indicates that sometimes the curses stood at the beginning in place of the historical prologue.

78. Ibid.

79. See *ANET*[3], pp. 199–203, where both the Egyptian and Hittite versions are translated side by side.

80. Remarks about the Egyptians' lack of a historical sense are particularly common in this regard.

81. See M. P. Nilsson, *Cults, Myths, Oracles, and Politics in Ancient Greece*, pp. 9–16.

ful limits could be drawn if one seeks to identify as historical thinking every single reference to the past and to generalize on that basis about the nation or people as a whole. Treaties are much closer in genre and function to legal texts and should not be included within a discussion of historiographic texts.[82]

Furthermore, arguments from precedent based upon the actions of a previous generation of rulers, which one finds in the treaty prologues, were quite common in the Near East during the era of Šuppiluliuma I. If we may judge from the diplomatic correspondence of the Amarna Age, the various major powers of the Near East, including the Hittites, often tried to build upon the goodwill established between that country and the previous rulers of Egypt in order to gain special privileges.[83] References to the past in these letters are functionally equivalent to the use of the past in the treaties. In both cases "history" is a diplomatic means of persuasion. The appeal to precedent as a means of political persuasion is used not only in treaties but also in edicts, such as the Proclamation of Telepinu, with its tacit comparison of Telepinu's own behavior and that of Ḫattušili I and the fact that the edicts are based upon, and intended to continue, that pattern of royal behavior. Now, history as precedent can be a significant motif in historiography, alongside an investigation into causes or a presentation of chronological sequence.[84] But the use of precedent as a motivation for human behavior, whether in political, legal, or other aspects of society, is so pervasive in so many cultures that to recognize it in one of its uses as strong evidence for an advanced historical consciousness is misleading.

A text that Hoffner characterizes as royal propaganda is the Apology of Ḫattušili III.[85] It is an autobiographical account of how the king as a child became a priest of the goddess Ishtar of Šamuha and how this goddess prospered his career in the face of many difficulties, first as a governor of the northern regions under his brother's rule and then as a rival of his nephew for the throne of all Ḫatti. Ḫattušili concludes that through all his military and "domestic" trials the goddess Ishtar gave him success, and for this reason she is worthy of perpetual honor within his royal family.

82. Kammenhuber (*Saeculum* 9:140–41) characterizes the treaties as historical documents but not history writing and, along with royal correspondence, emphasizes their purely practical character.

83. For editions of the Amarna letters see J. A. Knudtzon, *Die El-Amarna Tafeln*, 2 vols.; S. A. B. Mercer, *The Tell El-Amarna Tablets*, 2 vols. EA 17, a letter of Tušratta of Mitanni to Egypt, is interesting because it contains a brief autobiographical sketch not unlike the Hittite texts, especially the Apology of Ḫattušili III.

84. J. G. A. Pocock, "The Origins of Study of the Past: A Comparative Approach," *CSSH* 4 (1962):209–46, esp. pp. 232ff.

85. Hoffner, "Propaganda," pp. 49ff.; idem, *Orientalia* 49:315–16; see also H. M. Wolf, "The Apology of Ḫattušiliš Compared with Other Political Self-Justifications of the Ancient Near East." (Dissertation, Brandeis University, 1967); Sturtevant and Bechtel, *Chrestomathy*, pp. 42–99.

The form-critical problem of the Apology is acknowledged by almost everyone who deals with this text, and many different opinions have been expressed.[86] For instance, it is often identified as an autobiography because it traces the career of Ḫattušili from childhood through to his enthronement as the great king. But the designation *autobiography* is so vague that it hardly reflects very formal characteristics beyond first-person narration. To this extent the annals, as well as many other forms, are also autobiographical.

The work is also commonly designated an "apology" because of Ḫattušili's justification for claiming the throne from his nephew.[87] That there is a strong "apologetic" element in the work cannot be denied, but as one scholar has observed,[88] this is no more helpful than "autobiography" in identifying the specific form or genre of the work as a whole. One thinks of an apology as implying a legal context with a fairly clearly defined "jury" and one's status or life at stake. But this work is not directed to such a body as the senate or to any other political organ for a judgment. It gives no hint that the king's current status is threatened or in need of confirmation since it was written several years after his accession to the throne and since he seems quite capable militarily of dealing with any renewed threat to his authority. So if we continue to use the title Apology to identify this work it is only for the sake of maintaining a useful convention.

In terms of more formal criteria the work has some similarities with annals.[89] The roughly chronological treatment of events, the annalistic style of the military campaigns, and the language about divine guidance and protection all reflect a dependence upon the annalistic tradition. We can even find in the Ten-Year Annals of Muršili a similar apologetic tone. Nevertheless, the similarity can be pushed too far. Although Ḫattušili does mention the "first of his manly deeds," he generally neglects to mention most of them and even states that at some future time he will write about the countries he conquered when he was a young man on a separate tablet to be deposited in the temple, as if he had in mind an additional work that would be comparable to the Ten-Year Annals. In the Apology the chronology of events also tends to be confused. Whereas in the annals short digressions are used to give background to particular military actions, the Apology's digressions are lapses into generalizations that project into the king's later life; for example, the "first manly deed" is described after an earlier statement about the king's numerous military successes. In the greatest campaign of his career, the war with Egypt, in which Ḫattušili

86. See the review by Wolf, "Apology Compared," pp. 12–22.
87. Ibid., pp. 20ff.
88. M. Tsevat, in a review of Wolf, *JBL* 87 (1968):458ff.; cf. Gese, *ZThK* 55:139–40.
89. Kammenhuber, *Saeculum* 9:153.

claims a major role, the battle itself and the outcome are not even mentioned. The war with Egypt is merely used as a point of reference for
other, nonmilitary matters. The Apology is clearly not a record of the
king's "manly deeds."

The Apology also has much in common with the edict form, especially
with that of the Proclamation of Telepinu.[90] The works are similar because both rulers were usurpers and felt compelled to set forth a justification of their actions. The histories in the two texts are quite different in
that one deals with several generations while the other covers only one
generation. But the function of the histories is the same since they provide
the background for the edicts. The edict at the end of the Apology establishes certain cultic rights and properties for the goddess Ishtar of Šamuha,
and obligates descendants of the royal family toward the upkeep of this
cult.

The apologetic character of the text is directly related to this edict.
Ḫattušili is not explicitly justifying his right to rule but is setting forth the
reasons why this particular goddess should receive elevated status and why
certain extensive properties, those from the family of Armadattus, now belong to this deity's estate. The text is meant as a document for future generations. Its historical background is intended to constitute the "legal" record in support of the edict for all time, and only implicitly for the king.
Thus Cancik's description of the genre as an "endowment document"
comes close to the mark.[91] Just as treaties had historical prologues that
were part of the treaty itself, so this edict had its necessary prologue even
though it seems disproportionately long in comparison with the edict at
the end. Undoubtedly this prologue is also a unique literary creation,
drawing upon the annals tradition, the Proclamation of Telepinu, and the
special circumstances of the king.

The nature of the edict as cultic endowment has a bearing on the perspective from which the account is written. The king's piety is similar to
Muršili's veneration of the sun goddess of Arinna in the Ten-Year Annals.
In the Apology it is the Ishtar of Šamuha who is honored, and everything
is related to the special election and revelations by this goddess and to her
divine guidance and protection. Because the Proclamation of Telepinu
deals with a much different order of law—an almost secular process of
succession—it makes only a few oblique references to divine aid and judgment.

The Apology of Ḫattušili raises the question whether or not historiogra-

<hr/>

90. Hoffner, "Propaganda," pp. 51ff.
91. *Grundzüge*, pp. 41ff. Yet one should not assume that there were many endowment
documents with precisely this form. Cancik's comparison with the annalistic text of
Šuppiluliuma II has some justification, but they certainly do not belong to the same genre.

phy implies a particular form and intention. Is there a form that we can call a history and is the intention of history to lay the past open for judgment? An edict is not what one would ordinarily call a history. The historical preamble of this text, however, and the one in the Proclamation of Telepinu, share with historiography the attempt to evoke a judgment about a set of past events. This is reflected in the author's (the king's) statement of objection in the Apology:

> "If any one speaks as follows: 'Why did you formerly establish him (Urḫitešub) on the throne? And why are you now declaring war upon him?' (I answer, 'Very well), if he had never started hostilities with me.' Would (the gods) have subjected a great king (who was) upright to a small king? Now because he started hostilities with me, they subjected him to me in the trial."[92]

The author tries to present the events in a manner showing that the king's actions are fully justified and that his behavior is in accordance with the regulations of the Telepinu edicts as well as with the support of the goddess. But this is the special "defense" of an interested party in a quasi-legal context, and although the analogy between the court of law and history may be strong,[93] one cannot thereby include all texts recording legal judgments under the rubric of historiography. Other nonapologetic texts do not attempt to evoke any such judgments about the activities of the king or past events.[94]

In spite of many assertions to the contrary, the compiling of early official Hittite historical records seems to have been indebted to Mesopotamian historiography. The Anitta text can best be explained as a compilation of royal inscriptions that did not differ very much from their Mesopotamian counterparts. Such inscriptions may have been known from the region of northern Syria. Because the Anitta text became a part of the official scribal tradition of the Old Kingdom, it may well have served as a major impulse in the development of annals under Ḫattušili I. Another important Mesopotamian influence upon the early annals was the histor-

---

92. Table III, ll. 73–79, translation from Sturtevant and Bechtel, *Chrestomathy*, pp. 77, 79. See also Hoffner, *Orientalia* 49:315.

93. Cf. the remarks by R. G. Collingwood, *The Idea of History*, pp. 249ff.

94. Gese, *ZThK* 55:139, makes this statement about the *Apology*: "Der Begriff der Geschichte als Folge menschlichen Tuns ist überall gewahrt" (The concept of history as the consequence of human action is constantly upheld). This seems a rather forced way of construing the intention of the text. What it says is that the gods who act as the supreme judges of men's actions vindicate the righteous over the wicked. The theological use of the legal analogy is common in Mesopotamia and ancient Israel as well, but whether it manifests historical thinking is highly debatable.

ical epic tradition of the Akkadian kings. Not only does Ḫattušili I make an explicit reference to Sargon the Great and the King of Battle epic, he even compares one of his own "manly deeds" with Sargon's accomplishment in a manner typical of later Assyrian inscriptions.[95] This strongly suggests that Ḫattušili compiled his annals or "manly deeds" to justify his right to the title of Great King and that other Hittite kings simply followed his example. So often, as in the annals of Muršili II, the Deeds of Šuppiluliuma, the Apology of Ḫattušili III, and the text of Šuppiluliuma II, the references to "manly deeds" suggest that they are part of the nature and legitimation of the royal office. A king with no manly deeds is no king.

If the annals had a tendency to become more detailed in time, then they may have acquired the additional function of serving as archival records, as in the case of the Detailed Annals of Muršili II, which could then have been used for composing other texts of various kinds. But this genre never developed into a history of the state for its own sake. There is no evidence that the state maintained any chronicles or careful chronological records apart from such royal annals.

The Hittites were more interested in using the past than in recording it, and they used it for a variety of purposes. In the Old Kingdom under Ḫattušili I there was a strong tendency, as we have seen, to use the past for didactic purposes. The past supplied examples of good and bad behavior for the nobility and officials of the court. The past could be used to justify exceptional political actions and behavior or it could provide a precedent to support a continuity of royal rights and privileges. In this the Hittites seem to be no different from their Near Eastern contemporaries, as the Amarna correspondence shows. They use the same epistolary style and make the same kind of historical references as we find in the letters of the other major powers. The use of historical persuasion by the Hittites in their treaties with other states suggests that this kind of historical thinking was common also among these states. Nevertheless, historical references used in edicts, treaties, prayers, letters, or other genres do not make any of these genres histories. The fact is that there are no Hittite histories, and there is no indication that the Hittites were interested in simply tracing the course of their past from the earliest king down to later times. Neither the kingship as such, nor the state or the people, was the focus of any Hittite author's concern. The only possible exception is the Proclamation of Telepinu, where kingship is the theme of the historical prologue but only insofar as it leads up to an edict on royal succession. For the purpose and

95. It is a common topos of Assyrian royal inscriptions to mention that the loyal subject went beyond the limits traversed by any of his predecessors. See the Naram-Sin text in *ANET*³, p. 269.

propagation of the edict the presentation is very narrow and schematized and does not encourage the continuation of any subsequent historical record. The Hittites' use of the past here as elsewhere is too pragmatic to give rise to actual history writing.

Much has been made of the principles of causality among the Hittites,[96] but this causality is evident only because the historical events are embedded in genres that seek to use the past for religious, political, or legal purposes. On the other hand, it is quite wrong to deny that the same sense of causality is present in Mesopotamia. Gese's suggestion that for "Mesopotamian man" history was only sequence and not consequence because certain genres of historiography such as king lists and chronicles illustrate only sequence is highly misleading.[97] The Babylonians and Assyrians did believe in the consequences of human actions totally apart from any consideration of divine intervention, as is evident in their law codes. It is pointless to cite here the countless letters and records of legal transactions from Mesopotamia that could illustrate the plain fact that people were held accountable for their actions. At the same time many Mesopotamian texts suggest divine intervention in human affairs as a way of accounting for past events.[98] If history is, at least in part, the extension of the principles of "divine" justice and human accountability (Herodotus's *aitia*) on a much broader basis in both time and space than the individual, then it does not seem to me that the Hittites were any more concerned with history than the Mesopotamians.

As we have seen above, Cancik has put the issue of historiography in terms of the development of a particular form of prose narration with a focus upon the texts of the empire period. Although the genetic approach to the problem of historiography as literature corresponds to my own interest, there are two basic problems with his work. First, he cannot account for the development of this prose style into later forms of historiography and he makes little attempt to do so. Second, his thesis rests upon the view that Hittite prose style is quite distinct from Mesopotamian and the only possible precursor of the Hebrew and Greek prose styles. This position must now be examined more closely.

At least two genres of Mesopotamian historical texts, overlooked by

---

96. A. Malamat, "Doctrines of Causality in Hittite and Biblical Historiography: A Parallel," *VT* 5 (1955):1–12. Malamat makes much of the so-called Plague Prayers of Muršili II. This king endeavors to find in the previous generation the causes of the plagues that beset his land. He attributes the disease to an act of the gods as punishment for the violation of a treaty oath and a neglect of the cult in the previous generation. I do not find this view of causation very different from that reflected in the Weidner Chronicle or the Tukulti-Ninurta Epic or any number of other Mesopotamian texts.

97. *ZThK* 55:131ff.

98. See Albrektson, *History and the Gods*, and the discussion below, 7c.

Cancik, should be considered here, the historical epic and the Neo-Assyrian letter to the god. These texts go well beyond the mere listing of events or simple accounting of royal deeds.[99] The two examples discussed in detail in the previous chapter—the Tukulti-Ninurta Epic and the Sargon Letter to the God—are highly artistic presentations of rather important political events.[100] I have drawn attention to their thematic unity and their possible use as political propaganda in a fashion not too different from the Apology of Ḫattušili III.

The Tukulti-Ninurta Epic and the Sargon Letter to the God pass the test of *Literarizität* that Cancik lays down as well as do any of the Hittite texts.[101] Intended for specific audiences and public presentation, they are clearly literary works that became part of the scribal tradition. They were the result of at least some "research" or use of a variety of sources, and they represent a carefully planned and executed composition rather than mere compilation.

A few features of *Erzählformen*, outlined by Cancik,[102] call for special consideration. It is instructive to consider especially the Tukulti-Ninurta Epic because it falls so close in time to the texts of the Hittite empire. Very important for Cancik is the use, in the Hittite historical texts, of "background" (*Vorgeschichte*), in which various events are given a perspective based on previous relations between the Hittites and the states involved. This parallels very closely the historical prologues of the state treaties, which have the same function. In fact, Cancik suggests that the form of historical background in the historiographic texts has its *Sitz im politischen Leben* in the treaty form. The Tukulti-Ninurta Epic has as its point of departure and overall theme the violation of a treaty relationship between Assyria and Babylon by the Kassite king, and it goes to great lengths to make this point clear.[103] It even goes back into previous generations of rulers for at least a century to deal with the relationship between the two states. Here much of the language is similar to that in the Hittite texts with special emphasis on the element of divine judgment. In fact, the theme of ordeal by battle (III A, 13′f) in which the victor is the righteous one and the loser is the evildoer—is clearly indicated.[104] Machinist is correct in identifying these elements as influence from Near Eastern treaties.[105] It is therefore reasonable to assume that treaties with historical prologues such as are known from the Hittites were common in this period through-

99. *Grundzüge*, pp. 13ff.
100. See above, 3a and e.
101. Cf. *Grundzüge*, pp. 52ff.
102. Ibid., pp. 18ff.
103. See P. Machinist, *The Epic of Tukulti-Ninurta I*, pp. 39–45.
104. Ibid., p. 232 and n. 162, where the Hittite parallels are also cited.
105. Ibid., pp. 214ff., 510–11.

out the Near East and that such a historical prologue was part of the treaty between the Assyrians and the Babylonians. Thus in a piece of political historiography that seeks to prove the accountability of the Babylonians for the conflict it would be only natural that these features would appear prominently in the account. Although the text is fragmentary, we still find a lengthy account of various types of violations and reasons for the hostilities and for the ultimate defeat of the enemy.

Because of the broken condition of the Tukulti-Ninurta text, we cannot be entirely certain about several features, but one that is prominent is the use of speeches.[106] These are employed to great effect in classical Greek historiography, and Cancik notes the occurrence of speeches, messages, and the like in Hittite historical texts. But as we have seen above, these are very stereotyped, especially in the sending and receiving of messages; the episode of Šuppiluliuma's exchange with the Egyptian queen is the only exception. In Tukulti-Ninurta Epic, however, many speeches and messages are exchanged between the two opposing kings. Particularly striking is the use of soliloquy on the part of the Kassite king to admit his own guilt. This is part of a remarkable two-sidedness (*gleichzeitige Handlung*) to the presentation of the events that comes closer to the classical model than anything in the Hittite texts.[107]

The Sargon Letter to the God is in a different genre and from a different period and does not use speeches as does the Tukulti-Ninurta Epic.[108] On the other hand, prior to many of the military attacks it does include brief statements of historical background (*Vorgeschichte*) that indicate previous encounters with the same enemy or acts of rebellion justifying the pacification or the "liberation" of territories of allies that had been unjustly seized by the king of Urartu. The violation of the loyalty oath by Urzana of the city of Muṣaṣir (§169) is emphasized as the reason for capturing this holy city. All these "background" statements give justification for the campaign as a whole and the way in which it was conducted.

Another prominent feature of classical historiography—digression—is used to great effect in this work.[109] Cancik notes that there is limited use of digression in Hittite historiography but denies that it even exists in Mesopotamian historical texts.[110] Yet we have already seen that the Sargon Letter makes remarkable and varied use of digressions far beyond anything

---

106. Ibid., pp. 39ff.
107. Cf. Cancik, *Grundzüge*, pp. 20, 120–21, 163ff. His Hittite examples are weak in comparison with the Tukulti-Ninurta Epic, and his statement that *Gleichzeitigkeit* does not appear in Mesopotamian historiography is wrong.
108. Note, however, the use of speeches in the Esarhaddon letter and Oppenheim's comment, *JNES* 19:144.
109. See Oppenheim, *JNES* 19:138ff.
110. *Grundzüge*, p. 35.

in the Hittite texts. Other similarities between the Sargon Letter and early Greek prose have already been noted.

The conclusion to be drawn from this survey is that Cancik's thesis will not stand up to scrutiny because he has not compared the right Mesopotamian texts with the Hittite texts. Historical narration, in both poetic and prose genres, was far more advanced and complex than he supposes and provides a much more likely prospect for comparison with early Hebrew prose. Whether Hittite historiography had any influence upon Mesopotamian forms, such as the annals, cannot be debated here, but the development is largely a parallel one, with considerable evidence that Mesopotamian culture had a clear impact upon Hittite culture rather than the other way around.

CHAPTER FIVE

EGYPTIAN HISTORIOGRAPHY

To include a discussion of Egyptian historiography within a comparative study of this kind would appear questionable to some scholars and calls for some justification. Many studies of Egyptian civilization portray its ideology of kingship and the state in such a way as to emphasize the static character of Egyptian thought, with the result that any idea of history and progress through time becomes a complete contradiction. Thus scholars of Near Eastern historiography feel quite justified in leaving Egypt out of the picture altogether. Gese, in his survey on historical thinking in the Near East,[1] dismisses Egypt from consideration on the authority of a statement by L. Bull that the Egyptians had no idea of history in the modern sense.[2] Cancik also fails to make any comparison between Hittite and Egyptian forms of historiography even though he asserts the great superiority and originality of Hittite historiography over that of Egypt.[3] Is there any justification for this neglect?

In his article on the idea of history in ancient Egypt, Bull concluded:

> In the writer's view it seems fair to say that the ancient Egyptians cannot have had an "idea of history" in any sense resembling what the phrase means to thinkers of the present age or perhaps of the last 2,400 years.[4]

Now this statement does not deny that the Egyptians had a great interest in, and reverence for, the past, as Bull makes clear throughout his discussion. Furthermore, the statement can be applied with equal justification to the Hittites and the cultures of Mesopotamia. But what is significant is that the statement is more a remark about the theoretical impossibility of

---

1. H. Gese, "Geschichtliches Denken im Alten Orient," *ZThK* 55:128.
2. L. Bull, "Ancient Egypt," in *The Idea of History in the Ancient Near East*, p. 32.
3. H. Cancik, *Grundzüge*, p. 3. Only in the notes, and in one brief discussion on p. 130, does Cancik make occasional reference to Egyptian historical sources. The treatment is hardly adequate.
4. See n. 2, above.

historiography among the Egyptians than a conclusion based upon data collected. Bull asserts that the Egyptians *cannot* have had an "idea of history" by emphasizing their static view of life. Since it has already been pointed out that Plato's philosophy cannot be used to reflect the thought of a Herodotus or a Thucydides, it is equally questionable to use Egyptian mythology to interpret all its historical texts as well. The fact is that the Egyptians were at pains to record important historical events for posterity and to preserve much of their past over very long periods of time. And it must also be remembered that the classical historians, beginning with Hecataeus and Herodotus, were immensely impressed with the Egyptian's preservation of his records of the past.

More important than the debate over the Egyptians' "idea of history" is the question whether or not they had any historiographic forms comparable to those of other neighboring states. Now, even a cursory survey of the literature would indicate that the Egyptians had such genres as king lists, annals, biographies, commemorative inscriptions, and historical narratives that warrant comparison with both Mesopotamian and Hittite texts. It is also interesting that E. Meyer, in his discussion of Egyptian historical texts, referred to a twofold source for Egyptian history, an official chronographic literature and a legendary source.[5] This division is similar to that formulated by Güterbock for Hittite historiography.[6]

The possibility of direct cultural contact between the major Near Eastern powers, especially in the Amarna Age, must also be taken seriously. For a considerable period of time the Egyptians exchanged envoys and diplomatic correspondence with the Hittites, the Mitannians, the Assyrians, and the Babylonians, as well as dominated the Levant politically. Evidence of Egyptian cultural influence can be seen, for instance, in the Hittite royal ideology of the empire period, which moves in the direction of deification of the king.[7] A new element in the royal titulary is the reference to the king as the "sun," and since in the Amarna correspondence the Syrian and Palestinian vassals call the king of Egypt their "sun-god," it is likely that this Hittite innovation derives from Egypt through this intermediate region. But then too the great historiographic texts of Egypt, such as the Annals of Thutmose III, on display in the capital, may have had some impact upon foreign diplomats.

One reason why scholars do not include Egypt in a survey of Near Eastern historiography may be that few comprehensive treatments are available for generalists to use. There is, of course, the large collection of histor-

5. *Geschichte des Altertums* II/1, p. 508. This general impression is strongly supported by both Herodotus and Manetho. However, an alternative explanation is suggested below.
6. See above, 4a.
7. Gurney, *Hittites*, pp. 64–65.

ical texts in English translation by James Breasted covering the period from earliest pharaonic times down to the Persian conquest.[8] While newly discovered texts and more recent editions of previously known works may supplement this collection, it is still representative of Egyptian historical texts. Since it is organized chronologically it must be used together with other studies in order to carry through a discussion of literary genre. Yet such studies are, at best, sporadic and do not yet give a very complete picture of Egyptian historiography. Studies on individual genres, such as A. Hermann's on the *Königsnovelle*[9] and E. Otto's on Late Egyptian biographies,[10] have been used to investigate biblical parallels. The king-list tradition has been treated by H. W. Helck,[11] and military annals of the Eighteenth Dynasty by A. Spalinger.[12] D. B. Redford has recently written a study of king lists, annals, and daybooks.[13]

In the article mentioned above, Bull stressed the Egyptians' intense interest "in making and preserving records of their past as a nation,"[14] and he illustrated this thesis with numerous examples from the whole pharaonic period. But since he was reluctant to concede in the end that the Egyptians actually wrote history, other scholars were not inclined to take the data seriously. In 1966 E. Otto published a "programmatic study" seeking to show that Egyptian historiography represents a tension between the world of facts and a historical ideal (*Geschichtsbild*).[15] Although the Egyptians were very conservative the ideal was far from static over the centuries. Otto discusses it in terms of two concepts, the notions of time and royal ideology. Now, it would be easy to place too much emphasis upon the presentation of the *Geschichtsbild* in the texts and to deny that the Egyptians had any interest in history, but Otto's study suggests that this would be, in fact has been, a serious error. Not only were the Egyptians conscious of a long history but they tried very seriously to come to terms with it. No Near Eastern society was more meticulous in its record keeping, as represented in the annals and king lists, and yet more ideological in its presentation of past events as they centered upon the king. An appreciation of this duality will constitute a basic principle in our study of the Egyptian texts.

8. J. H. Breasted, *Ancient Records of Egypt*, 5 vols.; abbreviated as *BARE*.

9. A. Hermann, *Die ägyptische Königsnovelle*.

10. E. Otto, *Die biographischen Inschriften der ägyptischen Spätzeit*.

11. H. W. Helck, *Untersuchungen zu Manetho und den ägyptischen Königslisten*.

12. A. Spalinger, "Aspects of the Military Documents of the Ancient Egyptians" (Dissertation, Yale University, 1974); idem, "Some Notes on the Battle of Megiddo and Reflections on Egyptian Military Writing," *MDAIK* 30 (1974):221–29; idem, "A Critical Analysis of the 'Annals' of Thutmose III (Stucke V–VI)," *JARCE* 14 (1977):41–54.

13. D. B. Redford, *King-Lists, Annals, and Day-Books* (forthcoming).

14. In *The Idea of History*, p. 3.

15. E. Otto, "Geschichtsbild und Geschichtsschreibung in Ägypten," *WO* 3 (1966): 161–76.

The tension between ideology and reality is more apparent, perhaps, in texts intended for political propaganda. The studies of G. Posener and others on this subject[16] have focused particularly upon the literature of the Twelfth Dynasty, with some expansion beyond this in the essay by R. J. Williams.[17] But examples of this kind of literature are much more numerous than these studies suggest.[18] Since political propaganda was an important feature in both Hittite and Mesopotamian historiography and since some regard it as an element of early Israelite historiography, we must consider it here.

In any study of Egyptian historiography form-critical questions concerning genre, function, and setting should be taken up. This is especially true of any comparative study of the "uses of the past" in the ancient Near Eastern cultures. In this regard, therefore, it must be kept in mind that most of the extant written materials from ancient Egypt are funerary.[19] This makes Egypt fundamentally different from both the Hittites and Mesopotamia.[20] One may legitimately expect a commemorative use of the past to predominate in a mortuary context, and it certainly does in the numerous personal biographies. Of course, the cult of the dead also plays a large part in such inscriptions. Other prominent sources for royal historical texts are the inscriptions on temple walls or stelae associated with sacred places, and in these cases the political events take on important religious significance or are interpreted as evidence of the close relationship between the king and the gods in the unfolding of historical events. This comes closer to a use well attested throughout the Near East. On the other hand, in contrast to both Mesopotamia and the Hittites, no large libraries or archives have been found,[21] even though Egyptian texts contain many references to their existence. The reason for this is obvious: the texts of such libraries and archives were written on papyrus or leather and only a few such texts have been preserved to the present day. Yet even monumental texts can reflect the use of archival source material. Genre and function are most important in any comparative analysis and diachronic study of these texts.

Another factor that limits any comparison with ancient Israel is the pau-

16. G. Posener, *Littérature et politique dans l'Égypte de la XIIᵉ dynastie.*

17. R. J. Williams, "Literature as a Medium of Political Propaganda in Ancient Egypt," in *The Seed of Wisdom*, pp. 14–30.

18. The dangers of this restricted view are evident in the comparisons with the biblical material by R. N. Whybray, *The Succession Narrative*, pp. 105ff.

19. See Gardiner, *Egypt of the Pharaohs: An Introduction*, p. 53.

20. However, note the use of funerary inscriptions by the Canaanite-Phoenicians, *ANET*³, pp. 661–62.

21. The cache of Amarna tablets from Akhenaten's capital is surely a good indication that such existed, that they contained foreign literary texts, and that the Egyptians had their own libraries in hieratic and hieroglyphic.

city of texts after circa 1100 B.C., the end of the Twentieth Dynasty. The reason for this is twofold. First, the decline of Egyptian civilization meant greatly diminished building activity, fewer texts having to do with international politics, and therefore fewer texts of historical interest. Second, because the petty rulers of the Twenty-first to the Twenty-sixth dynasties, with the exception of the Ethiopian kings, were located in various parts of the Nile Delta, their monuments have suffered more from the ravages of time than those of Upper Egypt. Yet the considerable number of texts and documents from the Late period makes it clear that the historiographic traditions of the earlier periods did not come to an end with the demise of the empire. There was a significant continuity of virtually every major genre down into classical times.

This survey will not attempt to deal with all the material represented by the five volumes of Breasted and all the historical texts published since his work. Nor is it possible to discuss in detail the problems of interpretation related to many of these texts. My chief purpose is to give a fairly accurate picture of the variety of historiographic genres in the broadest sense and some appreciation of their continuity and development or transformation through time. Since Egyptology lacks a comprehensive typological or form-critical analysis, my own classification must remain rather tentative, but I consider a sensitivity to the questions of the type and function of a text to be of utmost importance in evaluating its place in the historiographic tradition.

a. THE PALERMO STONE AND ITS ANTECEDENTS

A study of Egyptian historiography might do well to begin with a remarkable document of the Old Kingdom period, the Palermo Stone.[22] This large inscribed stone fragment was part of a historiographic work compiled at the end of the Fifth Dynasty (ca. 2350 B.C.) that covered at least seven centuries of history. Although most of the monument is missing, it is still possible to reconstruct the basic form of the work. Originally, it was a large, freestanding block of stone about seven feet long and two feet high and inscribed on both sides. It contained a number of horizontal rows, with each row divided vertically into compartments. Each compartment in the top row of the front contained the name of a predynastic ruler, those of Upper Egypt being identified by a hieroglyphic figure wearing a white crown, those of Lower Egypt by a red crown, and at least six rulers wearing combined crowns signifying control of both regions. These rulers

22. *BARE*, vol. 1, §§ 76–167; Gardiner, *Egypt*, pp. 62ff.; Bull, *Idea of History*, pp. 4–5.

presumably all belonged to the period of Egyptian history prior to the "final" unification of Upper and Lower Egypt under Menes (ca. 3100 B.C.). In subsequent rows front and back, very likely beginning with Menes although his name is not preserved, each compartment represents one year of a particular king's rule. The name of each king is inscribed under his year section in the space between the rows. For the earliest dynastic kings the year compartments contain one or two events for each year, while the later compartments of the Old Kingdom are larger and often include a number of items. Most often the events were of a religious nature, having to do with the cult or its images or festivals, but they could include military victories, building activities, mining expeditions, and other matters. When the monument was complete it very likely contained the names of the rulers of Egypt from predynastic times to the end of the Fifth Dynasty, and it was possible to ascertain the length of each king's reign. The text also constitutes a brief religious and political chronicle for the period from Menes onward.

Some scholars believe that the individual year compartments originate in a system of year-names for dating purposes like the one in Mesopotamia. This is corroborated by the finding of wooden and ivory labels of the Early Dynastic period on which such year-names were inscribed.[23] These labels often contain the same hieroglyphic signs for years as those used to separate the year compartments from each other in the Palermo Stone. It would appear from this that "annals" developed in Egypt out of the practical expedient to keep a list of year-names and then to supplement such a list with other useful data. An argument against this view, however, is that already by the Second Dynasty another dating system arose that replaced that of the year-names. Every second year a census was taken of livestock and other commodities and it became the practice to refer to a certain year within a particular king's reign as the "*n*th occurrence of the counting of cattle" or "the year after the *n*th counting." Such a system is reflected in the Palermo Stone and finds its counterpart on documents of the Old Kingdom. In fact, only the early entries of the Palermo Stone resemble the date-list form while the later ones are quite different.

The problems of the document's form, how or why it was composed, and why there appears to be no real continuation of an annalistic tradition in the subsequent periods all raise serious difficulties for any view that sees the Palermo Stone as the product of a gradual and continuous development of an annalistic style or genre. While its precise purpose and *Sitz im Leben* are unknown to us, it seems evident that such a fine monument was not an archival document but was meant to be put on display for a special function and occasion. It is also unlikely that it was simply the current edi-

23. W. B. Emery, *Archaic Egypt*, pp. 38–104.

tion of a "running account of history" from the archives. Rather, it seems to have been put together from various sources. The old king lists of the first register were very likely based upon sources separate from the rest. The bulk of the Early Dynastic materials may come from date-lists. The annual height of the Nile, recorded in its own rectangle at the bottom of each year component, is probably derived from yet another source. The form of the Fifth-Dynasty entries, on the other hand, suggests that they are derived primarily from dedication inscriptions that simply list the royal benefactions to the various cults for any given year.[24] Such material was drawn from accounting records and reflects the "daybook" tradition, which is known from later periods of Egyptian history. Thus the latter part of the work is far less "annalistic" in character than the earlier part, with its "date-list" tradition.[25]

The Palermo Stone is, therefore, not a set of annals in the strict sense but a work composed as a product of "research" in order to reflect the great antiquity of the monarchy and to review its successive deeds with whatever materials were available. While it is difficult to authenticate its presentation, it would appear to be remarkably free from ideological bias and to represent its sources faithfully. It did not give rise to an annalistic tradition but it did have an important continuation in the king-list tradition, as we shall see below.

The antecedents to the brief historical statements about the early dynasties in the Palermo Stone may be seen in the pictorial presentations of political events in monuments from the very beginning of dynastic history.[26] On ceremonial slate palettes, maceheads, and knife handles one finds carved in relief scenes of warfare between the two major regions of Upper and Lower Egypt or against foreign neighbors. The royal figures are identified by hieroglyphic signs but beyond that the scenes must be interpreted by "reading" the emblematic standards for various regions, the stylized presentation of various figures, and the various symbolic gestures and actions.

The most famous of these objects, but by no means the first, is the Narmer Palette.[27] King Narmer is often identified with Menes, whom Manetho tells us was the first king of Egypt to unite Upper and Lower

---

24. On the form of these see below, 5d.

25. Cf. Redford, *King-Lists*, chap. 4 (on *gnut*). There are too many problems to permit us to simply maintain that a form of annals (*gnut*) was created in the Old Kingdom or earlier and continued in existence throughout the Pharaonic period. The term *gnt* itself is rare in the Old Kingdom and is not used in the plural until the Middle Kingdom.

26. Gardiner, *Egypt*, pp. 392ff.; Emery, *Archaic Egypt*, pp. 38ff.

27. Gardiner, *Egypt*, pp. 402ff., plates xxi, xxii; Emery, *Archaic Egypt*, pp. 43ff. See also *ANEP*[2], no. 296–97; H. Frankfort, *The Birth of Civilization in the Near East*, pp. 91–92 and figs. 27, 28.

Egypt. This palette is frequently interpreted to be a record of this event.[28] On one side the king, wearing the white crown of Upper Egypt, has a captive by the hair whom he is about to strike with a mace. Above the kneeling captive is a bearded human head with a body in the form of a papyrus marsh as a symbol for the Delta. A cord attached to the nose of the head is held by the falcon god, Horus, the royal symbol of Upper Egypt. In the bottom register two figures flee before the king. The message that the king of Upper Egypt has conquered Lower Egypt seems clear.

The opposite side of the palette, in three registers, suggests the same theme of conquest but with the additional element of the unity of the two regions. In the top register the king, clearly identified by two hieroglyphs as Narmer but wearing the red crown of Lower Egypt, marches in procession behind four standard-bearers and a royal official. Before them are ten bound and decapitated figures of the enemy. The middle register has two lions, with serpentine necks twisted about each other, held in check by two keepers. They suggest the unity of the two separate regions. The bottom register shows a bull as royal symbol trampling a northerner and destroying his fortress. The name of Narmer is in a special enclosure at the top on both sides of the palette.

There is little doubt that an attempt is being made to commemorate in pictorial form an important historical event at a time when hieroglyphic writing was not sufficiently developed to provide an adequate interpretive narrative. Only a few hieroglyphic signs are inserted in the scenes of these early monuments as captions for names of a few persons and places. But in the ivory and wooden labels of the First Dynasty we can see the transition from symbolic representation to hieroglyphic narrative.[29] At the same time there seems to be a decided decline in the commemorative scenes, with only the dating labels carrying on the tradition. On the other hand, the symbolic scene of the king smiting the enemy became a stereotype, with the northerner usually identified as an Asiatic.

As we have seen above, the Palermo Stone takes up the historical tradition at the point at which it is translated into year-names corresponding to those found on the wooden and ivory labels. How early in the First Dynasty the primitive hieroglyphic records could be rendered in a continuous annual series is a moot point that cannot be debated here. By the time of the Old Kingdom the interest in commemorating great events, whether on monuments or in archival records, seems to have passed, and in its place we have merely the records of an elaborate bureaucratic administration concerned primarily with annual income and expenditures.

28. Cf. Emery (*Archaic Egypt*, pp. 31–37), who does not equate Narmer with Menes and presents arguments against such an identification.
29. See Emery, *Archaic Egypt*, pp. 49ff.

b. THE TURIN CANON AND OTHER KING LISTS

The so-called Turin Canon of Kings is a king list written on papyrus in the time of Ramesses II, around the thirteenth century B.C., that is now in very fragmentary condition in the Turin Museum.[30] It originally contained the names of more than three hundred kings of Egypt down to the end of the Second Intermediate period, ca. the mid-sixteenth century B.C. The extant text, therefore, was not the original composition but a copy of an earlier text composed at the beginning of the Eighteenth Dynasty. It begins with names of gods and demigods who ruled before Menes, all with very long reigns, and here the parallel with the Sumerian king-list tradition of Mesopotamia is obvious.[31] The Turin Canon then proceeds with a list of royal names and the precise length of each reign. It also includes numerous headings and summations that group kings together in a series, and although the headings are often fragmentary or missing it is clear that the work tries to make some significant historical distinctions in the long line of kings. A good example is the designation of six rulers within the Second Intermediate period as "foreign rulers" (Hyksos). Occasional bits of historical information are included although there is no attempt at annal writing. Mesopotamian king lists also have brief historical statements scattered throughout. Another practice of the Turin Canon is to include a notation with the various sums, or within a series of names, using the term *wsf* followed by a measure of time. Redford has recently suggested that the term means "suppressed" and that it was used in those cases where the name of the king was anathematized but his period of rule was retained in order to keep a correct tally.[32]

A comparison of the Turin Canon and the Palermo Stone for the early part of the list is noteworthy. The Turin Canon lists in the predynastic period a group of gods, the Greater and Lesser Ennead, the "glorified spirits" (*'ḫw*), and groups of mythical kings all with very long reigns in place of the mere listing of the predynastic rulers in the Palermo Stone. Otto has recently called attention to the significant difference in historical perspective represented by this change.[33] The Palermo Stone presents quite clearly the historical reality that prior to the First Dynasty there was a separate group of kings in both Upper and Lower Egypt and then for a time a number of kings who controlled both regions. There is no suggestion in this docu-

---

30. Gardiner, *Egypt*, pp. 47–48; idem, *The Royal Canon of Turin*; H. W. Helck, *Untersuchungen zur Manetho und den ägyptischen Königslisten*; D. B. Redford, *King-Lists, Annals, and Day-Books* (forthcoming).
31. See above, 3b.
32. *King-Lists*, s.v. "Turin Canon."
33. "Geschichtsbild und Geschichtsschreibung," WO 3 (1966): 169–70.

ment that gods ruled on earth before human kings. In fact, the Old Kingdom period appears to have kept the realms of gods and men quite separate. The Turin Canon gives evidence of a radical shift in the historical
perspective with the complete mythologizing of prehistory so that now
there was an original unified rule under successive periods of gods and heroes before the historical period. This same tradition is later reflected in
Manetho and is able to completely supplant the historical tradition. This is
one of many instances in which, as Otto has shown, the perspective of history (*Geschichtsbild*) has been influenced by theology and royal ideology
and has led to a significant revision of the historiographic tradition.

Otto sees this tendency toward the mythologization of history in a prior
historicization of mythology in which a genealogy of the gods is developed
as part of an elaborate cosmology that was then made continuous with
history. The historicization of mythology also played a part in the royal
ideology in which the king was the embodiment of Horus, son of Osiris.[34]
But the mythologization of early history probably did not come about until after the end of the Old Kingdom. Only in the First Intermediate period
do we begin to find references to the "time of the god Horus" or the like
as the earliest period of history. Such references become very common in
later texts and inscriptions.

The construction of a temporal continuity from theogony and the time
of heroes and first rulers to later history by means of genealogical connections is also part of early Greek historiography. Whether Egypt had some
influence upon this Greek development, along with the Mesopotamian antediluvian tradition, is hard to say.[35]

The Turin Canon also seems to follow the Palermo Stone tradition in
making no distinctions or special groups of kings within the names from
Menes to Unas, although Manetho divides them into five dynasties with
eight or nine kings each. The precise criterion for these divisions is not
known, although he may have taken as his pattern the nine divine kings of
the Greater and Lesser Enneads.[36] Manetho's preference for the number
nine is apparent in later dynastic divisions as well.

For the period subsequent to the Fifth Dynasty the question of sources
for the Turin Canon becomes more difficult, since the names of the First
and Second Intermediate periods often represent more than one line of
kings ruling simultaneously. These could hardly have been taken from one
continuous annalistic source. But as the Palermo Stone suggests, annual

34. The common practice of interpreting the conflict of Horus and Seth euhemeristically
as representing a prehistoric struggle between the two regions of north and south is anachronistic and hardly justified.

35. See the discussion by P. Walcot, *Hesiod and the Near East*, pp. 77–78.

36. See Redford, *King-Lists*, s.v. "Turin Canon."

records of royal benefactions to the gods were probably kept at the major temple sites, such as Memphis, Heliopolis, and Thebes. Rivaling royal families might well have honored only the major temples in their region during a period of divided rule. It is also possible that in certain periods, such as the Twelfth Dynasty, precise records of the king's accession date were kept for administrative and dating purposes and that notations from such records found their way into the Turin Canon.

Where the remains of the Turin Canon preserve any indication of the reason for royal groupings, they are based upon such criteria as the location of the royal residence, genealogical continuity, or foreign rule. But these divisions likewise suggest that the sources for the Turin Canon are multiple. As Redford concludes, there is little evidence that "the *Vorlage* to Turin involved anything like a running king-list, kept up without interruption; the Turin Canon is a product of the first half of the New Kingdom."[37] This clearly makes it a historiographic work meant to encompass the whole course of the monarchy from its origin down to the time of the author, with distinctions, summations, and comments where the author felt they were necessary. Furthermore, it has a continuous historiographic tradition down to the time of Manetho. Redford and Helck have firmly established that Manetho's work cannot be understood apart from this king-list tradition.

If we use Manetho to understand the post-Turin king-list tradition, then it is evident that the same criteria for distinguishing dynasties were used. In the Late period also the king-list tradition was handed down at the temple sites of Memphis and Saïs, which were inclined to preserve the names of those kings recognized by these centers but to ignore other major rulers who were not honored there even if they controlled Thebes and much of the country. It was also the priests of these centers of Memphis, Heliopolis, Saïs, and Thebes who were able to impress Hecataeus and Herodotus with their ancient records, and it was as one of these priests that Manetho wrote his history. The continuity of this historiographic tradition from the Palermo Stone through the Turin Canon to Manetho cannot be denied.

The term king list is often wrongly used, as Redford points out, for "those groupings of ancestral royal names or images which occur in temple contexts."[38] The most frequently cited lists are the Abydos Lists of Sety I and Ramesses II, the Karnak List of Thutmose III, and the Ramesseum List, all made by kings, and the Saqqarah List in a private tomb of a high temple official. These "lists" are found in scenes, either as rows of names in cartouches or as the pictorial representation of royal statues. In

37. Ibid.
38. *King-Lists*, chap. 4. Cf. Gardiner, *Egypt*, pp. 48ff.

any case, they depict special cultic usage. In the actual ceremonies to which the scenes refer, statues of the dead kings were carried in procession like the cult images of the gods. In many instances, such as the Abydos and Karnak lists, the scenes represent the presence of royal ancestors at an offering ceremony in a state or mortuary temple in which offerings are being given to the dead kings. The Saqqarah List, in a private tomb, is an imitation of the royal ceremony by a private official as a show of piety. In the Ramesseum List the royal ancestors are present to witness the renewal of kingship at the king's coronation and to thereby affirm his legitimacy. In any event these lists, and others like them, point to the strong practice of venerating ancestors, and, depending upon the occasion, more or fewer ancestors were included in the group. Many of the lists went back in time, albeit selectively, to the first king Menes, then to the founders of dynasties, and above all to the genealogical line of their own immediate succession. On the other hand, they invariably suppressed the reigns of Hatshepsut and Akhenaten, who were anathematized by their immediate successors.

The relationship of the cult assemblages to real king lists like the Turin Canon is not entirely clear. In contrast to the king list the cult assemblages did not include any precise data on the length of reigns, although the rulers' names are usually in correct chronological order. They did not clearly signify change of dynasty or change in residence. They did not contain nearly the same number of names, excluding most of the ephemeral rulers of the First and Second Intermediate periods and especially the rule of the Hyksos. Nevertheless, they occasionally contain a few names that are not found in the Turin Canon. In the cultic lists, kings who established new eras or were otherwise significant were often selected for inclusion. Since there was no complete uniformity in the lists themselves, we can only conclude that a broad historical tradition lies behind them and that the Turin Canon represents one of a number of attempts to reconstruct this historical tradition of the royal line back to the beginning. The cultic assemblages and other such lists were a secondary use of the list tradition for cultic or political purposes. The king list itself was noncultic and nonpolitical and showed a strong historical concern for the completeness of the record based upon the sources available to the author.

c. ROYAL INSCRIPTIONS

There are so many royal inscriptions from ancient Egypt that we can give only a very selective presentation. What is also needed for any faithful overview is a comprehensive genre analysis, but as this has not yet been carried out by Egyptologists my suggestions at classification are tentative at best. For the Old and Middle kingdoms I have treated the relatively few examples in roughly chronological order. I suspect that many of the texts belong to broader genres or types, but this cannot always be demonstrated for want of additional examples. Because texts from the New Kingdom are much more numerous, it seems preferable to classify them into types and genres. In the Late period, historical texts are again scarce, but it will be enough to show how earlier historiographic forms are continued in this period.

Alongside the royal inscriptions are many private inscriptions from the Old Kingdom onward, and for the period before the New Kingdom many of these are more useful to the historian than the royal inscriptions because they recount important political events. While Breasted's collection classifies them all together as historical texts, the private inscriptions have a different place in the development of Egyptian historiography and must be considered separately.

The inscriptions of the Old Kingdom (ca. 2700–2200 B.C.) are very few and those that do exist hardly contain any detailed information on events of the day. This has often led to explanations emphasizing the development of a rigid ideology of kingship that presents the permanence of the monarchy with little room for change and is primarily concerned with the mortuary cult.[39] But the paucity of historical texts may be due more to archaeology's heavy concentration on the pyramids of the Old Kingdom rather than on such Old Kingdom sites as Memphis.

The witness of later times is contradictory on this question. On the one hand, the Greek historians Herodotus and Diodorus assert that these early kings accomplished nothing noteworthy, which may be explained by the fact that, besides the pyramids, few Old Kingdom monuments and stelae survived into later times.[40] On the other hand, the Middle Kingdom (2050–1800 B.C.) and subsequent periods down to classical times frequently refer back to the great kings of the Old Kingdom, and a rich lore of popular tales grew up about them.[41] Certainly more public information was passed on about these kings than now meets the eye.

Some brief inscriptions do exist in out-of-the-way places. The Sinai turquoise mines were opened up in the Old Kingdom, and Snefru of the Fourth Dynasty was particularly associated with work in this region.[42] He is represented on a relief as smiting an Asiatic, but the text contains only his name and titulary. This kind of scene is repeated frequently by other

39. Gardiner, *Egypt*, p. 55.
40. See Redford, *King-Lists*, chap. 4.
41. See material collected in D. Wildung, *Die Rolle ägyptischen Könige im Bewusstsein ihrer Nachwelt*.
42. A. H. Gardiner, T. E. Peet, and J. Černý, *The Inscriptions of Sinai*, 2 vols.

Old Kingdom pharaohs who worked these mines. Leaders of the expeditions often left records of their own as to how they carried out their commissions. One leader from the late Middle Kingdom compares the achievements of his commission with those of Snefru: "Never had the like been done since the time of the King of Upper and Lower Egypt, Snefru, triumphant."[43] For this writer that was about eight hundred years before his own time and represented hoary antiquity. Brief Old Kingdom inscriptions in the southern borders of the land signify the control of the region by these pharaohs, and inscriptions in the quarries of Hammamat and Hetnub begin a long tradition of leaving records of commissions and activities there.

One further type of royal monument that deserves some mention here is the reliefs in the mortuary temples portraying the life and activities of the king. These are, perhaps, partly biographical and partly typical and not strictly intended to commemorate historical occasions. Nevertheless, the scenes in the mortuary temple of Sahure of the Fifth Dynasty do appear to represent specific events, such as the king's victory over the Libyans and the expedition to Byblos for a load of cedarwood.[44] The scenes are supplied with brief captions giving names but no extended text and strongly suggest a continuation of that "illustrated history" known from the Narmer Palette. However, we are sobered by the knowledge that such scenes were sometimes plagiarized by later pharaohs even to the point of repeating the same foreign names in the captions. There is in the Egyptian material, as Otto has suggested,[45] the constant problem of distinguishing real events from those that have become part of the pharaonic ideal and are simply copied and repeated in later monuments.

Few royal monuments have survived from the Middle Kingdom, although the tradition of royal inscriptions at Sinai and the quarries of Hammamat was resumed, with the rise of the Middle Kingdom, under Menthotpe III. Of special note is the inscription of Senwosret I dealing with the building and dedication of a temple in Heliopolis.[46] The original stela inscription was not preserved, but a copy of the first part of it made on a leather roll in the Eighteenth Dynasty is extant. The inscription takes the form of a long poem describing how the king took counsel with his court in order to plan for the building of the temple. After the king reveals his desire to build the temple, the courtiers concur in the wisdom of his plan and orders are given to carry it out. The ceremonial "stretching of the

43. *BARE*, vol. 1, § 731.
44. Gardiner, *Egypt*, p. 57.
45. In "Geschichtsbild und Geschichtsschreibung," *WO* 3:161.
46. *BARE*, vol. 1, §§ 498–506; Lichtheim, *AEL*, vol. 1, pp. 115–18; Erman, *The Ancient Egyptians*, pp. 49–52.

line" to begin work is described, but the rest is missing. One interesting statement is the king's acknowledgment of his motive in building these monuments—that he will be remembered: "The king dies not, who is mentioned by reason of his achievements." That does not reflect the royal ideology of the king as the living Horus who becomes Osiris at death but the desire for historical actuality, which is expressed by other rulers as well.

A number of inscriptions by Senwosret III relate to his southern frontiers and his activities against the Nubians.[47] In one text he claims, "I have made my boundary beyond that of my fathers,"[48] and this becomes a regular cliché of the Empire period. He gives advice about the necessity of vigilance against the enemy, tells of his conquests, and affirms with an oath that he is telling the truth, another practice of later pharaohs. He ends by stating that future generations should be prepared to fight for the boundary that he has established by his statue and inscription. This suggests that the setting up of such stelae and statues on foreign soil was deemed as a claim upon that territory.[49]

From Abydos comes a long inscription on a stela by Neferhotep, of the Thirteenth Dynasty. It follows the pattern of the Senwosret I stela in its extensive use of dialogue between king and courtiers and in its commissioning of messengers. The theme is the restoration of the cult of Osiris at Abydos. The king summons his courtiers and together they carefully examine the ancient mythological records. The king then tells of the execution of his plans and concludes with an exhortation to the priests to maintain the correct worship of the god.[50]

d. DEDICATION INSCRIPTIONS

Among the most numerous royal inscriptions of Egypt, the dedication inscriptions usually begin with the king's titulary followed by the statement "he made it as a monument for GN." Many of them name the object or structure dedicated, such as a temple building, portable shrine, obelisk, etc.[51] A list of gifts or offerings could also be included. Many titularies were expanded into a long encomium on the pharaoh, containing mostly conventional epithets but sometimes also references to military exploits of

47. *BARE*, vol. 1, §§ 640–72.
48. Ibid., § 657.
49. See also the stelae of Thutmose I and Thutmose III on the Euphrates.
50. A comparison is suggested with the reform of Josiah in 2 Kings 22–23.
51. Cf. the form of the Assyrian dedication inscriptions (3a above), in which accounts of military exploits develop out of the royal titulary, and military accounts precede the description of the temple construction.

the recent past.[52] Some inscriptions were accompanied by a scene at the top of the stela or on the temple wall, showing the king making an offering before the appropriate god.[53] Sometimes one inscription contains a list of several structures with their descriptions, details of construction, and, as in the long inscription of Amenhotep III, a hymn of praise to the god.[54] Stelae were often set up at the Station of the King[55] within the holy of holies to mark the official dedication of the temple itself. In the case of Amenhotep II the occasion was his return from victorious Asiatic campaigns, and his stela portrayed the sacrifice of enemy princes.[56] In the Amenhotep III stela the king addresses the deity and tells of his buildings and offerings.[57] To this the god Amon replies, as well as the Divine Ennead. A dedication inscription by Ramesses II for the great Karnak temple[58] contains, as a digression within the dedication formula,[59] a speech by Amon in the divine council in which he blesses Ramesses.

It should be apparent from this description that there is considerable variation in the dedication form from the simple statement of dedication to the elaborate combinations with other elements and forms. The form is already attested in the Palermo Stone for the Fifth-Dynasty kings,[60] with a few extant examples from the Middle Kingdom.[61] It is very common throughout the Empire period and continues down to the end of the Late period.[62]

In two examples of dedications of the Middle Kingdom, those of Senwosret I at Heliopolis[63] and Neferhotep at Abydos,[64] we observe an entirely different form, a discursive narration telling of the circumstances under which a particular building project or cult reform was undertaken.[65] The Abydos example begins a tradition of such a form at the sanctuary of

52. Many examples may be found in *BARE*, vols. 2 and 3.

53. Note the dedication scene on Thutmose III's *Hymn of Victory* stela. A good photograph may be found in J. Ruffle, *Heritage of the Pharaohs*, p. 155.

54. *BARE*, vol. 2, §§ 878–92.

55. For an explanation of this term see *BARE*, vol. 2, p. 61, note b.

56. *BARE*, vol. 2, §§ 791–98.

57. *BARE*, vol. 2, §§ 904–10.

58. *BARE*, vol. 3, §§ 509–13.

59. The use of a digression within a larger unit is a common literary technique in ancient Egyptian monumental inscriptions and literary works.

60. *BARE*, vol. 1, §§ 153–67.

61. *BARE*, vol. 1, §§ 484–85; 500; 644; 767.

62. *BARE*, vol. 4, §§ 1008–12.

63. *BARE*, vol. 1, §§ 498–506; Lichtheim, *AEL*, vol. 1, pp. 115–18.

64. *BARE*, vol. 1, §§ 753–65.

65. To call these etiologies, as is sometimes done, is misleading since they are virtually contemporary with the events themselves. Compare, e.g., the reform program of Josiah, 2 Kings 22–23.

Osiris that is used in later periods. Thus a stela of Thutmose I (1525–1512 B.C.) from Abydos[66] employs the same dialogue between king and priests about the king's intentions to restore and beautify the temple and its cult objects, expresses the same purpose to perpetuate his name through such monuments, and ends with a similar exhortation to the priests. The long Abydos inscription by Ramesses II (1290–1224 B.C.) also follows the same pattern.[67] It begins with a speech by Ramesses expressing both his love for Osiris after the example of the divine Horus and his concern for his own deceased father, Seti I. This is followed by the account of his inspection of the Abydos temple complex, begun by Seti but now in a ruinous state. Ramesses summons his court and lays out his plans for restoration. In the course of his proposals he makes a long digression on the themes of his divine birth, his youth, and his appointment as coregent,[68] after which he returns to his theme of completing his father's work as a good son should. The court replies with long eulogies; the work on the temple is then completed, as well as additional construction and endowments to Seti's mortuary cult. Ramesses then offers a long prayer to Seti setting forth his numerous benefactions and asking him to intercede for him with the gods. The dead king replies with a blessing and a promise to petition the gods on his behalf. The result is a combination of a dedication to the god Osiris and to the dead Seti.[69]

If we understand this inscription as, in part, a mortuary dedication by Ramesses to his father, then a comparison might be made with an Abydos stela of Ahmose I (1570–1546 B.C.),[70] of the early Eighteenth Dynasty, that contains a discursive dedication of mortuary buildings for the queen ancestress Tetisheri. The style is that of a story instead of a precisely dated event. The opening scene finds the king and queen in the palace conversing about the offerings for the dead. The king, Ahmose, indicates his desire to build new mortuary buildings for his ancestress. There is a statement of his plans and prompt execution of them, with a concluding prayer to the gods on her behalf. The remark is made: "His majesty did this because he so greatly loved her, beyond everything. Never did former kings the like of it for their mothers." Both the Ramesses and Ahmose texts give strong emphasis to the love of the parent or ancestor as the motivation for the building activity.

66. *BARE*, vol. 2, §§ 90–98.
67. *BARE*, vol. 3, §§ 251–81.
68. For similar use of digression see above, n. 59.
69. On the level of royal ideology Osiris and Seti are the same, but in practical terms they must be dealt with quite distinctly, and the quality of Seti's divinity depends very much upon Ramesses' actions on his behalf.
70. *BARE*, vol. 2, §§ 33–37.

Also in the Abydos tradition, although not a dedication inscription as such, is a stela of Ramesses IV (ca. 1162 B.C.)[71] containing a prayer to Osiris: "Thou shalt double for me the long duration, the prolonged reign of King Ramses II, the Great God; for more are the [mighty—*translator's restoration*] deeds, and the benefactions which I do for thy house . . . during these four years [of his reign thus far] than those things which King Ramses II, the Great God, did for thee in his sixty-seven years." Whatever one might think of the king's theology or the truth of his claims, the texts manifest an interesting use of precise historical data from the past.

Reference to the building activity of previous rulers may also be found in dedication inscriptions that mention the renovation of older sanctuaries. An inscription by Thutmose III, in a Nubian temple of Semneh,[72] recounts how the king rebuilt the temple of Senwosret III. He preserved the original dedication inscription and offering lists of Senwosret, treated him as a god, and recognized his prior military achievements in the area. In a similar example, from the time of Ramesses IX, the priestly quarters connected with a temple of Senwosret I at Karnak were said to have been renewed by the high priest of Amon, Amenhotep.[73]

Another type of discursive inscription concerns the discovery of water by digging a well on the desert road. A series of three inscriptions were set up by Seti I (1302–1290 B.C.) in a Nubian desert temple at the site of a well.[74] The first relates how he was on the desert route in search of gold when the need for water arose for the expedition. Guided in mind by a god, Seti discerned where water was to be found and dug a successful well. Consequently a settlement and temple were built at the site and the inscription set up so that all future generations should give thanks to god on his behalf. This text may be viewed as an extension of the Abydos tradition since the expeditions to the mines were for the purpose of supplying the Osiris temple of Abydos. The second inscription is a series of blessings and curses addressed to the workmen and the future kings, and commands them to maintain the endowments established for supplying the Abydos temple with gold.[75] The third is a dedication inscription, using the regular formula, to the god Amen-Re and to the Divine Ennead. A final blessing upon Seti is put in the mouth of the people and speaks again of their gratitude for the well. Thus the same series of inscriptions have the discursive

71. *BARE*, vol. 4, §§ 469–71. One might compare the form of this stela with private biographic monuments of the Late period (see below, 5h), which are often dominated by a concern for rewards from the god.

72. *BARE*, vol. 2, §§ 167–76.

73. *BARE*, vol. 4, §§ 486–89.

74. *BARE*, vol. 3, §§ 162–98.

75. The pattern of "historical prologue," declaration of decrees and endowments, and blessing and curses is similar to the Late Bronze treaty pattern discussed above, 4b.

dedication and the formal dedication styles. A similar story about the discovery of a well in Nubia on the desert road is told by Ramesses II.[76] Here it is entirely the godlike character of Ramesses that brings about the miracle of discovery where other kings had failed. There is no hint of dedication to a god, only the naming of the well after Ramesses and the discursive account commemorating the discovery.

The dedication inscriptions thus follow two main types, the formal style with the direct statement of dedication and the discursive style narrating the circumstances inspiring the gifts or monuments. Yet the use of discursive narration does not change the function of the dedication or its setting as a monumental inscription. Nor does this style originate in a fixed story pattern outside of the dedication function, although in a few instances folktale motifs may inspire some parts of the accounts. The discursive style gave rise to the same kind of imitation and scribal borrowing that we find in formal inscriptions, and so we may speak, as we have above, of an Abydos tradition or a "water-discovery" story. These may be within the dedication genre or borrowed from another broad genre. Discursive style by itself, however, is not a genre but only one element or technique that may be used in a variety of literary forms.[77]

e. COMMEMORATIVE INSCRIPTIONS

At the end of the Second Intermediate period and throughout the period of the Empire we encounter texts whose primary function was to commemorate the great deeds of the king for posterity. Frequently the text includes a commission to record the royal deeds upon an enduring monument and an appeal to future generations to "hear" all that the king has done. Although such monuments are most often found in or near temples and usually have a deeply religious quality, they are not "reports to the deity" or directed at the god in the same way that dedication inscriptions are.

The origin of this genre is probably obscured because so few royal monuments have survived from the Middle Kingdom. The earliest example, the Kamose Stelae, is already so developed in form and narrative style that it cannot have been the first attempt at such a work. This is so because the stelae may derive ultimately from the biographical or commission inscriptions of high-ranking officials and local monarchs, especially since the Seventeenth Dynasty arose from the local princes of Thebes. This genre of private inscriptions will be taken up later. One cannot entirely rule out

---

76. *BARE*, vol. 3, §§ 282–93.
77. The issue will be taken up in more detail below, under the heading *Königsnovelle*.

foreign influence during the period of Hyksos domination, but we have no evidence from their sparse monuments to support such speculation.

To trace a precise genetic development of this genre through its whole period of use into the Late period would be risky. What I offer instead is a suggestion of certain lines of continuity and influence. To ascertain the content and details of these works the reader must refer to the sources, since my concern is only to identify certain historiographic features that are helpful in the general discussion.

The Kamose Stelae

The earliest commemorative inscription appears on the twin stelae of Kamose (ca. 1580), last king of the Seventeenth Dynasty, on which he records his war with the Hyksos ruler of Avaris.[78] The text states that it was commissioned by the king and it gives the name of the author, Neshi, who was also a highly placed official of the court. This indication of authorship is a rare occurrence for such accounts, whether in Egypt or the rest of the Near East.[79]

The text opens with a simple date, the year 3, followed by the titulary of Kamose and an account of events told by the king. The story begins with a discussion in the council chamber between the king and his grandees as to why the prince of Thebes should tolerate the division of power with a Nubian to the south and an Asiatic ruling Lower and Middle Egypt. His councillors recommend against changing the peaceful status quo, but the king rejects their advice and prepares for war. He sails downstream, is victorious over the confederates of the northern ruler, and is soon in the vicinity of Avaris, the Hyksos capital. Interspersed in the action are royal speeches directed against the enemy. A captured letter sent by the Hyksos ruler for aid from Nubia is also quoted. Kamose, after doing much damage and taking much booty, returns in triumph to Thebes.

The rather vague chronology and imprecise record of events and booty suggest that the account is based primarily upon recollection shortly after the event and not upon military records. Yet the excerpt from the captured correspondence does resemble international diplomatic correspondence known from Mesopotamian sources of the Old Babylonian period and the Amarna letters.[80] So it is likely to be a fairly close copy of such a document. On the other hand, the council scene before the war is certainly a stereotype and intended to put the king in the best possible light as the wisest and most courageous.

78. ANET³, pp. 232–33, 554–55; L. Habachi, *The Second Stela of Kamose and His Struggle against the Hyksos Ruler and His Capital.*
79. But see below on The Battle of Kadesh.
80. J. Van Seters, *The Hyksos: A New Investigation,* pp. 165–70.

The Annals of Thutmose III

The military exploits of Thutmose III (1490–1436 B.C.) were commemorated on many of his monuments, not only at Thebes but as far away as the town of Napata at the fourth cataract of the Nile, the southern border of the empire. The fullest account is given in the Annals of Thutmose III, which were inscribed on the walls within the great Karnak temple of Amen-Re.[81] The style is clear and succinct, in third-person narration, and not as bombastic as is typical of most pharaonic inscriptions. The main source of information for the Annals was military field reports that were systematically kept from day to day, thus providing a very careful record. Concerning the capture of Megiddo the Annals state:

> Now everything which his majesty did to this town and to that wretched enemy and his wretched army is set down by the individual day, by the individual expedition, and by the individual [troop] commanders. . . . They [are] set down on a roll of leather in the temple of Amon to this day.[82]

This is confirmed by a remark in one of the tomb biographies of the period in which a certain army scribe named Tjaneni tells us that his task was to record such military exploits in the field.[83] The Annals themselves reflect this practice by the frequent reference to precise year, month, and day of the event being described.

According to the prologue and epilogue the Annals were commissioned by Thutmose III to be set up on a monument in the temple of Amen-Re as a record of his deeds covering all the seventeen campaigns over a twenty-year period. This is similar to the commission in the epilogue of the Kamose Stelae. The degree of detail in recounting the various campaigns is uneven, with a major part of the text devoted to the first campaign while brief treatment is given to most of the rest. In fact, the text clearly acknowledges abbreviation of the account at certain points "in order not to multiply words." The reader is referred to "a daybook of the palace" for more complete information.[84] This appears to be a second source, an economic record of income and expenses, and not the leather scroll of military activity. At least one implication of these references to sources is the Annals' verifiability, since commemorative inscriptions often express concern for the credibility of the record.

81. *BARE*, vol. 2, §§ 391–540; see partial translations in Lichtheim, *AEL*, vol. 2, pp. 29–35; *ANET*[3], pp. 234–41. See also the recent studies by Spalinger, n. 12, above.

82. *ANET*[3], p. 237.

83. See *BARE*, vol. 2, § 392.

84. *BARE*, vol. 2, §§ 393, 472; *ANET*[3], p. 239b.

One must also take into consideration the function of the Annals within the context of the temple inscriptions themselves. This is to provide an introduction to the extensive lists of feasts and offerings to the god Amun that were the direct result of the Asiatic campaigns.[85] For this reason considerable space is taken up with the rather precise recording of booty, much of which was committed to the estate of Amun. The texts sometimes include income and tribute from the south that were clearly not related to the Asiatic campaigns. This must have resulted from the practice of entering items from the income lists of the palace "daybook" for that particular year, whether they had anything to do with a campaign or not.

Accompanying the Annals was a list of the cities captured in the campaigns, an element of the genre repeated by later pharaohs. This evidence of onomastic and encyclopedic learning is evident within the Annals themselves in that Thutmose III included scenes upon the walls of the Festival Hall depicting the various strange plants of Syria.[86]

The most impressive narrative portion of the whole Annals is the description of the victory at Megiddo.[87] The background to the first campaign is the widespread rebellion against Egypt by the princes of Palestine and Syria. The pharaoh and his forces march by stages until they come to Yehem, where they hold a council of war concerning the assault on Megiddo. This discussion permits the author both to present Megiddo as the crucial battle, since it represents the focal point of the coalition of all the Syro-Palestinian forces against Egypt, and to describe carefully the region's topography and the appropriate military strategy. It is clear that there are three major routes through the Carmel mountain chain, two broad and one narrow. The scouting reports apparently indicated that the broad ones were well guarded but the narrow one was not, so it was decided to risk the narrow road. Of course, as in the Kamose Stelae, this decision is presented as the courageous action of the pharaoh against the more conservative suggestions of the councillors, but discounting this element the presentation seems to be fairly accurate.

The alignment for the decisive battle is described, and the victory is swift. The flight of the enemy into the confines of Megiddo is given with almost humorous detail since many were hauled up the walls by their clothing. At this point the author criticizes a breakdown in the discipline of the Egyptian army:

> Now if his majesty's troops had not set their hearts to plundering the possessions of the enemies, they would have [captured] Megiddo at

85. *BARE*, vol. 2, §§ 541–73.
86. Gardiner, *Egypt of the Pharaohs*, p. 188.
87. *BARE*, vol. 2, §§ 408–43; *ANET*[3], pp. 234–38; Lichtheim, *AEL*, vol. 2, pp. 29–35. See also Gardiner, *Egypt*, pp. 189–92.

this moment, when the wretched foe of Kadesh and the wretched foe of this town were being pulled up hurriedly so as to admit them into their town.[88]

The result was a long siege. Again in a speech Thutmose emphasizes the significance of taking Megiddo. Since so many kings and princes were involved in the battle, "the capture of Megiddo is the capture of a thousand towns." The final submission is recorded and the booty taken is carefully listed; there is also an interesting note on the harvest of the region carried out during the siege.

This account of the first campaign, made twenty years after the event, is remarkable in the way in which it still gives the greatest weight to the earliest battle and has a strong sense of its significance. The other versions of the deeds of Thutmose confirm the importance with which Megiddo was regarded, but in many other ways these inscriptions are quite different. The Armant Stela and the Napata Stela[89] are much shorter versions of the wars and not in annalistic form. The events are not mentioned in chronological order, and precise details such as dates and lists of booty are excluded. The Armant Stela makes a virtue of its brevity by stating in the prologue that it is only a "summary of the deeds of might and victory which this good god performed," since "if one were to mention each occasion by name, they would be too numerous to put into writing."[90] It then organizes the deeds into at least two groups, those having to do with hunting and Thutmose's military exploits. The Napata Stela, dated five years after the Annals, mentions only three events: the campaign against Mitanni, the elephant hunt in Niy, and the battle of Megiddo, in that order! It also includes a number of speeches of self-praise by the king and the court's responses. It is set out entirely in first-person narration like the Kamose Stelae instead of the third-person form of the Annals. The details of the eighth campaign are much fuller in the Napata Stela than in the Annals, which must mean that the author consulted the "official record" as a basis for his inscription. What is clear from a comparison of these versions is that a great deal of flexibility in the use of sources was possible, depending upon the purpose of the account.

A Hymn of Victory, which was not part of the Annals but which dealt with the same subject, was set out on a stela.[91] It was found in the great Karnak temple. Cast in the form of an address, the god Amon emphasizes

88. Lichtheim, *AEL*, vol. 2, p. 32.

89. R. Mond and O. H. Myers, *Temples of Armant, A Preliminary Survey: The Text*, trans. M. S. Drower, pp. 182ff.; G. A. Reisner and M. B. Reisner, "Inscribed Monuments from Gebel Barkal." Pt. 2: "The Granite Stela of Thutmose III," *ZÄS* 69 (1933): 24–39. See also the excerpts in *ANET*[3], pp. 234–41.

90. Mond and Myers, *Temples*, p. 183.

91. *BARE*, vol. 2, §§ 655–62; Erman, *The Ancient Egyptians*, pp. 254–58; *ANET*[3], pp. 373–75; Lichtheim, *AEL*, vol. 2, pp. 35–38.

to Thutmose III that he was the one behind all the king's achievements. The hymn was a favorite with later pharaohs and parts of it were often "borrowed."

A comparison of the Annals of Thutmose III and the Ten-Year Annals of Muršili II of Ḥatti might be helpful in the light of Cancik's assertion that nothing in the ancient Near East is comparable to the Hittite annals.[92] The following similarities are worth noting:

1. Both have a prologue and epilogue stating that the annals contain the campaigns conducted within a certain period of years, ten years for Muršili and twenty years for Thutmose.

2. The reason for starting both campaigns is rebellion against the imperial authority. In the Hittite annals the king receives an oracle of confidence from the deity that he will be victorious, and the account regularly refers to this divine assistance. In the Egyptian annals the pharaoh does allude to a command of Amen-Re but much less is made of divine intervention on the king's behalf. Yet in the other versions of Armant and Napata and in the Hymn, as well as in later examples of the commemorative genre, divine intervention often plays a major role. Divine appearances in dreams and oracles giving confidence of victory before battle are also common.

3. The Hittite annals indicate the yearly sequence of events in a rather vague way, sometimes indicating the season of the year but usually stating only that certain actions were accomplished in the course of that year. The Egyptian annals, however, are very specific about dating to the day, month, and year of the king's reign, both for the start of the campaign and for various stages and events within it.

4. The taking of prisoners and booty is set down in a rather general and stereotyped fashion in the Hittite annals but is described very precisely in the Egyptian records.

5. The degree of detail on the battle of Megiddo concerning the nature of the terrain, the strategies used, the course of the battle itself, and its significance is far greater than any account of a battle given in the Hittite annals.

6. The highly stereotyped exchange of messages between Muršili and the regions he is attacking compares rather unfavorably with the vivid and

92. Cancik's brief and one-sided remarks (*Grundzüge*, p. 130) are certainly unacceptable. His single point of comparison is between the "staff meeting" by Thutmose III before the battle of Megiddo, which he dismisses as a fictitious element from the so-called *Königsnovelle*, and the motif in the annals of Muršili of the king taking counsel with himself (lit. "speaking with his heart"). First, since the latter motif is frequently found in Egyptian texts, it is not distinctive of Hittite historiography. Second, there is no reason to suppose that the "staff meeting" is in any way a fictitious motif, but even if it were it is a common device used by the later Greek historians and hardly discredits their historiography.

dramatic dialogue in the Egyptian annals. As we shall see below, this becomes even more marked in such later works of this genre as the Battle of Kadesh under Ramesses II and the Piankhy Stela.

7. The Hittite annals frequently refer to the past history of relations with a certain king or nation under Šuppiluliuma, the father of Muršili. This reference to *Vorgeschichte* is understandable from the point of view of the introduction, which seeks to demonstrate that Muršili is his father's true successor, with comparable deeds and worthy of respect. The Egyptian annals have less need for such an apologetic tone. Nevertheless, there is one reference to Thutmose III setting up his stela in the north country beside that of his grandfather, Thutmose I, and so at least equaling the latter's achievement.

8. Both the Hittite and the Egyptian kings were concerned with publishing their manly or divine deeds for posterity, and the annalistic style arose in both cases as one way of doing this. There seems to have been no other reason for compiling such field reports and annals, and their successors also found other forms in which to present their deeds.

On balance it seems to me that the Egyptian annals are more sophisticated historiographic works than the Hittite annals, at least within the limits of the genre. Given the rather restrictive medium of inscribing on stone as compared with writing on clay, the Egyptian texts are, nevertheless, remarkably full at certain points. If the actual leather scrolls that were the sources for these inscribed texts were extant, the comparison might be even more one-sided in favor of the Egyptian annalists. Yet the lack of close political relations between the two regions at the time when such annals arose makes it unlikely that the origin of such a genre was a result of direct cultural influence in either direction.[93]

The Annals of Amenhotep II

The annals tradition had its continuation in the time of Amenhotep II (1439–1406 B.C.), who set up stelae in Memphis and Karnak.[94] In them he gives a consecutive record of his first and second campaigns in his seventh and ninth years respectively, and in a style similar to the Annals of Thutmose III. The focus, however, is on the personal exploits of the pharaoh himself, some of which seem frivolous. Because the annals genre appears to have been closely bound to the reporting of military campaigns on a regular basis, when the latter practice declined toward the end of Amen-

93. It is possible that Hittite envoys of later times could have visited the capital and witnessed the annals on public display, but it seems more likely to me that both are the result of internal literary development.

94. *ANET*[3], pp. 245–47; E. Edel, "Die Stelen Amenophis II aus Karnak und Memphis," *ZDPV* 69 (1953):98–176.

hotep's reign and in the reigns of the subsequent pharaohs, annals as a genre disappeared. When campaigning by the pharaohs was revived in the Nineteenth Dynasty, the reporting of these events took a somewhat different form. Of course, the notion of inscribing stelae with vague statements and clichés about great military achievements, whether real or imaginary, continued. But this was a convention meant to maintain the pharaonic image and it had little influence on historiography.

Commemorative Scarabs

A unique way of "publishing" special events during the reign of Amenhotep III (1398–1361 B.C.) was to issue large scarabs with events narrated in hieroglyphs on the flat side.[95] These consist of the following five series:

1. The full titulary of the pharaoh and the Great Royal Wife Tiyi, the names of the queen's parents, and the boundaries of the empire. This series is often called the "marriage scarab" because it may have been issued on such an occasion, but that is just speculation. It is undated but probably belongs to Amenhotep's first year.

2. The wild-bull hunt in year 2.

3. The lion hunts, consisting of the total number of lions bagged in the first ten years of his reign.

4. The arrival of a Mitanni princess at the court in year 10.

5. The digging of an artificial lake in year 11.

These scarabs were produced in abundance and were found not only in Egypt but in Nubia and Syria-Palestine as well.

Commemorative Reliefs

Special events could also be publicized and commemorated through pictorial reliefs. Earlier examples of this were noted in the mortuary temples of the Old Kingdom, particularly that of Sahure.[96] With the scenes on the great mortuary temple of Queen Hatshepsut (1486–1468 B.C.) at Deir el-Bahri, this tradition of reliefs seems to have been revived. One group of scenes depicts the transporting of two great obelisks from Elephantine to the temple at Karnak.[97] Another series, of ten scenes, portrays the successive stages in the royal expedition to Punt (Pwene) in Hatshepsut's ninth year.[98] Here the illustrations are given in considerable detail, with interest in the diverse flora and fauna of the region, in the appearance of the inhabitants, and in their customs and style of living. Captions are provided

95. BARE, vol. 2, §§ 860–69; C. Blankenberg-van Delden, *The Large Commemorative Scarabs of Amenhotep III.*

96. ANEP², nos. 41, 42; Gardiner, *Egypt*, pp. 88–89.

97. BARE, vol. 2, §§ 322–36.

98. BARE, vol. 2, §§ 246–95.

for explanation with the inclusion of some longer texts for divine and royal speeches. Additional series of scenes portray the supposed divine birth of the queen and her accession to the throne.[99] The last two series have a strong propagandist character which will be discussed below. The scenes were intended to be biographical, presenting great moments in the queen's life.[100]

Commemorative Inscriptions of the Nineteenth and Twentieth Dynasties

At the beginning of the Nineteenth Dynasty the presentation of important events through pictorial reliefs is taken up by Seti I. These reliefs depict a series of three campaigns, two Asiatic and one Libyan, presented in twenty scenes on the walls of Seti's additions to the great Amun temple at Karnak.[101] While only one date is given, viz. the year 1, in connection with the initial scene, it is possible to determine by the groupings of scenes the departure and eventual return of each of the three campaigns. Like the earlier pictorial reliefs, the scenes bear short captions to identify principal figures and geographic locations, but their historical content is meager. Most of the captions, even those associated with the battles, contain stereotyped language. In one text, a speech by the god Amun to Seti, long passages were "borrowed" from earlier inscriptions. That the whole work functioned as a religious statement is clear from the way in which the series climaxes in the scenes of sacrifice and presentation of the spoils to Amun.

With Ramesses II comes an important innovation: the pictorial relief is combined with a full text account of a campaign to give a complete presentation of a significant event. It is clear that for Ramesses the battle of Kadesh against the Hittites in his fourth year was as momentous in his early career as was the battle of Megiddo for Thutmose III.[102] There are two different versions of Ramesses' Battle of Kadesh, the Bulletin or Record and the Poem. Both were repeated in several copies on various temple walls; the Bulletin occurs seven times and the Poem eight times. The latter is also found on fragments of two hieratic papyri, while the former is regularly appended to a series of pictorial reliefs with explanatory captions. The accounts of the battle of Kadesh were well publicized![103]

99. BARE, vol 2, §§ 187–212, 215–42.
100. The use of reliefs in tomb biographies will be dealt with below.
101. BARE, vol. 3, §§ 80–156. These scenes are no longer on the mortuary temple and therefore move away from the biographical origins.
102. BARE, vol. 3, §§ 296–351; A. H. Gardiner, *The Kadesh Inscriptions of Ramesses II*; Lichtheim, *AEL*, vol. 2, pp. 57–72.
103. There are important differences between Gardiner and Lichtheim in the treatment of these texts. Gardiner regards the Bulletin as part of the reliefs which he then describes as the

The two versions are not simply two different accounts, or even a long edition with an abbreviated version. They are complementary works that must be taken together to give the whole picture.[104] Even the reliefs add significant information not included in the written accounts. The result is a very detailed description of a great battle, perhaps the most complete record of such a battle prior to the time of Herodotus.

The Poem states in the proem that the theme of the work is Ramesses' victory over the Hittites and the members of the coalition. It then includes a poetic encomium extolling the virtues of the king, which is typical of many victory hymns.[105] However, it subsequently lapses into sober prose describing the king's preparations for the campaign, the precise date and departure from Egypt, and the rapid progress of the forces until they reached the region of Kadesh. At this point there is a shift in viewpoint to describe the enemy. The members of the Hittite coalition are named; their composition and strength is given and the text suggests that they were paid mercenaries of the Hittites. The enemy had taken up a position northeast of Kadesh, hidden from the view of the Egyptians, and it is carefully explained that the Egyptians advanced in a most vulnerable formation with the divisions of the army strung out in a line and open to attack, while all the while the Hittites reacted to the Egyptian advance with movements of their own. The surprise attack upon the Egyptians, throwing them into panic and confusion and completely surrounding Ramesses, is then described. At this point the prose prologue breaks off and the poetic description, in the first person, of Ramesses' heroic action in battle takes up the main body of the work. Here, for the first time in Egyptian literature, all the elements of epic narration are present.[106] In the face of this great danger Ramesses appeals in a long prayer to Amun and receives a word of encouragement in return. At that point the tide is turned and Ramesses proceeds to slaughter the enemy. He also encourages his dispirited forces. An interesting comparison is drawn between the warring Ramesses and the king of the Hittites, who, surrounded by a large band of infantry, remains at a distance watching the battle. The poetic narration continues to the point where the battle is won by Ramesses and his troops. Then the ac-

---

Pictorial Record. The Poem Gardiner describes simply as the Literary Record and denies that it is poetic. Lichtheim's literary interpretation of the texts is the one adopted here. The difference between these two scholars, however, is not crucial to my argument.

104. This unity is strongly emphasized by Gardiner (*Kadesh*, pp. 46–47) and Lichtheim (*AEL*, vol. 2, p. 59).

105. This poetic portion is omitted from Breasted's translation. The distinction between poetry and prose throughout the work is clearly indicated in Lichtheim's translation and is important for understanding the composition of the text.

106. See Lichtheim, *AEL*, vol. 2, 59.

count reverts to prose: the Hittites appeal for a truce, which the Egyptians grant. They withdraw from the region and return to Egypt.

The Bulletin recounts more precisely the circumstances leading up to the battle itself. For the most part the account is in third-person narration, with a final unit reverting to a first-person statement by the king about his victory. The report begins almost immediately, after giving the date, with an explanation of how the Hittites attempted to draw the Egyptians into a trap by a ruse; two Bedouin (Shasu) were to pose as deserters and deceive the Egyptians into thinking that the Hittites had withdrawn north of Aleppo, while in fact they were concealed behind the city mound of Kadesh. The nature of the ruse is carefully set forth in a digression within the general description of the action. What is revealed in the Poem but not in the Bulletin is that the Egyptians proceeded north toward Kadesh, in a long, drawn-out column of four divisions with some distance between them, so that the first division of Amun with the pharaoh was already setting up camp northwest of Kadesh while the others were still on the road. The Bulletin then describes the capture and interrogation of two enemy scouts, who reveal the true position of the Hittites. In a council of war the leaders are severely criticized for their lack of military "intelligence," and riders are sent to summon the lagging divisions. At this point the enemy engage the second division of Re and attack the camp itself, surrounding the king and his personal force. Ramesses, however, breaks out of the encirclement and rallies his forces for the counterattack. Reverting to a somewhat poetic style, the Bulletin then describes the military conduct of the pharaoh in an idealized form that conceals the exact nature of the event's conclusion.

On the other hand, the pictorial reliefs accompanying the Bulletin give further details that are not in either the Bulletin or the Poem. In contrast to the Seti reliefs, the remarks are vivid and informative, reflecting specific moments in the battle. They show, in one scene, the method of interrogating the Hittite scouts by beating them. Another depicts more clearly the surprise attack on the camp itself. The scenes also indicate that in the battle the pharaoh did get aid from two sources: the vizier who had gone in a chariot to get the third division and had managed to bring it quickly into action, and an unexpected arrival of "recruits" from Amurru who surprised the Hittites attacking the camp and effected a rescue there. These details are not included in either written account so as not to detract from the singular accomplishments of the pharaoh himself. One scene also lists by name several prominent officers of the defeated Hittites while it shows the Hittite king himself standing aloof from the battle, protected by a large body of infantry.

It is clear from scholarly reconstructions of the event based upon the prose portions of the Poem, the Bulletin, and the scenes with their captions that a single superior report and analysis lies behind these works.[107] It is not just a military log but the total presentation of the battle seen in retrospect from whatever sources were available. It exhibits remarkable detail, critical evaluation of events as they unfold, candor about the mistakes of the Egyptian forces, and a clear sense of the whole episode. As it now stands, the work in its various forms suffers not only from its "fragmentation" in the Bulletin and the Poem but also from the limitations of these genres, which must present the pharaoh in all his godlike qualities, the invincible victor in the heat of battle. The tension between the royal ideal and historiography could not be more sharply drawn. Given the limitations within which any scribe of Ramesses had to work, the accomplishments are remarkable.

But what are we then to make of the poetic first-person account within the Poem? Is it by another hand? We have already noted that this poetic unit is a significant innovation of epic narration that exactly fits the work as a whole because it uses poetry for the complete idealization of Ramesses' role in the event. There is no reason to doubt that the whole work is not by the same author, although it is certainly an exceptional person who could be so skillful in historiographic prose, an innovator in poetic narration, and a director of the artistic reliefs.[108] It is doubtful whether any later Egyptian work before Hellenistic times attained such a level of historiographic reporting of an important historical event.

The practice of making both prose and poetic versions of an event is carried on by the court of Merneptah (1224–1214 B.C.). A prose account of the invasion in Merneptah's fifth year by a coalition of Libyans and sea peoples contains a long introduction and conclusion with two speeches of self-praise by Merneptah full of stereotyped phrases.[109] But unlike the Battle of Kadesh there is little treatment of the battle scene itself, and the quality of reporting is far inferior. The poetic version, after giving the date, royal titulary, and formal encomium, gives no prose context but launches immediately into a description of the defeat.[110] In formal poetic technique it is similar to the Kadesh Poem, but it is inferior to the Poem in epic nar-

107. See esp. Gardiner, *Kadesh*, pp. 46ff.

108. Note that the Papyrus Sallier III has a colophon naming three persons as responsible for the work. This may refer not to the Poem alone but to the entire composition of reliefs, Bulletin and Poem as a whole (cf. the conclusion of the Kamose Stelae). Yet even so these three court officials cannot be identified for certain as its "authors" in the strict sense.

109. *BARE*, vol. 3, §§ 572–92.

110. This is called the "Israel" stela because it contains a reference to Israel and an Asiatic campaign. See *BARE*, vol. 3, §§ 602–17; *ANET*[3], pp. 376–78; Lichtheim, *AEL*, vol. 2, pp. 73–78; Thomas, *DOTT*, pp. 137–41.

ration because it really presents a series of scenes rather than actions. After the initial description of Libya's devastation there is a scene reflecting the divine court of the gods *before* the battle begins. In it Merneptah is formally appointed the executor of righteousness and is given the sword by Ptah while the chief of Libya is condemned for his crimes against the sacred places. The war has thus become an ordeal by battle in which the guilty party has been punished. It is noteworthy that this theme occurs at about the same time among the Hittites and Assyrians as well. The final scene is that of the peaceful conditions in Egypt brought about by the victory.

In the temple of Medinet Habu, built by Ramesses III (1195–1164 B.C.), we again find presentations of pictorial scenes and accompanying inscriptions, covering the fifth to the twelfth years.[111] These were not annals composed at one time, like the campaigns of Thutmose III, but were added successively after each series of events and with the progressive expansion of the building itself. The combination of prose and poetry in the Battle of Kadesh seems to have degenerated, in the inscriptions of Medinet Habu, into a highly figurative and flowery form of narration that is neither prose nor poetry and that results in a total lack of a sense of order and progress in the presentation of events.[112] Thus it is often difficult to understand exactly what took place and where in the various campaigns. In the Medinet Habu texts the scenes with their captions are usually more informative than the long inscriptions.

The Piankhy Stela

About five hundred years after the demise of the Egyptian empire another account of a military campaign is composed by an Egyptian king that is comparable to Thutmose III's account of his first campaign or Ramesses' Battle of Kadesh. This is the great stela of Piankhy (ca. 747–716 B.C.), an Egyptianized Ethiopian ruler and founder of the Twenty-fifth Dynasty.[113] The stela was found in a temple of Amun in the capital city of Napata in the far south, at the fourth cataract of the Nile. At the height of the Egyptian empire this was regarded as the southern border of the province of Kush, and it was here that Thutmose III had earlier set up a version of his own victories on a stela dedicated to Amun. Control of the region by Egypt had largely come to an end after ca. 1200

111. *BARE*, vol. 4, §§ 21–138.
112. See esp. the remarks by Breasted, ibid., pp. 12ff. See also Gardiner, *Egypt*, pp. 283ff.
113. *BARE*, vol. 4, §§ 796–883. See also Gardiner, *Egypt*, pp. 335–40; K. A. Kitchen, *The Third Intermediate Period in Egypt (1100–650 B.C.)*, pp. 358ff.; G. A. Reisner, "Inscribed Monuments from Gebel Barkal," *ZÄS* 66 (1931):89–100. For a new translation with notes and bibliography, see M. Lichtheim, *Ancient Egyptian Literature*, vol. 3: *The Late Period*, pp. 66–84.

B.C., but the region remained strongly Egyptian in culture and devoted to the cult of Amun. By the middle of the eighth century all of Nubia was under the control of the kings of Napata, and Piankhy extended his protection over Thebes, the holy city of Amun, and made an alliance with many of the princes of Upper Egypt. There is no doubt that Thutmose's Napata Stela influenced Piankhy, who early in his career had adopted Thutmose's titulary. But the texts and monuments of Thebes itself must have been the greatest source of inspiration for the king and his gifted chronicler.

The text was characterized by Breasted as the "clearest and most rational account of a campaign which has survived from Egypt,"[114] and this statement is probably still true today. This certainly applies to the general narration of events as they unfold in the course of the campaign. On the other hand, many speeches by Piankhy and the petty dynasts whom he is fighting are cast in a rather elevated and poetic style, somewhat reminiscent of the first-person sections of the Battle of Kadesh. It is as if poetry is regarded as the language of kings and gods. The stela has a scene at the top that includes the deities Amun and Mut, the king Piankhy, and a number of petty kings and princes who make their submission to him as a result of his several victories. While the scene primarily illustrates the surrender of Nimlot at Hermopolis, the inclusion of the other princes makes it a composite representation of Piankhy's victory over the whole region of Middle and Lower Egypt.

It is not necessary to describe the text in detail, but some remarks on its content might be helpful. The work begins with a date and short titulary. The king commands the readers, "Hear of what I did, more than the ancestors,"[115] and then gives an encomium on his divinity. The political background to the beginning of the war is introduced by the common statement, "one came to say to his majesty. . . ." It is then reported that a powerful ruler of the Delta region has formed a coalition of princes and is endeavoring to gain control of the whole of Egypt. Piankhy's first action is to send his subordinates to deal with the trouble. They are quite successful in their first encounters, but since they allow the leaders themselves to escape, Piankhy now takes over the direction of the campaign. The successive capture of various cities is accomplished either by breaching the wall or by siege warfare. Nimlot's surrender at Hermopolis is described in considerable detail. Once this city fell, many others quickly capitulated. The campaign and siege against Memphis are described at length. First it is told how the enemy prince Tefnakhte entered the city under cover of night and urged resistance, detailing the resources of the city to maintain a siege. He

114. *BARE*, vol. 4, p. 414.
115. Quotations are taken from Breasted's translation.

then left, promising to return with help. The next day a discussion takes place in the opposing camp on the best military strategy for capturing the city. After several proposals are made Piankhy himself suggests a way by which the weakest part of the defenses on the river may be penetrated, and the city is taken. The rest of the account deals with his march north, his visit to the holy of holies in the temple of Re, and the submission of all the petty rulers of the Delta including Tefnakhte. All these rulers Piankhy magnanimously allows to live. He then returns home amid much rejoicing.

The Piankhy Stela raises the problem of genre. The style of the work is not that of a compilation of military field reports since many of the marks of such reports are missing. It does not use exact dates but only general narrative connectives, such as "next morning," "after many days." Nor do we have exact lists of prisoners or booty but only general statements about the kinds of treasure that the surrendering princes showered upon Piankhy. We get many glimpses of Piankhy's character: his deep piety, his love of horses, his generosity toward his enemies. The result is a well-constructed composition. The whole campaign is seen as a unity, from the initial instigation of the conflict by Tefnakhte and the defection of Nimlot to the defeat of these two principals and their confederates. The events are weighted in the discourse according to their significance. Thus Nimlot's surrender is a turning point and the capture of Memphis the real defeat of Tefnakhte. The event at Heliopolis in the temple of Re is the symbolic acknowledgment of Piankhy's complete supremacy. The work certainly has dramatic action and dialogue with many flowery speeches, but it is not an epic. It is basically a commemorative inscription recording a great achievement and represents the best in the Egyptian tradition of historiographic prose. It may have been a text intended for delivery at a particular celebration like the almost contemporary Sargon Letter to the God, but its archaic use of language and lack of colloquial style would speak against this. The work is all the more remarkable since it stems from such a distant "provincial" region and from a time when Egyptian culture is generally regarded as at a rather low ebb.

The historiographic tradition continues, as is evident in the Dream Stela of Tanutamon,[116] the last of Piankhy's dynastic line, but it does not attain to the quality of the Piankhy Stela. Nevertheless, it is quite possible that the Saite kings of the Twenty-sixth Dynasty who succeeded the Ethiopian rulers inherited their tradition of historiographic prose. Although the records of this period are sparse, a badly worn stela of Amasis does give

116. *BARE*, vol. 4, §§ 919–34; Gardiner, *Egypt*, p. 347; Kitchen, *Third Intermediate Period*, p. 393.

evidence for such a continuity.[117] This, then, was the nature of the "official" historiographic tradition in Egypt on·the eve of those visits by the earliest Greek historians, Hecataeus and Herodotus.

f. THE HISTORICAL NOVEL

The one genre of Egyptian literature that has long been regarded as having the most bearing upon Israelite historiography is the historical novel. There are two types, those having to do with the king and those whose subject is a high-ranking government official. Many examples have been cited for the former group, which are called *Königsnovellen*. There are primarily two examples of the latter, the Story of Sinuhe and the Journey of Wenamun, which are best treated individually.

The Königsnovelle

A. Hermann, in a 1938 study, regarded several texts as having sufficient features in common that they could be considered a distinct literary genre, the *Königsnovellen*.[118] He cited examples of this form from the Middle Kingdom to the Late period. The genre was widely accepted by Egyptologists, who drew comparisons between it and certain texts of the Old Testament. There is, however, good reason to question the existence of such a genre, or, at any rate, the usefulness of the designation.

Hermann described the form as an account of a state event in which the king summons his council and tells them of his plan to construct a temple or to carry out a military expedition. The council responds with words of praise and the plan is carried through to completion. Now this schema hardly represents a story or novella and is certainly not comparable to the stories of Sinuhe and Wenamun or the many other tales in Egyptian literature. The only example that comes close to being a story is the Bentresh Stela,[119] and that is because it was a complete fabrication of the Late period. Its author tries to imitate inscriptions of the time of Ramesses II but is guilty of a number of woeful mistakes. However, his account was not written as a story on papyrus. Instead he attempted to pass it off as a commemorative stela with scenes at the top and inscription below. Its purpose was not entertainment but religious propaganda for the god Khonsu.

Another problem arises if we accept as a *Königsnovelle* every text in

117. *BARE*, vol. 4, §§ 996–1007; Gardiner, *Egypt*, p. 361. See also the victory stela of King Psamtik II in Lichtheim, *AEL*, vol. 3, pp. 84–86.
118. A. Hermann, *Die ägyptische Königsnovelle*. See also S. Herrmann, "Die Königsnovelle in Ägypten und in Israel," *Wissenschaftliche Zeitschrift der Karl-Marx Universität Leipzig*, Gesellschafts und Sprachwissenschaftliche Reihe, 3/1 (1953/54): 51–62.
119. *BARE*, vol. 3, §§ 429–47; *ANET³*, pp. 29–31; Lichtheim, *AEL*, vol. 3, pp. 90–94.

which a discussion in council occurs between the king and his followers. Such a scene is present in the Annals of Thutmose III before the battle of Megiddo. Does that make the whole of the Annals a *Königsnovelle*? The same question can be raised for the accounts of the Battle of Kadesh, the Piankhy Stela, and many other such texts. To include them all is to make the form meaningless, to exclude them is to be rather arbitrary in one's selection.

Furthermore, the genre allows for excessive variation and flexibility in form and content. For instance, the council may disagree with the king's proposal, in which case the events themselves must prove his superior wisdom. In many examples there is no council at all. In the Ahmose Stela recording the building of the mortuary chapel and tomb for Queen Tetisheri, a conversation takes place between the king and his royal consort in which he lays out his plans. In this case neither approval nor disapproval is expressed by the queen; the text records only that the plan was immediately carried out. In the Sphinx Stela of Thutmose IV there is no counseling with anyone, only a dream-vision from a god that provides the motivation for the subsequent activity. The action of the king is often said to be motivated simply by the arrival of a messenger with bad news which may or may not lead to the summoning of a council. This motif, however, is so common that it would also cause the inclusion of many commemorative inscriptions within the genre and would thereby dilute the genre's form-critical usefulness.

It is likewise questionable whether those texts that are discussed below under the heading of political propaganda should be considered *Königsnovellen*. Two examples are the divine birth and coronation of Hatshepsut and the coronation text of Thutmose III. Both in terms of their function as propaganda to legitimize the claim to the throne and in their general form and content they are so different from dedication inscriptions or commemorative texts, which celebrate the king's victories, that it seems quite forced to lump them all together. It is even more questionable, however, to see in every allusion to a divine origin and birth or to divine election in the introductory encomium of an inscription a reference to a *Königsnovelle*.[120] Given all the possible motifs that are used as evidence for the *Königsnovelle*, it becomes difficult to exclude from the genre any but the very briefest of royal inscriptions. The designation is thus rather meaningless and it should be replaced by more appropriate categories based on content and function such as we have suggested above.

In order to illustrate these problems with the *Königsnovelle* it might be helpful to consider a frequently cited example, the Sphinx Stela of Thut-

120. See S. Herrmann, "Die Königsnovelle," pp. 51–52.

mose IV (1406–1398 B.C.).[121] The stela begins, like most royal inscriptions, with a formal titulary and a short encomium on the king's godlike qualities. Then follows an account of how, as crown prince, he was accustomed to shooting, hunting, and riding with his two companions in the region of the Sphinx at Giza, and how one day while resting at the foot of the Sphinx he fell asleep and had a vision of the Sphinx as a god speaking to him. The god promised him the crown but also laid upon him the obligation to clear away the sand that threatened to bury the image. The prince awoke and, without revealing the vision to anyone, brought back appropriate offerings to the god. The rest of the text is missing but presumably it told how, when Thutmose became king, he carried out the will of the god and then set up his stela.

Before discussing the form or the text, the following points should be noted. First, the date of the text itself is unknown since in its present form it belongs to the Late period, but whether it was composed or merely "restored" at that time is difficult to decide.[122] Second, it is clear, in any case, that the inspiration for the text and most of the details are drawn from an earlier Sphinx stela belonging to Amenhotep II.[123] This too begins with a titulary and a somewhat more elaborate poetic encomium, followed by a narrative describing the crown prince's athletic prowess and his exercising horses in the vicinity of the Sphinx. There he conceived the idea of building a monument in honor of the pyramid builders, Khufu and Khafre. This plan he kept secret until he became king and brought it to completion. The only major difference between the two versions is the dream revelation, which is clearly an innovation, but it is also the only thing that allows us to call the Thutmose IV text a *Königsnovelle*. Now, while dream revelations are not unknown for the Eighteenth Dynasty they are certainly not developed to the degree that we find in the Late period.[124] The dream also has another function that makes the inscription quite different from its model. It is propaganda, not so much to legitimize Thutmose IV as pharaoh, since only he knew of the revelation until he was king, but to raise the esteem of the god Harmakhis represented by the Sphinx. In this regard its function comes close to that of the Bentresh Stela. On the other hand, the stela of Amenhotep II is purely commemorative of his youth, as he states.

S. Herrmann has taken up A. Hermann's suggestion that a number of

---

121. *BARE*, vol. 2, §§ 810–15; *ANET*[3], p. 449.

122. See introductory remarks by Breasted and Wilson in works cited in n. 121.

123. See Lichtheim, *AEL*, vol. 2, pp. 39–43; *ANET*[3], pp. 244–45 (only a partial translation).

124. Cf. esp. the dream in the Bentresh Stela and so-called Dream Stela of Tanutamon, *BARE*, vol. 4, §§ 919–34.

parallels to the *Königsnovelle* are extant in the Old Testament, especially in texts that have to do with the United Monarchy period.[125] Herrmann goes so far as to suggest that it was precisely the conditions created by the Davidic empire and the close relations between Egypt and Israel in the Solomonic period that account for the use of this genre at this place in the biblical literature.[126] One of the primary texts that Herrmann discusses is the dream revelation of Solomon at Gibeon in 1 Kings 3:3–15 and its parallels with the *Königsnovelle*, especially the Sphinx Stela of Thutmose IV.[127] Let us consider some of these parallels.

1. Herrmann makes much of the reference in verse 7 to Solomon's youth and associates it with the references to Thutmose IV's youth and similar references in other royal inscriptions. However, the difference could not be greater. The point of the biblical passage is to stress the young king's humility and lack of experience. It is not a legitimation of Solomon since he is already king. In the Sphinx stelae of both Amenhotep II and Thutmose IV the king is a crown prince in his youth. Yet there is no suggestion of humility but only of all his godlike qualities, which outdo even the best of mature men.

2. Herrmann points to the offering of sacrifices after the vision in both the Egyptian and biblical accounts. However, in the Sphinx Stela the sacrifices are meant to recognize the deity of the Sphinx. In the biblical story Solomon offers sacrifice at Gibeon *before* the dream but only in Jerusalem after it. In fact, verse 15 implies some criticism of the offering of sacrifice earlier at Gibeon.

3. The nature of the dream revelation is quite different. It is not the deity who confirms Solomon's election but Solomon himself who reaffirms it. Nor does Solomon do anything for the deity. Instead he receives the wisdom for which he asks and many things for which he does not ask.[128]

4. The only real similarity is in the notion of a dream revelation, but this is not so exceptional in the Old Testament, in Egyptian literature, and in Near Eastern and Greek materials in general.

There is no useful parallel between the Sphinx Stela of Thutmose IV and the biblical text of 1 Kings 3:3–15, and the effort to find one has seriously obscured the fact that the latter is thoroughly Deuteronomistic in style and

125. See work cited in n. 118 above.
126. The possible Egyptian influence in the United Monarchy period has been greatly exaggerated by scholars. See D. B. Redford, "Studies in Relations between Palestine and Egypt during the First Millennium B.C.," in *Studies in the Ancient Palestinian World*, pp. 141–56.
127. Herrmann, "Die Königsnovelle," pp. 53ff. His other major biblical parallel is 2 Sam. 7. This need not be discussed here, but for a critique see F. M. Cross, *Canaanite Myth and Hebrew Epic*, pp. 247–49.
128. One is reminded of the prayers in the Late biographical stelae, which are concerned with health, long life, and prosperity.

belongs to a theological pattern and structure of such texts throughout the Solomonic narrative.[129] To this we will return below.

The only merit in the discussion of the genre *Königsnovelle* is the observation that within a variety of different types of royal inscriptions the Egyptians employed a number of novelistic features, many of which became rather common stereotyped motifs. Since the Egyptians did not have the genre of "historical epic," these embellishments served to make the texts more vivid and dramatic, and the number of such motifs could vary a great deal from text to text. The same was true of the use of poetry in such inscriptions, as we have already seen. The so-called *Königsnovelle* simply represents a recognition of a wide range of storytelling motifs.[130] The error was to try to make a specific genre out of them.

If one wishes to speak about the use of dramatic and novelistic motifs as a technique of historiography and to compare this practice with the historiographies of other regions, that is quite another matter. The use of sending and receiving messages, the use of dialogue between king and subjects or between two adversaries, the reception of omens or dream revelations are all known to some degree in the historiographies of all the regions covered thus far and in the Old Testament as well. To what extent such techniques, or the particular motifs themselves, were transmitted from one region to another is a question that perhaps will never be satisfactorily answered.

The Story of Sinuhe

The Story of Sinuhe is a literary work of the Middle Kingdom that may be justly described as a classic of ancient Egyptian literature.[131] It was frequently recopied and was well known in later periods. Its extant remains are represented by five papyri and more than twenty ostraca. The basic theme is the flight of a court official into exile in Asia, his life there for many years, and his eventual return. The fact that this theme was frequently used in later literary works probably testifies to the popularity of the Sinuhe story. Unlike many other Egyptian tales it avoids all mention of the fantastic and gives a presentation and insight into the political affairs of the early Twelfth Dynasty that is of the greatest interest to modern historians. But our special concern here is its literary character and the ex-

---

129. The same can be said for 2 Sam. 7.

130. It does not, however, have anything to do with etiologies as Herrmann suggests, "Die Königsnovelle," p. 51. A dedication inscription set up at the time a temple was built cannot be regarded as etiological any more than a cornerstone inscription!

131. For translations see *BARE*, vol. 1, §§ 486–97; Erman, *The Ancient Egyptians*, pp. 14–29; M. Lichtheim, *AEL*, vol. 1, pp. 222–35. Wilson's translation in *ANET*[3], pp. 18–22, omits certain poetic passages which makes it less useful for literary study.

tent to which the Story of Sinuhe may be viewed as a work of Egyptian historiography.[132]

Of primary importance is the question of the work's form. Its various elements correspond rather well to the genre of tomb autobiographies. The story begins with the titles that Sinuhe had at the end of his life, his name, and the introductory formula, "he says." His concluding statement, that he was blessed with royal favors until the day of his death, and the enumeration of these gifts are also features of the tomb texts. The inclusion of a poem in praise of the king is common enough, and the narration of the events of his life does not contain anything that is incompatible with the genre of a mortuary autobiography.

Nevertheless, it is clear that this is not a copy of a tomb text. The various elements of that genre receive a very obvious literary transformation. The introduction with Sinuhe's titles is very brief and does not contain a eulogy of his character, as compared with the long narrative that follows. It is the story that portrays the qualities of the man. The panegyric to the king Senwosret I is not an extraneous addition but an important part of the story itself. There is no prayer for offerings or appeal to the public to recognize all of Sinuhe's good works and piety. In fact, very little is said about the gods or their worship in the entire work. The construction of the tomb itself is described, which is hardly necessary in the case of a tomb inscription. On the other hand, the offerings are not listed at the end but enumerated in a letter that the king sends to Sinuhe while he is still in the foreign land. Furthermore, letters and decrees from the king were often included in tomb biographies as memorable events, but the Story of Sinuhe includes Sinuhe's reply as well. G. Posener has noted a tendency in Egyptian literature to use a genre with a precise *Sitz im Leben* as a model and literary vehicle for a completely fictitious construction. He states:

> It is thus legitimate to think that a writer, having thought up the story of Sinuhe, was able to choose, for its form, the model of a tomb inscription which was admirably suitable to his subject and which answered to his desire to give a veracious and realistic character to his account.[133]

Yet having said this it still remains to ask to what extent the story reflects historical fact. On the basis of historical criticism it is possible to conclude that the story does represent rather accurately both the political conditions in Egypt at the beginning of the reign of Senwosret I—the unsettled period following the assassination of Amenemhet I—and the resto-

---

132. See especially Posener's study, *Littérature et politique*, pp. 87–115; also Williams, *Seed of Wisdom*, pp. 22ff.

133. *Littérature et politique*, p. 92 (my own translation).

ration of tranquillity and political security by the end of his reign. The general good relations with Asia reflected in the story seem to conform to other historical information from these times. But the specific historicity of Sinuhe himself cannot be precisely determined, and the vague information that the text contains on Asia can be of little use here. While it remains entirely possible, as Posener suggests, that the basic text was derived from an actual tomb inscription that then received literary reworking with fictional elaborations, nothing can prove that such was actually the case. If such a text did exist there is no way to go behind the extant literary form to suggest what elements may or may not have belonged to it.

Although the author is anonymous it is possible to say something about the work's date and the milieu out of which it came. Posener argues from the treatment given Senwosret I that it must almost certainly be dated to the last few years of this king's reign. The favorable attitude expressed toward the monarchy and the treatment and description of the court also make it likely that the author was closely associated with this stratum of society. Yet Posener does not believe that it was a commissioned work of political propaganda. Rather, it was written by someone genuinely appreciative of the stability and prosperity that Senwosret had brought to Egypt; it was not a work intended to bolster a questionable claim to the throne.

If the work is a novel, then strictly speaking it cannot be a work of historiography no matter how much it reflects the age in which it was written. Nevertheless, some observations on the nature of the narration may be important for the later development of historical narrative. First, the exaggerated formal stereotypes expressing the royal ideology are put into poetic passages or into the formal correspondence of Sinuhe with the king. This language emphasizes the godlike and exalted character of the king and his belligerent domination of foreign lands. On the other hand, the story itself emphasizes the king's human and compassionate qualities and the real friendship expressed between Asiatic rulers and Egypt in this period. In other words, the author has found a way to deal effectively with the tension between the idealization of the monarchy and its formal image and the historical reality that he wishes to communicate. Second, he can construct a skillful argument. In the conversation between Sinuhe and the foreign prince the latter wants to know how to appraise the situation in Egypt at the death of Amenemhet I. Sinuhe replies with a panegyric on the new king's qualities but he also makes it clear that these were tested while the previous ruler was alive and Senwosret was only coregent. He had already proved his royal worth.[134] Third, the author has a way of describ-

134. One might compare this concern with that in the Annals of Muršili. However, it should be noted that the author is able to look back over thirty years and correctly reconstruct this concern at the beginning of Senwosret's reign. By the time the story was written such a problem was long past.

ing rather delicate political events, such as those surrounding the assassination of the king, with great sensitivity. Yet he also knows that there are situations in which the event cannot be fully reported. Thus, when Sinuhe tells the prince in Asia the reason for his flight he adds parenthetically, "But I spoke in half-truths," and does not disclose everything that happened. And he uses the same obscure manner in his letter of reply to the pharaoh.

Furthermore, the author has equal facility with prose and poetry, and when he reverts to poetry in the course of his narration it is for a particular heightened or dramatic effect. These poetic units do not derive from other sources, nor do they reflect an earlier level or stratum of storytelling such as an oral tradition. They are merely one facet of the writer's literary art. He can also imitate forms within forms, as he does for the royal decree and the correspondence between Sinuhe and the king.

While the work is a skillfully written composition not dependent upon a long tradition, it utilizes storytelling motifs like, for instance, the scene of single combat between Sinuhe and the ruler of Retenu.[135] The resemblance to an epic style of portraying single combat between heroes is quite clear and in no case should the scene be understood as the actual style of warfare in that period. The same is true of the royal audience scene in which Sinuhe receives his final pardon and has difficulty being recognized by the queen whom he once served because he now resembles an Asiatic and must be transformed by means of all the amenities of civilization back into an Egyptian.

Composed in the twentieth century B.C., the Story of Sinuhe came before the long development of historiographic prose in Egypt as reflected in the commemorative and annals inscriptions. It is likely, therefore, that its great popularity in later times and its realistic and highly political subject influenced later historical prose.

The Journey of Wenamun

The Journey of Wenamun[136] reads like an adventure story although the events are in no way fantastic and could correspond to the activities by a high religious official of the god Amun sent on a commission in the first quarter of the eleventh century B.C. The text tells how the official, Wenamun, set out for Byblos from Thebes with funds and instructions to obtain a load of lumber with which to construct the great bark of

---

135. The parallel with the story of David and Goliath, 1 Sam. 17, has often been noted. See the discussion by R. de Vaux, "Single Combat in the Old Testament," in *The Bible and the Ancient Near East*, pp. 122–35, esp. p. 129.

136. For translations of the work see *BARE*, vol. 4, §§ 557–91; *ANET*[3], pp. 25–29; Gardiner, *Egypt*, pp. 306–13; Erman, *The Ancient Egyptians*, pp. 174–83; Lichtheim, *AEL*, vol. 2, pp. 224–30.

Amen-Re. Many difficulties, misunderstandings, and other misfortunes beset the official, causing his work to be unduly delayed. The account ends abruptly when the hero is blown off course on his homeward journey, beached on the island of Cyprus and trying to talk his way out of a threatening situation with the local inhabitants. The original story must have told how Wenamun eventually returned with his cargo to Egypt.

As in the Story of Sinuhe, the problem of form is most important for the literary study of this text. Some scholars regard it primarily as a literary work while others insist on viewing it as a "report," an administrative document in the strictest sense. In the most recent extensive study of the text H. Goedicke states that "the late Jaroslav Černý was able to show that the text in its preserved form agrees fully with the peculiarities of official documents of the late New Kingdom and concluded that it is not a literary work but an administrative document."[137] Without any further discussion of Černý's arguments Goedicke regarded the question of form as settled, and his subsequent treatment of the text is based upon the conclusion that the work is an administrative report.

The matter, however, is worthy of some reconsideration. Černý, in describing the use of papyrus in ancient Egypt,[138] explains how the scribe wrote in columns on the inside of the papyrus roll along the horizontal grain of the papyrus fibers and with the joins between the papyrus sheets running vertical and at right angles to the writing. This was the standard practice for a literary work in all periods. On the other hand, from the middle of the Eighteenth Dynasty onward it became customary to write some administrative texts parallel to the end of the roll and the joins and thus at right angles to the papyrus fibers. In this way the scribe would simply use the amount he needed for his letter or accounts and then cut the piece off, thus saving papyrus. Since the latter technique was used to compose the text of Wenamun, Černý concludes (1) that the text was an administrative report and not a literary text, and (2) that the extant papyrus was the original version and not a later copy.

The difficulty is that the first conclusion has some weight only if the second is true, but the second conclusion does not follow from the paleographic argument and must be established on other grounds. Yet if the extant document is a copy then the author of the original may indeed have written it in the usual literary manner while only a copyist was responsible for the extant orientation of the writing. Now Goedicke himself has

---

137. *The Report of Wenamun*, p. 4. See also W. F. Albright, "The Eastern Mediterranean about 1060 B.C.," in *Studies Presented to David Robinson*, vol. 1, pp. 223–31; idem, *CAH*[3], vol. 2, pt. 2, p. 519, n. 3; Breasted, in *BARE*, vol. 4, p. 274, also insists that it is a genuine report but at the same time acknowledges that it is unique. Cf. the views of Gardiner, *Egypt*, p. 306, and Wilson in *ANET*[3], p. 25.

138. J. Černý, *Paper and Books in Ancient Egypt*, pp. 21–22.

strongly argued that the surviving manuscript is a copy and not the original.[139] First, he points to an obvious copyist's error in the text at 2, 63 which has created a serious lacuna. He then argues that the present text is incomplete, not because the last part was destroyed but because the copyist stopped writing in the middle of a sentence even when he had more space to fill. Finally, he points out that the term *ḥt*, meaning "copy," occurs at the very end of the text.

Goedicke's own arguments therefore undermine what is essential to Černý's conclusions. In fact, Goedicke inadvertently suggests a plausible explanation for why the copyist adopted the administrative style in this instance, namely, that he had no intention of copying the whole work. He included only the part that was of particular interest to him and then cut the roll off at that point. Consequently, there is no reason to conclude, on the basis of the technical style of writing in the extant copy, that the Journey of Wenamun is an administrative report rather than a literary work.

Egypt had a long tradition of private inscriptions in which a high-ranking public official relates how he faithfully carried through to completion a commission laid upon him by the king. Such reports were inscribed upon stelae or rock surfaces and are frequently found at the sites of mines and quarries.[140] They date the event and give a record of their service, often telling of some difficulty or unusual event that took place in the course of the work. Nevertheless, in scope and degree of literary skill and polish none of these reports approaches the Journey of Wenamun. A more likely possibility is that a public stela describing the completion of a commission to obtain lumber from Lebanon formed the basis and inspiration for a literary treatment of the subject. This would be analogous to Posener's proposal for the Story of Sinuhe, discussed above, and seems to me to be the most likely possibility.

The work's literary quality is evident upon a close reading of the text, even in translation, but the judgment of M. Lichtheim will be quoted here as confirmation of this opinion.

What makes the story so remarkable is the skill with which it is told. The Late-Egyptian vernacular is handled with great subtlety. The verbal duels between Wenamun and the prince of Byblos, with their changes of mood and shades of meaning that include irony, represent Egyptian thought and style at their most advanced. What *Sinuhe* is for the Middle Kingdom, *Wenamun* is for the New Kingdom: a literary culmination.[141]

139. Goedicke, *Report*, pp. 5–6.
140. See especially the Sinai and Wadi Hammamat inscriptions.
141. Lichtheim, *AEL*, vol. 2, p. 224.

A comparison of the Story of Sinuhe and the Journey of Wenamun on their whole outlook and purpose is suggested at a number of points. As noted above, Sinuhe is sympathetic to the ideals of the monarchy in the Middle Kingdom and toward the ruler Senwosret I in particular. In Wenamun the ruler of Egypt, Ramesses XI, is not even mentioned and the initial date is given as the fifth year of the Renaissance Era.[142] The other principal authorities of Egypt, Herihor the high priest of Thebes and Smendes the ruler of Tanis, are referred to when necessary but without titles or praise. This is a vastly different view of political authority from that of the older period of history, in which a public official could scarcely do anything of significance without associating its initiative and purpose with the will and pleasure of the king.

The relationship between Egypt and Asia is also viewed in an entirely different way in Sinuhe and Wenamun. It is not just that Egyptian power in Asia has declined by the eleventh century B.C., with the result that Egyptian officials are no longer held in the same esteem as previously. What is remarkable is that, after so many years of state propaganda that spoke of such complete and universal domination of the world by Egypt, an Egyptian writer was now able to represent that relationship in a way that was so humiliating for Egypt. At his first stop in Asia, the Tjeker town of Dor, Wenamun is robbed of a very large sum by one of his own sailors. Wenamun adopts a typical Egyptian imperialistic attitude, that the prince of Dor must be held responsible because it happened in his port. This is ridiculed as a completely unjust demand, but it does not interfere with his hospitable reception. However, after Wenamun departs he retaliates by pirating one of the Tjeker ships. The amount he gets does not do him much good, and the future trouble it causes him makes it clear that the action was foolish and completely unjustified.

Wenamun's relations with the prince of Byblos also put him in a bad light. He has to sit in his tent by the harbor while the prince sends him orders to leave which he cannot follow since he has no ship. This goes on for a month until he is finally summoned by the prince only to reveal that he has no money and no credentials to support his mission. At virtually every point in the dialogue he is bettered by his foreign host. Wenamun employs the official Egyptian dogma that Asiatic rulers are to do the bidding of Egypt and that since the god Amun is lord of these lands as well their resources belong to him. All this counts for little with the prince of Byblos. He wants payment before delivery and he gets it. The prince also makes it clear that Byblos has been dealing with Egypt on the basis of payment for

142. This was an independent means of dating begun by the high priest Herihor in the nineteenth year of Ramesses XI. For further discussion see Gardiner, *Egypt*, pp. 304–05.

material and not just "gifts" such as are mentioned in Sinuhe. Furthermore, envoys from Egypt in the past have not always fared so well, some
never returning to Egypt but finding their tombs in Byblos.

The attitude toward Egyptian religion is also noteworthy. Wenamun
makes a fuss about the traveling-Amun image, which he must hide in a
hole in his tent for protection or try to sneak on board a boat at night. But
it does not impress the prince of Byblos at all, even after its presence has
been revealed by a local ecstatic at the last minute. The prince is not irre-
ligious and can recognize Amun as the supreme deity alongside, and with
the aid of, Seth (= Baal), but this religious mission is regarded as foolish. Wenamun also tries to propound the new Theban dogma that the
kings of Egypt no longer dispense life and health, that this is solely in the
hands of Amun and his administrators, but this makes little impression
upon the prince. He wants payment. Wenamun also suggests to the prince
that he ought to make a stela for himself, stating on it all that he did for
the god Amun, and thereby receive long life from the god and praise from
men, without, however, indicating on such an inscription that he was paid
for this service. The prince accepts the suggestion as a good idea, but it
surely makes a mockery of dedication or mortuary inscriptions and the
prayers for offerings on such stelae.

There are certainly other points in the story where Egyptian belief and
customs are held up for ridicule, or at least for some examination, in a
way that is completely absent from Sinuhe. The whole outlook and intention of the Journey of Wenamun could not be more opposed to the highly
favorable view of Egyptian life, culture, the political system, and the mortuary cult found in Sinuhe. Wenamun is a political and religious satire on
the "official" view of the state and state religion, which the author knows
to be completely contrary to reality and which can be so painfully exposed
by a journey abroad. Wenamun represents the public official who struggles
hopelessly to cope with the world as it is while still trying to live with the
old ideology. To take the work as an actual report and then to try to explain away this aspect of it as totally unintentional seems to be a most unlikely prospect.[143]

We must now return to the question of genre and the place the Journey
of Wenamun has in Egyptian historiography. The work may be called a
"historical novel," but it is certainly not a precise report of events in the
recent past. Yet when we consider it in the light of the tension in the Egyptian historiographic tradition between state ideology and actual events, the
work bears witness to a critical mind that perhaps goes beyond that in any
other work in the Egyptian corpus we have considered. The form may be

143. See Goedicke in *Report*.

autobiographical but in fact it is a genuine third-person perspective with the freedom from "archaic simplicity" that is the mark of the later Greek historiographic spirit.

It is hard to say what impact the work had upon its own day or later times. It was not nearly as popular as Sinuhe and survived in only one copy dating from perhaps a century or so later. Even this may have been copied for reasons other than its literary merits since the whole work was not included. At present we cannot trace any genetic literary or historiographic development to later times, or even discern any significant decline in the "official" political or religious attitudes of later periods.

g. THE USE OF THE PAST AS PROPAGANDA

If propaganda is the attempt to influence the general public to support the governing institution and its programs, then a large part of the court-produced literature of Egypt might be understood as propagandist.[144] This would certainly include many of the dedication inscriptions and commemorative texts that present a certain image of the monarchy and its achievements for popular consumption. What I want to consider under this heading, however, are those works that make a clear attempt to sway public opinion in the face of opposition, rival claims, or questions of legitimacy. These situations arose in times of political disunity, or when the hereditary line of male successors was interrupted, or when a usurper seized the throne to begin a new dynasty. The propaganda used during these times takes a variety of forms in the literature, but we are concerned here only with those that use the past to influence public opinion.

Since the Old Kingdom pharaohs did not indulge in setting up historical inscriptions, this period need not concern us. In fact, it has been argued that the royal ideology was, by and large, so secure that it did not need to furnish texts in support of its authority. But with the breakdown of this absolutism into the anarchy of the First Intermediate period (ca. 2200–2050 B.C.), persuasion became a necessary art of the court or courts now that the country was divided into regions. A plurality of kings ruling simultaneously made a mockery of the traditional ideology. The various districts, or nomes, were fairly autonomous, governed by their own noble families with only nominal allegiance to a pharaoh.

144. No general survey of this function of literature exists within Egyptology. The primary focus of such studies in the past have been upon the 12th Dynasty. See esp. G. Posener, *Littérature et politique dans l'Égypte de la XIIᵉ dynastie*; R. J. Williams, "Literature as a Medium of Political Propaganda in Ancient Egypt," in *The Seed of Wisdom*, pp. 14–30. This last study extends the survey to some earlier and later periods. See also the literature cited in these works.

The Tenth Dynasty, with its center in Heracleopolis, had regained control of Middle and Lower Egypt but was still opposed in the southern region of the land by the princes of Thebes. One ruler of this dynasty expressed his view of the monarchy in a document called Instructions for Merikare.[145] The work is written in the Old Kingdom style of advice given by a sage to his students, and in this case a king at the end of his career advises his son and heir Merikare. Since the text itself clearly indicates that the aged king is dead, the work must be by Merikare himself. Why was such a fiction used? The nature of the supposed advice was to review the accomplishments of Merikare's father, Khety III, and to urge a continuation of these policies on the authority of the predecessor. On the other hand, Khety is made to confess to certain faults, particularly concerning his conflict with the rulers of Thebes over control of the regions of Thinis. The "advice" given is to practice compromise and accommodation instead of hostility, and in this way Merikare is really putting forward a new policy. The presentation of a political program that represents both continuity and discontinuity with past practice, both praise and censure of the preceding regime, in a fictional literary form that is specially adopted for the purpose of persuasion is surely a remarkable piece of propaganda.

The beginning of the Twelfth Dynasty provided quite a different situation and a different response.[146] The first ruler, Amenemhet I, was a usurper who had no real claim to the throne through any hereditary connection with the previous royal family. The land had been unified by the pharaohs of the Eleventh Dynasty, more by force and the domination of Thebes over the other regions than in any spiritual sense. So Amenemhet I and his successors set out consciously to win the support of the whole land in a rather diverse program of literary propaganda. Here we will consider only one of these works, the Prophecy of Neferty.[147]

The Prophecy was written down during the reign of Amenemhet I but purports to be the work of a famous sage and lector-priest named Neferty who lived under Snefru of the Fourth Dynasty. The prologue tells how, at Snefru's request, Neferty entertains the king with a prediction of the future that is then put into writing. The prediction describes the coming chaos and trials of the First Intermediate period and the way in which they will come to an end. He states: "In fact, a king will arise in the south, Ameny by name, the son of a woman of To-Seti. He is a child of Upper Egypt. He

145. Williams, in *The Seed of Wisdom*, pp. 16–19. See also *ANET*[3], pp. 414–18; Lichtheim, *AEL*, vol. 1, pp. 97–109; Erman, *The Ancient Egyptians*, pp. 75–84.
146. See esp. the remarks by Posener, *Littérature*, pp. 1–20.
147. Ibid., pp. 21–60; *ANET*[3], pp. 444–46; Williams, in *Seed of Wisdom*, pp. 19–21; Lichtheim, *AEL*, vol. 1, pp. 139–45; Erman, *The Ancient Egyptians*, pp. 110–15.

will receive the white crown, will don the red crown."[148] The text, of course, refers to Amenemhet, and it goes on to describe his royal qualities as a savior and his accomplishments. The prophecy is a case of *vaticinia ex eventu*, and the fiction was intended to persuade the population to accept the rule of Amenemhet. The motif of the true ruler who arises after a period of chaos to set order in the land continues as a means of legitimation into later periods as well. Of course, this text conveniently overlooks the fact that Mentuhotep II had already united the land some fifty years earlier. So the work probably appealed to the region of Lower Egypt, where the Eleventh Dynasty had not been very popular and was perhaps never truly recognized.[149]

The situation at the end of the Second Intermediate period differed from that of the First Intermediate period in that the rulers of Thebes were in a rivalry with the Hyksos of Lower Egypt, who were foreigners. Thus the princes of Thebes could pose as the liberators of the land from foreign domination and to this extent the inscription on the Kamose Stelae is certainly a piece of propaganda.[150] Thus, beginning with the Kamose inscription, the king as conqueror of foreign peoples becomes a major element of the royal image and a theme of propaganda whenever it was needed.

When Hatshepsut aspired to the sole rule of Egypt after the death of her husband, Thutmose II, much about her rule was anomalous.[151] The legitimate heir Thutmose III was a minor who could be controlled for a time but not dismissed. To retain her authority Hatshepsut had to make a strong case for her legitimacy, and perhaps no other reign is so filled with propaganda. A few of the primary examples will suffice.

On the facade of a cliff-temple in Middle Egypt (called Speos Artemidos by the Greeks) is an inscription that contains the enumeration of Hatshepsut's pious works.[152] She states in a concluding summary:

> Hear ye, all people and the folk as many as they may be. I have done these things through the counsel of my heart. I have not slept forgetfully, but I have restored that which had been ruined. I have raised up that which had gone to pieces *formerly*, since the Asiatics were in the midst of Avaris in the Northland. . . . They ruled without Re, and he (the king) did not act by divine command down to (the reign of) my majesty. (Now) I am established upon the thrones of Re.[153]

148. Williams, in *The Seed of Wisdom*, p. 21.
149. Compare the Mesopotamian prophecy texts of a much later period, 3f above.
150. For literature see n. 78, above.
151. See Gardiner, *Egypt*, pp. 183ff.; also the recent study by D. B. Redford, *History and Chronology of the Eighteenth Dynasty of Egypt: Seven Studies*, pp. 57–87.
152. *BARE*, vol. 2, §§ 296–303; *ANET*³, p. 231 (only a partial translation).
153. *ANET*³, p. 231.

The import of this text is clear. Hatshepsut is claiming to be the divinely appointed savior who restores order after the destruction brought about in Egypt by the Hyksos many years earlier. The inscription completely overlooks the intervening reigns in the application of the model of the true ruler who sets the land in order again after evil times.

On the walls of Hatshepsut's mortuary temple at Deir-el-Bahri is a series of pictorial reliefs meant to represent the queen's divine birth.[154] A precedent for this account exists in a popular story about the divine birth of three children whom a priest's wife bore to Re and who grew up to become the first three kings of the Fifth Dynasty. However, it is uncertain whether any monarch ever understood his own birth as the result of a direct union between the god and the queen before the time of Hatshepsut.[155] She, at any rate, completely historicized the ideological conception of the ruler as the "offspring of Re" and told the story in her reliefs of how she was the product of a union between the queen Ahmose and Amen-Re, the god being in the semblance of Thutmose I. The subsequent scenes deal with her being fashioned by the god Khnum, her actual birth and nurture by the goddess Hathor.

A second series of scenes continues from the first series and shows Hatshepsut's coronation.[156] These reaffirm her divinity and Amun's choice of her as future ruler. But they go on to tell the story of how on a certain occasion when she was a young woman she made a trip to Heliopolis with her father Thutmose I in order to be designated crown princess and co-ruler by her father. The scenes portray an elaborate state ceremony in which Hatshepsut underwent the full ritual of the coronation. The date for the ceremony was put on New Year's day, although on other monuments she reckoned her accession from a different day of the year. The text of the coronation ceremony itself was copied directly from the account of the coronation of Amenemhet III of the Middle Kingdom. There was, in fact, no such coronation during Thutmose I's lifetime, and Hatshepsut's claim to be ruler of Egypt was first made only after the death of her husband and ruler, Thutmose II, and always as co-ruler with Thutmose III. As Breasted states, "It is clear that this entire coronation of Hatshepsut, like the supernatural birth, is an artificial creation, a fiction of later origin, prompted by political necessity."[157]

Thutmose III too had reason to justify his claim to the throne.[158] He was the son of Thutmose II, not by the King's Great Wife, Hatshepsut, but

---

154. *BARE*, vol. 2, §§ 187–212.
155. The language in the Heliopolis Stela of Senwosret I (*BARE*, vol. 1, § 502) may be taken to suggest this but it is still very vague.
156. *BARE*, vol. 2, §§ 215–42.
157. Ibid., p. 95.
158. See Gardiner, *Egypt*, pp. 181–82; Redford, *History and Chronology*, pp. 74ff.

by a concubine of much lesser status. Since Hatshepsut did not have a son, Thutmose III did have considerable support for his claim that could be suppressed during his minority but not denied. In a text that probably dates to the period of his sole rule, inscribed on the walls of the Karnak temple, Thutmose III tells of an episode during his youth in which the god Amun recognized him as king.[159] He was serving in the temple as a young priest when he received a divine oracle during a religious procession in which the god Amun, and possibly also the reigning king Thutmose II, designated him as the future king. After this he speaks of an ascent to heaven during which the deity himself crowned Thutmose as king and fixed his titulary. The rest of the inscription, to which the coronation account is the "historical" prologue, concerns the dedication of monuments and offerings to the deity.

Whether this narrative of events was original with Thutmose III or a copy of an earlier version related by Thutmose I, whose claim to the throne was rather weak, cannot be determined with certainty.[160] However, its political character is clear. It is another example of an attempt to historicize the mythology of divine election as in the texts of Hatshepsut cited above. It is not just a claim to divinity or to divine recognition but an effort to tie that claim to a precise event in the past in order to give it credibility.[161]

Haremhab (1342–1303 B.C.) was another king without the necessary genealogical connection with the previous line of kings. So he too has a coronation inscription telling the story of his divine election—a collaboration between the god Horus and the great god Amen-Re, with the other gods joining in.[162] No precise dates are given for the event, the whole account being an artificial creation to justify his position as king.

A common feature of many royal inscriptions is the designation of a particular event as the greatest such achievement since the monarchy began. At the same time these kings solemnly testify that what they stated was the truth. Of all the Egyptian kings perhaps none was so conscious of his image of greatness as Ramesses II. Not content just to glorify his own accomplishments, he put his name upon the monuments of many of his predecessors. It also seemed important for the public image of the king as the supreme ruler on earth to completely falsify the nature of his relations between Egypt and other foreign nations. Thus diplomatic exchanges of gifts between the courts of the major powers, such as is reflected in the

159. *BARE*, vol. 2, §§ 131–66.
160. See Redford, *History and Chronology*, pp. 75–76.
161. In time these stories become stereotype motifs and just part of the accumulative image of the king. See, e.g., the application of the divine birth theme to Amenhotep III (*BARE*, vol. 2, § 841).
162. *BARE*, vol. 3, §§ 22–32.

Amarna letters, become construed in the Egyptian monuments as tribute received from these regions as signs of their submission to the suzerainty of Egypt.[163] Nothing is ever said about the gifts that Egypt sent to the foreign ports in exchange.

Nowhere is this falsification of the true political situation more apparent than in Ramesses II's relations with the Hittites. With the cessation of war between the two powers and the establishment of peace, a treaty was concluded; a copy has been found in Boğazköy and an Egyptian version was inscribed on the walls of the Karnak temple and the Ramesseum.[164] The treaty views the two parties as being on equal footing, with peace and brotherhood sworn between the two rulers. Yet on his monuments Ramesses continued to represent himself in a most belligerent fashion as the complete conqueror of the Hittites.[165] At the same time the Egyptian court negotiated with the Hittite rulers the marriage of a Hittite princess to Ramesses, but this too is presented on the monuments in a most derogatory fashion. The princess is described as part of a great tribute that the Hittites brought to Egypt with which to appease the disfavor of Ramesses and to complete the submission of their realm to Egypt. Again the event is characterized as "a great, mysterious, marvellous, and fortunate affair. It was unknown, unheard of from mouth to mouth, not mentioned in the writings of the ancestors."[166] It seems that Egyptian historiography was more interested in the unprecedented event, the Hittites in historical precedents.

One document that comes out of very troubled times is the Great Harris Papyrus.[167] It is a mortuary text giving a detailed statement of Ramesses III's benefactions to gods and men during his reign of thirty-one years. It was compiled at his death by his son Ramesses IV and was intended to present to the gods a record of the father's good works to ensure him happiness after death. P. Harris has four main sections, stemming from the three major cult sites of Thebes, Heliopolis, and Memphis, with a final section including the smaller temples. After the gifts to each appropriate god are listed, Ramesses III prays to the god on behalf of his son, Ramesses IV, to establish him upon the throne and to make his reign great. It seems that Ramesses IV was motivated out of some self-interest in compiling a record of his father's deeds, namely, to encourage a favorable attitude toward himself by gods and men alike.

163. See M. Liverani, "Memorandum on the Approach to Historiographic Texts," in *Approaches to the Study of the Ancient Near East*, pp. 191ff.
164. See *ANET*³, pp. 199–203.
165. *BARE*, vol. 3, §§ 392–491; see also Gardiner, *Egypt*, pp. 264ff.
166. *ANET*³, p. 258.
167. *BARE*, vol. 4, §§ 151–412; see also Williams, in *Seed of Wisdom*, pp. 27–29.

The final section of the work, only a small fraction of the whole, contains a historical epilogue. This is addressed not to the gods but to the people of Egypt. It gives a historical survey, beginning with a period of anarchy under a foreign ruler—the interregnum at the end of the Nineteenth Dynasty. This period came to an end with Setnakht, who founded a new dynasty and who was soon succeeded by his son Ramesses III. There is a lengthy recitation of all his accomplishments—administrative, military, and economic. The description of these achievements is in much plainer prose than that of Ramesses III's Medinet Habu inscription, but still they are not dated or in any chronological order. The piece ends with a reference to the king's death and an exhortation by the dead king to recognize and give homage to his son Ramesses IV.

The reign of Ramesses III was during a very troubled time and he ruled with some severity.[168] A serious attempt was made on his life by a palace conspiracy involving many members of the royal family and highly placed officials who were subsequently brought to trial. The historical summary mentions nothing of this or any other problems during the reign. Instead it casts the best possible light upon the period. We certainly get the impression from this unit that a case is being made, in politically difficult times, for the legitimacy of the royal line as a whole and the succession of Ramesses IV in particular.

The Chronicle of Prince Osorkon[169] was a long text written by the eldest son of King Takelot II of the Twenty-second Dynasty, who held important religious, political, and military posts under his father and his father's successor Shoshenk III during the latter part of the ninth and the early eighth centuries B.C. The Chronicle was inscribed on the walls of the Bubastite Gate of the great Temple of Amun at Karnak. Actually, since the work consists of two separate texts, the term *chronicle*, or even *annals*, as it is sometimes called, might be misleading.[170] One text narrates events only in Takelot's eleventh year and was inscribed shortly thereafter. The second text deals with events beginning in Takelot's twelfth year and continues for several decades, with the result that the second part of the Chronicle was not actually completed until Shoshenk III's twenty-ninth year. The first text has an opening date and the second text two dates near the beginning, but the relationship of these dates to the actual events is not at all clear, and the lack of precise dates in the second text makes the chronology of events difficult to follow. One has the distinct impression that the opening date has become a somewhat artificial convention. It is hardly evidence that a strong chronicle tradition lies behind the text.

168. For background see Gardiner, *Egypt*, pp. 288ff.
169. See now the fine edition by R. Caminos, *The Chronicle of Prince Osorkon*.
170. Caminos's definition (ibid., p. 1, n. 1) does not convince me.

The historical circumstances in Egypt during the period to which these texts date are not well known. Yet it is clear that the rulers of Egypt, whose residence was now at Tanis in the Delta, had difficulty maintaining political control over the region of Upper Egypt, especially the southern districts that centered around Thebes. This city was a semiautonomous principality, a kind of theocratic state, under the authority of the high priest of Amun. From time to time these high priests even adopted the trappings of royalty. It was therefore expedient that a member of the northern royal family fill this post to maintain political unity, and this was the case with prince Osorkon, the eldest son of Takelot II. He also held the military and political offices that were necessary to administer the whole region of Upper Egypt. Now, such appointments to the high priesthood could be viewed as an infringement upon the local autonomy and were often contested. Hence the reference in the Chronicle to revolts and unrest in the region. With this background in mind it is not hard to interpret the function of Osorkon's inscriptions as propagandistic. They are intended to justify his position and his actions in the face of rather constant opposition. His presentation is based upon a long tradition of ideological legitimation, used by former rulers of Egypt. Let us briefly consider the chief features of the two inscriptions.

The first text is surmounted by two symmetrically balanced scenes with labels, each containing the god Amen-Re embracing the king, Takelot II, followed by Osorkon the hereditary prince with the goddess Mut. The main text begins with a date, the eleventh year of King Takelot, then the titles of Osorkon, his royal lineage, and his strong assertion of loyalty to his father. This is followed by the description of a revolt and Osorkon's successful restoration of peace. He proceeds to Thebes to receive recognition from Amun and the acclamation of the populace as the savior of the land. Thereupon he administers justice upon the rebels, makes new appointments of loyalists, and gives decrees for the temples. The epilogue states:

> I have acted for Amūn with willing heart on [behalf of] the life, prosperity, and health of my father, the son of Rēʿ Takelothis . . ., [in order] to cause his spirit to rejoice until I am upon his throne.[171]

This is followed by a blessing upon those who maintain his decrees and a curse upon those who violate them.

It is clear that Prince Osorkon fully expected to succeed his father on the throne, something that in fact he never did even after his father's death. In anticipation of his coronation he presents himself as the one chosen by the

171. Ibid., § 257.

god to restore order out of chaos, to execute justice, and to care for the cult—actions befitting royalty. Yet all this is done with complete loyalty toward his father, the current ruler of the land.

The second text provides some significant differences from the first. It is also surmounted by two symmetrically balanced scenes, but in these Osorkon appears alone before the god Amen-Re as high priest with no reference to the reigning king, Shoshenk III. The main text begins with the date in the twelfth year, the first month, and the ninth day of Takelot II, but it is difficult to understand the reason for this date since the paragraph that goes with it mentions as eventful three trips to Thebes in the course of the year to celebrate festivals and nothing else. For the rest, this section is full of stereotyped motifs and phrases in a long encomium such as is usually reserved for royalty. The text then mentions another date in the fifteenth year of Takelot II, when a serious civil war broke out that involved the whole of Egypt in conflict for several years. Osorkon claims credit for having effected a reconciliation that brought peace to Egypt. But certain personal enemies were able to oust him for a time from the high priesthood as well as to deprive him of the succession, which went to Shoshenk III.[172] However, in fulfillment of a promise by Amun he is eventually restored to the high priesthood, and he ends his Chronicle by listing his benefactions to the gods from the eleventh year of Takelot to the twenty-ninth year of Shoshenk III. The epilogue contains a blessing and curse similar to those in the first inscription.

In the second text Osorkon makes his claim to the high priesthood on a different basis from the first text. He is no longer high priest by virtue of his relationship to the ruling king as hereditary prince but rather because of his divine qualities through his royal birth. There was, of course, some precedent for the claim to divinity by the high priesthood of Amun. Osorkon justifies his claim also through his actions, since he is able to keep the peace between the various rivaling factions in the land to the benefit of Thebes. His final claim is based upon an oracular promise by the god Amun that actually restored him to his office without force of arms.

This combination of historical and ideological justification is the result of a long tradition in the use of such themes. The election of the supreme deity manifested through some oracle or sign at a certain point early in the recipient's career was used by Hatshepsut and Thutmose III as well as by Osorkon. The theme of the true king who restores the land after a period of chaos and hard times is also common ever since the Prophecy of Neferty and recurs frequently. It is evident in the Great Harris Papyrus and in both texts of the Chronicle. The king as the guardian of the cult places and the

---

172. See Kitchen's speculative suggestions in *The Third Intermediate Period*, pp. 332–33.

epitome of true piety is also a recurrent theme, as well as the king who is the good shepherd of his people. These themes are already prominent in the Middle Kingdom, frequent in the Empire period, and find expression in the Great Harris Papyrus and the Chronicle of Prince Osorkon.

In the discussion of Hittite historiography we gave considerable attention to those texts, such as the Proclamation of Telepinu and the Apology of Ḫattušili III, in which various rulers were concerned to legitimize their usurpation of power.[173] Egypt differs from the Hittites in its heavier reliance upon the mythology of royal ideology for its tradition of succession—i.e., the Horus-Osiris myth or the king as the offspring of Re —while the Hittites evolved a set of rules to govern succession. But precisely because of the tension between the mythological ideal and the exigencies of historical reality, the Egyptian monarchy was faced with an even greater need to legitimize authority, to historicize the myth when necessary, and to use forms of historical persuasion whenever possible. The result is not a great difference between the two cultures. The themes of the restoration of order after a period of chaos, as in the Proclamation of Telepinu, and of divine election, guidance, and protection, as in the Apology of Ḫattušili, are both common to Egyptian literature. Even the combination of the religious and political offices and the attaching of cultic endowments and benefactions, with threat of prosecution or curse for violators, to a historical review of one's behavior in office make the Chronicle of Prince Osorkon and the Apology of Ḫattušili similar in form and function.[174]

Yet it would nonetheless be quite wrong to propose any direct influence by one historiographic tradition upon the other. And this ought to caution us about reaching conclusions too quickly when we deal with Israelite literature on the monarchy that may suggest the theme of political legitimation.

h. BIOGRAPHIES

In contrast to the other countries of the ancient Near East, Egypt has yielded many private inscriptions that are biographical. It became customary early in Egyptian history to decorate the tombs of leading state officials with painted scenes or scenes in relief depicting family portraits, the funerary banquet, daily life, and state affairs. Alongside these scenes were

173. See above, 4b.
174. For a quite different and rather limited comparison of Egyptian and Hittite sources, see H. M. Wolf, *The Apology of Ḫattušiliš Compared*, pp. 99–106.

inscriptions with their autobiographies or obituaries.[175] Because of the status enjoyed by these officials within the kingdom, many of the texts contain historical information. In fact, in view of the paucity of royal inscriptions in the Old Kingdom and Middle Kingdom periods, the biographies often constitute the most important historical source for these periods. Although they are personal in perspective and therefore rather limited as historiographic documents, there is reason to believe that they had a strong influence on the development of royal inscriptions and thus upon Egyptian historiography in general.[176]

In the Old Kingdom the earliest private tomb inscriptions consisted of honorific titles and lists of offerings to be given to the dead. In time the lists were changed to prayers for offerings while the titles were sometimes expanded to include an account of how at least some of the offices and honors of the deceased were achieved. By the Sixth Dynasty some of the tomb inscriptions had become quite autobiographical, reflecting two major concerns.[177] First, the content of the texts was completely dominated by the association of the deceased with the king. Those activities and services that were rendered on the king's behalf and for which some royal honor was received were mentioned above all else, and the inscriptions belabor the point that the deceased was constantly held in the highest love and esteem by the king, as if nothing else in life counted. The texts also speak, in a rather conventional fashion, of the exemplary behavior of the deceased, who occasionally passes his moral teaching on to his remaining offspring.

The second concern that dominates these biographies is their perspective on the afterlife. They were intended to present the deceased in the best possible light, to influence not only the gods but also the living in the hope that they would make regular offerings for their funerary cult. The deceased was dependent upon the king for regular offerings and even for certain materials in the construction of the tomb itself. Frequently, the tomb was built during the lifetime of the official himself but it may have been completed by his heirs. Because the biographies are obituaries intended to present the deceased in the most favorable light for king, family, and public, they therefore contain nothing critical about the deceased or the state.

From the Eleventh Dynasty onward tomb stelae were set up in the mortuary chapels attached to private tombs as well as in the great temple of Osiris at Abydos so that the god of the dead who is judge in the afterlife

---

175. See general remarks by Gardiner, *Egypt*, pp. 57–60; and Lichtheim, *AEL*, vol. 1, pp. 3–5.

176. Gardiner (*Egypt*, p. 58) estimates that less than 5 percent of the private tombs of high officials actually contain biographies.

177. See the biography of Weni, *BARE*, vol. 1, §§ 291–94, 306–15, 319–24, 325–36, 350–54, 355–85; *ANET*[3], pp. 227–29; Lichtheim, *AEL*, vol. 1, pp. 15–27.

may be reminded of the deceased's good works.[178] Many of these stelae refer to those who might visit the temple and read the stelae, and as a consequence they utter a prayer for offerings on behalf of the deceased, especially if the visitor was favorably impressed with what he read.

The decentralization of the First Intermediate period produced a significant change in style in funerary biographies. The various administrative districts or nomes into which Egypt was divided had gradually come under the domination of certain noble families toward the end of the Old Kingdom, and the office of nomarch had become a hereditary princedom. These nomarchs continued the practice of inscribing their tombs with biographies, but by the time of the First Intermediate period they were ruling their own districts with only a nominal acknowledgment of any pharaoh, and this is reflected in their biographies.[179] These now become a record of their own rule. Even with the reunification of the land in the Middle Kingdom the pharaohs of the Twelfth Dynasty felt it expedient to continue the semiautonomous privileges of these hereditary nomarchs and to incorporate them into the administration of the realm as much as possible.[180]

Belonging to this period are some remarkable family tomb groups of the nomarchs with colorful scenes painted on the tomb walls accompanied by inscriptions. In one such tomb, that of Knumhotep II of the Oryx nome (Beni Hasan),[181] the deceased nomarch carefully outlines the past history of the nome and his family's control over it, with special emphasis upon the establishment of the nome's boundaries under his grandfather by the ruler Amenemhet I. He himself had been confirmed in his office by Senwosret II and mentions the appointment of his sons to the administration of yet other nomes, the result of intermarriage between noble families. This is an instance in which hereditary rights and historical precedent lead to the creation of a historical text covering several generations, which is quite unusual for Egyptian biographical texts. It anticipates by several centuries the similar historical prologues of the Hittite treaties of the late second millennium B.C., in which the Hittite ruler confirms the hereditary succession of the ruler of a vassal state and pledges to continue the relationship between the two states as established by previous generations. Yet this historical form does not appear to have any successors in later periods in Egypt because the power of the nomarchs was severely curtailed by Senwosret III in the latter part of the Middle Kingdom.[182]

178. Lichtheim, *AEL*, vol. 1, pp. 120–30.
179. *BARE*, vol. 1, §§ 391–414; Lichtheim, *AEL*, vol. 1, pp. 83–93.
180. Gardiner, *Egypt*, pp. 128–29; W. C. Hayes, *The Scepter of Egypt*, pp. 171ff.
181. *BARE*, vol. 1, §§ 619–39.
182. See W. C. Hayes, "Notes on the Government of Egypt in the Late Middle Kingdom," *JNES* 12 (1953):31–39.

After the Second Intermediate period the Eighteenth Dynasty again con-
solidated authority in the hands of the pharaoh and a cadre of civil servants, so that the noble families became less prominent. Nevertheless, because of the wealth of the empire many of the private tombs of court
officials were lavishly decorated with scenes and inscriptions, illustrating
and narrating the various careers of the persons buried in them. The tomb
biographies of military men feature their own accounts of exploits on the
battlefield on behalf of their king, and the honors they received. Some of
these recollections are not in chronological order and contain information
not found in the "official record."[183] The tomb of the vizier Rehmires
gives an elaborate description of his investiture and duties, well illustrated
by numerous scenes.[184] These tomb paintings and texts illuminate so
many facets of Egyptian life that they constitute the primary source for our
knowledge about Egyptian society in this period.

The Late period of Egyptian history down to the Persian conquest continues this tradition of private biographies but with some modification.[185]
They still include only the upper level of society, such as the major religious leaders, generals of the army, and high government officials. The
physical form, however, has changed somewhat so that most of the texts
are from statues that were set up in various temples. The stela form is also
found in the temple but more frequently in the necropolis, while inscriptions on the inside of tombs become quite rare. A number of the statues
were set up by those still alive at the time, but in most respects these are no
different from those inscribed on behalf of the deceased.

The literary forms of the inscriptions have also changed from the earlier
period. The combination of a biographical narrative as an expansion of
the titles and honors of the deceased followed by a prayer for offerings becomes quite rare. Instead, the entire inscription is set forth as a direct
speech to the hearer (or reader) and is not restricted just to the prayer for
offering as previously. The lives of those in the biographies are then presented as lessons for posterity, as examples of piety and good conduct. The
purpose of the whole biography becomes strongly didactic. Furthermore,
in place of the request for offerings we frequently find the desire to be remembered and to have one's name repeated in perpetuity by those who
view one's statue or stela. Often an appeal is made to the deity to remember the good works that the deceased has done for the deity and to reward

---

183. *BARE*, vol. 2, §§ 574–92; *ANET*³, pp. 240–41.
184. *BARE*, vol. 2, §§ 663–759; N. de G. Davies, *The Tomb of Rekh-mi-rēʿ at Thebes*, 2
vols.
185. E. Otto, *Die Biographischen Inschriften der ägyptischen Spätzeit*; Lichtheim, *AEL*,
vol. 3, pp. 13–65.

him accordingly. For the living these benefits would have to do with this life, for the dead the hope of being remembered in perpetuity and for a life beyond.

There are several reasons for believing that tomb biographies had a considerable influence upon royal inscriptions and therefore indirectly upon the Egyptian historiographic tradition.[186] Texts containing a recital of historical events, especially military campaigns, occur in tomb biographies long before they make their appearance in royal inscriptions in the Kamose Stelae. The fact that the Seventeenth Dynasty was directly descended from a noble family of Thebes may have been an important factor in the development of such commemorative inscriptions by royalty. The term for recording events in the Annals of Thutmose III is "to make a feast," and according to Otto this comes from the tomb biographies, where the representation of the deceased at a banquet is a prominent feature.[187] The setting up of stelae for public display of a man's deeds is also first of all a tradition of the tomb biographies, and it is a small step to have such royal stelae set up in the temple of Amun as a parallel to mortuary stelae in the temple of Osiris. The tradition of scenes with labels in royal mortuary temples was already practiced in the Old Kingdom, but whether it was continued through the Middle Kingdom and early Empire period cannot be known with any certainty due to a lack of monuments. But since it is clear that the tradition was kept alive in the private tomb murals throughout the intervening periods, the commemorative reliefs of the Eighteenth and Nineteenth dynasties must be a continuation of this genre.

Tomb biographies and royal inscriptions share a large measure of common terminology. Both frequently appeal to the Egyptian people and to future generations to regard one's great deeds and works of piety favorably. Both often include a fervent attestation that what is stated in the inscription is the truth. And what is most important for form-critical considerations, both private biographies and royal inscriptions often have the same complex structure with a variety of genre elements included within the same work, each appropriate to the general *Sitz im Leben* in which it is used. Prose narration may be combined with poetic forms, especially hymns and prayers. Both genres may contain lists or legal enactments, and even elements of wisdom. The fact is that various genre elements could be used in a variety of settings and made appropriate components of that larger unit without being "original" to anything else. The same scribes who put together private tomb texts and scenes could also compose royal

186. See the remark by Gardiner, *Egypt*, p. 56.
187. Otto, "Geschichtsbild und Geschichtsschreibung," *WO* 3:174.

inscriptions and adapt their literary forms accordingly. So it is not difficult to see how what was a traditional element in one setting became a part of a larger form in another. At any rate, on the basis of present evidence, it seems reasonable to suggest that tomb biographies, in their development of the narration of past events, did influence the rise of the royal commemorative inscription and, ultimately, of Egyptian historiography.[188]

The matter can perhaps be taken one step further. In a recent study G. von Rad has shown that certain features of the Memoirs of Nehemiah have a remarkable resemblance to those of the Egyptian biographies of the Late period.[189] Quite apart from the autobiographical style used in both, some other similarities may be noted:

1. The Egyptian biographies, after a short introduction naming the subject of the text, begin with the statement "he says," followed by the body of the inscription. The Book of Nehemiah opens with the heading "The words of Nehemiah the son of Hacaliah," followed by narration in the first person.

2. Both texts have the same kind of religious and social concerns: the restoration of buildings and monuments, the protection of the rights of the weak, the reform and purification of religious institutions, etc. The subject of the text is described as going about his duty to set things right in much the same way.

3. Nehemiah represents a high court official with the same status as the officials in the Egyptian biographies, with similar responsibilities and a similar relationship to the ruler.

4. The statement, "Remember for my good, O God, all that I have done," and the like, which occurs frequently in Nehemiah, corresponds to the petitions for rewards from the gods by the authors of the Egyptian biographies.

5. Nehemiah states that God put it into his heart to undertake his tasks, and this theme is also common to the biographies.

We do not need to minimize the differences between Nehemiah's Memoirs and the Egyptian biographies in order to be convinced that the degree of similarity cannot be fortuitous.[190] Nehemiah, of course, had no cultural contact with Egypt since he came from Susa, a long way in the opposite direction. So we must assume that this style of biographical inscrip-

188. Cf. below (6b) the discussion of the memorial inscriptions of rulers of the Levant, a form that seems to have characteristics of both the commemorative inscription and the memorial biography.
189. Von Rad, "Die Nehemia-Denkschrift," *ZAW* 76 (1964): 176–87.
190. Von Rad, ibid., pp. 186–87, is careful to point out the differences as well as the similarities.

tion was known and used in the Levant as a consequence of Egyptian cultural influence there.[191] If this is the case then the genre of Egyptian biography made a contribution, however indirect, to Israelite historiography and perhaps to that of other regions as well.

191. The extant tomb inscriptions from the Levant are few and mostly quite brief, but since most of the Egyptian tomb inscriptions are not biographical this is not surprising. However, note the interesting statement about Absalom setting up a memorial for himself as a way of perpetuating his memory, 2 Sam. 18:18.

CHAPTER SIX

TEXTS AND INSCRIPTIONS
OF THE LEVANT

In this chapter I consider historiographic texts and inscriptions from the regions of southern Anatolia, Syria, Phoenicia, and Moab. For the second millennium B.C. this limits us to two major sites, both located in the northern part of the region under consideration, Ugarit on the Mediterranean coast and Alalakh on the Orontes. For the first millennium down to about 500 B.C., we include texts in Phoenician and Aramaic, or closely related dialects, but not including the Old Testament. We add to these also works that purport to be from much earlier times but are now preserved in texts of the Greco-Roman period, namely, the Annals of Tyre and the *Phoenician History* of Philo Byblius. The texts that we have from both early and late periods are so few and fragmentary that it is difficult to reconstruct any continuity in the historiographic tradition within the region. To facilitate this effort it seems advisable, therefore, not to consider these texts in a strict chronological sequence but to trace two lines of possible development or continuity of historiographic genre from earliest to latest: first, the royal inscriptions and annals tradition from Alalakh to the Annals of Tyre, and second, the epic and mythological texts from Ugarit to Philo Byblius.

a. THE STATUE OF IDRIMI

The story of the career of Idrimi, king of Alalakh from the mid-fifteenth century B.C., is inscribed upon the front surface of his statue.[1] This remarkable text has no clear literary relationship to the historiographic traditions of the king's contemporaries—the Hittites, Mesopotamians, and Egyptians—although certain features of the work are still worthy of some comparison with the writings of these other regions. Its form is autobio-

---

1. Sidney Smith, *The Statue of Idrimi*; with a translation by A. L. Oppenheim in *ANET*[3], pp. 557–58 (quotations are taken from this translation). A photograph of the statue may be found in *ANEP*[2], p. 156, no. 452.

graphical, beginning with the words "I am Idrimi, the son of Ilimilimma, the servant of Adad, of Hepat and of Ishtar, the Lady of Alalakh, my lady." This identifies both the statue and the subject of the story. The actual scribe, who is very likely the author, is mentioned at the end of the text, and this corresponds to certain Egyptian practices, most notably on the Kamose Stelae. It is also likely that the text was composed after Idrimi's death since it gives the length of his reign and strongly suggests that his son Adadnirari has succeeded him on the throne.

The story begins with an unspecified disaster in Idrimi's ancestral home of Aleppo and the flight of his family to Emar. It tells of his subsequent departure from there and his journeys and adventures until he was eventually established on the throne of Alalakh. During his reign he became reconciled to the Hurrian overlords of the region, was victorious in a campaign against seven Hittite towns, built a palace with the booty, honored the cult of the gods, and reestablished the ancestral ways. The chronology for all these achievements is vague and confusing and no firm dates are given, although it is clear that the events extend over the course of a lifetime.

In his recent remarks on the story of Idrimi, M. Liverani points to the "fairy-tale character" of the account, which is evident both in the preformed pattern of the hero who overcomes adversity to gain the throne and in the use of typical details.[2] Examples of the latter are the expression "seven years" to indicate a long period of time and the contrast between Idrimi's setting out with his groom to make his fortune and his older brothers' inactivity in exile. This is not to deny that historical events do lie behind the story, but it suggests that the account is written to give the king a heroic character, to make his name and his reign especially memorable.

The fact that Idrimi usurped the throne of Alalakh, although he never says so directly, suggests a comparison with the Apology of Ḫattušili III.[3] Both texts are autobiographical in form, dealing with events from their heroes' early youth to their ascent to the throne and some of their subsequent accomplishments and cultic endowments. Both record the events in a rather vague chronological sequence, a significant departure from the previous annalistic style in the case of the Ḫattušili text. However, the differences are also significant. Idrimi makes little reference to divine intervention, mentioning only the favorable omens sent by the god after seven years of wandering, whereas Ḫattušili makes divine guidance and protection by the goddess the constant theme of his work. Idrimi does not mention the previous ruler of Alalakh, whom he replaced, or the reason for his long conflict with his Hurrian overlords, which must have been related to

2. "Memorandum on the Approach to Historiographic Texts," *Orientalia* 42 (1973): 182–83.
3. See above, 4b.

his usurpation of power. His legitimation of power rests upon his final recognition by the Hurrian king Barattarna, confirmed by a treaty. Ḫattušili,
on the other hand, explicitly names his protagonists and rivals and gives
elaborate explanations to justify his seizure of the throne. There is much
less use of obvious folktale models in the Ḫattušili text, although it is no
less biased in the telling.

The folkloristic element in the story of Idrimi calls to mind the so-called
Königsnovelle of Egypt.[4] It does not fit any of the specific story models
usually associated with the *Königsnovelle* but it does suggest the same
tendency to combine folktale elements with historical records of events for
a specific purpose, usually to enhance the "image" of the king. The work
is not propagandistic in the narrow sense of trying to win public support
for any specific actions of the king, but it has a general political function in
projecting an image of the founder of a new dynasty.

A recent study by Jack Sasson takes the question of the insertion of
folktale elements in a historiographic work one step further.[5] Sasson regards the story of Idrimi as a "simulated autobiography," the creation of
Šarruwa the scribe based on his rather slim knowledge of a king of a by-
gone day. Most of the story Sasson regards as invented by the author two
centuries or so after the time it purports to portray. While the story
glorifies the king as hero and founder of a dynasty, it does so through the
mediums of folktale and legend and not by describing his known political
achievements.[6]

If Sasson is correct in his historical and literary assessment, then his
study raises some serious questions about historiography in the Levantine
region since several of the later memorial inscriptions resemble this work.
The story of Idrimi suggests that it was possible for a scribe in a high place
to invent a lifelike portrayal of a dynastic founder in a historical text and

4. For a discussion of this form and the literature on the subject see above, 5f.
5. Jack M. Sasson, "On Idrimi and Šarruwa, the Scribe," in *Studies on the Civilization
and Culture of Nuzi and the Hurrians*, pp. 309–24.
6. The reasons for Sasson's view are numerous and persuasive.
(1) The historical details of the text have always been difficult to fit into the known historical
background of the period of Idrimi's rule.
(2) The story resembles in several features the genre of pseudoautobiography that is known
from Mesopotamia.
(3) The story also makes use of the model of memorial inscriptions that came into vogue at
the end of the Late Bronze and the Early Iron ages.
(4) The art of the statue and the throne also belongs to this late period and not to an earlier
time.
(5) The archaeological data of the statue's find confirm that it belonged to Alalakh IB and the
last phase of the Ishtar temple, in which it occupied a place of honor. It must have been destroyed ca. 1200 B.C. with the city's final destruction.
(6) It is also hard to see how such an anti-Hittite statue could have survived the earlier period
of Hittite hegemony prior to ca. 1250 B.C.

to do this in the interests of nationalism and political propaganda. The story was certainly intended to be taken as fact by the populace, and no doubt the king was greatly venerated because of the exploits recounted in it.

The Old Testament also contains stories of the founders of dynasties, especially Saul and David, who performed legendary exploits in their rise from obscurity to the monarchy. While scholars have drawn parallels to the Idrimi story in arguing for the historicity of early Hebrew historiography, the comparison may more correctly point in the opposite direction. The similarities between the story of Idrimi and the biblical stories should not be pressed too far; however, they do at least suggest that heroic and folkloristic elements could quite easily be applied to such founding monarchs and become part of the historiographic tradition.

b. MEMORIAL INSCRIPTIONS IN THE LEVANT

The statue of Idrimi represents a genre of memorial inscription whose formal and stylistic features have a long tradition in western Asia. Examples of this genre are the Hittite text of Šuppiluliuma II and subsequent Hittite hieroglyphic texts; Phoenician and Aramaic texts from Karatepe, Zinjirli, Byblos, and Hamath; and the Moabite Stone. The following features may be noted:[7]

1. The texts begin with the statement "I am RN_1, son of RN_2, king. . . ." This is unlike the usual Egyptian royal inscription, which begins with a date, or the Hittite annalistic texts, which have the form of an edict: "Thus says RN. . . ." Middle Assyrian royal inscriptions, however, have a form that is much closer to this western style.

2. The introductions frequently contain a statement about the favor of the deity and the king's accession to the throne through divine election. This is not a part of the Idrimi inscriptions, perhaps because the body of the text tells how he gained the throne. But it is a common feature of introductions to Egyptian and Mesopotamian royal inscriptions.

3. The body of the text deals with royal deeds. No attention, however, is paid to chronology or dating of events. Thus the texts show no evidence that an annalistic tradition was used in their composition. They were not written to commemorate a specific accomplishment or victory in battle but, as Miller stresses,[8] they have the character of a memorial inscription

---

7. See especially the form-critical discussion of Max Miller, "The Moabite Stone as a Memorial Stela," *PEQ* 104 (1974): 9–18. The present discussion is indebted to his many important observations.

8. Ibid., pp. 9, 12–13.

composed after a considerable period of time. This is also supported by their inclusion of a list of the king's virtues and a statement of his desire to be remembered after death in perpetuity.

4. Some texts contain a blessing upon those who remember the name of the king or a request for blessing from the god, and most include a curse upon anyone who does harm to the inscription or obliterates the name in it. Although such blessings and curses are sometimes found in Egyptian commemorative and biographical stelae, they are a regular feature of Assyrian royal inscriptions.

With these general features in mind let us look at some of the individual inscriptions in greater detail.

From Karatepe comes a bilingual inscription in Phoenician and Hittite hieroglyphs, dating from the late eighth century B.C.[9] In it Azitawadda, king of Adana, tells of his establishment of peace and prosperity in his own time ("in my days"), his military prowess and the security of the borders, and especially his building of a city named after himself at the command of the gods.[10] He appeals for a blessing from the gods upon the royal house and pronounces a curse upon anyone who removes the inscriptions with the king's name from the gateway of the city.

The presence of the hieroglyphic text establishes the cultural continuity of the region of Adana with the Neo-Hittite culture of North Syria and southern Anatolia, but this text has little in common with the older Hittite annalistic tradition. In some respects it is closer in style to Egyptian biographical stelae, many of which contain similar appeals to the gods for blessings because of piety and good deeds and a concern to perpetuate one's name.[11]

At the site of Zinjirli a number of Phoenician and Aramaic inscriptions from the ninth and eighth centuries B.C. have been found. In the earliest a certain Kilamuwa[12] compares his own accomplishments with those of several of his predecessors and claims to have surpassed them all. He also presents himself as a great boon to his people and concludes with a curse upon any who might destroy his monument. In a recent study F. M. Fales, following Liverani's treatment of Idrimi, draws attention to the literary qualities of this text.[13] He points out that an effort is made, not only in this work but in most of the texts in this genre, to present the king in a highly favorable light so that his own days always seem much better than

9. Donner and Röllig, *KAI*, no. 16; *ANET*[3], pp. 653–54.
10. This is a common feature of Assyrian royal inscriptions from Tukulti-Ninurta I onward.
11. See above, 5h.
12. Donner and Röllig, *KAI*, no. 24; *ANET*[3], pp. 654–55.
13. Fales, "Kilamuwa and the Foreign Kings," *WO* 10 (1979): 6–22. See also Sasson, "On Idrimi," pp. 320–22.

the past and so that he seems in many respects greater, wiser, and more deserving of honor than his foreign contemporaries. To agree with Fales in regarding such texts as propaganda may be stretching the term too far, but they do have some of the same rhetorical qualities as political propaganda. In most cases, however, the concern seems to be less to promote a king's policies and more to ensure that future generations will regard his name highly.

About a century later comes the inscription of Panammu I on the colossal statue of Hadad.[14] It tells how the king in his youth received from the gods the authority to rule and how subsequent prosperity led to successive building, including the setting up of the statue of Hadad and its cult place. The king hopes that a future son and heir will both honor the cult of Hadad and remember the "soul" of Panammu with offerings, and he invokes a curse upon any successor who does not do these things. The final part of the text is concerned with the problem of regular and legitimate succession and especially the elimination of violence within the royal household. In this regard it is reminiscent of the Proclamation of Telepinu,[15] but the similarity is perhaps only fortuitous. This inscription raises another issue, noted by Miller,[16] namely, that it belongs also to the genre of dedication inscriptions. But many of these texts from the Levant combine the element of dedication or votive inscription with commemoration or memorial, as do the Egyptian and Mesopotamian texts.

A few generations after Panammu I, Barrakab dedicated a statue to his father, Panammu II,[17] in which the opening line, "This statue Barrakab has set up for his father," does not follow the usual form, "I am RN. . . ." Nevertheless, it is clearly a memorial inscription written after the death of Panammu II. It tells in vivid terms how the royal family, and with it the whole land, went through a severe crisis during a period of civil strife, but Panammu II survived and regained the throne. He returned the country to prosperity and gained honor with his Assyrian overlord. The inscription further recounts Panammu's death and Barrakab's succession, at which point the regular form is used: "And I Barrakab, son of Panammu. . . ." It ends with a statement about the setting up of his father's memorial (zkr). It is striking how similar the form of this text is to the Hittite memorial text of Šuppiluliuma II for his father, Tudḫaliya IV, which also speaks of the king setting up a special monument for his father with his great deeds inscribed on it.[18] Barrakab composed a second text using the regular form

14. Donner and Röllig, *KAI*, no. 214; Gibson, *SSI* II, no. 13.
15. See above, 4b.
16. *PEQ* 104:10ff.
17. Donner and Röllig, *KAI*, no. 215; Gibson, *SSI* II, no. 14.
18. H. G. Güterbock, "The Hittite Conquest of Cyprus Reconsidered," *JNES* 26 (1967):73–81.

in which he speaks of his construction of a new palace and further follows the usual pattern of comparing himself favorably with all his predecessors.[19]

From Byblos comes a votive inscription of Yehawmilk dated to the fifth or fourth century B.C.[20] Yet it begins with the opening line of a memorial inscription: "I am Yehawmilk, king of Byblos, son of . . . whom the mistress, the Lady of Byblos, made king over Byblos." The text is taken up with a description of the votive objects and it concludes with a curse upon anyone who removes the king's name from these gifts. However, there is also a short unit calling upon the goddess to bless and prosper the king because "he is a righteous king." This theme occurs also in memorial inscriptions, as we have seen.

The Stela of Zakkur, king of Hamath from the late ninth or early eighth century B.C., is dedicated in the opening line to the god Ilwer.[21] But this indicates only the place of its safekeeping in the god's temple and not its genre, which is a memorial stela of the usual type. Most of it seems to commemorate a remarkable deliverance from a siege in the royal city of Hadrach by the god Baalshamayn. In the siege Zakkur was opposed by a coalition of sixteen kings, led by Barhadad of Damascus. Subsequent to this, at the lowest point in his fortunes, he firmly reestablished his position and carried out much building. The text also ends with a curse upon anyone who removes the stela from its place.

The Moabite Stone also belongs to the genre of memorial inscriptions, as Miller has clearly demonstrated.[22] It dates to the mid-ninth century B.C. and was set up by Mesha, king of Moab, in honor of the god Chemosh and as a review of the king's thirty-year reign. Mesha portrays the bad times under his father's rule, when Chemosh was angry with his land[23] and it was subject to Israel, and the complete reversal of fortune during his own reign ("in my days"), in which he won numerous victories and achieved complete liberation. Mesha also tells of his building of a citadel in Dibon as well as other construction projects, with the result that the text represents a lifetime of achievements. Since the temporal relationships between events are unclear, as in the other texts, and no dating of events is indicated, even the order of events may not be chronological. Miller has

19. Donner and Röllig, *KAI*, no. 216; *ANET*[3], p. 655; Gibson, *SSI* II, no. 15.
20. Donner and Röllig, *KAI*, no. 10; *ANET*[3], p. 656.
21. Donner and Röllig, *KAI*, no. 202; *ANET*[3], pp. 655–56; Thomas, *DOTT*, pp. 242–43; Gibson, *SSI* II, no. 5.
22. See above, n. 7. For the text and translations see Donner and Röllig, *KAI*, no. 181; *ANET*[3], pp. 320–21; Thomas, *DOTT*, pp. 195–203; Gibson, *SSI* I, pp. 71–83.
23. Compare the situation in the statue for Panammu II set up by Barrakab, which seems to suggest a curse upon his father's household from which his father was delivered (see Gibson, *SSI* II, p. 82, note to line 2). See also the Plague Prayers of Muršili (*ANET*[3], pp. 394–96).

pointed to a number of parallels, both in phraseology and in the themes treated, with the other texts of this group, especially the Karatepe inscription of Azitawadda.[24]

The general uniformity of these memorial texts in the Levant, especially in the ninth and eighth centuries B.C. from Karatepe in the north to Moab in the southeast, suggests that such texts were probably not unknown in Israel and Judah, even if none has yet been found. They bear some resemblance to the Assyrian display inscriptions but there is no evidence that they rest upon an annalistic tradition comparable to the Assyrian annals. They functioned primarily as memorials of a king's career, with highlights upon a few important events and building achievements but with no attempt to establish a chronological framework.

c. THE ANNALS OF TYRE

The Annals of Tyre are mentioned only in the works of Josephus.[25] He says they were translated into Greek by a certain Menander of Ephesus, who probably lived in the second century B.C., and from this source Josephus occasionally quotes the Annals. He also mentions a work by Dius, a historian of the Phoenicians,[26] but it is doubtful that it constitutes an independent witness to the Annals since plagiarism of another's history without due credit was a common practice among Hellenistic historians.[27]

It is not appropriate here to enter into a critical evaluation of the use of these sources for the reconstruction of Phoenician and Israelite history. The only question that must be raised is whether the transmission of the Annals through what is obviously a complex process to what remains of them in Josephus is reliable.[28] A basic problem is that Hellenistic and Greco-Roman historians sometimes quote ancient authorities directly and sometimes paraphrase and interpret them in a biased and inaccurate fashion. This can be illustrated from Josephus's use of the Annals. At times he refers to their content indirectly, suggesting that they contain references to biblical material, such as the building of Solomon's Temple. But when he

24. *PEQ* 104:13ff.
25. *Antiquities of the Jews* VIII:144–46; 324; IX:283–87; *Contra Apionem* I:116–25, 155–58. The text editions used were those in the Loeb Classical Library by H. St. J. Thackeray and R. Marchus.
26. *Ant.* VIII:147–49; *Contra Ap.* I:112–15.
27. Cf. H. J. Katzenstein, *The History of Tyre*, pp. 78–79, where he treats both Dius and Menander as separate witnesses to the Annals.
28. See Katzenstein, ibid., pp. 78, 88–89. One has the distinct feeling that Josephus has used the work of Eupolemus to supplement his remarks about Solomon's relations with Tyre. On Eupolemus see B. Z. Wacholder, *Eupolemus: A Study of Judaeo-Greek Literature*, esp. pp. 52–57.

quotes the Annals directly in support of his statements it is clear that the Annals do not contain any information about Solomon's Temple.

In his attempt to demonstrate the antiquity of the Jewish nation, Josephus wants to show that the construction of the Temple can be dated precisely to 143 years and 8 months before the founding of Carthage, a datum that was used as a benchmark in Greco-Roman historiography.[29] To do this he excerpts statements from the Annals giving the length of life and reign of each king from Hiram's accession to the end of the reign of Pygmalion (see table), and since Carthage was founded in this king's seventh year the total that Josephus obtains is 155 years and 8 months. He then states that since the Temple was built in the twelfth year of Hiram he arrives at the figure of 143 years and 8 months.[30]

Chronology of Kings of Tyre according to Josephus
(with emendations suggested by Albright [A] and Katzenstein [K])

King's Name	Age at Death	Length of Reign	Age at Accession
Hiram	53	34	19
Balbazer (son)	43	17	26
Abdastratus (son)	39 (29-A)	9	30
	break in dynasty		
Methusastartus	54	12	42
Astharymus (brother)	58	9	49
Phelles (brother)	50	8 months	50
	break in dynasty		
Ithobal	48 (68-A,K)	32	16
Balezor (son)	45	6	39
Metten (son)	32	29 (9-A,K)	3
Pygmalion (son)	58	47	11

Scholars have been quick to recognize the many problems with this section, and various solutions have been proposed. First, it seems doubtful that the Annals contained any reference to Solomon's Temple, let alone a precise date in Hiram's reign for its completion. Katzenstein notes that since 1 Kings 6:38 indicates that the Temple was completed in Solomon's eleventh year and dedicated in his twelfth year (1 Kings 8:2), this accounts for Josephus's dating of the Temple's completion in Hiram's eleventh or twelfth year.[31]

Second, the Annals, as quoted by Josephus, state that Balbazer (Baalezer) lived 43 years and reigned 17 and that he was succeeded by his son Abdastratus, who lived 39 years and reigned 9. This would make the latter 30 years old at his father's death, which means that his father was only

29. On the founding of Carthage see G. C. and C. Picard, *The Life and Death of Carthage*, pp. 28–35, for a critical evaluation of the evidence.
30. *Contra Ap.* I:121–26.
31. Katzenstein, *Tyre*, p. 83.

13 years of age when he was born. Albright reduces Abdastratus's age by 10 years;[32] Katzenstein, on the other hand, suggests that Abdastratus was really the son of Hiram and the brother of Balbazer.[33] The latter solution is unlikely since the Annals elsewhere are careful to specify when a brother succeeded to the throne. It is easier to suggest that the numerals have become corrupted, but changes in any of them are rather arbitrary.

Third, the text points to a series of usurpers of the throne, all brothers, but only three are subsequently listed with names, ages, and lengths of reigns. Scholars have been undecided as to whether a fourth ruler should be added, and if so, how long he reigned. At least one version does add an additional 12 years.[34]

Fourth, Ithobal is said to have lived 48 years and reigned 32, which would make him 16 years old when he gained the throne by assassinating the previous ruler. Because he was the "priest," that is, the high priest, of Astarte it is highly unlikely that he was only 16. Both Katzenstein and Albright add 20 years to his life.[35] Some emendation is demanded by the figures given for the next king, Balezor, because as the text stands he was 39 at his father's death, which, if that figure remains at 48, would create a problem with the father's age at Balezor's birth. The next king, Metten, is said to have lived 32 years and reigned 29, but that would make him only three at his accession. Katzenstein and Albright deduct 20 years from this reign on the basis of some versional evidence. Katzenstein then adds this 20 years to Balezor's reign, which would make his father 49 years old at his birth.[36] Albright, on the strength of an Assyrian royal inscription, proposes inserting an additional king, Baalmanzer, into the list after Balezor and giving him the 20 years deducted from Metten.[37]

It is not my intention to debate the merits of each of these emendations. However, the proposals of both Katzenstein and Albright suggest that there is some value in retaining the total of 155 years and 8 months given by Josephus. But since we cannot be certain that corruptions were kept out of the transmission process prior to Josephus's text, that figure has little importance. With the text of the Annals suspect at so many points, it can be used only with the greatest caution in any historical reconstruction.[38] This is not to deny that the Annals fragments in Josephus preserve some-

32. W. F. Albright, "The New Assyro-Tyrian Synchronism and the Chronology of Tyre," *AIPHO* 13 (1953):6.

33. *Tyre,* pp. 126–27.

34. Albright, *AIPHO* 13:6, n. 1.

35. Katzenstein, *Tyre,* p. 129; Albright, *AIPHO* 13:7.

36. Katzenstein, *Tyre,* p. 119.

37. Albright, *AIPHO* 13:2ff.

38. Albright's chronological scheme for the history of Israel, also reflected in the work of John Bright, *A History of Israel,* 2d ed., p. 190, n. 28, p. 206, n. 65, is heavily dependent upon the accuracy of this 155 years.

thing of their original historiographic form and genre. But if there is good reason to suspect some corruption in the transmission, then the only way to evaluate the Annals' form and character is by comparing them with known and extant historiographic genres.

It is surprising how often the view is expressed that the form of the Annals is self-evident. Scholars assume that all the courts of the Near East kept annals and that whatever Josephus says is in the Annals of Tyre is appropriate to such a form.[39] They cite the reference in the Journey of Wenamun to the "journal rolls" of the kings of Byblos as evidence that annals were kept at Phoenician courts since the second millennium.[40] Even if we take this reference as a historical, and not just a fictional, statement it probably refers to nothing more than economic accounts and records. Such "daybooks," maintained on papyri, were known from ancient Egypt, just as in Mesopotamia elaborate economic records were kept on clay tablets. To assume that because the peoples of the Fertile Crescent kept such economic records they also kept annals of their rulers is unwarranted.

To what extent do the Annals of Tyre really reflect the genre of annals as we know it from Egypt, the Hittites, and Mesopotamia? Katzenstein suggests, on the basis of a reference to the "deeds of Ithobalos, King of Tyre," that these annals were the compilation of the annals of the individual kings.[41] First, in those regions where annals of kings were composed, such a compilation would not furnish the precise length of a king's reign or the length of his life. This kind of information could be gained only from a document such as a king list, which both Assyria and Egypt also kept but which so far has not been found among the ruins of the Hittites.

The second observation that we can make about the Annals is that events within the reign of a particular king are rarely dated, whereas we would expect precise dates in annalistic texts. The only date that would appear to come from the Annals is, "in the seventh year of his [Pygmalion's] reign his sister took flight and built the city of Carthage in Libya." This is indeed a strange entry to find in a royal annal and very likely derives from a popular etiological tale long after the founding of the city.[42] The more direct detailed quotations from the reigns of Hiram, Ithobal, and Elulaios attach no dates to the events enumerated. The dates given for the siege of Tyre by Nebuchadnezzar and the rise of Cyrus to power do not come directly from the quotation of the "Phoenician record"

39. See Katzenstein, *Tyre*, p. 77.
40. On Wenamun see above, 5f.
41. *Tyre*, p. 117.
42. *Contra Ap.* I:125. It is quite likely that Josephus or his source knew the popular story told by the fourth-century B.C. historian Timaeus and reflected in the Roman historian Justin (XVIII, 4–6) on the dating of the founding of Carthage and did his own calculation. See G. C. and C. Picard, *The Life and Death of Carthage*, pp. 30ff.

but appear to be part of Josephus's own calculation, which may be no more trustworthy than his earlier dating of the Temple's completion.[43] At any rate, Near Eastern annals have a love for precise dates, and these are conspicuous by their absence in the Annals of Tyre.

The fragment of the Annals that speaks about the deeds of Hiram, apart from the anecdote over Solomon's riddle contest, and the two quotations dealing with Ithobal and Elulaios could have come from the same kind of memorial inscription discussed above. Since Tyre suffered very little destruction over a long period, it is possible that at a late date in Persian or Hellenistic times a historian could have made summaries of a number of such monuments and combined them with a king list. As we have seen above,[44] such king lists could supply the length of reign, filiation, and even short notices on changes in dynastic succession and usurpation of power through assassinations.[45]

This still leaves open the question of when anecdotal material such as the story about the riddle contest between Hiram and Solomon and the reference to the founding of Carthage were added. They may have been added when the "history" was first put together or in the Hellenistic period, when such cultural connections and borrowings were very much in vogue. At any rate, the Annals of Tyre do not give us information about the keeping of annals per se in the Levant from the tenth to the sixth centuries B.C. But they may suggest how nationalistic histories were composed when such histories came into literary vogue throughout the Near Eastern and Hellenic world.

d. THE LITERATURE OF UGARIT

It is an open question whether or not the literature of ancient Ugarit merits any place in a volume on historiography.[46] The literary texts are chiefly mythological or legendary, composed in a rather uniform epic

43. *Ant.* IX:154–59.
44. See 3b, on the Assyrian king lists.
45. What cannot be derived from the Mesopotamian or Egyptian type of king list is the length of a king's life. But we will see below (9a) that the Judean king-list tradition did preserve this kind of information.
46. Cf. most recently N. Wyatt, "Some Observations on the Idea of History among the West Semitic Peoples," *UF* 11 (1979): 825–32. Wyatt regards both the ʿAnat-Baal myth cycle and the Keret texts as historiographic works. But only by a rather euhemeristic interpretation of the former and a rather forced interpretation of the latter can they be considered historiography. The literature on the Ugaritic texts has become voluminous and there is little point in citing numerous works here. For a guide to bibliography see M. Dietrich, *Ugarit-Bibliographie*, AOAT 20. A convenient collection of some of the major alphabetic literary texts may be found in *ANET*[3], pp. 129–55; Thomas, *DOTT*, pp. 118–33.

style.[47] Apart from these poetic narrative texts little else that has been found can be regarded as belonging to any historiographic genre. Yet some scholars would argue that the roots of at least some later Hebrew, Phoenician, and even Greek historiographic concerns lie in the kind of epic material represented by the Ugaritic texts. This is really a continuation of the issue raised much earlier, that epic is viewed by some scholars as the precursor of historiographic prose.[48] Nothing thus far in the literary remains of ancient Greece, Mesopotamia, the Hittites, and Egypt has pointed to such a conclusion. But because the advocates of this view place most of their emphasis upon the close linguistic and literary association between the Ugaritic and Hebrew literatures,[49] we must give some attention to the matter here.

The legend of King Keret is the story of a king of Khubur, a demigod ("son of 'El"), who has met with a series of disasters in which his wife and all his children have died.[50] While in deep despair he receives a dream vision from 'El who reveals to him how he may obtain a new wife and hence new offspring by conquering the realm of Udum and marrying the defeated king's daughter. All this comes about and Keret again has numerous offspring. But it appears that he has forgotten some of his vows in the process, and the result is the working out of a curse by which he becomes ill and is about to die. Once again 'El intervenes and creates a woman who has the power to heal him, which she does. At this point Yassib, the eldest son, who thinks that Keret is still sick, approaches his father in order to persuade him to give up his throne. Keret replies with a curse, at which point the text breaks off.

According to a colophon the text was composed by a certain Elimelech in about the mid-fourteenth century B.C., although some scholars think it is much older.[51] Keret has been identified with a Kirta, the founder of the Mitanni Kingdom in the sixteenth century B.C., but the location of the land of Khubur is uncertain, and if the story did have such a foreign origin nothing in it points any longer to Keret as the founder of a dynasty. Nor is there any hint of a connection with the city of Ugarit. Since nothing suggests that the story relates to the people's past or constitutes an identity-

---

47. See W. F. Albright, *Yahweh and the Gods of Canaan*, pp. 4ff. Albright uses the term epic for both the mythological and the legendary texts. F. M. Cross, *Canaanite Myth and Hebrew Epic*, pp. viii–ix, appears to distinguish between the Canaanite myths and epic. He continues to use the term epic for the Keret and Aqhat stories but only the term myth for the Baal cycle. The distinction, however, is based not on form but on content and what Cross regards as the religious function of the text.
48. See above, 2b, and below, 7b.
49. As in the works of Albright and Cross cited in n. 47.
50. *ANET*³, pp. 142–49.
51. Albright, *YGC*, p. 5, n. 9.

tradition,[52] it cannot be construed to function historiographically in a way that was certainly the case for the *Iliad* of Homer.

This point needs to be stressed because recently F. M. Cross has tried to see in the story of Keret an epic that functions much like the patriarchal stories of Genesis.[53] He makes the connection, first of all, on the level of a supposed similarity between the god 'El in the Ugaritic texts and *'el* in the Genesis stories. The notion of an "'El, god of the fathers" in the patriarchal stories, however, is debatable and Cross's dependence upon such late texts as Gen. 14 and 17 is unacceptable.[54] Second, the fact that both Keret and Abraham are in need of offspring is a slim basis upon which to compare these stories. Gunkel could cite much closer parallels to this theme from classical folktales.[55] Cross also makes much of a nocturnal or dream revelation to the heroes, but this is such a common motif in the ancient world that its use of both stories is hardly significant. We have already seen that there is no *a priori* reason for assuming that epic sources must lie behind the prose narratives of Genesis, so that the difference between the prose form of the one and the epic form of the other is significant.[56] Furthermore, the patriarchal stories do function as identity-traditions in portraying for the Israelite who he is and where he came from. Abraham's role as the progenitor of the people and the beginning of their history is altogether different from that of Keret, who is merely the hero of a foreign domain in a vague past. Whether the story was intended to be anything more than a piece of entertainment can no longer be determined.

It seems likely that the people of Ugarit did venerate the ancestral kings of the city. A king list in alphabetic script has been published, and in spite of lacunae it suggests entries for about thirty names of kings.[57] They are all introduced with the designation "god," indicating that they are deceased, which is similar to Egyptian and Hittite practice. Since the list does not give any chronological data or filiation, its function is clearly cultic.

K. Kitchen has recently discussed the list and comes to the conclusion that the order of names is not from the oldest to the youngest but from the most recent back to the "founder."[58] He also suggests that the list's func-

---

52. By the term *identity-tradition* I refer to a story like the Exodus by which a people explain who they are in terms of their origins and their constitution as a people. For a discussion of the role of identity-traditions in ancient Israel see J. Van Seters, "Tradition and Social Change in Ancient Israel," *Perspectives in Religious Studies* 7 (1980):96–113.

53. Cross, *Canaanite Myth*, pp. 182–83.

54. See my discussion in "The Religion of the Patriarchs in Genesis," *Biblica* 61 (1980): 220–33.

55. H. Gunkel, *Genesis*, s.v. "Griechisches und Römisches," in the *Sachregister*.

56. See below, 7b.

57. M. Dietrich, O. Loretz, and J. Sanmartín, *Die keilalphabetischen Texte aus Ugarit*. Pt. 1: *Transcription*, AOAT 24, p. 119, text 1.113, verso.

58. K. A. Kitchen, "The King List of Ugarit," *UF* 9 (1977): 131–42.

tion was to venerate the dead kings. For both proposals there are Mesopotamian and Egyptian parallels. Kitchen also believes that the list represents
only one dynasty, but since no filiation is given this is far from certain. The
cultic lists of Egypt certainly contain sequences of kings that belonged to
more than one dynasty, and both Hittite and Mesopotamian rulers often
refer back to "founding" kings as their ancestors.[59]

If Kitchen's interpretation of this list is correct then it is clear that Keret
did not play a role in any such ancestral veneration. Kitchen has tried to fit
him into the scheme by placing him before the entire list, which would put
Keret by Kitchen's reckoning into the third millennium B.C.[60] However, if
it is correct that the name Kirta is Indo-Aryan and associated with the
kingdom of Mitanni then this suggestion is hardly possible.[61] There is,
therefore, at present no evidence to suggest that Keret was an ancestor or
royal model for the people of Ugarit.

It might not be immediately apparent how the mythological epics have
any relevance for the question of historiography, but these have become
associated more and more with the theogonic and cosmogonic texts of
early Greece, as well as with the *Phoenician History* of Philo Byblius. As
we have seen above,[62] the earliest Greek "historians," the so-called logographers, made use of this material in an attempt to construct a bridge between the creation of gods and men and the known history of the Greek
and neighboring peoples. The association of the Ugaritic myths with these
later writings is based upon the resemblance of a number of motifs and
story elements, and it may very well be that through a long and complex
tradition-history the older mythological material was transmitted to later
times. But what still remains at issue is whether or not a cosmogony is reflected in the Ugaritic myths.

Cross has recently argued in favor of a cosmogony in these texts for two
reasons. First, he interprets those elements in the various myths that resem-

59. The so-called dynastic seal with the name of the founder, "Yaqaru, son of Niqmad,"
on it, which Kitchen (p. 132) identifies with the oldest name on the cultic list, may have been
used in later periods to maintain the *fiction* of continuity. Cf. the useful article by A. F.
Rainey, "The Kingdom of Ugarit," *BA* 28 (1965):102-25.

60. Kitchen, *UF* 9:140-41.

61. Cf. Albright, *YGC*, p. 5, n. 9; p. 118, n. 19.

62. Cross (in *Canaanite Myth*, p. 41) makes the following suggestion:

The particular wars of 'Ēl are to establish his headship in the family of the gods. His
wars are against his father Šamêm, "Heaven," in behalf of his wronged mother Arṣ
"Earth"; the two, Heaven and Earth are the last of the theogonic pairs. 'Ēl takes his sis-
ters to wife and emasculates his father.

This is a reconstructed theogony that does not correspond to any known text and is not
found in the Ugaritic myths. Indeed, if the title 'ēl qōnê 'arṣ, "'El, creator of earth," is an
old epithet, then it can scarcely be squared with this reconstruction.

ble the stories in Hesiod or Philo Byblius as having the same cosmogonic significance. But there is not the slightest clue within the Ugaritic texts themselves that either in part or as a whole they must be so interpreted, and to do so entails a rather severe dismemberment of the stories.[63] Furthermore, since the same story motifs are not used in the same way or with the same or corresponding deities in all the parallel sources, their significance is hardly consistent. For instance, Baal's struggle with Prince Yam ("Sea") cannot have the same meaning as Marduk's victory over Tiamat, which is clearly cosmogonic.

The second way in which Cross finds cosmogony in the Ugaritic texts is to redefine cosmogony.[64] He suggests that whereas theogony uses the language of time, cosmogony may or may not do so. This argument is intolerable since it merely defines the critical term in such a way as to overcome the major objection to its use for the Ugaritic texts. Cosmogony has to do with the origin, structure, and development of the universe, and that entails movement. In the Ugaritic texts there is no creation, no development, no movement from one stage to another whatsoever. It is true that there are older gods such as 'El and younger ones such as Baal, but no text shows any transition from one generation of gods to another. We can say exactly the same for the gods in the *Iliad,* but no one would suggest that the *Iliad,* with all its divine rivalries, is a cosmogony.

Cross's position would be more persuasive if evidence could be found apart from the Ugaritic myths for a cosmogony or theogony in the religious traditions of the West, in Phoenician and Aramaic texts. Indeed Cross finds such evidence in the list of divine witnesses in the Sefire treaty inscription.[65] It is important for this discussion to quote the full text of gods (i A 7–12):

> This treaty, which Barga'yah has concluded, [he has set up in the presence of . . . . . .] and MLŠ, in the presence of Marduk and Zarpanit, in the presence of Nabu and [Tashmet, in the presence of Irra and Nus]k, in the presence of Nergal and Las, in the presence of Shamash and Nur, in the presence of Sin [and Nikkal . . . . . .], in the presence of NKR and KD'H, in the presence of all the gods of the open country and the cultivated ground, [in the presence of Hadad of] Aleppo, in the presence of the Seven, in the presence of El and Elyon, in the presence of Heaven [and Earth, in the presence of Abyss] and Springs, in the presence of Day and Night.[66]

63. Cross, *Canaanite Myth,* pp. 113ff.
64. Ibid., p. 120.
65. For the text see Donner and Röllig, *KAI,* no. 222; *ANET*[3], pp. 659–60; Gibson, *SSI* II, no. 7.
66. Gibson, *SSI* II, p. 29.

Cross comments upon the ordering of this list as follows:

After listing the major patron deities of each party of the treaty, the text then names the high god 'El-and–'Elyon and then goes on to list primordial pairs. . . . Similar sequences are familiar in the Hittite treaties. It will be noted that in the list of witnesses the theogonic sequence is reversed, moving behind the "executive" deities to more fundamental structures that bind even the gods.[67]

Is this interpretation of the text necessary, or even plausible? All the gods listed before 'El and 'Elyon can scarcely be grouped under the rubric of patron. The pairs of old Mesopotamian gods hardly belong to the native cults of the parties involved. The "gods of the open country and the cultivated ground" and the "Seven" (demons?) also represent yet other types of deities. Cross's reference to the Hittite treaty parallels is also instructive.[68] These have gods in a similar sequence but not cited in pairs, and the "older gods"[69] are not the last group, as Cross suggests, but the term used for the gods who are not associated with a particular place within the realms of the treaty partners. The list of natural phenomena at the end contains some obvious pairs but also some names that are not in pairs. There is no evidence here or in any other Hittite text of a cosmogony or theogony involving such elements of nature.[70] Since treaties in this form were also common in the Levant from the last half of the second millennium onward, it is obvious that the form with the gods in this order derives from this source.

Furthermore, it is natural to view the lists as beginning with the most important witnesses to the treaty and moving to the most trivial and obscure. The pair 'El and 'Elyon, which are not male and female, cannot be interpreted as one god, as Cross has done.[71] They are simply two "foreign" gods or terms for deity that are given a rather insignificant place in the list. The three pairs do not make a theogonic or cosmogonic scheme that is otherwise known, and other treaties vary the list. The Esarhaddon treaties suggest that the list of natural elements is just another way of saying "all the gods of heaven and earth" and no more than that.[72] One

---

67. *Canaanite Myth*, pp. 40–41.

68. For convenience see the examples translated by A. Goetze, *ANET*[3], pp. 201–06.

69. So rendered by Goetze, ibid., p. 205a. See also the opening lines of the Kumarbi myth, in which these same gods are also spoken of as the "olden gods" (*ANET*[3], p. 120).

70. The Kumarbi myth (*ANET*[3], pp. 120–21), which appears to be Hurrian in origin, is a theogony that begins with the generations of Alalus and Anu, the olden gods, and the latter's contest with Kumarbi. It does not deal with any earlier theogonic or cosmogonic stage. It is, perhaps, significant that Kumarbi does not appear in the Hittite witness list.

71. See my discussion in *Biblica* 61:227–29.

72. See *ANET*[3], pp. 533–41; D. J. Wiseman, *The Vassal-Treaties of Esarhaddon, Iraq* 20 (1958), pt. 1.

would have to find something much more specific than lists of gods in treaty texts on which to build a case for a theogonic or cosmogonic tradition in the Levant.

e. THE *PHOENICIAN HISTORY* OF PHILO BYBLIUS

Any discussion of the *Phoenician History* by Philo Byblius involves a great deal of controversy and debate which cannot be fully reviewed here. Fortunately, the recent studies by James Barr and R. A. Oden give an excellent survey of past discussion and provide the basis for the remarks that follow below.[73]

The title *History* may be somewhat misleading for the modern student of history because, from what is now known of the work, it does not resemble in the least the Annals of Tyre or deal with political events in historical time. Instead it consists of myths and legends that its author Philo claims to have taken from the works of a certain Sanchuniathon (Sakkunyaton),[74] whom he dates to the time before the Trojan War. The subject matter includes a cosmogony, a technogony (or history of culture),[75] and a history of the rule of Kronos and his successors, understood as mortal rulers who were deified at death. Other passages that may belong to Philo's work deal with the origins of child sacrifice in the time of Kronos and the divine nature of snakes,[76] but these are not important for the present discussion. The themes of cosmogony and technogony, however, were of considerable interest to the early prose writers of ancient Greece as well as to the authors of the early chapters of Genesis, and it is therefore important to consider whether the Canaanite-Phoenician world played a major role in encouraging the treatment of these themes in ancient historiographic writing.

The first issue is the transmission of the text.[77] Most of what we know of the work of Philo Byblius comes to us through quotations in Eusebius's *Praeparatio Evangelica*, which, though extensive, still represent only a small fraction of the whole. Nevertheless, a fair assessment of the nature of

---

73. James Barr, "Philo of Byblos and His 'Phoenician History,'" *BJRL* 57 (1974):17–68; R. A. Oden, "Philo of Byblos and Hellenistic Historiography," *PEQ* 110 (1978):115–26. See also, most recently, A. I. Baumgarten, *The Phoenician History of Philo of Byblos: A Commentary*, 1981. These works contain excellent bibliographies on the subject.

74. Sakkunyaton is the Phoenician form of the name. For discussion of the name with literature see Oden, *PEQ* 110:117–18.

75. The term *technogony* is from Barr. See his useful chart (*BJRL* 57:62–63), which contains a good summary of this selection.

76. See Barr, *BJRL* 57:30. This material is not included in Eusebius.

77. See Barr, ibid., pp. 33–40.

the work seems possible on the basis of these fragments, and scholars generally agree that Eusebius's transmission of Philo is highly trustworthy.

An evaluation of how Philo used his sources, however, produces no such unanimity. Scholars still disagree about whether he actually used an older work by a Phoenician sage, Sanchuniathon, or whether this figure is a literary fiction.[78] The device of adopting a figure and projecting him into the distant past, to the founding period of nations and peoples, is such an obvious ploy for literary authority used by Hellenistic writers that the reference to such an ancient authority here must be considered highly suspect. The fact that Sanchuniathon does happen to be a Phoenician name, although not nearly as old as Philo suggests, cannot be made to bear the whole weight of Philo's reliability.

Biblical scholars, most notably W. F. Albright and O. Eissfeldt,[79] have been moved to put great confidence in the existence and basic reliability of such a figure as Sanchuniathon by the correspondences that they find between the mythological material of the Ugaritic texts and the statements in the *Phoenician History*. Barr, however, has been justifiably critical of the eclectic and fragmentary way in which such correspondences have been found,[80] and it still remains to be demonstrated that any Canaanite-Phoenician tradition of cosmogony existed comparable to what we find in the Greek world, or even in Mesopotamia and Egypt. The latter, according to Oden, still seems to be the best source for the cosmogonic character of the *History*.[81] On all counts it would appear that Philo's *History* represents a highly eclectic and syncretistic work of the Roman period and that the source "Sanchuniathon" represents in a vague way the body of Phoenician tradition as Philo knew it and used with considerable flexibility in his own work.

That the *Phoenician History* is a typical work of Hellenistic historiography is the most important thesis of Oden's study, and he suggests five characteristics of histories in the Greco-Roman age by which to judge Philo's work.[82] One is the appeal to ancient and esoteric sources which can refute later corruptions in the tradition, just as Philo uses "Sanchuniathon." The other characteristics are the euhemeristic treatment of the gods as deceased kings and culture heroes; "the impulse to write history

---

78. The latter opinion was recently expressed by W. Speyer, *Die literarische Fälschung im heidenischen und christlichen Altertum*, pp. 157–58.

79. Albright, *YGC*, pp. 223ff.; O. Eissfeldt, *Sanchunjaton von Berut und Ilumilku von Ugarit* and many additional studies as set out in Barr's bibliography. For a discussion of their views see Barr, *BJRL* 57:19–20; Oden, *PEQ* 107:116–17; Baumgarten, *The Phoenician History*, pp. 1–6.

80. Barr, *BJRL* 57:58–59.

81. Oden, *PEQ* 110:124ff.; see also Baumgarten, *The Phoenician History*, pp. 261ff.

82. *PEQ* 110:118ff.

on a universal scale," both chronologically and geographically; the patriotic concern to demonstrate the nation's antiquity and achievements; and the antagonism toward Greek culture and claims, and the propensity to correct Greek authors.

That Philo can be seen to fit all these criteria seems clear, and yet this does not necessarily impugn all his source material any more than in the case of Manetho and Berossus. But it does mean that we must be cautious and critical whenever we might suspect these tendencies of affecting his presentation. This is particularly true of the euhemerism that may have been responsible for the particular arrangement of the material in its present order.[83] But the real problem is to judge the degree to which these characteristics were already anticipated by certain tendencies in the Near Eastern world before the rise of Hellenism. For instance, there is the long tradition in western Asia, attested among the Hittites and at Ugarit, that kings became deified at death, and within the Mesopotamian and Egyptian king-list tradition gods and demigods are listed as reigning before mortals. If we add to this the tradition of a Late Babylonian theogony,[84] in which successive generations of gods who rule as kings are murdered and then buried in their own city, it takes a rather small step for a rationalistic thinker to give a euhemeristic interpretation to mythologies and cosmogonies.

Universalism is another characteristic tendency in pre-Hellenistic material. The Mesopotamian and Egyptian traditions certainly manifest a universalism of time although not of geography. But the Yahwistic and Priestly sources of the Pentateuch manifest both and would have to be judged as fitting Oden's criterion. Nowhere else in the Near East is there any such comparable example of universalism within a historiographic work. Was there such a tendency within Phoenicia contemporaneous with the Pentateuchal sources?

The characteristics of patriotic history and of polemic against a rival culture may also fit biblical historiography. The Yahwist can be interpreted in several places as engaged in a *Kulturkampf* with both Babylonian and Canaanite civilizations, not only in the obvious cases of the Tower of Babel story and the curse of Canaan but in a number of more subtle examples throughout his work in which he handles comparable traditions. However, Philo's patriotism and polemic against the Greeks seem to be clearly a product of Hellenism and the typical attitude of cultural minorities within the Roman Empire.

The ordering of the material in Philo's *History* is curious, with the the-

83. Barr, *BJRL* 57:33–34.

84. W. G. Lambert and P. Walcot, "A New Babylonian Theogony and Hesiod," *Kadmos* 4 (1965):65–72; cf. Albright, *YGC*, pp. 93ff.

ogony coming after the technogony and not related to or part of the cosmogony. In fact, Philo insists that the names Ouranos ("heaven") and Gē ("earth") are not to be understood cosmogonically. This also fits the combination of Earth, Sea, and River with other gods in the Babylonian theogony, where the text is not a cosmogony. Furthermore, there is a degree of overlap among the three sections. Thus, for instance, we find *Samēmroumos*, "high heavens," in the sixth generation of the technogony and Ouranos, "heaven," in the second generation of the theogony, whereas we might have expected them to come before both of these sections in the cosmogony. It would appear, instead, that the three sections really represent three different types of traditions. The cosmogony reflects Egyptian cosmogonic traditions, the theogony Babylonian, and the technogony more native Phoenician with its large incidence of Semitic terms.

The gods (deified mortals) in the technogony represent a curious mixture of divine epithets, elements of nature, classes or groups and professions, qualities, and personal names.[85] One has the impression that these are all viewed as minor deities and that the elements of nature cannot be extracted and derived from a cosmogony. Thus the four mountains —Kassios, Lebanon, Antilebanon and Brathu—which are said to be four deified giants who gave their names to mountains, correspond to the divine mountains in the treaty witness list. But the whole work is so eclectic in character that it would be impossible to reconstruct a tradition-history of its various parts. Yet it would be useful to keep in mind its general pattern of cosmogony, technogony, and theogony, interpreted as the most primitive history, when we consider the histories of Genesis.

We have good reason to believe that Phoenicia was a highly literate society that produced works of literary merit, but if this was so then the extant remains are a great disappointment. They allow us to say very little with certainty about Phoenicia's role in the rise of historiography. Not only are we lacking the native historiographic traditions of the region, but we are also unable to appreciate fully the role that Phoenicia very likely played as the broker for those forms and traditions of Mesopotamia and Egypt. We may be reasonably certain that Tyre and other major centers had their own king-list traditions. They also erected memorial and dedication inscriptions and placed inscriptions upon their tombs and sarcophagi. But whether the Phoenicians had any pre-Hellenistic annals tradition is much more doubtful. The Annals of Tyre cannot be used uncritically to support such a view. It is equally uncertain whether the Phoenicians engaged in efforts to construct a primeval history, such as we find in Philo Byblius, at any time contemporaneous with the Old Testament.

85. See Barr's discussion (*BJRL* 57:41ff.).

CHAPTER SEVEN

ISRAELITE
HISTORIOGRAPHY

a. THE CRITICAL ISSUES

Because the subject of Israelite historiography has become highly diversified and the terminology increasingly ambiguous and confusing, the same
terms are used in quite different ways. Historiography may mean, first, the
evolution of a form of prose narration about historical events. The focus
of scholars is on the homogeneous unit within large literary works, and the
method of analysis is form critical. Historiography may also be concerned
with the nature and composition of biblical histories, i.e., by the Yahwist,
the Deuteronomist, etc. Here scholars are interested in the larger works,
often very heterogeneous in character and inclusive of many smaller units.
Source-critical analysis is used in the evaluation of these works. Finally,
historiography is a designation awarded to certain works that reflect a degree of historical thinking regardless of the form in which it is expressed.
The primary concern of scholars is to trace the evolution of mental states,
namely, Israel's overcoming of mythical approaches to reality, usually in
contrast to her neighbors. This spiritual evolution may or may not be correlated with the evolution of genres. The method may involve the history
of ideas, or biblical theology, or even the anthropological study of primitive societies.

These various meanings of historiography are not so easy to integrate or
relate to one another, and it is not surprising that some of the approaches
have gone their own way. The resulting gaps that exist between many of
the discussions on the subject make it difficult to review them in a chronological or systematic fashion. For the sake of our survey of the main lines
of the discussion, it seems best to organize the material primarily in terms
of these three broad areas of interest: the evolution of literary forms, the
development of histories, and the advancement of historical thought in ancient Israel.

The issues involved in the current discussion of history writing in ancient Israel arise primarily out of the views developed by H. Gunkel and

H. Gressmann.[1] This is certainly true for twentieth-century German biblical scholarship and to a lesser extent for Old Testament studies in general.
There is no need to elaborate here all the changes or minor differences
within or between the works of these two scholars. Instead I will outline in
a simplified form the basic scheme that they evolved.[2] They acknowledge
a certain dependence upon the historian Eduard Meyer by accepting his
high esteem for the quality of historical narrative in the history of the Davidic period,[3] and this point becomes an important focus of their discussion. For the most part, however, their views grew out of the relatively
new form-critical investigation of narrative genre.

Gunkel, in his article on history writing in the Old Testament,[4] begins
by asserting that history writing arises only under certain social and political conditions at the height of a culture. It is thus a *"gelehrte Gattung"*; it
exists only in writing for a limited circle of like-minded, literate persons;
and it combines the critical spirit with a philosophy of history. Obviously the model for this view is Greece, with its evolution of critical historiography out of the Ionic "enlightenment," and not the advanced cultures
of the ancient Near East. Even though the Near East produced a great
mass of "historical documents," these did not in themselves lead to history
writing. To be sure, Israel adopted some of these "historical" forms and
incorporated them into its histories, and Gunkel in fact believed that they
were one of the two sources out of which history writing developed. However, in the later views of Gunkel and Gressmann, and especially in statements made by the latter,[5] history writing did not owe anything to these
forms and in its earliest appearance did not make use of documents. The
impetus toward historical narrative came from another direction, from the
development of the art of narration in *Sagen,* "legends."

Gunkel and Gressmann, in their numerous studies on the art of narration in the Pentateuch,[6] developed a theory about the evolution of narrative forms from the most primitive, the *Märchen* or fairy tale, to history
writing. Thus the *Märchen,* which gives free reign to fantasy and imagina-

1. H. Gunkel, "Geschichtsschreibung im A.T.," *RGG* II, pp. 1348–54; idem, *RGG²* II,
pp. 1112–15; idem, "Die israelitische Literatur," in *Die orientalischen Literaturen* (1906,
1925²), pp. 53–112; H. Gressmann, *Die älteste Geschichtsschreibung und Prophetie Israels*
(1910, 1921²). See also H. Schmidt, *Die Geschichtsschreibung im Alten Testament* (1911).

2. For a fuller discussion of these points see W. Klatt, *Hermann Gunkel: Zu seiner
Theologie der Religionsgeschichte und zur Entstehung der formgeschichtlichen Methode,*
FRLANT 100 (1969); Jay A. Wilcoxen, "Narrative," in *Old Testament Form Criticism,* pp.
58–79.

3. See E. Meyer, *Geschichte des Altertums,* vol. 2, pt. 1, pp. 285–86.

4. See n. 1, above.

5. *Die älteste Geschichtsschreibung,* p. xiii.

6. See esp. H. Gunkel, *Genesis* (1901, 1910³); idem, *The Legends of Genesis;* H.
Gressmann, *Mose und seine Zeit,* FRLANT 1 (1913). See also Wilcoxen, "Narrative," pp.
69ff.

tion by the "primitive," moves on to legend, in which the timeless stories are associated with specific peoples and places. The oldest level of this material is reflected in the patriarchal legends (*Vätersagen*), which explain the origins of a people in terms of a family—an explanation also found in other cultures. The subject matter dealing with the time of the ancestors, the frequent use of etiological motifs to explain origins and practices, and the form of short individual story units all point to the legend's early place in narrative development. These legends underwent an evolution in the course of time by being combined into a series and by the use of a more expansive narrative style, corresponding to a higher level of culture. The form of the Joseph story, for instance, has been transformed into a novella.

Alongside these *Vätersagen* were legends about heroes (*Heldensagen*), also called "historical legends" because they dealt with public figures such as Moses and Joshua or Saul and David. However, the treatment of these figures was still dominated by the typical and the ideal, and details about individuals and events were exaggerated. Since Gunkel can include figures from Moses to Elijah within the same group, it is not clear how this genre fits into the history of literature. Perhaps this explains why Gressmann was inclined to regard the "prophetic legend" as a separate and latter offshoot of the *Sage* for religious or devotional purposes, i.e., *Legende* in German.

Historical narrative or history writing arises out of a legend whose focus is upon the public figure, as in *Heldensagen*, but the political events themselves and not preformed *Märchen*-like episodes are seen as providing the story. Such a development, in Gunkel's view, cannot take place before the rise of the state. For this reason his earliest example is the story of Abimelech in Judges 9, the first attempt to establish a monarchy. But the real flowering of history writing comes with the rise of the monarchy under Saul and David, the finest example being the account of the revolt of Absalom (2 Sam. 13–20 in Gunkel, or 15–20 in Gressmann).[7] Gressmann characterizes this kind of writing as *Geschichts-Novelle*. Both Gunkel and Gressmann stress the continuity of history writing with legend as seen in the similarity of the technique used in both forms of narrative.[8] But the difference is that the historian tells "how it actually was" and therefore excludes wonders and direct appearances and "physical" intervention by the deity. History is thus profane although not godless, since the hand of the deity may be discerned indirectly in the events.[9] Thus the historian may refer to

---

7. Gunkel and Gressmann disagree as to the limits of this work. Rost later proposed new limits in his discussion of the Succession Story.

8. In Gressmann's view "epic laws" would be equally applicable to both even though history writing was written and nonfictional. See *Die älteste Geschichtsschreibung*, p. xiv, § b.

9. Gunkel compares the OT with Herodotus at this point.

the word of a prophet or an oracle or the wondrous "coincidence of circumstances" (*Fügungen des Schicksals*). He also retains an objectivity
about his subject and is reserved in his judgments. The favorite example is
again the revolt of Absalom (Court History of David). Gressmann stresses
that history writing deals with recent events, whereas the subject of legend
is persons and events of the more distant past.[10]

Gressmann further observes that since the border line between legend
and historical narrative is unclear, it is not always easy to assign a particular narrative to one genre or the other. He also asserts that in antiquity, at
least for the Old Testament, an individual legend was not transformed by
rationalization into a historical narrative.[11] Thus the primeval time was
represented by myth, the older periods by legends, and recent events by
historical narrative. And by means of a chronological framework one
could put these together in a series to construct a more wide-ranging presentation without greatly affecting the nature of the material included in
such a work. Only in this way does legend become a part of history. On
the other hand, a historical narrative, as the event moves into the past, can
in a certain sociological context acquire the character of legend through
the addition of fairy tale and legendary motifs. Those works that are "half-
way" between historical narrative and *Sage* Gressmann describes as *Ge-
schichts-Legende*.

A few observations on this general scheme may now be made. First,
Gunkel's attempt at a classification of narrative genres seems both legitimate and reasonable and it has been followed with modification by many
scholars. However, the possibility of constructing a history of literature
from *Märchen* or myth to legend and eventually to history writing is much
more questionable. Although the forms did continue to exist side by side
and to be composed in the same periods, they performed different functions, thus making a strict evolutionary scheme difficult to sustain. Such
genres as the "prophetic legends" create serious problems for any simple
reconstruction of the history of literature.

Even more debatable is Gunkel's effort to relate his literary history to
sociopolitical levels of development in ancient Israel. This becomes obvious from Gunkel's own treatment when he admits that fairy tales, myths,
and legends came into Israel from its neighbors and were "Israelitized."
But if these cultures were more advanced, then these forms do not reflect
preliterate levels of society and may have been adopted at any time prior

10. What seems to lie behind Gressmann's statement is the model of Thucydides, with his
critique of the older "logographers," including Herodotus, and his own justification for dealing with the recent war.
11. This statement would certainly not hold true for early Greek historiography, where
rationalization of myths and legends was a common practice.

to the date of the biblical writing in which they are found. To date a unit
of narrative by its form alone, for example, the legends of Genesis to the
premonarchy period, is a dubious procedure. If we take seriously Gressmann's statement that in antiquity myths are always the genre used for talk-
ing about primeval times, whereas legends are used for the distant "historical" past and historical narrative for the recent past, then there is little
point in attempting a sociological correlation for each of the forms.[12]

Once it became accepted that the monarchy produced history writing
because it gave rise to historical consciousness and offered the most appropriate subject matter for historiography, then Gunkel had to explain why
the other Near Eastern monarchies did not produce such histories. Subsequent studies return to this question and give a variety of answers, none of
which seems very convincing. In many respects the model for Israel's
historiographic development was ancient Greece, yet here the political
background was altogether different. Hecataeus of Miletus lived during
the period in which the Ionian states had lost their independence to Persia,
and Herodotus of Halicarnassus spent much of his life in foreign ports.

In the subsequent period of German biblical scholarship a consensus developed that supported the general scheme of literary history proposed by
Gunkel and Gressmann. This can be seen in G. von Rad's essay "The Beginning of Historical Writing in Ancient Israel," published in 1944.[13] Von
Rad affirms the view that only in Greece and Israel did a "historical sense"
arise that was able to apply causational thinking to sequences of political
events. He describes both the Egyptians and Mesopotamians as limited in
their treatments of the past to the making of lists and other historical documents that "lacked the power to meet the task of presenting the history
of the nation in a unified and orderly form."[14]

Von Rad takes as the first predisposing factor toward this historical
sense in Israel, and therefore among the Israelites, the use of the etiological
legend in the Old Testament. Since etiologies explain present conditions by
a past event, they may be said to reflect "historical thinking." Here von
Rad has taken up the notion of continuity between legend and history
writing presented by Gunkel and Gressmann, but he views the continuity
not so much in terms of narrative techniques as in the kind of thought pro-

12. Cf. the remarks by M. P. Nilsson, *Cults, Myths, Oracles, and Politics in Ancient
Greece*, pp. 9–16.

13. In *The Problem of the Hexateuch and Other Essays*, pp. 166–204.

14. P. 167. Von Rad is impressed by Israel's strong interest in the question of its origins
and in the possibility that it might have had documents or genuine historical traditions going
back to the beginnings of its nationhood. This interest in origins Gunkel had *not* regarded as
unique but rather as typical of many peoples. As for the records of a nation's beginnings one
would have to credit Egypt, Assyria and Babylonia, and the Hittites with having such documents about their past.

cess involved. Yet Gunkel and Gressmann had stressed the unhistorical character of the manner of thinking behind legends. One must seriously question whether von Rad is justified in calling such etiological connections historical thinking.[15]

The second predisposing factor von Rad mentions is the development of a simple and terse narrative style that presumably makes for good, dispassionate historical prose. Von Rad does not account for how this style came into being and to what extent it grew out of the storytelling stage of legends. To the extent that such a terse style is found in the historical books it may reflect the influence of "official" documents and a scribal convention that are quite different from the more colorful storytelling forms of folktale and legend.

Von Rad's third predisposing factor is the theological orientation of the Israelite historians to the understanding of political events as "a most powerful organizing principle."[16] In fact, von Rad considers their "belief in the sovereignty of God in history" as the most important factor in Israel's development of its historiography. For Gunkel this factor would correspond to the prophetic influence upon the later historiography, which he regarded as the ruination of the old "profane" historiography. Furthermore, von Rad has combined the diachronic form-critical scheme of Gunkel and Gressmann with a discussion about Israel's "idea of history," which is synchronic and quite unrelated to the development of form. Von Rad wants to say that Israelite historiography is both the evolution of a literary form and the "revelation" of a particular way of thinking about the past.[17]

Von Rad takes up the question of the hero legend and its role in the development of history writing in much greater detail than did Gunkel and Gressmann. He asserts that, unlike the patriarchal legends of Genesis, "their heroes stand in the full light of history."[18] Considering the fact that he sees stories from Joshua to 1 Samuel as belonging to this genre, his evaluation of their historicity may be overly optimistic. For purposes of illustration von Rad takes up the story of Gideon. This account portrays a series of events related to one another from the beginning of a crisis to its

15. For a quite different assessment of etiology and history see the recent article by B. S. Childs, "The Etiological Tale Re-examined," *VT* 24 (1974):387–97. Cf. von Rad's recent discussion of "saga" and history in *Old Testament Theology*, vol. 2, pp. 419ff. A reconsideration of etiology and history will be taken up below.

16. "Historical Writing," p. 170.

17. Von Rad's statement that this principle of divine activity in history makes the OT "totally different from the Greek conception of history" (ibid., p. 170) must be taken as an overstatement. Von Rad admits that Herodotus was willing to recognize a large measure of divine intervention in human affairs and it is questionable that he dismisses this as easily as he does. On divine intervention in Near Eastern historical texts see below.

18. "Historical Writing," p. 172.

resolution, but closer examination reveals that they are "a conglomeration of very diverse sagas."[19] Von Rad analyzes the unit in Judg. 6:11–24 as a typical cult legend that has been made to serve as a call story associated with the figure of Gideon, with the result that "the material of an aetiological cult-saga has been subsequently transformed into a hero-saga."[20] The theme of the charismatic call has two effects upon the work as a whole. It establishes a connection between an originally separate unit of legend and a wider context of events, thus giving to the whole a compositional complexity not evident in single-unit etiological legends. It also makes God the deliverer and focus of attention as much as Gideon. Other episodes and motifs, such as 6:25–32, 7:24–25, 8:22–28, whose origins seem to reflect etiologies, have a slender connection with the "heroic" events in the story. Even the two main units recounting the mighty deeds of Gideon and his men (7:1–23 and 8:4–21) appear to refer to two quite different traditions and occasions.

The fundamental question, which von Rad does not attempt to answer, is how all these units were drawn together. Is it the nature of the hero legend to combine disparate materials and to transform etiological legends into building blocks for larger hero legends, or is this evidence of a sophisticated process more akin to the activity of the writers of historical works? The latter possibility seems to me to be the more likely, and the call narrative is directly related to the broader theme of the historical work, not just to the story of Gideon.[21] Von Rad, in fact, seems to admit that these combinations are editorial when he says that the story within 7:1–23 is "a typical hero saga, and was never anything else."[22] The same is true of 8:4–21, another hero legend that was combined with the former one only through "editorial handling."[23]

When von Rad deals with 7:1–23 he admits that 7:2–8 "was not a part of the saga in its earliest form." Its function was to "enhance the miraculous nature of the events" and to show "that at bottom it is Yahweh alone who acts."[24] He regards this addition as significant because it places so much emphasis upon divine intervention alongside heroic exploits. He then compares this miraculous element in hero legends with its absence in history writing, where the activity of the deity is handled in a much more

19. Ibid.
20. Ibid., p. 173.
21. W. Richter, in *Traditionsgeschichtliche Untersuchungen zum Richterbuch*, pp. 319–43, ascribes the assembling of the diverse traditions to an author of the northern kingdom, probably during the Jehu dynasty (mid-ninth to eighth century B.C.), which would be a problem for von Rad's thesis. Whether one can even speak, as Richter does, of a predeuteronomistic *Retterbuch* in Judges is still an open question. See below, 10e.
22. "Historical Writing," p. 173.
23. Ibid., p. 175.
24. Ibid., p. 174.

subtle fashion. Here we must object to von Rad's reasoning. If the miraculous element is secondary it is not a feature of the hero legend but of the later "historian" of the larger work, as was the call narrative, and the basis for his comparison of legend and history writing is vitiated. Furthermore, his third predisposing factor—the activity of God in human affairs—cannot be found in this instance at the level of hero legend.

Von Rad turns next to the Succession Story, which he says "must be regarded as the oldest specimen of ancient Israelite historical writing."[25] The limits of this work and its general characterization by von Rad follow very closely the treatment by L. Rost.[26] Von Rad distinguishes the nature of the narration, with its complex series of interwoven scenes and episodes, from the simple paratactic style of the collection of legends that we encounter in the Gideon story. Such an advance in literary technique and sophistication can arise only out of a political state of some magnitude and stature. Saul's limited kingdom could not produce a work of this kind. But with the empire, "all at once it is there, mature and artistically fully developed to an extent which makes it impossible to envisage further development in this direction."[27] Von Rad follows Rost in making the basic themes of the historian's work the problems of political succession and of the newly emergent political institution.

Von Rad is convinced by the brilliance of the character portrayal that the author was doubtless a member of the court and that his account of events is entirely reliable. Especially noteworthy is the author's lack of praise or blame of David as compared with the judgments so common in the Deuteronomistic history. Nevertheless, the principle of retribution plays a major role in the accounting of events. Divine activity is presented not in the form of miraculous and intermittent intervention but in the discerning of God's hand in the realm of profane and quite ordinary events. Such a work was possible, according to von Rad, only in the international court of the Solomonic "enlightenment," which could break with the archaic forms and cult legends and absorb a "flood of secular ideas."[28]

It is not necessary to examine von Rad's interpretation of the Succession Story in detail. What must be questioned, however, is whether von Rad or any other scholar can so easily date the work to the Solomonic era, and whether that era was, in fact, one of "enlightenment." Concerning the former question, serious literary problems remain, which make an early

25. Ibid., p. 176 (also p. 192). However, see *Old Testament Theology*, vol. 1, pp. 48–56, esp. p. 49.

26. *Die Überlieferung von der Thronnachfolge Davids*, BWANT III/6, reprinted in *Das kleine Credo und andere Studien zum Alten Testament*, pp. 119–253. A detailed discussion will be given below, 8d.

27. "Historical Writing," p. 193.

28. Ibid., p. 203.

date for the work difficult to maintain, and without a firm dating in the United Monarchy the whole scheme fails. As for the Solomonic "enlightenment," its only analogue is the Ionic enlightenment that produced the earliest Greek historians. The political atmosphere of Ionia in the late sixth and early fifth centuries, however, was more akin to the Israelite exile than to the Israelite "empire." How could Israel receive a "flood of secular ideas" and a profane attitude to the past when such a viewpoint hardly characterizes the neighboring kingdoms and certainly not Egypt, thought to be the source of so much of Israel's wisdom at this time?

In a more recent work von Rad attributed two other historical works to this age of "enlightenment," the history of David's rise to power (1 Sam. 16:14–2 Sam. 5:12) and the Yahwist's history.[29] These works could hardly be viewed as manifesting a very secular outlook on life. Of the three works, von Rad regarded the Story of David's Rise as the oldest and the Yahwist as the most recent.[30] This now made the Story of David's Rise the oldest piece of history writing. Such a position represents a clear shift away from the opinion that narrative evolved from the short legend to the historical novella of the Succession Story.[31] Von Rad's emphasis is now upon Israel's new ability "to shape history into great complexes" and to be able to make historical connections. The Story of David's Rise was much more a collection of materials than a well-integrated novella like the Succession Story. In fact, von Rad seems to undercut the argument of an evolving style by dating examples of the so-called expansive style of legend, like Gen. 24, to the era of the Yahwist himself.

Von Rad's shift is significant because if history writing means the collection and integration of a number of pieces of tradition of diverse origin, what we are really describing is a "historical work." History writing is the development of both a style of prose and a method of accumulating and organizing information about the past. The next question is how a historical work like the Story of David's Rise relates to the larger history in which it is found as well as to the Succession Story, since they appear to dovetail with each other, although they are quite different in their literary character.

M. Noth was responsible for the third-edition revision of Gunkel's ear-

29. *Old Testament Theology*, vol. 1, pp. 48ff.
30. Ibid., p. 49, n. 25.
31. Cf. Gressmann, *Die älteste Geschichtsschreibung*, p. xv, where he states: "Mit der Geburt der Geschichts-Novelle beginnt die Geschichtsschreibung." Only with the Dtr Historian did he consider the rise of "historical works." See also R. Rendtorff, "Beobachtungen zur altisraelitischen Geschichtsschreibung Anhand der Geschichte vom Aufstieg Davids," in *Probleme biblischer Theologie*, p. 438, where he states, as an amplification of von Rad's position, that the Story of David's Rise did not develop out of the *ausgeführten Geschichtserzählung* in the same way that the Succession Story did.

lier article on history writing in *Die Religion in Geschichte und Gegenwart*.[32] He follows Gunkel in considering history writing a literary form distinct from the oral forms of *Sage* and *Legende*, and he relates it to its sociological context. But Noth does not distinguish so sharply between legend and history with respect to their use of the past, especially as the legends now exist in the large collections in the Old Testament. Thus biblical authors or editors organized originally separate oral units of legend into a collection with a historical perspective, using the smaller units as sources. Noth clearly has in mind here the sources of the Pentateuch and the Yahwist in particular, and these collections represent something more than schools of storytellers. But whether they are on the same level as the Deuteronomistic historian is not clear from the article.

Noth follows the older scholars in the belief that the ancient Near East, while it produced historical documents in great abundance, did not produce works of history. These other nations did not get beyond the stage of merely keeping lists, even lists of notices about historical events. They dealt only in the raw material of history. This applies to the annalistic presentations of wars and building projects in royal inscriptions, to king lists, and to chronicles. Noth includes here the "fictional historical narratives out of the past," which do not relate actual historical events. He sees the presentation, in Near Eastern historiography, of cycles of prosperity and disaster as based upon a mythological scheme and not as an account of historical succession.[33] Noth's separate remark on Hittite historiography seems to acknowledge an understanding of historical continuity, but he denies that this nation is any exception to the lack of history writing in the Near East.[34]

Noth recognizes that Israel also had similar historical documents, some going back earlier than the rise of the monarchy but most of them the result of court bureaucracy. Yet with Gunkel, Gressmann, and von Rad, he asserts that history writing did not grow out of these documents even if they were used to write political history. History writing begins with the rise of the monarchy only because the society reached a certain *geistige Niveau* at this time, which made such a literary form possible. Noth regards it as a process that is parallel to the literary and theological forma-

32. "Geschichtsschreibung im A. T.," *RGG*[3], Vol. 2, pp. 1498-1504.
33. There is an implied comparison here on the level of "historical thinking" between a Near Eastern mythological perspective and an Israelite "historical" perspective that at least prejudices any comparative approach on the literary level. In anticipation of the discussion below it may be noted that Assyriologists deny any clearly cyclical view of history in Mesopotamian historiography. On the other hand, patterns of recurrence that do play a role in Near Eastern historiography are also rather common in the OT.
34. Noth had much more material at his disposal than his predecessors did, but he did little more than reiterate the same basic viewpoint.

tion of the Pentateuch and suggests that the two developments are related, although the question of priority is difficult to answer. He proposes that the fixation of the basic historical traditions of Israel that resulted from a long transmission process (*Überlieferungsvorgeschichte*) had been reached just at the point when the significance of contemporary history was also being appreciated. Thus the history of Israel began as contemporary history.

Noth also follows von Rad in placing strong emphasis upon the theological interpretation of historical events, even if the way this is done in the two bodies of material, the older tradition and the contemporary events, is quite different. Noth thus sees the roots of Israel's historiography in Israel's understanding of divine guidance and its particular form of historical consciousness. This is for him the way to explain the difference between Israel and the rest of the ancient Near Eastern world. He does not see Israel's history writing as inspired by political awareness or development, thereby eliminating one of von Rad's predisposing factors. Nor is he as certain as his predecessors in what circles this kind of history writing arose.

Noth follows A. Alt[35] in regarding the Story of David's Rise (1 Sam. 16:14–2 Sam. 5:25) and the Succession Story (2 Sam. 7; 9–20; 1 Kings 1–2) as historical works of the highest order. He takes them both as written shortly after the events themselves. He also considers shorter historical narratives such as Judg. 9 and 2 Kings 9–10, but he does not really indicate the date of the former and how it would fit into his general picture of development. Noth gives little comment about the "historical works" such as the Deuteronomistic history and the Chronicler except to say that they incorporated the older contemporary history. Noticeably missing here are Gunkel's derogatory remarks about these works, but Noth still follows the older position in not dealing with them as history writing.

Noth adds some remarks about the genre of biography, which was not included in Gunkel's earlier article. This genre is reflected in Nehemiah and Jeremiah and is regarded as an offshoot of history writing. It has some anticipation in the prophetic vision reports and in the collections of oral legends about the preclassical prophets. But how this branch of history writing is related to the older historiography or to biographical forms in the rest of the Near East is nowhere discussed.

It is important to note that the basic scheme of Noth's predecessors has begun to come apart somewhat. Not only is there no step-by-step progression from legend to history writing, but the interest has shifted to the

---

35. A. Alt, *Die Staatenbildung der Israeliten in Palestina,* 1930, reproduced in *Kleine Schriften,* vol. 2, pp. 1–65 (see p. 15).

movement from the legends to the "collections" which are their end products. Because the small units of history writing in Samuel become sources in the same way for the historical work of the Deuteronomist, the real issue is the origin of the Yahwist in the Pentateuch and of the Deuteronomist in the Former Prophets, and the relationship between the two. This issue Noth addressed in his earlier studies, to which we will return below. Noth also places much weight upon Israel's belief in the sovereignty of Yahweh over history as a basic source for historical thinking and therefore for historiography. The confusion among the three aspects of the discussion of historiography mentioned at the outset, that is, the history of the genre, the origin of the histories, and the idea of history in Israel, has become complete. By the time of Noth's article the discussion of historiography has become so diversified that it seems best to consider further developments in the subject under the headings "Narrative Forms," "The Histories of the Old Testament," and "The Idea of History in Israel."

b. NARRATIVE FORMS

What has recently become a basic issue in the general discussion of historiography is the nature of the various historiographic genres and their genetic relationship, if any, to the rise of history writing. The "classical" scheme of Gunkel was not everywhere adopted, either in the precise definition of the individual genre or in the construction of a literary history of these genres from legend to "history writing."[36] An important dissenter to the scheme was O. Eissfeldt in the arrangement of his form-critical material for his *Introduction*.[37] Under the rubric of historical narratives Eissfeldt includes both reports derived from official sources, such as annals or chronicles, and "popular history," which is what Gunkel would regard as historical narrative and history writing as a distinct form and level of literary achievement. Eissfeldt does not have a genre called "history writing." On the contrary, he brings the treatment of Israelite forms more into line with the broader Near Eastern study of historiography, in which his basic distinction between official and popular seems to follow the work of H. Güterbock.[38] Eissfeldt's classification and discussion of oral forms is separate from his treatment of the development of the Pentateuch and the historical books, and he does not propose an evolutionary scheme to get from one type of material to the other.

---

36. See the useful discussion by Wilcoxen, "Narrative," pp. 79–88, where he deals with a broader survey of opinion on narrative genre than can be given here.
37. O. Eissfeldt, *The Old Testament: An Introduction*, pp. 47ff.
38. H. Güterbock, "Die historische Tradition und ihre literarische Gestaltung bei Babylonian und Hethitern bis 1200," *ZA* 42 (1934):1–91; 44 (1938):45–149.

The same criticism by classification can be seen in the more recent *Introduction* by G. Fohrer.[39] In his form-critical discussion of narrative genre he deals with myth, fairy tale, novella, anecdote, "saga," and legend under one rubric of "narrative literary types," and lumps together lists, annals and chronicles, historical narrative and historiography, biography, and dream narrative under the heading "reportorial literary types," with no discussion of a relationship between them. Here, at least, he appears to be following the lead of Eissfeldt. Furthermore, Fohrer's discussion of the development and subsequent use of "sagas" (legends) in Israel points not to their contribution toward a historical sense and history writing, but to a didactic and theological function.

Fohrer's discussion of historical narrative per se begins with a group of self-contained units dealing with fairly circumscribed events, such as Abimelech's kingship (Judg. 9) and Saul's deliverance of Jabesh Gilead (1 Sam. 11). Belonging to a second type of historical narrative are the works called the "Book of the Acts of Solomon" and the "Book of the Chronicles of the Kings of Israel/Judah," which he describes as compendia drawn from court annals. As a third type Fohrer accepts the category of "historiography proper," to which belongs the Court History of David. He accounts for the rise of this work by dating it to "the period of awakening national consciousness based on the religious foundation of Yahwism during and after the reign of David."[40] It is fair to say that at this point Fohrer has accepted, in piecemeal fashion, the older scheme in the von Rad version.

These scholars—Eissfeldt, Fohrer, and others—represent by their classification and discussion the problem of genetic relationship between genres. But there is also the problem of defining the individual forms. Since Gunkel, the major preoccupation of scholars who are concerned with "preliterate" forms of prose narrative has been the genre of *Sage*, or legend.[41] Gunkel had identified the element of etiology as its most important characteristic and the basic motivation for the creation of such stories. He classified the legends into various subtypes depending upon the kinds of etiological interests that they manifest. But etiology as such was a sure indicator of the primitive character of the traditions and their early date in the literary history. While adjustments and refinements to the literary categories were made by a number of scholars, they did little to change the basic scheme of Gunkel's *Literaturgeschichte* until a challenge was given to de-

---

39. G. Fohrer, *Introduction to the Old Testament*, §§ 12–13.
40. Ibid., p. 98.
41. There has been a tendency for some time to translate the German *Sage* by the English word "saga," even though the more correct rendering is "legend" and it is the one that I use throughout. The use of saga is misleading, as will be explained below. See also the discussion in *Abraham in History and Tradition*, pp. 131–38.

fining the legends on the basis of etiology. The studies of J. Fichtner, B. S. Childs, and B. Long,[42] among others, raised serious form-critical arguments against viewing the etiological element in the legends as primary and constitutive of the form as a whole. Instead, the etiological elements, or at least the formulae that were thought to be clear indicators of etiology, were judged to represent "redactional commentary on existing traditions."[43]

This undermining of the criteria by which one is able to identify what is legend in the early traditions of Israel has far greater consequences than its proponents seem to imagine. First, it threatens to destroy the basis upon which one can actually identify these traditions as preliterate and premonarchical in Gunkel's scheme. If the etiological elements do not mark them as primitive, then the stories may belong to any period prior to their use in the extant literary works. Furthermore, if one cannot assume that etiologies are the oldest form of the Pentateuchal traditions, then there is no way to reconstruct a tradition-history from the supposed early etiological form through all its subsequent modifications. This leaves in limbo a large body of traditio-historical discussion on the Pentateuch. It is hard for me to see how the Gunkel–von Rad reconstruction of the rise of historiography can survive this attack without drastic modification.

The implications of this critique have not gone unnoticed, and an attempt has been made to give to the genre of *Sage* a new understanding that does not depend upon etiology and that will also be able to maintain its preliterate and premonarchic characteristics. In his work *Einfache Formen* (1930)[44] Andre Jolles had suggested that *Sage* was not what was commonly understood by the term in German folklore studies. Instead it was to be identified with the Norwegian term *saga,* particularly as it is found in the collections of Icelandic sagas.[45] Jolles went so far as to identify the patriarchal stories of Genesis with this form of *Sage,* a suggestion that was

42. J. Fichtner, "Die etymologische ätiologie in den Namengebungen der geschichtlichen Bucher des AT," *VT* 6 (1956): 372–96; B. S. Childs, "A Study of the Formula 'Until this Day,'" *JBL* 82 (1963):279–92; Burke O. Long, *The Problem of Etiological Narrative in the Old Testament,* BZAW 108 (1967).
43. Childs, *JBL* 82:290; quoted with approval by Long, *Etiological Narrative,* p. 85. Childs found considerable similarity between the form and function of such formulaic elements in the work of Herodotus and in the OT, but he did not pursue the implications of this in terms of the historiographic character of the biblical narratives. "Redactional commentary" is a rather meaningless phrase. In the work of Herodotus it means Herodotus himself and refers to at least one aspect of his work as a historian!
44. A. Jolles, *Einfache Formen* (1930, 1958²), pp. 62–90.
45. This is the real derivation of the English term *saga*. According to standard usage in folkloristic studies the German *Sage* should be rendered by the English word "legend": see W. D. Hand, "Status of European and American Legend Study," *Current Anthropology* 6 (1965):439–46. I continue to use this rendering of "legend" for *Sage* below. See also *Abraham,* pp. 131–32.

taken up by German Old Testament scholars, notably C. Westermann and K. Koch.[46] Jolles's proposal was particularly attractive because the set of characteristics that he attributed to the Icelandic sagas so nearly fitted what was needed to revise and bolster Gunkel's scheme. The Icelandic sagas were regarded as originating in oral tradition at the time of the island's settlement. The oldest of these sagas were thought to be the so-called family sagas, which had a long prehistory before the rise of the so-called king sagas, which dealt with political events of the Norwegian state.

It was not hard for Westermann to fit these characteristics to the biblical material. He identified the early traditions, particularly the patriarchal stories, with the family sagas, and the stage of history writing in the early monarchy with king sagas. The category of *Heldensagen,* which for von Rad had been the transition from etiological legend to history writing, was played down by Westermann as not really a part of the biblical tradition. More recently, Westermann has pursued the matter a stage further by pointing out that the Court History of David still exhibits a strong interest in family history and thereby betrays a continuity with the older form.[47] Using this revised scheme we can identify the oldest layers of the tradition by their domestic themes and have some basis for a tradition-history and redaction criticism of the stories themselves, as well as a literary history of Israelite historiography very similar to Gunkel's.

However, some formidable problems make this proposal untenable. First, Jolles's highly unconventional definition of *Sage* is unacceptable to folklorists who deal with the genre.[48] Second, his characterization of Icelandic saga goes back to the work of Andreas Heusler (1914), and almost every point that he sets down is now disputed or at least debatable.[49] This includes whether family sagas reflect any oral tradition or are simply written compositions, as well as problems of dating and their relationship to king sagas. Third, family sagas are not what their name implies—simple, short domestic tales—but are usually long and involved struggles between two parties and their families, and the English word saga correctly reflects this complex feature of the work.[50] What is most damaging to Westermann's view is that he did not attempt to actually describe a particular ex-

46. C. Westermann, "Arten der Erzählungen in der Genesis," *Forschung am Alten Testament,* pp. 36–47; K. Koch, *The Growth of the Biblical Traditions: The Form-Critical Method,* pp. 148–58.
47. "Zum Geschichtsverständnis des Alten Testament," *Probleme Biblischer Theologie,* pp. 611–19.
48. Cf. C. W. von Sydow, "Kategorien der Prosa-Volksdichtung," in *Selected Papers on Folklore,* pp. 61ff.; L. Petzoldt, ed., *Vergleichene Sagenforschung,* p. vii.
49. For a history of saga criticism which includes an evaluation of Heusler, among others, see T. A. Andersson, *The Problem of Icelandic Saga Origins.*
50. For a useful discussion of the Icelandic saga's structure and content see T. A. Andersson, *The Icelandic Family Saga: An Analytic Reading.*

ample of an Icelandic saga and then compare it with the stories in Genesis. If he had, the inappropriateness of the comparison would have been self-evident.

Another aspect of Westermann's study of the Genesis narratives that calls for some discussion is his definition of the term narrative (*Erzählung*). He states that "in a narrative an event is related in which a tension [*Spannung*] leads to a resolution [*Lösung*]."[51] Using this definition, Westermann can separate the true and original narratives from redactional additions and modifications, and this in turn becomes the basis for his traditio-historical treatment of the promise theme in the patriarchal stories.

Here again the definition is highly questionable.[52] A narrative may be a story, in which case the statement might hold. But it is quite possible to have a historical narration of events which does not begin with a tension and does not have a resolution, just as it is possible to have a series of such episodes in one work. By using his special definition of a narrative, Westermann has attempted to recover Gunkel's small unit, but there is no justification on this basis for doing so. The Yahwist's narrative may contain various dramatic episodes that may or may not go back to self-contained stories, as well as scenes that contain only divine speeches related to the larger whole. All of it is narration and its form gives little indication of its date or literary prehistory.

Another way of dealing with the development of early Hebrew historiography is to speak of the biblical histories as "epics" or as the prose versions of "underlying epics" and then to compare them with epic literature elsewhere, or at least to attribute the qualities of epic literature to the biblical material. Recently, C. Conroy has made a survey of the use of the term epic by biblical scholars as a description for various parts of the historical traditions.[53] He concludes:

> The term "epic" has been used in a bewildering variety of ways with reference to early Hebrew literature. Not only has the whole Pentateuch as it stands been called an epic, so too have various parts of the present Pentateuch (the Patriarchal narratives, even the Joseph story), as well as the Yahwistic work (J), the *Grundlage* or common basis of J and E, and various compositions said to underlie parts of the Pentateuch (Creation epic, Exodus epic, etc.); scholars have also spoken of

51. "Arten der Erzahlung," p. 33.
52. Even if one could accept the definition, the application by Westermann is faulty. He describes Gen. 18:1–15 as a "Promise Story" (pp. 18–19), but this part of the test only deals with the tension since the promise is itself the problem. The resolution comes with the birth of the child in 21:2ff., as is clear from the parallel story in 2 Kings 4:8–17. For a more detailed discussion see *Abraham*, pp. 202–08.
53. "Hebrew Epic: Historical Notes and Critical Reflections," *Biblica* 61 (1980):1–30.

existing or underlying epics in the books of Joshua, Judges, Samuel, Kings and Job. The Israelites, it appears, had royal epics and national epics, large epics and small epics, as well as epic style and epic tonality.[54]

There is no need to repeat Conroy's excellent survey on the use of epic here. Yet the views of a few scholars call for some comment because of their continued influence up to the present time. W. F. Albright, providing the leadership for much American biblical scholarship, held the view that behind the prose narrative of Genesis lay an older epic form of poetic narration by which the early traditions of Israel were preserved. He adopted a notion that was rather widespread in classical studies in the nineteenth and early twentieth centuries, that all the earliest forms of folk traditions were composed and handed down orally in "epic" verse.[55] In his recent work, *Yahweh and the Gods of Canaan*, Albright devoted a whole chapter to this thesis, entitled "Verse and Prose in Early Israelite Tradition."[56] He pointed out that fragments of poetry are often preserved together with the prose accounts in the traditions of early Israel, and he took this as evidence that older Israelite epics, similar to the "Canaanite" epics of Ugarit, originally preceded the prose versions of the Pentateuchal sources. This position is now often reiterated as virtual dogma without any supporting discussion by several of Albright's former students.[57]

Since Albright also believed that the poetic form could preserve the ancient historical tradition more faithfully than prose, this view of an epic original went hand in hand with an elaborate attempt to demonstrate the origins and close "fit" of the patriarchal stories in the early second millennium. Some support could also be found in the early writings of Gunkel, which reflect the view that poetic traditions, although not epics, preceded prose forms.[58] But Gunkel later abandoned this position in his dispute with Sievers over a poetic original to the book of Genesis, and it never became a part of the German treatment of *Sagen* in general.[59] At the same time, Albright and his student J. Bright objected strongly to the emphasis placed upon the etiological element in the *Sagen* as constitutive of the

54. Ibid., p. 14.

55. *From the Stone Age to Christianity*, p. 35.

56. *Yahweh and the Gods of Canaan*, pp. 1–52.

57. For the views of D. N. Freedman and F. M. Cross, see above, 2b. This view is also reflected in the works of C. H. Gordon. For references see Conroy, *Biblica* 61:6–7, 11.

58. See W. F. Albright's introduction to H. Gunkel's *The Legends of Genesis* (1901) in the reprinted version by Schocken Books, New York, 1964, pp. xi–xii. In the light of Gunkel's later views Albright's statement must be regarded as rather misleading.

59. *Genesis, übersetzt und erklärt*, 3d ed. (1910), p. xxvii and n. 4. See also Wilcoxen, "Narrative," p. 63. Gunkel never did subscribe to the notion of a national epic and it plays no role in his discussion of Hebrew literature.

form, since this threatened the historicity of the traditions.[60] With the relegation of etiology to a secondary role by the recent studies mentioned above, it would appear that Albright's position stood a chance of filling the gap and of offering a new way of dealing with the early traditions and the rise of history writing. Yet attempts to date the patriarchal traditions in the second millennium B.C. have not proved very successful under close scrutiny. Their antiquity cannot be authenticated by the use of Near Eastern parallels, and much of the data in these stories speak against it.[61]

A similar notion of "underlying epics" to the biblical traditions was taken by U. Cassuto.[62] Like Gunkel, he followed E. Meyer in asserting that Israel pioneered history writing in the time of David, five hundred years before Herodotus. Yet he saw the process of a development toward history writing as quite parallel to one in ancient Greece and he outlined a theory of historiographic evolution as follows. He suggested that first of all came short, epic-lyric poems dealing with single episodes—events worthy of commemoration. From these grew "heroic poetry of great imaginative sweep"—the epic—like the Homeric poems of the *Iliad* and the *Odyssey* and the poems of Hesiod. Based on epic poems as well as folktales in prose and genealogies, the logographers of Greece developed narrative prose that was still a quite uncritical collection of materials. Finally, Herodotus applied to this prose tradition his critical skills of historical evaluation.

Cassuto sought a parallel literary evolution in ancient Israel. He points to poems within the Pentateuch as epic-lyric works (for example, the Song of Deborah) and regards such accounts as the stories of Creation, the Flood, and the Exodus as based upon epics similar to Near Eastern models. He regards the Pentateuchal narrators as on a par with the Greek logographers, and the texts of the United Monarchy as representing true history writing itself. Cassuto differs from Albright in that he does not seem to regard the Patriarchal traditions as based upon an epic but upon legends, much like Gunkel. As might be expected, Cassuto's views have been quite influential among Israeli scholars.[63]

Cassuto's main argument for the theory that epic poetry underlies at least some of the prose in the Pentateuch is the fact that many verses or

---

60. See esp. J. Bright, *Early Israel in Recent History Writing*.

61. See my *Abraham in History and Tradition*, pt. 1, pp. 7–122; also T. L. Thompson, *The Historicity of the Patriarchal Narratives: The Quest for the Historical Abraham*, BZAW 133 (1974).

62. "The Beginning of Historiography among the Israelites," *Biblical and Oriental Studies* I, pp. 7–16. See also idem, "The Israelite Epic," in *Biblical and Oriental Studies*, vol. 2, pp. 69–109; and the remarks by Conroy, *Biblica* 61:9ff.

63. One dissenting voice here has been that of S. Talmon, "The 'Comparative Method' in Biblical Interpretation—Principles and Problems," SVT 29 (1978):352–56.

parts of verses have poetic characteristics. He states: "These verses are easily explained if we assume that in the prose reworking of an ancient poem there were cited here and there a few verses in their original form."[64] Cassuto also offers some other arguments, but these are not so much for the existence of an epic form as for traditions that could have been in a number of different folkloristic genres.

The thesis, put forward by both Albright and Cassuto, that epic forms of poetic narration lie behind the prose versions is originally derived from classical scholarship, as might be deduced from their parallels. But, as we have already seen, this view was promulgated in the nineteenth and early twentieth centuries and has been under attack for more than fifty years. It scarcely represents the views of classical scholars today.[65] Suffice it to say here that in my view these "schools" of Old Testament studies do not provide a readily acceptable alternative to the German positions on early Israelite historiography.

c. THE HISTORIES OF THE OLD TESTAMENT

The question just where the histories of the Old Testament fit into the rise of historiography often receives quite different answers. Gunkel and Gressmann distinguished between "history writing" and "historical works." By the former they meant a particular genre that was a single unit of narration, such as the Rebellion of Absalom. A number of such units and others of different genres made up the larger complex historical works in the books of Samuel and Kings. Gunkel and Gressmann restricted the designation "historical works" to the Deuteronomistic redaction of the Former Prophets and to the Chronicler. As far as the Pentateuch was concerned, they regarded the older sources of the Yahwist and the Elohist merely as collectors or "schools of story-tellers" (Erzählenschulen) because their subject matter was virtually all myths and legends. Gunkel disparaged the historical works because he saw them as coming under the influence of prophecy. To him this was one of two "catastrophes" that befell history writing, the other being the end of the state and the establishment in its place of a priestly hierarchy, which was enough to condemn both the Priestly Writer of the Pentateuch and the Chronicler. So the form-critical task of narrative research for Gunkel was to rescue the old historiography out of the collections in the historical books.[66]

Gressmann, on the other hand, gave to prophecy and its subsequent in-

---

64. "Beginning of Historiography," p. 11.
65. See above, 2b.
66. See esp. *RGG*, vol. 2, p. 1354.

fluence on historiography a much more positive assessment.[67] It is prophecy with its uses of the past, recalling the old traditions in order to deliver a moral critique and encourage reform, that stimulated history writing anew. It gave birth to the Deuteronomic reform, which in turn provided the ideological basis for the Deuteronomistic redaction of the traditions. But the real achievement of the Deuteronomistic history writing was the skillful way in which the material was organized within a framework and a chronology. All the various elements—legends, historical narratives, anecdotes, annals, and religious legends—make up its flesh and blood so that the past comes alive. And all is brought under the control of a particular idea.[68] By modern standards it may be somewhat primitive, but for Gressmann it was a step in the right direction—to organize the material in such a way as to uncover the deeper meaning in the bare events. In this case, that meaning is the religious idea that the deity speaks to his people through events, and by means of the good or evil destiny that befalls them he guides them in the right way.

Those scholars who were inclined to follow the lead of Gunkel and Gressmann henceforth dealt with the sources of the Pentateuch in a way quite different from the historical books of Samuel and Kings. This can be seen in von Rad's "Form-Critical Problem of the Hexateuch" (1938).[69] Von Rad acknowledged the labors of his predecessors who had divided the Hexateuch into its "sources" as well as into the smaller components of genre analysis. He now asked the question: how did the work receive the particular shape into which all the diverse materials are placed? He observed that this shape is that of a history from creation to the conquest and that such an organization of traditions cannot be fortuitous. Now, it does not greatly matter if one describes this history as "salvation history"; what is important is the historical orientation of the Pentateuch, even in its earlier source, the Yahwist.

Von Rad identified the main themes of this *Heilsgeschichte* as the basic components of Israel's faith. Its origin one finds in the creedal formulas reflected in Deut. 26:5–9 and Josh. 24:2–13, as well as in some "free adaptations" in the Psalms. Von Rad regarded the form as associated with, and preserved in, certain cultic contexts. The earliest form, which he called the "settlement tradition," celebrated the deliverance from Egypt and the bringing of Israel into the Promised Land. Originally quite separate from

67. *Die älteste Geschichtsschreibung,* pp. xvi–xvii.

68. Gressmann seems to reject Gunkel's criticism that this is merely a philosophy of history.

69. *Das formgeschichtliche Problem des Hexateuch,* BWANT 26/4 (1938) [*Gesammelte Studien zum Alten Testament,* pp. 9–86]; translated as *The Problem of the Hexateuch and Other Essays,* pp. 1–78.

this tradition, and not found in the "credos," was the tradition about the giving of the law on Sinai. Von Rad saw this tradition as the focal point of a different liturgical celebration. According to von Rad, it was the Yahwist who used the settlement tradition as the fundamental framework for his collection of ancient materials into which he fitted the Sinai tradition. The patriarchal traditions were developed and interpreted as a prologue to the settlement tradition, and the primeval history was composed and integrated thematically with the patriarchal stories as an introduction to the whole. The result is that the Yahwist is a historian of quite remarkable scope. For him the whole movement of history is under the guidance and activity of God.

Von Rad's most recent discussion of the rise of historiography[70] fits more closely his treatment of the form-critical problem of the Yahwist. In it the Story of David's Rise is viewed as a historical work that was prior to, and a model for, the Yahwist's history. This kind of history writing, as the integration and thematic orientation of a complex of originally heterogeneous traditions, von Rad saw as evolving out of the confessional, historical summaries. The spirit of the age, reflected in the Succession Story, affected the Yahwist's style at a number of points in his work, but it was the *method* of the author of David's Rise that was most influential in the Yahwist's development of a historical work for the earlier period of Israel's history.

Many questions and issues have been raised by von Rad's study of the form-critical problem of the Hexateuch, and all cannot be reviewed here. It is important, however, to point out a few problems. First, since we cannot easily dismiss the thoroughly Deuteronomic character of the credos, their primitive character as original credos is in doubt.[71] They may be merely summary statements of the traditions within the Deuteronomic circles.[72] Second, if we do not regard the dating of the Yahwist in the Solomonic age as assured, then the relationship of his work to the Deuteronomic tradition must be raised anew.[73] This is especially so since his history contains a much more elaborate and comprehensive scheme of events than anything suggested by the Deuteronomistic summaries. Criticisms of von Rad's study have not solved the basic problem: where did the form of the Pentateuch (Hexateuch) come from? Is it the work of a historian or the result of some other process? On this issue there is a strong difference of opinion among biblical scholars.

70. *Old Testament Theology*, vol. 1, pp. 48–56.
71. G. Fohrer, *Introduction to the Old Testament*, p. 118.
72. See esp. the form-critical study by B. S. Childs, "Deuteronomic Formulae of the Exodus Traditions," SVT 16 (1967): 30–39.
73. See my *Abraham*, pp. 148–53, 249–78; H. H. Schmid, *Der sogenannte Jahwist*.

M. Noth took up the task of making a comprehensive study of the historical traditions. Turning his attention first to the corpus of writings from Joshua to Kings,[74] he departed from the older approach of literary criticism, which merely extended the method of source analysis beyond the Pentateuch and into the historical books as well. He attributed the same kind of redactional combining of independent literary sources that characterized Pentateuchal criticism to Deuteronomistic redactors of the Former Prophets. Now Gressmann had already proposed that a greater appreciation of this corpus as history writing was necessary, and Noth's work reflects this reappraisal. He first limits the Pentateuchal sources, J, E, and P, to the Tetrateuch (Genesis to Numbers) and sees in the Former Prophets a comprehensive history compiled by a single author, having as its prologue the book of Deuteronomy, to which the author furnished a new introduction (Deut. 1:1–4:43). The work consists of many oral and written tradition pieces that have been brought together. Most of them were independent of each other, not part of earlier comprehensive literary works, before they were collected, reworked, and systematically presented by the Deuteronomistic historian (Dtr). In order to create a thematic unity out of such materials, the author used certain editorial pieces or speeches to introduce or give some explanation of, or judgment on, events that he records. The date of Dtr, to judge by where the work comes to an end, must be around the middle of the sixth century B.C.

Before pursuing this thesis further, and the various reactions to it, it is important to note its implications for Pentateuchal studies, which Noth outlined in a subsequent monograph.[75] Noth had already suggested, on source-critical grounds, that there was a break between the Tetrateuch and the following historical books. He went on, however, to suggest that the difference was much greater, having to do with the very nature of the Pentateuch's formation. Unlike the Dtr history, which was the work of an author compiling his source material, the Pentateuch did not have such "authors" but was rather the result of a process that was responsible for the basic form. Noth states:

> This form was already given in the beginning of the history of the traditions in a small series of themes essential for the faith of the Israelite tribes. These themes in turn constituted the content of more or less definitely formulated "confessions" which were customarily recited at particular cultic celebrations. The thematic outline so given in the early cult was then richly and variously filled out by the gradual addition of innumerable individual traditions.[76]

74. M. Noth, *Überlieferungsgeschichtliche Studien*, vol. 1.
75. *A History of Pentateuchal Traditions [Überlieferungsgeschichte des Pentateuch]*.
76. *Pentateuchal Traditions*, p. 2.

The result is the formation of a "Pentateuchal tradition" containing most of the essential elements now found in the Pentateuch and in their present relationship to each other.

This proposal rests, first, upon von Rad's suggestion, mentioned above, that not only the individual stories but also the thematic framework, in the form of cultic confessions, comes from the preliterate period of Israelite life. Noth, however, breaks up the credo series used by von Rad and simply lists a series of five originally independent themes: guidance out of Egypt, guidance into the arable land, promise to the patriarchs, guidance in the wilderness, and revelation at Sinai. The process by which these themes came together was complex, but it eventuated in the "salvation history" which forms the basis of the Pentateuchal tradition. At the same time, these individual themes were filled out with popular traditions of the legends and legend-cycles investigated by Gunkel and Gressmann. It was no longer the basic stories that were preliterate or a confessional statement which included allusion to one or more themes, but the whole process of amassing and combining diverse materials within a series of thematic structures that is the work of a preliterate community. Noth gives this product his own rather precise sociological correlation (*Sitz im Leben*)—the amphictyonic league of the premonarchy period.[77]

Where is the Yahwist, the earliest source of the Tetrateuch, in all this? For von Rad, the Yahwist was still the creative genius who combined the various themes, filled them out, and gave the theological perspective to the whole. Noth, however, makes him responsible for the addition of the primeval history (Gen. 2–11) and the connection between this and the theme of the patriarchal promises (Gen. 12:1–3).[78] For the rest J accepted the Pentateuchal tradition with no substantial alteration. At the same time, J is not a name for a ninth-century school of storytellers, as Gunkel and Gressmann held, since the function of assembling such stories has been transferred to the preliterate and premonarchical community.

An extended critique of Noth's method and conclusions is not possible here,[79] but a few remarks on their implications for historiography are in order. First, it remains a curious fact that since the primeval traditions cannot be construed as confessional for the twelve-tribe league, the Yahwist is made responsible for their collection, arrangement, and thematic treatment but does nothing with the rest of the Pentateuchal traditions except record them. It is also left entirely unexplained how the hypothetical amphictyonic community could carry out this complex task of collecting, combining, and giving comprehensive thematic and structural unity to the Pentateuchal tradition in a way that strongly resembles the work of a historian

77. Ibid., pp. 42ff.
78. Ibid., pp. 236ff.
79. See my remarks in *Abraham in History and Tradition*, pp. 143–48.

and theologian—all on a preliterate level. This traditio-historical process would then be the real origin of history writing, a process that cannot be observed and is completely *sui generis*. History writing would not be the result of literacy or the cultural achievement of the monarchy.[80] The Yahwist, dated only as a matter of convenience to the Davidic-Solomonic period, would merely be the earliest recorder and supplementer of a prior historical work.

Since the prerequisite studies of Gunkel, Gressmann, and von Rad pose problems regarding the methods of identifying preliterate forms and primitive thematic confessions, Noth's work is subject to the same difficulties. His hypothetical *Sitz im Leben* of an amphictyonic league that produced this early history is also under grave suspicion.[81] But quite apart from these weaknesses it is difficult to see why anyone should be persuaded that the Pentateuch developed any differently from the Dtr history. Both are collections of highly diverse materials, systematically and thematically arranged, with all the marks of a literary editorial process. To admit that, at least for part of the material in Genesis, the Yahwist did the same kind of historical editing as Dtr, and with much the same outlook, is surely to eliminate all reason for viewing the works as entirely different in their formation. If J and Dtr are viewed as written much closer in time to each other, this would also work against Noth's view.

Returning to Noth's thesis of a single Dtr history, we find that the reactions to it vary from qualified approval to rather strong rejection.[82] Without going into great detail at this point it would nevertheless be helpful to mention where some of the major questions and problems lie. A. Jepsen, who restricts his discussion to the books of Kings,[83] gives qualified approval to Noth's thesis but raises some questions about the redactional process identified by the designation Dtr. He differs from Noth in proposing as many as three redactors, although the last one makes only a few additions. The basis for the earliest work was a synchronistic royal chronicle and an annalistic work containing the most important events during the monarchies of Israel and Judah. These official documents were combined by a priestly redactor (RI) in his presentation of a "cult history."

80. To be sure Noth asserts (op. cit., p. 44) that historiography appeared only with the rise of the state and that it replaced the "saga tradition." But it seems pointless to deny that the "Pentateuchal tradition" as Noth understood it was a "history," and not just a collection of stories.

81. For criticisms of this notion see G. Fohrer, "'Amphictyony' und 'Bund,'" *TLZ* 91 (1961), cols. 801–16, 893–903; R. de Vaux, *Histoire ancienne d'Israël*, vol. 2, pp. 67–86; C. H. J. de Geus, *The Tribes of Israel*.

82. See the recent survey by A. N. Radjawane, "Das deuteronomistische Geschichtswerk, ein Forschungsbericht," *ThR* 38 (1974):177–216.

83. *Die Quellen des Königsbuches*.

This was followed by a prophetic redaction (R II) which extended the work back to the time of Moses and is equivalent to Noth's Dtr. The third redactor (R III) simply represents some later additions which Noth also recognized. The problem raised by Jepsen for Kings could also be illustrated by recent discussion about Judges, that is, whether or not Dtr combined a number of pre-Dtr literary works in his larger corpus.[84]

On the other hand, some scholars continued to hold the position that the Pentateuchal sources extended beyond the limits of the Tetrateuch. Some, such as von Rad and Fohrer,[85] argued that the very nature of the Pentateuchal themes, with the promise of land to the fathers, demanded that the story of the conquest also be told. Consequently, they looked for the end of the Pentateuchal sources in Joshua and Judges 1. Noth's explanation, that the Priestly Writer was not interested in the conquest and therefore left out the account by J and E, is rejected by von Rad and Fohrer as highly improbable.

Other scholars argue that the Yahwist and the Elohist were indeed historians and that it is inconceivable that J and E ended their histories at a point so far in the past.[86] Thus their works continued from an account of Israel's beginnings up to their own time. For the Yahwist this meant the United Monarchy or shortly thereafter, and for the Elohist, some time later during the Divided Monarchy. Eissfeldt's comment on this point is significant:

> All the analogies suggest that Israelite historical writing began when Israel had reached or just passed its zenith, i.e., under or soon after David and Solomon; and that it did not restrict itself to the immediate present or to a section of the past closely connected with it, but presented the whole development of the people from its beginning, linked with the beginning of the world and of mankind, right down to the contemporary scene.[87]

84. See Richter, *Traditionsgeschichtliche Untersuchung zum Richterbuch*.

85. See Radjawane, *ThR* 38:200ff., 208ff.

86. G. Hölscher, *Geschichtsschreibung in Israel: Untersuchungen zum Jahwisten und Elohisten*. A more recent version of Hölscher's position is presented by H. Schulte, *Die Entstehung der Geschichtsschreibung im Alten Israel*, BZAW 128 (1972). Also O. Eissfeldt, *The Old Testament: An Introduction*; see also Radjawane, *ThR* 38:192–200.

87. *Introduction*, p. 247. "All the analogies" in this quotation comes down to one, that of the Maccabean period. Thus Eissfeldt states (p. 140): "An experience like the rise to power under David happened to Israel again only in the victorious rebellion of the Maccabees, and at that time too there immediately arose a great writing of history appropriate to the greatness of the subject. Thus it is a natural assumption, and one that has often been made, that it was David's deeds or the recollection of them which first led a particular individual to set out a presentation of Israel's history linking it with the history of humanity." I do not find the analogy in the least persuasive. It does not provide a good model for J as Eissfeldt would define this work and I do not believe that it is a "natural assumption" that history writing arose with David. It seems "natural" only because it has been repeated so often.

Whether we agree with Eissfeldt's position on the Pentateuchal sources or not, it must be admitted that he is raising an important issue. Why would anyone write a history of a period in the distant past, especially one so comprehensive in scope as the Yahwistic work, if it did not make any connection with the Yahwist's own time? Either we must adopt the solution of Eissfeldt and Hölscher, or we must presuppose that a history covering the years from the settlement to the monarchy had already been written.

The ambiguities and differences in perspective on the subject of Israelite historiography become quite apparent in S. Mowinckel's 1963 article.[88] As we have seen above, those scholars who followed the lead of Gunkel distinguished between "genuine" history writing and the larger "collections," or "historical works," in which this older history writing was preserved. Other scholars, such as Hölscher and Eissfeldt, prefer to speak of historians and history writing only in terms of the larger literary works, such as the Yahwist or the Deuteronomistic history. Mowinckel appears to do away with this separation at one stroke by redefining the term saga, which had come to be used somewhat erroneously in biblical studies as the English equivalent of the German *Sage,* in its Norwegian meaning—"an old historical work." Mowinckel does not describe the characteristics of "saga" in detail, but he does not limit it to oral or preliterate works and he applies the term directly to both the Yahwist and the Deuteronomist. In fact, he goes so far as to substitute the term "Deuteronomistic sage" for Noth's *deuteronomistische Geschichtswerk* in his discussion of Noth's study of this literary work. As a result, he attempts to shift the whole discussion to a consideration of the nature and composition of these larger historical works.

It should be immediately obvious that Mowinckel's use of the word saga is entirely different from Westermann's, even though they both refer to the same parallel material, the Norwegian and Icelandic sagas. Mowinckel's direct familiarity with these works, however, makes his application of them to the larger, more complex histories much more appropriate. Even so, the parallels are so slender and the whole history of their development so different from the Israelite forms that it is best to avoid the comparison altogether. Certainly Mowinckel's attempt to develop "laws" on the basis of how an author of one of the Norwegian sagas developed his work is a debatable procedure. It is also noteworthy that for Westermann this redefinition of saga enabled him to stay within Gunkel's scheme of development from the stories of Genesis to the Court History of David. For Mowinckel, on the other hand, it allows a shift to the histories in which the Yahwist and Dtr are viewed in largely the same way.

88. "Israelite Historiography," *ASTI* 2 (1963):4–26.

Another fundamental departure by Mowinckel is his quite different assessment of the role of "official" documents in the rise of history writing.[89] He discusses the references in the books of Kings to the "Annals of the Kings of Israel, or Judah" and the "Annals of Solomon," and finds in these works a "popular and narrative 'edition'" of the official records which could then be used as a framework for the addition of other nonofficial materials. Consequently, Mowinckel asserts that "in the annals lies the point of departure for a historiography."[90] He gives no indication in his remarks how radical his departure from Gunkel is. In fact, he seems to minimize this difference by immediately adding, "It is a wellknown fact, that Israel is the only people in the whole ancient Near East, where annalistic writing developed into real historiography."[91] This way of putting it would clearly not be acceptable to many scholars, even though his judgment on the works from Mesopotamia, Egypt, and the Hittites is virtually identical with that of Noth. Mowinckel's explanation for why "real historiography" evolved in Israel but not in these other regions is the same as von Rad's "third predisposing factor," the theological orientation of Israelite historians with their belief in the sovereignty of God in history.

Mowinckel does not begin with "J's saga," which he regards as a great synthesis and the culmination, rather than the beginning, of history writing. Instead he turns to the more modest beginnings. In this way he need say nothing about the etiological sagas of Genesis. He enunciates two "laws" for the origin and rise of history writing. First, storytellers and early historians focus on individuals and their great deeds before they develop a synthetic construction on a broader scale. Second, "all real historical writing has come into existence in connection with the political life of its time,"[92] and by implication, the only significant political life of early Israel was the United Monarchy. Since Mowinckel's first "law" looks very much like von Rad's discussion of *Heldensagen,* it is possible to see in these "laws" a conflation of two stages. At any rate, Mowinckel only begins with a discussion of the stories about David and Solomon.

Mowinckel takes exception to the reconstruction of a "succession story" by L. Rost and its subsequent use by von Rad. Against all the earlier opinions going back to Gunkel, he does not regard this as the beginning and apex of historiography. Instead he sees in the "History of Solomon" (his rendering of *sēfer dibrē šelōmōh* in 1 Kings 11:41) a reference to the earli-

89. Note Mowinckel's important earlier comparative study, "Die vorderasiatischen Königs- und Fürsteninschriften," *Eucharisterion, Festschrift Gunkel,* vol. 1, FRLANT 36 (1923) pp. 278–322.
90. *ASTI* 2:7.
91. Ibid., p. 8.
92. Ibid., p. 9.

est written historiographic work containing not only official annals but also "more 'popular' tales about the deeds and the 'wisdom' of the king." This work was written by one of the "history-minded" officials of Solomon's court and comprised the major part of 1 Kings 1–10. Only after such a political history was written was there any motivation to trace back the "family saga" of David's court and the earlier associations with Saul and Samuel and to gather them into one great collection. Consequently, Mowinckel regards this second stage of historiography as constituting a historical saga that includes the books of Samuel in their entirety.

The traditions of the Pentateuch, some of which Mowinckel regards as older than the early historiography, were preserved and had their function in an ongoing cultic *Sitz im Leben* in Jerusalem. The Yahwist, under the influence of "profane" historiography, put these traditions into their present historiographic form, and to him Mowinckel attributes the notion of an overall theological conception of history which was then found in later works. But J itself he dates as late as the end of the ninth or early eighth century B.C.[93] The materials of Joshua and Judges are viewed as supplementing the Yahwist or filling the gap between the time of the conquest and the "Saul-David saga." Thus hero tales contributed toward early historiography only at a relatively late stage in the process.

At this point Mowinckel takes up the "Deuteronomistic saga" primarily as it has to do with the books of Kings. For him it is based largely upon one work, "a synchronistic history of the kings of Israel and Judah,"[94] which corresponded also to a popular version of the state annals of Judah. Mowinckel has no difficulty in including within such a source the prophetic legends and other stories of a popular sort. To a large extent its formation parallels that of the earliest work on Solomon. Dtr's function seems to be primarily that of a redactor of the various sagas or parts thereof from the time of Moses (that is, Deut. 1) to the end of the monarchy.

Mowinckel's treatment of Israelite historiography raises a number of questions. As we have already indicated, his use of the Norse-Icelandic analogy of saga formation needs more justification than its usefulness to his argument and reconstruction. To explain one unknown by what to most Old Testament scholars is another is hardly useful.

Mowinckel's use of Near Eastern parallels is also curious. On the one hand, history writing is derived from annals, which he regarded as a com-

---

93. Here Mowinckel accepts Hölscher's dating of J (ibid., p. 15) but not the character or limits that Hölscher attributes to the work. His reasons for the dating are very slim.

94. Ibid., p. 18. While he does not say so, Mowinckel has in mind the analogy of the Synchronistic History from Assyrian historiography. Its nature, however, is altogether different. For a discussion of this work see above, 3d.

mon Near Eastern phenomenon. Yet at the same time Mowinckel argues that popular versions of such annals are the real form-critical stepping-stone to history writing, but these apparently are not found elsewhere. If these popular annals are also "profane" and lack the theological factor that separates Israel from its neighbors, then why are they not found else-where and how did they arise? Norwegian analogies aside, why is there any good reason to believe that they existed in Israel? The statements about the "Books of the Chronicles of the Kings of Israel/Judah" do not suggest any such content.

Mowinckel's rather quick dismissal of Rost's treatment of the Succession Story and his argument for one "saga" covering all the books of Samuel cannot be accepted without a more sustained literary discussion. In fact, Samuel clearly does not constitute a literary unity and represents a very weak link in Mowinckel's general scheme. This is all the more so since Mowinckel has abandoned any sociological scheme which says that oral tales are preliterate and developed in the premonarchy period. If popular and oral tales of all types persist alongside written works, then the Gunkel-Gressmann-von Rad reconstruction is not very useful. The combination of traditions may be the result of influence from history writing rather than its cause, and the collectors may be active historians and not merely passive transmitters of past lore. Mowinckel keeps the date of the United Monarchy as the beginning of history writing, but he no longer has a strong reason for doing so.

d. THE IDEA OF HISTORY IN ISRAEL

The third way of approaching Israelite historiography is to discuss "historical thinking" or the "idea of history" in the Old Testament, usually in contrast to the rest of the Near East. Already in his essay "Geschichtsschreibung im A.T." Gunkel had discussed briefly why history writing arose in Israel but not in Mesopotamia or Egypt.[95] He stated that in the latter regions the absolutism of the political system and the rule of the priesthood destroyed the freedom of spirit necessary for true history writing. How Gunkel could be sure that such "freedom of spirit" existed in the Davidic-Solomonic period is not clear. Gunkel did not give any positive assessment to a theological understanding of history. On the contrary, he regarded such a prophetic interpretation of history as a catastrophe. Gressmann, on the other hand, saw the prophets' use of history as the source of rejuvenation of historiographic interest in the late monarchy and

95. *RGG*, vol. 2, p. 1353.

exilic period as seen in the works of Deuteronomy and the Dtr redactor. On the whole, however, both Gunkel and Gressmann were concerned more with the origin of form and less with the nature of historical thinking.

Von Rad's treatment of historiography signals an important change in perspective. For him, three "predisposing factors" explained the origin of the historical sense among the Israelites which was lacking in their neighbors. For von Rad the theological factor was the most important, and it applied not only to prophecy and therefore to late historiography but also to the earliest "profane" historiography as well. This represents a rather substantial reversal of Gunkel's original position. Von Rad states emphatically: "The Israelites came to a historical way of thinking, and then to historical writing, by way of their belief in the sovereignty of God in history."[96] This dictum is found rather frequently in subsequent studies.

In his contribution to the volume *The Idea of History in the Ancient Near East,* M. Burrows surveys the uses of the past that may be found in the Old Testament as reflections of Israel's idea of history.[97] His examination includes not only the simple legends and larger "historical narratives," such as the Succession Story and the histories of J and Dtr, but also prophecy and apocalyptic literature. He concludes that "the basic, distinctive presupposition of all ancient Hebrew ideas about history is the conviction that in human history the one eternal, living God is working out his own sovereign purpose for the good of his creatures, first for his chosen people, and through them for the rest of mankind."[98] This position is similar to von Rad's but it includes a much more comprehensive theological statement. One has the feeling that Burrows has made a careful selection of concepts and put them together to formulate his own biblical theology, which he then attributes to the Hebrew people as a whole in all periods of their history. This, of course, is the fallacy of speaking about *the* Hebrew idea of history and then comparing it with *the* Greek idea or *the* Mesopotamian idea.[99]

H. Gese draws a comparison between "historical thinking" in the Old Testament and in the rest of the Near East, primarily in Mesopotamia and

96. *The Problem of the Hexateuch,* p. 170. Von Rad puts this statement in italics for emphasis.
97. M. Burrows, "Ancient Israel," in *The Idea of History in the Ancient Near East,* ed. R. C. Dentan, pp. 99–131.
98. Ibid., p. 128.
99. In fairness to Burrows it should be pointed out that since the Yahwist and Second Isaiah have much in common in their theological perspective, if these are viewed as the two poles in time within which most of the remaining material lies, then such a uniform theological outlook seems justified. If the Yahwist and Second Isaiah are contemporaries, however, this forces a quite different evaluation upon the whole question.

the land of the Hittites.[100] He suggests that for these cultures history is understood as the consequence of human actions. The gods, however, do not intervene on behalf of those whom they favor, but they bring immediate doom upon any who break the divine ordinance. Israel remained aloof from these neighboring cultures and so developed its own unique conception of history, based upon its particular understanding of a covenant with Yahweh. Following von Rad and Noth in their proposal of primitive "historical" confessions, Gese suggests that Israel's covenant was based upon the confession of a series of historical events: the exodus, desert wanderings, entry into the arable land, and the concluding of the covenant at Sinai. To this the patriarchal traditions were related as promise leading to fulfillment in the subsequent events. This gave to Israel's conception of history the sense of destiny. Furthermore, not only did the violation of the covenant result in doom but, because of the element of divine promise, the misfortune that Israel experienced was interpreted as punishment and correction. Thus Israel viewed history as divine judgment. The covenant relationship is a process toward ultimate fulfillment—a plan of salvation.

Gese believes that all this was part of Israel's primitive conception, its basic "predisposing factor," to use von Rad's term, and that this gave rise to "historiographic works." He briefly surveys the Succession Story, the Yahwist, and Dtr to show how this conception of history lies behind their work. He also deals with the prophetic view of history, which he sees as developing, out of this basic Israelite conception, an eschatological view in which history comes to an end in the Kingdom of God.

If we cannot accept von Rad's thesis about a primitive historical confession, and if the Yahwist, who is Gese's primary witness to the early traditions, cannot be dated so early in the monarchy, and if the covenant notion is really Deuteronomic,[101] then the whole scheme needs rather drastic revision. Gese feels confident in setting forth Israel's conception of history without referring to textual evidence or explicating clearly datable pieces as he does for the Near Eastern materials. It then seems rather circular argumentation to find this primitive concept of history behind the texts that he subsequently examines. It is doubtful whether his scheme—history as a plan of salvation—really works for Dtr, and his treatment of the early prophets is forced.

Whenever comparative historiography has centered on the idea of history in Mesopotamia and ancient Israel, as in Gese's study, the result has been to emphasize the contrast between the two. There is a rather pervasive opinion that Israel was unique in the ancient world in its understand-

100. "Geschichtliches Denken im Alten Orient und im Alten Testament," *ZThK* 55 (1958): 127–45, esp. pp. 41ff.
101. See now L. Perlitt, *Bundestheologie im Alten Testament*, WMANT 36 (1969).

ing of history and in its formulation of theology as revelation through history. The contrast was sharpened by characterizing the Mesopotamian world as polytheistic and therefore mythical and cyclic in its view of nature and history.[102] For this reason, it could have no sense of history and no history writing.

This view, however, has been strongly challenged by B. Albrektson in his recent book.[103] He suggests that in the texts of Mesopotamia and the Hittites the gods are presented as intervening in the affairs of men, directly affecting the historical process. Thus the outcome of historical events, such as wars, is attributed to the activity of the gods, often as a direct consequence of human behavior, whether pious or impious. The king is frequently represented as an agent of the deity in such activity and designated with an appropriate title of subordination. The deity's word has the inherent power to command the forces governing nature and the affairs of men, and to affect the outcome of battles, as well as changes in nature. Consequently, we could speak about revelation through history even to the extent that the gods were seen as always supporting the righteous and the pious king and therefore just in their actions, or as merciful in bringing about a return to prosperity after a period of hardship. The greatness of the gods was reflected in the success of the nation with whom they were primarily associated (for example, Ashur among the Assyrians and Marduk among the Babylonians), as well as in the powers of nature that they represented.

At each point in the discussion Albrektson makes a comparison with the Old Testament and finds very little difference in outlook. At times, quite similar formulae are used to express the notion of divine intervention. Thus he points out: "The phrase which the king here uses to express the belief that the course of events was directed by the gods and that his victory over the enemies was a divine gift, 'the gods delivered it into my hand,' seems to have spread all over the ancient Near East and is found in texts from different ages and different areas."[104] He furnishes examples of this formula for the divine handing-over of the enemy from the Hittite Old Kingdom, the Amarna period, an inscription of Nebuchadnezzar II, and numerous references in the Deuteronomistic corpus of the Old Testament.

102. See M. Eliade, *Cosmos and History: The Myth of the Eternal Return.*
103. *History and the Gods: An Essay on the Idea of Historical Events as Divine Manifestations in the Ancient Near East and in Israel.*
104. Ibid., p. 38. This phraseology "Yahweh will deliver/has delivered the enemy into your hand" has often been taken in the past as a basic theme of Israel's holy war tradition from its earliest days, but see most recently the comparative study of M. Weippert, "'Heilige Krieg' in Israel und Assyrien: Kritische Anmerkungen zu Gerhard von Rads Konzept des 'Heiligen Krieges im alten Israel,'" *ZAW* 84 (1972):460–93.

Of course, Albrektson does concede that a great difference exists between a theological world view in which there are numerous gods, each
with their different, and often competing, spheres of activity, and the monotheism of the Old Testament, in which all supernatural activity is subordinated to the will and direction of the one deity. It seems, therefore, that
just this difference would be most apparent in the notion of a divine plan
in history, and many scholars have emphasized the distinctiveness of Israel's thought precisely at this point. Albrektson's response is to say that the
notion of a divine plan of history in the Old Testament has been greatly
overstated. Such a view does not appear to be the perspective of the historical books, at any rate. The Deuteronomistic History and the Chronicler
do not point to any universal goal in history. Whether or not such a view
is present in the Yahwist depends upon a rather disputed interpretation of
the divine promise of blessing to all the families of the earth. In the prophetic literature Albrektson finds only a vague plan of salvation or restoration for Israel, which he describes as a rather diluted sense of the idea of a
"plan of history." Only in the apocalyptic literature of Daniel can one
speak in terms of a fixed plan for universal history.

It is at this point that Albrektson's work has come in for criticism.
W. G. Lambert,[105] while admitting that there is not much difference between the Deuteronomistic and the Babylonian view of history, nevertheless argues strongly that in the Yahwist as well as in the prophets there is
an eschatology and a movement in history toward a goal. Yet it is doubtful
that any of the Old Testament histories, including the work of the Yahwist, contains an eschatology. The notion of the election of Israel, upon
which Lambert places considerable weight, is not so different from the notion of divine election of the king, which is common in Mesopotamian
thought.[106] We can even speak of a certain democratization of royal ideology if we compare the language of Second Isaiah—being chosen from
the womb—with that of the Assyrian and Babylonian royal ideology.[107]
Historical thinking does not have to be teleological in order to produce
historiographic works, as is evident from the classical histories.

Nevertheless, Lambert's review does point to a serious problem. As we
have seen, he is not alone in identifying the Yahwist as the chief source for
a comprehensive theology or philosophy of history. If the Yahwist is given
an early tenth-century date, then it is only to be expected that scholars
would regard his idea of history as lying behind the prophets and all subse-

---

105. See his review in *Orientalia* 39 (1970):170–77; also idem, "Destiny and Divine Intervention in Babylon and Israel," *OTS* 17 (1972):65–72.

106. See H. Frankfort, *Kingship and the Gods*, pp. 239–40.

107. See also my discussion of such a democratization in the Yahwist, in *Abraham in History and Tradition*, pp. 275–76.

quent history writing and historical works. Yet Albrektson is justified in finding little evidence of such a comprehensive theology before the time of Second Isaiah and is therefore inclined to doubt that it really exists in the Yahwist. The obvious answer to the riddle is a reassessment of the Yahwist's date and the possible assignment of the work to the exilic period, contemporary with that of Second Isaiah—the time in which a more comprehensive theology of history evolved.

Albrektson's book, it seems to me, goes a long way toward breaking down any prejudice against the comparative study of Israelite and Mesopotamian or other Near Eastern historiography. He need not prove that all Mesopotamian ideas of history are the same as all Israelite views. What they have in common in their "theologies" of history is enough to warrant a comparison of historiographic genres as well.[108]

This point has also been made in a recent article by J. J. M. Roberts,[109] who indicates his agreement with Albrektson and objects to the widely held position that true historiography first developed in Israel. He seeks to counter a definition of historiography that might be particularly appropriate for Israel's historical corpus in its final form but would exclude the rest of the Near East from consideration. He rightly warns against the confusion of "a *literary* category (historiography), which could include more than one genre, with a particular, though not self-evident *philosophical* concept of history,"[110] or what we have referred to above as the idea of history. Within the literary category of historiography, Roberts would include several genres—king lists, chronicles, annals, epics, royal apologies, among others[111]—and in this he is in agreement with A. K. Grayson.[112] His own work, however, does not pursue the literary side of the study but carries forward Albrektson's program, to compare the ideas of history in Israel and Mesopotamia.[113]

Another explanation of Israel's "historical consciousness," along a quite

108. See also most recently, H. W. F. Saggs, *The Encounter with the Divine in Mesopotamia and Israel,* chap. 3, "The Divine in History," pp. 64–92.
109. "Myth *versus* History: Relaying the Comparative Foundations," *CBQ* 38 (1976): 1–13.
110. Ibid., p. 3.
111. Ibid., p. 3, n. 15.
112. On the extensive study of Mesopotamian historiographic genres by Grayson see above, 3a.
113. See also J. J. M. Roberts, "Nebuchadnezzar I's Elamite Crisis in Theological Perspective," in *Essays . . . in Memory of J. J. Finkelstein,* pp. 183–87; P. D. Miller and J. J. M. Roberts, *The Hand of the Lord: A Reassessment of the "Ark Narrative" of 1 Samuel*; N. Wyatt, "Some Observations on the Idea of History Among the West Semitic Peoples," *UF* 11 (1979): 825–32.

different line, has recently been put forward by M. Weippert.[114] He attempts to correlate the emergence of historical thinking in Israel with certain historical, sociological, and political realities in a way similar to Gunkel's treatment of the history of literary genres and their sociological contexts. Weippert thus refrains from any ahistorical predisposing factor and takes a thoroughly historical approach to this aspect of the subject. Yet it may be viewed as a way of revitalizing the older Gunkel–von Rad scheme of the rise of history writing without getting caught up in the problems of genre, about which Weippert has little to say.

Weippert begins by citing from numerous texts the twofold conviction that the Israelites had about themselves: (1) that the land in which they lived was a great benefit (*Heilsgutes*), and (2) that originally it did not belong to them—they came in from without and dispossessed the autochthonous population. The land was in fact a gift from Yahweh and this was expressed in the kerygmatic formula "The land that Yahweh swore to give to the fathers, to Abraham, Isaac, and Jacob." This notion of coming into the land from without was reflected in old traditions of the conquest and in the patriarchal traditions, as well as in statements found in the earliest prophets.[115]

Weippert notes that these basic convictions reflect a certain historical reality. Following the thesis of A. Alt,[116] he correlates the notion that in the Late Bronze Age nomads gradually settled in Palestine with clues from the stories of Genesis, and he shows how, because of their settlement in the hill country away from the main cultural centers, the Israelites made the transition to settled life without much assimilation, retaining their consciousness of not being Canaanites. However, the rise of the monarchy and the empire under David and Solomon changed this whole picture. With the absorption of the Canaanite population and all its institutional trappings, including the worship of foreign deities such as Baal, conflict arose between the old class of Israelite farmers and the new order. It is out of these circumstances, Weippert suggests, that the historical works of the Yahwist and the Elohist arose.

114. "Fragen des israelitischen Geschichtsbewusstseins," *VT* 23 (1973):415–42. The citation of recent literature on historiography, particularly on p. 415, n. 1 and 416, n. 3, is most useful.

115. Weippert makes a great deal out of Israel's consciousness of not being autochthonous and cites Amos 9:7, but the point of this text is that the notion was quite common among a number of peoples so that they all shared this same kind of "historical" consciousness. Furthermore, some of the Greeks also did not regard themselves as autochthonous and stories about migrating ancestors were rather common.

116. For an extensive demonstration of support for Alt's thesis of a gradual settlement in the land see M. Weippert, *The Settlement of the Israelite Tribes in Palestine*.

Weippert interprets these works as the historical presentation of the course of events from creation or the call of Abraham through the promise of land to the fathers, the sojourn in Egypt and the Exodus, the making of the covenant at Sinai, to the settlement in the Promised Land. He concludes from this content that J-E is a great *Ätiologie des israelitischen Kulturlandbesitzes*[117] whose point is to make clear that Israel received the land from Yahweh and not from Baal. The work is thus to be construed as a piece of polemic against the new order and propaganda for the old. To be sure, behind these works lies the kind of tradition-history suggested by von Rad, and the particular combination of law and history stemming from two different cultic traditions may have been influenced by the Hittite treaty pattern. But the rise of the empire and its challenges was the occasion that made these traditions center on the theme of settlement in the land.

One major problem that Weippert immediately takes up is the apparent lack of a conquest-settlement theme in J-E, but he is able to recover fragments of this theme in Num. 21:21–31 and Judg. 1:1–2:5, which he attributes to these early sources. On this basis he affirms that the Conquest tradition was the real nucleus of these Pentateuchal works. Weippert then draws a parallel development for the Deuteronomistic history of Joshua to 2 Kings, which he interprets as a great *Ätiologie des Landverlustes*[118] written in the time of another crisis, the exile.

There is no need at this stage to deal with Weippert's literary proposals for the composition and redaction of the historical books. The point at issue is whether history writing arose from the sense of historical consciousness as he reconstructs it. There are many difficulties with his hypothesis. First, J and E represent a strange kind of polemic when they do not even name Baal or make the worship of foreign gods an issue. This comes out only in the Deuteronomic tradition, and with great frequency. Weippert has transported the whole controversy of Hosea back into the Davidic period, but scarcely any trace of such an issue can be found there. To interpret the Yahwist as a polemic against Baal worship seems to me far-fetched.

It is likewise most curious that Weippert fills the court of David and Solomon with foreigners—Canaanites—who have no historic sense because they are autochthonous, and claims that the Yahwist writes against them and their program. Yet he can later turn around and attribute to this same courtly class the complex of stories about Samuel, Saul, and David, including the Succession Story, and account for their high quality of historiogra-

117. *VT* 23:428.
118. Ibid., p. 435.

phy because the empire had reached such a height of self-assurance. But these writers were obviously Israelites and Yahwists, not Canaanites, and their writings do not reflect any such cultural or religious struggle within the court. There appears to be a serious contradiction here. It is also note-worthy that Weippert has made no effort to retain the Gunkel–von Rad scheme of genre development from the *Sage* embodied in J-E to the history writing of the Succession Story. In fact, two quite independent groups and causes appear to give rise to somewhat different forms of historiography at the same time.

In his recent discussion of Israel's interest in the past,[19] H.-P. Müller deals, first, with the religious character of Israel's treatment of history, what he calls the *religionsmorphologischer Hintergrund*. He regards the relationship of myth to history in Israel as similar to that in the rest of the Near East—a marked departure from previous treatments, back to the time of Gunkel. Thus we find in Israelite literature the twofold movement of a mythologization of history and a historicization of myth. The former allows the deity to intervene in human affairs through "wonders" as signs of his presence. This makes possible the mythologization of history, as seen especially in the so-called *Heilsgeschichte* of Israel's early history. Müller refers to this as the *Heilsgeschichtsmythos* and traces its actualiza-tion in various literary genres, i.e., *Sagen, Legende, Märchen, Chronik*, and *Königsnovelle*.

Müller gives the greatest attention to the movement of historiography from *Sage* to its final collection in the Yahwistic source of the Pentateuch. This is where the *Heilsgeschichtsmythos* is most fully embodied. He views J primarily as a collector of the tenth century B.C. whose work reflects the empire period. The stories of the early monarchy, especially the Succession Story, are characterized as a secularization of the *Geschichtsmythos* (di-vine activity in human affairs) which reflects the "humanism" of the Solo-monic era. In this form the thesis of continuity from legend to history writ-ing is maintained.

Müller's use of *Heilsgeschichtsmythos* is similar to von Rad's treatment of the "predisposing religious factor," but in the former the emphasis is upon continuity with the general Near Eastern mentality. This part of Müller's treatment would seem to be compatible with Albrektson's study, although the latter's work is not mentioned by Müller. The understanding of myth as any rendering of divine activity in human affairs and its rela-tionship to the presentation of historical events in Israelite literature will continue to be much-debated issues. Yet the discussion of the relationship

119. J. Krecher and H.-P. Müller, "Vergangenheitsinterresse in Mesopotamien und Israel," *Saeculum* 26 (1975): esp. pp. 30–44.

between myth and history can be advanced only by comparing the use of mythologization within like historiographic genres by Israel and its neighbors.

Apart from raising this important issue, the value of Müller's study is limited to the degree to which one is willing to subscribe to the various genres or literary categories, their dating and characteristics, that Müller has taken over largely from earlier scholarly discussions. The questions and criticisms raised in the previous remarks apply to his work also. One rather surprising omission is the complete lack of any treatment of the Deuteronomist and the function of mythologization in the historical works in general—except for J and his use of *Sage*.

Throughout this survey we have focused upon the scheme inaugurated by Gunkel and Gressmann which, in spite of all subsequent modifications, has persisted up to the present time. Simply put, it holds that Israelite historiography evolved from early preliterary forms of the tradition to a sophisticated way of thinking and writing about the past, whether recent or more distant, by the time of the United Monarchy. The modifications of this view have to do with whether the focus is upon the evolution of narrative form and a proper definition of that form, the development of a way of thinking about the past, or the kinds of social, cultural, and religious influences that gave rise to both form and thought. All these presentations interpret the Court History of David (or Succession Story) as a piece of "contemporary history," and, while dating the Yahwist to the same period, understand J as a collection of traditions from the premonarchy period. It is safe to say that virtually none of the studies or essays on Hebrew historiography reviewed above could survive a serious attack on these two tenets. Yet they are far from certain and in need of thorough reconsideration.

The second feature worth noting about these studies is the very weak attempt made in them to take account of the form of history writing in Kings or the "Dtr Historian" within the context of a discussion of the rise of history writing. So different is the work of this historian, with his collecting and editing of sources, from the development of the early traditions that were thought to give rise to history writing, and so separate in time from the early monarchy, that it is as if we are dealing with two quite independent origins of history writing. The earlier one has nothing in common with the rest of the Near East, the later one is closely related to Near Eastern historiographic forms and builds directly upon them. Most of the scholars following Gunkel simply ignore or give little attention to the origin of this "later" history writing. Mowinckel, as we have seen, tries to overcome the problem by seeing the earliest work, the "History of Solomon," and the latest, the Dtr history of Kings, as two works of the same kind, both based upon official records and dated at either end of the spectrum with the other historical "sagas" arranged in between. The integration of the two kinds of historiography seems forced and not very satisfactory. It is most unlikely that the author of the "History of Solomon" is different from the author of the "History of the Kings of Israel and Judah," and if this separation into two works cannot be maintained, then his scheme falls apart. For the rest, the complete dichotomy between the supposed early and late history writing remains rather inexplicable.

A third common feature in the study of Israelite historiography is the real ambivalence of scholars toward a comparative approach. On the one hand, Israel and Greece are linked together as the two nations in antiquity within which history writing arose. Herodotus and Thucydides represent standards of comparison for evaluating the quality of certain pieces of Israelite prose. In a few instances, parallel features are cited between the two regions. Nevertheless, on the whole a comparative study of early Greek historiography with that of the Old Testament has not been undertaken. Biblical studies have almost completely ignored the scholarly literature in classical studies on the rise of history writing in ancient Greece and have seemed more interested in the "sagas" of Iceland of the twelfth century A.D.

Comparative treatment of the historiography of the Near East with ancient Israel has fared only a little better. This comparison has been carried on almost entirely under the supposition that the cultures and their ways of treating the past are for the most part radically different. Because the comparison has been of mental states, not of form, the surveys often appear haphazard and do not adequately represent the kind of material that does exist for thorough examination. Even when it is recognized that Israel did share certain historiographic forms with its neighbors, scholars are rarely concerned with comparing or elucidating the important features of such genres, so that terms like "annals" and "chronicles" are used in a rather questionable fashion. Too many statements made about Near Eastern forms in these studies are misleading or untenable.

The heart of the discussion of Hebrew history writing lies in the literary analysis of the books of Samuel and, in particular, of the Story of Saul, the Story of David's Rise, and the Succession Story (or Court History). To what extent can these be regarded as independent literary works close in time to the events they portray? If they are independent, how do they relate to the larger Dtr work in which they are found? It will become apparent in the discussion below why I have serious differences with the earlier assessment of a "primitive" historiography of the early monarchy period and therefore why the whole subject of Hebrew history writing needs such a complete reexamination.

In contrast with the uncertainties about the early traditions in Samuel is the historiography of the books of Kings. The structure of the latter is clear and gives to the whole a sense of being the work of a historian. The author's references to "official" sources allow for a comparison with other Near Eastern historiographic genres, and his work is fairly closely dated to the mid-sixth century. While the historian's method is revealed through the structure of Kings and the way in which the author combines "official" and "popular" sources, the work's thematic concerns open up the important question of the relationship of Kings to the books of Samuel.

Once the continuities between Samuel and Kings have been clarified, the place of Joshua and Judges in the larger history can be taken up. Which older sources were used by the author (or authors) and what later additions were made to his work? The relationship between what Noth calls the Dtr history and other possible histories (the Pentateuchal sources J and P) must also be determined. This is not a trivial issue. It goes to the very heart of what history meant in ancient Israel and therefore to the questions how and why the histories were written. To throw some light on this subject is the purpose of this study.

CHAPTER EIGHT

HISTORIOGRAPHY IN THE BOOKS OF SAMUEL

While Israel may have had counterparts to some of the genres of the various civilizations discussed above, we must adopt a different approach in studying Israelite historiography. In Israel the historical "streams of tradition" have come together in the form of histories—a literary form that is paralleled only in the historiography of Greece. In order to see how the historiographic genres of the Near East may have contributed to a biblical history, and to better understand the form of the history itself, I will focus special attention upon one of these histories, that of the Deuteronomistic Historian (Dtr) in the biblical books from Joshua to 2 Kings.

It is important to recall the definition of history set forth at the outset of this study, namely, "the intellectual form in which a civilization renders account to itself of its past." The critical questions in the rest of the study will be in what way Dtr is a history according to this definition and whether or not history writing existed in any form or at any stage prior to Dtr. The absence of such an inclusive form of history writing from the other civilizations of the ancient Near East means that we cannot begin with the notion that in Israel history was a self-evident form of national consciousness and identity. If we deem something in Joshua to 2 Kings to be a piece of history writing prior to, and apart from, the history as a whole, then we must be prepared to show how it could function by itself as a comprehensive identity tradition. Since the rise of history writing in Israel is most often associated with various parts of the books of Samuel, it is here that we must begin our investigation.

Our survey of the study of Israelite historiography indicated that the books of Samuel have long been regarded as showing the emergence, out of its earlier form of legend-narrative, of the finest example of history writing before Herodotus—the Succession Story. According to such views, the Dtr is credited with only a rather minor role in the compilation process, primarily in his supplementation of the traditions of Samuel and Saul. For these figures only *Heldensagen* existed, which had to be edited to give them some shape and coherence. The Story of David's Rise and the Court

249

History, on the other hand, are believed to be documents, reflecting the old historiography, which were incorporated by Dtr into his history with little modification. Such general theories, however, run up against a number of serious literary problems as soon as we begin to examine more closely the various groups of stories and their relationship to each other. Intensive study of the individual parts and of their interrelationships must inevitably have important consequences for theories about the development of history writing as a whole in Samuel.

a. THE STORY OF SAUL

Since the time of J. Wellhausen, the stories about Saul have been divided into two blocks of material, often characterized as the Early Source and the Late Source.[1] The Early Source comprises the stories in 1 Sam. 9:1–10:16 and chapters 11, 13, and 14, and within this source are the oldest traditions about Saul's monarchy. The Late Source, consisting of 1 Sam. 8, 10:17–27, and chapters 12 and 15,[2] is usually ascribed to a Dtr editor and is regarded as having few early traditions behind it. M. Noth modified this position by regarding the Dtr source as part of the larger historical work of Dtr from Joshua to 2 Kings.[3] In his view, the stories of the Early Source were incorporated into the Dtr history as independent traditions and not as a continuous source document. In some recent studies of the Saul stories, scholars have suggested either that the earliest traditions do form a continuous early narrative about Saul[4] or that a pre-Deuteronomic edition of the Saul stories was composed before the final Dtr version.[5]

These revisions of Noth's position rest largely upon the ability to see within the Late Source evidences of early traditions. Thus it is suggested

1. J. Wellhausen, *Prolegomena to the History of Ancient Israel*, pp. 245–72. For recent surveys on the history of the discussion see F. Langlemet, "Les récites de l'institution de la royauté (1 Sam. VII–XII): De Wellhausen aux travaux récents," *RB* 77 (1970):161–200; B.C. Birch, *The Rise of the Israelite Monarchy: The Growth and Development of 1 Samuel 7–15*, pp. 1–10; F. Crüsemann, *Der Widerstand gegen das Königtum*, WMANT 49, pp. 1–17; P. Kyle McCarter, *1 Samuel: The Anchor Bible*, pp. 12–30.

2. However, some scholars, including Wellhausen (*Prolegomena*, pp. 258–59), regard chap. 15 as early.

3. *Überlieferungsgeschichtliche Studien*, pp. 3–110. See also H. J. Boecker, *Die Beurteilung der Anfänge des Königtums in den deuteronomistischen Abschnitten des 1. Samuelbuches: Ein Beitrag zum Problem des "Deuteronomistischen Geschichtswerkes,"* WMANT 31; K.-D. Schunck, *Benjamin: Untersuchungen zur Entstehung und Geschichte eines israelitischen Stammes*, BZAW 86 (1963), pp. 80–108.

4. See especially J. Maxwell Miller, "Saul's Rise to Power: Some Observations Concerning 1 Sam. 9:1–10:16, 10:26–11:15, and 13:2–14:46," *CBQ* 36 (1974):157–74; Crüsemann, *Der Widerstand*, pp. 54ff.; McCarter, *1 Samuel*, pp. 26–27.

5. Birch, *Rise of the Monarchy*, pp. 131ff.; McCarter, *1 Samuel*, pp. 18–23.

that the naming of Samuel's two sons and the locality of their activity in 1 Sam. 8:1–3 allows us to recognize an old tradition behind these verses.[6] My own view, however, is that these verses, with the rest of the chapter, are a late fiction. The notion that Samuel appointed his two sons as judges over Israel and that they then held office in Beersheba cannot be reconciled with the early period of Israel's history. Is it conceivable that Samuel ruled as judge over an area so large that it included southern Judah? Beersheba became an important administrative center only in the late Judean monarchy, so the setting for the events in chapter 8 is anachronistic. The office of judge as both administrator and magistrate would also fit quite well with the late period, since judges were used in these roles at Tyre in the Neo-Babylonian period.[7] Furthermore, the two sons of Samuel who corrupt their office as judges parallel the two sons of Eli who abuse their station as priests, and in neither case can the father control his sons in his old age. The scene has been invented to explain the people's demand for a change in the form of government.

The description of the "customary behavior of the king" (mišpaṭ hammelek) in 8:11–17 is likewise identified as an early source directed against emulating the rule of foreign kings.[8] It is further suggested that since Dtr condemned kings primarily for their apostasy, this characterization of the king must represent an independent tradition. But 8:18 makes it quite clear that this is a description of later Israelite kings. Furthermore, Deuteronomy and Dtr recognize that the institution of kingship is foreign (see Deut. 17:14ff.) and that it is therefore susceptible to corruption in two ways, by the aggrandizement of the court—which leads to the enslavement of the people—and by the apostasy of religion. If the description of the monarchy in this text is thought to resemble the court of Solomon, Deut. 17:14ff. does even more so.[9] It should also be noted that the story of Naboth's vineyard in 1 Kings 21 illustrates very well Dtr's concern about the

---

6. Crüsemann, Der Widerstand, p. 61; Birch, Rise of the Monarchy, pp. 22–23. The latter advocates an early source for vv. 1–7, but the subtle distinction he sees between v. 7 and vv. 8ff. is not persuasive. His early dating of vv. 4–7 seems to be dictated by his pre-Dtr dating of 10:17ff. See also McCarter, 1 Samuel, pp. 159ff., who seems to regard the whole chapter as belonging to a pre-Dtr "prophetic edition," with only v. 8 as a Deuteronomic interpolation.

7. Josephus, Contra Ap. I, 156ff.

8. I. Mendelsohn, "Samuel's Denunciation of Kingship in the Light of Akkadian Documents from Ugarit," BASOR 143 (1956): 17–22; Crüsemann, Der Widerstand, pp. 61–62; cf. R. E. Clements, "The Deuteronomistic Interpretation of the Founding of the Monarchy in 1 Sam. VIII," VT 24 (1974):398–410; Birch, Rise of the Monarchy, pp. 24–25.

9. McCarter, 1 Samuel, pp. 161–62, points to the strong parallel between 1 Sam. 8:1–22 and Deut. 17:14–17 but does not conclude the obvious, that the former is Dtr. Instead he proposes that the Deuteronomic tradition is derived from a proto-Deuteronomic prophetic history. Since his views for such a "prophetic edition" are heavily dependent upon Birch, the latter's views must be examined below.

social evils of the monarchy reflected in this text. The particular evils of
kingship are emphasized here because Samuel is trying to dissuade the people from choosing a king. Once a king has been chosen, it is appropriate to
warn both king and people about the danger of apostasy, as Samuel does
in 1 Sam. 12. I see no reason why this list of abuses could not have been
composed by Dtr.[10]

Several scholars, following O. Eissfeldt, have also suggested that 1 Sam.
10:17–27 is not a unity but a combination of two separate and conflicting
traditions about Saul's election to the monarchy. It is argued that in one
tradition (verses 20–21bα) Saul is chosen by lot, whereas in the other
(verses 21bβ–24) Saul is revealed by divine oracle.[11] Thus B. Birch states
that the nature of lot casting was such that "one who was not present
could not be chosen by the lot as the present text seems to indicate."[12]
But this is certainly not the case. As J. Lindblom has shown, one method
of drawing lots was to put several names into a container and then draw
one out. The process envisaged here is quite simple.[13] In order to handle
only a limited number of inscribed lots at one time, the names of the tribes
were first entered and one chosen. Next, the clans within the chosen tribe
were entered, then the families, the households, and the eligible males, until out of this last group one *name* was drawn. In this process an individual
did not need to be present to be chosen. But Saul's apparent absence from
the assembly seemed to call into question his selection by lot; thus the situation required a further oracular inquiry by which his presence was in fact
revealed. In this way the story of Saul's selection by lot is simply embellished with a little drama and character portrayal. There is no reason to
speak here of any source division, nor is there any evidence that an old tradition lies behind the account as it stands. If 10:17–27 is a unity and if

10. See Birch, *Rise of the Monarchy*, p. 25: "Thus far it may be said that there is clear evidence of a Deuteronomistic hand in the chapter . . . and that this same hand is probably responsible for the use of the stereotyped description in vss. 11–17." On the other hand, Clements's attempt to prove (*VT* 24: 407) that the Deuteronomists recognized only the Davidic
monarchy as legitimate is much too forced. Even if he could explain away the election of
Saul, the stories of Jeroboam's election (1 Kings 11:29ff.; 14:7ff.) and Baasha's (1 Kings
16:1ff.) clearly show the possibility of other non-Davidic kings being elected by Yahweh.

11. O. Eissfeldt, *Die Komposition der Samuelisbücher*, p. 7. He assigns 10:17bα to his E
source and 10:21bβ–27 to his L source, but few follow him in this source division. Others
who nevertheless see two traditions in this unit are Birch, *Rise of the Monarchy*, pp. 42–54;
idem, "The Choosing of Saul at Mizpah," *CBQ* 37 (1975):447–57; Crüsemann, *Der Widerstand*, pp. 54ff.

12. Birch, *Rise of the Monarchy*, p. 44.

13. J. Lindblom, "Lot-casting in the Old testament," *VT* 12 (1962):164–78. Birch's appeal to Lindblom is quite misleading since Lindblom, by his own explanation, sees no tension
between vv. 21 and 22 (pp. 165, 170). On the preference for reading with LXX instead of
MT in vv. 21–22, see McCarter, *I Samuel*, p. 190.

none of it belongs to the older level of the tradition, then it becomes difficult to construct an early continuous history of Saul.

In his study of the Saul traditions Birch has advocated the position that prior to the Dtr editing, which was rather slight by his analysis, there was a "prophetic edition" of these stories. The crux of Birch's argument comes in 10:17–27, where he is forced to show that no part of this unit belongs to Dtr.[14] His position, however, becomes rather weak at this point, for 10:17–19 strongly resembles the Dtr "prophetic" speech in Judg. 6:7–10.[15] Furthermore, 1 Sam. 10:19 recapitulates chapter 8 and follows on from 8:22. The literary device of dismissing all the people in 8:22 and reconvening them again in 10:17 allows for the incorporation of the material in 9:1–10:16 as a kind of digression. The text in 1 Sam. 10:25, with its mention of the "statute of kingship" (*mišpaṭ hammᵉlukāh*),[16] very likely refers to Deut. 17:14ff., and Samuel follows the Deuteronomic model of Moses writing a book of laws and depositing it before Yahweh (see Deut. 31:24ff.).

Birch also has the larger problem of designating more precisely the limits of a "prophetic edition" beyond those texts that he has identified within the Saul story. He points to some rather definite continuities within the story of David and its culmination in 2 Sam. 7. The nature of this editorial work therefore cannot be resolved until these links are fully identified, but the fact that 2 Sam. 7 is increasingly viewed as a central text in the Dtr history raises serious questions for Birch's work.[17] Furthermore, Birch's hint that the "prophetic edition" may extend into the books of Kings as well raises a related problem. He dates the "prophetic edition" by comparing Samuel's role in this source to the role of the preclassical prophets as portrayed in the books of Kings. But if, in fact, all these prophetic portraits are Dtr, then the case both for the early dating of the "prophetic edition" and for its distinctiveness from Dtr cannot stand. The position taken here is that the entire Late Source is part of the Dtr editing of the stories of Saul.

14. Birch, *Rise of the Monarchy*, pp. 47–54.

15. Birch argues (ibid., pp. 45–46) that none of the phrases cited by W. Richter as Dtr in Judg. 6:7–10 is found in 1 Sam. 10:17–19 (see *Die Bearbeitungen des "Retterbuches" in der deuteronomischen Epoche*, BBB 21, p. 106). However, the rest of the phraseology in both texts and the practice of citing the *Heilgeschichte* prior to the pronouncement of an accusation are clear indications of Dtr authorship. For the numerous additional parallels see G. F. Moore, *Judges*, ICC, pp. 181–82.

16. The phrase is not the same as *mišpaṭ hammelek* in 8:9. It is the difference between the institution itself, subject to regulations, and the occupant of the office, who may behave in a customary, but unlawful, fashion. The wordplay may be deliberate, but the differences do not argue for a different authorship.

17. For a discussion of 2 Sam. 7 see below, 8c.

In turning to the Early Source, we find a broad scholarly consensus that the first story in 1 Sam. 9:1–10:16 is not a unity.[18] While some difference of opinion remains on a few details, it is generally agreed that the oldest story simply dealt with Saul's recovery of his father's asses and that a later redactor introduced into this story the theme of Saul's divine election and anointing. Without reviewing all the variations on this proposal, I will simply set forth my own division of the text with the original story and the redactional additions.[19]

The original story in 9:1–8, 10–14, 18–19, 22–27aαβ; 10:2–6, 9–13 has all the stylistic marks of a folktale.[20] A clear situation of need is resolved through the fortunate intervention of a holy man. The story strongly resembles the genre of *legenda* in which the "man of God," a seer, has the power of clairvoyance.[21] Saul and his servant seek a seer's aid for a small fee when their resources are gone. The unnamed seer turns out to be Samuel, who tells Saul that he will take care of his concerns the next day; but first, Saul must be his guest at a banquet. Following this, Samuel provides Saul with sleeping quarters for the night and then sends him on his way the next morning. Before Samuel lets Saul go, however, he tells him about three episodes that will occur to him on his return home: in the first he will receive news that his father's asses have been found; in the second he will be given provisions for their homeward journey; and in the third he will encounter a band of ecstatics who will induce in him a fit of ecstasy. The first two events occur without comment, but the third is described in detail in order to explain a popular saying: "Is Saul also among the prophets?"—a somewhat derogatory view of the *nᵉbiʾîm*. At the conclusion of the story Saul arrives home.[22] In this form the story is a self-contained entity with a consistent focal concentration upon Saul. Like the *legenda* it is a wonder story, with "signs" but with very little theological interest.

18. B. C. Birch, "The Development of the Tradition on the Anointing of Saul in 1 Sam. 9:1–10:16," *JBL* 90 (1971): 55–68; idem, *Rise of the Monarchy*, pp. 29–42; Crüsemann, *Der Widerstand*, pp. 57ff.; L. Schmidt, *Menschlicher Erfolg und Jahwes Initiative: Studien zu Tradition, Interpretation und Historie in Uberlieferungen von Gideon, Saul und David*, WMANT 38, pp. 58–102. These various analyses are similar. Cf. Miller, *CBQ* 36:157–61.

19. My basic difference with Birch is that I include 9:25–27aβ, 10:5–6, 10–13 in the original story and vv. 14–16 as part of the addition. In contrast to Crüsemann and Schmidt, I would include 10:5–6 and 10–13, and exclude 10:7. Against Miller, I regard the reference to the Philistine garrison (*nᵉsîb*) in 10:5 and the instructions in 10:8 as redactional links to chap. 13 and not part of the original.

20. Birch, *JBL* 90:58–61.

21. On prophetic *legenda*, see A. Rofé, "The Classification of the Prophetical Stories," *JBL* 89 (1970):427–40. A fuller discussion will be given below, 9b.

22. The ending has been somewhat obscured in MT with the statement, in v. 13, that after Saul finished prophesying he came "to the high place," *habbāmāh*. This does not make any sense in the context and I would therefore emend it to read "to his home," *habbaytāh*.

A number of redactional additions to this story have radically changed its character and intention. These are found in 9:9, 15–17, 27aγ, b; 10:1, 7–8, 14–16. The first indication of this change is the editorial comment in 9:9 suggesting a very different view of prophecy and a considerable span of time between the story the editor has received and his own treatment of it. The addition in verses 15–17 creates a digression that seriously interrupts the action of the story at a crucial point. It creates a disunity in time by referring back to the previous day and it introduces an entirely new situation of need, that is, the Philistine oppression, which makes the problem of the lost asses trivial. This new crisis is drawn from the broader context of the books of Samuel and it makes this story the first scene in a number of subsequent events. The digression also shifts the focus from Saul to Samuel, who now assumes the central role, and a new theme is given to the story, that of the election of Saul to kingship. The story receives a theological orientation in that it is about God's intervention to rescue "his people" by the designation of a "prince," *nāgîd*.[23] Samuel, as prophet, is the means by which the divine will and activity are set in motion. His clairvoyance is now explained as the result of divine revelation, so that the prophet is primarily the medium of the word of God. This is precisely the same contrast that exists between the *legenda* and Dtr's view of the prophet in the books of Kings.[24]

The theme and perspective of verses 15–17 are carried through in the other editorial additions. An obvious tension is created between verse 19 of the original story, in which Samuel tells Saul that he will deal with his problem the next day, and verse 20, the addition, in which Samuel immediately dismisses the problem of the lost asses as trivial and substitutes for this the theme of Saul's election, verses 20–21. This makes the revelation that the asses have been found, in 10:2, entirely redundant. The theme of Saul's election culminates in his secret anointing, 9:27aγ, b–10:1(LXX).[25] Samuel's words in 10:1, following the anointing, reiterate the theological themes of 9:15–17. The language about the salvation of God's people is reminiscent of the Dtr themes in Judges,[26] and the reference to Israel as Yahweh's "inheritance," *naḥᵃlāh*, is a distinctive Dtr concept.[27] The series of events—"signs" (*'ōtôt*) in the sense of wonders (10:9)—is also in-

23. The important term *nāgîd* will be discussed in greater detail below.

24. See below, 9b.

25. On the text of 10:1, see most recently McCarter, *I Samuel*, p. 171. It is possible that the invitation to the meal in 9:22–24 has been embellished to suggest that Saul, as the future king, had the place of highest honor, in which case the remark of the maiden in v. 13, "afterwards those eat who are invited," would also be an addition. But this suggestion is less certain and not so important to the whole discussion.

26. Judg. 2:16ff. This will be discussed below.

27. G. von Rad, "The Promised Land and Yahweh's Land in the Hexateuch," in *The Problem of the Hexateuch*, pp. 80ff.

terpreted as an indication of Yahweh's election of Saul, thus creating a pattern similar to the call and election of Gideon in Judges 6.[28]

Within the predicted events in 10:2–6, a seemingly casual reference is made in verse 5 to a garrison of the Philistines at Gibeah.[29] This has no significance for the "sign" itself but harks back to 9:16, which refers to the Philistine oppression. It also anticipates the remark in 10:7, "do whatever your hand finds to do, for God is with you," which then relates to Saul's later attack on the Philistine garrison in chapter 13. This military action is meant to follow closely his reception of the "spirit of Yahweh," as it so often does in Judges. The rather strange instructions directing Saul to wait for Samuel seven days at Gilgal relate to nothing that immediately follows but provide a link to events in 13:8ff., as we shall see below.[30] The final scene in 10:14–16 is related to the theme of the secret anointing, for the point of the scene is that Saul did not divulge Samuel's remarks about his kingship to anyone, not even to members of his own family.[31]

Saul's rescue of the people of Jabesh-Gilead in chapter 11 is a self-contained story[32] that is probably the oldest account of how Saul was crowned king.[33] His rise to a position of leadership is based on a singular act, as is so often the case in the stories of the Judges. To this account have been added verses 12–14 (along with the reference to Samuel in verse 7), which make of this coronation a "renewal" of kingship. The connections between 10:26–27 and the remarks in verses 12–13 are obvious. They

28. The parallels between the two stories are the result of common authorship and not evidence for a preprophetic call pattern, as some have suggested. Cf. Birch, *JBL* 90:61–67; idem, *Rise of the Monarchy*, pp. 35ff.; N. Habel, "The Form and Significance of the Call Narratives," *ZAW* 77 (1965):297–323; W. Richter, *Die sogenannten vorprophetischen Berufungsberichte: Eine literaturwissenschaftliche Studie zu 1 Sam. 9, 1–10, 16; Ex. 3f. und Ri. 6,* 116–17, FRLANT 101.

29. Miller (*CBQ* 36:159ff.) argues that this is part of the original account, but see n. 19, above.

30. The simple remark in 10:6 about Saul being turned into a different person as a result of an ecstatic experience is interpreted by the redactor in v. 9aβ rather pietistically to mean that God changed his heart. See also 10:26.

31. See also Miller, *CBQ* 36:160.

32. The introduction to this story in 4Q Sam[a] makes this even more apparent than in MT. The following is a translation taken from McCarter, *I Samuel*, p. 198:

Now Nahash, the King of the Ammonites, had been oppressing the Gadites and the Reubenites grievously, gouging out the right eye of each of them and allowing Israel no deliverer. No men of the Israelites who were across the Jordan remained whose right eye Nahash, king of the Ammonites, had not gouged out. But seven thousand men had escaped from the Ammonites and entered into Jabesh-gilead. About a month later . . .

33. For recent treatments of 1 Sam. 11, see Birch, *Rise of the Monarchy*, pp. 54–63; Schunck, *Benjamin*, pp. 90–91. Cf. Miller (*CBQ* 36:165ff.), who argues against any redactional additions in 11:12–14 and takes the link with 10:27 as original. I do not find his position convincing.

represent a redactional link and not an old tradition of opposition to the monarchy. The victory in chapter 11 is interpreted by the redactor as proof and confirmation of the divine choice in 10:20ff. Again in this redactional addition the rather "secular" story is given a theological perspective through the words of Saul,[34] "today Yahweh has won a victory in Israel."

The account of Saul's warfare with the Philistines in 13:2–14:46 contains a number of indications that the history of its development and transmission may be complex.[35] It has no obvious original connection with the preceding stories, since Saul is no longer a young man but now has a full-grown son, Jonathan, who is also a field commander. The beginning of the account is somewhat defective, but the events can be reconstructed as follows. An attack on the Philistine garrison at Gibeah (Geba) leads to war. Some of the Israelites desert, but Saul is able to maintain a force of six hundred with Jonathan at the captured fort of Gibeah, where they face the enemy camp across the valley at Michmash. A brave attack on the enemy garrison by Jonathan and his companion begins the final assault, which leads to victory. In the course of battle, however, Jonathan inadvertently places himself under his father's curse but is subsequently rescued by the people from his father's hand.[36]

Into this story has been fitted an episode about Samuel (13:4b, 7b–15a) that takes place away from the scene of action at the sanctuary of Gilgal. The statement, in verse 8, that Saul "waited seven days, the time appointed by Samuel," cannot be taken as part of the original story but instead constitutes a redactional connection with 10:8. It allows no time whatever for the events in between or for the great differences in Saul's age between the two events. Its only function is to serve as a literary link between the story of Saul's election and that of his rejection. Saul is accused of breaking the command of Yahweh, which must refer merely to Samuel's earlier injunction to wait seven days. Presumably Saul could otherwise have legitimately offered sacrifices through his own priest (14:18ff., 34ff.). In this way Saul is said to have forfeited the right to have his kingship continue on in perpetuity after him. In his place Yahweh would designate another "after his own heart" to be a prince, *nāgîd*, over his people, one who would keep his commandments. It is clear that the addition of the scene of Gilgal is from

34. Or Samuel, as in LXX.
35. See Birch, *Rise of the Monarchy*, pp. 74–94; Miller, *CBQ* 36:161–65; Schunck, *Benjamin*, pp. 91–93.
36. Birch characterizes the primary material in 13:2–7a, 15b–18, 23 as "annalistic" (*Rise of the Monarchy*, p. 84) and distinct from the story in chap. 14. But there are no clear features that point to such a characterization on the basis of the Near Eastern annals considered above. It is best to consider these verses as merely introductory to the story of Jonathan's exploits in chap. 14.

the same hand as that of the secret anointing of Saul. But whereas in the earlier unit the editor looked back to the time of the judges, here he looks forward to the history of David and sets forth the themes that will be decisive for that history too.

The editorial process that absorbed these three stories of Saul into the larger whole is instructive for the discussion of historiography. It would appear that the editor found these stories already in fixed written form and felt under some constraint to retain them as they were. Only by supplementation did he seek to reinterpret them and to fit them into his larger thematic framework, even at the expense of creating obvious tensions and absurdities. Samuel does not have a place in the early Saul traditions, except perhaps in the first story of Saul's youth. The connection is developed by Dtr in order to make the description of Saul's relationship to Samuel similar to his other descriptions of prophet-king relationships in Kings. For the rest, he seems to have composed his pieces in chapter 8, 10:17–27, and chapter 12 rather freely. Dtr has Samuel dismiss the people in 8:22, only to reconvene them in 10:17, so that 9:1–10:16 serves as a kind of digression. The final admonitory speech is reserved for chapter 12, after the "renewal" of kingship but before Saul's rejection. It picks up the themes of the people's demands for a king, the divine election and anointing, and the threats about disobeying Yahweh's commands. This redactional process—a mixture of free composition and the creation of redactional links between independent blocks of material of different types and genres—is the basis of historiography in Samuel and Kings. The individual legends about Saul, which cannot be easily dated, do not by themselves point to a stage of narrative development or historical consciousness that could be construed as a stage in the development of Israelite historiography.

Quite different from the other stories of Saul is the one about his war with the Amalekites in 1 Sam. 15.[37] There has been considerable diversity of opinion about whether it is early or late and how it relates to the other stories.[38] Many scholars think that the work represents, at the very least, early traditions about holy war in the time of Saul that were later "reworked." However, serious questions may be raised about the account of the war, questions that discredit its historicity, credibility, and antiquity. First, the story suggests that Saul had complete control over both Israel and Judah, but there are many reasons to doubt this.[39] Second, the description of the obliteration of the Amalekites is in conflict with the account of David's campaign against this group later on.[40] Finally, the

37. See Birch, *Rise of the Monarchy*, pp. 94–108; Schunck, *Benjamin*, pp. 82–85.
38. See J. H. Grønbaek, *Die Geschichte vom Aufstieg Davids (1. Sam. 15–2. Sam. 5): Tradition und Komposition*, pp. 37–68.
39. The Story of David's Rise does not seem to recognize control of Judah by Saul.
40. 1 Sam. 30.

oldest stories about Saul in the previous texts show that Samuel had no historical role in Saul's monarchy, that this was only created by a later redactor. The story in chapter 15 has all the marks, in form and theme, of a late fabrication.

As for the story's form, Birch has recently analyzed the components according to C. Westermann's forms of prophetic speech.[41] He finds that the story fits the type that Westermann calls the "judgment-speech to the individual," albeit in a rather drawn-out narrative style. In this respect it is similar to 13:7b–15a. Birch also follows Westermann in dating such a form to the period *before* the classical prophets and in agreeing that "a few examples extend into the time of the writing prophets only to disappear completely after that."[42] This allows Birch to attribute this chapter, along with other parts of the redactional additions, to a "prophetic editor" of the late eighth century. The fallacy of Westermann's early dating of this form lies in the fact that all the texts he cites are narratives and many of them refer to the early periods of Israelite history.[43] But most of them can be said to belong to the Dtr history or to a Dtr redaction of the prophetic books. That some of the examples of the form can be so clearly dated as late casts serious doubt upon the early dating of any of them.[44]

If, on the other hand, this story is compared with Rofé's classification of prophetic *legenda*, then it certainly belongs to the late didactic or theological type, which is altogether different from the style of simple *legenda* in the original story of 9:1–10:16.[45] Thus it teaches the lesson that "obedience is better than sacrifice," a well-known theme of classical prophecy. The story also portrays the prophet as the medium of the divine word, a type of portrayal consistently used by Dtr in Kings and by the redactor in the stories of Saul. Contrary to the opinion expressed by Westermann, this is the view of prophecy that was formulated in the postclassical prophecy period.[46]

The language of this chapter also reflects the Dtr tradition. Thus we find

41. Birch, *Rise of the Monarchy*, pp. 98ff. See C. Westermann, *Basic Forms of Prophetic Speech*, pp. 129–63.

42. Westermann, *Basic Forms*, p. 138.

43. Ibid., p. 137.

44. A clear example is in 1 Kings 13:1–3, where the reference in v. 2 to Josiah establishes it as a late text. On the dating of this text see A. Rofé, "Classes in the Prophetical Stories: Didactic Legenda and Parable," SVT 26 (1974):158ff.

45. On didactic *legenda* see Rofé, SVT 26 (1974): 145ff. For the broader discussion of Rofé's classification see below, 9b.

46. Westermann's argument (in *Basic Forms*, pp. 129ff.) for the early dating and preservation of prophetic speech forms in Kings is most curious. He states that "the versions of the prophetic speeches in Chronicles are so different from those in Kings that, because of this difference, those in Kings quite automatically give the impression of having a greater proximity to the actual prophetic speeches." Given that Chronicles was probably written two centuries after Kings, this comparison says nothing about King's preservation of early forms. Kings simply stands closer to the *end* of classical prophecy than does Chronicles.

such expressions as, "to heed the voice of Yahweh/his or my voice," *sm^c l^e qôl (dibrē) yhwh/b^e qôlô* or *l^e qôlî;*[47] "thus says Yahweh of hosts," *kōh 'āmar yhwh ṣ^e bā'ôt;*[48] "the word of Yahweh came to . . .," *way^e hî d^e bar yhwh 'el;*[49] "he did not confirm/obey my word" (verse 11), *w^e 'et d^e bāray lō' hēqîm.*[50] Also common in Dtr is the reciprocal judgment statement: the king (people) rejects Yahweh, he rejects him (them).[51] The reference in verse 2 to Amalekites opposing the Israelites on the road when they came out of Egypt is similar in language to Deut. 25:18. Likewise Saul's act of tearing Samuel's cloak, in verses 27–28, as a symbol of Yahweh's tearing the kingdom from Saul and giving it to David, is repeated in 1 Kings 11:29–31, where Ahijah's torn garments represent the northern kingdom torn from the house of David and given to Jeroboam (see also 2 Kings 17:21). All these features point strongly to the Dtr character of 1 Sam. 15.

The story in chapter 15 provides a transition from the Saul traditions to those of David. Yet its relationship to the preceding Saul stories and to the following Story of David's Rise has been a matter of some confusion. On the one hand, the account of Saul's rejection seems to lead directly into the story of David's anointing as successor in 16:1–13. But it also has strong connections with the Saul stories that precede it. For example, 15:1 refers directly back to 10:1. The verbal similarity is so great that literary dependence can hardly be disputed. Similarly, 15:7 contains an allusion to Saul's initial meekness in 9:21 when he was offered the kingship over Israel. On the other hand, chapter 15, with its theme of Saul's rejection, seems to be a doublet to the episode in 13:7b–15a. The following features are common to both stories. Saul's rejection arises out of a command by Samuel to Saul that is not *totally* obeyed.[52] The scene of rejection in both cases is set in Gilgal and includes the offering of sacrifices, of which Saul's are rejected. When Samuel arrives at the scene, Saul greets him (*brk*) as if nothing is wrong. Samuel rebukes Saul with an accusing question and Saul immediately makes an excuse expressing fear or weakness. Samuel then tells Saul that he has disobeyed the divine command and as a consequence has been rejected by God in favor of another, bringing his own kingdom to an end. The two men part company and go their separate ways. While the divine command and the subsequent offense by Saul are somewhat different in

47. See Deut. 1:34; 5:28; 8:20; 9:23; 13:5, 19+; Judg. 2:2, 20; 6:10; 1 Sam. 12:14, 15; Jer. 3:13, 25; 7:23+. Yahwistic texts of the Pentateuch influenced by Dtr style that contain this expression are Gen. 22:18; 26:5; Exod. 5:2; 15:26; 19:5.

48. See 2 Sam. 7:8; this phrase also occurs frequently in the prose of Jeremiah.

49. See 2 Sam. 7:4; this phrase also occurs frequently in Dtr stories of prophets in Kings, and in Jeremiah and Ezekiel.

50. Deut. 27:26; Jer. 34:28; 35:14, 16.

51. 2 Kings 17:15–20.

52. Cf. the treatment of this theme in the story of the man of God from Judah, 1 Kings 13. See Rofé, SVT 26:158–63.

the two versions, the theme that "obedience is better than sacrifice" is still implicit in the first story and explicit in the second.

Practically every aspect of the first episode is paralleled in the second, even though the context of the larger story is entirely different; such a degree of similarity cannot be fortuitous. Either these episodes are the work of the same author or the author of one is directly dependent upon the author of the other for the story's structure and theme. Yet is is difficult to see why the same author would tell of Saul's rejection twice, giving virtually the same reason for rejection in both stories. Presumably no author would have so awkwardly inserted the scene of Saul's rejection into the larger story of Saul's warfare if he were planning later to present the scene as a separate episode. Birch attributes both stories to one author, who he feels had a different purpose in each account; he maintains that in the first, 13:14, only Saul's dynasty is discontinued, whereas in the second Saul himself (15:26) is rejected, leading to David's anointing.[53] The wording of the two accounts, however, does not allow for such a distinction. In both cases it is said that Saul's kingship (*mamleket/meml*^e*kût*) has been taken from him and given to another, better than he. In fact, in the subsequent story of David, Saul's kingship is not immediately ended and Saul views David as a threat not to his own rule but to the succession within his own household.

One solution to this problem would be to adopt the view that the doublets belong to different literary sources.[54] It has been suggested that the story of Saul's monarchy concludes with the summary statements about his career and his family in 14:47–52, and that a new literary work—which has as its theme David's rise to power—begins with the story of Saul's rejection in chapter 15 and leads directly into the anointing and election of David in 16:1–13. Yet the long episode about Saul's rejection in chapter 15 seems a strange way to begin a separate literary work about David, and it still leaves unsolved the problems of apparent literary dependence between the two accounts of rejection and the role of Dtr in the compilation of both the Saul and David stories.

In order to put chapter 15 in its proper place in the development of the present literary corpus, I think we must examine its sequel, the story of the witch of Endor in 28:3–25. There may be an anticipation of this episode in the ambiguous remark that "Samuel did not see Saul again until the day of his death" (15:35). The remarks in 28:17–18, however, clearly refer back to the story in chapter 15 and leave no doubt about the link between

---

53. *Rise of the Monarchy*, pp. 105–06; McCarter, *I Samuel*, pp. 270–71, n. 4.
54. Grønbaek, *Aufstieg Davids*, pp. 37ff. See also the discussion of this problem by A. Weiser, "Die Legitimation des Königs David: Zur Eigenart und Entstehung der sogen. Geschichte von Davids Aufstieg," *VT* 26 (1966):325–54.

the two stories.[55] Samuel's speech, with its repetition of the judgment and the final details of doom, is the climax of this story, just as the divine judgment was the climax of chapter 15. Here again the question of context arises. The opening verses (3–5) set the scene, but they have a number of curious features. The statement recounting the death and burial of Samuel is certainly necessary for what follows, but it repeats 25:1. It is not clear why the same author would state the same facts twice.[56] The introduction also mentions a religious reform by Saul, comparable to that of Josiah (2 Kings 23:24), which is important to the circumstances of the story. Now if this story were part of a Dtr compilation, it would be remarkable for Saul not to receive commendation for his reform. A third difficulty has to do with the setting of the story. In verses 4–5 the Philistines gather for battle at Shunem, and the Israelite troops are on Mt. Gilboa, from which Saul views the enemy below and becomes afraid. But the geography of this scene creates a problem for 29:1, which is a direct continuation of 28:2. In 29:1 the Philistines are still some distance away at Aphek,[57] while Israel is already encamped in the plain, not on the mountain slopes. Only after David and his men are dismissed in 29:11 do the Philistines proceed to Jezreel. We cannot solve the problem of context by simply transposing the story to a position after chapter 30.[58] All these facts would indicate that 28:3–25 has been added by a second author to the original episode in 28:1–2, 29:1–11. However, 28:3–25 was not an independent tradition but was dependent upon the previous compilation of the Story of David's Rise.

55. See Wellhausen, *Prolegomena*, pp. 259ff.; also Schunck, *Benjamin*, pp. 94–96. Some have suggested that 28:17–18 should be taken as a later gloss, but against this is the form of prophetic speech used in vv. 16–19. It begins with an accusing question and a reference to past disobedience (16–18a), followed by the phrase *'al-kēn*, introducing judgment, and then the judgment speech (18b–19). It would be difficult on form-critical grounds to view only part of this speech (vv. 16 and 19) as original and exclude the rest.

56. The inversion of subject and verb at the beginning of 28:3 would suggest that the author wished to point to some time in the past (a reference to 25:1) but also to a fact important for the present story. Note also the inversion at the beginning of v. 3b.

57. There are at least three towns with the name Aphek, and this raises considerable confusion about the geography of the war. It is usual to identify this Aphek with the one in the Plain of Sharon because of its general proximity to the Philistine territory (so also in the story of the Ark in 1 Sam. 4:1). But this makes the confrontation in the Plain of Jezreel rather peculiar (see the map in McCarter, *I Samuel*, p. 438). A second choice would be the Aphek in the Plain of Acco, which would fit the story better. But it still does not explain why both armies were so far north for this confrontation. The third Aphek is in the region east of the Sea of Galilee. Now, in the time of the kings of Israel, this Aphek was the staging site for the Aramaean wars against Israel, and Jezreel was the second capital of the northern kingdom (1 Kings 20:16ff.; 2 Kings 13:17). It would appear that the geography appropriate to this later period has been anachronistically applied to the time of Saul.

58. If 28:3–25 is placed after chap. 29 or 30, then the position of Israel in 28:4 compared with 29:1 would represent a retreat up the slopes of the mountain before the battle was even engaged. But this is not what the story suggests.

It would appear from this that both 15:1–16:13 and 28:3–25 are by the same hand and are additions to the combined stories of Saul and David, supplementing them in the same way.[59] Both later additions present a view of Saul different from that of the earlier compilations. The primary difference between the rejection account in chapter 15 and its doublet in 13:7b–15a is that the former contains Saul's admission of guilt and plea for forgiveness, which is completely refused. Saul must still meet his fate.[60] The story of Samuel's ghost in 28:3–25 carries forward the same theme. In spite of Saul's piety in purifying the land of false practices, God refuses to answer him and his death is sealed. The author presents Saul with great sympathy as a pathetic and broken man for whom Samuel weeps (15:35, 16:1) and for whom the witch of Endor tenderly prepares a final meal. This is in contrast to the mad and ruthless Saul in the Story of David's Rise, who is only a foil for David himself.

Once chapter 15 is acknowledged as secondary, we must consider the relationship of the story of David's anointing in 16:1–13 to the previous story of Saul. The transition from 15:35 to 16:1 is obvious. There is even a shift in terminology from that of the earlier redactor (Dtr) to that used by the author of chapter 15: in 16:12 Samuel anoints David as king (*melek*) rather than *nāgîd* over Yahweh's people, Israel (cf. 15:1, 26). Yet the story is patterned after the anointing of Saul. In both there is a sacrifice at a local sanctuary to which certain persons are invited, God reveals his choice directly when Samuel sees the elected one, and there is a secret anointing with oil, although here David's family is apparently aware of it. The anointing of David also involves a process of elimination until the right choice is found, parallel to 10:17–27. Yet here we find an interesting contrast. The eldest son is rejected because he is tall and handsome, whereas in Saul's case this is confirmation of his election. The story makes the point that "man looks on the outward appearance but Yahweh looks on the heart." As this religious maxim indicates, this story has the same kind of didactic and theological character as chapter 15. Finally, just as the spirit of Yahweh came to Saul after his anointing (10:6) as a sign of his election, so David also receives the spirit (16:13).

If 15:1–16:13 is secondary to the combined accounts of Saul and David, then the Story of David's Rise begins with 16:14. This would follow directly from the concluding summary of 14:47–52 and the statement, "Whenever Saul saw any warrior or well-bred person he would attach him to himself." Such a remark is a fitting introduction to how David joined the service of Saul. It is also clear that the rest of the story of David never

---

59. See also Schunck (*Benjamin*, pp. 84–85), who makes these texts the work of the same author with a secondary addition by R₂ (whom he identifies as Dtr).

60. Compare Dtr's approach to repentance in the story of Ahab, 1 Kings 21:27–29.

refers again to this anointing scene and the author appears to know nothing about it.[61]

b. THE STORY OF DAVID'S RISE

The notion of an independent literary work known as the Story of David's Rise to power has become important for recent theories about early Israelite historiography.[62] The idea was first put forward by L. Rost as part of his study of the Succession Story, but he provided no literary analysis to support it.[63] Nevertheless, subsequent scholars have become so convinced that such a work existed[64] that literary criticism of the books of Samuel has usually been tailored to accommodate the theory.[65] Yet serious questions remain about the limits of the work—where it begins and ends—and the extent to which it has been subject to one or more redactors.[66] These issues are so important that the way they are decided can change the whole nature of further discussion about Israelite historiography.

We have already seen that scholars disagree about where the story of Saul ends and the story of David begins. Following the lead of Wellhausen, who regards 1 Sam. 16:1–13 as a later addition, many scholars are inclined to begin the story of David with 16:14.[67] A. Weiser, however, argues that 16:1–13 is an integral part of the work and he therefore begins the story with 16:1.[68] Recently Grønbaek has argued that because 1 Sam. 15 cannot be separated from 16:1ff., and because 14:47–52 contains an

61. The references to Saul as the "anointed of Yahweh" in 1 Sam. 24:7, 11; 26:9, 11, 16, 23, and to David's own anointing as king in 2 Sam. 2:4; 5:3, suggest that the story of David's secret anointing is secondary.

62. See above, 7a.

63. L. Rost, *Die Überlieferung von der Thronnachfolge Davids*, BWANT III/6 (1926), reprinted in *Das kleine Credo*, pp. 119–253. See especially pp. 125, 238; see also E. Meyer, *Die Israeliten und ihre Nachbarstämme*, pp. 483ff.

64. H.-U. Nubel, *Davids Aufstieg in der frühe israelitischer Geschichtsschreibung*; F. Mildenberger, *Die vordeuteronomistische Saul-Davidüberlieferung*; J. H. Grønbaek, *Die Geschichte vom Aufstieg Davids*; A. Weiser, "Die Legitimation des Königs David: Zur Eigenart und Entstehung der sogen. Geschichte von Davids Aufstieg," *VT* 16 (1966):325–54; T. N. D. Mettinger, *King and Messiah: The Civil and Sacred Legitimation of the Israelite King*, pp. 33–47. Mettinger follows closely the works of Grønbaek and Weiser.

65. See the commentaries of H. W. Hertzberg, *I & II Samuel*; P. K. McCarter, *I Samuel: The Anchor Bible*.

66. To be sure, some scholars have not accepted the existence of such a work, but they usually belong to those holdouts for a style of literary analysis that still divides these books into sources similar to, or identical with, the sources of the Pentateuch. See O. Eissfeldt.

67. See G. von Rad, *Old Testament Theology*, vol. 1, pp. 49, 309.

68. Weiser, *VT* 16:325–29.

obvious conclusion, the story of David must actually begin with the account of the rejection of Saul.[69] Yet in another study of the story of David, Mildenburger has argued that the story of Saul cannot be separated from the story of David; the whole work thus begins with 1 Sam. 9.[70]

My own analysis above has suggested that 1 Sam. 15:1–16:13, along with 28:3–25, has been added to the combined stories of Saul and David. I have also argued that the story of Saul was put together by a Dtr editor, and that it was this editor-historian who was responsible for the themes of Saul's special election, anointing, and rejection. The short unit in 14:47–52, a Dtr summary of Saul's career, provided a transition to the story of David, which then commenced in 16:14–23.[71] If the redactional activity in the Saul story is by Dtr, then the combined works may begin even before 1 Sam. 9. Furthermore, the opening statement in 16:14, "Now the spirit of Yahweh departed from Saul and an evil spirit from Yahweh tormented him," makes the connection with the account of Saul's rejection. How else would such a statement make any sense? At the same time, the whole unit is meant to anticipate the following presentation of Saul. The unit 16:14–23 also provides a transition from Saul, who is the primary figure at the beginning of the unit, to David, who becomes the center of focus by the end of it. He is characterized as a musician, an able warrior with all the courtly virtues, and a shepherd boy, all in anticipation of later parts of the story. The scene describes how David entered Saul's service, but it really serves as a redactional introduction to the larger story that follows.

There is a fairly broad consensus that the Story of David's Rise expresses the theme of David's legitimate and rightful succession to the throne of Saul, not through any overt act of his own but through Yahweh's election of David and his rejection of Saul.[72] This theme is supported by the way in which David gradually rises in the estimation of all Israel and Judah, and Saul steadily declines until he is unworthy of the throne. God's election of David as Saul's successor is frequently expressed by the notion that "Yahweh is with him," in contrast to Saul, whom Yah-

69. Grønbaek, *Aufstieg Davids*, pp. 25–29.
70. Mildenberger, *Saul-Davidüberlieferung*, pp. viff.
71. For some notion about the redactional continuity between the stories, see H. J. Stoebe, *Das erste Buch Samuelis*, p. 309; McCarter, *I Samuel*, p. 256; cf. Birch, *Rise of the Monarchy*, pp. 93, 146–50. Weiser (*VT*, p. 350) also sees some dependence of the Story of David's Rise upon the Saul tradition, especially 1 Sam. 10:1; 13:13–14, but he does not indicate the nature of this dependence. He prefers to explain it in terms of Alt's notions about an early form of charismatic or elective kingship, but this theory is itself based entirely upon a selection of Dtr texts.
72. See especially Weiser, "Die Legitimation des Königs David," *VT* 16:325–54; see also the works of Grønbaek, Stoebe, and McCarter cited above.

weh has abandoned.[73] Yahweh's presence ensures David's military success in Saul's service.[74] Even after he leaves Saul's service, he continues to be successful.[75] David completely replaces Saul as the one who fights the "wars of Yahweh" (18:17; 25:28), which is the primary role of the *nāgîd*.[76]

Once Yahweh has abandoned Saul (16:14; 18:12) and an evil spirit has come to trouble him (16:14; 18:10; 19:9), we can trace a development in Saul's condition through various stages. At first it is only a stage of melancholy, which can be relieved by David's playing on the lyre (16:23). But then it becomes jealousy (18:9), fear (18:12, 15, 29), and hatred of David himself, with numerous plans to kill David, either by means of making heroic demands upon David for the hand of the king's daughter in marriage (18:17–27) or by trying to incite Jonathan against him (19:1; 20:30–31). David's music, of course, no longer has the power to soothe Saul since he is the cause of Saul's ill temper, so the latter tries to kill David with his spear in the course of his playing (18:10–11; 19:9–10). On David's account Saul even threatens Jonathan with his spear (20:33).[77]

This evil spirit from Yahweh manifests itself in a form of ecstatic prophesying (*wayyitnabbē'*, 18:10). But such prophetic rapture also comes to Saul when he seeks to take David from the presence of Samuel (19:18–24). This episode is parallel to the earlier one in 10:10–12, with the same proverb applied to both. The parallel, however, is not the result of two variant traditions but a deliberately composed contrast: the second episode was put forward by Dtr, the author of the Story of David's Rise, to negate the positive attribution of the first.[78] He wants his readers to interpret the saying "Is Saul also among the prophets?" in the most derogatory fashion as madness and disgusting behavior. In the end Saul, forsaken by God, falls at the hands of the Philistines at the very time that David is successful in a "holy war" against the Amalekites (1 Sam. 30:7–8, 23, 26).

Furthermore, in contrast to Saul's growing hatred of David, all others come to love David—the people, Saul's servants, and Saul's children.[79] Jonathan, Michal, and Samuel all risk their lives to save David, and the priestly house of Ahimelek suffers a cruel massacre on his behalf. An exception to this support of David is Doeg, the Edomite, but his willingness

---

73. 1 Sam. 16:18; 18:12, 14, 28; 20:13; 2 Sam. 5:10. See the remarks by Weiser, *VT* 16:334–35.

74. 1 Sam. 18:5, 13–19, 27, 30; 19:8.

75. 1 Sam. 23:1–5; chap. 30; 2 Sam. 5:9–10, 17–25.

76. See Cross, *Canaanite Myth*, p. 220, although the evidence for the meaning "commander" still seems inclusive to me.

77. Note the other references to Saul's spear in 22:6; 26:7ff.

78. Cf. L. Schmidt, *Menschlicher Erfolg*, pp. 103–19.

79. 1 Sam. 18:2–3, 5, 16, 22, 28, 30; 19:4; 20:3.

to slaughter the priests of Nob and their families makes his loyalty to Saul contemptible. The only other person who shows disdain for David is Nabal, the Calebite (chapter 25), who meets a sad fate, while his gracious wife receives David with honor and eventually becomes his wife and queen.

By describing these expressions of love and favor toward David, by stressing David's noble qualities, and by emphasizing the theme of divine election as *nāgîd* (13:14), Dtr is presenting the case for David's right to the throne. Because of the divine presence, all those around David come to recognize that he is to be the future king. When he first enters the service of Saul, David's many regal qualities are enumerated (16:18). His marriage to Saul's daughter makes him a son-in-law of Saul and thus next in line for the throne after the death of Saul and his three sons. Jonathan is the first of Saul's household to see David as future king in place of himself (18:4; 20:13–16; 23:17). Eventually Saul himself concedes that David will be the future ruler (20:31; 23:17); such concessions climax the scenes in which David spares Saul's life (24:20–21; 26:25). In these two episodes David does nothing against Saul because Saul is still "Yahweh's anointed," although he cannot pass this status on.[80] Even the Philistines recognize David as a "king of the land" (21:11). In the story of Abigail (chapter 25) the climax of Abigail's speech to David centers upon the theme of David as the one whom Yahweh has "appointed" as "*nāgîd* over Israel" (verse 30). This language goes back specifically to 13:14 and the rejection scene of Saul. There is also a reference to a "sure house," *bayit ne'ᵉmān*, which was denied Saul, and there are various allusions to Saul's pursuit of David. Abigail's words not only refer back to Samuel's prediction in 13:14 (how Abigail could know this does not trouble the author) but also foreshadow David's military success and the whole of his later career as king. Consequently, Abigail's efforts to restrain David from taking action against the household of Nabal are viewed as preserving David's future destiny as monarch and his dynasty from the curse of blood guilt.[81]

All the scenes and episodes in the Story of David's Rise are governed by

80. One view of these two stories is to see them as different versions of the same tradition (see K. Koch, *The Growth of the Biblical Tradition*, pp. 132–48). Another is to consider one account a redactional adaptation of the other (see McCarter, *I Samuel*, pp. 385–87). It is our view that both accounts are by the same hand.

81. It is too simple to say that vv. 28–31 are an interpolation by Dtr or some other redactor. V. 26 makes a double prediction about both Nabal and David's enemies, particularly Saul, so that it is the same kind of prediction as vv. 28ff. It also deals with the question of vengeance, but the reason for not shedding blood is given in vv. 28ff., and this is what persuades David, vv. 32ff. It is possible to exclude all of vv. 26, 28–34, but this would make the account rather trivial. The ominous note in v. 34, which repeats v. 22, would also be missing, and it seems required for the denouement. The brief remark in v. 31b also anticipates the ending in v. 42.

the theme of David as Yahweh's ruler-designate, replacing the rejected Saul. This theme is not merely additional to otherwise independent tradition but seems integral to each episode. This is a basic form-critical difference between the story of Saul and the story of David. We have already seen that the compiler of the Saul stories introduced his perspective into a number of Saul traditions largely by way of editorial additions, thereby creating considerable literary tension between the additions and the stories themselves. These traditions in their basic form do not have any real connection with each other, nor do they presuppose the events or situations presented in the earlier stories. But in the Story of David's Rise each unit contributes to the thematic interest of the whole and is composed with this larger theme in mind. Scarcely a single episode can be considered in isolation from the rest of the story. Whatever the nature of the traditional material behind the Story of David's Rise, it has been used with complete freedom by the author, making it virtually impossible to distinguish between the received traditions and the elements of his own composition.[82] There is only one notable exception to this unity: the story of David and Goliath in 1 Sam. 17, which must have been a self-contained didactic/theological legend. The author of the story of David incorporated it into his larger work, but not without creating numerous tensions with the rest of his account. Nevertheless, it is now so thoroughly integrated into the story at various points that it cannot be construed merely as a late redactional addition.[83]

The conclusion often drawn from a comparison of the story of Saul and the Story of David's Rise is that the difference represents a development in historiographic technique, from merely collecting separate episodes to creating a unified account. But in fact the same author employs both techniques in both stories, though in somewhat different proportions. One must clearly identify this author-redactor and the true extent of his work before making any comparative judgments.

Another literary technique used in the Story of David's Rise is the repetition of short scenes, motifs, and the like to reinforce the overall theme and unity of the work. This has often been interpreted as an indication of a plurality of sources or traditions, but such an explanation does not work very well. The doublets in the story of David are of an entirely different character from those in the Pentateuch, because in the latter the differences in the story's style and purpose regularly point to different authors. The story of David, however, has a uniform style and all the episodes appear to

82. See especially the remarks by Grønbaek, *Aufstieg Davids*, pp. 16–18.
83. See the various treatments by Grønbaek, *Aufstieg Davids*, pp. 80–100; Hertzberg, *I & II Samuel*, pp. 142–55; McCarter, *I Samuel*, pp. 284–309.

be directed to the same purpose.[84] All the episodes bear the same thematic concern for legitimizing David's role as successor to Saul and for putting Saul in an unfavorable light. Thus on three occasions David plays for Saul on the lyre, and on two of these occasions Saul tries to kill him with his spear.[85] At various points in the narrative David's military activity is described, sometimes rather generally, at other points more specifically.[86] There are two offers of marriage by Saul and two sets of negotiations.[87] On two occasions Jonathan speaks with his father on David's behalf. Both involve David hiding in the field—for no apparent reason, since David speaks with Jonathan directly afterward.[88] Jonathan's solemn commitment to David is also stated on several occasions.[89] David makes two attempts to enter the service of King Achish of Gath.[90] Details about David's flight from Saul are repetitious, especially in the two episodes in which he spares Saul's life.[91] The author of David's Rise also often splits scenes and events, for example, the marriage of David to Michal and her subsequent aid in his escape,[92] David's receiving aid from the priests of Nob and their massacre by Saul,[93] the advance of the Philistines against Saul and the account of Saul's defeat and death.[94] The techniques of splitting or repeating scenes and episodes, when few of these scenes constitute a complete story in themselves, create with this interweaving and repetition a degree of progression and unity that greatly reinforces the theme of the whole. The story shows little concern for exact chronology and makes little attempt to overcome inconsistencies and contradictions in the compilation of its scenes and episodes. No amount of source analysis, tradition criticism, or redaction criticism can solve what is basically the result of this author's particular literary techniques.

Weiser has pointed to another feature of the story that is worthy of consideration. As part of the evidence of divine guidance and protection, David regularly consults the oracle of Yahweh, the ephod that was in the possession of the priest Abiathar, a fugitive who had joined David's band.[95]

---

84. Cf. Koch, *Growth of the Biblical Tradition*, pp. 138–41, who treats the doublets in the Story of David's Rise as "heroic sagas" (*Heldensagen*) as compared with the simple "sagas" (*Sagen*) in Genesis. Koch here follows the Gunkel-von Rad scheme of literary development (see above, 7a).

85. 1 Sam. 16:23; 18:10–11; 19:9–10.

86. 1 Sam. 18:5, 13–19, 27, 30; 19:8.

87. 1 Sam. 18:17–27.

88. 1 Sam. 19:1–7; chap. 20.

89. 1 Sam. 18:1, 3–4; 20:12–17, 41–42; 23:16–18.

90. 1 Sam. 21:11–16 (ET 10–15); 27:1–4.

91. 1 Sam., chaps. 23–24; 26.

92. 1 Sam. 18:20–27; 19:11–17.

93. 1 Sam. 21:2–10 (ET 1–9); 22:6–23.

94. 1 Sam. 29; 31.

95. See 1 Sam. 23:2, 4, 9ff.; 30:7ff.; 2 Sam. 2:1; 5:19, 23 (see also 1 Sam. 22:15, 20ff.).

Saul also consults the oracle by means of the ephod.[96] However, after David enters the story Saul is not represented as consulting an oracle again. Indeed, the story of Samuel's ghost in 28:3–25, which I view as an addition, indicates that God would not give Saul an answer by dreams, lot, or prophet. David also receives guidance from the prophet Gad in 1 Sam. 22:5, which Weiser states "scarcely stems from an old tradition."[97] The theocratic interpretation of history is reinforced not only by these technical means of divine guidance but also by the various predictions of Jonathan, Abigail, and even Saul about David's future greatness.[98] The Court History, by contrast, contains no reference whatever to the use of oracles or other forms of divine guidance.

The Story of David's Rise is not a self-contained work. It depends heavily upon the prior story of Saul and especially upon those thematic elements introduced by the redactor-author, Dtr. He uses similar methods of developing the stories about the two kings, except that he seems to have used more preformed traditions in the case of Saul than of David. In no case, however, can we trace a development from the *Heldensagen* of Saul to the story of David as a major stage in the rise of historiography. The history of the early monarchy, as evidenced by both editorial technique and thematic unity, is the work of the Dtr Historian.

There is considerable disagreement about where the Story of David's Rise ends. Most scholars believe its conclusion is in 2 Sam. 5, although they often select different points in the chapter. Stoebe notes a distinct change in the character of the material in 2 Sam. 2ff., so he ends the account earlier, in 2 Sam. 1.[99] On the other hand, the three important studies of Weiser, Mildenberger, and Nubel all end the work later, in 2 Sam. 7.[100] The arguments for this ending rely on the strong thematic and philological continuities between 2 Sam. 7 and the Story of David's Rise. The arguments against its inclusion result either from a commitment to the place this chapter has in Rost's analysis of the Court History (Succession Story) or from the judgment that the chapter belongs to Dtr and therefore cannot be part of the Story of David's Rise—an argument that would carry no weight in the present discussion.[101] The text 2 Sam. 7 is impor-

---

96. 1 Sam. 14:3, 18–19, 36–37.

97. Weiser, *VT* 16:335.

98. One is reminded here of the use of oracles and other forms of prediction in Herodotus, and the oracles in the Sargon Letter to the God.

99. *Das erste Buch Samuelis*, pp. 296ff.

100. Weiser, *VT* 16:342ff.; Mildenberger, *Saul-Davidüberlieferung*, p. x; Nubel, *Davids Aufstieg*, pp. 81–82; Mettinger, *King and Messiah*, pp. 41ff.

101. Mettinger (*King and Messiah*, pp. 31, 41ff.) attempts to have it both ways with some form of the Nathan oracle included in both works.

tant for the whole study of early historiography and calls for detailed examination.

c. THE DYNASTIC PROMISE: 2 SAMUEL 7

Scholars have paid so much attention to this chapter that a wide diversity of opinion exists about its date, its authorship, and its relationship both to older sources and to its present literary context.[102] The older literary approach has usually regarded the chapter as late, influenced by messianism and Deuteronomistic language and notions.[103] In an important and influential study L. Rost has observed that there are numerous points of tension or breaks in continuity within the chapter; thus, in his analysis, it consists of fragmented traditions from the early monarchy period, continuously reworked, with only minor Dtr additions.[104] S. Herrmann's form-critical study, by associating this chapter with the so-called *Königsnovelle* of Egypt, suggests that the text as a whole, and not just a small fragment of it, reflects a royal document of the United Monarchy period.[105] On this basis Noth is willing to argue for the essential unity of the whole chapter, maintaining that it reflects an early source with only minor Dtr phrasing added in verses 22–24.[106] Noth discounts some of the tensions in the text referred to by Rost and others as the result either of poor textual transmission or of slight redactional alteration. In contrast to the older literary-critical method, Noth's traditio-historical approach stresses the thematic unity of the whole and the way in which the chapter reflects the period out of which it arose.

Weiser, in a recent study, uses the work of Herrmann to argue for the existence of an original royal document, and he maintains that such a document provided the basis not only for this chapter but also for the Story of David's Rise as a whole.[107] The thematic unity explored by Noth is thus

102. For recent bibliography see F. M. Cross, *Canaanite Myth*, p. 241, n. 95; L. Schmidt, *Menschlicher Erfolg*, p. 146, n. 1. See also L. Perlitt, *Bundestheologie im Alten Testament*, pp. 47–53; Mettinger, *King and Messiah*, pp. 48–63, esp. n. 1; T. Veijola, *Die ewige Dynastie*, pp. 68–79.

103. See H. P. Smith, *The Books of Samuel*, pp. 297–302.

104. "Thronnachfolge," in *Das kleine Credo*, pp. 159–83.

105. "Die Königsnovelle in Ägypten und in Israel," *WZK-MUL* 3/1 (1953/54):51–83. See above, 5f.

106. "David and Israel in II Samuel VIII" (1957), in *The Laws of the Pentateuch and Other Studies*, pp. 250–59.

107. "Die Tempelbaukrise unter David," *ZAW* 77 (1965): 153–68; idem, *VT* 16:349ff. See also Mettinger, *King and Messiah*, pp. 52ff. However, since Mettinger argues that the name theology of 2 Sam. 7:13 may well be Solomonic, there is no longer any reason for him to view any of the chapter as Dtr. This approach is unacceptable.

extended over a much broader body of material. However, the *Königsnovelle*, which provides the basis for Noth's and Weiser's view of a primitive source, has recently come in for sharp criticism.[108] As I have noted above, the very notion of a *Königsnovelle* is highly doubtful.[109] Thus the form-critical character of 2 Sam. 7 has not been adequately explained.

A different attempt to get back to primitive sources in the chapter has been made by F. M. Cross.[110] His method of analysis is to look for poetry behind the prose "reworking" of the text, and then to extract archaic elements from the admittedly later work.[111] He suggests that in this chapter two original poetic oracles may be recovered from the prose text. In order to derive poetry from the text, however, Cross must eliminate some words and supply others, a rather arbitrary methodological procedure. In no case does the present text contain good synonymous parallelism, the hallmark of Hebrew poetry. The complementary or contrastive word pairs that occur in these passages are such a common feature of prose that they scarcely count as evidence for an original poetic source.[112] Furthermore, an appeal to Ps. 89 or 2 Sam. 23:1–7 is no help in this matter because, as L. Perlitt has recently argued, these pieces are quite late and directly dependent upon 2 Sam. 7.[113] Even Ps. 132 bears the stamp of the Dtr outlook. The reconstructed poetic fragments that Cross is able to find in the text do not correspond to any specific form or genre and give no help whatsoever in the form-critical analysis of the chapter.[114]

The form of 2 Sam. 7 is prose narration, the report of a royal audience, that has been influenced by a number of forms and conventions. The work begins with the remark that Yahweh has given the king rest from his enemies as an introduction to David's stated desire to build a temple. This is in keeping with the widespread Near Eastern literary convention, particularly evident in the Assyrian annals, of dealing with the king's wars prior to describing his temple-building projects. The main body of the text (verses 4–17), however, is the report of a prophetic oracle of the type com-

---

108. Cross, *Canaanite Myth*, pp. 247–49.

109. See above, 5f.

110. *Canaanite Myth*, pp. 254ff. An earlier attempt to see poetry in this chapter is in Smith, *Samuel*, pp. 299–301.

111. The weakness of this method of searching for poetic "epic" sources has been noted above, 2b, 7b. Another attempt to find primitive oracles behind the Dtr reworking has been suggested by Veijola, *Die ewige Dynastie*, pp. 72–74.

112. Even a casual reading of the parenetic passages of Deuteronomy should put this matter to rest. It is simply a feature of the elevated style of divine speech which any prose writer could easily produce.

113. *Bundestheologie*, pp. 50–52.

114. To ascribe the words of David in 7:2 to an "old poetic oracle of Nathan" (*Canaanite Myth*, p. 255) seems very confusing to me and form-critically doubtful. Vv. 1–7 contain dialogue belonging to narrative and not prophetic oracles.

mon in the redactional additions to the Saul story and in the Dtr presentation of the prophets in the books of Kings. Many of these oracles begin with a question and are followed by an account of God's dealings in the past with either the king or the people.[115] Because most oracles end in judgment, scholars have been quick to interpret their first part in a negative sense. But the form can also be used as an oracle of salvation. The clue to interpreting the oracle in this way is in the divine pronouncement in verse 10: "I will assign a place for my people, Israel; I will plant them and they will settle in their own place and they will not be disturbed again, nor will violent men ever again oppress them as in the past." The language of this text sounds as if it were borrowed from the salvation oracles of the prose of Jeremiah.[116] Since the oracle does not conclude in judgment but in salvation, the initial question, "Would you build me a house to dwell in?" cannot be interpreted as an accusation, as is often done.

This means that we cannot reconstruct an earlier oracle of Nathan against building the Temple out of verses 4–7 and then view verses 8ff. as an addition by a later redactor to give it a more positive character. On form-critical grounds the two parts of the oracle must be taken together so that the oracle as it stands, with its affirmation of David's plan to build the Temple, is a unity and the most original version of the account that we possess.

The last part of the chapter, verses 18–29, is also often attributed to a redactor. These verses are described as a prayer, $t^e fillah$ (verse 27), a term usually signifying a lament or petition, but the form here is that of a prose hymn, similar to 1 Kings 8:22–26. In the more common report of a judgment oracle, one would expect the response of prayer to take the form of a lament or petition for forgiveness.[117] But since the report concerns an oracle of salvation, it is most appropriate to have instead a prayer of thanksgiving. From the point of view of form criticism there is no reason why the whole chapter cannot be considered the work of one author.

Once the unity of the chapter is affirmed on form-critical grounds, a different interpretation of these texts is necessary. The question in verse 5b, "Would you build me a house to dwell in?" is not accusatory but ambig-

115. Here both king and people are included together, but this is a mark of Dtr literature and not the result of redaction (contra M. Weinfeld, *Deuteronomy and the Deuteronomic School*, p. 38n.). A similar combination of people and leader may be found in Deut. 31 and 1 Sam. 12.

116. Note the almost exclusive use of *nt'*, "to plant," referring to the people of Israel as the object of God's planting in Jeremiah (Jer. 1:10; 2:21; 18:9; 24:6; 31:28; 32:41; 42:10; 45:4; cf. also Amos 9:15; Exod. 15:17).

117. See examples of the report of judgment in 1 Sam. 15:10ff.; 1 Kings 21:17–29. Cross (in *Canaanite Myth*, p. 254, n. 154) considers the prayer to be "a free Deuteronomistic composition presuming the Dtr oracle in vv. 1–17 without clear evidence of the use of earlier sources."

uous—one need not interpret it as antitemple. In verse 7 God asks rhetor-
ically whether he ever required or expected of the judges *in the past* that
they build for him a house of cedar. The implied answer is negative. But
this does not mean that he prohibited such a dwelling at any time. What is
suggested is a comparison of the time of the judges and the time of the
monarchy under David. Under temporary rulers Yahweh's abode was
transitory. Only with the establishment of the monarchy (verse 8) and the
subjugation of Israel's enemies (verse 9), so that Israel is fixed in its own
place (verse 10), will God establish a dynasty, "a house," and have the
first member of the dynasty build him "a house." A comparison with the
time of the judges, when the people did not have rest from their enemies, is
repeated in verse 11, making this interpretation certain. Admittedly, the
expression of ideas in verses 11ff. is somewhat awkward, but this is because the author attempts to interweave a number of different themes and
present them all in one oracle.

Not only is 2 Sam. 7 a unified work, it also has many strong thematic
links with what has gone before, which suggests that it is an important
part of a larger whole. The most immediate connection of 2 Sam. 7 with
its context is as a continuation of the Ark Narrative in 6:17–19, where the
Ark has been brought to Jerusalem and placed in a "tent that David had
pitched for it." David, in 7:2, compares this resting place of the Ark in a
tent with his own palace of cedar, and this establishes a further link with
the statement in 5:11 about Hiram of Tyre building a palace of cedar for
David. And the reference, in 7:1, to David's having rest from his enemies
recalls the Philistine wars in 5:17–25. These seemingly peripheral connections could be explained as merely editorial, but there is also extensive thematic continuity between 2 Sam. 7 and the stories of Saul and David.

One theme that runs throughout 2 Sam. 7 is the understanding of Israel
as the religious community of Yahweh, expressed by the phrase "my/thy
people Israel." Noth points out that this cannot be a reference to the political state because both Israel and Judah were related to David by separate
agreements with little religious significance (2:4; 5:3).[118] Therefore, Noth
takes the phrase as a reference to the prior amphictyonic community to
which the promise and the legitimation in the Nathan oracle were being
related. Apart from the fact that Noth's views on such an amphictyony
have been seriously challenged, this explanation seems quite unnecessary
in the present chapter.[119] In 7:23–24, a text that is acknowledged as

118. *Laws of the Pentateuch*, pp. 253ff.
119. For recent critiques of the amphictyony thesis, see R. de Vaux, *Histoire ancienne
d'Israël*, vol. 2, pp. 19–36; C. H. J. de Geus, *The Tribes of Israel: An Investigation into Some
of the Presuppositions of Martin Noth's Amphictyony Hypothesis*, with a survey of earlier
criticism on pp. 54–68.

thoroughly Dtr, one finds repeated reference to "thy people Israel," so that this same language throughout the chapter simply reflects the well-known Dtr theme of Yahweh's election of Israel.[120]

Closely associated with the theme of the people's election is the divine choice of David as ruler, *nāgîd*, over God's people Israel. Noth regards the title *nāgîd* as a special function "assigned to David in Israel as the ancient tribal confederacy" and draws attention to the fact that Saul was thus appointed.[121] But as we have already seen, the term *nāgîd* is used only in the redactional additions to the Saul story, where the language is strikingly similar to 2 Sam. 7. In 1 Sam. 9:16 and 10:1, Saul is referred to as "*nāgîd* over my/his people," "over his inheritance," and in 13:14 Saul will be replaced by another who will be *nāgîd* over Yahweh's people. In the Rise of David the term occurs in 1 Sam. 25:30, where Abigail says that Yahweh's promise to make David *nāgîd* over Israel will come true. Abigail also predicts (verse 28) that Yahweh will establish for David a dynasty ("sure house"), as described in 2 Sam. 7:11ff., and will destroy his enemies, 2 Sam. 7:9 (see also 1 Sam. 20:15). Finally, the term *nāgîd* is used in 2 Sam. 5:2, where a reference is made to God's past promise to David that he would be both shepherd and *nāgîd* over Israel (cf. 2 Sam. 7:7).[122] The author of the combined work of the story of Saul and David's Rise is consistent in his use of the term *nāgîd* to express the divine choice of a ruler over the people of Israel.

In addition to the strong thematic continuity between 2 Sam. 7 and the preceding story of Saul and David are the many linguistic connections and references to the earlier story line. The text emphasizes Yahweh's presence and his guidance of David (2 Sam. 7:3, 9). Weiser regards this theme as the leitmotiv of the Story of David's Rise,[123] and the fact that it is stated in a retrospective manner ("I have been with you wherever you went") points directly to this theme in the earlier story. There are also references to Saul's rejection (verse 15), to David's origins as a shepherd (verse 8),

120. The whole question of the "all Israel" concept as a religious entity and inclusive of both Judah and Israel has been a matter of much discussion with the demise of Noth's theory of a twelve-tribe league. See S. Herrmann, "Autonome Entwicklungen in den Königreichen Israel und Juda," SVT 17 (1969):139–59. My own view is that the "all Israel" concept did not arise before the demise of the northern kingdom. When Israel as a *political* state came to an end, Israel as a *religious* community came into being.
121. Noth, *Laws of the Pentateuch*, pp. 254ff. See also W. Richter, "Die nāgīd-Formel: Ein Beitrag zur Erhellung des nāgīd-Problems," *BZ* 9 (1965):71–84; L. Schmidt, *Menschlicher Erfolg*, pp. 141–71.
122. The dependence of 1 Sam. 25:28–30 and 2 Sam. 5:2 upon 2 Sam. 7 is strongly argued by Schmidt, *Menschlicher Erfolg*, pp. 121–26, 158. However, Schmidt (pp. 159ff.) regards the reference to nāgīd in 1 Kings 1:35 as an early primary witness to the use of the term. See also E. Lepinski, "Nāgīd, der Kronprinz," *VT* 24 (1974):497–99, who suggests the meaning "crown prince" on the basis of 1 Kings 1:35. On this last text, however, see below, 8d.
123. Weiser, *VT* 16:335.

and to his frequent military successes (verse 9). The use of the verb ṣiwwāh (verses 7, 11) in the sense of the deity "appointing" the judges, is also found in 1 Sam. 13:14 and 25:30 in connection with God "appointing" David as nāgîd. As indicated above, Weiser argues persuasively that the Story of David's Rise reaches a fitting climax only in 2 Sam. 7,[124] and this would appear to be confirmed by our observations here.[125].

Furthermore, 2 Sam. 7 must be viewed in a still wider context than the stories of Saul and David since it has been increasingly recognized as an important Dtr text. A comparison of its language and phraseology with that of the Dtr corpus reveals how completely this is the case.[126] In a recent study D. J. McCarthy goes so far as to suggest that 2 Sam. 7 is central to the whole structure of the Dtr history.[127] The Dtr scheme of dividing Israelite history into three periods—the exodus and conquest, the age of the judges, and the rise of the monarchy (1 Sam. 8:8; 10:18–19; 12:6ff.)—is basic to 2 Sam. 7. In particular, as McCarthy points out, "the concept of the judges as official leaders of all Israel and the picture of their era as a time of regularly recurring troubles is . . . specifically deuteronomistic."[128] "My servant David" (verse 8) is a title that frequently occurs in the thematic framework that Dtr constructs for the rest of his history of the monarchy;[129] it parallels his use of the title "my servant Moses." Dtr thus sets apart these two figures as the dual founders of the nation and marks off two important eras in Israel's history.[130] Moses as the servant of Yahweh was the one who delivered to Israel the covenant by which the people and their kings were to live. David, on the other hand, is the recipient of the promise of a perpetual dynasty—the real founder of the state—because of his obedience (cf. 1 Sam. 13:14); thus the title "my servant David" thereafter means both the recipient of the promise and the model of obedience to the Mosaic covenant.[131] One can, in fact, go further and assert that the notion of the Davidic promise of a perpetual dynasty is a basic ideological construction that is no older than the Dtr history.

124. Ibid., pp. 242ff.
125. I cannot follow McCarter (I Samuel, pp. 16–17, 27–30), who takes all the thematic and predictive texts as later additions.
126. See the useful collection of parallels from the Dtr corpus in Cross, Canaanite Myth, pp. 252–54.
127. "II Samuel 7 and the Structure of the Deuteronomic History," JBL 84 (1965): 131–38.
128. Ibid., p. 133. See also Noth, ÜS, pp. 20–21, 53.
129. See below, 9c.
130. See Josh. 1:2, 7; cf. Deut. 34:5; Josh. 1:1, 13; 22:2. To a lesser extent there is also a parallel with Joshua, the "servant of Yahweh" (Josh. 24:29//Judges 2:8), who gave "rest" to Israel through the conquest just as David gave it rest through his reign.
131. See Perlitt, Bundestheologie, pp. 47ff., especially the statement (47–48) "Dtr kunt (noch) keinen überlieferten David-Bund. 'Nur' eine David-Verheissung steht im DtrG der mit dem Gericht rechnenden dt בְּרִית-theologie retardierend gegenüber."

The way in which 2 Sam. 7 is thematically central to the later Dtr history of Kings will be taken up below. But if this chapter is the centerpiece for the larger history, it has important implications for the discussion of the limits of the Story of David's Rise. One objection that Grønbaek raises to considering 2 Sam. 7 as concluding David's Rise is that the chapter introduces the theme of building the Temple, a theme that has no place in the earlier story of David.[132] This criticism, however, no longer carries any weight if 2 Sam. 7 is not the end of a literary work but a transition to a new subject and a new series of historical events.

Yet a most important question remains to be considered—how the Nathan oracle and the Dtr history as a whole relate to the Court History of David, since in the canonical form of the text the Court History is part of the immediate context of 2 Sam. 7. Only after clarifying this issue can we further consider the Dtr's thematic structure.

d. THE COURT HISTORY OF DAVID

The Court History of David in 2 Sam. 9–20 and 1 Kings 1–2, also known as the Succession Story, has long been regarded as the pinnacle of Israelite historiography. As noted above, it forms the basis for the view that history writing began in the time of the United Monarchy. The Court History is commonly thought to be the work of a member of David's court, set down in the early years of Solomon's reign. It is often compared favorably with the classical histories of Greece, which it preceded by several hundred years.[133]

The most important study of this story is that of L. Rost, whose observations and conclusions have been widely accepted.[134] Against the views of older scholars he argues for the unity of the whole story with the exception of the report on the Ammonite war (1 Sam. 10:6–11:1, 12: 26–31).[135] This account, he feels, was an older source from the time of David that the author of the Succession Story used. The author also relied upon a version of the Nathan oracle, preserved, according to Rost, only in 2 Sam. 7:11b, 16. Only a few glosses, which Rost attributes primarily to

---

132. *Aufstieg Davids*, pp. 29ff.

133. See above, 7a.

134. "Die Überlieferung von der thronnachfolge Davids," in *Das kleine Credo*, pp. 119–253.

135. Ibid., pp. 212ff. The unity of the work has recently been questioned in the studies by J. J. Jackson, "David's Throne: Patterns in the Succession Story," *CJT* 11 (1965):183–95; and J. W. Flanagan, "Court History or Succession Document? A Study of 2 Samuel 9–20 and 1 Kings 1–2," *JBL* 91 (1972):172–81. As described in these studies, I do not find the use of symmetrical structure as a method of literary criticism very convincing.

the Dtr editor, were added to the Succession Story at a later time.[136] Rost sees the theme of the work as embodied in the question, "Who will sit on the throne of my Lord the King after him?" (1 Kings 1:20, 27)—hence the name Succession Story. He points out how each episode in the story is related to the theme of succession. Rost also carefully analyzes the style of the story and shows that, unlike most other parts of Samuel and Kings, the work is not simply a combination of various older sources but a skillful homogeneous literary masterpiece, perhaps the finest prose in the entire Hebrew Bible.

On matters of unity and style I have little argument with Rost's treatment. But a disturbing question remains unanswered, either by Rost or by any of the more recent studies of the Court History. If, as is now generally assumed, the Dtr Historian incorporated the Court History into his own work, how could he consistently maintain that David was the ideal ruler and the model that all the kings of Israel and Judah should follow? The Chronicler's solution to this difficulty in his source material was simply to omit the Court History so that his account of David's excellence would be consistent. If the Dtr also had this problem with his sources, why did he not do the same thing? It is generally assumed that the Court History was a self-contained work of early date that was added to other sources or fitted into its present context by a redactor, perhaps Dtr. In the process, some parts of the original work may have been lost, omitted, or even slightly rearranged. Since problems raised by a consideration of the work's limits are invariably solved by the "redactor," some scholars scarcely bother to discuss the limits of the Court History,[137] while others invoke a redactor to an almost excessive degree.[138] In either case the principle of the Court History as an originally independent story is maintained. This approach, however, does not really solve the literary problems or explain why a Dtr redactor would seek to incorporate into his work a source that so seriously contradicted his own view of David.[139]

It is necessary to begin the discussion of literary problems at those points where redactional connections between the Court History and its

136. According to Rost ("Die Überlieferung von der thronnachfolge Davids," pp. 214–15), the additions would consist of 2 Sam. 12:7b–12; 14:25–27; 18:18; 1 Kings 2:2–4, 11, 27b. I see no reason to attribute the first three references or the last reference to the Dtr. On the other two, see below.

137. As in the recent study by R. N. Whybray, *The Succession Story*, where these questions are rather quickly dismissed (p. 8).

138. See D. M. Gunn, *The Story of King David: Genre and Interpretation*, especially chap. 4.

139. For a recent review of the unity of the Court History, its limits and its relationship to the larger context, see Peter R. Ackroyd, "The Succession Narrative (so-called)," *Interpretation* 35 (1981):383–96. Would not the problems Ackroyd raises concerning the place of the Succession Narrative in Dtr take on an entirely different character if it were viewed as an addition to Dtr and not part of his source?

context must be assumed. There is a fairly broad consensus that the conclusion of the whole story is in 1 Kings 2:46b: "So the kingdom was established in the hand of Solomon." But serious difficulties arise earlier in the chapter. The unit in 2:1–4, in which David gives parting moral advice to Solomon, has been recognized by all as Dtr. It follows the pattern of Moses giving his charge to Joshua (Deut. 31:7ff.), Joshua instructing the people (Josh. 23), and Samuel giving his warning to king and assembly (1 Sam. 12).[140] In each case the leader is aged and about to die,[141] and the instructions about keeping the law are in typical Dtr terminology. The introductory language used in the installation of Joshua is particularly significant: "Yahweh said to Moses, 'Behold your time to die has come. Summon Joshua and [both of you] stand in the tent of meeting that I may commission him [$wa^{\prime a}\d{s}awwennû$]'" (Deut. 31:14a). Compare this with 1 Kings 2:1: "David's time to die came so he commissioned [$wayy^e\d{s}aw$] Solomon his son, saying. . . ." This comparison makes it quite clear that the whole of 2:1–4 is Dtr; thus verse 1 cannot be construed as original to the Court History, as some have tried to argue.[142]

On the other hand, the speech by David that continues in verses 5ff. does belong to the Court History. David advises Solomon to take certain actions after his death, which he carries out. If 2:1–4 is removed as an addition, then the subsequent speech by David is left hanging in the air, for verse 5 begins with w^egam, "and furthermore," which assumes a previous statement. The obvious conclusion must be that the Dtr unit is primary and the Court History has been built around it.

In 2:10–12 we encounter formulae that were frequently used by Dtr as the framework for his history to signify the transition from one reign to another.[143] While this framework usually includes the statement "PN reigned in his stead," this formula appears to have been deliberately altered by Dtr to read: "David lay down with his fathers . . . and Solomon sat upon the throne of David, his father, and his kingdom was firmly established." This conforms to the promise in the Nathan oracle (2 Sam. 7:12), where the wording is similar: "When your time has come and you lie down with your fathers I will raise up your offspring after you . . . and I will establish his kingdom." If 2:10–12 is viewed as secondary just because it is Dtr, this creates a problem, for the action described in verses 13ff. assumes the statement about David's death.[144] We are left with the conclusion that verses 10–12 existed *prior* to the Court History and origi-

140. See also D. J. McCarthy, "An Installation Genre?" *JBL.*
141. It is true that Samuel, although aged, does not immediately die. But a new age is inaugurated and he gives up his leadership role.
142. Rost, "Thronnachfolge Davids," pp. 197–200.
143. See below, 9a.
144. Various attempts have been made to divide up vv. 10–12 between the Dtr and the Court History to overcome this obvious problem, but none of them is satisfactory.

nally went with 2:1–4 as the Dtr ending to the history of David. The Court History merely used this unit in two parts.[145]

The beginning of the Court History is also problematical. The narrative could hardly begin with 2 Sam. 9, although this is the limit set by most scholars. One simple solution would be to conclude that the beginning was lost in the process of redaction, but such a solution is hardly adequate.[146] First, Solomon, in 1 Kings 2:24, makes such a direct reference to the dynastic promise in the Nathan oracle that Rost feels certain part of it must have preceded the Court History. Rost also points out that 2 Sam. 6:23 contains a concluding remark to the effect that Michal, Saul's daughter and David's wife, was childless to the day of her death.[147] This remark and the scene as a whole fit the theme and style of the Court History very well, and Rost takes 6:16, 20–23 as part of the story. But the scene is not a self-contained unit. It is very dependent upon the Ark Narrative, although it could not have been original to it since it is quite different. Nor is it so easy simply to regard the scene as a displaced fragment from another context.[148] It must have been added to the pre-existing Ark Narrative.

Rost's proposal for the beginning of the Court History does not solve the problem; it only postpones it. What was the literary form of the Ark Narrative and the Nathan oracle when the author of the Court History took them up? As we have seen above, Rost's analysis of 2 Sam. 7 cannot be maintained, and the chapter as a whole must be viewed as the work of the Dtr. Furthermore, chapter 7 is connected to the Ark Narrative in chapter 6, not primarily by the reference to Michal's childlessness in verse 23 but by David's statement about building a house of cedar for the Ark

145. However, cf. Veijola, *Die ewige Dynastie*, pp. 19–26. Veijola considers the whole of 2:1–12 to be Dtr and post-Dtr additions to the original Court History. This creates a problem for him, that there is nothing in the original Court History, as he reconstructs it, about the death of David although it must certainly be assumed. Veijola must also assign many other texts to Dtr in his reconstruction, both in 1 Kings 1–2 and in other parts of the Court History, but their designation as Dtr additions rests heavily upon his assignment of the whole of 2:1–12 to Dtr. Mettinger (*King and Messiah*, pp. 27–32) disputes the claim by Veijola that the whole of 1 Kings 2:1–12 is a Dtr addition and returns to the position that 2:5–9 belongs to the Succession Narrative. He must then resort to a lost beginning to David's speech to accommodate the Dtr texts 2:1–4.

146. Cf. Whybray, *Succession Narrative*, p. 8.

147. "Thronnachfolge Davids," p. 215. For a recent treatment of the Ark Narrative see A. F. Campbell, *The Ark Narrative (1 Sam. 4–6; 2 Sam. 6): A Form-Critical and Traditio-Historical Study.* Campbell describes these verses (pp. 127, 163–64) as an "epilogue" to the Ark Narrative, but he does not discuss their place in the Court History.

148. See Gunn (*King David*, pp. 73–75), who also adds vv. 5 and 14a as part of the Court History source. All these texts (6:5, 14a, 16b, 20–23) Gunn suggests originally belonged after 5:1–3, but he believes that a later redactor (for no apparent reason) removed them from this context and scattered them in the Ark Narrative. This kind of literary criticism makes little sense to me.

(7:2), which follows naturally after the celebration of bringing the Ark to the *tent* in Jerusalem (6:17–19). This connection was made prior to the addition of the little scene in 6:16, 20–23, since the latter seriously interrupts the continuity of subject matter and is incongruous with the tone of the chapter that follows. For these reasons it may therefore be argued that the Court History used the Dtr history and not vice versa.

Some scholars feel that Rost may not have carried his examination of the Court History's beginning far enough because he defined the theme of the literary work too narrowly in terms of the problem of succession. An older view that has recently been revived is that much of 2 Sam. 2–4, namely, the account of David's warfare with Ishbosheth, also belongs to the Court History and therefore is not a part of the Story of David's Rise.[149] The most obvious question that this account raises is, where did Ishbosheth come from? It would appear fairly clear that Dtr considered Saul to have three sons (1 Sam. 14:49), all of whom were killed by the Philistines (1 Sam. 31:2).[150] To consider Ishbosheth to have been a minor and therefore not involved in the battle, contrary to the statement in 2 Sam. 2:10, is to circumvent the literary problem by substituting historical speculation. Another problem is the present sequence of events in 2 Sam. 2, which leaves the episode in 2:4b–7 hanging in the air. The gesture by David to Jabesh-Gilead is surely meant as an invitation by him to become king over Israel as well as Judah while giving special notice to those of Jabesh-Gilead who had been most loyal to Saul that they should become David's valiant warriors too.[151] The natural sequel to this would be 5:1ff. A third point of tension between the Ishbosheth story and the one preceding it is the geography over which Ishbosheth is said to exercise his rule (2:9).[152] One area mentioned is Jezreel, but in the previous account of the Philistine's victory it is stated that after the Israelites were defeated they abandoned the region of Jezreel and the Philistines occupied it (1 Sam. 31:7ff.). In fact, the story of Ishbosheth's rule completely ignores the Philistine problem, although it

149. See H. P. Smith, *The Books of Samuel*, pp. xxvi, 267–68; and most recently, Gunn, *King David*, pp. 75ff.

150. The variant in the name of the second son, Ishvi/Abinadab, whatever the reason for it, does not allow for the survival of a fourth son in this story. The fact that 1 Chron. 9:39 names four sons of Saul simply points to this author's "correction" of the record subsequent to the addition of the Court History.

151. This gesture to the men of Jabesh-Gilead becomes most incongruous in the Court History when the latter states that David was a long-standing and loyal friend of Nahash, king of the Ammonites (2 Sam. 10:2; cf. 1 Sam. 11).

152. The various areas designated are not altogether clear in terms of the nature of Saul's monarchy. In particular, the designation "Assurites" = Assyrians is puzzling and for this reason has often been emended. But perhaps it reflects the late development of the use of the term "Syrians," which arose as a consequence of Assyria's provincial domination of the West.

is a dominant concern throughout the Story of David's Rise both before and after this unit.[153]

These inconsistencies between the account of the war with Ishbosheth and the Story of David's Rise suggest that 2 Sam. 2:8–4:12 is a part of the Court History instead. The lines of continuity are numerous and significant. Joab's murder of Abner in 2 Sam. 3:22ff., with David's protestation of innocence and his curse upon Joab's head, is specifically recalled in 1 Kings 2:5, 32, and Solomon's execution of Joab seems to be the eventual working out of this curse. Furthermore, in the words of David and Solomon, the murder of Abner is coupled with that of Amasa. Both assassinations are carried out in the same way, by stabbing the unsuspecting victim in the stomach (*ḥōmeš*), 2 Sam. 3:27; 20:10. The death of Abner is also linked to that of Asahel, who died of a spear thrust in the stomach (*ḥōmeš*), 2:23. Both Asahel and Amasa die while pursuing the enemy, and in both cases the sight of the dead commander distracts passers-by (2:23, 20:11ff.). In the conflict following each of these two deaths, the fighting finally ends when Joab sounds the trumpet to recall the troops and they then disperse (2 Sam. 2:28ff.; 20:22; see also 18:16). In accounts of battles outside the Court History, the trumpet sounds to begin the fighting (see Judg. 3:27).[154]

There is another link between these two parts of the Court History: the references in 9:3, 13 to the fact that Mephibosheth was crippled in his feet or lame (*nᵉkēh raglayim* and *pissēaḥ*) take us back to 4:4, where it is explained with the same terms how Mephibosheth became lame. The brief remark in 4:4 seems to have no other purpose than to anticipate the story in chapter 9; thus it must belong to the same author. Also, since it sits rather loosely in its present context, some scholars have suggested transposing it to the beginning of chapter 9. But this suggestion presents problems—the immediate transition from young child to full-grown man doesn't work well, and it is difficult to explain why some later editor

153. One argument that might be used to suggest that the account of Ishbosheth's rule was part of the Dtr corpus is the presence of the dating formulas in 2:10–11. As we shall see below, such formulas form part of the historical framework for Dtr. But in this case there is some indication that these formulas are not a genuine part of this framework but only an imitation. The dating pattern used for Ishbosheth, with the statement of his age at the time of his accession and the numerical elements of the formula coming first in the sentence order, is the standard form for the kings of Judah, whereas Ishbosheth was only a king of the north. He would never have been included in a Judean king list. The formula used for David's rule over Judah, on the other hand, while somewhat anomalous, follows more closely the northern pattern. Dtr's formula for introducing David's rule, which uses the true Judean pattern, actually occurs in 5:4.

154. See my earlier discussion of these in "Oral Patterns or Literary Conventions in Biblical Narrative," *Semeia* 5 (1976): 147–48, in criticism of Gunn, "Narrative Patterns and Oral Tradition in Judges and Samuel," *VT* 24 (1974):303–11, and Gunn's turnabout in *King David*, p. 80.

would have displaced this passage from an original connection with chapter 9 to its present location. Its position in the text must be viewed in a wider context.

The author of the Court History had a special interest in the household of Saul and its relationship to David.[155] This can be seen in David's demand that Michal, Saul's daughter, be returned to him as his lawful wife (3:13–16). The event obviously raises speculation about David's claim to Saul's realm, a claim further established by the death of Ishbosheth. The encounter between David and Michal in 6:20–23 is the sequel to the earlier event and points to the fact that David will not establish his dynasty together with the house of Saul.[156] It is in this light that we must view the remarks about Mephibosheth in 4:4. Just before the death of Ishbosheth, the last claimant to the throne of Saul, the author mentions another surviving Saulide—Mephibosheth, son of Jonathan—albeit a lame one. This raises the question how David will eventually deal with this possible claimant to the throne. Consequently, the notation about Mephibosheth in 4:4 seems to have been placed by the author in its present position in the Court History for specific dramatic purposes.

Another argument for including 2:8–4:12 within the Court History has to do with the work's distinctive literary qualities. Rost, in his study, stresses the skillful treatment of characterization throughout, of both major and secondary figures. This same quality of character portrayal is found in 2:8–4:12, but it is completely lacking in the Story of David's Rise. There, for instance, David is a man of transparent principles who does not strive in any way for the crown and who always leads his men personally into battle against the enemy. He has complete control over all his men and he dominates virtually every scene except where Saul is presented as his foil and opposite. This continues to be the case in the series of reports in 2 Sam. 5 and 8 as well. But in the war with Ishbosheth, David sits at home in Hebron while his men do all the fighting, a pattern that is consistent in the Court History.[157] David is also no longer in complete control of his own men or affairs. He begins to show that weakness so characteristic in the Court History.

The figure of Joab is particularly important. He is mentioned previously only in 1 Sam. 26:6 as the brother of Abishai. But in the account of the war with Ishbosheth, Joab is a well-known figure who needs no introduction, and he exhibits the ruthlessness, power, and domination of David

155. Besides 2:8–4:12, where this element is constant, it occurs in 6:20–23; chap. 9; 16:1–13; 19:15–30; 1 Kings 2:8–9, 36–46.

156. Weiser (*VT* 16:344) also points to the close connection between 3:13–16 and 6: 20–23 but concludes from this that the latter must be part of the Story of David's Rise. I would suggest instead that both belong to the Court History.

157. The exception is 2 Sam. 10:15–19a, but this originally belonged to chap. 8.

that are typical of the Court History.[158] Similarly, the figure of Abner, who is just mentioned by name in 1 Sam. 26:7, 14–15, is developed into a cunning and ambitious warrior in the unit 2:8–4:12 and plays a major role as a counterpart to Joab. Other characters, such as the weakling Ishbosheth and the swift and brash Asahel, also receive their due. There is no comparable portrayal of such secondary characters in the Story of David's Rise, whereas this style is completely consistent with the Court History.

Another aspect of style is the intricate development of the plot over the course of several scenes, giving a close-knit unity to the whole account of the war with Ishbosheth. There is also a mastery of descriptive detail, as in Asahel's pursuit of Abner (2 Sam. 2:18–23), the funeral procession of Abner (3:31ff.), and the murder of Ishbosheth (4:5–7a). This manner of presentation is consistent with that of the Court History but quite different from that of the Story of David's Rise.[159]

It has often been noted that in the Court History the historical course of events is presented with little reference to the deity or to divine intervention in political events.[160] This same "secular" manner characterizes the unit 2:8–4:12: the author does not comment on what part the deity had in these events.[161] In the Story of David's Rise the author (Dtr) frequently asserts that Yahweh is with David[162] and that David constantly receives divine guidance for all his military and political actions.[163] This is because he is fighting the "wars of Yahweh" (1 Sam. 25:28). But David's struggle with the house of Saul contains no hint whatsoever of this perspective.

In all these ways the account of David's war with Ishbosheth (2 Sam. 2:8–4:12) seems to stand apart from the Story of David's Rise and to form part of the Court History. Yet it is also dependent upon the previous Story of David's Rise. The defeat of Saul by the Philistines and David's establishment of power in Hebron over Judah is presupposed (2:8–10; 4:4). In 3:13–16 a specific reference is made back to David's marriage to Michal (1 Sam. 18:20–27) and to Saul's giving of Michal to another husband

158. It would appear that in the original account of the taking of Jerusalem (2 Sam. 5:6–9; 1 Chron. 11:4–9), Joab became commander of the army only at that time. Yet the Court History in 2 Sam. 2:8–4:12 presents Joab as already commander-in-chief while David is still in Hebron.

159. For further discussion of style see Gunn, *King David*, pp. 76ff.

160. Von Rad, *Problem of the Hexateuch*, pp. 196ff.

161. Stoebe, *Das erste Buch Samuelis*, pp. 296ff., argues that the Story of David's Rise ends at 2 Sam. 1. He regards 2 Sam. 2ff. as quite distinct from the Story of David's Rise in its pragmatic, rather than theological, perspective.

162. 1 Sam. 16:18; 18:12, 14, 28; 20:13; 2 Sam. 5:10.

163. 1 Sam. 22:5, 9–15; 23:1–5, 9–13; 30:7–8; 2 Sam. 2:1–2; 5:10, 12, 19, 23–25.

(25:44). Consequently, in its beginning the Court History was a secondary addition to the earlier history of David.

The connection between David's reaction to the murder of Ishbosheth in 2 Sam. 4:9ff. and his treatment of the messenger from Saul's camp on the death of Saul and his sons in 2 Sam. 1 is quite different.[164] A long-standing difficulty has existed in the discrepancies between the details of Saul's death given in 1 Sam. 31 and 2 Sam. 1. This difficulty, however, lies entirely in the Amalekite's story in 2 Sam. 1:5–10, 13–16, which can easily be removed as secondary, leaving a harmonious continuity. It would appear that the addition was made by the same hand that was responsible for the account of Ishbosheth's death in chapter 4, the author of the Court History. If this is the case, then the Court History must be a later addition to the Story of David's Rise. As we shall see, the intention of the addition is clear enough. It changes the whole character of David's reaction to the news of Saul's death.

Furthermore, the unit 2:8–4:12 leads up to the crowning of David as king of the Israelite tribes (in 5:1ff.) and his move to Jerusalem.[165] Certainly everything that follows in chapters 9ff. presupposes these events, even though no scholars reckon chapter 5 as part of the Court History. Now, scholars have often noted that there appears to be a doublet in 5:1 and 5:3 in which first the *tribes* of Israel come to David to make him king and then the *elders* come to make a covenant with David. This may be most easily explained by the fact that in 3:12–13, 17–21, Abner is shown as a mediator trying to bring about a covenant between the *elders* of Israel and David. Thus 5:3a would be a gloss by the author of the Court History to tie the earlier episode to chapter 5 and at the same time to interpret the relationship between David and Israel as a political agreement. The original unit would have stated simply that the Israelite tribes, on recognizing David's divine right to rule, anointed David as their king in a manner completely parallel to that of Judah in 2:4.

The latter part of the Court History also contains references to the Rise of David or to the larger Dtr history. First, the reference in 2 Sam. 9:1, 7 to David's showing kindness to Saul's household "for Jonathan's sake" presupposes a knowledge of the friendship and covenant between the two and of the oath regarding Jonathan's descendants (1 Sam. 20:14–17). Second, there is a similarity between the foodstuffs that Abigail brings to Da-

---

164. Gunn, *King David*, p. 75, recognizes the force of this connection but can suggest nothing to account for it.

165. Gunn, *King David*, pp. 74–75, also feels the need to include 5:1–3 in the Court History, but he expresses considerable uncertainty as to how to make it fit. So many scholars attribute 5:1–3 to the Story of David's Rise (and therefore to Dtr), as a parallel to 2:4, that the issue of its authorship cannot be ignored. Certainly 5:4–5 presuppose the preceding verses, and they (vv. 4–5) contain the Dtr dating formula.

vid and his men in 1 Sam. 25:18 and those that Ziba brings to David and
his men in 2 Sam. 16:1. D. M. Gunn[166] accounts for this similarity on the
basis of oral conventions in storytelling. Direct literary dependence, however, seems to me a preferable explanation. Third, in the circumstances
surrounding the death of Uriah the Hittite his death is compared in 2 Sam.
11:21 with the death of Abimelech (Judg. 9:50ff.). Finally, many scholars
have suggested that 1 Kings 2:27, which relates Abiathar's expulsion from
the priesthood, is an addition to the Court History by the Dtr. The original
prediction, however, had a much more immediate fulfillment in the death
of Hophni and Phinehas (1 Sam. 2:34) and never envisaged the situation in
1 Kings 2:27. This is just another instance of the author of the Court History making a connection with the previous history. The statement in 1
Kings 4:4 makes it doubtful that any such expulsion ever took place.

As mentioned previously, Rost suggests that the Ammonite war in 10:
6–11:1; 12:26–31 was a source that the writer of the Court History had
used for his work. However, I can see no break in continuity between 10:6
and what precedes it. The campaign against the Ammonites, led by Joab
and Abishai in David's absence, is quite in keeping with the other military
descriptions in chapters 2, 18, and 20, all part of the Court History. Only
the unit in 10:15–18a is different since it mentions that David is in charge,
instead of the two generals, as in chapters 5 and 8. The name of the Syrian
king, Hadadezer, links this unit directly with 8:3–8 and very likely belonged originally to it. This would suggest that the author of the Court
History used this unit in its present location as another way of making a
connection with a previous story about David, that is, the Dtr version.

Up to this point I have suggested that the Court History made use of,
and supplemented, the Dtr history and not vice versa, as so many scholars
have held. This theory has many implications for how the work is to be
understood. It must be considered first and foremost a literary composition that was written to augment a pre-existing larger historical work. It is
doubtful, therefore, that we can use the genre designation "traditional
story" recently proposed by Gunn.[167] Nor is it any kind of contemporary

166. *VT* 24 (1974):301–02; *King David*, pp. 50–51. For my earlier criticism of all these
"oral conventions," see *Semeia* 5:139–54. Gunn surely misses the point. If the Court History
is subsequent to Dtr's Story of David's Rise and built into it, then one can hardly argue that
the pattern of provisions in 2 Sam. 16:1 is an independent narrative pattern. It is far easier to
suppose that it was copied from the earlier work (1 Sam. 25:18) if the author had it in front
of him, whether or not we can say why he did so. Gunn fails to mention the fact that the list
of provisions in 2 Sam. 17:28–29 is altogether different.
167. *King David*, pp. 38ff. Gunn objects to Whybray's designation of the work as a
"novel" on two accounts: (1) "the term implies an essentially written as opposed to an oral
genre," and (2) "it implies also a particularly high degree of autonomy of the author over his
style and subject matter." I must, however, reject Gunn's objections because both of these
features are true of the Court History. It is a written work and therefore novelistic even

historical reporting or political propaganda of the early monarchy.[168] Since the date of the work cannot be earlier than the mid-sixth century, the events may all be imaginary.[169]

The question of the Court History's genre, however, cannot be finally answered until we consider the theme of the work. The usual understanding is that it is a succession story, whose purpose was to legitimize Solomon's rule and thus to associate it with an intimate of the court from a time early in his reign. But this interpretation surely runs counter to the obvious fact that Solomon's rise to power is the result of a palace intrigue and cold-blooded murder on very flimsy pretexts. More recent studies, by L. Delekat[170] and E. Würthwein,[171] have proposed the opposite understanding, namely, that the work reflects an antimonarchical tendency during the reign of Solomon and a questioning of the royal ideology. This antimonarchical interpretation seems to me to be much closer to the mark, although the dating to the Solomonic period is neither necessary nor even plausible in view of the relationship of the Court History to Dtr discussed above. Gunn's latest work gives up entirely on any historical context for

---

though it could incorporate within it "oral" or "traditional" features such as colloquialisms, proverbs, songs, a short tale, etc., features quite common in novels—and also in the *Histories* of Herodotus. Its very late date and highly uniform style and many other features observed above suggest that the author was quite creative with his material and subjects. Gunn's own suggestion of "traditional story" is really no genre designation at all. The adjective "traditional" is highly ambiguous. It could mean that the theme or content of the story is traditional. Thus, for instance, most of the Greek tragedies are traditional stories, i.e., based upon a body of fairly well known tradition. But that still allowed the various tragedians a great deal of flexibility in style and the treatment of their subject matter. On the other hand, Aeschylus's *Persians* was not traditional even though the theme of the great war had been dealt with before. The genre of tragedy made use of, but did not demand, traditional stories. The adjective "traditional" can also refer to form or genre. Here again one can speak of Greek tragedy as being "traditional" in form, although it was by no means rigidly fixed. But a traditional genre does not make a traditional story.

On neither account can the Court History be described as a "traditional story." We have no evidence whatsoever that the family life of David was the subject of a long tradition of storytelling. This is the only example that there is, and it does not follow any traditional mode of telling the story. It is unique within the Bible and has no close parallel outside it. The designation "traditional story" is therefore unwarranted.

168. Whybray, *The Succession Narrative*, pp. 50–55.

169. This late dating and novelistic character effectively remove the Court History from any useful comparison with the Hittite historical texts. Cf. H. Cancik, *Grundzüge der hethitischen und alttestamentlichen Geschichtsschreibung;* H. M. Wolf, *The Apology of Ḫattušilis Compared with Other Political Self-Justifications of the Ancient Near East.* See above, 4a and e.

170. "Tendenz und Theologie der David-Solomon-Erzählung," in *Das ferne und nahe Wort,* BZAW 105 (1967): 26–36.

171. *Die Erzählung von der Thronfolge Davids—theologische oder politische Geschichtsschreibung?* Würthwein argues for many redactional additions to the work, but I do not find these suggestions very convincing. See also Crüsemann, *Der Widerstand gegen das Königtum,* pp. 180–93.

the work and chooses to interpret the work as it is, whatever the author might have intended.[172] That particular approach, whether it is legitimate or not, ignores the problem posed at the outset—the relation of the Court History and its view of David to the Dtr history.

The meaning or interpretation of the Court History must be seen in terms of its relation to the prior Dtr Rise of David and to its theme. We have already noted above that the theme of God's election of David as prince, *nāgîd*, and of his promise of a perpetual dynasty in 2 Sam. 7 were known and used by the author of the Court History. But it is precisely the *way* in which he did this that reveals the purpose of the work. In the palace intrigue of 1 Kings 1, Solomon's right to rule is based upon a very dubious promise which the king is said to have made to his mother, Bathsheba, but which was actually invented by Nathan.[173] This is in contrast to the promise by divine revelation to Nathan in 2 Sam. 7. After the whole shady plot is hatched, it is arranged, again without oracle or revelation, that Zadok the priest and Nathan the prophet will anoint Solomon and then have him sit on the royal throne to be king in his father's place while David is still alive to ensure his right to rule. David's final statement in this arrangement is, "I have designated him *nāgîd* over Israel and Judah" (verse 35). In the Dtr stories of David and Saul only God makes this statement, as an indication of the ruler's divine election. Finally, the military commander states, "Amen. May Yahweh the God of my lord the king say thus. As Yahweh has been with my lord the king, even so may he be with Solomon. . . ." Since Benaiah enforces the executions for Solomon to ensure his throne, this statement clearly makes a mockery of the whole divine election theme.

The divine promise of 2 Sam. 7 is also referred to in 1 Kings 2:24. It is placed in the mouth of Solomon in the context of an oath that his elder brother be put to death on mere suspicion of his intentions. Then, after the further murders of Joab and Shimei and the expulsion of Abiathar, the account concludes: "So the kingdom was established in the hand of Solomon" (1 Kings 2:46). This repeats the statement of the Dtr formula in 1 Kings 2:12, but in the case of 2:46 the allusion to the divine promise to David that his kingdom would be established is full of irony.

Early in the Court History, in 2 Sam. 6:21, David speaks of himself as being chosen by Yahweh as *nāgîd* over the people of Yahweh. This is a

172. *King David*, pp. 87–88. Gunn's interpretation of the Court History is what he chooses to see in the work, what it means to him in the twentieth century. He feels no need, as he says, to "stick with the author." Why, then, he imputes his own private meaning to the author (p. 111) is not at all clear to me. In my own attempt to "stick with the author" I have found quite a different meaning to the story.

173. See Würthwein, *Thronfolge Davids*, pp. 13ff.

taunt thrown in the face of Michal, Saul's daughter, in order to silence her reprimand. David states that since he is Yahweh's elect, he may behave with all the maidens in any way he pleases without regard for her views. Abner speaks of God's election and promise to David in much the same way in 2 Sam. 3:9–10, 17–18. In the first instance it comes out in an angry dispute between Abner and Ishbosheth that Abner intends to fulfill the divine promise by switching loyalties and by political maneuvering. While the reference is meant to recapitulate the rejection of Saul, it also reflects more nearly the oracle of Nathan, particularly 2 Sam. 7:15. This use of the promise as a threat or taunt against the house of Saul, as in 6:21, tends to belittle the element of divine activity in the accomplishment of this goal. Abner again employs the theme of divine revelation to David (3:18) to persuade the elders of Israel to throw in their lot with David and to make a deal (covenant) with him as the best one to save them from their enemies. In point of fact, the terms of this revelation are more nearly those made about Saul through Samuel (1 Sam. 9:16; 10:1 LXX), so that Abner seems to have shifted them to David purely for his own political reasons. By contrast, when Abner comes to David he does not make any confessional recognition of David's divine right to rule, such as Jonathan, Abigail, and others expressed in the Story of David's Rise. Instead he speaks of his own ability to deliver all Israel to David, and this David is ready to accept. David's own political aspirations are described by Abner as "all that your ambition craves" (verse 21).[174] The story suggests that the theme of divine election may be used as a guise and justification for dishonorable political action.

If, as I have previously suggested, the stories of Saul and David within the Dtr history were intended to present the legitimation of the royal house of David, then the Court History has been added as an antilegitimation story, referring to the same theme of divine promise but in an entirely different way.[175] This negative theme is brought out not only in the nature of the succession but also in the description of the inauguration of David's

---

174. kol *a*šer t*e*'awweh nafšekā. The combination of verb or noun of the root 'wh with nefeš usually has the sense of bodily appetites (see Num. 11:4, 34), hence the somewhat stronger rendering "ambition" in place of the rather mild "all that your heart desires," RSV. In a parallel text in 1 Kings 11:37, the same phrase is used by the prophet Ahijah in speaking to Jeroboam. In this case it is the deity who, through the prophet, is promising the northern kingdom of Israel to Jeroboam. Since the divine promise is qualified by the condition of obedience to the law, in language that clearly marks the whole section as Dtr, the remark does not carry a strongly negative connotation. When the author of the Court History has the same words come from a defecting military leader without any religious qualification, they have an entirely different impact on the reader.

175. Some scholars, such as Weiser (VT 16:338ff.), have included all the references to the promise theme within the same source without reckoning with the fact that the two sources are so different in their presentation of the theme.

rule and of the various revolts through which he maintained his power.[176] The Court History is a bitter attack upon the whole royal ideology of a "sure house" for David. David gains control over his kingdom by direct military action, by political scheming, and by assassinations. All this is in strong contrast to Dtr, who simply had David peacefully succeed Saul at the invitation of the northern tribes. According to the Court History, David's household is nothing but turmoil and intrigue, infidelity and murder, hate and suspicion. David is a moral and spiritual weakling who does not fight the battles of Yahweh but takes the wife of his bravest warrior while the latter is on campaign with the Ark. It is also deeply ironic that Nahash, the king of the Ammonites, is described in 2 Sam. 10:2 as having enjoyed a close friendship with David. This is the same king who is described in the story of Saul as a cruel and bitter foe of the eastern tribes of Israel, and over whom Saul had won a great victory in the name of Yahweh.

There is scarcely anything exemplary in David's actions in the whole of the Court History. It is, therefore, inconceivable to me that Dtr would have included such a work virtually unedited in his history when his whole perspective was exactly the opposite. For him David is the ideal monarch who always did what was right in the eyes of Yahweh and according to whom all the actions of the later kings are judged. The qualification added in one instance (1 Kings 15:5), "except in the matter of Uriah the Hittite," is so incongruous to the praise of David that it is surely a later gloss. The Chronicler, who also supported the royal ideology of David as the ideal, simply omitted the whole of the Court History from his history.

We may conclude from these observations that the Court History is a post-Dtr addition to the history of David from the postexilic period. In this period the theme of the divine promise to David in 2 Sam. 7 tended to develop into an "eternal covenant" with strong messianic overtones.[177] The Court History must be seen, therefore, as the product of an antimessianic tendency in certain Jewish circles at this time. This would mean, of course, that by itself the Court History was not a piece of history writing, although it involved a close scrutiny of the pre-existing Dtr history as a source. There is no reason to believe that any other sources, traditional or archival, were at the author's disposal when he composed the various scenes and episodes of his work. They may all be contrived. The notion of

176. Jackson's suggestion (in *CJT* 11:183–95), which would ascribe the themes of legitimation and succession to two different literary levels or sources, seems to me quite unnecessary. Both are part of the same issue—the way in which David and his house gained the throne of Judah and Israel. Gunn's treatment of this twofold aspect (*King David*, pp. 94–111) as David being given the throne by others and David giving up the throne is also inadequate. David's manner of gaining the throne is intended to be just as negative as his efforts to maintain it and to pass it on.

177. See Perlitt, *Bundestheologie*, pp. 50–52.

an eyewitness account of events has to be abandoned and with it the standard reconstruction of the rise of history writing in Israel. There is no such historiography in Samuel-Kings prior to the work of the Dtr Historian.

CHAPTER NINE

STRUCTURE, GENRE, AND THEME IN THE BOOKS OF KINGS

While many scholars recognize that the author or authors of the books of Kings used "official" records in composing the work, few acknowledge that the use of such sources was essential to the development of historiography, since most scholars trace the rise of Israelite historiography to the period prior to the divided monarchy.[1] Nevertheless, for the books of Kings, court documents appear to have been an important source of information as well as part of the structural framework for the presentation of royal deeds in chronological order. The characterization of such documents is often quite loose: scholars use terms like annals, chronicles, and synchronistic history which do not correspond to genres with the same names in the Near East generally. In addition, the relationship of more popular, "unofficial" sources to the official documents is seldom clarified. It is necessary, therefore, to consider the variety of such genres and their place within the books of Kings. Included within the framework of Kings, but also in longer editorial digressions and in speeches placed in the mouths of Israel's leaders, are statements that reflect the work's "philosophy of history." These thematic texts explain the basis for selection of material and the author's intention for the work as a whole. It seems reasonable, therefore, to investigate the historiography of Kings by examining both those features of the work that give it its historiographic structure and those passages that reflect thematic and ideological continuity throughout the work as a whole.

a. CHRONICLES, KING LISTS, AND ANNALS

The historian[2] of Kings cites what appear to be official records when he refers to "the book of the deeds of Solomon" (sēfer dibrē šᵉlōmōh)[3] and

1. See the discussion above, 7a.
2. For convenience I will refer to this author in the singular and discuss below the issue of the plurality of authorship.
3. 1 Kings 11:41.

"the book of the chronicles of the kings of Israel/Judah" (*sēfer dibrē hayyāmîm lᵉmalᵉkē yiśrā'ēl/yᵉhûdāh*)[4] as sources of information for his history. It has been suggested that these works were daybooks or diaries, or summaries made from such works.[5] Some scholars have pointed to the *mazkîr*, one of the court officials, as the royal archivist whose responsibility it was to maintain such records.[6]

Egyptian examples of record keeping provide the model for the court daybook.[7] From the end of the Middle Kingdom (eighteenth century B.C.) comes a document, P. Boulaq 18, that appears to be a royal diary of the Theban court, recording the daily affairs of the palace.[8] Its content varies greatly from matters of business to formal affairs of state. In the annals of Thutmose III statements are made to the effect that more information about military campaigns or income from booty can be obtained from daybooks kept in the temple or palace respectively.[9] The Journey of Wenamun, from the eleventh century B.C., refers to the king of Byblos consulting the records of his fathers to see what financial dealings they had with the pharaohs.[10] Redford has recently conducted an extensive investigation of all such possible Egyptian daybooks.[11] He notes that they represent the precisely dated daily record of activity in important institutions such as the court, the temple, the courts of law, and the necropolis; they even include the logs of sailing ships. The content of the Egyptian daybooks covers the whole range of record keeping: economic and legal matters, military and administrative affairs, even astronomical observations. Their purpose was completely utilitarian; they were not created to preserve a historical account for posterity, so they do not belong to historiography proper. These records do not differ greatly from the archives of business, legal, and administrative documents kept in Mesopotamia, except that the latter are written on tablets instead of scrolls. It is likely that Israel too had its archives of scrolls for the day-to-day business of the kingdom. However, none of the Egyptian examples suggests a work containing a summary of the principal deeds of a series of kings, or even of each king, such as the biblical references seem to indicate. By themselves the Egyptian parallels do not take us very far in identifying the historical genre in question.

4. 1 Kings 14:19, 29.

5. See Hugo Gressmann, *Geschichtsschreibung*, p. xi. His view has been frequently repeated in later commentaries.

6. J. A. Montgomery, *The Book of Kings*, p. 31. However, R. de Vaux, *Ancient Israel: Its Life and Institutions*, p. 132, strongly disputes this meaning and prefers the rendering "royal herald."

7. Gressmann, *Geschichtsschreibung*, p. xi.

8. *CAH*³, vol. 2, pt. 1, pp. 48–49.

9. See above, 5e.

10. See above, 5f.

11. Redford, *King-Lists, Annals, and Day-books*, s.v. "Day-books."

Other parallels for daybooks have been cited from the late Persian and Hellenistic periods.[12] Ezra 4:15 contains a reference to "the book of the records [dokrānayyā] of your fathers," meaning the archival record of the Persian kings. The existence of such a book in this instance appears to be a fiction: the Persians certainly could not have had a record of Israelite history covering the whole period of the monarchy, which is what is clearly suggested in verses 15, 19, and 20, since none of the monarchy was contemporaneous with the Persian Empire. But by the time of the author of Ezra, the notion of histories under the rubric of dokrānayyā was well known.

Esther 2:23 contains a reference to a book of chronicles (dibrē hayyāmîm) in which an important public event is recorded. The same book is referred to in Esther 6:1 by two expressions, "the book of memorial deeds" (hazzikrōnôt) and "chronicles" (dibrē hayyāmîm). It seems that here the two expressions are synonymous. The first term, hazzikrōnôt, is very likely the Hebrew equivalent of the Aramaic dokrānayyā of Ezra 4:15. The Greek term in 2 Esdras 4:15 is hupomnēmatismoi, which is also the term in the Hellenistic period for official journals and record keeping.[13] The confusion in the late period between general record keeping and chronographic works may go back to an earlier time, but this is not at all certain. Neither is it certain that chronicles arose merely as a natural extension and development of record-keeping practices. Egypt, for instance, had daybooks of various kinds throughout the second and first millennia B.C., but it never developed a true chronicle tradition.[14] One cannot assume that chronicles were kept in all the courts of the Near East throughout the first millenium B.C. and then make Israel a part of this supposed practice.

The closest analogy to the chronographic works referred to in the books of Kings is the Babylonian Chronicle Series. As we have seen above,[15] the recording of important political events with precise dates in strict chronological sequence from one monarch to another seems to have been the special development of the Neo-Babylonian kings, beginning with the dynastic founder, Nabu-nasir, in 747 B.C. I have also argued that such a form of chronicle did not exist in either Babylon or Assyria before the Neo-Babylonian period. Grayson has suggested that the chronicles were derived from diaries containing records of astronomical or meteorological matters,

12. Gressmann, Geschichtsschreibung, p. xl.
13. See also Macc. 2:2, 13. U. Wilcken, "'Υπομνηματισμοί," Philologus 53 (1894):80ff., discusses examples of such daybooks down to the time of Roman Egypt.
14. The Palermo Stone may be an exception, but its form of record keeping never survived beyond the Old Kingdom (see above, 5a).
15. 3d.

market prices, and river heights; they also contained references to current political events, which were extracted for a special series. According to Grayson, at some time early in the Neo-Babylonian period the transition was made from merely keeping daily records to composing royal chronicles from them.

When we compare the Babylonian chronicle style and form with the Old Testament, it appears that only in 2 Kings 25, in the account of the fall of Jerusalem and subsequent events, was this chronicle style taken up in its full form in the historical books. There we find a strict and careful recital of events dated precisely by year, month, and day, just as in the Babylonian chronicles. We also find the chronographic style in the texts of Jeremiah that deal with these same events, and it becomes a distinctive feature of Ezekiel's prophecy. These works were composed when the Judean scribes, after 597 B.C., came most directly under the influence of Babylonian conventions.

The difficulty with suggesting any influence from the Babylonian Chronicle Series is that the biblical "chronicles" cover most of the history in the books of Kings, a history that goes back long before the Babylonian Chronicle Series began. Before offering a solution to this problem, I would like to consider two other Mesopotamian parallels to Kings which do not have this limitation. Many scholars have referred to the Assyrian Synchronistic History as a close parallel to the books of Kings.[16] The scope of this work is comparable to that of the books of Kings; it goes back at least to the fifteenth century B.C. Also, the way it synchronizes the reigns of certain Assyrian kings with their Babylonian counterparts is similar to such synchronisms in Kings. But there the resemblance ends. The Synchronistic History deals only with border disputes, warfare, and subsequent treaties between Assyria and Babylonia, and it is written from the Assyrian perspective as rather blatant political propaganda. It does not give a continuous history of the two regions and it does not synchronize the chronologies. Thus, its comparison with Kings is not very useful. Nevertheless, as noted above, the author of the Synchronistic History did make use of inscriptions on monuments still extant in his own day to compose his history, and this work in turn became a source for later chronicles.

A second text often cited as a parallel to Kings is the Weidner Chronicle.[17] Like the Synchronistic History, it is highly tendentious, in this case on behalf of the Marduk cult of Babylon. But while it purports to cover a period of ancient history, its references throughout to the cult of Marduk are anachronistic and represent attitudes prevalent at the time of composi-

16. On the Synchronistic History, see above, 3d.
17. On this work, see above, 3d.

tion many centuries later. Only the names used in the text are historical, taken very likely from king lists; thus the Weidner Chronicle is a fabrication with little historical value, hardly a chronicle in the true sense. However, it does have points of similarity to the biblical books of Kings. The author of Kings has an anachronistic perspective on the Jerusalem cult and passes judgment upon the various kings of Israel and Judah on the basis of the cultic injunctions of Deuteronomy. Also, the nature of divine retribution is similar in the two works; but for the rest, the style of presenting the history of the nation is so different that further comparison is not profitable. In any event, neither the Synchronistic History nor the Weidner Chronicle solves the problem of how Israel could produce chronicles that dealt with the whole period of the monarchy; nor can either work tell us the form such chronicles took.

Three Babylonian chronicles, however, are relevant. As we have seen above,[18] the Chronicles of the Early Kings, Chronicle P, and the Eclectic Chronicle all deal with the period before the time covered by the Babylonian Chronicle Series and all seem to have been produced by "historical" research. The result is a continuous history from earliest times down to the beginning of the Neo-Babylonian period. It is significant that these works made use of both the Synchronistic History and the Weidner Chronicle, as well as of other historiographic works like king lists and omen texts. As I have suggested above, these Babylonian chronicles were composed no earlier than the Neo-Babylonian period; the Babylonian Chronicle Series inspired "historical" research and provided the form in which materials about the early period would be presented, even though its precise system of dating could not be used.

We should also consider the western tradition of chronographic writing as it is preserved in the Annals of Tyre.[19] When the original chronicle was written is not known, but the parts used by Josephus indicate that it covered the period at least from the tenth to the sixth centuries B.C. In my earlier discussion of this work I argued that, like the three Babylonian chronicles mentioned above, the Annals were probably constructed out of a king list, supplemented by material from commemorative inscriptions and popular traditions. A number of similarities between the Annals of Tyre and the chronological statements in the books of Kings may be observed. In both the Annals and the Chronicles of the Kings of Judah the age of the king is given along with the length of his reign—a practice not found in other Near Eastern king lists.[20] Second, in both the Annals and the books

---

18. See above, 3d.
19. On this work, see above, 6c.
20. In the Bible the age of the king is given at the time of his accession, whereas in the Annals the total length of the king's life is recorded.

of Kings the length of a king's reign is always given *before* the account of his reign and not as a summation at the end, as in the Babylonian chronicle tradition. Third, any irregular succession to the throne was also noted in the chronological framework in both the Annals and Kings. This evidence of similarity in form suggests that, in spite of the transformation the Tyrian Annals may have suffered in the process of transmission to the Roman period, the genre of royal chronicles used by the author of Kings was not a unique phenomenon in the west. A similar form also developed in Phoenicia, very likely as a response to influence from the Babylonian chronicle tradition. Whether the "chronicles" mentioned in the books of Kings were constructed out of king lists and other official documents remains to be considered.

Throughout the books of Kings the various rulers of Israel and Judah are introduced by a formula dealing with the king's accession to the throne and the length of his reign. This chronological framework has often been attributed to the author of Kings, together with the formulae dealing with religious judgments on the reign, but there is reason to believe that the chronology derives ultimately from two separate king lists in Israel and Judah. In a recent study S. R. Bin-Nun has argued that the formulae represent two distinct styles in the two kingdoms which can be explained only as derived from independent sources.[21] According to Bin-Nun, the appearance of greater homogeneity in the series of introductory formulas is created by the synchronisms drawn between the two reigns of contemporary kings in Israel and Judah, but these synchronisms, with a few possible exceptions, are the work of the later author of Kings. Once these are removed, the distinct styles become apparent. The formula for the Israelite kings is:

A (the son of B) reigned over Israel in (Tirzah/Samaria) *n* years

or

And he (name previously mentioned) reigned over Israel *n* years in (Tirzah/Samaria).

In this formula the length of reign is always given at the end, whether additions or synchronisms are added to the formula or not.[22] In the case of the Judean kings, however, the order is inverted, with the number of years always given first:

And *n* years reigned he in Jerusalem.

21. "Formulas from Royal Records of Israel and Judah," *VT* 18 (1968):414–32.
22. 1 Kings 15:25, 33; 16:8, 29; 22:51; 2 Kings 3:1; 13:1, 10; 14:23; 15:8, 13, 17, 23, 27; 17:1.

This statement is also regularly preceded by the age of the king at his accession and the name of the queen mother, items not given for the Israelite kings.[23]

This scheme cannot be made to work very well for the early kings from Saul to Solomon, where the formula manifests a certain variation on the two styles, as does the formula for Jeroboam and Jehu. It is my view that these formulas should be left outside the king-list scheme.[24] The rest of the formulas suggest two separate king lists for Israel and Judah, maintained from the time of the division of the kingdom onward. Furthermore, it is not surprising that the formulas, especially those of the Judean list, resemble so closely the chronological formula in the Annals of Tyre.[25] The formulas in Kings, like those in the Annals of Tyre, sum up the total years of a king's reign *before* recounting his deeds, thus producing an illogical sequence that is otherwise unknown in chronicles. This suggests that the formulas belonged originally to separate king lists rather than to annals or chronicles and that these king lists were used as the framework for the later reconstruction of the two chronicles.

If the Assyrian King List and the Annals of Tyre can be taken as models, then the king lists of Israel and Judah may also have included unusual circumstances in the process of succession, such as a violent seizure of the throne or an assassination of the king, and this seems to be the case for the succession formulas in Kings. It also seems likely that these official records included some reference to the royal burial place.[26] For any king who did not die violently there is usually the statement that he "slept with his fathers and was buried in [place name, usually the capital]," and that a successor reigned in his place.

These two king lists for Israel and Judah provided a framework that could be expanded into the two literary works, "the chronicles of the kings of Israel" and "the chronicles of the kings of Judah." If this is the case, then such chronicles could not have been "contemporaneously constructed" during the course of the monarchy[27] but were much later works created by supplementing the king lists with records from other historical sources, such as the commemorative or memorial inscriptions.

It is entirely possible that the kings of Israel and Judah left behind records of their achievements in the form of commemorative or memorial inscriptions, even though none has been found. As we have seen above,[28]

23. 1 Kings 15:1, 9; 2 Kings 8:16, 25; 9:29; 14:1; 15:1, 32; 16:1; 18:1.
24. Cf. Bin-Nun, VT 18:422–23.
25. Note similar variations between the Assyrian and Babylonian King Lists, discussed above, 3b.
26. See especially the Dynastic Chronicle, discussed above, 3d.
27. Montgomery, *Kings*, p. 31.
28. See above, 6b.

such inscriptions have come to light throughout the Levant. They usually contain a first-person recitation by the king of his mighty deeds accomplished with the aid of the deity. They deal with military affairs, frequently making comparisons with periods of hardship or servitude that preceded the particular king's reign. This theme of a return to order and piety also appears in Egyptian and Hittite texts. Common to many inscriptions are references to royal building activity: construction of cities, palaces, temples, and other works. These accounts often review the deeds of the king through several years with little concern for specific dates or proper chronological order. As in the Mesopotamian inscriptions, the accounts of military campaigns usually precede those of building activity, although sometimes the two subjects are mixed. Whether these states also had more detailed records on perishable materials cannot be known.

Apart from the Annals of Tyre, whose form and content must remain somewhat suspect, there are no extant "histories" from the Levant with which to compare the biblical histories. Mesopotamian historiography, on the other hand, did produce literary works—king lists, the Synchronistic History, and chronicles of olden times—that did make use of historical sources such as inscriptions and prior literary works in the scribal tradition. Primary archival records, however, were seldom if ever consulted for periods in the distant past.[29] Consequently, many historical works dealing with earlier centuries contain a heterogeneous mixture of genres, a quality also reflected in the books of Kings.

J. A. Montgomery has suggested that it is possible to find in the books of Kings traces of archival sources,[30] by which he means dated annals recording the deeds of the various kings of Israel and Judah. Such a suggestion is now widely accepted in the literature, but it harbors some serious misconceptions about Near Eastern historiography. We must first of all distinguish between archives and the scribal tradition (the library).[31] Archives are records of day-to-day business or legal transactions that were preserved because of their usefulness in the affairs of state. They were not preserved for their own sake, and if the material on which they were recorded was perishable, they did not last very long. Anything that became part of the scribal tradition, however, was transmitted through subsequent copying for the benefit of posterity. Royal annals and commemorative inscriptions were not archival documents. Nor, on the whole, were they part

29. This is also the case with classical historiography, as A. Momigliano has pointed out. See "Historiography on Written Tradition and Historiography on Oral Tradition," in *Studies in Historiography*, pp. 211–20.

30. "Archival Data in the Book of Kings," *JBL* 53 (1934): 46–52; idem, *Kings*, pp. 31–37.

31. See A. L. Oppenheim, *Ancient Mesopotamia*, p. 13.

of the library collections—the literary tradition. Rather, they were either monumental or votive, although some school-text copies were sometimes made of them.

Furthermore, annals have been erroneously understood as

> . . . records . . . of important events arranged by year. They were intended to preserve the memory of these events, and were therefore stored in archives. They represent a true reportorial literary type. Annals were recorded since the earliest times, especially at the royal court, less commonly at sanctuaries.[32]

In point of fact, annals are restricted to the Hittites, the Egyptians of the empire period, and the Assyrians. They deal almost entirely with successive annual military campaigns, but they were originally produced only by kings who campaigned frequently. Thus Muršili II, the Hittite, and Thutmose III of Egypt are the primary examples of kings who published annals in the second millennium. The Assyrians, on the other hand, furnish numerous examples of annals, but they developed the fiction of recording campaign years even when there was no military activity. Unless one supposes that Judean and Israelite kings campaigned annually, there is no reason to speak of Israelite "annals," at least not on the analogy of parallel Near Eastern materials. So G. Fohrer's remarks, quoted above, must be modified in the light of these considerations.

Apart from the chronicle style at the end of Kings, the evidence for sources with precisely dated events is slim indeed. Montgomery, in trying to make up for this lack, argues that the Hebrew construction 'az, "then," with the verb in the perfect (in place of the usual 'az + imperfect) really stood for a precise date in the original annals.[33] But this suggestion suffers from two weaknesses: (1) 'az with the perfect also occurs in prose passages where an annalistic source is doubtful;[34] and (2) in West Semitic inscriptions no annalistic texts have been found, only the more general memorial inscriptions. Montgomery also argues that such expressions in Kings as "in those days," "at that time," "in his days," and the like are typical of Assyrian and West Semitic royal inscriptions. This is quite true.[35] But since these phrases occur in prose throughout the whole Deuteronomistic corpus, they can scarcely be used to identify those parts of it that may go back to official records. These and other features of scribal style may in fact indicate that historical narration in inscriptions influenced biblical historiographic prose in general. As we have seen, in the Near East unofficial or

32. G. Fohrer, *Introduction to the Old Testament*, p. 97.
33. *JBL* 53:49–51.
34. Josh. 10:33; 22:31b; Judg. 8:3b; 13:21; 2 Sam. 21:17.
35. See Mowinckel, "Die vorderasiatischen Königs und Fürsteninschriften," in *Eucharisterion*, vol. 1, pp. 278–322.

completely fictional accounts were sometimes cast in the form of official historical narration, and this may have happened in the Old Testament as well.

Those texts most closely associated with the chronicles of the kings of Israel/Judah include accounts of military campaigns and building activity, information that could have been taken from memorial inscriptions.[36] Texts having to do with the payment of tribute and servitude to Assyria may have survived on foreign stelae set up by these kings in Samaria and Judah. Detailed accounts of conspiracies also seem to derive from official records and are common in Near Eastern sources generally. In two instances historical events are dated, at least as to year (1 Kings 14:25–28; 2 Kings 18:13–16), and in both the events may be corroborated by evidence from either Egypt or Assyria. In both cases the accounts record the payment of tribute from the Temple treasury; a number of other episodes involving Temple funds and artifacts may also be cited. Some scholars have suggested a Temple "chronicle," but the term may be misleading. It is, however, possible that a record of Temple income and its use was retained and was accessible to a chronographer or historian of a later day. The "history" of the Temple may have become a subject of interest in Judah as it did in a somewhat different way in Mesopotamia.

Another "official" source used by the historian of Kings for his account of the United Monarchy is the "book of the deeds of Solomon" (1 Kings 11:41). The extent and character of this work are difficult to assess, but we should *not* assume that it is the same type of work as the other two chronicles. I would suggest that it is a collection of the records of Solomon's reign, especially inscriptions, that were extant in the time of the compiler. It is reasonable to suppose that a commemorative or memorial inscription would mention the building of the Temple and palace, possibly with dates (although this would be unusual), and would provide a few details about their construction. However, the elaborate description of these buildings seems odd and reads like a memory of things past, as if it had been written after these structures were destroyed. This is also true of the list of bronze furnishings for the Temple (7:13–46), which may represent some Temple inventories. Evidence that bronze vessels were extensively used in Solomon's day seems incontrovertible. Whether Solomon's trading ventures in the Red Sea (9:26–28, 10:11–12) or his visit from the Queen of Sheba and his trade in horses and chariots can be accepted is a matter of some debate.[37]

One reference to Solomon's building activities that may reflect an offi-

36. 1 Kings 12:25; 14:19; 16:24; 22:39; 2 Kings 13:24; 14:15, 28. See Noth, *ÜS*, pp. 74–75; Montgomery, *Kings*, pp. 35–36.
37. On these see below.

cial source is found in 9:15, 17b, 18, 23. It begins with the statement, "This is the record of the forced labor which king Solomon raised to build the house of Yahweh. . . ." It looks very much like an official accounting list in an inscription, but the editor of Kings deliberately omits the numbers and instead inserts a remark (verse 20) about the use of the indigenous population in the construction projects, a remark contradicted by many other statements. However, verse 23 does give the total for the officers in charge as 550. But in 5:27–32 (ET 13–18) the figure for the labor force on the Temple alone is 30,000, while the number of officers is set at 3,300, six times the number in 9:23. It is possible that the whole section 5:15–32 is an attempt by the historian of Kings to write a historical narrative based on a number of official records.

Other units, derived from official records, that may have belonged to the "deeds of Solomon" are the lists of Solomon's high officials (4:1–6) and the division of the land into taxation districts with their officers (4:7–19 and 5:2 [ET 4:22]).[38] The purpose of the twelve-part division was to provide the royal court with its daily provisions, one month for each district.[39]

The various references to building activity, inventories, and lists that seem to have made up the main content of the "book of the deeds of Solomon" do not constitute a royal chronicle. In spite of the specific dates given for the building of the Temple and palace, the material is unchronological in its arrangement. It is also doubtful that much of it came from commemorative or memorial inscriptions such as are typical in the Levant. Thus the work clearly differs from the "chronicles of the kings of Israel/Judah." When such a compilation of "Solomonic" records was made is difficult to say, but we have several reasons for suspecting that some of these elements were attributed to Solomon anachronistically. Although the question of historicity does not directly concern us here, it is clear, nevertheless, that the various lists themselves and the "book of deeds" as a whole can hardly be regarded as a form of history writing. The "book of deeds" becomes a source for historiography only when the historian of Kings uses it in particular ways to present a broad portrayal of the Solomonic era as a whole.

---

38. Why is it that only the administrative officers of Israel are given? It cannot be that the list from Judah is missing because the twelve districts supply the court for twelve months. Either Solomon taxed only Israel and not Judah, which would certainly explain the northern revolt, or the list comes from a later period of the northern kingdom.

39. See D. B. Redford, "Studies in Relations between Palestine and Egypt during the First Millennium B.C.," vol. 1: "The Taxation System of Solomon," in *Studies in the Ancient Palestinian World*, pp. 141–56.

b. THE PROPHETIC LEGENDS

The books of Kings contain a number of popular stories, many of which are derogatory to the monarchy. It is therefore unlikely that these emanate from the court or any official historiographic sources. This large corpus of material, usually referred to as "prophetic legends," is regarded as based upon oral traditions that one or more historians incorporated into Kings. According to Gunkel and Gressmann, these religious legends, best exemplified in the stories of Elijah and Elisha, form a line of development from *Sagen*—one that did not end in historiography but retained the more fanciful aspects of the older form.[40] Just as *Sagen* represent the oral traditions of the preliterate period of political life before the rise of the monarchy, the prophetic legends mark the preliterate period of prophecy before the rise of the classical prophets.

And yet this scheme, which is still widely accepted, does not do justice to the diversity of the prophetic stories or to their role within the historical works of which they are a part. In two recent studies, A. Rofé has offered a new analysis and classification of the prophetic legends in the books of Kings, as well as some suggestions about the relationships between the types thus identified—a kind of *Gattungsgeschichte* of prophetic stories.[41] His point of departure is the discovery of a model in the medieval *legendae*, stories whose theme is the veneration of pious men, Christian saints and Jewish rabbis; he sees this model as basic to a number of types of prophetic stories.[42] The primary form is the "simple *legenda*," which centers upon a "man of God" and recounts a single miracle as a means of showing his greatness. Examples of miracle stories are the healing of the spring (2 Kings 2:19–22), the curse and slaughter of the disrespectful children (2:23–24), the multiplication of oil to pay a widow's debt (4:1–7), the healing of the stew (4:38–41), the multiplication of bread to feed a large company (4:42–44), the floating of the ax head (6:1–7), and the resurrection of a dead man thrown into the prophet's grave (13:20–21). Each story moves from a situation of need and despair to a miraculous solution without any development of the central character or plot. The form has all the marks of popular oral tradition, recorded in concise written form. Also to be associated with this level of oral tradition are the *Vitae*, biographical details about the beginning and end of the holy man's life with special interest in the point in life, at birth or by special commission, at which he re-

---

40. See above, 7a.
41. "The Classification of the Prophetical Stories," *JBL* 89 (1970):427–40; idem, "Classes in the Prophetical Stories: Didactic Legenda and Parable," SVT 26 (1974):143–64.
42. *JBL* 89:429–30.

ceived his unusual powers setting him apart from his fellows.[43] These *Vitae* usually arise only after the great reputation of the holy man is established. Such elements are particularly prominent in the Elisha cycle.[44]

According to Rofé, some prophetic stories are the product of literary composition and creativity, even if they have been inspired by the *legenda* model or a specific *legenda* tradition. One such type is the "elaborated *legenda*," which contains an artistic presentation of character, a subtlety of psychological motivation, and a complex elaboration of plot.[45] All this betrays the careful reflection and composition of a literary work in which any original folk *legenda* cannot be easily isolated from the literary activity. Rofé's primary example is the story of the Shunemite woman, the miraculous birth of her son, and his death and restoration to life (2 Kings 4:8–37).[46] A second literary form of prophetic story is the "didactic *legenda*."[47] Here the focus is not upon the miracle or on special veneration of the prophet but on the way the event is intended to be a witness to the greatness of the God of Israel. This does not have the artistic concern of the elaborated *legenda* but presents religious beliefs and moral concerns through speeches by stereotyped characters. Furthermore, its attitude to the popular *legendae* may be quite negative or critical of the way the miraculous is presented. Such stories may be attempts to refine popular *legendae* or they may be more elaborate theological compositions in which the element from oral tradition is minimal. The examples of this type discussed by Rofé are the stories of Naaman the leper (2 Kings 5), Elijah and the widow of Zarephath (1 Kings 17:8–24), and the healing of Hezekiah (2 Kings 20:1–11).

A third literary form is designated by Rofé as the "parable."[48] This is like the didactic *legenda* in its concern to teach a moral or religious truth, but it goes beyond it in being a literary composition without any basis in a prior tradition or *legenda*. The most obvious example of this type is the story of Jonah, but Rofé also ascribes to this type the story of the man of God from Judah in 1 Kings 12:33–13:32.[49]

Rofé's classification does not exhaust the prophetic stories. Other stories involve the prophet not so much as wonder-worker but as the medium of

43. Ibid., pp. 435–49.
44. 1 Kings 19:19–21; 2 Kings 2:1–18; 13:14–21.
45. *JBL* 89:433–35.
46. Could we also consider the ascension of Elijah in 2 Kings 2 an elaborated *vita*?
47. SVT 26:145–53.
48. Ibid., pp. 153–64.
49. This classification seems much superior to the rather confusing characterization of "prophetic midrash in saga style" by J. Gray, *I & II Kings*, p. 294. The designation "midrash" has a limited justification in the sense that the story takes the episode of the making of the golden calves, found in Dtr, as its point of departure. But this does not seem to be the way in which Gray uses the term.

the divine oracle.[50] In some cases the oracle has been solicited by a king or public figure;[51] in others it is sent by Yahweh to an official, with the prophet as messenger.[52] The delivering of an oracle may be the focal point of a whole story or merely a schematic element within a larger complex. The degree to which such stories contain legendary elements varies greatly. This prophetic type often has a strong didactic or theological character insofar as the fulfillment of the oracle demonstrates the power of Yahweh to bring this about. Such a story type or motif has a strong affinity to the oracular function of classical prophecy, with its primary emphasis upon the prophetic word of judgment or promise.

Within the larger context of the books of Kings the various types of prophetic stories fall into certain fairly clear groups. In fact, the Elisha stories in 2 Kings 2, 4–7; 8:1–15; 9:21 are a loose collection tied together by statements of the prophet's itinerary from one point to another.[53] The story of the the seven-year famine (2 Kings 8:1–6) not only refers back to an earlier story (4:18ff.) but also suggests a collection of such stories. In verses 4–5 the king inquires of Gehazi, Elisha's servant, "about all the great things Elisha had done." This is not an independent *legenda* but a rather artificial creation to give a sense of unity, which the collection otherwise lacks. The stories in 2 Kings 3 and 9, however, stand outside this collection. Here the prophet plays a minor role, primarily as the messenger of Yahweh, quite different from the stories within the Elisha collection.

The collection of Elisha stories, excluding 2 Kings 3 and 9, has not been integrated in any way into the Deuteronomist's history, nor does it show any signs of his editing. Yet according to Rofé's analysis, which we follow here, there has been considerable literary and theological development from one type to the other. It is also noteworthy that whenever the king of Israel is mentioned he remains anonymous. According to the canonical placement of the stories, this would have to be during the reign of Jehoram, a son of Ahab. Yet the prophet seems to be on fairly cordial terms with him. The Elijah stories of 2 Kings 17–19, 21, and 2 Kings 1 are quite different. These are not only integrated into the general chronological framework but also bear the stamp of the Dtr concern about the incursion of the Canaanite cults and the Dtr aversion for the house of Ahab, elements completely lacking in the Elisha collection. On the other hand, 2 Kings 3 and 9–10 fit the patterns and themes of the Elijah stories and do

---

50. B. Long, "2 Kings III and Genres of Prophetic Narrative," *VT* 23 (1973):337–48.

51. Besides 2 Kings 3, Long also cites the examples of 2 Kings 8:7–15, 1 Kings 14:1ff., and 22:4ff. with elements also present in 2 Kings 1:1–17, 22:13ff., 1 Sam. 9:1ff., and Gen. 25:21–34.

52. See 1 Kings 21; also common in the prose narration of prophetic books.

53. On the use of the itinerary as a literary device for combining stories, see G. W. Coats, "The Wilderness Itinerary," *CBQ* 34 (1972):135–52, especially the remarks on pp. 147ff.

belong within the work of Dtr. All the *legendae* in Dtr are theological-didactic, even those with a close parallel to the *legendae* of the Elisha story. Dtr has presented Elijah and Elisha as messengers of the divine oracles and not as wonder-workers in their own right. The wonders affirm the claims of Yahweh and are performed in response to prayer or as fulfillment of an oracle.

It seems to me that the Elisha collection was not a part of the original Dtr history but was added to it only at a later stage. Yet it may very well have existed as a separate literary work known to Dtr and used by him in order to compose his story about the widow of Zarephath, since there is strong evidence of literary dependence. In any event, Dtr exercised a great deal of liberty with the *legenda* form whenever he took over prophetic legends or composed his own in order to express his own theological concerns and conception of the prophetic office. This would further point to considerable flexibility and freedom in his use of other "unofficial," or popular, sources. Subsequent to the formation of the Dtr history there was a propensity to increase the number of prophetic legends, both for the sake of including wonder stories as well as for theological and didactic purposes. That a history could include such uncritical tales should not be deemed surprising for antiquity, since Herodotus's work too contains many such stories for popular appeal.

A further implication of the classification of prophetic legends is the realization that elements and motifs clearly belonging to these genres are not restricted to the books of Kings.[54] They are also found in the books of Samuel, supposedly at the stage of *Heldensagen* and primarily in connection with the figure of Samuel. In the Pentateuch they almost completely dominate the presentation of the figure of Moses. There are *legendae* about Moses as wonder-worker in the plague stories and wilderness traditions, and *vitae* in connection with his birth, calling, and death. But Moses is supremely the bearer of the divine oracle, the messenger of Yahweh. Yet all these genres have been combined and utilized by a single narrative source, the Yahwist. Contrary to Gunkel and Gressmann, one cannot trace a line of literary development from these Pentateuchal stories to later prophetic legends. The influence is in the opposite direction. Only at a rather late stage, when Moses and Samuel were deemed great prophets, were such *legendae*, *vitae*, and the like associated with them. Even Abraham becomes a prophet who can pray for the healing of a king's wives—a rather weak *legenda* motif.[55]

54. See remarks by Rofé, SVT 26:164.
55. See Gen. 20. The didactic and theological character of this story is clear. See J. Van Seters, *Abraham in History and Tradition*, pp. 171–75.

c. THEMATIC CONTINUITY IN SAMUEL AND KINGS

Once the extent of Dtr's handiwork in the stories of Saul and David is appreciated (excluding, of course, the Court History), then its thematic continuity with Dtr's treatment of the career of Solomon and the rest of the books of Kings can be properly understood. It is wrong to view Dtr as one who simply added pious and didactic phrases to pre-existing units.[56] Rather, he subordinated his received material or completely reshaped traditions to conform to his thematic concerns and perspectives. It is difficult to know how much he invented and what might have come to him from official records or popular traditions. This is certainly the case with Dtr's presentation of the deeds of Solomon.[57]

The transition from the story of David to that of Solomon is given by Dtr in 1 Kings 2:1–4, 10–12, which, as we have seen above, represents his original conclusion to the reign of David. This unit reiterates the theme of the divine promise to David and gives the first step in the fulfillment of that promise, indicating that Solomon has succeeded David, his father, as king and is firmly established on the throne. David's last words also have the form of a commission in which the success of the monarchy and the continuation of the dynasty are made conditional upon obedience to the law of Moses.[58] This link between obedience to God and the succession is basic to the story of Saul's rejection and David's election, and, as we shall see, it is frequently repeated in the story of Solomon. Admittedly, there is greater stress on obedience to the law in the account of Solomon's reign than is suggested by the reference to possible punishment in 2 Sam. 7:14, but this is mostly a matter of context. David himself is never directly exhorted to obedience because Dtr regarded him as always having kept the law of God. Solomon, on the other hand, failed badly in spite of repeated warning. There is thus no reason to suggest a plurality of Dtr redactors to explain this difference in emphasis between the two kings.

Immediately following the original unit of 2:1–4 and 10–12 in the Dtr history came the account of the divine theophany to Solomon in 3:1–15. The notion of a nocturnal appearance by the deity to a king to disclose to him his destiny, whether for good or ill, is common in antiquity, and there is no warrant for seeing in this example a special genre such as the *Königsnovelle*.[59] Nor can we use this story form as evidence that the tradition behind the extant written version is early and contemporary with the

---

56. Such, for instance, is the approach of John Gray, *I & II Kings*, pp. 111ff. He does little to explain Dtr's contribution to the presentation of Solomon in his historical work.

57. See Noth, *ÜS*, pp. 66–67.

58. See Deut. 17:14ff. and also the parallel commissioning of Joshua in Deut. 31.

59. See above, 5f.

events.[60] The account of the theophany in 3:1–15 is thoroughly Dtr, just as is the Nathan oracle of 2 Sam. 7, and the themes of the two units are very similar. The folkloristic element in the episode is the granting of a wish, which is made to account for all of Solomon's great success and fame. He made the right choice—wisdom—and he made it in the spirit of humility. This motif of wish making and wish granting is certainly not presented in typical fairy-tale style but is totally subordinated to Dtr's interests and religious perspective. In requesting wisdom Solomon acknowledges, first of all, the fulfillment of the divine promise in 2 Sam. 7 as a result of David's piety and obedience. Solomon then makes a show of humility similar to that in David's prayer in 2 Sam. 7:18ff.,[61] and he finally requests wisdom in order to "govern this thy great people." Also characteristic of Dtr is the emphasis upon God's election of his people and the close connection between the fate of people and king, as in 2 Sam. 7:8ff., 23ff. The divine reply enumerates the gifts that made Solomon great, in addition to wisdom, but it also ends on a note of exhortation to keep the law of God. The close association between wisdom and the divine law is characteristic of Deuteronomy;[62] it is not just an afterthought but very much a part of the whole.

What is the source of the tradition of Solomon's wisdom in the Dtr narrative? R. B. Y. Scott has given close attention to this question[63] and concludes that it cannot be derived from the account of Solomon's wisdom and greatness in 1 Kings 5:1–14 or in the story of the Queen of Sheba in 10:1–10, 13ff., since these verses have all the marks of being very late and post-Deuteronomistic. Scott also points out that the conception of wisdom in the Dtr account of chapter 3 involves primarily the capacity to govern well and to make sound judgments, as is illustrated by the story in 3:16–28. The answer to the question of the origin of this tradition may be in the royal ideology, especially as expressed in Ps. 72, where the ability to govern wisely is linked with fame, prosperity, peace, and great wealth. In Isa. 11:2ff. wisdom and understanding are also associated with correct judgment. Since the power and greatness of the monarchy were at their zenith early in Solomon's reign, it is only natural that Dtr associated this kind of wisdom with this period of his rule. Furthermore, the notion of a

60. Cf. Gray, *I & II Kings*, pp. 117–18.
61. The contrast between the humility expressed in 1 Kings 3:6ff. and chap. 2 of the Court History could not be more sharply drawn. In the latter, David speaks of Solomon's wisdom in knowing how to get rid of his enemies and this Solomon does with great self-assurance. As a later addition it makes a mockery of Solomon's prayer.
62. Deut. 4:6.
63. R. B. Y. Scott, "Solomon and the Beginnings of Wisdom in Israel," in *Wisdom in Israel and in the Ancient Near East*, SVT 3 (1955):262–79. See also in the same volume, M. Noth, "Die Bewährung von Salomons 'Göttlicher Weisheit,'" pp. 225–37. Gray's treatment of Scott's arguments (in *I & II Kings*, pp. 138–39) is unacceptable.

"Solomonic enlightenment," which depends rather heavily upon the tradition of wisdom origins in Solomon's time, is seen to have a slender basis in fact.

Solomon's career is dominated, on the other hand, by his construction of the Temple. Even the earliest event of the theophany is set by Dtr against the backdrop of this achievement; he tells us that it took place in the time before the Temple was built, when the people were still sacrificing at the high places and when Solomon himself used the great high place at Gibeon. After the theophany we are reminded that the Ark of the covenant of Yahweh was in Jerusalem; Solomon's festive celebration before the Ark recalls David's in 2 Sam. 6:17–19 and anticipates the later events of chapter 8. Dtr further suggests in 5:15ff. (= ET 5:1ff.) that preparations for the Temple were begun almost immediately after Solomon became king. In the negotiations with Hiram of Tyre for supplies, Solomon repeats the mention of the divine promise of David regarding this succession and the building of the Temple (verses 17–19 = ET 3–5), and Hiram acknowledges this also in his response in verse 21 (= ET 7).[64] The wisdom theme of chapter 3 is also carried through here (verses 21, 26 = ET 7, 12) as a fulfillment of God's promise to Solomon.[65]

Following the provisions made for the materials of the Temple, the description of the actual construction is begun in chapter 6. By dating the Temple 480 years after the exodus (verse 1), Dtr suggests the beginning of a new era, just as in 2 Sam. 7 he contrasts the whole period from the exodus up to the time of David with the building of a fixed abode. Within the description of the Temple is a digression that includes an oracle of Yahweh (verses 11–13). It confirms once again David's promise concerning the dynasty and Yahweh's commitment to begin a new mode of "tenting" among his people.[66] But both promises are conditional upon obedience to the law. Some scholars have argued that these verses are later editorial additions, but the repetition of verses 9a and 14a would indicate that the work has been carefully constructed to accommodate this digression.

Concerning the description of the Temple itself, many scholars believe that it is based upon a document from the Solomonic period.[67] No useful

64. It is arbitrary to identify vv. 17–19, 21 as later Dtr additions to an early source when there is no evident tension or inconsistency with their context. The strong grammatical connective w^e'$att\bar{a}h$ (v. 18) makes it difficult to eliminate what has gone before. See Montgomery, *Kings*, p. 133; Gray, *I & II Kings*, pp. 142–43.

65. The description of this preparation is hardly an "official" account, whatever its sources might have been. On the exaggeration of the numbers of workers involved, see above.

66. For comments on the use of *škn*, "to tent," see Cross, *Canaanite Myth*, pp. 245–46. I am not inclined to see some of its uses in poetry, such as in 1 Kings 8:12, as any different or any more archaic than the reference in 1 Kings 6:13.

67. See Montgomery, *Kings*, p. 142: "We actually possess in these chapters concerning the construction and furnishing of a temple the fullest and most detailed specifications from

analogy or parallel to such a text, however, has ever been suggested. Dedication inscriptions, which often mention the building of a temple, do not describe these structures in detail because the appearance of the structure with which the inscription is associated is self-evident. Such an elaborate description is necessary only when the structure itself cannot be seen, either because it is located in a distant land (as are the monuments of Egypt described by Herodotus) or because it no longer exists. What Dtr is trying to do in his descriptions in chapters 6 and 7 is to recapture the glories of the past *after* the Temple was destroyed in 586 B.C.[68] The description of the Temple is completely the work of Dtr, gilding and embellishing his own recollections of the Temple (or those of his contemporaries) after its destruction.

The transfer of the Ark of the Covenant from its temporary location in Zion where David had placed it (2 Sam. 6:16ff.) to the new Temple is for Dtr the climax of Solomon's career. The whole account is composed from this perspective and scarcely reflects any other document source. It again ties the time of Moses and the giving of the law with the Temple of Solomon by describing the Temple as the abode of the Ark, which contains the two tablets of stone (verse 9).[69] Elements of the desert theophany of the "cloud" (verse 10) are also associated with the event, although they do not again occur in connection with the Temple.[70] The whole occasion from beginning to end (see verses 62–66) is one in which Solomon offers sacrifices and celebrates a great feast, just as David does in 2 Sam. 6.

In blessing the people, Solomon recalls the theme of the promise to David in 2 Sam. 7. Again Solomon makes a contrast between the era without a temple—which extended from the time of the exodus to that of David —and the new era under the Davidic dynasty, in which there is a permanent abode for the "name" of Yahweh (verses 14–21).[71] Solomon, in his prayer to Yahweh, (verses 22–26) emphasizes the divine promise of dynas-

the ancient oriental world." The obvious reason for this is that such records and descriptions were not made for any official documents. See also Gray, *I & II Kings*, p. 149, where he speaks of a writer's use of "temple-archives" and his own visual experience to compile a contemporary document; such a writer would have had to have been a priest. What the purpose of such a document might have been one can scarcely imagine, and how it came into the final author's hand is also unclear.

68. Note also the almost verbatim repetition of some of the elements in the description of the Temple's furnishings in 2 Kings 25:13–17 (cf. 1 Kings 7:15–26, 40). Similarly, all our descriptions of Herod's temple come from the time after its destruction in A.D. 70, in Josephus and the tractate Middoth in the Mishnah. The result is a number of irreconcilable differences in the descriptions.

69. Cf. Deut. 10:1–5.

70. Deut. 31:15; Exod. 33:7–11.

71. Note that the negative statement in v. 16 is the equivalent of 2 Sam. 7:6–7. However, it cannot here be interpreted as a condemnation of building a temple. In both cases it is a matter of contrasting two eras. See also vv. 54–61.

tic succession tempered by the condition of obedience to the law. The rest of the prayer is a statement of Dtr theology on the presence and power of the divine name and an anticipation of the later history of the people down to the time of the exile.

The deity's response to Solomon is given in a vision (chapter 9)[72] that refers directly to the consecration of the Temple and the promise to David. But God also threatens punishment and exile for king and people if they disobey the divine laws, with the added threat of the destruction of the Temple.

After Dtr records some of Solomon's achievements (9:10–28),[73] he concludes with an account of Solomon's downfall (chapter 11), his love of foreign women. This picks up an earlier theme, Solomon's early marriage to a daughter of Pharaoh (3:1; 9:16, 24). The suggestion that marriage to foreign women leads to apostasy and the ultimate destruction of the state is thoroughly Deuteronomic, so that Solomon becomes an object lesson of this principle. He makes this the fundamental reason for the division of the kingdom, namely, Yahweh's rejection of the dynasty of David over Israel, although for David's sake and for Jerusalem the house of David will continue to rule Judah (1 Kings 11:9–13). Solomon's rejection leads directly to Jeroboam's designation by the prophet Ahijah as the future king of the northern tribes (verses 26–40). The pattern is exactly the same as in the Story of Saul and the Story of David's Rise. Jeroboam is also promised a "sure house as I built for David" and rule over Israel if he proves to be obedient to the divine commands, as David was. For the duration of Solomon's reign Jeroboam has to take refuge in a foreign realm (11:40), just as David did from Saul.

To sum up the Dtr account of Solomon's reign, we would have to say that the whole presentation is a rather elaborate reconstruction by Dtr based upon very little prior material. He is concerned, first and foremost, to see in Solomon's reign the fulfillment of the divine promise to David of a "sure house" and at the same time the completion of David's aspiration to build a temple for Yahweh. The account is also a climax to the Deuteronomic theme of Yahweh's choice of a place for the permanent abode of his name; this theme joins Deuteronomy and the law of Moses, as well as the whole history from the exodus to Solomon, to the construction of the Temple. In this way the centralization and purity of worship become the touchstones of true obedience to Yahweh for all future rulers. On the negative side, Solomon's marriages, which lead him to religious apostasy, re-

---

72. Note the freedom that the author takes with the chronology, since Solomon's building activities were not completed until long after the Temple was finished.

73. These are only partly based upon his sources, which are liberally augmented with his own comments. Chap. 10 is secondary, as we have seen above.

sult in a divine judgment that becomes the first of a series of judgments against religious deviation in the following reigns.[74]

A strong continuity between Samuel and Kings can be seen in the theme of the divine election and rejection of the ruler. In Dtr's account of the rejection of Jeroboam, 1 Kings 14:7–16, the prophet Ahijah recapitulates Yahweh's election of Jeroboam as a *nāgîd* over his people, Israel (verse 7). The language is the same as that used in the election of both Saul and David. At the same time, the incident of Ahijah's prior secret designation of Jeroboam as the future king, in chapter 11, is recalled by the reference to the imagery of tearing the kingdom of Israel from the house of David, so that it is clear the two episodes must be taken together as composed by a common author. The standard of comparison is David, against whom Jeroboam is judged, just as Solomon had also been judged in the previous situation in chapter 11. It is announced that the "house of Jeroboam," namely, his dynasty, will be brought to an end and that "Yahweh will raise up" a new king to take his son's place (verse 14). Here the pattern of rejecting the ruler and his "house" because of his sins and the designation of a future king is parallel to that in the stories of Saul and David, even to the point of continuing the use of the term *nāgîd*. The same pattern is repeated in the case of Baasha (16:1–4), in which the prophet Jehu recalls that Baasha was elevated by God "from the dust" and set as *nāgîd* over "my people, Israel." Baasha is then condemned for his sins in following the example of Jeroboam, and the same curse is applied to his "house." The pattern of divine election and then rejection of the king and his house—from Saul, to Solomon, to the first northern kings—is a literary artifice created by Dtr in order to make a bridge between the period of the judges, with its own schematic pattern, and the period of the dual monarchy.[75] This technique of creating patterns in the prose material is the basis of paratactic style, whether it be in Mesopotamian literature or in the prose of Herodotus. The repetitive pattern creates a sense of unity and movement in the longer work.

Into this thematic pattern of election and rejection is introduced another scheme, that of the judgments on each king's reign. The highest standard of excellence is David, who becomes the model against which the kings of Judah are judged. The northern kings, on the other hand, are judged pri-

74. See H.-D. Hoffmann, *Reform und Reformen*, pp. 47–58. Hoffmann sees in the remarks about apostasy and reform in the books of Kings an essential thematic structure of Dtr. More on this below.

75. A. Alt, in his study of the early form of the Hebrew monarchy (see *Essays*, pp. 183ff.; 241ff.), construes this literary technique as an actual political pattern; hence his notion of a "charismatic" form of kingship in Saul, which he also attributes to the northern kingdom. Cross argues in a similar fashion (*Canaanite Myth*, pp. 219ff.). The passages cited, however, are all texts of Dtr and the pattern is a purely theological one of his own creation.

marily on the basis of their continuity with the behavior of the first northern king, Jeroboam, who led Israel to sin. Just as Dtr's life of David served
as the basis for the judgments about his complete obedience to God, so the
story of the golden calves becomes the basic point of departure for judgments on the northern realm. Obviously, then, for Dtr's assessment of the
northern kingdom, this episode is important and must be given further
consideration.[76]

The biases of Dtr in the story of the golden calves are quite clear.[77] He
believed that from the time the Temple of Solomon was built, worship was
centralized in Jerusalem, with all Israel making regular annual pilgrimages
to the Temple. He therefore blames Jeroboam for destroying this practice
for the northern tribes at the beginning of his reign, out of weakness and
political expediency. There is no reason to believe that worship was centralized, for amphictyonic or any other purposes, prior to the Josianic reform, so the basis for the story is anachronistic and Jeroboam's actions are
deprived of their primary motivation.

But Dtr goes much further than this. The actions of Jeroboam are set
forth in sequence as a studied violation of the Dt Code. He attributes to
Jeroboam the making of molten images—calves of gold—not to represent
foreign deities but to serve as substitutes for the God of Israel, to be venerated by the perverted confession, "Behold your gods, O Israel, who
brought you up out of the land of Egypt." Jeroboam introduces his own
pilgrimage festival to Bethel on the wrong day of the wrong month. He is
held responsible for building shrines on the high places and for conse-
crating non-Levitical priests to these temples. But what is especially revealing is the statement that he then installed in Bethel these same non-

76. The literature on the golden calves has become extensive. However, see particularly
M. Noth, "Zur Anfertigung des 'Goldenen Kalbs,'" VT 9 (1959):419–22; I. Levy, "The
Story of the Golden Calf Reanalysed," VT 9 (1959):318–22; S. Lehming, "Versuch zu Ex.
xxxii," VT 10 (1960):16–50; M. Auerbach and L. Smolar, "Aaron, Jeroboam and the
Golden Calves," JBL 86 (1967): 129–40; J. Debus, Die Sünde Jerobeams; G. W. Coats, Re-
bellion in the Wilderness, pp. 184–91.

Many studies give a historical explanation of the story, presupposing that a basic historical
kernel of ancient tradition can be extracted from the narrative of 1 Kings 12:25ff. In my recent study of Israelite historiography I offer a number of arguments against this position
(Orientalia 50 [1981]: 170–74), which I summarize below.

(1) There are serious difficulties in reconciling the details and perspective of the story with the
probable historical background of the early part of Jeroboam's reign.

(2) The story of the man of God from Judah contains obvious anachronisms and cannot be
used as a witness to support an early date. Recent scholarship has even argued that it is post-
Dtr, so that the sequel is the Dtr story of 1 Kings 14.

(3) Exod. 32, often considered a witness to the event, is dependent upon 1 Kings 12:26ff. and
is Dtr or post-Dtr in date. See also Hoffmann, Reform und Reformen, pp. 306–13; Perlitt,
Bundestheologie, pp. 207ff.

77. See Noth, Überlieferungsgeschichtliche Studien, pp. 100–10; and recently, Hoffmann,
Reform und Reformen, pp. 59–73.

Levitical priests whom he had appointed to the high places. This statement by itself makes little sense, for why should the priests of the high places serve at the "central" sanctuary of Bethel unless the high places were abolished, which is certainly not what the author intends his reader to conclude. One would have expected Jeroboam simply to appoint new priests to Bethel. Dtr has in mind the regulation of Deuteronomy allowing priests of the local sanctuaries to serve at the central temple since in the Josianic reform the high places were to be abolished. Yet Dtr also knows that in the reform such priests were not allowed to serve at the altar in Jerusalem. By creating this close analogy with a "centralized" apostate, Bethel, the author is suggesting that since the time of Jeroboam the credentials of local priests have become suspect, thereby justifying the Josianic deviation from the Dt code.

Besides anticipating the reform of Josiah in the most explicit way, the story also serves to inaugurate a new era in Israel's history, the history of the northern kingdom. Every king of the north as well as the people themselves followed the practice of Jeroboam and therefore suffered the ultimate consequence (2 Kings 17:21–23). We cannot remove this *Tendenz* of Dtr as a gloss and still retain a historical tradition. The story about Jeroboam and the golden calves is so thoroughly anachronistic and propagandistic that we must suspect it of being a complete fabrication. It is the literary creation of Dtr and functions in much the same way for the account of the northern kingdom as 2 Sam. 7 does for Judah. In this respect also, the story of the golden calves in its Dtr form should not be considered as an isolated unit but as closely associated with the story of the illness of Jeroboam's son in chapter 14, which served as the original prophetic judgment on the apostasy. It is here above all that the full scope of the episode is indicated as including not only the "house of Jeroboam" (13:34; 14:10–14) but also the whole of the northern kingdom (14:15–16; cf. 2 Kings 17:21–23).

It would appear from this that the thematic unity of the Dtr history in the books of Kings consists in the development not only of one simple theme but of a complex of themes; these have to do with the one dynasty of Judah and the many dynasties of Israel, as well as the divine election of Jerusalem and the founding of the one temple there, in contrast to the establishment or recognition of a plurality of cults and sanctuaries in Israel. All these themes are interrelated in various ways and grow out of the ideological and thematic basis developed and articulated for them already in the books of Samuel in Dtr's treatment of the stories of Saul and David.

d. THE JUDGMENTS UPON THE KINGS OF JUDAH AND ISRAEL

The Dtr Historian gives additional continuity to his treatment of the monarchy by employing a chronological and theological framework into which all the reigns of the two kingdoms are fitted. As we have seen, the chronology is not his own (except for the synchronisms) but is borrowed from two sources to which he frequently refers, namely, "the chronicles of the kings of Israel/Judah."[78] But the theological judgment that Dtr passes on each reign is part of his own thematic framework and gives unity to the work as a whole. The language of these judgments is highly stereotyped. Thus, for the good kings of Judah one finds the statement: "He did what was right in the sight of Yahweh as his father PN (as David his forefather) had done, only the hill shrines were not removed but the people continued to sacrifice at the hill shrines."[79] The qualifying statement at the end did not, of course, apply in the case of Hezekiah and Josiah (2 Kings 18:3; 22:2). The unworthy kings of Judah and all the kings of Israel receive the judgment that "he did what was evil in the sight of Yahweh, as his father(s) had done, *or* proceeding in the ways of his father."[80] For the northern kings Dtr adds, "and in the sins that Jeroboam had committed and into which he led Israel, provoking Yahweh, the God of Israel."[81] The two sons of Ahab and the two Judean kings related to the Ahab dynasty by marriage are compared with Ahab and Jezebel or the house of Ahab, a comparison repeated in the case of Manasseh.[82]

These judgments allow for considerable variation in the choice or combination of stereotyped clichés, and they are often augmented with specific details relating to a particular king. Furthermore, such words of judgment are not restricted to the editorial framework that appears at the beginning and end of a reign. They also occur frequently in a much fuller form as part of scenes containing prophetic oracles addressed directly to the king. This, in turn, produces a pattern of prophetic speeches of judgment and fulfillment, with the result that a considerable number of texts become directly related to the presentation of the author's theme.[83] The result is an

78. See above, 9a.

79. 1 Kings 15:11; 22:43–44; 2 Kings 12:3–4; 14:3–4; 15:3–4, 34–35. A slightly different wording is used in 1 Kings 3:3. The formula is used in the negative in 1 Kings 11:33, 38; 14:8; 15:3–4; 2 Kings 16:2, 4.

80. 1 Kings 14:22; 15:26, 34; 16:19, 25–26, 30–31; 22:53–54; 2 Kings 3:2–3; 8:18, 27; 13:2, 11; 14:24; 15:9, 18, 24, 28; 21:2, 15, 16–17, 20–21; 23:27, 32; 24:9, 19.

81. In addition to those in n. 80, see also 2 Kings 10:29, 31; 13:6; 17:22. See also 1 Kings 14:16; 15:3, 30; 16:2, 13; 21:22.

82. 1 Kings 22:43–44; 2 Kings 3:2–3; 8:8, 27; 21:2–3.

83. The following are examples of divine speeches or prophetic speeches in which these judgment formulas occur: 1 Kings 11:1–13, 29–39; 14:7–16; 16:1–4; 21:20–27; 2 Kings 10:30–31; 21:10–16; 22:14–20. See also the statements in 1 Kings 15:30; 2 Kings 13:6; 17:7–23; 23:15.

extensive network of interconnections that does not easily permit the kind of redactional divisions that have so often been suggested.[84]

The judgments cannot be viewed in isolation but are closely related to a number of thematic speeches and episodes. These refer back rather frequently to Jeroboam, first king of the north, or to David for the kings of the south, and these two kings are mentioned in such a way that their lives and reigns are viewed as having important consequences for all that followed. It seems reasonable to assume, therefore, that Dtr included in his work the central episodes of 2 Sam. 7, 1 Kings 6–8, and 1 Kings 12:26ff., together with the judgments that depend so heavily upon them. Nor do these judgments make any sense unless they presuppose the Dtr presentation of the life of David, the building of the Temple, and the apostasy of Jeroboam. We have seen how the promise theme of 2 Sam. 7 is taken up in 1 Kings 3:2ff. and 1 Kings 11. But worked into these texts are typical statements of judgment (3:2–3; 11:4ff.; 33). Such judgments also occur in the election/rejection pattern in 11:29ff., 14:7–16, and 16:1–4, so that the patterns overlap.[85] Furthermore, only with the first of the northern kings,

---

84. Principal examples of a redactional approach are: A. Jepsen, *Die Quellen des Königsbuches*; W. Dietrich, *Prophetie und Geschichte: Eine redaktionsgeschichtliche Untersuchung zum deuteronomistischen Geschichtswerk*; H.-C. Schmitt, *Elisha: Traditionsgeschichtliche Untersuchungen zur vorklassischen nordisraelitischen Prophetie.*

Recently H. Weippert (in "Die 'deuteronomistischen' Beurteilungen der Könige von Israel und Juda und das Problem der Redaktion der Königsbucher," *Biblica* 53 [1972]: 301–39) has suggested that the various styles of judgment statements reflect at least three redactions of the books of Kings. The problems with this proposal are numerous, but a few general remarks will suffice here. First, in dealing with the styles characteristic of each redactor, Weippert must often eliminate phrases from one text assigned to R I because they are more characteristic of R II or R III. Note, for instance, the close similarity in style between 1 Kings 22:53–54 (ET 52–53), ascribed to R II, and 2 Kings 3:2–3, which is R I. The latter verses also refer back to 1 Kings 16:32–33 (R II). To try to eliminate all these connections as secondary additions seems arbitrary. Similarly, 1 Kings 22:43 (R I) cannot be separated from 15:11–14 (R II) since the former text clearly presupposes the statements made in the latter. Many other such examples could be cited. Second, Weippert proposes that R I began his history with Jehoram in the north and Jehoshaphat in the south, and carried it through to the fall of the northern kingdom and the time of Hezekiah. Apart from the fact that the judgment statements on Hoshea and Ahaz do not fit the right patterns for R I, this is a strange history indeed. Why would a history begin with Jehoram and Jehoshaphat, especially when their respective evaluations presuppose earlier reigns? Furthermore, if the theological statements are closely tied to the chronology, drawn from the pre-existing "chronicles," which went back to the beginning of the divided monarchy, why would R I not begin where his sources began, especially when he refers back so often to Jeroboam I? I do not find this multiplication of redactors in the books of Kings the least bit convincing. Consequently, I regard all the thematic statements of praise or blame as the work of a single Dtr historian.

A much less radical division into two redactions, a pre-exilic and an exilic redaction (Dtr[1] and Dtr[2]), has been proposed by Cross, *Canaanite Myth*, pp. 274–89. I am not convinced of the arguments for such a division.

85. Note also that the formula referring to the kings' or the peoples' sins provoking Yahweh to anger, which is so often a part of the judgment statements, has a much wider use within the Dtr corpus. See D. McCarthy, "The Wrath of Yahweh and the Structural Unity of the Deuteronomistic History," in *Essays in Old Testament Ethics*, pp. 97–110.

Jeroboam, is the comparison made with David, a pattern otherwise reserved for the southern kings. But precisely because Jeroboam was the first of his line, he could be compared, only in a negative fashion, with David.

In rather marked contrast to the work of H. Weippert a new study has just appeared—a dissertation by Hans-Detlef Hoffmann—that seeks to examine all the reforms and alterations in the cult mentioned in Kings from the time of Solomon to the great reform of Josiah. These statements about reform he regards as the product of only one Dtr.[86] Since most of these cultic reforms are mentioned in close conjunction with the judgments on the kings, a detailed study of all the judgments having to do with cultic reform is important to the understanding of Dtr's historiography.[87] Hoffmann's examination indicates that most texts do not seem to reflect an actual tradition of cult reform or preserve any annalistic record of such reform. Instead they represent the religious concerns of the Dtr, reflected most fully in the account of Josiah's reform and read back into the history of earlier times. This interest in reform is built into a scheme of both positive and negative changes in the cult, of which the apostasy of Jeroboam is a primary example, as we have already noted. The artificiality of such a historical scheme of reform is evident in many features, not the least of which are the seven positive and seven negative reforms as well as a carefully devised movement back and forth between the positive and negative poles. This pendulum swing is most evident in the case of the late Judean kings, where the whole scheme reaches a climax in Ahaz, Hezekiah, Manasseh, and Josiah.

Hoffmann also points out that Dtr often interprets certain political events, such as the marriage of foreign princesses,[88] the division of the kingdom, the political revolutions of Jehu and Jehoiada, and the subservience to the Assyrians by Ahaz and Manasseh, as having religious consequences although Dtr probably had no traditions or other evidence to support his conclusions. In this way the religious reforms (or apostasies) create the subdivisions in the historical periods and the sense of movement from one to the other, whereas the political fortunes of the states are often obscured.

The cultic reform notices also provide the opportunity for numerous interconnections and recapitulations that help create a sense of unity. The most obvious type of connection is the comparison with an immediate

86. Hans-Detlef Hoffmann, *Reform und Reformen: Untersuchungen zu einen Grundthema der deuteronomistischen Geschichtsschreibung.*

87. The texts under special consideration in Kings as listed by Hoffmann, *Reform*, p. 27, are: 1 Kings 11:1–13; 12:25–33; 14:21–24; 15:9–15; 16:29–33; 22:41–47, 52–54; 2 Kings 3:1–3, 9–10; 11:1–20; 12:1–17; 13:1–9; 15:32–38; 16:1–4, 10–18; 17:7–23, 24–41; 18:1–6; 21:1–16, 22–23.

88. Solomon's Egyptian queen, Jezebel, and Athalia, who is certainly regarded as a foreigner although this hardly does her justice.

predecessor. But there are references to other precursors as well, notably the cultic apostasies of Solomon, Jeroboam, Ahab, Ahaz, and Manasseh. These receive their fullest expression in the reform reports of Manasseh and Josiah.

The account of Josiah's reform, 2 Kings 22–23, calls for special attention. First, after the word of commendation (22:2) there is a description of the repairing of the Temple (22:3–9), which cannot be separated from the earlier account of the reform of Temple finances in 2 Kings 12:5–17 (4–16). The inauguration of the system of Temple financing in the time of Joash is entirely presupposed in the later Josiah account.[89] However, this system of collecting funds and the references to the "high priest" and to other Temple personnel all suggest close association with the Priestly source of the Pentateuch and the period of the second Temple.[90] Furthermore, the connection between the discovery of the book of the law and the repairing of the Temple is weak (22:8–10) and suggests that the original account had only the discovery of the book of the law by Hilkiah "the priest" and its transmission to the king.[91] In this way, in the original account everything is motivated by the discovery and reading of the book of the law.[92]

The oracle of Hulda the prophetess in 22:15–20 has often been used as an argument that there were at least two Deuteronomists, the first during Josiah's reign and the second in the exilic period.[93] The oracle states (verse 20): "Therefore, behold I will gather you to your fathers, and you shall be gathered to your grave in peace, and your eyes shall not see all the evil which I will bring upon this place." This reference to dying in peace seems at first sight to be contradicted by Josiah's violent death at the hands of Necho (2 Kings 23:29). Hence the notion of an early Dtr. Yet, as Hoffmann points out,[94] the reference to being gathered to one's grave in peace does not preclude a violent death. It means only that the king would be buried in his own tomb (23:30), which in fact was the fulfillment of the

89. The strong linguistic parallels are given by Hoffmann, *Reform*, pp. 192–96.

90. Hoffmann (*Reform*, pp. 118–24) points to these late elements in the text but still regards it as a Priestly work that was taken up by Dtr into his own work. Apart from the difficulty of dating Dtr so late—after the second Temple—his proposal still leaves the Priestly work in limbo. It is surely preferable to see the Priestly text as a later addition to Dtr than vice-versa.

91. Hoffmann, *Reform*, pp. 192ff., sees this as all the work of Dtr. But he has not really made a strong case for the unity of 2 Kings 22.

92. Note how drastically the Chronicler has rewritten the account in 2 Chron. 34:8–18 to try to overcome the problem of the loose connection between the restoration and discovery of the law book.

93. Cf. F. M. Cross, *Canaanite Myth and Hebrew Epic*, p. 286, n. 45, and R. E. Friedman, *The Exile and Biblical Narrative: The Formation of the Deuteronomistic and Priestly Works*, p. 25, where the attitudes to dating are ambivalent.

94. *Reform*, pp. 170–89.

Hulda prophecy.[95] There are no grounds here for conjecturing more than one Dtr historian.

The covenant-making ceremony in 2 Kings 23:1–3 has close affinities with the revolution of Jehoiada in 2 Kings 11:13–20. In both there is an assembly of the people with the king standing beside the pillar in the Temple (11:13–14, 23:1–3). In both a covenant is made between Yahweh and the king and people (11:17, 23:3). In both the covenant ceremony is followed by the religious reform as its natural consequence. The Dtr language and its intention to recapitulate the notion of covenant renewal, so prominent in Deuteronomy, make them both the obvious creation of Dtr.

The Passover that follows the reform program, in 2 Kings 23:21–23, is also performed according to "the book of the covenant"—Deuteronomy. This gives Dtr the opportunity to look back over the whole sweep of his history: "For no such Passover had been kept since the days of the judges who judged Israel, or during all the days of the kings of Israel or of the kings of Judah." As we have noted previously, the judges and the monarchy constitute for Dtr the two major eras in the history of Israel.

The heart of Hoffmann's thesis concerning the theme of reform in Dtr is in his assessment of the account of Josiah's reform. He disputes the claim that precise documents are reflected in the text of 2 Kings 23:4–20. At most this text depends upon some vague historical traditions about a politically and prophetically inspired reform in Josiah's time. The episode of the discovery of the law book is, at any rate, pure fiction. Hoffmann also seeks to demonstrate that the list of reforms is a collection in one place of all the references to reform from the other reform notices as well as from Deuteronomy. It is Dtr's conception of the purification of the cult in keeping with the first and second commandments of the decalogue. The list of reforms is a mixture of generalized clichés and some with precise geographic qualifiers or associations with particular kings and officials. But the reforms that include such precise details do not constitute an independent and more reliable source. They simply follow a style of creating such fictional elements in historiographic dress, which is found throughout the Dtr's account of cultic reform.[96]

Hoffmann concludes that the Dtr work is a history of the cult presented in an artful composition using prologues, introductions, the structuring of epochs with precise markers and turning points, and a system of cross-references binding the texts together. The cultic notes and reports of reform representing the dynamic element of the history do not reflect re-

95. Cf. the case of Ahab in 1 Kings 21:17–29 where Ahab's contrition led to a lessening of the judgment against him but did not preclude his own violent death.

96. See, e.g., the curious reference to Ahab's pillar of Baal in 2 Kings 3:2 and Hoffmann's discussion of it, *Reform*, pp. 84ff.

ceived tradition so much as they do a device of Dtr to structure the course of history and to conceive it theologically. Hoffmann also sees more unity and uniformity in the work and thought of Dtr than scholars have seen in recent years, and in this respect he represents a return to the position of Noth in viewing Dtr as a historian.[97]

In one important respect, however, Hoffmann represents an even more basic revision in the current image of Dtr. Contrary to the view, held even by Noth, that Dtr was primarily a compiler and redactor of various official sources and popular traditions, Hoffmann argues that Dtr is an author and a storyteller who composed his literary work with a great deal of freedom and creativity. This applies not only to the extensive material on cult reform in the framework of Kings but also to his use of actual historical material and prophetic traditions. So completely are many of his "sources" reworked that it is no longer possible to retrieve most of them from the text by literary analysis. Furthermore, the tendency to separate Dtr's framework from the transmitted materials, as if Dtr's work was to be found only in the former, must also be given up. There is, in fact, a reciprocal relationship between the thematic framework and the received material such that Dtr left very little of it as it was. He could also freely construct analogous fictional traditions if he felt the need to do so.

Up to this point Hoffmann's conclusions come very close to the observations made above in this study. Also, in terms of our definition of history as "an intellectual form whereby a people render an account to itself of its past" one would have to say that the theme of cult reform is a good example of such an evaluation of the past. Nevertheless, it seems to me that Hoffmann has still understood the basic theme of Dtr and the genre of history too narrowly. A considerable body of material in Dtr, largely ignored by Hoffmann, points to the author's rendering an account of the past in the sense of articulating the people's identity. While the record of the monarchy in Kings focuses on evaluating the progress of people and their kings from the time of Solomon until the end, this appraisal does not make sense without the story of the rise of the monarchy, the enunciation of the divine promise to David, and the establishment of the true cult center in Jerusalem under Solomon. The author must first set out these constitutional elements of the Israelite state by which all the "reforms" must be judged. It remains to be seen whether the earlier era from Moses to the end of the judges is structured in the same way.

The conclusion to be drawn from the study of Dtr's thematic continuity in Samuel and Kings is that the unity of the work does not rest upon a

---

97. See especially Hoffmann's conclusions, *Reform*, pp. 315–18. His treatment of Judges will be dealt with below.

single theme or thesis and its subsequent demonstration or argumentation.[98] Rather, the author has tied together blocks of material of uneven
length by means of a number of unifying devices characteristic of the paratactic style. These include patterns and analogies, repetition of formulaic
statements in a framework, prophecies and their fulfillment, and contrasts
between major figures like David and Saul or David and Jeroboam.[99]
Techniques such as these allow the historian to carry forward a number of
different concerns in a loose association with each other and to incorporate into his work a great variety of source materials of different styles. To
break each pattern or scheme apart into a separate redaction or source is a
serious mistake. No single scheme is imposed upon the whole since the periods and subjects do not easily lend themselves to such uniformity of
treatment. Nevertheless, the interweaving and overlapping of patterns and
formulas make the sense of unity clear enough. Thus Dtr is an example of
early historiographic prose in the paratactic style that is vital to the study
of parataxis in prose in the rest of the Old Testament as well.[100]

98. Cf. Chronicles, which achieves its unity by greatly simplifying his theme and the range
of his subject matter to the Kingdom of Judah from David to the exile and the hope of restoration in the edict of Cyrus.

99. Hoffmann, throughout his study, has taken pains to point out the many techniques
used by Dtr to create his sense of unity, but see especially *Reform*, pp. 38–46.

100. On parataxis in Herodotus, see above, 2c.

CHAPTER TEN

THE DEUTERONOMIST
FROM JOSHUA
TO SAMUEL

The literary problems of the books of Joshua and Judges are so numerous and complex that no comprehensive review of the present state of scholarly discussion can be attempted here. Nevertheless, this study would not be complete without seriously considering Noth's proposal that a substantial amount of Joshua and Judges belongs to a Dtr history stretching from Moses (Deuteronomy) to the end of the monarchy (2 Kings). In these introductory remarks I shall focus upon the debate between those who advocate the continuation of the Pentateuchal sources into Joshua (and Judg. 1)[1] and Noth, whose thesis is that such sources end in the Tetrateuch and that Joshua derives from a completely different literary corpus and process, namely, Dtr.[2]

The argument by those scholars in Old Testament literary criticism who still advocate the notion of a Hexateuch is simple but telling. Both the Yahwist and Priestly source of the Pentateuch contain the theme of the Promised Land, to which both accounts point forward. It would appear inconceivable that such sources did not conclude with a treatment of the conquest. Advocates of this view attempt to find Yahwist and Priestly versions of the conquest in Joshua and in Judg. 1.

The argument for Noth's position, which many scholars have adopted, is that since Joshua is so closely integrated with Deuteronomy and follows it as its natural continuation, it is difficult to accommodate Joshua to the usual view about the growth of the Pentateuchal traditions. What earlier scholars regarded as overwhelming evidence of the Priestly source in Joshua

---

1. Among the many advocates of this view, we note in particular the views of G. von Rad, "The Form-Critical Problem of the Hexateuch," in *The Problem of the Hexateuch*, pp. 1–78; idem, "Hexateuch oder Pentateuch?" *Verkündigung und Forschung* 1947/48, 1–2 (1949):52–56; S. Mowinckel, *Tetrateuch-Pentateuch-Hexateuch: Die Berichte über die Landnahme in den drei altisraelitischen Geschichtswerken*, BZAW 90 (1964).

2. In addition to Noth's *Überlieferungsgeschichtliche Studien*, see also *Das Buch Josua*. For a recent review of this issue, see A. N. Radjawane, "Das deuteronomistische Geschichtswerk," *ThR* 38 (1973/74):177–216; and J. H. Hayes and J. M. Miller, *Israelite and Judean History*, pp. 217ff.

is set down by Noth as merely a few late glosses in the Priestly Writer's style. On the other hand, those who oppose Noth's thesis tend to limit the Dtr influence in Joshua and Judges to some late Deuteronomistic redaction of the Hexateuchal material. This view, however, still makes it difficult to understand how later material from an independent Priestly source could have been added to the work.

The problems that result from having to choose between these two positions are alleviated when it is understood that the need for the choice arises out of only two tenets of Pentateuchal criticism that are currently under attack.[3] The first is the view that the various Pentateuchal sources are independent of each other and were combined only by later redactors. Increasingly scholars are coming to view the Priestly source as both author and redactor, whose work supplements earlier sources of the Pentateuch.[4] The second tenet being criticized is the early date of the Yahwist. Some scholars now advocate a much later date than previously suggested, and J may, in fact, be post-Dtr.[5] While this is not the place to deal with the whole discussion of Pentateuchal criticism, the implications of these two changes are great for resolving the debate between the advocates of a Hexateuch and the supporters of a Dtr history. To accept these changes would mean to acknowledge that Deuteronomy and the Dtr history were written first. The Yahwist and the Priestly Writer looked upon the conquest as portrayed in Joshua as the fulfillment of their land promise theme, and thus composed the rest of the Pentateuch (the Tetrateuch) in two stages as additions to the earlier history. There was consequently no need for them to produce their own accounts of the conquest-settlement tradition *de novo*. Of course it was still possible for the Yahwist and the Priestly Writer to supplement the Dtr conquest narrative with additional material in their own style and perspective, and I hope to show that they did so.

I do not intend to solve here all the literary problems of the Pentateuch, although I believe that an analysis of Joshua is an important part of that solution. Instead I shall focus upon the Dtr history and its proper delineation in Joshua, Judges, and the early chapters of 1 Samuel. This task has been obscured by the debate over a Hexateuch as well as by the quest for early historical documents and a multiplication of Dtr redactions. We will examine all these issues in the following pages.

3. See J. Van Seters, *Abraham in History and Tradition*, pp. 148–53; also idem, "Recent Studies on the Pentateuch: A Crisis in Method," *JAOS* 49 (1979):663–73.

4. See also F. M. Cross, *Canaanite Myth*, pp. 293ff.

5. In addition to works in n. 3 above, see also H. H. Schmid, *Der Sogenannte Jahwist: Beobachtungen und Fragen zur Pentateuchforschung*; H. Vorländer, *Die Entstehungszeit des jehowistischen Geschichtswerkes*; H. C. Schmitt, *Die nichtpriesterliche Josephsgeschichte: Ein Beitrag zur neuesten Pentateuchkritik*, BZAW 154 (1980); M. Rose, *Deuteronomist und Jahwist*.

a. JOSHUA 1–12

Joshua[6] begins by establishing a continuation with Deuteronomy: "After the death of Moses, the servant of Yahweh. . . ." The divine speech that follows in verses 1b–9 recapitulates the language and themes of Joshua's prior commissioning for leadership by Moses (Deut. 31:7–8, 23–24; 32:44).[7] The dimensions of the Promised Land in verse 4 correspond to those given in Deut. 11:24b, and the exhortations accompanying it in verses 3 and 5 are similar in language to Deut. 11:25. There are repeated references to God's commands and promises to Moses, and especially to the "law" (tôrāh) and to the "book of the law" (sēfer hattôrāh), verses 7 and 8, which clearly refers to Deuteronomy. It is the ruler's obligation to consult this law constantly (verse 8; see Deut. 17:18ff.), and by doing so he will have great success (Deut. 5:32ff.; 29:8 [ET9]; also Josh. 23:6–7).

Joshua's command to the officers (verses 10–11) sets the stage for the following action (3:2ff.) and provides the chronological framework for these events. The speech refers to both crossing the Jordan and taking possession of the land—the themes of the whole book. It also repeats the divine command of verse 2 and the subject of Joshua's commissioning in Deut. 31:2ff. Joshua's further exhortation to the Reubenites, the Gadites, and the half-tribe of Manasseh in verses 12ff. picks up on the theme and language of Deut. 3:18–20, stating that the eastern tribes were to serve in the army of conquest with their western brethren. This theme is recapitulated at various points in Joshua.[8] One significant difference from the earlier account is that in verses 16–18 the tribes make a reply to Joshua, whereas in Deut. 3:18–20 no such response is given to Moses.[9]

From the evidence of heavy dependence upon Deuteronomy, it may be safely asserted that Josh. 1 is a thoroughly Deuteronomistic introduction which does not include within it any other source. It is not just an editorial prologue attached to an otherwise independent story or series of stories but the true beginning of the whole basic account of the conquest. Without it, the rest of the story of Joshua would be badly fragmented. This realization puts the other pieces of the Joshua puzzle in proper perspective. Instead of taking the customary approach of considering Dtr as secondary and a redactional addition to an older substratum, I am suggesting that Dtr is the author of the conquest narrative.

6. In addition to the works mentioned in n. 2 above, we should perhaps mention the recent commentary by J. A. Soggin, Joshua. However, this work adds little in the way of original literary analysis beyond that proposed by Noth.

7. D. J. McCarthy, "An Installation Genre?" JBL 90 (1971):31–41.

8. Josh. 4:12–13; 22:1–6.

9. On the other hand, the P account in Num. 32 has developed the response into a lengthy dialogue between Moses and the tribes.

The story of Rahab, the harlot, and the spies (in Josh. 2) presents a major literary problem. Apart from the many internal problems that the story contains, there is the special difficulty of how the story fits into its context. First, it does not agree with the chronology indicated in 1:11 and 3:2, since the time required would be more than three days. Second, in the story of the fall of Jericho in chapter 6 nothing that the spies could have learned from Rahab would in any way assist in the capture of the city. The exercise of spying was entirely unnecessary. To see this as some alternate tradition of the taking of the city is highly speculative and unconvincing.[10] The point of the episode is entirely theological, centering on the confession, by the non-Israelite Rahab, of faith in the God of Israel. Nothing of military significance is discussed or even suggested. Rahab's mention of the divine deliverance at the Red Sea and the defeat of Sihon and Og points to a strong connection with the Pentateuch and with the Yahwist in particular. This whole story is secondary and not part of the original Dtr stratum. The episode was contrived and added in order to articulate a more universalistic perspective on Israel's religion. This leads me to my second principle in the study of Joshua: if Pentateuchal sources are to be found in Joshua, whether J or P, they are all secondary additions made directly onto the original Dtr work.

The account of the crossing of the Jordan in Josh. 3 and 4 presents us with a text that has been greatly complicated by such secondary additions, which were probably made in two stages.[11] The original Dtr presentation of the crossing begins in 3:2–3 as a direct continuation of chapter 1. The notation in 3:1 is an itinerary notice by the P source of the Pentateuch.[12] It disturbs the chronology of the "three days" and is thereby disclosed as an addition. The statement in verse 4a, "However, there is to be a distance between you and it [the Ark] of about two thousand cubits, do not come near it," is another addition, one that seems to contradict the whole point of the people following the Ark, namely, "in order that you may know the way you are to go, for you have not passed this way before" (verse 4b). The concern for a large space is the Priestly Writer's concern for the Ark's holiness. To this source also belongs the injunction in verse 5 to the people to sanctify themselves, since the reference to "tomorrow" is again out of keeping with the context: the crossing takes place the same day. The rest of the Dtr account I would identify as found in 3:6–7, 9–11, 13–16; 4:10b, 11a, 12–14. The story thus reconstructed has Joshua indicate to

---

10. See Soggin, *Joshua*, pp. 37ff. If this was an old source, as Soggin suggests, why did Dtr do such a poor job of integrating it into his overall chronology and scheme of events?

11. For an entirely different division of the text in which Dtr is regarded as secondary, see Soggin, *Joshua*, pp. 43–46, and Noth, *Josua*, pp. 26–39.

12. G. W. Coats, "The Wilderness Itinerary," *CBQ* 34 (1972): 135–52.

the people that the miracle of the dividing of the Jordan's waters is proof to them that Yahweh will give them victory over their foes. This is followed by a simple description of the miracle and the crossing of the people, including the eastern tribes. The reference to the eastern tribes makes the connection back to 1:12ff.[13] A second theme, the exaltation of Joshua (3:7; 4:14), rounds out the episode.

In Dtr's account, as set forth above, the author does not make any reference to a memorial of stones.[14] Since two such versions do occur, it is evident that they belong to two subsequent additions to the story. The first type of modification is in the activity and position of the priests. In Dtr the priests carrying the Ark simply move to the edge of the river, at which point the waters are "cut off" upstream and the whole procession crosses the river. In the additions the priests bearing the Ark remain standing in the river on dry ground while all the people cross, and then the stones are taken from the riverbed at the point where the priests stood. Here the two additions also part company. In the earlier addition the stones are taken from the river to the place where the people lodge for the night, namely Gilgal (3:8, 12, 17; 4:1–5, 8, 20–24). In the second addition a memorial is also set up in the river itself as a "memorial forever" (4:6–7, 9–10a, 11b, 15–19).[15]

A few observations may be made about these additions. First, they depend entirely upon the basic Dtr account; in no way can they be viewed as the conflation or editorial combination of independent sources or traditions. Second, the additions suggest some continuity with the sources of the Pentateuch. The first addition makes a strong connection with the Red Sea event, as in Josh. 2:10, with its emphasis upon the crossing on "dry ground," the characteristic motif of J. The setting up of twelve stones for the twelve tribes is also paralleled by Moses' action at Sinai in Exod. 24:4 (J). The author of the second addition, when it is taken together with 3:4a, 5, would appear to be the Priestly Writer. He emphasizes the great sanctity of the Ark, the stones as a "sign" ('ôt) and "memorial" (zikkārôn) in perpetuity ('ad 'ôlām), and the precise dating of events (as is his custom with wilderness wanderings). It is also likely that it is he who portrayed

---

13. Soggin (Joshua, p. 45) assigns 4:12–13 to the pre-Dtr author, although he has previously attributed 1:12–18 to Dtr. This kind of source analysis is highly questionable.

14. Given the Deuteronomic animosity toward standing stones, it would be surprising if Dtr made any mention of them. Both J and P, however, have a way of turning such Maṣṣēbôt into memorial stones.

15. It is possible that the second addition developed as a midrashic interpretation of 4:5b and understood the text to mean: "And you are to raise for yourselves each one stone upon its shoulder [i.e., one upon the other] according to the number of Israelite tribes." This would produce a column, not a row of stones, which would then be visible above the surface of the water.

the division of the waters at the Jordan as a great wall of water, just as he represented it in his description of the Red Sea event.[16] The children's questions also have their closest parallels in the J and P sources.[17]

The various units of chapter 5 do not belong to Dtr. The opening verse, 5:1, is directly connected with the preceding J addition of 4:23–24 and is parallel as well to 2:9–11. It serves to make the response of the nations to the two miracles—the Red Sea and the Jordan crossings—similar, and to emphasize their greatness.[18] On the other hand, 5:1 is somewhat awkward in the present context because it does not serve to introduce any new event, as one would expect. Its only purpose seems to be to make a theological statement. The descriptions of the circumcision, verses 2–9, and of the keeping of the Passover, verses 10–12, are priestly texts. The episode in verses 13–15 dealing with Joshua's encounter with the "commander of Yahweh's host" looks like a parallel to Moses' theophany on Sinai in Exod. 3 and is probably the work of J.[19]

The conquest of Jericho in chapter 6 should be viewed as the direct continuation of the Jordan crossing in 4:12–14 (Dtr). This chapter also presents a number of points of confusion in the extant version of the story. The source of this confusion is that P has attempted to turn the rather simple procedure, set forth by Dtr, of marching around the wall seven days in silence with only a shout at the sign of the shofar, into an elaborate procession.[20] The addition of all the trumpet-playing priests has ruined the effect of the one blast on the horn and the great war cry. Connections have also been made with the spy story in verses 17b, 22–23, 25.[21]

The story of the conquest of Jericho appears to end on a positive note: "Yahweh was with Joshua and his fame was throughout the land." It is surprising, therefore, to find in 7:1 that all was not well and that Yahweh was, in fact, angry with his people. The story of Achan concerns a matter of holiness, and there is much here that is reminiscent of such issues in the

16. The rather awkward phrases *nēd 'eḥad* (v. 13) and *qāmû nēd eḥad* (v. 16) may well represent explanatory glosses supplied by P. See especially the studies of B. S. Childs, "Deuteronomic Formulae of the Exodus Traditions," SVT 16 (1967):30–39; idem, "A Traditio-Historical Study of the Reed Sea Tradition," VT 20 (1970):406–18; G. W. Coats, "The Traditio-Historical Character of the Reed Sea Motif," VT 17 (1967):253–65; idem, "The Song of the Sea," CBQ 31 (1969):1–17.

17. Exod. 12:26–27 (P); 13:8–10 (J); cf. Deut. 6:20–24.

18. Cf. also Exod. 15:14–16.

19. As this episode now stands, it looks strangely incomplete. One solution would be to suppose that the rest of the account was lost (cf. Soggin, *Joshua*, pp. 76–78). The other would be to see it as an introduction to the divine speech of 6:2, with 6:1 treated as a parenthetical statement. In this case 5:13–15 is regarded as a secondary addition to the divine speech of 6:2ff. in order to supply Joshua with a theophany parallel to that of Moses.

20. This can be seen by isolating 6:1–3, 4aβ, 5, 6a, 7 (omitting *wayyō'mer 'el hā'ām*, "and he said to the people"), 10–11, 14–16aα, b, 17a, 20b, 21, 24a, 26–27.

21. The additions in vv. 18, 19, 24b will be dealt with below.

Pentateuch, especially the rebellion of Korah in Num. 16.[22] I would consider the story of Achan an addition by P with connections to the preceding account in 6:18, 19, 24b, where the reference to the "treasury of the house of Yahweh" seems to be an anachronism.

With the battle of Ai in chapter 8 we return again to the Dtr history. The introduction in verses 1–2 makes the story a sequel to the conquest of Jericho. Verses 3–9, however, are directly related to chapter 7 in that they refer to the previous attack upon Ai. The problem with these verses is that they form a doublet with those that follow and are unnecessary to the sense of the story. When they are removed as part of a later addition, there is no longer any suggestion of an earlier defeat.

The building of the altar at Ebal and the reading of the law in 8:30–35 seem to represent a digression that does not easily fit in with the geography of the campaign. The actions portrayed here are directly related to the injunctions of Moses in Deut. 11:29–30 and in chapter 27, but both of these passages are also secondary within Deuteronomy. The regulations concerning the altar in Deut. 27:5–7 and Josh. 8:31 correspond to the law given in Exod. 20:25 (J). Likewise, the location given in Deut. 11:30 as "beside the oak of Moreh" at Shechem recalls the same location sanctified with an altar by Abraham (in Gen. 12:6) and the place where Jacob buried foreign gods under the oak (in Gen. 35:4). These associations strongly suggest that the additions to Deuteronomy in 11:29–30 and chapter 27, as well as in Josh. 8:30–35, were all made by the Yahwist.[23]

The treaty with the Gibeonites in chapter 9 is a story that presupposes the law of warfare in Deut. 20:10ff.; this law is a completely artificial and ideological creation and was never an actual institution of Israel in this form. Consequently, there can be no doubt that the story as a whole is a thoroughly Deuteronomic invention. Within the story, however, some literary complexity has been created by later additions. On the one hand, Joshua has the role of leadership and enters into an agreement with the Gibeonites (verses 15a, 16, 22, 24–26, 27). This is the original version of Dtr. To it has been added the version that shifts the blame for the agreement with the Gibeonites onto the "leaders of the congregation," who did not take the trouble to inquire of Yahweh. This addition is to be found in verses 14, 15b, 17–21, 23, and in some glosses in verse 27. The language

22. The story of the rebellion of Korah, Dathan, and Abiram has usually been divided between the J and P sources (see Noth, *Numbers*, pp. 120–22), but I can find little justification for such a division. J is otherwise quite disinterested in the priesthood, and the story has as its main concern the controversies over the priesthood of the postexilic period.

23. On these texts see Perlitt, *Bundestheologie*, p. 248, n. 3, where he is quite critical about the suggestions that these texts contain early premonarchic covenant traditions. On Josh. 24, which many scholars associate with Josh. 8:30–35, see below.

and the repetitious style of composition are characteristic of P,[24] but this is not a separate, self-contained version of the story. It is an addition that was primarily intended to shift the blame from Joshua to the "leaders."[25]

The story of Joshua's defeat of the "southern coalition" in chapter 10 presents no great problems. It continues on from chapter 9 and clearly presupposes the events there. The one interruption in the narrative is the unit about the sun standing still, along with a short poem in it said to have been derived from the "Book of Jashar."[26] Since Dtr again quotes from this source in 2 Sam. 1:18ff., the verses in Josh. 10:12–14 are probably from Dtr also. The reference in verse 15 to Joshua's return to camp, however, is clearly out of place, since the pursuit of the enemy is still in progress. The flight of the kings in verses 16ff. really follows closely from verse 10. For the rest, there is no reason to see any other hand in the work.

The campaign against Hazor and the "northern coalition" in chapter 11 is also thoroughly Dtr, with few, if any, later glosses. The presentation of the battle, preceded by the oracle of salvation to Joshua before the battle itself, is quite typical of Dtr style. Deuteronomy envisages the complete success of the conquest and the use of the ban (*ḥērem*) against the inhabitants, and the summary statements in Joshua 11 indicate that these measures were successfully carried out. Also, the theme of God hardening the heart of the enemy so as to lead them into war in order to destroy them (11:20) is typical of Dtr, as in Deut. 2:30.

The list of defeated kings on both sides of the Jordan in chapter 12 does not contain anything that is distinctive of the Dtr source, and I agree with Mowinckel[27] that it is from the hand of P. It could be explained only as corresponding to P's love of lists, which he displays so prominently throughout the Pentateuch. At various points it does not entirely agree with the previous Dtr account.

To sum up my observations about the first half of Joshua, I have suggested that the original version of the conquest was composed by Dtr. There is, to my mind, no evidence of an earlier *Sammler* which constituted

24. For a treatment of the priestly style, see S. E. McEvenue, *The Narrative Style of the Priestly Writer.*

25. It is in this latest priestly addition to the story that some scholars like Soggin (*Joshua,* pp. 113–14) want to find the *oldest* traditions and a historical background to the story. From the literary perspective, such a viewpoint is questionable.

26. On the meaning of the poem, see J. S. Holladay, Jr., "The Day(s) the Moon Stood Still," *JBL* 87 (1968):166–78. As indicated by Holladay, the poem is based upon an omen of a rather common type in Near Eastern texts in which the position of the heavenly bodies was regarded as propitious (or unpropitious). Dtr, however, construed the text to mean a rather miraculous event. Whether the original poem was associated with Joshua, as Holladay suggests, is much more difficult to say.

27. Mowinckel, *Tetrateuch,* pp. 59–60.

a pre-Deuteronomic source. This proposal by Noth[28] replaced the older critical position that the early Hexateuchal sources continued on into Joshua and were simply edited by Dtr. The fact is, as I have tried to show, that the sources J and P both made *post*-Dtr additions to the basic Dtr presentation as supplements or modifications of the earlier work. Thus these Hexateuchal sources did not need to present their own conquest narrative as a completion of their Tetrateuchal compositions. They simply built on to the Dtr history of the conquest and settlement their own prehistory of these events and modified the older Dtr history where they felt it desirable to do so. If this analysis is correct, it accounts for the critical points in favor of a Hexateuch that have been raised against Noth by von Rad and Mowinckel, but it keeps intact Noth's fundamental observation that Dtr is not just a redactor of older sources but an author-historian in the full sense of the word.

The Dtr Historian interpreted the tradition of the entrance into the arable land as a great military conquest along the lines of the frequent invasions that Israel and Judah had experienced at the hands of the Assyrians and Babylonians. In these cases Israel and Judah had often been party to coalitions that sought to resist the invader, usually to no avail. In the presentation of Joshua's invasion the coalitions of the native inhabitants, both the southern and northern groups of kings, are defeated and the various cities destroyed.

Furthermore, the Dtr narrative has a basic similarity to the accounts of such military campaigns in the Near Eastern inscriptions, particularly those of the Assyrian annals and the "letters to the god."[29] The latter often give special attention to a few major battles or conquests of important cities while summarizing the overthrow of many others in a stereotyped series. They may also highlight at the outset of a campaign the overcoming of a special physical barrier, such as a river in flood or a mountain range. Before an important battle the king often receives an "oracle of salvation" from a deity who promises to deliver the enemy into his hand.[30] Sometimes envoys come from a great distance to sue for peace and submit to terms of servitude in order to avoid destruction. It is also not unusual during the course of a campaign to consult or rely upon omens in order to predict the ultimate outcome of the war. General descriptions of sieges or military stratagems; summary treatments of attack and flight of the enemy and the burning of cities; enumerations of participants of coalitions, kings

28. *Das Buch Josua*, p. 13.
29. For a discussion of these texts, see above, 3a.
30. See the recent study by M. Weippert, "Heiliger Krieg in Israel und Assyrien: Kritische Anmerkungen zu Gerhard von Rads Konzept des 'Heiligen Krieges im alten Israel,'" *ZAW* 84 (1972):460–93.

defeated, or cities taken; lists of casualities and the amount of booty; dedications of victory and of spoils to the god—all occur with great regularity. In the royal inscriptions of the Assyrians and Babylonians the native peoples of Syria-Palestine are all lumped together under the rubric of "Amorites" or "Hittites." Also, the borders given in these inscriptions for the "land of the Amorites/Hittites" correspond closely to those in Josh. 1:4.[31] Once we isolate the basic Dtr account of the conquest, without the stories of Rahab (chapter 2) or the sin of Achan (chapter 7) and the other additions of J and P (especially chapter 5), then it is remarkable how closely Dtr's work has been made to correspond with the literary pattern of military campaigns in the Assyrian royal inscriptions. Even the "installation" of Joshua as the leader who succeeds Moses suggests that the conquest is the first victorious campaign of the new regime.

This treatment of the migration into the land does not seem to be reflected in the "gift of the good land" theme in the prophetic tradition.[32] Instead it grows directly out of the militant "puritanical" reform of Deuteronomy, in which the obliteration of everything un-Israelite in Israel's religious practices is justified on the basis of an "original" command by God to obliterate the indigenous population and all their alien forms of worship. Israel's very right to the land requires its purification. The Dtr Historian has turned this theological principle in Deuteronomy into a great invasion and campaign of victory under the leadership of Joshua. The continuity between Deuteronomy and Joshua seems to be firmly established at numerous points in the first eleven chapters of Joshua, and especially in the opening chapter of the book. This is not the place to debate the degree to which the Dtr Historian edited Deuteronomy and made additions to it, especially in chapters 1–4 and 29–34. Nevertheless, it seems reasonable to assume that if a Dtr history did exist as an extended work of one author, then Deuteronomy was incorporated into it as its prologue and statement of guiding principles. Joshua's conquest is the initial carrying out of those principles by cleansing the land of Amorites.

b. THE LAND DIVISION: JOSHUA 13–24

The designation of sources for the second half of Joshua is a hotly debated issue. Most scholars are willing to admit that the division of the land among the tribes is secondary to the original conquest narrative. However,

31. J. Van Seters, "The Terms 'Amorite' and 'Hittite' in the Old Testament," *VT* 22 (1972):64–81.

32. The only exception to this would appear to be Amos 2:9–10, but 2:9–12 is suspect as a Dtr addition. See J. M. Ward, *Amos and Isaiah: Prophets of the Word of God*, p. 67, n. 3.

whereas Noth would attribute it to a second Dtr redactor, Mowinckel and von Rad ascribe it to the Pentateuchal sources, because there is little evidence throughout most of the material of any Dtr influence. Noth's counter to this is that the Dtr redactor employed documentary source materials from various periods without altering them, only reworking them to fit them into his own general scheme. Several scholars have followed this proposal with their own suggestions about the time and function of such hypothetical documents.[33]

All this evidence of documents, however, has been created by scholars *ex nihilo,* because there are no such extant lists, nor is there any reason to suppose that such records ever existed. No comparable records can be produced from the ancient Near East such that the originals can be reconstructed out of what we have in these chapters. The artificial and idealized character of the lists has been frequently noted, and yet to attribute this to editorial reworking while at the same time using the theory of documents to explain the lack of a particular editorial hand is contradictory. The evidence by which to identify the author is abundant and cannot be easily ignored or explained away.[34]

First, let us consider what can be attributed with some certainty to Dtr. The unit in 21:43–45 contains a summary of the complete victory that is very similar to 11:15, 23, and while it seems somewhat redundant, it is nevertheless thoroughly Dtr in character. The following unit, 22:1–6, in which the eastern tribes are dismissed by Joshua and permitted to return home, completes a theme begun in Josh. 1:12–18 and mentioned again in 4:12–13. The language also is typical of Dtr. What follows in 22:7–35 is quite different. The farewell speech by Joshua in chapter 23 is so clearly in the style of Dtr that there seems little need to demonstrate this fact. But the attribution of any other texts in this part of Joshua to Dtr, beyond these few, remains questionable.[35]

Most of the latter half of Joshua is dominated by the allotment of land to the various tribes. Von Rad, in his study of this theme, suggests an important distinction between the Deuteronomic notion of the inheritance of the land and that used by P.[36] This distinction is that while Dtr "speaks almost exclusively of the inheritance of *Israel*" as a whole,[37] P refers to

33. See the discussion and bibliography in Hayes and Miller, *Israelite and Judean History,* pp. 235–36.

34. See Mowinckel's critique in *Tetrateuch,* pp. 62–67.

35. It will be shown below that the appointment of the cities of refuge in chap. 20 (with the exception of v. 6 and the last phrase in v. 9) also belongs to Dtr.

36. "The Promised Land and Yahweh's Land in the Hexateuch," in *The Problem of the Hexateuch,* pp. 79–93.

37. Deut. 4:21, 38; 12:9; 15:4; 19:10; 20:16; 21:23; 24:4; 25:19; 26:1.

the inheritance of the individual tribes and the families within the tribes.[38] This means that for Dtr it was enough to suggest that Joshua, through his leadership in the conquest of the land, had brought the people as a whole into their inheritance. The Priestly Writer, however, developed this theme to delineate the precise inheritance of each of the tribes and of the families within each tribe, and so greatly expanded the conquest/settlement theme in this direction. There is no reason to conjecture a second Dtr redactor for this material (as Noth does) when it corresponds so closely with the Priestly program as laid out in Numbers. In this program P indicates first that the census of the tribes by families was undertaken with a view to the future division of the land by lot among the various tribes and the families within each tribe (Num. 26:52–56; 33:54). Closely related to this is the description of the general boundaries of the land of Canaan, which is to be divided by lot (Num. 34). This is followed by the injunction about the cities for the Levites, into which are incorporated the laws for the cities of refuge.

A comparison of the Priestly program with Joshua shows how it was carried out in the land of Canaan, and there is no need to suppose that it was put together by any other hand than P. This author was still confronted with the task of integrating his material into the original Dtr text of Joshua. He did this partly by way of commentary. For instance, it has often been remarked that Josh. 13:1a shows a close similarity to 23:1b, but this observation is never carried far enough. If we set down the parallel texts, we can make some observations about them.

Joshua 23:1–5 (Dtr)	Joshua 13:1–7 (P)
1. A long time afterward, when Yahweh had given rest to Israel from all their enemies round about, and Joshua was old [and] well advanced in years,	1. And Joshua was old [and] well advanced in years. And Yahweh said to him, "You are old [and] well advanced in years and there remains much land to be possessed.
2. Joshua summoned all Israel . . . and said to them, "I am now old [and] well advanced in years. . . .	2. (This is the land that remains . . .).
4. Behold I have allotted to	6b. I will dispossess them from before the Israelites.

38. Num 18:21, 24; 26:53–54, 56; 36:3. Based on the fact that Deut. 10:6–9 is clearly a later P addition to Deuteronomy, I would also suggest that all the remarks about Levi having no portion or inheritance (ḥēleq weⁿaḥᵃlāh) in Israel in Deut. 12:12; 14:27, 29; 18:1ff. are later P additions, so that the distinction in usage between D and P is even more consistent than von Rad had suggested.

you as an inheritance for your tribes those nations that remain, along with the nations that I have already cut off, from the Jordan to the Great Sea in the west. 5. Yahweh your God will push them back before you. . . ."	Only allot it to Israel as an inheritance as I commanded you. 7. Now therefore divide this land for an inheritance to the nine tribes and the half tribe of Manasseh."

From this comparison we can observe that P has borrowed his introduction in 13.1 from 23:1b–2 (in spite of the chronological problem arising from 23:1a); but P's main concern is with 23:4. According to Dtr, Joshua is committing to the people all the territory within the idealized boundary, including what he has conquered for them; it remains for them gradually to realize this inheritance to the full by pushing these nations back the whole distance from the borders of Egypt to the Euphrates. P distinguishes quite carefully between the lands that remain to be conquered (which he defines by a long geographic digression in the middle of the divine speech) and the lands that are already conquered, which must be allotted. This then becomes the point of departure for his treatment of the specific allotments to the individual tribes, in which he uses his own terminology (13:7ff.).[39]

A brief comparison of the two versions of the division of the land among the eastern tribes, in Josh. 13:8–33 and Deut. 3:8–17, is instructive.[40] The version in Deuteronomy begins with a general description of the total area of the land taken in the defeat of the two kings (verses

39. In a recent study R. Smend has suggested that 13:7, along with v. 1abα, belongs to the original Dtr and that Josh. 23 is to be attributed to a late redactor, DtrN. Without going into detail on this proposal it may be pointed out, on the basis of von Rad's study of terminology in n. 36 above, that it seems most difficult to see how Smend can find any basis for 13:7 in the Dtr corpus. Nor does 13:7 appear to me to follow very readily from v. 1abα. The land division does not finally come about because of Joshua's advanced age but as a result of the conquest. The *weʿattāh* (v. 7) is a very imprecise editorial connective no matter how one views this pericope. Furthermore, Smend makes no attempt to show how the following division of the land to the nine and a half tribes can be so easily integrated into the original Dtr, which is what 13:7 implies. In fact, everything speaks against this, and Smend's suggestion fails on this account. It is more likely that those texts that contain an overwhelming preponderance of Deuteronomic phraseology, such as Josh. 1:1–9 and chap. 23, are part of the primary Dtr, and those that contain little or none are secondary. See R. Smend, "Das Gesetz und die Völker," in *Probleme Biblischer Theologie*, pp. 494–509. In this tribute to von Rad one might have expected Smend to pay more attention to von Rad's article on the subject, which he does not even mention!

40. For a recent discussion of these texts, see M. Wüst, *Untersuchungen zu den siedlungsgeographischen Texten des Alten Testaments. I. Ostjordanland*. The traditio-historical method employed in this work is not compatible with the results of the literary analysis used here.

8–10). This land is then distributed in two parcels corresponding to the two kingdoms (verses 12–17). The northern parcel goes to the half-tribe of Manasseh, and the southern area is given to both the Reubenites and the Gadites, with no attempt to draw boundaries between them. There is, throughout this description, no reference to any method of division, such as the use of lots, or any indication of inheritance distributed to smaller subdivisions, such as families. By contrast, Josh. 13:8ff., after repeating the general dimensions of the land for no apparent reason, divides up the land fairly precisely, according to the principle laid down in P—the division to be made according to the families of the tribes, with the boundaries and the cities clearly designated.[41] This sets the pattern for the rest of the land division from chapter 14 onward, in which the allotment for the western tribes is made.

The first general allotment of territory to the tribe of Judah and the house of Joseph, in chapters 14–17, seems to be interrupted by, or to include, short narrative portions in a somewhat different style from the rest of the material.[42] These are the allotment of land to Caleb (in 14:6–15) and his conquest of it within the territory of Judah (in 15:13–19), and the tribe of Joseph's complaint about lack of space at the conclusion of their allotment (in 17:14–18). Also, parallels are drawn between these units and a similar case in Num. 32:39–42. This type of narrative digression does not seem to me (as it does to most scholars) to signify a separate source, and the passages contain some features that are characteristic of P.[43] Consequently, I am inclined to see the entire allotting of territory in chapters 14–17 as constructed by the hand of P.

The allotment in chapters 18–19, which deals with the last seven tribes, is also the work of P.[44] The manner in which the assembly is convened at Shiloh and the procedures laid down for the land division are characteristic of the P style. This has long been recognized and there seems to be no good reason to dispute it.[45] The allotment of the cities of refuge in chapter 20 is a more complex matter. On the one hand, it seems to correspond to the instructions in Deut. 4:41–43 and 19:1–13, rather than to the P provisions in Num. 35:6–34. For this reason I would add it to the list of Dtr texts in the second half of Joshua. Josh. 20:6 and the final phrase in verse

41. Note the reference to a specific P tradition in 13:21b–22 = Num. 31.

42. See a similar digression in Deut. 3:14.

43. Mowinckel (*Tetrateuch*, pp. 44ff.) ascribes all these texts to the Yahwist, but much in them is not compatible with this source designation. It also makes difficult an explanation of how such J fragments became scattered throughout the P source in chaps. 13–19.

44. J. G. Vink, *The Date and Origin of the Priestly Code in the Old Testament*, OTS 15, pp. 63–73.

45. Noth's remarks (*ÜS*, pp. 183ff.), that we have to do only with some glosses in a priestly style and phraseology, are forced and unconvincing.

9bβ, however, are modifications by the Priestly Writer. The designation of the cities for the Levites in 21:1–42 corresponds only to the P injunction in Num. 35:1–8 and so belongs to P.[46]

As noted above, 22:1–6 belongs to Dtr and fits well with the other statements about the eastern tribes. On the other hand, verses 7ff. constitute a new beginning, and the whole story about the altar of witness of the eastern tribes, in which Phineas the priest and the "chiefs of the congregation" play a leading role, has much that is characteristic of P's style and vocabulary. The whole of 22:7–34 belongs to P, as do the final notations in 24:32–33.

The pericope in 24:1–27, however, is another matter.[47] It constitutes a second farewell speech by Joshua, and it hardly seems likely that both would come from the same hand. I have considered chapter 23 as more likely the work of Dtr; but even though there are some Deuteronomic phrases in chapter 24, it is a post-Dtr addition. The historical recitation of events is a significant clue to its authorship. It seems to correspond to a summary account of J's version of the Pentateuch,[48] especially in the statements about the patriarchs, in the description of the Red Sea event, and in the Balaam story, while containing nothing that is distinctively P. The nature of Joshua's covenant making is also similar to the covenant ceremony of Moses in Exod. 24 and the witnessing scene in Genesis 31: 43–54. Josh. 24:1–27 was added to chapter 23.

To summarize the source analysis of the latter half of Joshua (13–24), we would suggest as the original Dtr text Josh. 20:1–5, 7–9; 21:43–22:6; 23:1–16. To this, at the first stage of supplementation, the Yahwist added 24:1–27. P then added the rest in chapters 13–19; 20:6, 9bβ; 21:1–42; 22:7–34; 24:28–33. The meaning of this analysis is that Dtr included within his story of the conquest only the setting up of the cities of refuge on the "west bank"—paralleling Moses' actions on the "east bank" in compliance with Deuteronomic law—and the dismissing of the eastern tribes, which completes their original recruitment in Deut. 3:18ff. The farewell speech in chapter 23 also parallels Moses' final admonitions and

46. Noth's treatment of this chapter (*ÜS*, pp. 189–90) typifies the problem with his analysis. Since this is a Priestly addition to the Dtr version of Joshua, it must belong to a P redactor and not to the P source itself, which Noth regards as an independent literary work. However, if P, even in the Pentateuch, was only a supplement to the other sources, then Noth's approach to the problem of P in Joshua suffers from a misunderstanding of the nature of this source.

47. See the study of Perlitt, *Bundestheologie*, pp. 239–84, for his critique of earlier approaches. Even so, his own solution to this chapter is not entirely convincing. It is not an "ur"-dt work but a post-Dtr work.

48. See the recent discussion by B. S. Childs, "Deuteronomic Formulae of the Exodus Tradition," *SVT* 16 (1967):30–39. Here Childs discusses the so-called credos as historical summaries—not as old liturgical texts, as von Rad had proposed.

provides the transition to the next period of history. This basic Dtr account in Joshua has the appearance of a tightly composed, unified whole, with strong literary continuity to Detueronomy on the one hand and to Judges on the other.

At the first stage of supplementation, what could be the purpose of the Yahwist's addition of Josh. 24 to Dtr's account? It cannot be just a conclusion to the story of Joshua, which was already provided in the earlier work. Josh. 24 is the summing up in credo form, after the model in Deut. 26:5–9, of the Yahwistic presentation of the Pentateuch from Abraham to the conquest; it is thus the concluding chapter of the Yahwist's entire work. It also provides J's final challenge of faith to his own exilic audience—whether in the homeland or in the Babylonian exile—to serve Yahweh rather than the gods "in the region beyond the River, or the gods of the Amorites in whose land you dwell" (Josh. 24:15). Each household must now make that decision for itself. A more fitting conclusion to the Yahwist's history could scarcely be proposed.[49]

The major addition by P to the conquest story is the precise but artificial and idealized division of the land to the tribes and clans, or families. This shows a historiographic concern for geographic precision about the settlement of individual tribes and about the boundaries of the "Promised" Land as a whole, and it parallels P's concern for chronological precision in the Pentateuch, which is greater than J's. But we cannot fully appreciate the purpose of P's additions until we give some consideration to the literary problems of Judges.

c. JUDGES 1:1–2:5

The fundamental problem of the Hexateuch is, perhaps, how to view Judg. 1:1–2:5 and its relationship to what comes before and after it.[50] Since the days of E. Meyer literary critics have commonly ascribed this unit to the early Pentateuchal sources, preferably J, and have viewed it as J's counterpart to the conquest narratives in the first half of Joshua.[51] They have considered it older because it seemed to represent a view of the

49. Is it too much to suggest that in Joshua's second writing of the law one can see J's legitimation of his own second presentation of the law after Deuteronomy?

50. For a survey of the current literary discussion see Hayes and Miller, *Israelite and Judean History*, pp. 236–69. Note also the commentaries of C. F. Burney, *The Book of Judges: With Introduction and Notes*; G. F. Moore, *A Critical and Exegetical Commentary on Judges*. Special attention will be given to C. H. J. de Geus, "Richteren 1:1–2:5," *Vox Theologica* 36 (1966):32–53; and M. Weinfeld, "The Period of the Conquest and of the Judges as Seen by the Earlier and Later Sources," *VT* 17 (1967):93–113.

51. See Moore, *Judges*, pp. xxxii–xxxiii, 3–100; Mowinckel, *Tetrateuch*, pp. 17–33.

settlement as piecemeal and incomplete, and therefore closer to the actual facts than the Dtr presentation of a single invasion, as in Joshua. This judgment, in turn, has had great implications for the assessment of the second half of Joshua, since the latter has parallels or excerpts that are almost identical to those in Judg. 1. It therefore becomes necessary to assign at least some of the texts on the division of the land to J. The result is a highly fragmentary separation of sources for Josh. 13ff.[52]

The primary difficulty with this approach is the recognition by all scholars that Judg. 1:1–2:5 is an intrusion in its present context. The literary mechanism for making this addition is the repetition of Judg. 2:6ff. in Josh. 24:28ff. This means that scholars have had to try to explain why Dtr set aside the Yahwist version of the conquest and a later redactor reintroduced it. None of their proposals seems satisfactory. Noth, who opposed the notion of a Hexateuch, simply regarded the unit as a later redactional addition that made use of unspecified early sources—a conglomerate of various materials but not a Pentateuchal document.[53] In spite of Noth's view of the matter, scholars have persisted in finding a connection between Judg. 1:1–2:5 and the Pentateuchal sources.[54] In my view the issue has not yet been resolved.

In analyzing Judg. 1 the first point to observe is that, except for a few possible additions, the chapter is a unity.[55] The first part, verses 1–21, deals with the settlement of the southern tribes, and the second part, verses 22–35, with the northern tribes. Any traditions or other "sources" that may have existed behind the present account[56] are fully integrated into the perspective of the whole, and no redactional framework can be removed without destroying the sense of the individual elements. Second, any analysis must take seriously the close relationship between this chapter and the latter half of Joshua. Not only is the general time frame set "after the death of Joshua," but the unit presupposes the allotment of the land. Since the whole allotment scheme is also considered secondary to Dtr, the question arises whether Judg. 1 is part of the same supplemental source. Third, the work in Judg. 1 shows the influence of a broad range of biblical texts. Its terminology and its specific historical allusions indicate familiarity with the Pentateuch, and it also contains information taken from the historical books. In its variety of style and use of literary genres, in the range of its sources, and in its use of editorial comment, the work repre-

---

52. Mowinckel, *Tetrateuch,* pp. 67ff.
53. Noth, *ÜS,* pp. 7–10.
54. See Weinfeld, *VT* 17:93–113.
55. See de Geus, *Vox Theol.* 36:43.
56. The notion of archival documents, so dear to many scholars, is highly speculative. Just what historical genre would correspond, in whole or in part, to the material in Judg. 1: 1–2:5?

sents a rather advanced historiography. Let us consider some of these issues in greater detail.

As indicated above, Judg. 1 presupposes the distribution of the land by lot (gôrāl). This is the terminology and perspective of the Priestly Writer, and there is no reason to suppose that any other author held such a view of the settlement.[57] It is further assumed in Judg. 1:3, 17 that the allotments of Judah and Simeon were closely tied to one another, as set forth in Josh. 19:1–9. The same close association is true of Judah and the Calebites. When it is recognized that Judg. 1:20 is out of place and should come directly after verse 10,[58] then the pericope of Judg. 1:10, 20, 11–15 forms a sequel to the allotment scene in Josh. 14:6–15, just as the parallel version does in Josh. 15:13–19. There is no point in trying to decide which of the two almost identical versions is the original, because both are from the same hand. They merely serve slightly different functions in the two different contexts. P was never shy about repeating himself. The combination of the people of Judah with the Kenites (verse 16), on the other hand, does not go back to Joshua but to the Pentateuch, Num. 10:29–32, where Hobab the Midianite (Kenite), Moses' father-in-law, receives a promise from Moses that he will be treated well and allowed to share the land with Israel. Furthermore, it would appear that the allotment of land in Joshua is treated by P only as an unfulfilled promise, so that the individual tribes must claim their land by their own military actions. This pattern of allotment before conquest can be seen in Josh. 14:6–15 and 15:13–16, and it exemplifies the more general pattern of Judah's allotment in Josh. 14–15 before its conquest of the territory in Judg. 1:1–21. Similarly, the "house of Joseph" receives its allotment in Josh. 16–17 before it conquers the region in Judg. 1:22–26.

This brings us to the matter of the parallel texts, in which Judg. 1:21 = Josh. 15:63, Judg. 1:27–28 = Josh. 17:11–13, and Judg. 1:29 = Josh. 16:10. It is usual to assume that these texts are primary in Judg. 1 and secondary in Joshua, since the series of unconquered territories continues with the other tribes as well in Judg. 1:30–33, and these have no counterpart in Joshua.[59] Yet in Josh. 13:13 we find a similar qualification—that the eastern tribes "did not drive out the Geshurites and the Maacathites, but Geshur and Maacath dwell in the midst of Israel to this day." The language and style of the statement are reminiscent of Judg. 1. Yet this is hardly a stray Yahwistic text, as some have suggested, since it

57. See von Rad, *The Problem of the Hexateuch*, p. 82, where he presents a list of all the texts. Von Rad attributes some of the instances to JE, but all of these are in Josh. 13–17 or Judg. 1, texts that we do not regard as part of the JE corpus.

58. See de Geus, *Vox Theol.* 36:37.

59. Cf. ibid., pp. 39–40; Mowinckel, *Tetrateuch*, pp. 15–16, 24.

fits well in its context and provides the pattern for the subsequent texts of this kind in Joshua. Furthermore, the remarks in Josh. 19:47 about Dan losing its primary holdings and moving to the north complement the statement in Judg. 1:34 that the Danites were not successful in conquering the Amorites in their southern allotment. Again, we cannot suppose that Josh. 19:47 does not belong originally with the whole allotment pericope of verses 40–48.

These facts are best explained by assuming that the same author, P, composed both the Joshua and Judg. 1 texts. In his description of both the initial distribution of the land and the subsequent taking of it, the Priestly Writer wanted to stress that the promise was not entirely kept. The information about the cities that were not conquered comes partly from the Dtr history, which provided information about the later conquest or acquisition of Jerusalem and Gezer, and about the local population being put to forced labor.[60] The presence of non-Israelites in the land could also represent the author's own experience in a later day, when the urban population in the northern region of Israel was an ethnic mixture of Israelite and non-Israelite.

The antiquity of the particular events presented in the anecdotes in Judg. 1:4ff. and 22ff. is rather questionable. The story about Adonibezek seems to have as its point of departure Joshua's campaign against Adonizedek of Jerusalem in Josh. 10.[61] The totally artificial character of the name Adonibezek, and his association with both Bezek and Jerusalem, give the show away as a rather *ad hoc* creation. The story of the capture of Bethel, like the Jericho story, combines such simple motifs as the use of spies, leniency to the informer, and the secret entrance to the city—but it is hardly convincing.[62]

It is not difficult to suppose that all of Judg. 1 could be the work of P. If this identification is accepted, then it becomes clear that the account of Joshua's death was repeated in Josh. 24:28ff. because that was the only way to fit the new material into its context. The reference to the burial of Joseph's bones in verse 32 draws on information from the Pentateuch, but it also creates a parallel to P's account of the burial of other patriarchs at

---

60. 1 Kings 9:20–21. This text is interesting for two reasons. It speaks of the Israelites' inability to destroy the remaining inhabitants, although in Dtr this inability is clearly the result of disobedience. Second, Dtr, following D, prefers the terminology of extermination, *ḥrm*, while the author in Joshua 13ff. and Judg. 1 consistently uses the verb *yrš*, "to dispossess."

61. See de Geus, *Vox Theol.* 36:35–36.

62. Cf. ibid., pp. 40–41. I am not convinced by de Geus's statement, "Het is duidellijk, dat de auteur van Ri. 1 in vv. 22–26 weer een oudere overlevering heeft benut." Saying so does not make it so, and why should all the signs of lateness, e.g., "the house of Joseph," be regarded as only editorial?

Hebron. The notation on the death and burial of Eleazar, the priest in verse 33, also fits well with P authorship. The rather full list of cities not taken by the Israelites, the love of antiquarian information about ancient peoples and place names, and the concluding geographic digression[63] are all characteristics of the Priestly style.

This brings us to a consideration of Judg. 2:1–5. Here an angel of Yahweh accuses Israel of violating the command not to make a covenant with the inhabitants of the land but to expel and dispossess them; he warns that they will suffer the consequences. Because this theme has a number of precursors in different sources, it is not easy to identify the author. Primary among these thematic precursors is Deut. 7, but since Deuteronomy nowhere mentions any "angel of Yahweh," it would be difficult for an author who used Deuteronomy to introduce such a figure without explanation. Another precursor of this text is Exod. 23:20–33 (J).[64] Here the "angel of Yahweh" is introduced as a guiding and directing force but is never actually presented as a person.[65] Rather, he seems to represent the spiritual presence of Yahweh, as appears to be the case in Gen. 24, where divine providence is the activity of the "angel of Yahweh." If Judg. 2:1–5 is dependent upon Exod. 23:20–33, the author has made a rather literal interpretation of the angel's function of admonishing the people (verses 21–22). It is unlikely that Judg. 2:1–5 can be reconciled with the Yahwist's perspective.

The third text that is relevant here is Num. 33:50–56 (P). In this passage Moses charges the people to take possession of the land, to dispossess all its inhabitants, and to destroy all their cult objects and places of worship. They are solemnly warned that leaving the task incomplete will have dire consequences. Nothing is said here about Yahweh (D) or the "angel of Yahweh" (J) going before the people to give them victory. Also, the task of dispossessing the inhabitants is closely combined with the process of distributing the land by lot, clearly implying that each tribe is responsible for taking possession of its own allotted inheritance.

The events described in Judg. 1:1–2:5 seem to fulfill the threat of dire consequences in Num. 33. The individual tribes attempt to claim their allotments, but they are only partly successful since many enclaves of indigenous inhabitants remain in the land. This leads to the reprimand by the angel of Yahweh that the people have not been obedient and therefore will

63. Note 1:36. Cf. Num. 34:3–5; Josh. 15:1–4 (P). See the discussion by Burney, *Judges,* pp. 33–35.

64. See also Exod. 32:31; 33:2; 34:16: Num. 20:16. Because I do not subscribe to a distinctive E source in the Pentateuch, I regard all these texts as J. Cf. the discussion by Burney, *Judges,* pp. 35–36. That this is not an early usage of the "angel" is evident from Mal. 3:1ff.

65. The theophanic use of the "angel of God/Yahweh" in Genesis and in Exod. 3 and Josh. 5 is another matter.

have to suffer the consequences. It seems reasonable to conclude that Judg. 2:1–5 is the work of P. The reference to God establishing his covenant with the fathers "forever" (*l^e ʿôlām*) further confirms this, since it clearly employs P terminology. The suggestion in the admonition that the people also made a covenant with the inhabitants of the land likewise seems to point back to Josh. 9 and the P addition of verses 14, 15b, 17–21, and 23, where the tribal leaders are clearly culpable for their actions. Finally, descriptions of the people weeping in response to bad news are also found in the testing stories of the wilderness journey, particularly in the P versions (Num. 11:4ff.; 14:1). There seems little reason to doubt that Judg. 2:1–5 belongs to P, along with chapter 1.[66]

d. JUDGES 2:6–16:31

The Dtr historian continues his history in Judg. 2:6ff. by moving from the life and activity of Joshua to the time of the judges in such a way as to make Joshua the first judge. He interprets the period of the judges as a cyclic repetition of events in which the people fall away from serving Yahweh to take up the worship of the gods of the nations around them. As a result, they are not able to continue their conquests by defeating these nations but instead become oppressed by them or subservient to them. Then, from time to time, Yahweh sends relief through a "judge" or "deliverer," but the people's renewed allegiance to Yahweh during the judge's rule is only temporary: they repeat their old ways after the judge's death, with the result that Yahweh vows not to complete the conquest of the land that was left upon the death of Joshua. Up to this point (2:6–21) the pattern is in agreement with the statements of warning found in Josh. 23. But 2:22–3:4 introduces a new element that is not consistent with what has gone before. It suggests that the remaining nations were intended even before Joshua's death to be a test of Israel's obedience to Yahweh; therefore, the fact that they remain unconquered does not represent a change in the divine plan (verses 22–23; 3:1a, 4; cf. 2:21).[67] A second reason for the nations to remain in the land was so that the people might practice the arts of war (3:1b–2). Both reasons, which are compatible with each other, give an entirely positive purpose to the presence of the nations and mitigate the notion that they function as a punishment. The list of the nations that re-

66. This also means that P was responsible for the repetition of Judg. 2:6ff. in Josh. 24:28–31 in order to allow for the addition of Judg. 1:1–2:5. He also appended the special notices of Josh. 24:32–33 at the same time.

67. See also Deut. 7:22 and Exod. 23:29–30, where a gradual conquest is suggested but not for the reason stated in Judg. 2:23; 3:4. Therefore I cannot agree with Weinfeld's inclusion of 2:22–3:4 within Dtr (*VT* 17:97ff.). The Dtr language in 2:22–23 and 3:4 is borrowed primarily from the immediate context, so its presence is no surprise.

main (3:3) corresponds to the geography of the Promised Land as set forth in Josh. 13:2–6—a section that we assigned above to P. For this reason I regard 2:22–3:4 as a further addition by P to the Dtr prologue of his history of the judges.[68]

The recognition that Judg. 1:1–2:5 and 2:22–3:4 are the work of P puts into perspective the priestly texts on the division of the land in Joshua. P is concerned not only with the ideal dimensions of the Promised Land but also with the problem of why these dimensions were never realized. This problem is considered on two levels. The first has to do with the peoples who remained within the allotted tribal boundaries. These were the responsibility of the tribes, who failed to carry out fully their assignment to dispossess these peoples.Within the larger idealized boundaries, however, were other nations purposely left by God as a means of testing and training for the Israelites. With these additions in Judges, the whole Priestly scheme of the settlement is complete and it is evident that P made no further additions to Dtr's work.[69]

The Dtr introduction in 2:11–21 and 3:5–6 is used as the theological framework by which the various episodes of the "judges" or "saviors" are incorporated into the history. The Dtr may speak of his heroes as judges who save the people from their enemies or saviors who judge the people. Efforts to reconstruct a pre-Dtr "Book of Saviors," whom the Dtr only later made into judges, cannot sustain such a distinction between these two uses in the text. The fact is that Dtr could even speak on occasion of the kings of Israel as saviors whom God provided for his people to deliver them from their enemies in response to their cry for help (see 2 Kings 13:4–5; 14:26–27). Furthermore, we cannot separate the story of the first "savior," Othniel, from the Dtr introduction. The whole account is an artificially constructed model of deliverance made up of elements taken from the introduction with no ancient tradition whatever behind it.[70] The stories of the other judges in Dtr are then made to correspond in their introductions and conclusions to this model.[71]

The rest of the stories of the judges or deliverers seem to derive a certain amount of their material from old folk legends, and various attempts have been made to reconstruct their earlier forms in order to reproduce a pre-Dtr collection.[72] In most cases, however, the framework of Dtr has been so thoroughly integrated into the story itself that it is surely Dtr who is re-

68. Josh. 3:5–6 reverts back to the language of Dtr and is the continuation of 2:21, the original Dtr prologue (cf. Weinfeld, VT 17:98).

69. But see below, n. 79.

70. See Moore, *Judges,* pp. 84–85; Burney, *Judges,* pp. 64–65. Efforts to salvage some historical kernel in the story have hardly been convincing.

71. See Hoffmann, *Reform,* pp. 272–74.

72. See the recent studies by W. Richter, *Traditionsgeschichtliche Untersuchungen zum Richterbuch; Die Bearbeitungen des 'Retterbuches' in den deuteronomistischen Epoche.*

sponsible for the present collection. This can be seen, for instance, in the story of Ehud. The theological framework—the people's apostasy, the divine handing over of the people into the power of the enemy, their oppression and appeal for help, God's sending of a deliverer—is interwoven with the political background of the story so completely in 3:12–15 that it is difficult to extract an original literary stratum. The same is true for the story of Deborah and Barak, where the theological framework and the narrative setting are completely integrated in the introduction (4:1–4).[73]

In the case of Gideon too the political background to his exploits has been combined with the stereotyped themes of Dtr theology (6:1–6). But, in addition to this, Dtr has introduced the words of a prophet (6:7–10) who recounts the sacred history and issues a warning against the worship of the "gods of the Amorites."[74] This also has an interesting parallel in Samuel's words to the people on the occasion of their election of a king (1 Sam 10:17–29). What happens in both instances is the subsequent divine election of a leader to rescue the people from their enemy.[75]

Gideon is responsible, early in his career, for a cultic reform (6:25–32). The description of pulling down the altar of Baal and cutting down and burning the Asherah so clearly follows the language and prescriptions of Deuteronomy and Dtr that Hoffmann is justified in viewing it as a purely Dtr construction.[76] Later in his career Gideon introduces another cultic change by making an ephod from the golden objects taken in battle. But the ephod led to apostasy by causing the people to "play the harlot after it" so that it "became a snare" to Gideon's family (Judg. 8:27). Again the language is thoroughly Dtr and part of Dtr's larger history of cultic reform. Gideon represents a premonarchic example of both positive and negative cultic reform that anticipates the actions of the later kings of Israel and Judah. Further, the story of Gideon concludes with the people's apostasy and judgment (8:33–35), thus completing the cycle of the people's typical behavior as outlined in 2:11ff.

The theological framework introducing the story of Jephthah in 10:6–16 is much more extensive than in the previous stories.[77] Here Dtr elaborates on the theme of Israel's apostasy in the service of foreign gods, which results in Yahweh's anger and the Israelites' subsequent servitude to the Philistines and the Ammonites. Since these two powers dominate Israel's concerns until the time of David, the unit encompasses this larger history as well. Because of this oppression the people cry to Yahweh and in

73. Hoffmann, *Reform*, p. 273, n. 6.
74. For the Dtr character of this text (*contra* Richter) see Hoffmann, *Reform*, p. 275. Hoffmann regards the whole of Judg. 6:1–8:35 as a carefully constructed work of Dtr.
75. See also above, 8a.
76. *Reform*, pp. 275–78.
77. Ibid., pp. 280–87. Especially noteworthy are the comparisons that Hoffmann makes with 1 Sam. 12.

response they receive a divine oracle, much as in the case of the prophet's word in 6:8ff. At the same time the unit serves as a recapitulation and reenforcement of the themes of 2:6–21, which again are part of the larger cult history of Dtr.

Yet it would be wrong to view the introduction in 10:6–16 as merely an editorial digression or late addition, for the author is careful in 10:7–9 to set forth the political situation of Ammonite supremacy. This state of affairs is again picked up in 10:17–18, which provides the bridge to Jephthah's election as the people's leader in 11:4ff. Furthermore, the device of narrating negotiations between the two warring parties in 11:12–28 allows Dtr to once again recapitulate the sacred history of the exodus and conquest and to fully integrate the exploits of Jephthah into his history.

In addition to the theological framework, the author, Dtr, also assumes a chronological framework, a forty-year generation of rest from war after deliverance by a judge. Within this scheme are periods of various lengths, between the death of one judge and the "raising up" of another, during which the Israelites were under servitude to a foreign power. The analogy for such a chronological scheme is the chronological framework of the monarchy, so that Dtr had his chronological and theological framework for both the judges and the kings. We are reminded here of our earlier discussion of Herodotus and other early Greek historians, who, in the absence of a precise chronology for early Greek history, used an average length of 30, 33 ⅓, or 40 years per generation to complete their chronology.[78] Outside the Dtr scheme in Judges, and somewhat in tension with it, are the so-called minor judges of Judg. 10:1–5 and 12:8–15. These are secondary and should not be allowed to confuse the pattern.[79] It has also long been recognized that chapters 17–21 stand outside Dtr's work as later additions. They interrupt the continuity of the work from the time of Samson to the story of Samuel in 1 Sam. 1–7, and they will not be considered any further here.

The Dtr created the period of the judges out of his collection of hero stories by suggesting that during this time, between Israel's entrance into the land and the rise of the monarchy, a succession of magistrates ruled the people. Dtr was familiar with a type of magistrate known as a "judge" (šōfēt), who was more than the one who presided in a court of law. During periods of interregnums some of the Phoenician cities had apparently been governed by a nonhereditary officeholder with this title.[80] The application

---

78. See above, 2a.

79. These additions may be the hand of P. See especially the remarks of Burney, *Judges*, pp. 289–90.

80. Josephus, *Contra Ap.* I, 156ff. See also S. Moscati, *The World of the Phoenicians*, pp. 29, 132–33, 209–10. The fact that two judges were often appointed to one city may explain why both of Samuel's sons were associated with Beersheba (1 Sam. 8:1–2).

of such an institution to premonarchy Israel may be both anachronistic and artificial, since it presupposes a highly unified state, but it was Dtr's way of trying to come to terms with a little-known period of Israel's history. On the other hand, he made no effort to create any real uniformity among the rather broad diversity of persons who were thought to fill the ranks of the judges of this period, apart from the fact that they act in some way to deliver the people from their enemies—and even this needs qualification in some cases.

It is clear that for Dtr the story of Samson is not really the end of the line of judges, since both Eli and Samuel are to follow. These stories of heroes or deliverers were never intended as a self-contained collection. There would appear to be little point in such a collection since it is not the portrayal of a heroic age, such as we find in Homer. The so-called "pragmatic" theme would have little relevance by itself in a later age of the monarchy. The period of the judges could have significance only as part of a larger history, and that larger history of Israel could not be written without the history of the monarchy. The history of the books of Kings is the intellectual prerequisite for the history of the judges. Individual stories about events and persons could exist in the past, but to construe these events as related to each other in both a chronological and an ideological way is to make a conscious effort to write history.

e. 1 SAMUEL 1–7

The chapters in 1 Sam. 1–7 confront us once again with the question of the nature of Dtr's history. Was the material that he took up largely preformed, or did he extensively reshape the traditions for his own purposes? Is the hand of Dtr evident in only a few minor "redactional" additions, or does the material as a whole conform to his basic thematic concerns? How does this unit function as a bridge between the period of the judges and that of the monarchy?

It is easy to see how the subjects dealt with in these chapters fall into two blocks of material that can then be explained as separate sources or traditions having only a loose connection or secondary integration with each other.[81] One group of stories describe the birth and childhood of Samuel (1 Sam. 1:1–2:11, 18–21, 26; 3:1–4:1a) and his career as deliverer and judge (1 Sam. 7:3–16). A second set deals with the Ark of Yahweh and the fate of the priests who were in charge of it (1 Sam.

---

81. This is now the position of most of the recent commentaries. See H. W. Hertzberg, *I & II Samuel;* P. K. McCarter, *I Samuel, the Anchor Bible;* H. J. Stoebe, *Das erste Buch Samuelis.* Cf., however, the earlier commentaries, such as H. P. Smith, *Samuel,* where no such division is observed.

2:12–17, 22–25, 27–36; 4:1b–7:2). But these two subjects do not simply come together as two documents compiled and interwoven by an editor. They are not self-contained entities, and a different explanation is needed to understand their relationship to each other.

Let us first consider the story of Samuel. The narrative of Samuel's birth would certainly seem to be appropriate as a pious *vita* of a famous holy man, telling about his dedication to Yahweh from birth.[82] The one disturbing detail in this story, however, is the etymology given for his name in verse 20, which appears to derive it from the verb *š'l*, "to ask." This is reinforced by the frequent repetition of the verb in verses 27–28 and has led scholars to speculate that the birth story was originally about Saul, whose name is in fact derived from the verb *š'l*.[83] But since nothing in the story in any way fits Saul the king, there is no reason to suppose that a tradition about Saul's birth lies behind it.

It seems better to follow McCarter's suggestion, that the author really finds the etymology of the name Samuel ($\check{S}^e m\bar{u}'\bar{e}l$)in the phrase "from Yahweh" (*mē yhwh*), as if the name meant "the one who is from God" ($\check{S}e$ $m\bar{e}'\bar{e}l$).[84] Such etymological mistakes and shifts in pronunciation are not at all uncommon in biblical name etiologies. The further play on the verb *š'l* would then have to do, not with his name, but with his future destiny. The designation of a child's destiny is a common element in such birth stories.[85] Thus it is not necessary to see a connection with a possible Saul tradition.

There is therefore no need to separate Samuel's birth story on any literary or traditio-historical grounds from the subsequent account of his youth. The oath to dedicate Samuel is fulfilled in his subsequent employment under Eli in the temple (1 Sam. 2:11, 18–21, 26; 3:1–4:1a). This immediately raises the problem of the relationship of the account of Samuel's boyhood in the temple to the other texts about the sons of Eli. The texts about Samuel, when put together, do not read like an independent source; rather, their interpretation depends heavily upon how one understands this second block of material.

According to L. Rost, the story of the capture and return of the Ark —often called the Ark Narrative—originally existed as a separate document.[86] Rost believes this work included not only 1 Sam. 4:1b–7:2 but

82. On the *vita* of a holy man, see A. Rofé, "The Classification of the Prophetical Stories," *JBL* 89 (1970):435–39.
83. Note especially *hû' šā'ûl leyhwh*, v. 28.
84. McCarter, *I Samuel*, p. 62.
85. R. Neff, "The Birth and Election of Isaac in the Priestly Tradition," *Biblical Research* 15 (1970):5–18.
86. L. Rost, "Die Überlieferung von der Thronnachfolge Davids," in *Das kleine Credo*, pp. 122–59. Other recent studies that use Rost's work as a point of departure for their own

also 2 Sam. 6, which tells of David bringing the Ark into Jerusalem. He considers this document an early source used by the author of the Succession Story, since the latter added 2 Sam. 6:16, 20–23 in order to incorporate the Ark Narrative into his own work. For Rost this means that the Ark Narrative must have been a document of the early monarchy, since he dates the Succession Story to the Solomonic era. This early dating has caused any signs of lateness in all subsequent treatments of the Ark Narrative to be judged as editorial additions. In the previous discussion, however, I questioned the early dating of the Succession Story, which I called the Court History; this removes the major argument for viewing the Ark Narrative as an early source.[87]

A recent study by P. D. Miller and J. J. M. Roberts poses some serious questions about the limits of the Ark Narrative as defined by Rost.[88] The basic issue for Miller and Roberts is whether or not the Ark Narrative could simply begin with 1 Sam. 4:1b, without prior dependence on, or connection with, what has gone before. They correctly conclude that this cannot be the case. The events recounted in chapter 4 raise the obvious questions of why Israel suffered this great defeat at the hands of the Philistines and why special attention is given to the calamities of the household of Eli. For the reader, these questions have already been answered by the previous descriptions of the impious actions of the priests Hophni and Phinehas (the sons of Eli) in Sam. 2:12–17 and 22–25 and the subsequent prediction of disaster upon the household of Eli in 1 Sam. 2:27–36.[89] Since the remarks about the sacrilegious behavior of the sons of Eli and the description of their ultimate fate fit so well together, it does not seem persuasive to attribute these two groups of texts to different sources.

The addition of these verses (2:12–17, 22–25, 27–36) to the Ark Narrative, however, does not entirely solve the problem, for some introduction to the figure of Eli is demanded not only by chapter 4 but also by 2:12ff. Miller and Roberts have responded to this problem by suggesting that some additional introductory material has been lost or displaced in the process of connecting the story of the Ark with the story of Samuel.[90] But this explanation seems unnecessarily complicated, since the preceding pe-

---

analysis are: F. Schicklberger, *Die Ladeerzählung des ersten Samuel-Buches: Eine literaturwissenschaftliche und theologiegeschichtliche Untersuchung*; A. F. Campbell, *The Ark Narrative (1 Sam. 4–6; 2 Sam. 6): A Form-Critical and Traditio-Historical Study.*

87. See above, 8d.

88. P. D. Miller, Jr., and J. J. M. Roberts, *The Hand of the Lord: A Reassessment of the "Ark Narrative" of 1 Samuel.*

89. McCarter (*I Samuel*, p. 26) concurs with the analysis of Miller and Roberts, with the qualification that 2:27–36 is a later Deuteronomistic addition. But this has rather serious consequences for the basic thesis of Miller and Roberts, which McCarter too easily ignores.

90. *The Hand of the Lord*, p. 19. The technique of the "lost beginning" or "lost ending" is a frequently used, but quite dubious, method of literary criticism.

ricope in 1 Sam. 1:1–2:11 does provide a suitable introduction to the figure of Eli. In fact, 2:11 leads directly into 2:12. Furthermore, if we put together all the remarks about Eli—his age, his eyesight, his position as seated at the door of the Temple or the gate of the city—we find a remarkable consistency that goes beyond the necessity of redactional integration.[91] The major argument against the unity of the story of Samuel and the Ark Narrative is that Samuel does not figure in the action of 4:1b–7:2. Yet, given the circumstances described in the Ark Narrative, it is hardly suitable for him to have any place in the narrative at this point.

Where the Ark Narrative ends has also become a disputed issue. Rost views 2 Sam. 6 as the climax to the Ark Narrative, but this has recently been questioned by Miller and Roberts.[92] They point to an obvious break in continuity between 1 Sam. 7:1 and 2 Sam. 6:1, as indicated by a change in the name of the place where the Ark was kept, from Kiriath-jearim to Baalejudah, and a change in the names of those in charge of the Ark, from Eleazar to Uzzah and Ahio (although all three are called sons of Abinadab). The alternative proposed by Miller and Roberts is that the Ark Narrative ends in 1 Sam. 7:1. But this hardly seems an adequate ending to the story. The Ark is only temporarily housed, with one consecrated priest in attendance. This scarcely fulfills what they regard as the whole point of the story, the prophecy of the "faithful priest" and his "sure house" who "shall go in and out before my anointed forever" (2:35). This prediction must surely refer to the establishment of an important priestly family to be in charge of the Temple in Jerusalem.[93]

The problem with this debate is the assumption by all these scholars that the Ark Narrative is a self-contained story. If, however, this is no more the case for the end of the story than for the beginning, then the lack of direct continuity between 1 Sam. 7:1 and 2 Sam. 6 is no difficulty. The latter text would take for granted that some time had elapsed between the two parts of the story, and this is just what is indicated in 1 Sam. 7:2.[94] Furthermore, the similarities between the two parts of the Ark Narrative greatly outweigh the minor differences.

It has already been noted above at several points that the Ark theme played a vital role in the Dtr history beginning with the crossing of the Jordan, which is the first miracle produced by the Ark. This is followed immediately by the conquest of Jericho, which results from the simple procession with the Ark around the city. Then the ark theme disappears from view until the episodes of the Ark Narrative. Immediately following the

91. See 1:9, 12ff.; 2:22; 3:2; 4:13, 15, 18.
92. *Hand of the Lord,* pp. 22–26.
93. See McCarter, *I Samuel,* pp. 91–93.
94. Miller and Roberts (*Hand of the Lord,* p. 20) regard this text as redactional.

restoration of the Ark and its location in Jerusalem is the divine promise to David, which is closely related to his wish to properly house the Ark in a temple.[95] But the climax for Dtr is not reached until the Ark finds its permanent resting place in the Solomonic Temple.[96] The Ark Narrative is just part of the wider theme of the Ark as the symbol of the divine presence; implicit in the one Ark are the notions of unification and centralization of worship.

It is widely recognized that Dtr often referred to the Ark as the "Ark of the Covenant of Yahweh/God" because he regarded it as the respository of the covenant laws of Deuteronomy.[97] Thus the term is used frequently in Dtr's story of the Jordan crossing along with the more abbreviated forms. When this Dtr designation occurs in 1 Sam. 4:3–5, however, it is dismissed as a redactional addition, although it is hard to explain, if this were the case, why this change was not made throughout. From the viewpoint of the story it makes sense to use the longer form at the beginning, and especially in conjunction with the Israelites' hope that the presence of the Ark will save them. In enemy territory the Ark would scarcely be recognized as "the Ark of the Covenant." Instead, the phrase "the Ark of the God of Israel" comes to the fore, especially in the mouths of the Philistines, revealing the author's sensitivity for the appropriateness of the terminology he employs.

Of special interest is the author's designation in 1 Sam. 4:4—"the Ark of the Covenant of Yahweh who is enthroned on the cherubim." This designation is similar to the one in 2 Sam. 6:2—"the Ark of God, which is called by the name of Yahweh of hosts who is enthroned on the cherubim"—and calls for special comment. The title of God as the one enthroned upon the cherubim is very likely derived from the liturgical tradition and refers to God as king upon the heavenly throne.[98] According to the Dtr's description of the Temple, great cherubim were constructed in the holy of holies in such a way that the Ark could be placed under the outstretched wings; together they were regarded as the seat of the deity.[99] Thus Dtr is responsible for the juxtaposition of the Ark as the portable throne of the deity with the symbols of the cherubim and the special divine title of the one "enthroned on the cherubim." Dtr goes further and also associates the "glory," kābôd, with the Ark, both in 1 Sam. 4:21–22 and in

95. 2 Sam. 7:1ff.
96. 1 Kings 8.
97. Deut. 10:1–5.
98. See Pss. 80:2; 91:1; Isa. 6:1–2.
99. 1 Kings 8:6–7. The P version in Exod. 25:10–22 seems to have taken the development a step further by actually making the cherubim and the "mercy-seat" a part of the Ark itself.

the description of the placing of the Ark in the Temple in 1 Kings 8:11.[100]

Furthermore, once it is admitted that 1 Sam. 2:27–36 is part of the Ark Narrative, then the case for Dtr authorship of the whole becomes very strong indeed.[101] There is no question that the notion of Yahweh's election of his people while they were in Egypt, and the special election of one place out of all the tribes as a place of worship, are Deuteronomic themes. Here Dtr adds to these, using the same terminology, the special election of a priestly house. This is not the house of Aaron, of which Dtr knows nothing.[102] Instead it is the priestly office that continued from the time of the Exodus through the period of the judges to the very beginning of the monarchy. This original priesthood, like the Davidic monarchy, had been assured a perpetual succession, but now through the disobedience of Eli's sons it is rejected, and the author has the deity declare: "I will raise up for myself a faithful priest, who shall do according to what is in my heart and in my mind; and I will build him a sure house, and he shall go in and out before my anointed forever." The pattern here is exactly the same as that used in the rejection of Saul and the election of David to replace him. It also parallels the promise to David of a "sure house" and clearly refers to the Zadokite priesthood established by David for the service of the Jerusalem Temple. A new era is marked not only by the election of David and the building of the Temple but also by the beginning of a new priestly line.[103] We cannot maintain that this unit contains only a few phrases of Dtr editing. The whole conception suggests the same Dtr hand that we have seen before, the same schematization of history, the same election and rejection dependent upon obedience to the law.[104]

100. Cf. Isa. 6:1–5 with its combination of Yahweh of hosts enthroned as king, winged seraphim, and the "glory."

101. See also McCarter's arguments (*I Samuel*, pp. 91–93) for Dtr authorship. On the other hand, the arguments for associating this prediction in 2:27–36 with the outcome of events in chap. 4 are equally convincing. McCarter (p. 98) is also forced to suggest that 3:11–14 has been revised to accommodate 2:27–36. All these problems would be solved by admitting that chaps. 2–4 were by the same author.

102. The reference to Aaron in Deut. 9:20 appears to me to be secondary and presupposes the story in Exod. 32. The unit in Deut. 33:48–52, in which the name of Aaron occurs (v. 50), is also secondary. In the rest of Deuteronomy Aaron and a special Aaronic priesthood play no role.

103. The notion of beggar priests (Levites), 2:36, who were disinherited, coming to the Jerusalem priesthood for employment is a direct allusion to the consequences of the Josiah reform. See also McCarter, *I Samuel*, p. 93.

104. The reference in 1 Kings 2:27, on the other hand, does not belong to Dtr but to the later Court History, as I have argued above (8d). The connection of Abiathar with the house of Eli is a weak one and may be entirely artificial and of late polemical intent. The genealogical line is traced back through 1 Sam. 22:20 and 14:3, but this last reference is rather curious, because only by identifying Ahitub as Ichabod's brother is the line traced back to Eli. Yet why was it necessary to mention Ichabod at all, since the latter must have been a younger brother to Ahitub, if we are to believe this statement? The connection of Ahitub with the

If 1 Sam 2:27–36 is indeed the work of Dtr and is part of the larger Ark Narrative as well, then the question of the meaning of the Ark Narrative must be addressed anew. Miller and Roberts are correct in stressing that the Ark Narrative, at least in chapters 4–6, is primarily concerned with the theological question of whether or not the capture of the Ark as the symbol of the divine presence really signaled the defeat of Yahweh. They bring forward a considerable body of comparative Near Eastern material to suggest that the capture and carrying off of one's gods was a common subject of religious texts among the ancients; such an event called forth a variety of responses, both on the occasions of defeat or victory and when the gods were returned to their rightful owner. From this they argue that the Ark Narrative represents a document written on the occasion of the actual return of the Ark from the hands of the Philistines as portrayed in this account. Yet at this point their argument seems rather weak, especially since they exclude 2 Sam. 6 from consideration. It is difficult to believe that the occasion for the Ark Narrative may be found in the remarks about the return of the Ark to its temporary lodging in the house of Abinadab and to see in Eleazar the "faithful priest" (1 Sam. 7:1; cf. 2:35).

Once the story is seen in its larger Dtr context, however, another major concern immediately comes to mind—the exile. It is precisely at this time that "the glory has been *exiled* from Israel" (1 Sam. 4:21, 22).[105] What happened to the Ark at the time of the fall of Jerusalem is unknown, but there is no reason to doubt that it was part of the booty taken from the Temple. Yet the larger question that was being addressed in this story about an earlier capture of the Ark was whether the deity was now subject to the foreign gods or still in control of the affairs of men. In somewhat different, though related, ways, Dtr and Ezekiel answer this question by affirming the latter.

This brings us to a consideration of 1 Sam. 7:3–17.[106] This pericope, as we have it, presupposes the prior introduction of Samuel in the previous chapters. It also takes for granted that the Israelites have suffered defeat and are subservient to the Philistines, and that "all the house of Israel lamented after Yahweh" (7:2). This last verse is not just a transition to a new unit but a necessary introduction to what follows. In this chapter

---

priestly family of Eli looks forced indeed, but it is hard to say who was responsible for it. It probably grew out of the postexilic controversies over priestly authority.

105. The notion of the "glory" of Yahweh leaving the Temple and going into exile is also strong in Ezek. 8–10.

106. Noth (*ÜS*, pp. 54ff.) has identified this chapter as substantially the work of Dtr. Some recent studies have attempted to find some older traditional material within it. See A. Weiser, *Samuel: Seine geschichtliche Aufgabe und religiöse Bedeutung*, pp. 5–24; B. Birch, *The Rise of the Israelite Monarchy*, pp. 11–21.

Samuel fulfills the twofold role of prophet and deliverer-judge. In his capacity as prophet, he preaches to the people in Dtr style to repent from their worship of foreign gods and to serve Yahweh alone, as in the prologue of Judges. In his role as deliverer-judge, Samuel rescues the people from the hand of the Philistines.[107] One cannot fail to see that Samuel is being presented as the last of the victorious judges who was able to subdue the enemy and bring peace to the Israelites during his period of office.[108] The victory at Ebenezer also provides a contrast to the earlier Israelite defeat there, and so properly completes this series of episodes. At the same time Samuel's career brings to a close the era of the judges, since the story of Samuel would have followed from the end of Samson's career in Judges 16.[109]

1 Sam. 1–7 is the work of Dtr combining two themes, the story of Samuel and the Ark Narrative. These were never independent documents, and it is scarcely possible, in my view, to recover earlier stages in the tradition of these themes, if they ever existed. The way they are presented, however, provides not only a continuity with the age of the judges but also a strong link between the age of Moses/Joshua on the one hand and David/Solomon on the other, with the Ark serving as the primary connection. This means that we can affirm Noth's basic thesis that one continuous history runs through the period from Moses to the end of the monarchy.

107. Samuel's role in battle is not unlike Joshua's, especially in Josh. 10, where the victory is won through the prayer of the leader.

108. There is admittedly some inconsistency between 7:13 and the later suggestions of Philistine domination in chaps. 9ff. But 7:13 is so obviously stated in terms of the Dtr formula that its lateness can hardly be doubted. The pattern of judgeships being quite separate from each other, as in Judges, breaks down with Eli, Samuel, and the careers of Saul and David. The pattern has thus been made to fit material that was not entirely suitable for it. The author (Dtr) really regards the "days of Samuel" as closed at the end of chap. 7 but must have a new situation of need to account for the rise of Saul.

109. I do not think that we can speak of 1 Sam. 7 as a prophetic story that has been supplemented and reworked by Dtr (see McCarter, *I Samuel*, pp. 149ff.). I find no evidence of an earlier stratum distinct from the work of Dtr, and unless this can be demonstrated more convincingly, I view it all as the work of Dtr.

CHAPTER ELEVEN

CONCLUSIONS

The search for the intellectual form of history in ancient Israel has taken us through a maze of critical discussion and historiographic works of great variety. It remains for me now to draw together some of the implications and conclusions of this study. But even beyond the presentation of my own reconstruction of the development of Israel's history writing, it is my hope that this survey has opened up the study of historiography in the ancient world beyond the specialties of the scholar in any one area of this broad field.

I have focused this search on Huizinga's definition of history as an intellectual form of corporate self-understanding because I regard the question of genre as the key issue in the discussion, whether we are dealing with the biblical authors or the Greek and Near Eastern materials. Thus I have pursued an investigation of many traditional genres that make use of, or are interested in, the past and that might be related to the particular traditional form—history writing. A discussion about the "ideas of history," or causation in human affairs, or critical and objective reporting of past events, while not without some value, too often misses the mark.

The various chapters on the Greek and Near Eastern historiographic genres have provided a broad basis for comparison with biblical historiography, even if the similarities have not always been explicitly stated. This survey can also help us determine more clearly what particular streams of foreign influence and what possible set of historiographic genres played a role in the earliest histories. At the same time it should caution us against the abuse of such terms as annals, chronicles, and court histories, as if these genres existed in every Near Eastern state and their form and function were self-evident.

Noteworthy also are the many different ways in which public or political interest in the past can be expressed, often yielding much important historical information and insight. And yet for the Egyptians, the Hittites, and the nations of Mesopotamia these historiographic genres did not lead to true history writing. Insofar as the king, his dynasty, or even kingship itself was the focus of such texts, they did not develop into a form of tradition encompassing the people as a whole. To be sure, the king was both public and political and his deeds were of great significance to the nation. But only when the nation itself took precedence over the king, as happened in Israel, could history writing be achieved.

On the question of history's intellectual form, I have argued for a reevaluation of the Gunkel-von Rad· thesis, that history writing arose in Israel (and hence in Western civilization in general) in the Davidic-Solomonic period. Their proposed evolution of narration from legend to history writing is untenable, as is the combination of this literary scheme with a theory of sociological development from primitive tribalism to the unified political state.[1] In chapter 7 I have called into question the numerous modifications of their views proposed by subsequent scholars. Nor can I accept the alternative proposals that historiography developed out of an epic tradition or that the biblical histories correspond to sagas in the Norwegian sense of the term. The introduction raises serious questions in response to these suggestions on general theoretical grounds, and the subsequent examination of the biblical texts themselves finds no support for these views. The failure of previous theories concerning the rise of Israelite historiography is due largely to an inadequate treatment of the comparative literature, both classical and ancient Near Eastern.

Important to virtually all previous discussion of Israelite historiography has been the conviction that the books of Samuel contain a number of early historiographic works, such as the Story of Saul, the Story of David's Rise, and above all, the Court History or Succession Story. These supposedly independent works constitute, for many scholars, the high point of history writing during the United Monarchy, a level that was never again achieved in subsequent periods. This study has shown that the Court History was not contemporary historical reporting but a post-Dtr work of quite a different kind. Near-contemporary reporting of events in an objective manner cannot be the criterion for judging the existence of history writing in ancient Israel. As for the rest of the stories in Samuel, they are pieces within the larger Dtr work, much like the various *logoi*[2] of Herodotus's *Histories*. They never had an independent existence of their own.

This study also disputes the existence of "collections" (*Sammelwerken*) as a hypothetical intermediate stage in the development of history writing. This suggestion, in fact, contains a serious contradiction. It has often been

1. For the latest critique on Gunkel's treatment of legend, see S. M. Warner, "Primitive Saga Men," *VT* 29 (1979):325–35.

2. *Logos* is a technical term used in classical studies to designate a self-contained piece of prose such as a story or a section within Herodotus's history.

observed that the other Near Eastern civilizations were given to the making of lists and collections but never moved beyond this to history writing.[3] Yet in spite of the Near Eastern propensity for collections, we cannot find any that correspond to such collections of stories as have frequently been proposed in the analyses of Judges and Samuel. As is evident from the early Greek historians ("logographers"), and from Herodotus in particular, this kind of collecting arises only out of a much broader historiographic concern, namely, to create a historical continuum through a set period of time.[4] It was Dtr himself who collected his material and put it into the sequence and chronological scheme in which it now appears from Deuteronomy to 2 Kings.

The writing of history, in both ancient Greece and Israel, made use of several historical and chronographical genres, even though, strictly speaking, it did not directly evolve out of any one of them or all of them together. One of these genres is the king list, from which the chronologies of the histories are derived. When a history first correlated two separate king lists or other chronological schemes, a way of representing absolute historical time resulted. Nothing in the documents of the ancient Near East prior to the Dtr history contains such a correlation of chronologies.[5] In the event that a certain period of history was not represented by a king list, the historians of Greece and Israel had to resort to other means to make up the deficiency. Dtr, for instance, thought in terms of a succession of leaders (Moses to monarchy) and their corresponding generations, and gave a rough calculation of time in this way. Another method was the use of genealogies. However, these do not by themselves have an interest in time but only in genetic relationships, so they would not necessarily lead to the development of a chronology. Only in the interest of further lengthening a chronology that was already based upon some genuine chronographic source would a genealogy be converted into a way of measuring time and thus become useful for historiographic purposes. The early Greek historians and the Pentateuchal sources J and P both used this method in their historical works.

A second genre that probably contributed to the development of history writing is the royal inscription in all its varieties—annals, display or dedi-

---

3. See, e.g., the discussion by H. Gese, 7a.

4. In a somewhat similar fashion the late Babylonian chronicles dealing with early Mesopotamian history also put together a "collection" of various kinds of historical materials to create such a continuum (see above, 3d).

5. The Synchronistic History of the Assyrians is not a true example of this since it is not a continuous chronology and it correlates in only a general way the rulers of Assyria and Babylonia who were at war with each other. On this work see above, 3d. On the other hand, it was Herodotus who first produced a truly wide-ranging chronological correlation among a number of states.

cation inscriptions, letters to the god, memorial texts, etc. These set forth the great achievements of the ruler, primarily military campaigns and the building of temples and palaces. These texts have the appearance of contemporary reporting of great public events. Such inscriptions are usually presented in a highly stereotyped form, but at times the form gives way to real narrative drama, as in Thutmose III's Battle of Megiddo, Ramesses II's Victory at Kadesh, and the Eighth Campaign of Sargon II.

A third historical genre, and perhaps the most significant for historiography, is the chronicle. It combines precise chronology with the careful portrayal of political events. While the chronicle is not itself history writing, its form, at a certain point in its use, created the potential for the historical "research" and reconstruction of the past that is indispensable to the development of history writing. Babylonia, during the Chaldean renaissance, discovered that the chronicle form of the regular Babylonian Chronicle Series was a way of recreating the past from historical sources of various kinds. It is my belief that the nations of western Asia, and Israel in particular, followed this example. Examples of such chronicles containing antiquarian materials are the "Book of the Deeds of Solomon" and the "Chronicles of the Kings of Israel/Judah."

The past was used in many different ways and by means of many distinct forms to exercise an authority over institutions, customs, rights, and behavior.[6] An expansive portrayal of the past, however, could embody the explanation and the legitimation of all of these in one complex genre. The prestige of a dynasty, the primacy of a temple and its priesthood, the question of territorial rights and boundaries, civil and religious laws—all could be integrated and supported by one "history," instead of using a variety of forms, such as king lists, temple legends, priestly genealogies, treaty "histories," and law codes. The genius of the Dtr history is that it attempted such a wide-ranging integration of forms in order to set forth within one work the whole foundation of Israelite society.[7]

Israel's history writing, as represented by Dtr, is not limited to the integration into one work of a number of historical sources. It also represents the development of a narrative style that is able to incorporate much that is in the popular storytelling mode. It has much in common with oral forms, such as legends, but this does not mean that history writing itself evolved out of myths and legends, as earlier Old Testament scholars have proposed. Even though Herodotus was a great storyteller in his day, and

6. See the useful discussion on tradition by E. Shils, "Tradition," *CSSH* 13 (1971):122–59; also my earlier remarks in "History and Myth in Biblical Interpretation," *Andover Newton Quarterly* 8 (1968):154–62.

7. Compare this with the remarks by M. P. Nilsson (*Cults, Myths, Oracles, and Politics in Ancient Greece*, pp. 12–13) on the function of myth as the foundation of Greek society.

his history is replete with tales and legends, his work is not just a collection of folk traditions.[8] It has a design, a combination of disparate forms, a way of creating continuity, and a sense of unity and purpose throughout the whole, and these features do not derive from the stories themselves. In the same way Dtr makes use of many stories and popular traditions in his work, but he makes each fit his design for the whole. This is so clearly the case for so much of the material that indisputably belongs to him that if a story or episode does not fit, it must be suspected of not belonging to the original Dtr work.

Another parallel between Herodotus and Dtr is the way they combine popular stories into groups by means of a chronological framework or by a specific historical genre. Thus the Joshua narratives are shaped by the military invasion report while the judges' traditions are linked in chronological sequence, so that the judges resemble a succession of state magistrates. These blocks of material constitute *logoi* that have their own coherence; yet each forms part of the work as a whole. It might be tempting to view some of these—the conquest of Joshua, the stories of the judges, the Story of Saul, the Story of David's Rise, the Ark Narrative—as having had a life of their own. There is no more reason to believe that they did, however, than to dissect Herodotus's history and attribute all the pieces to prior "logographers."[9]

The comparative study of Herodotus and Dtr has also suggested that a variety of literary techniques were used in early historical prose narration to create a sense of unity in a long and complex work. These include parataxis (the repetition of a set formula or pattern as a connective) within a particular unit or *logos*; the use of speeches by major figures or the insertion of editorial comment to introduce or sum up the theme of a unit, or to provide a transition to the next unit; the periodization of history with the dovetailing of eras, themes, and *logoi*; the association of themes with principal figures—the law of Moses, the promise of David, the Temple of Solomon and its centralization by Josiah, the apostasy of Jeroboam; the pattern of prophecy and fulfillment, which may be used as two poles within a *logos* or as a link for quite widely separated units; and the use of analogies between the figures of history. An exhaustive list of such techniques cannot be given here. I have suggested throughout my comparative analysis that such literary devices were widely used both in the ancient Near East generally and in early Greek prose. What is sorely needed in the study of

8. For a useful discussion of the relationship between oral tradition and writing in ancient Greece (even though the study is now thirty years old), see W. C. Greene, "The Spoken and the Written Word," *Harvard Studies in Classical Philology* 9 (1951):23–59.

9. This is not to dispute that Herodotus made use of earlier writers as source material for his own work.

historiographic prose in the Old Testament is not the splitting up of prose works into various "traditions" in a highly speculative and uncontrolled fashion but a careful study of those literary qualities that the Old Testament shares with this large body of early prose works from antiquity.

Given the level of prose development for its time, the Dtr history is a literary work of superb accomplishment. It cannot be judged by the canons of narrative art as set down by Aristotle, or by the canons of historiography established by Thucydides, any more than it is reasonable to hold Herodotus to such standards. Dtr's unfortunate fate was that, unlike Herodotus, he remained anonymous, so that his work has been fractured into a number of canonical books or, worse yet, has been hopelessly dissected by modern scholars into numerous collections and redactions. Noth's recovery of this author is commendable, but Noth did not go far enough. He still attributed too little of the work to the author himself and too much to his sources and "traditions."

Once the Dtr history is divested of all its later additions, it has a remarkably uniform style and outlook. The history moves from the founding of the nation under Moses, through the conquest under Joshua and the rule of the judges, to the rise of the monarchy under Saul and David. The fortunes of the monarchy are traced from its height under Solomon, through its subsequent division and the unfolding fate of the two kingdoms, down to the exile and the author's own day. What is attempted is not merely a chronicle of events. Dtr's purpose, above all, is to communicate through this story of the people's past a sense of their identity—and that is the *sine qua non* of history writing. No other historical work of the ancient Near East reveals so broad a purpose as this.

The form of this national or corporate identity in Dtr's work is quite simple. It is expressed, first and foremost, in the Mosaic (Deuteronomic) covenant by which Israel became the people of Yahweh and Yahweh became their God. The birth of the nation was the exodus from Egypt, and the conditions for its life in the land of promise were the laws of Moses. Violations of those conditions and of loyalty to Yahweh could only result in death as a nation and expulsion from the land—which happened in the exile. Even after this disaster, Dtr did not alter his conception of the people's identity, and perhaps he harbored some hope for new national life through the people's repentance. Insofar as any of the other Near Eastern nations express a concept of identity through their historiographic forms, it is in the person of the king as the state. In Dtr the royal ideology is incorporated into the identity of the people as a whole ("*nāgîd* of my people, Israel"), so that the leaders of the people must always be obedient to the Mosaic covenant.

The question how this sense of the people's identity is so strong in the

Dtr's work deserves some further comment. The work is presented as the one integrating tradition[10]—the foundation for the whole society, laws and institutions, beliefs and social behavior—in place of the many separate traditions that legitimize beliefs and practices. The discovery of history writing is the discovery of the most comprehensive and authoritative genre of tradition. That Deuteronomy and Dtr were deeply concerned with the integration of tradition into a single authoritative form is evident in so much of the work—the emphasis on the one deity, the one ethical and religious code, the centralization of worship, the all-Israel orientation. Furthermore, a major task of Dtr's history appears to have been the combination and reconciliation of the northern Mosaic traditions, reflected in Deuteronomy, with the royal ideology of the house of David in the south. No one doubts that Deuteronomy was intended to be authoritative tradition. But the Dtr historian, by incorporating D into his expansive historical work, sought to be even more comprehensive in his formulation of the people's identity, which he saw as the foundation of their life.

One cannot just assume that ancient Israelites possessed some predisposing frame of mind that caused them to think in corporate terms about their past. Nevertheless, it is already evident that the eighth-century prophets addressed their message of moral responsibility to the people as a whole.[11] Hosea especially, by personifying Israel as a child or youthful bride in characterizing its early history, makes this corporate sense quite vivid.[12] Deuteronomy reflects the northern prophetic heritage but formulates this metaphorical language into a doctrine of Yahweh's election of Israel and of Israel's covenant commitment to Yahweh, handed down from the fathers to the sons. This prophetic sense of corporate responsibility, so strong in Deuteronomy, was the basis for the Dtr outlook as well.

The doctrine of Israel's election as the chosen people of Yahweh set the nation apart from other peoples. It was a special feature of its identity. All other callings and elections, whether to kingship, priesthood, or prophecy, were viewed in association with the choice of the people as a whole. Many of the Near Eastern historiographic documents that have to do with kingship deal with the special election of the king to rule, and even recount the divine providence by which he gained the throne and was victorious over his enemies. But nowhere outside of Israel was the notion of special election extended to the nation as a whole, such that the complete history of

10. I use the term *tradition* here in the broad sense as discussed by Shils (see n. 6, above).
11. See the remarks on the rise of popular prophecy by John S. Holladay, "Assyrian Statecraft and the Prophets of Israel," *HTR* 63 (1970):29–51. Holladay offers reasons for the suggestion that prophecy did not direct its message to the people as a whole, but merely to the king, until after ca. 750 B.C. Schmid (in *WuD* 13:16ff.) also sees the prophets as important in the rise of historiography.
12. Such images have a continuation into the late prophets, Jeremiah and Ezekiel.

the people could be viewed in this way. The fact that the theme of election gave the Dtr history a dominant theological orientation was enough reason, in Gunkel's view, to disqualify it as good historiography. All Hebrew historiography, however, is written from a theological perspective. Even the work of Herodotus has a strong interest in divine providence.

The Dtr history, as the authoritative "canonical" tradition, stimulated a variety of responses, as can be seen by the great diversity of additions that were made to the work. In some instances it provided the general context for short pieces with a moral or theological message;[13] in others it attracted the traditions of a specific group or faction, such as the Elisha cycle of stories. In the case of the Court History a rather drastic effort was made to reshape the history's perspective on the royal ideology, perhaps as a challenge to the use of the dynastic promise to David in postexilic messianism. The Court History is not more historical than Dtr because it reflects a greater verisimilitude to despotic oriental monarchies; the author simply has a different perception of the "historical" reality of monarchic rule and the relevance this view might have for his own time. These additions do not reflect upon the general question of Israelite identity but upon more specific theological and institutional lessons from the past. Consequently, they do not add anything directly to the discussion of the development of history writing in ancient Israel.

Yet other histories *were* written subsequent to Dtr's work and are directly related to it. One is the work of the Yahwist, who supplemented Dtr by extending the history back in time to the beginning of the world. This history has a different conception of corporate identity from that of Dtr and therefore makes a different selection of traditions and focuses upon a different period of history. J's use of the stories about the eponymous ancestors is meant to express a strong ethnic identity so important to a people scattered in exilic and diaspora communities.[14] In contrast to Dtr, J expresses this identity in a more universalistic fashion, both temporally and geographically, and as a positive relationship to "all the families/ nations of the earth."[15] P builds upon both J and Dtr a system of institutional and cultic identity that could be meaningful both for the diaspora Jews and for the renewed cultic community in Jerusalem. A strongly "revisionist" history is that of the Chronicler, who makes use of both the Pentateuch and the Dtr history (with additions) to rewrite the tradition.[16] He

13. See, e.g., 1 Kings 13.
14. See my treatment of this in "Confessional Reformulation in the Exilic Period," *VT* 22 (1972):448–59; and *Abraham in History and Tradition*, pp. 263–78; cf. Schmid, *WuD* 13:18ff., who also dates Pentateuchal historiography late.
15. Gen. 12:3; 18:18; 22:18; 26:4; 28:14.
16. See H. G. M. Williamson, *Israel in the Books of Chronicles*.

puts forward his own conception of David's founding of the Jerusalem religious community as the "kingdom of God," excluding or altering what is incompatible with this view.

A comprehensive study of these three histories still needs to be carried out. They employ historiographic styles and techniques that go beyond those observed in Dtr, and these also need to be compared with Greek and Near Eastern historiography. The relationship to, and comparison with, Dtr should also be explored much more fully than in these rather brief remarks. This is a rich lode to be mined in future research; only then can the full scope of Israel's early historiography be appreciated. Nevertheless, I hope I have demonstrated that the first Israelite historian, and the first known historian in Western civilization truly to deserve this designation, was the Deuteronomistic historian.

BIBLIOGRAPHY

Ackroyd, P. R. "The Succession Narrative (so-called)." *Interpretation* 35 (1981): 383–96.

Albrektson, B. *History and the Gods: An Essay on the Idea of Historical Events as Divine Manifestations in the Ancient Near East and in Israel.* Lund, 1967.

Albright, W. F. "The Eastern Mediterranean about 1060 B.C." In *Studies Presented to David Robinson,* edited by G. Mylonas, pp. 223–31. St. Louis, 1951.

———. *From the Stone Age to Christianity.* Baltimore, 1940.

———. "The New Assyro-Tyrian Synchronism and the Chronology of Tyre." *AIPHO* 13 (1953):1–9.

———. *Yahweh and the Gods of Canaan.* The Jordan Lectures, 1965. London, 1968.

Alt, A. "The Formation of the Israelite State in Palestine." Translated in *Essays on Old Testament History and Religion* by R. A. Wilson, pp. 173–237. Oxford, 1966. Originally published as *Die Staatenbildung der Israeliten in Palästina.* Leipzig, 1930.

Aly, W. *Volksmärchen, Sage und Novelle bei Herodot und seinen Zeitgenossen: Eine Untersuchung über die volkstümlichen Elemente der altgriechischen Prosaerzählung.* Göttingen, 1921.

Andersson, T. A. *The Icelandic Family Saga: An Analytic Reading.* Cambridge, 1967.

———. *The Problem of Icelandic Saga Origins.* New Haven and London, 1964.

Astour, M. C. *Hellenosemitica.* Leiden, 1967.

Auerbach, M., and Smolar, L. "Aaron, Jeroboam and the Golden Calves." *JBL* 86 (1967):129–40.

Baltzer, K. *Das Bundesformular.* 2d ed. WMANT 4, 1964. Translated by D. E. Green as *The Covenant Formulary in Old Testament, Jewish, and Early Christian Writings.* Oxford, 1971.

Barr, J. *Biblical Words for Time.* London, 1962.

———. "Philo of Byblos and His 'Phoenician History.'" *BJRL* 57 (1974):17–68.

Bartelmus, R. *Heroentum in Israel und seiner Umwelt: Eine traditionsgeschichtliche Untersuchung zu Gen. 6, 1–4 und verwandten Texten im Alten Testament und der altorientalischen Literatur.* AThANT 65. Zurich, 1979.

Baumgarten, A. I. *The Phoenician History of Philo of Byblos: A Commentary.* Leiden, 1981.

Baumgartner, W. *Zum Alten Testament und seiner Umwelt.* Leiden, 1959.

———. "Zur Form der assyrischen Königsinschriften." *OLZ* 27 (1924):313–17.

Benardete, S. *Herodotean Inquiries.* The Hague, 1969.

Bin-Nun, S. R. "Formulas from Royal Records of Israel and of Judah." *VT* 18 (1968):414–32.

Birch, B. C. "The Choosing of Saul at Mizpah." *CBQ* 37 (1975): 447–57.

————. "The Development of the Tradition on the Anointing of Saul in I Sam. 9:1–10:16." *JBL* 90 (1971):55–68.

————. *The Rise of the Israelite Monarchy: The Growth and Development of 1 Samuel 7–15*. Missoula, Montana, 1976.

Bittel, K. *Hattusha, the Capital of the Hittites*. New York, 1970.

Blankenberg-van Delden, C. *The Large Commemorative Scarabs of Amenhotep III*. Leiden, 1969.

Boecker, H. J. *Die Beurteilung der Anfänge des Königtums in den deuteronomistischen Abschnitten des 1. Samuelbuches: Ein Beitrag zum Problem des "Deuteronomistischen Geschichtswerkes."* WMANT 31, 1969.

Boman, T. *Hebrew Thought Compared with Greek*. London, 1960.

Borger, R. "Gott Marduk und Gott-König Šulgi als Propheten: Zwei prophetische Texte." *BiOR* 28 (1971):3–24.

Brandon, S. G. F. *History, Time and Deity*. New York, 1965.

Breasted, J. H. *Ancient Records of Egypt*. 5 vols. Chicago, 1906–07.

Bright, J. *Early Israel in Recent History Writing*. SBT 19. London, 1956.

————. *A History of Israel*. 2d ed. Philadelphia, 1972.

Brinkman, J. A. "Appendix: Mesopotamian Chronology of the Historical Period." In *Ancient Mesopotamia: Portrrait of a Dead Civilization*, by A. L. Oppenheim, pp. 335–52. Chicago and London, 1964.

————. "Comments on the Nassouhi Kinglist and the Assyrian Kinglist Tradition." *Orientalia* 42 (1973):306–19.

————. "Ur: 'The Kassite Period and the Period of the Assyrian Kings.'" *Orientalia* 38 (1969):310–48.

Brueggemann, W., and Wolff, H. W. *The Vitality of Old Testament Traditions*. Atlanta, 1975.

Bull, L. "Ancient Egypt." In *The Idea of History in the Ancient Near East*, edited by R. C. Dentan, pp. 1–34. New Haven and London, 1955.

Burney, C. F. *The Book of Judges, with Introduction and Notes*. 2d ed. London, 1930.

Burrows, M. "Ancient Israel." In *The Idea of History in the Ancient Near East*, edited by R. C. Dentan, pp. 99–131. New Haven and London, 1955.

Burstein, S. M. *The Babyloniaca of Berossus*. Malibu, Calif., 1979.

Butterfield, H. *The Origins of History*. New York, 1981.

Cambridge Ancient History, 3d ed. Vol. 2, pt. 1: *History of the Middle East and the Aegean Region c. 1800–1380 B.C.*, edited by I. E. S. Edwards, C. J. Gadd, N. G. L. Hammond, and E. Sollberger. Cambridge, 1973.

Cambridge Ancient History, 3d ed. Vol. 2, pt. 2: *History of the Middle East and the Aegean Region c. 1380–1000 B.C.*, edited by I. E. S. Edwards, C. J. Gadd, N. G. L. Hammond, and E. Sollberger. Cambridge, 1975.

Caminos, R. *The Chronicle of Prince Osorkon*. Analecta Orientalia 37. Rome, 1958.

Campbell, A. F. *The Ark Narrative (1 Sam. 4–6; 2 Sam. 6): A Form-Critical and Traditio-Historical Study*. SBL Dissertation Series 16. Missoula, Montana, 1975.

Cancik, H. *Grundzüge der hethitischen und alttestamentlichen Geschichtsschreibung*. Wiesbaden, 1976.

————. *Mythische und historische Wahrheit*. SB 48. Stuttgart, 1970.

Carter, H., trans. *The Histories of Herodotus of Halicarnassus*. 2 vols. New York, 1958.

Cassuto, U. "The Beginning of Historiography among the Israelites." In *Biblical and Oriental Studies*, ed. U. Cassuto. Vol. 1, pp. 7–16. Jerusalem, 1973.

———. "The Israelite Epic." In *Biblical and Oriental Studies*, vol. 2, pp. 69–109. Translated by Israel Abrahams. Jerusalem, 1975.

Cerny, J. *Paper and Books in Ancient Egypt*. London, 1952.

Chadwick, H. M., and N. K. *The Growth of Literature*. 3 vols. Cambridge, 1932–40.

Childs, B. S. "The Birth of Moses." *JBL* 84 (1965):109–22.

———. "Deuteronomic Formulae of the Exodus Traditions." In *Hebräische Wortforschung: Festschrift Walter Baumgartner*. SVT 16 (1967):30–39.

———. "The Etiological Tale Re-examined." *VT* 24 (1974):387–97.

———. *Memory and Tradition in Israel*. SBT 37. Naperville, Ill., 1962.

———. "A Study of the Formula 'Until this Day.' " *JBL* 82 (1963):279–92.

———. "Traditio-Historical Study of the Reed Sea Tradition." *VT* 20 (1970): 406–18.

Clements, R. E. "The Deuteronomistic Interpretation of the Founding of the Monarchy in I Sam. VIII." *VT* 24 (1974):398–410.

Coats, G. W. *Rebellion in the Wilderness*. Nashville and New York, 1968.

———. "The Song of the Sea." *CBQ* 31 (1969):1–17.

———. "The Traditio-Historical Character of the Reed Sea Motif." *VT* 17 (1967):253–65

———. "The Wilderness Itinerary." *CBQ* 34 (1972):135–52.

Cobet, J. "Fehling: Die Quellenangaben bei Herodot." *Gnomon* 46 (1974): 737–46.

Cogan, M., and Tadmor, H. "Gyges and Ashurbanipal: A Study in Literary Transmission." *Orientalia* 46 (1977):65–85.

Collingwood, R. G. *The Idea of History*. New York, 1956.

Conroy, C. "Hebrew Epic: Historical Notes and Critical Reflections." *Biblica* 61 (1980):1–30.

Creuzer, F. *Die historische Kunst der Griechen in ihrer Entstehung und Fortbildung*. 2d ed. Leipzig, 1845.

Cross, F. M. *Canaanite Myth and Hebrew Epic: Essays in the History of the Religion of Israel*. Cambridge, 1973.

Crüsemann, F. *Der Widerstand gegen das Königtum*. WMANT 49. Neukirchen-Vluyn, 1978.

Culley, R. C. "Structural Analysis: Is It Done with Mirrors?" *Interpretation* 28 (1974):165–81.

Curtis, E. L., and Madsen, A. A. *A Critical and Exegetical Commentary on the Books of Chronicles*. New York, 1910.

Davies, N. de G. *The Tomb of Rekh-mi-rēʿ at Thebes*. 2 vols. New York, 1944.

Debus, J. *Die Sunde Jerobeams*. FRLANT 93. Göttingen, 1967.

de Geus, C. H. J. "Richteren 1:1–2:5." *Vox Theologica* 36 (1966):32–53.

———. *The Tribes of Israel: An Investigation into Some of the Presuppositions of Martin Noth's Amphictyony Hypothesis*. Assen/Amsterdam, 1976.

Delekat, L. "Tendenz und Theologie der David-Solomon-Erzählung." In *Das ferne und nahe Wort*. BZAW 105 (1967):26–36.

Dentan, R. C., ed. *The Idea of History in the Ancient Near East*. New Haven and London, 1955.

Diakonoff, I. M. "A Babylonian Political Pamphlet from about 700 B.C." In *Studies in Honor of Benno Landsberger on his 75th Birthday, April 25, 1965*, pp. 343–49. Chicago, 1965.

Dietrich, M. *Ugarit-Bibliographie*. AOAT 20. Kevelaer, 1973.

Dietrich, M., Loretz, O., and Sanmartin, J. *Die keilalphabetischen Texte aus Ugarit*. Pt. 1: *Transcription*. AOAT 24. Kevelaer, 1976.

Dietrich, W. *Prophetie und Geschichte: Ein redaktionsgeschichtliche Untersuchung zum deuteronomistischen Geschichtswerk*. FRLANT 108. Göttingen, 1972.

Dossin, G. "L'inscription de fondation de Iaḫdum-Lim, roi de Mari." *Syria* 32 (1955):1–28.

Drews, R. "The Babylonian Chronicles and Berossus." *Iraq* 37 (1975):39–55.

———. *The Greek Accounts of Eastern History*. Washington, D. C., 1973.

Edel, E. "Die Stelen Amenophis II aus Karnak und Memphis." *ZDPV* 69 (1953): 98–176.

Eissfeldt, O. *Die Komposition der Samuelisbücher*. Leipzig, 1931.

———. *The Old Testament: An Introduction*. Translated by P. R. Ackroyd. New York, 1965. Originally published as *Einleitung in das Alte Testament*. 3d ed. Tübingen, 1964.

———. *Sanchunjaton von Berut und Ilumilku von Ugarit*. Beiträge zur Religionsgeschichte des Altertums, vol. 5. Halle (Saale), 1952.

Eliade, M. *Cosmos and History: The Myth of the Eternal Return*. New York, 1959.

Ellis, M. de J., ed. *Essays on the Ancient Near East in Memory of Jacob Joel Finkelstein*. Memoirs of the Connecticut Academy of Arts and Sciences, December, vol. 19. Hamden, Conn., 1977.

Ellis, R. S. *Foundation Deposits in Ancient Mesopotamia*. New Haven, 1968.

Emery, W. B. *Archaic Egypt*. Baltimore, 1961.

Erman, A. *The Ancient Egyptians: A Sourcebook of Their Writings*. Translated by A. M. Blackman, with introduction by W. K. Simpson. New York, 1966.

Evelyn-White, H. G., trans. *The Homeric Hymns and Homerica/Hesiod*. LCL. Cambridge, Mass., 1936.

Fales, F. M. "Kilamuwa and the Foreign Kings." *WO* 10 (1979):6–22.

Fehling, D. *Die Quellenangaben bei Herodot: Studien zur Erzählkunst Herodots*. Berlin and New York, 1971.

Fichtner, J. "Die etymologische Ätiologie in den Namengebungen der geschichtlichen Bücher des AT." *VT* 6 (1956):372–96.

Filippi, W. de. "A Reappraisal of the Ashurnasirpal Text in King's College, Halifax." *RA* 68 (1974):141–48.

Finkelstein, J. J. "The Genealogy of the Hammurapi Dynasty." *JCS* 20 (1966): 95–118.

———. "Mesopotamian Historiography." *PAPS* 107 (1963):461–72.

Finley, M. I., ed. *The Greek Historians: The Essence of Herodotus, Thucydides, Xenophon, and Polybius*. New York, 1959.

Flanagan, J. W. "Court History or Succession Document? A Study of 2 Samuel 9–20 and 1 Kings 1–2." *JBL* 91 (1972):172–81.

Fohrer, G. "'Amphictyony' und 'Bund.'" *TLZ* 91 (1961), cols. 801–16, 893–903.

———. *Introduction to the Old Testament*. Translated by D. E. Green. Nashville, 1968. Originally published as *Einleitung in das Alte Testament*. Heidelberg, 1965.

Fornara, C. W. *Herodotus: An Interpretative Essay*. Oxford, 1971.

Frankfort, H. *The Birth of Civilization in the Near East.* Garden City, N.Y., no date.
———. *Kingship and the Gods.* Chicago, 1948.
Frazer, J. G. *Folklore in the Old Testament.* New York, 1975.
Freedman, D. N. "Pentateuch." In *IDB,* vol. 3, pp. 711–27.
Friedman, R. E. *The Exile and Biblical Narrative: The Formation of the Deuteronomistic and Priestly Works.* Chico, Calif., 1981.
Fritz, K. von. *Die griechische Geschichtsschreibung.* Vol. 1: *Von den Anfängen bis Thukydides.* Text and *Anmerkungen.* Berlin, 1967.
———. "Herodotus and the Growth of Greek Historiography." *TAPA* 67 (1936): 315–40.
Gadd, C. J. "The Harran Inscriptions of Nabonidus." *AnSt* 8 (1958):35–92.
Gardiner, A. H. *Ancient Egyptian Onomastica.* 3 vols. London, 1947.
———. *Egypt of the Pharaohs: An Introduction.* Oxford, 1961.
———. *The Kadesh Inscriptions of Ramesses II.* Oxford, 1960.
———. *The Royal Canon of Turin.* Oxford, 1959
Gardiner, A. H.; Peet, T. E.; and Černý, J. *The Inscriptions of Sinai.* 2 vols. London, 1952–55.
Gelb, I. J. "Two Assyrian King Lists." *JNES* 13 (1954):209–30.
Gese, H. "Geschichtliches Denken im Alten Orient und im Alten Testament." *ZThK* 55 (1958):127–45. Translated by J. F. Ross as "The Idea of History in the Ancient Near East and the Old Testament." *Journal for Theology and the Church*[2] (1965):49–64.
Goedicke, H. *The Report of Wenamun.* Baltimore and London, 1975.
Goetze, A. *Hethitische Texte in Umschrift, mit Übersetzung und Erläuterungen.* Vol 6: *Die Annalen des Muršiliš* . M V–A G 38. Leipzig, 1933.
———. "Historical Allusions in Old Babylonian Omen Texts." *JCS* 1 (1947):265.
———. *Kleinasien.* 2d ed. Munich, 1957.
Goody, J. R., and Watt, I. "The Consequences of Literacy." In *Literacy in Traditional Societies,* edited by J. R. Goody, pp. 27–68. Cambridge, 1968.
Gray, J. *I & II Kings: A Commentary.* Philadelphia, 1963.
Grayson, A. K. *Assyrian and Babylonian Chronicles.* Locust Valley, N.Y., 1975.
———. "Assyrian and Babylonian King Lists: Collations and Comments." *Lišān mithurti. Festschrift W. von Soden.* AOAT 1, pp. 265–77. Neukirchen-Vluyn, 1969.
———. *Assyrian Royal Inscriptions.* 2 vols. Wiesbaden, 1972–76.
———. *Babylonian Historical-Literary Texts.* Toronto and Buffalo, 1975.
———. "Chronicles and the Akītu Festival." In *Actes de la XVIIe Rencontre Assyriologique Internationale,* pp. 160–70. Brussels, 1969.
———. "Divination and the Babylonian Chronicles." In *La Divination en Mésopotamie Ancienne et dans les Régions Voisines,* pp. 69–76. XIVe Rencontre Assyriologique Internationale. Vendôme, France, 1966.
———. "The Early Development of Assyrian Monarchy." *UF* 3 (1971):311–19.
———. "The Empire of Sargon of Akkad." *AfO* 25 (1974/77):56–64.
———. "Histories and Historians of the Ancient Near East: Assyria and Babylonia." *Orientalia* 49 (1980):140–94.
Grayson, A. K., and Lambert, W. G. "Akkadian Prophecies." *JCS* 18 (1964): 7–30.
Greene, W. C. "The Spoken and the Written Word." *Harvard Studies in Classical Philology* 9 (1951):23–59.

Gressmann, H. *Die älteste Geschichtsschreibung und Prophetie Israels.* SAT II/1. Göttingen, 1910; 2d ed., 1921.

———. *Mose und seine Zeit.* FRLANT 1. Göttingen, 1913.

Grønbaek, J. H. *Die Geschichte vom Aufstieg Davids (1 Sam. 15–2 Sam. 5):Tradition und Komposition.* AThD 10. Copenhagen, 1971.

Gunkel, H. *Genesis, übersetzt und erklärt.* HKAT I/1. Göttingen, 1901; 3d ed., 1910.

———. "Geschichtsschreibung im A.T." *RGG,* vol. 2, pp. 1348–54. *RGG²,* vol. 2, pp. 1112–15.

———. "Die israelitische Literatur." In *Die orientalischen Literaturen,* edited by P. Hinneberg, pp. 53–112. Leipzig, 1906; 2d ed., 1925. Reprinted as *Die israelitische Literatur.* Darmstadt, 1963.

———. *The Legends of Genesis.* Translated by W. H. Carruth. Chicago, 1901. Reprinted, with a new introduction by W. F. Albright. New York, 1964.

Gunn, D. M. "Narrative Patterns and Oral Tradition in Judges and Samuel." *VT* 24 (1974):303–11.

———. *The Story of King David: Genre and Interpretation.* JSOT suppl. 6. Sheffield, Eng., 1978.

———. "Traditional Composition in the 'Succession Narrative.'" *VT* 26 (1976): 214–29.

Gurney, O. R. *The Hittites.* 3d ed. London, 1961.

Güterbock, H. G. "The Deeds of Suppiluliuma as Told by His Son, Mursili II." *JCS* 10 (1956):41–50; 59–68; 75–85; 90–98; 107–30.

———. "Die historische Tradition und ihre literarische Gestaltung bei Babyloniern und Hethitern bis 1200." *ZA* 42 (1934):1–91 and *ZA* 44 (1938):45–149.

———. "The Hittite Conquest of Cyprus Reconsidered." *JNES* 26 (1967):73–81.

———. "Sargon of Akkad Mentioned by Ḫattušili I of Ḫatti." *JCS* 18 (1964):1–6.

Habachi, L. *The Second Stela of Kamose and His Struggle against the Hyksos Ruler and His Capital.* Glückstadt, 1972.

Habel, N. "The Form and Significance of the Call Narratives." *ZAW* 77 (1965): 297–323.

Hallo, W. W. "Akkadian Apocalypses." *IEJ* 16 (1966):231–42.

———. "Antediluvian Cities." *JCS* 23 (1970):57–67.

———. "Assyrian Historiography Revisited." In *Eretz-Israel: Archaeological, Historical and Geographical Studies,* vol. 14, pp. 1–7. Jerusalem, 1978.

Hand, W. D. "Status of European and American Legend Study." *Current Anthropology* 6 (1965):439–46.

Hanson, P. D. "Rebellion in Heaven, Azazel, and Euhemeristic Heroes in 1 Enoch 6–11." *JBL* 96 (1977):195–233.

Hayes, W. C. "Notes on the Government of Egypt in the Late Middle Kingdom." *JNES* 12 (1953):31–39.

———. *The Scepter of Egypt.* New York, 1953.

Hecker, K. *Untersuchungen zur akkadischen Epik.* AOATS 8. Kevelaer, 1974.

Heidel, A. *The Gilgamesh Epic and Old Testament Parallels.* 2d ed. Chicago, 1949.

Helck, H. W. *Untersuchungen zu Manetho und den ägyptischen Königslisten.* Berlin, 1956.

Hermann, A. *Die ägyptische Königsnovelle.* Leipziger ägyptologische Studien 10. Glückstadt-Hamburg-New York, 1938.

Herrmann, S. "Autonome Entwicklungen in den Königreichen Israel und Juda." SVT 17 (1969):139–59.

————. "Die Königsnovelle in Ägypten und in Israel." *Wissenschaftliche Zeitschrift der Karl-Marx Universität Leipzig* 3/1 (1953/54):51–62.

Hertzberg, H. W. *I & II Samuel*. Philadelphia, 1964.

Hoffmann, H.-D. *Reform und Reformen: Untersuchungen zu einen Grundthema der deuteronomistischen Geschichtsschreibung*. AThANT 66. Zurich, 1980.

Hoffner, H. A., Jr. "Histories and Historians of the Ancient Near East: The Hittites." *Orientalia* 49 (1980):283–332.

————. "Propaganda and Political Justification in Hittite Historiography." In *Unity and Diversity: Essays in the History, Literature, and Religion of the Ancient Near East*, edited by H. Goedicke and J. J. M. Roberts, pp. 49–62. Baltimore and London, 1975.

————. Review of *Der Anitta-Text*, by Erich Neu. *BASOR* 226 (1977):78.

Holladay, J. S., Jr. "Assyrian Statecraft and the Prophets of Israel." *HTR* 63 (1970):29–51.

————. "The Day(s) the Moon Stood Still." *JBL* 87 (1968):166–78.

Holscher, G. *Geschichtsschreibung in Israel: Untersuchungen zum Jahwisten und Elohisten*. Rev. ed. Lund, 1952.

Huizinga, J. "A Definition of the Concept of History." In *Philosophy and History: Essays Presented to Ernst Cassirer*, edited by R. Klibansky and H. J. Paton, pp. 1–10. New York, 1963.

Immerwahr, H. R. *Form and Thought in Herodotus*. Cleveland, 1966.

Irwin, W. A. "The Orientalist as Historian." *JNES* 8 (1949):298–309.

Jackson, J. J. "David's Throne: Patterns in the Succession Story." *CJT* 11 (1965): 183–95.

Jacobsen, T. *The Sumerian King List*. Assyriological Studies no. 11. Chicago, 1939.

Jacoby, F. "The First Athenian Prose Writer." *Mnemosyne* 3d series, vol. 13 (1947):13–64.

————. *Die Fragmente der griechischen Historiker*. Berlin, 1923–58.

————. "Griechische Geschichtsschreibung." (1926). In *Abhandlungen zur griechischen Geschichtsschreibung von Felix Jacoby*. Leiden, 1956.

Jepsen, A. *Die Quellen des Königsbuches*. 2d ed. Halle, 1956.

Jolles, A. *Einfache Formen*. 2d ed. Tübingen, 1958.

Josephus. Vol. 1: *Contra Apion*. LCL. London and New York, 1926.

————. Vols. 4–8: *Jewish Antiquities*. LCL. Cambridge, Mass., and London, 1926.

Kammenhuber, A. "Die hethitische Geschichtsschreibung." *Saeculum* 9 (1958): 136–55.

Katzenstein, H. J. *The History of Tyre*. Jerusalem, 1973.

Kitchen, K. A. "The King List of Ugarit." *UF* 9 (1977):131–42.

————. *The Third Intermediate Period in Egypt (1100–650 B.C.)*. Warminster, Eng., 1973.

Klatt, W. *Hermann Gunkel: Zu seiner Theologie der Religionsgeschichte und zur Entstehung der formgeschichtlichen Methode*. FRLANT 100. Göttingen, 1969.

Klees, H. *Die Eigenart des griechischen Glaubens an Orakel und Seher*. Stuttgart, 1965.

Kleingünther, A. *Protos Heuretes: Untersuchungen zur Geschichte einer Fragestellung*. Philologus suppl. vol. 26, no. 1, 1933.

Knight, D. A. *Rediscovering the Traditions of Israel*. Rev. ed. Missoula, Montana, 1975.

Knudtzon, J. A. *Die El-Amarna Tafeln*. 2 vols. Leipzig. 1915.

Koch, K. *The Growth of the Biblical Tradition: The Form-Critical Method.* Translated by S. M. Cupitt. New York, 1969.

Koresec, V. *Hethitische Staatsverträge.* Leipziger rechtswissenschaftliche Studien 60. Leipzig, 1931.

Kramer, S. N. *History Begins at Sumer.* Garden City, N.Y., 1959.

———. *The Sumerians.* Chicago, 1963.

Krecher, J., and Müller, H.-P. "Vergangenheitsinteresse in Mesopotamien und Israel." *Saeculum* 26 (1975):13–44.

Kuhl, C. "Die 'Wiederaufnahme'—ein literarkritisches Prinzip? *ZAW* 64 (1952): 1–11.

Lambert, W. G. "Ancestors, Authors, and Canonicity." *JCS* 11 (1957):1–14, 112.

———. "Another Look at Hammurapi's Ancestors." *JCS* 22 (1968): 1–2.

———. *Babylonian Wisdom Literature.* Oxford, 1960.

———. "Berossus and Babylonian Eschatology." *Iraq* 38 (1976): 171–73.

———. "Destiny and Divine Intervention in Babylon and Israel." *OTS* 17 (1972): 65–72.

———. "History and the Gods: A Review Article." *Orientalia* 39 (1970):170–77.

———. "The Reign of Nebuchadnezzar I: A Turning Point in the History of Ancient Mesopotamian Religion." In *The Seed of Wisdom: Essays in Honour of T. J. Meek,* edited by W. S. McCullough, pp. 3–13. Toronto, 1964.

———. "Tukulti-Ninurta I and the Assyrian King List." *Iraq* 38 (1976):85–94.

Lambert, W.G., and Millard, A.R. *Atra-ḫasīs: The Babylonian Story of the Flood.* Oxford, 1969.

Lambert, W. G., and Walcot, P. "A New Babylonian Theogony and Hesiod." *Kadmos* 4 (1965):64–72.

Langlemet, F. "Les récites de l'institution de la royauté (1 Sam. VII–XII). De Wellhausen aux travaux récents." *RB* 77 (1970):161–200.

Laroche, E. *Catalogue des Textes Hittites.* Paris, 1971.

Lattimore, R. "The Wise Adviser in Herodotus." *Classical Philology* 34 (1939): 24–35.

Lehming, S. "Versuch zu Ex. xxxii." *VT* 10 (1960):16–50.

Lepinski, E. "*Nāgīd,* der Kronprinz." *VT* 24 (1974):497–99.

Levine, L. D. "The Second Campaign of Sennacherib." *JNES* 32 (1973):312–17.

Levy, I. "The Story of the Golden Calf Reanalysed." *VT* 9 (1959):318–22.

Lichtheim, Miriam. *Ancient Egyptian Literature: A Book of Readings.* 3 vols. Berkeley, Los Angeles, and London, 1973–1980.

Lindblom, J. "Lot-casting in the Old Testament." *VT* 12 (1962):164–78.

Liverani, M. "Memorandum on the Approach to Historiographic Texts." *Orientalia* 42 (1973):178–94. Reproduced in *Approaches to the Study of the Ancient Near East,* edited by G. Buccellati. Rome, 1973.

Lloyd, A. B. *Herodotus, Book II. Commentary 1–98.* Leiden, 1976.

———. *Herodotus, Book II. Introduction.* Leiden, 1975.

Long, B. O. "2 Kings III and Genres of Prophetic Narrative." *VT* 23 (1973): 337–48.

———. *The Problem of Etiological Narrative in the Old Testament.* BZAW 108. Berlin, 1968.

Lord, A. B. *The Singer of Tales.* Cambridge, Mass., 1960.

Luckenbill, D. D. *Ancient Records of Assyria and Babylonia.* 2 vols. Chicago, 1926–27.

Machinist, P. B. "The Epic of Tukulti-Ninurta I: A Study in Middle Assyrian Literature." Dissertation, Yale University, 1978.

———. "Literature as Politics: The Tukulti-Ninurta Epic and the Bible." *CBQ* 38 (1976):455–82.

Malamat, A. "Doctrines of Causality in Hittite and Biblical Historiography: A Parallel." *VT* 5 (1955):1–12.

———. "King Lists of the Old Babylonian Period and Biblical Genealogies." *JAOS* 88 (1968):163–73.

McCarter, P. K. *1 Samuel: The Anchor Bible.* Garden City, N.Y., 1980.

McCarthy, D. J. "An Installation Genre?" *JBL* 90 (1971):31–41.

———. "II Samuel 7 and the Structure of the Deuteronomic History." *JBL* 84 (1965):131–38.

———. *Treaty and Covenant.* AnBib 21. Rome, 1963.

———. "The Wrath of Yahweh and the Structural Unity of the Deuteronomistic History." In *Essays in Old Testament Ethics,* edited by J. L. Crenshaw and J. T. Willis, pp. 97–110. New York, 1974.

McCullough, W. S., ed. *The Seed of Wisdom: Essays in Honour of T. J. Meek.* Toronto, 1964.

McEvenue, S. E. *The Narrative Style of the Priestly Writer.* AnBib 50. Rome, 1971.

Mendelsohn, I. "Samuel's Denunciation of Kingship in the Light of Akkadian Documents from Ugarit." *BASOR* 143 (1956):17–22.

Mendenhall, G. E. "Law and Covenant in Israel and the Ancient Near East." *BA* 17 (1954):26–46; 49–76.

Mercer, S. A. B. *The Tell El-Amarna Tablets.* 2 vols. Toronto, 1939.

Meyer, E. *Geschichte des Altertums,* vol. 2, pt. 1. Stuttgart, 1910.

———. *Die Israeliten und ihre Nachbarstämme.* Halle, 1906.

Mildenberger, F. "Die vordeuteronomistische Saul-David-überlieferung." Dissertation, Tübingen, 1962.

Miller, J. M. "The Moabite Stone as a Memorial Stela." *PEQ* 104 (1974):9–18.

———. "Saul's Rise to Power: Some Observations concerning 1 Sam. 9:1–10:16; 10:26–11:15 and 13:2–14:46." *CBQ* 36 (1974):157–74.

Miller, P. D., Jr., and Roberts, J. J. M. *The Hand of the Lord: A Reassessment of the "Ark Narrative" of 1 Samuel.* Baltimore and London, 1977.

Momigliano, A. "Friedrich Creuzer and Greek Historiography." In *Studies in Historiography,* pp. 75–90. London, 1966.

———. "Historiography on Written Tradition and Historiography on Oral Tradition." In *Studies in Historiography,* pp. 211–20. London, 1966.

———. "Time in Ancient Historiography." In *Essays in Ancient and Modern Historiography,* pp. 161–204. Middletown, Conn., 1977.

Mond, R., and Meyers, O. H. *Temples of Armant, A Preliminary Survey: The Text.* Translated by M. S. Drower. London, 1940.

Montgomery, J. A. "Archival Data in the Book of Kings." *JBL* 53 (1934):46–52.

———. *The Book of Kings.* ICC. Edinburgh, 1951.

Moore, G. F. *A Critical and Exegetical Commentary on Judges.* ICC. New York, 1895.

Moran, W. L. "Notes on the New Nabonidus Inscriptions." *Orientalia* 28 (1959):130–40.

Moscati, S. *The World of Phoenicians.* London, 1968.

Mowinckel, S. "Israelite Historiography." *ASTI* 2 (1963):4–26.

———. *Tetrateuch-Pentateuch-Hexateuch: Die Berichte über die Landnahme in den drei altisraelitischen Geschichtswerken.* BZAW 90. Berlin and New York, 1964.

———. "Die vorderasiatischen Königs–und Fürsteninschriften eine stilistische

Studie." In *Eucharisterion, Festschrift Hermann Gunkel dargebracht.* Vol. 1. FRLANT 19, pp. 278–322. Göttingen, 1923.

Myers, J. M. *I Chronicles: The Anchor Bible.* Vol. 12. Garden City, N.Y., 1965.

Myres, J. L. *Herodotus: Father of History.* Oxford, 1953.

Na'aman, N. "Sennacherib's 'Letter to God' on His Campaign to Judah." *BASOR* 214 (1974):25–39.

Neff, R. "The Birth and Election of Isaac in the Priestly Tradition." *Biblical Research* 15 (1970):5–18.

Neu, E. *Der Anitta-Text.* Studien zu den Boğazköy-Texten 18. Wiesbaden, 1974.

Nilsson, M. P. *Cults, Myths, Oracles, and Politics in Ancient Greece.* Lund, 1951.

Noldeke, T. "Zu Herodot 3, 119 (Sophokles Antigone 903–913)." *Hermes* 29 (1894): 155–56.

Noth, M. "Die Bewährung von Salomons 'Göttlicher Weisheit.' " In *Wisdom in Israel and in the Ancient Near East.* SVT 3 (1955): 262–79.

———. *Das Buch Josua.* HAT 7. 3d ed. Tübingen, 1971.

———. "David and Israel in II Samuel VII." (1957). In *The Laws of the Pentateuch and Other Studies,* ed. M. Noth, pp. 250–59. Edinburgh and London, 1966.

———. *Exodus.* Philadelphia, 1962.

———. "Geschichtsschreibung im A. T." RGG. 3d ed. Vol. 2, pp. 1498–1504.

———. *A History of Pentateuchal Traditions.* Translated, with introduction by B. W. Anderson. Englewood Cliffs, N.J., 1972. Originally published as *Überlieferungsgeschichte des Pentateuch.* Stuttgart, 1948.

———. *Könige 1.* BKAT ix/i. Neukirchen-Vluyn, 1968.

———. *Numbers.* Philadelphia, 1968.

———. *Das System der Zwölf Stämme Israels.* BWANT 4/1. Stuttgart, 1930.

———. *Überlieferungsgeschichtliche Studien.* Tübingen, 1943. Partly translated as *The Deuteronomistic History.* JSOT suppl. ser. 15. Sheffield, Eng., 1981.

———. "Zur Anfertigung des 'Goldenen Kalbs.' " *VT* 9 (1959):419–22.

Nübel, H.-U. *Davids Aufstieg in der frühe israelitischer Geschichtsschreibung.* Bonn, 1959.

Oden, R. A. "Philo of Byblos and Hellenistic Historiography." *PEQ* 110 (1978): 115–26.

Olmstead, A. T. "Assyrian Historiography." The University of Missouri Series, Social Studies Series II/1. Columbia, Mo., 1916.

Oppenheim, A. L. *Ancient Mesopotamia: Portrait of a Dead Civilization.* Chicago and London, 1964.

———. "The City of Assur in 714 B.C." *JNES* 19 (1960):133–47.

Otto, E. *Die biographischen Inschriften der ägyptischen Spätzeit.* Leiden, 1954.

———. "Geschichtsbild und Geschichtsschreibung in Ägypten." *WO* 3/3 (1964/ 1966):161–76.

Pearson, L. *Early Ionian Historians.* Oxford, 1939.

Perlitt, L. *Bundestheologie im Alten Testament.* WMANT 36. Neukirchen-Vluyn, 1969.

Petzoldt, L., ed. *Vergleichene Sagenforschung.* Darmstadt, 1969.

Picard, G. C., and C. *The Life and Death of Carthage.* New York, 1969.

Pischel, R. "Zu Sophokles Antigone 909–912." *Hermes* 28 (1893):465–68.

Pocock, J. G. A. "The Origins of Study of the Past: A Comparative Approach." *CSSH* 4 (1962): 209–46.

Posener, G. *Littérature et politique dans L'Égypte de la XIIᵉ dynastie.* Paris, 1956.

Prakken, D. W. *Studies in Greek Genealogical Chronology.* Lancaster, Pa., 1943.

Pritchard, J. B. *The Ancient Near East in Pictures Relating to the Old Testament.* 2d ed. with supplement. Princeton, N.J., 1969.

Pritchard, J. B., ed. *Ancient Near Eastern Texts Relating to the Old Testament.* 3d ed. with supplement. Princeton, N.J., 1969.

Rad, G. von. "The Beginnings of Historical Writing in Ancient Israel." (1944). In *The Problem of the Hexateuch,* pp. 166–204.

————. "The Deuteronomic Theology of History in *I* and *II Kings.*" (1947). In *The Problem of the Hexateuch,* pp. 205–21.

————. "The Form-Critical Problem of the Hexateuch." (1938). In *The Problem of the Hexateuch,* pp. 1–78.

————. "Hexateuch oder Pentateuch?" *Verkündigung und Forschung* 1–2 (1949):52–56.

————. "Job xxxviii and Ancient Egyptian Wisdom." (1955). In *The Problem of the Hexateuch,* pp. 281–91.

————. "The Levitical Sermon in *I* and *II Chronicles.* (1934). In *The Problem of the Hexateuch,* pp. 267–80.

————. "Die Nehemia-Denkschrift." *ZAW* 76 (1964):176–87.

————. *Old Testament Theology.* 2 vols. New York, 1962–1965.

————. *The Problem of the Hexateuch and Other Essays.* Translated by E. W. Dicken. Edinburgh and London, 1966.

Radjawane, A. N. "Das deuteronomistiche Geschichtswerk: Ein Forschungsbericht." *ThR* 38 (1973/74):177–216.

Rainey, A. F. "The Kingdom of Ugarit." *BA* 28 (1965):102–25.

Redford, D. B. *History and Chronology of the Eighteenth Dynasty of Egypt: Seven Studies.* Toronto, 1967.

————. "The Literary Motif of the Exposed Child." *Numen* 14 (1967):209–28.

————. "Studies in Relations between Palestine and Egypt during the First Millennium B.C. Pt. 1: The Taxation System of Solomon." In *Studies in the Ancient Palestinian World,* edited by D. B. Redford and W. J. Wevers, pp. 141–56. Toronto, 1972.

————. *King-Lists, Annals, and Daybooks.* Forthcoming.

Reiner, E. "The Etiological Myth of the 'Seven Sages.'" *Orientalia* 30 (1961): 1–11.

Reisner, G. A. "Inscribed Monuments from Gebel Barkal." *ZÄS* 66 (1931): 89–100.

Reisner, G. A., and Reisner, M. B. "Inscribed Monuments from Gebel Barkal. Pt. 2: The Granite Stela of Thutmose III." *ZÄS* 69 (1933):24–39.

Rendtorff, R. "Boebachtungen zur altisraelitischen Geschichtsschreibung Anhand der Geschichte vom Aufstieg Davids." In *Probleme biblischer Theologie,* edited by H. W. Wolff, pp. 428–39. Munich, 1971.

————. *Das überlieferungsgeschichtliche Problem des Pentateuch.* BZAW 147. Berlin, 1977.

Richter, W. *Die Bearbeitungen des 'Retterbuches' in den deuteronomistischen Epoche.* BBB 21. Bonn, 1964.

————. "Die nāgīd-Formel: Ein Beitrag zur Erhellung des nāgīd-Problems." *BZ* 9 (1965):71–84.

————. *Die sogenannten vorprophetischen Berufungsberichte: Eine literaturwissenschaftliche Studie zu 1 Sam. 9, 1–10, 16; Ex. 3f und Ri. 6, 11–17.* FRLANT 101. Göttingen, 1970.

——. *Traditionsgeschichtliche Untersuchungen zum Richterbuch.* BBB 18. Bonn, 1966.

Roberts, J. J. M. "Myth *versus* History: Relaying the Comparative Foundations." *CBQ* 38 (1976):1–13.

——. "Nebuchadnezzar I's Elamite Crisis in Theological Perspective." In *Essays on the Ancient Near East in Memory of J. J. Finkelstein,* edited by M. de Jong Ellis, pp. 183–87. Hamden, Conn., 1977.

Röllig, W. "Die Glaubwurdigkeit der Chronik P." In *Heidelberger Studien zum Alten Orient. Festschrift Adam Falkenstein zum (60 Geburtstag) 17 sept. 1966,* edited by D. O. Edzard, pp. 173–84. Wiesbaden, 1967.

——. "Zur Typologie und Entstehung der babylonischen und assyrischen Königlisten." *Lišān mitḫurti. Festschrift W. von Soden.* AOAT 1, pp. 265–77. Neukirchen-Vluyn, 1969.

Rofé, A. "Classes in the Prophetical Stories: Didactic Legenda and Parable." *SVT* 26 (1974):143–64.

——. "The Classification of the Prophetical Stories." *JBL* 89 (1970):427–40.

Rose, M. *Deuteronomist und Jahwist: Untersuchungen zu den Berührungspunkten beider Literaturwerke.* AThANT 67. Zurich, 1981.

Rost, L. *Die Überlieferung von der Thronnachfolge Davids.* BWANT III/6 (1926). Reprinted in *Das kleine Credo und andere Studien zum Alten Testament,* pp. 119–253. Heidelberg, 1965.

Rudolph W. *Chronikbücher.* HAT 21. Tübingen, 1955.

Ruffle, J. *Heritage of the Pharaohs.* Oxford, 1977.

Saggs, H. W. F. *The Encounter with the Divine in Mesopotamia and Israel.* London, 1978.

Sasson, J. M. "On Idrimi and Šarruwa, the Scribe." *Studies on the Civilization and Culture of Nuzi and the Hurrians,* edited by M. A. Morrison and D. I. Owen (in honor of Ernest R. Lachmanl), pp. 309–24. Winona Lake, Ind., 1981.

Schicklberger, F. *Die Ladeerzählung des ersten Samuelbuches: Eine literaturwissenschaftliche und theologiegeschichtliche Untersuchung.* Forschung zur Bibel, 7. Würzburg, 1973.

Schmid, H. H. "Das alttestamentliche Verständnis von Geschichte in seinem Verhältnis zum gemeinorientalischen Denken." *WuD* 13 (1975):9–21.

——. *Der sogenannte Jahwist: Beobachtungen und Fragen zur Pentateuchforschung.* Zurich, 1976.

Schmidt, H. *Die Geschichtsschreibung im Alten Testament.* Tübingen, 1911.

Schmidt, L. *Menschlicher Erfolg und Jahwes Initiative: Studien zu Tradition, Interpretation und Historie in Überlieferungen von Gideon, Saul und David.* WMANT 38. Neukirchen-Vluyn, 1970.

Schmitt, H.-C. *Elisa: Traditionsgeschichtliche Untersuchungen zur vorklassischen nordisraelitischen Prophetie.* Gütersloh, 1972.

——. *Die nichtpriesterliche Josephsgeschichte: Ein Beitrag zur neuesten Pentateuchkritik.* BZAW 154. Berlin and New York, 1980.

Schuler, E. von. "Staatsverträge und Dokumente hethitischen Rechts." In *Neuere Hethiterforschung,* edited by G. Walser, pp. 34–53. Wiesbaden, 1964.

Schulte, H. *Die Entstehung der Geschictsschreibung im alten Israel.* BZAW 128. Berlin and New York, 1972.

Schunck, K.-D. *Benjamin: Untersuchungen zur Entstehung und Geschichte eines israelitischen Stammes.* BZAW 86. Berlin and New York, 1963.

Scott, R. B. Y. "Solomon and the Beginnings of Wisdom in Israel." In *Wisdom in Israel and in the Ancient Near East.* SVT 3 (1955):262–79.

Shils, E. "Tradition." *CSSH* 13 (1971):122–59.

Shotwell, J. T. *The History of History.* Vol. 1. New York, 1939.

Sievers, E. *Metrische Studien.* Vol. 2: *Hebräische Genesis.* Leipzig, 1904–05.

Smend, R. "Das Gesetz und die Völker." In *Probleme biblischer Theologie,* edited by H. W. Wolff, pp. 494–509. Munich, 1972.

Smith, H. P. *The Books of Samuel.* ICC. Edinburgh, 1899.

Smith, S. *The Statue of Idrimi.* London, 1949.

Soggin, J. A. *Joshua.* London, 1972.

Sommer, F., and Falkenstein, A. *Die hethitisch-akkadische Bilingue des Hattušili I.* Abh. der Bayerischen Akad. der Wiss., Phil.-hist. Abt., N.F. 16. Munich, 1938.

Spalinger, A. "Aspects of the Military Documents of the Ancient Egyptians." Dissertation, Yale University, 1974.

―――. "A Critical Analysis of the 'Annals' of Thutmose III (Stucke V–VI)." *JARCE* 14 (1977):41–54.

―――. "Some Notes on the Battle of Megiddo and Reflections on Egyptian Military Writing." *MDAIK* 30 (1974):221–29.

Speiser, E. A. "Ancient Mesopotamia." In *The Idea of History in the Ancient Near East,* edited by R. C. Dentan, pp. 35–76. New Haven, 1955.

―――. "The Biblical Idea of History in Its Common Near Eastern Setting." *IEJ* 7 (1957):201–16.

Starr, C. G. *The Awakening of the Greek Historical Spirit.* New York, 1968.

―――. "Historical and Philosophical Time." In *History and the Concept of Time.* History and Theory, no. 6, pp. 24–35. Middletown, Conn., 1966.

Stoebe, H.-J. *Das erste Buch Samuelis.* KAT VIII/1. Gütersloh, 1973.

Strasburger, H. *Homer und die Geschichtsschreibung.* Sitzungsberichte der Heidelberger Akad. der Wissen. Phil.-hist. Kl. 1972, 1 Abh., pp. 5–44. Heidelberg, 1972.

Sturtevant, E. H., and Bechtel, G. *Hittite Chrestomathy.* Philadelphia, 1935.

Sydow, C. W. von. "Kategorien der Prosa-Volksdichtung." (1934). In *Selected Papers on Folklore,* ed. C. W. von Sydow, pp. 60–85. Copenhagen, 1948.

Speyer, W. *Die literarische Fälschung im heidnischen und christlichen Altertum.* Munich, 1971.

Tadmor, H. "Assyria and the West: The Ninth Century and Its Aftermath." In *Unity and Diversity: Essays in the History, Literature, and Religion of the Ancient Near East,* edited by H. Goedicke and J. J. M. Roberts, pp. 36–48. Baltimore and London, 1975.

―――. "The Inscriptions of Nabunaid, Historical Arrangement." *Assyriological Studies* 16 (1965):351–64.

―――. "Observations on Assyrian Historiography." In *Essays on the Ancient Near East in Memory of J. J. Finkelstein,* edited by M. D. Ellis, pp. 209–13. Hamden, Conn., 1977.

Talmon, S. "The 'Comparative Method' in Biblical Interpretation—Principles and Problems." SVT 29 (1977):320–56.

―――. "The Textual Study of the Bible—A New Outlook." In *Qumran and the History of the Biblical Text,* edited by F. M. Cross and S. Talmon. Cambridge, Mass., 1975.

Thompson, T. L. *The Historicity of the Patriarchal Narratives: The Quest for the Historical Abraham.* BZAW 133. Tübingen, 1974.

Ungnad, A. "Datenlisten." *RLA* 2:131–94.

―――. "Eponym." *RLA* 2:412–57.

Van Groningen, B. A. *In the Grip of the Past.* Leiden, 1953.

Van Seters, J. *Abraham in History and Tradition.* New Haven and London, 1975.
———. "Confessional Reformulation in the Exilic Period." *VT* 22 (1972):
    448–59.
———. "Histories and Historians of the Ancient Near East: The Israelites." *Orientalia* 50 (1981):137–85.
———. "History and Myth in Biblical Interpretation." *Andover Newton Quarterly* 8 (1968):154–62.
———. *The Hyksos: A New Investigation.* New Haven and London, 1966.
———. "Oral Patterns or Literary Conventions in Biblical Narrative." *Semeia* 5
    (1976):147–48.
———. "Recent Studies on the Pentateuch: A Crisis in Method." *JAOS* 99
    (1979):663–73.
———. "The Terms 'Amorite' and 'Hittite' in the Old Testament." *VT* 22
    (1972):64–81.
———. "Tradition and Social Change in Ancient Israel." *Perspectives in Religious Studies* 7 (1980):96–113.
Vaux, R. de. *Ancient Israel: Its Life and Institutions.* London, 1961.
———. *Histoire ancienne d'Israël.* Vol. 2: *La période des Juges.* Paris, 1973.
———. "Single Combat in the Old Testament." In *The Bible and the Ancient Near East,* ed. R. de Vaux, pp. 122–35. London, 1971.
Veijola, T. *Die ewige Dynastie: David und die Entstehung seiner Dynastie nach der deuteronomistischen Darstellung.* Annales Academiae Scientiarum Fennicae. Series B, vol. 193. Helsinki, 1975.
———. *Das Königtum in der Beurteilung der deuteronomistischen Historiographie: Eine redaktionsgeschichtliche Untersuchung.* Annales Academiae Scientiarum Fennicae. Series B, vol. 198. Helsinki, 1977.
Vink, J. G. *The Date and Origin of the Priestly Code in the Old Testament.* OTS 15. Leiden, 1969.
Vorlander, H. *Die Entstehungszeit des jehowistischen Geschichtswerkes.* Europaische Hochschulschriften XIII/109. Frankfurt, 1978.
Wacholder, B. Z. *Eupolemus: A Study of Judaeo-Greek Literature.* New York and Jerusalem, 1974.
Walcot, P. *Hesiod and the Near East.* Cardiff, 1966.
Ward, J. M. *Amos and Isaiah: Prophets of the Word of God.* New York and Nashville, 1969.
Warner, S. M. "Primitive Saga Men." *VT* 29 (1979):325–35.
Weinfeld, M. *Deuteronomy and the Deuteronomic School.* Oxford, 1972.
———. "The Period of the Conquest and of the Judges as Seen by the Earlier and the Later Sources." *VT* 17 (1967):93–113.
Weippert, H. "Die 'deuteronomistischen' Beurteilungen der Könige von Israel und Juda und das Problem der Redaktion der Königsbücher." *Biblica* 53 (1972):
    301–39.
Weippert, M. "Fragen des israelitischen Geschichtsbewusstseins." *VT* 23 (1973):
    415–42.
———. "'Heiliger Krieg' in Israel und Assyrien: Kritische Anmerkungen zu Gerhard von Rads Konzept des 'Heiligen Krieges im alten Israel.'" *ZAW* 84 (1972):
    460–93.
———. *The Settlement of the Israelite Tribes in Palestine.* SBT 2/21. Translated by J. D. Martin. London, 1971.
Weiser, A. "Die Legitimation des Königs David: Zur Eigenart und Entstehung der sogen. Geschichte von Davids Aufstieg." *VT* 16 (1966):325–54.

————. *Samuel: Seine geschichtliche Aufgabe und religiöse Bedeutung*. FRLANT 81. Göttingen, 1962.

————. "Die Tempelbaukrise unter David." *ZAW* 77 (1965):153–68.

Wellhausen, J. *Prolegomena to the History of Ancient Israel*. Gloucester, Mass., 1973.

West, M. L., ed. *Hesiod: Theogony*. Oxford, 1966.

Westermann, C. "Arten der Erzählung in der Genesis." In *Forschung am Alten Testament*. TB 24, pp. 36–47. Munich, 1964.

————. *Basic Forms of Prophetic Speech*. Philadelphia, 1967.

————. "Zum Geschichtsverständnis des Alten Testaments." In *Probleme biblischer Theologie*, edited by H. W. Wolff, pp. 611–19. Munich, 1971.

Whallon, W. *Formula, Character, and Context: Studies in Homeric, Old English, and Old Testament Poetry*. Cambridge, Mass., 1969.

Whitman, C. H. *Homer and the Heroic Tradition*. Cambridge, Mass., 1958.

Whybray, R. N. *The Succession Narrative*. SBT 2/9. London, 1968.

Wilcken, U. "Ὑπομνηματισμοί." *Philologus* 53 (1894):80–126.

Wilcoxen, J. A. "Narrative." In *Old Testament Form Criticism*, edited by J. H. Hayes, pp. 58–79. San Antonio, 1974.

Wildung, D. *Die Rolle ägyptischer Könige im Bewusstsein ihrer Nachwelt*. Berlin, 1969.

Williams, R. J. "Literature as a Medium of Political Propaganda in Ancient Egypt." In *The Seed of Wisdom: Essays in Honour of T. J. Meek*, edited by W. S. McCullough, pp. 14–30. Toronto, 1964.

Williamson, H. G. M. *Israel in the Books of Chronicles*. Cambridge, 1977.

Wilson, J. A. *Herodotus in Egypt*. Leiden, 1970.

Wilson, R. R. *Genealogy and History in the Biblical World*. New Haven and London, 1977.

————. "The Old Testament Genealogies in Recent Research." *JBL* 94 (1975): 169–89.

Wiseman, D. J. *Chronicles of the Chaldean Kings (625–556 B.C.) in the British Museum*. London, 1956.

————. *The Vassal Treaties of Esarhaddon*. London, 1958.

Wolf, H. M. "The Apology of Ḫattušiliš Compared with Other Political Self-Justifications of the Ancient Near East." Dissertation, Brandeis University, 1967.

Wood, H. *The Histories of Herodotus: An Analysis of the Formal Structure*. The Hague and Paris, 1972.

Würthwein, E. *Die Erzählung von der Thronfolge Davids: Theologische oder politische Geschichtsschreibung?* Theologische Studien 115. Zurich, 1974.

Wüst, M. *Untersuchungen zu den siedlungsgeographischen Texten des Alten Testaments. I: Ostjordanland*. BTAVO, B/9. Wiesbaden, 1975.

Wyatt, N. "Some Observations on the Idea of History among the West Semitic Peoples." *UF* 11:825–32.

GENERAL INDEX